Intersecting Health, Livability, and Human Behavior in Urban Environments

Roberto Alonso González-Lezcano
Universidad CEU San Pablo, Spain

IGI Global
PUBLISHER of TIMELY KNOWLEDGE

A volume in the Advances in Religious and Cultural Studies (ARCS) Book Series

Published in the United States of America by
IGI Global
Information Science Reference (an imprint of IGI Global)
701 E. Chocolate Avenue
Hershey PA, USA 17033
Tel: 717-533-8845
Fax: 717-533-8661
E-mail: cust@igi-global.com
Web site: http://www.igi-global.com

Library of Congress Cataloging-in-Publication Data

Names: González-Lezcano, Roberto Alonso, 1971- editor.
Title: Intersecting health, livability, and human behavior in urban environments / edited by Roberto Alonso González-Lezcano.
Description: Hershey, PA : Information Science Reference, [2023] | Includes bibliographical references and index. | Summary: "Intersecting Health, Livability, and Human Behavior in Urban Environments considers how to improve the quality of the environment and healthy living in contemporary and future urban environments. Covering key topics such as environmental health, smart cities, and urban health, this premier reference source is ideal for policymakers, government officials, scholars, researchers, academicians, instructors, and students"-- Provided by publisher.
Identifiers: LCCN 2022056947 (print) | LCCN 2022056948 (ebook) | ISBN 9781668469248 (hardcover) | ISBN 9781668469255 (paperback) | ISBN 9781668469262 (ebook)
Subjects: LCSH: City planning--Health aspects. | Urban ecology (Sociology) | Urban health.
Classification: LCC RA566.7 .I58 2023 (print) | LCC RA566.7 (ebook) | DDC 362.1/042--dc23/eng/20230125
LC record available at https://lccn.loc.gov/2022056947
LC ebook record available at https://lccn.loc.gov/2022056948

This book is published in the IGI Global book series Advances in Religious and Cultural Studies (ARCS) (ISSN: 2475-675X; eISSN: 2475-6768)

British Cataloguing in Publication Data
A Cataloguing in Publication record for this book is available from the British Library.

For electronic access to this publication, please contact: eresources@igi-global.com.

Advances in Religious and Cultural Studies (ARCS) Book Series

Nancy Erbe
California State University-Dominguez Hills, USA

ISSN:2475-675X
EISSN:2475-6768

Mission

In the era of globalization, the diversity of the world and various cultures becomes apparent as cross-cultural interactions turn into a daily occurrence for individuals in all professions. Understanding these differences is necessary in order to promote effective partnerships and interactions between those from different religious and cultural backgrounds.

The **Advances in Religious and Cultural Studies (ARCS)** book series brings together a collection of scholarly publications on topics pertaining to religious beliefs, culture, population studies, and sociology. Books published within this series are ideal for professionals, theorists, researchers, and students seeking the latest research on collective human behavior in terms of religion, social structure, and cultural identity and practice.

Coverage

- Sociology
- Gender
- Impact of Religion on Society
- Politics and Religion
- Cross-Cultural Interaction
- Cults and Religious Movements
- Human Rights and Ethics
- Cultural Identity
- Social Stratification and Classes
- Stereotypes and Racism

IGI Global is currently accepting manuscripts for publication within this series. To submit a proposal for a volume in this series, please contact our Acquisition Editors at Acquisitions@igi-global.com or visit: http://www.igi-global.com/publish/.

The Advances in Religious and Cultural Studies (ARCS) Book Series (ISSN 2475-675X) is published by IGI Global, 701 E. Chocolate Avenue, Hershey, PA 17033-1240, USA, www.igi-global.com. This series is composed of titles available for purchase individually; each title is edited to be contextually exclusive from any other title within the series. For pricing and ordering information please visit http://www.igi-global.com/book-series/advances-religious-cultural-studies/84269. Postmaster: Send all address changes to above address.

Titles in this Series

For a list of additional titles in this series, please visit: www.igi-global.com/book-series

Reconstructing Perceptions of Systemically Marginalized Groups
Leslie Ponciano (Hope Education Research Solutions, USA)
Information Science Reference • © 2023 • 338pp • H/C (ISBN: 9781668468982) • US $215.00

Perspectives on Critical Race Theory and Elite Media
E. Thomas Lehner (Bronx Community College, USA)
Information Science Reference • © 2023 • 207pp • H/C (ISBN: 9781668452219) • US $190.00

Analyzing Black History From Slavery Through Racial Profiling by Police
Janelle Christine Simmons (Independent Researcher, USA)
Information Science Reference • © 2023 • 202pp • H/C (ISBN: 9781668485415) • US $215.00

Implications of Marginalization and Critical Race Theory on Social Justice
Harish C. Chandan (Independent Researcher, USA)
Information Science Reference • © 2023 • 300pp • H/C (ISBN: 9781668436158) • US $215.00

The Depathologizing of Black Masculinity Within Legacy and New Media
William R. Robinson (North Carolina Central University, USA)
Information Science Reference • © 2023 • 300pp • H/C (ISBN: 9781668424537) • US $215.00

Handbook of Research on Managing the Urban-Rural Divide Through an Inclusive Framework
Ayobami Abayomi Popoola (University of KwaZulu-Natal, South Africa) Hangwelani Hope Magidimisha-Chipungu (University of KwaZulu-Natal, South Africa) and Lovemore Chipungu (University of KwaZulu-Natal, South Africa)
Information Science Reference • © 2023 • 396pp • H/C (ISBN: 9781668462584) • US $270.00

Hamas in Power The Question of Transformation
Qossay Hamed (Al-Quds Open University, Palestine)
Information Science Reference • © 2023 • 294pp • H/C (ISBN: 9781668443088) • US $205.00

Urban Poetics and Politics in Contemporary South Asia and the Middle East
Moussa Pourya Asl (Universiti Sains Malaysia, Malaysia)
Information Science Reference • © 2023 • 330pp • H/C (ISBN: 9781668466506) • US $215.00

IGI Global
PUBLISHER of TIMELY KNOWLEDGE

701 East Chocolate Avenue, Hershey, PA 17033, USA
Tel: 717-533-8845 x100 • Fax: 717-533-8661
E-Mail: cust@igi-global.com • www.igi-global.com

Editorial Advisory Board

Table of Contents

Detailed Table of Contents

Several smart cities have been established all over the world and versatile infrastructure is being developed to enhance the resident experience. Environmentally friendly urban infrastructure development is critical for societal health and overall development. Solar smart benches are now gaining popularity in smart cities and indeed considered as part of essential infrastructure for futuristic smart cities. They produce electricity during the daytime and provide various services to users. This chapter presents engineering design and analysis of solar smart benches. Contemporary smart features have been considered and design alternatives have been developed. Technical specifications for the designs have been provided. Suitable information and communication technologies have been identified for putting the infrastructure to use. Solar smart benches have the potential to revolutionize the smart city ecosystem.

A sedentary lifestyle is a global and complex problem that, nevertheless, finds a very natural solution: movement. However, promoting physical activity among the population is not a simple task. It requires great efforts from individuals, society, and, particularly, from the urban environment. The concept of an active city arises as a response to make more livable and healthier cities. An increasing number of cities are committing to the active cities model. One of the most advanced is Hamburg. The Hanseatic city counts on a comprehensive strategy involving its entire territory. In this research, the main characteristics of the active city model of Hamburg will be presented and discussed, and the case of two urban interventions that show how the model can be applied to different urban settings: HafenCity and Oberbillwerder. The object of investigating the Hamburg case is to build evidence and references so that other cities can direct their urban policies and actions.

This study intends to analyze the impact of environmental regulation and incentives in socio-ecological and green technological innovation. It departs from the assumption that environmental regulation affects the performance of socio-ecological and green technological innovation in organizations. The method employed is critical analytical and reflective based on the theoretical, conceptual, and methodological literature. It is concluded that the analysis confirms that there is a direct relationship between the incentives of environmental regulation and the socio-ecological and green technological innovation in organizations.

The interest of the buildings analysed lies in the possibility of reusing and adapting them for other uses, as versatile examples that can be transformed into public, social and cultural centres. The time frame in which the study is framed is from the 17th century, with the creation of the first Tobacco Factory in Seville in 1620, to the present day, when the old factories and the urban environments in which they are located continue to be transformed. The enormous versatility of industrial architecture has allowed these factories to survive the passage of time and to adapt to changes in use. The reasons why they have been preserved are due to their dimensional characteristics and the fact that many of them were included in the historic city centres. These buildings can be considered as astute infrastructures because they are useful, sustainable, and functional.

Architects need the freedom to design their projects with the assurance that they will be inspiring aesthetic as well as healthy places, i.e., buildings, streets, parks, avenues, and squares that offer a complete living experience in an environment that takes into account light, sound, vibration, climate, and all those aspects that can disturb people's well-being. We know that prolonged exposure to noise can cause discomfort and sleep disorders, which affect the quality of life. This noise is not the only pollutant as there are other sound waves such as infrasound and ultrasound that are not perceptible but potentially harmful to health. Not forgetting electromagnetic waves, the light that reaches our bodies and which has regulated our lives throughout the existence of the species. The invention of electric lighting had the consequence that people spend practically all day indoors. Days are poorly illuminated, and the nights have too much light. On the other hand, the intensity of artificial light is a fraction of that of daylight and the spectral composition is also different.

Since the 1960s, a more rational and modern construction has been sought in line with industrialisation. In addition, due to the shortage of housing, professionals in the construction sector have been looking for solutions. The industrialisation of construction was first attempted after the Second World War through prefabrication. Today, it is moving towards more open concepts, making the industrial development of its products compatible with a construction that is still archaic and in need of updating. On the other hand, architects have reviewed the programmes and needs of users and citizens, in housing, workplaces, commerce, leisure and cities, and have proposed more contemporary solutions, with greater flexibility.

Preface

This book aims to improve environment quality and healthy living in contemporary and future urban environments. It welcomes submissions on a broad range of topics: scientific and technical information on environmental health and healthy living in the urban settings; knowledge around health effects related to urbanization, urban development, and urban renewal; empirical works on the sociocultural, political, economic, and health impacts of policies and interventions aiming to improve the health of living styles; assessments on the distributional characteristics, equality. and justice of health services and facilities in cities; and theoretic or evidence-based explorations on the effectiveness, people's inclusion, and improvement directions of the governance of healthy cities.

The promotion of sustainable urban development and livable cities in the past three decades has effectively merged the themes of urban health, urban sustainability, and urban livability into an integrated research field. As more people are predicted to live in a relatively confined space, the balance between the physical/built environment, social environment and urban dwellers becomes more delicate. Urban system evolves to be more complex than ever during this process. While complex systems often offer relative stability, delicate balance requires carefully designed plans and management to avoid collapse. It is hence of great interest and importance to know what the future sustainable and livable cities look like.

This research book will update the current state of knowledge on the subject, since the authors of the chapters are all be researchers and professors from prestigious universities. It is not a theoretical book, but is based on where current research is taking us in terms of environmental health, health systems, livability, smart cities, smart health, sustainable development, urban health, urban management and urban planning.

Intersecting Health, Livability, and Human Behavior in Urban Environments considers how to improve the quality of the environment and healthy living in contemporary and future urban environments. Covering key topics such as environmental health, smart cities, and urban health, this premier reference source is ideal for policymakers, government officials, scholars, researchers, academicians, instructors, and students.

The book has been divided into the following chapters:

Chapter 1

Anthropological Ecology and Ecological Anthropology as a Framework for the Analysis of Socio-Ecological Sustainable Development

José Vargas-Hernandez, María Higuera-Cota, Omar Vargas-González

This study is aimed to analyze the anthropological ecology and the ecological anthropology as a framework approach for the analysis of socio-ecological sustainable development. It departs from the assumption that sustainable development requires a socio-ecological approach sustained by anthropology and ecology. The method used is the analytical reflection based on the conceptual, theoretical, and empirical literature review. The study concludes that anthropology and ecology combine elements to sustain the anthropological ecology and ecological anthropology approaches to develop the framework for the analysis of a socio-ecological sustainable development.

Chapter 2

Anthropological Perspective of the Implications Between the Environment and Sustainability

José Vargas-Hernandez, Jorge Zamudio-Abdala, Omar Vargas-González

This study aims to analyze some of the theoretical, conceptual, and methodological implications between the anthropology and the environment and sustainability. Departing from the assumption that anthropological and ethnographic analysis and interpretive research on organizational anthropology has an emergent and symbolic role rooted in social processes and with no a priori assumptions, with explanations and categories defined by the organizational actors, which had an impact on sustainability and the environment through the green marketing practices. The method employes is based on an analytical and descriptive issues from the theoretical and empirical literature review leading to reflective analysis. It is concluded that the ethnographic and anthropological methodology is pertinent to be used in the analysis of its interactions between anthropology, the environment and sustainability as a new specialty in organizational studies. Also, the study proposes the implementation of green marketing habits and practices on the sustainability drawing from the organizational anthropology.

Chapter 3

Designing a Futuristic Solar Smart Bench for Smart Cities: Towards Developing the Futuristic Urban Infrastructure

Rodney Chakwesha, K.S. Sastry Musti

Several smart cities have been established all over the world and versatile infrastructure is being developed to enhance the resident experience. Environmentally friendly urban infrastructure development is critical for societal health and overall development. Solar smart benches are now gaining popularity in smart cities and indeed considered as part of essential infrastructure for futuristic smart cities. They produce electricity during the daytime and provide various services to users. This chapter presents engineering design and analysis of solar smart benches. Contemporary smart features have been considered and design alternatives have been developed. Technical specifications for the designs have been provided.

Suitable information and communication technologies have been identified for putting the infrastructure to use. Solar smart benches have the potential to revolutionize the smart city ecosystem.

Chapter 4

Hamburg at the Forefront of the Active Cities

Carlos Lahoz Palacio, José Antonio Blasco

Sedentary lifestyle is a global and complex problem that, nevertheless, finds a very natural solution: movement. However, promoting physical activity among the population is not a simple task. It requires great efforts from individuals, society and, particularly, from the urban environment. The concept of Active City arises as a response to make more livable and healthier cities. An increasing number of cities are committing to the Active Cities Model. One of the most advanced is Hamburg. The Hanseatic city counts on a comprehensive strategy involving its entire territory. In this research, it will be presented and discussed the main characteristics of the Active City Model of Hamburg and the case of two urban interventions that show how the model can be applied to different urban settings: HafenCity and Oberbillwerder. The object of investigating the Hamburg case is to build evidence and references so that other cities can direct their urban policies and actions.

Chapter 5

Organizational Socio-Ecology and Green Technological Innovation

José Vargas-Hernandez, María Higuera-Cota, Omar Vargas-González

This study intends to analyze the impact of environmental regulation and incentives in socio-ecological and green technological innovation. It departs from the assumption that environmental regulation affects the performance of socio-ecological and green technological innovation in organizations. The method employed is the critical analytical and reflective based on the theoretical, conceptual, and methodological literature. It is concluded that the analysis confirms that there is a direct relationship between the incentives of environmental regulation and the socio-ecological and green technological innovation in organizations.

Chapter 6

Reuse of Spanish Industrial Architecture From Tobacco Factories to Cultural and Public Spaces

Tamar Awad

The interest of the buildings analysed lies in the possibility of reusing and adapting them for other uses, as versatile examples that can be transformed into public, social and cultural centres. The time frame in which the study is framed is from the 17th century, with the creation of the first Tobacco Factory in Seville in 1620, to the present day, when the old factories and the urban environments in which they are located continue to be transformed. The enormous versatility of industrial architecture has allowed these factories to survive the passage of time and to adapt to changes in use. The reasons why they have been preserved are due to their dimensional characteristics and the fact that many of them were included in the historic city centres. These buildings can be considered as astute infrastructures because they are useful, sustainable, and functional.

Chapter 7

Sound and Light Waves in Healthy Environments: Architecture and the Health of People Through the Stages of Life – Healthier Cities, Multidisciplinarity as a Solution

Daniel Arranz-Paraiso, David Baeza-Moyano, Roberto Alonso González-Lezcano

Architects need the freedom to design their projects with the assurance that they will be inspiring and aesthetic as well as healthy places, i.e., buildings, streets, parks, avenues, and squares that offer a complete living experience in an environment that takes into account light, sound, vibration, climate and all those aspects that can disturb people's well-being. We know that prolonged exposure to noise can cause discomfort and sleep disorders, which affect the quality of life. This noise is not the only pollutant as there are other sound waves such as infrasound and ultrasound that are not perceptible but potentially harmful to health. Not forgetting electromagnetic waves, the light that reaches our bodies and which has regulated our lives throughout the existence of the species. The invention of electric lighting had the consequence that people spending practically all day indoors. Days are poorly illuminated and the nights have too much light. On the other hand, the intensity of artificial light is a fraction of that of daylight and the spectral composition is also different.

Chapter 8

Sustainability in Construction, Housing, and the City

Tamar Awad, Jesús Guardiola, Mariano Jiménez, Roberto Alonso González-Lezcano

Since the 1960s, a more rational and modern construction has been sought, in line with industrialisation. In addition, due to the shortage of housing, professionals in the construction sector have been looking for solutions. The industrialisation of construction was first attempted after the Second World War through prefabrication. Today, it is moving towards more open concepts, making the industrial development of its products compatible with a construction that is still archaic and in need of updating. On the other hand, architects have reviewed the programmes and needs of users and citizens, in housing, workplaces, commerce, leisure and cities, and have proposed more contemporary solutions, with greater flexibility. Sustainability can be seen in a techno-biological environment, where artificial activity is integrated with the life and resources of the environment, in a new balanced ecological system. The methodology implemented is based on Systems Theory, according to tools specifically developed in construction, for proposals and designs around the industrialisation of housing.

Chapter 9

Sustainable Acoustics for a Better Livability and Wellbeing

Laura de Azcárate

Acoustics is being addressed as a part of the LCA methodologies in construction, hence research in new acoustic materials is being developed on the benefit of natural materials that can be an alternative to traditional materials. It´s important to consider its acoustic performance as a key parameter in the choice of sustainable building materials. The Impact of applying sustainable acoustic materials for a particular space function and typology can be measured, defined and quantified when creating healthy and comfortable spaces for a better acoustic comfort and wellbeing. The use of environmentally-friendly acoustic materials in architecture, as well as the rest of the aspects that combined define a sustainable practice for a business, contribute to merge health, livability in urban environments. Human health and wellbeing is a consequence of a designer's intention, where acoustics plays an important role. Applying sustainable acoustic strategies embedded in the rest of the disciplines is a key factor to deliver holistic and appropriate architectural environments.

Chapter 10

Sustainable Cities With Gamification: How Gamification Can Help Improve Citizen Health and Reduce Carbon Footprint

Vinod Bijlani

This chapter talks about multi-dimensional sustainability by emphasizing the importance of people-participation through behavioral change and persuasive design via gamification technology to bring about a change for good. It describes the criticality of a sustainability performance information platform that brings together all the aspects of a sustainable cities, social, economic, and environmental qualities through intelligent management and operations. This chapter is an attempt for a framework that will lead to greater collaborative efforts towards more intelligent, sustainable cities with improved citizen health.

Chapter 11

The Application of Serviqual Tool to Improve Clients' Satisfaction in a Health Facility: Service Quality in a Health Center

Noluthando Matsiliza, Skhumbuzo Gcabashe

The use of SERVQUAL as a tool to measure service quality in healthcare facility is a giant step towards effectiveness and efficiency in health management and in public affairs. The purpose of this chapter is to assess the extent to which service standards in a health facility like Rietvlei Hospital is applied to improve service provision and the quality of lives of the customers. Although government adopted health policies in South Africa, there are still gaps in quality of services rendered by public healthcare institutions. The implementation of healthcare policies can demonstrate that they are fragmented. The key dimensions of service quality were investigated at Rietvlei and SERVQUAL was used as a tool to measure the effectiveness of service quality using a mixed methodology. Data was drawn from a probabilistic sample using mainly questionnaires and interviews.

Chapter 12

The Extent of New Technologies in Urban Environments: Virtual Reality, Lighting, and Accessibility

Daniel Arranz-Paraíso, Sandra Arranz-Paraíso

The United Nations estimated in 2018 that 68% of the population would live in urban areas in 2050. At the time of the estimate, the percentage was 55%, which would mean an increase of 13% in 32 years. Furthermore, according to their calculations, there will be 43 megacities with more than 10 million citizens by 2030. To ensure that the development of city dwellers takes place in the best possible conditions, the United Nations is committed to a sustainable urban design that guarantees the quality of life of city dwellers. The use of new technologies comes into play in the design of the urban environment to guarantee access to decent housing, employment, the inclusion of people with disabilities, transportation, energy systems, lighting, and other types of infrastructure, as well as essential services such as health, culture, and education. Considering all these challenges and their complexity of resolution, modern architecture must be constituted, planned, and made up of multidisciplinary groups that embrace the interrelationships between human beings and the environment as a whole.

Chapter 13

The Urban Context as a Support for Energy Efficiency: Mild Climate Cities

Jesica Fernandez-Agüera, Samuel Domínguez-Amarillo, Miguel Ángel Campano, Pedro Bustamante

This chapter focuses on the impact that urban development has had on mid-climate cities, with high consumption of natural resources, significant waste production and environmental impact, and encroachment on productive or wild territories. In these cities, buildings are dependent on considerable energy consumption to achieve internal comfort and habitability. Considering cities as urban ecosystems allows us to study them in a way that allows us to propose new strategies to improve the efficiency of urban systems, reducing their impact on the habitability of buildings and the city itself, as well as reducing their ecological footprint. In this chapter, we will discuss aspects of the urban climate that affect the well-being of citizens inside and outside buildings, such as natural lighting, sunlight, natural ventilation, and wind, and how planning can improve them.

Chapter 14

The Waste of Today's Architecture Will Become the Materials for the Architecture of the Future

Anya Pulido Cavada

Today, 55% of the world's population lives in large cities or dense urban areas, large concrete jungles whose constructions are responsible for between five and ten percent of the world's carbon dioxide. It is estimated that by 2050 this proportion will grow to 68%. Is the society of this decade prepared to deal with this congestion? And society 30 years from now? Inequality, waste generation, consumption, and resource depletion in front of the headline that has been sold in recent years: 'Smart cities, zero emissions and technologies that surpass science fiction'. 'The residues of today's architecture will be the materials of the architecture of the future' This headline makes us reflect on whether we are really thinking, not only about the reuse of materials and the design of mobile structures, but also about the great cost of returning to the environment that have a large part of the materials used in the architecture of the 21st century.

Chapter 15

Urban Health as a New Vector to Characterise Vulnerable Neighbourhoods: Zaramaga Neighbourhood in Vitoria-Gasteiz (Spain)

Emilia Román López, Ester Higueras García, Rafael Córdoba Hernández, Elisa Pozo Menéndez

For decades, public administrations have been working on rigorous analysis to identify and delimit vulnerable neighbourhoods, in order to prioritize their regeneration and rehabilitation actions. The progress and improvements have been significant, mainly in Euskadi (Spain), thanks to an alignment of economic investment with an exhaustive knowledge based on the articulation of indicators that integrate social, economic, environmental and urban data into a digital open access platform (Geo Euskadi). However, despite all these plans and actions, most vulnerable neighbourhoods continue having these challenges.

This situation has made the Government of Euskadi contract a pilot plan with the aim of establishing a new methodology to characterise vulnerable residential areas. The new methodology has focused on urban health and well-being, combining quantitative and qualitative data and the analyses for this goal are presented in this chapter.

In this book, we look for a range of innovative research and evidence-based policy ideas that demonstrate the importance of health, livability and human behavior in urban environments and in urban and environmental policies to guarantee health and well-being.

Roberto Alonso González-Lezcano
Universidad CEU San Pablo, Spain

Chapter 1
Anthropological Ecology and Ecological Anthropology as a Framework for the Analysis of Socio-Ecological Sustainable Development

José G. Vargas-Hernandez
Instituto Tecnológico Mario Molina, Mexico

María Fernanda Higuera-Cota
https://orcid.org/0000-0001-8285-1076
Autonomous University of Sinaloa, Mexico

Omar C. Vargas-González
https://orcid.org/0000-0002-6089-956X
Tecnológico Nacional de México, Ciudad Guzmán, Mexico

ABSTRACT

This study is aimed to analyze the anthropological ecology and the ecological anthropology as a framework approach for the analysis of socio-ecological sustainable development. It departs from the assumption that sustainable development requires a socio-ecological approach sustained by anthropology and ecology. The method used is the analytical reflection based on the conceptual, theoretical, and empirical literature review. The study concludes that anthropology and ecology combine elements to sustain the anthropological ecology and ecological anthropology approaches to develop the framework for the analysis of a socio-ecological sustainable development.

DOI: 10.4018/978-1-6684-6924-8.ch001

INTRODUCTION

Ecology is adopted by various disciplines, geography, economics, psychology, behavioral ecology, sociology, anthropology, anthropological ecology, cultural ecology, urban ecology, political ecology, urban political ecology, urban planning and design, ecological planning and design, landscape architecture (Lyle, 1985; McHarg, 1969; Ndubisi, 2002, Ndubisi, 2014; Palazzo, 1997; Steiner, 2001, Steiner, 1991, Steiner, 2016; Thompson & Steiner, 1997; Van der Ryn & Cowan 2007). The concept of human ecology evolved to embrace disciplines, such as economics, geography, land use, psychology, sociology, socioecology, socio-technology, sociobiology, anthropology, cultural ecology, anthropological ecology, etc. (Petterson, Kensek & Noble, 2017). This is due to the growing need to study the interaction between human beings and their environment with the aim of making this relationship sustainable.

In the same line of study of the relationships between the human being and its environment is anthropological ecology, which seeks to study the wide range of human responses to environmental problems. In turn, it has theoretical and practical implications on organizational sustainability through the integration of social and environmental dimensions. Sociology and anthropology are integrated into the organizational management aimed at co-evolution sustainability. The ecology of sustainability is a resource available to manage environmental changes in areas such as market forces, technology, geographical locations, natural resources, etc. Anthropology as well as psychology, medicine and social sciences have been interested in the study of diet in health and environmental effects of ecological adaptations (Montgomery, Bennett, & Scudder, 1973; Netting, 1974).

The engagements of urban political ecology with the public health crisis of Covid-19 led to important anthropological and biological insights. This is because through urban political ecology it is possible to explore the interactions between social, political, economic and natural factors both in the production and reproduction of urban environments. As a result of the health crisis, it was possible to become aware not only of its effects on health, economy, and social development, but also the impact of human beings on earth, where industrialization, massive deforestation, extensive use of pesticides in the Agriculture, consumerism, the indiscriminate use of plastics, among other practices, are present and deepen the environmental disorders linked to climate change, which originate from human action.

Focus on climate change brings vulnerabilities with unsustainable development practices with impacts through material changes in socio-ecosystems driven by climate processes (Barnett & Adger, 2003). Anthropological and ethnographic ecology are used in policy making in climate change, considered a biophysical phenomenon. The ethnographic analysis of the human-centered efforts is directed towards a sustainable environment and ecological and relations. Comparative analysis of ecological anthropology uses cross-cultural datasets in ecological dynamics influencing human population size, land ownership, environmental impact, social behavior, social inequality, etc. (Bliege Bird & Codding, 2022).

Anthropological ecology framework of cultural ecology is used for analytical and theoretical approach of organizational phenomena (Weick, 1969). Biocultural perspectives in anthropology aim to analyze the deterministic bases of the economic, social, environmental, cultural, and ecological factors influencing human biology and wellbeing (McElroy, 1990; Elith, 2006; Leonard, 2020; Alland, 1966). Biocultural perspectives are necessary when analyzing organizational phenomena, since the organizational phenomenon is framed within a represented complexity, where the context is understood as a whole, in which inside, the individual, the Society, the State, shareholder, environment, are interrelated and interact in different ways. Therefore, conservation actions in a biocultural approach that sustain the biophysical and sociocultural components of dynamic and interdependent socio ecological systems are necessary.

Cultural studies refer to nature-culture more than ecocultures nurturing the linkages between the ecological and social environments in biocultural diversity, different concept of bio culture in biocultural studies (Daryl Slack, 2008; Giblett, 2012; Böhm, Bharucha & Pretty, (Eds.) 2015; Simberloff, 2018; Davis & Morris, 2007; Ehlers, & Krupar, (Eds.); Krupar & Ehlers, 2020). Biocultural diversity is all biological, environmental, cultural, and linguistic manifestations interrelated to life diversity adapted to a complex socio-ecological system. Biocultural perspectives in anthropology aim to analyze the deterministic bases of the economic, social, environmental, cultural, and ecological factors influencing human biology and wellbeing (McElroy, 1990; Elith, 2006; Leonard, 2020; Alland, 1966).

Biocultural studies in ecological anthropology are a term used in biocultural diversity to explain co-evolving socio-ecological systems and implications with cultural dimensions (Mercon, et al., 2019). The term biocultural has overlapping descriptions used in biocultural diversity in the context of its usage being different from biocultural studies within anthropology. Biocultural studies in anthropology are a term used in biocultural diversity to explain co-evolving socio-ecological systems and implications with cultural dimensions.

Socio-ecological systems focus on international policy and planning of sustainable economic development to contribute to human wellbeing and health (European Commission, 2017; Food and Agriculture Organisation, 2017; United Nations Environment Program, 2012; United Nations General Assembly, 2017). The research design of biocultural studies includes human biology, medical ecology, and social, cultural, and behavioral variables (McElroy, 1990). Biocultural diversity is all biological, environmental, cultural, and linguistic manifestations interrelated to life diversity adapted to a complex socio-ecological system.

Biocultural studies within biological anthropology assumes humans as biological, social, and cultural beings (Elith, 2006) with connecting synergies to ecological and medical anthropology and political economy (Fletcher & Fortin, 2018; Fourcade, Engler, Rödder, & Secondi, 2014), evolutionary theory, political economic analysis and biocultural studies in anthropology (McElroy, 1990; Wiley & Cullin, 2016; Hoke & Schell, 2020; Hoke & Schell, 2020; Willermet, 2016; Farahmand, Nahrevanian, Shirazi, Naeimi, Farzanehnejad, 2011; Ghatee, Taylor & Karamian, 2020). Indigenous peoples have been unwilling subjects regarding science in anthropological, ecological and medical studies because they have been used in resource extraction (Schnarch, 2004).

Evolutionary anthropology is related to the abundance of resources, structure and distribution that have implications on the socio-ecological adaptive conditions leading to variability of resources on subsistence economies mediated by the interpersonal human violence (McCool, et al., 2022). Socio-ecological sources and methods of management policies to assess species recovery, restoration and conservation towards sustainable socio-ecological systems in operating social space (Raworth, 2012).

Development of new sustainable economic activities is an eco-restructuring process. These activities seek to increase social well-being by promoting responsible consumption through economic practices that are respectful of the environment and committed to society. It is in eco culturalism where the cultural and ecological dimensions are linked, such as biocultural diversity (Cajee, 2014). Issues such as economic development and social development are relevant for the exploitation of sustainable tourism and the regulation of territorial and urban development. Understanding sustainable tourism as the vehicle for regional and local socioeconomic development (Zan, Lusiani, 2011).

Previous research proceeds separately and must be integrated under sustainable development. Public welfare has been linked with private profits and was formulated on the assumptions of "trickle down" theory of the economics sustainability growth and development. Research and development of science and technology innovation is a fundamental factor in creating economic growth, social value, and environmentally sustainable development

After this introduction to the study, the analysis continues delimiting the interrelationships between anthropological ecology and ecological anthropology as a conceptual, theoretical, and empirical framework leading to continuing with socio-ecological sustainable development. Finally, some conclusions are given

ANTHROPOLOGICAL ECOLOGY AND ECOLOGICAL ANTHROPOLOGY

Anthropological wisdom considers humanity as an element of existence distinguishing from ecological wisdom that advocates an interdisciplinary approach to sustainable lifestyles development referring to the willingness of an embedded place in an ecosystem deciding the behavior in relation to the quality of life (Weston, 2009). Organizational sociology and ecological anthropology are at the forefront of ecology and natural resources management to integrate organizational sustainability development and conservation. The multidisciplinary approach combines the perspectives of organizational sociology and ecological anthropology in the integration of sustainability in organizational ecology.

Ecological anthropology is the foundation for sustainable development programs linking economic growth with sustainable community development. Ecological anthropology takes for granted these assumptions and categories to subject the analytical concept and current anthropological thinking and analyses of culture in organizations, providing a historical perspective of the development of organizational anthropology studies and the analytical methods used in research.

Organizations involved in local communities practice the anthropological perspective of sustainability and ownership, sponsoring public culture, and public recreational events, etc., always involved in local sustainability and social development programs. (Esty and Winston, 2006). The socio-ecological crisis of the communities supposes multiple challenges that go from the environment to the reproduction of patterns of social inequality, a situation that leads to biocultural crises. Ecocultural communities prioritize ethical principles to nurture ecological and sociological and economic well being, considering humans in nature to sustain human and social capital (Böhm, Bharucha, Pretty (Eds.) 2015; Yongming, 2010).

A critique consistent with the current ecological crisis argues that the sustainable macromarketing entails the comprehensive consumption fostering corporate profit maximization in the market and a take-making waste ecology reliant un unsustainable demand of raw natural resources and energy (Borland & Lindgreen 2013; Kilbourne et al., 1997; Prothero et al., 2011; Slater & Tonkiss, 2001; O'Neil et al., 2018; Stiglitz, 2015; Temesgen et al., 2021; Wallace-Wells, 2019). In other words, the extractivist model is questioned, as well as its cultural patterns of consumption and entertainment. It is believed that both agents, articulations and States could be emissaries of change as long as their efforts are aimed at reducing poverty and guaranteeing quality development for present and future generations without compromising the planet's resources. Socio-ecological issues is the starting point of the sustainable marketing process and not as a set of constraints and externalities (Belz & Peattie, 2010)

The macro relational perspective treats socio ecological issues as the marketing mix process focusing on the transformational potential of institutional change for sustainable production, distribution, consumption and reproduction free of externalities (Belz & Peattie, 2010; Kemper & Ballantine, 2019).

Ecological anthropology assumes that sustainable accounting and reporting addresses natural resources management and conservation consistent with local cultures aimed to promote sustainable development. Resource management of communities are challenged to measure the socio-ecosystem changes with the acknowledgement of archaeological and anthropological data to identify changes of socio-ecological observations beyond the time scales (Pauly, 1995; Dayton and others 1998). Ecological anthropology and organizational disciplines benefit from sustainable accounting reporting (Kottack, 1999; Stone, 2003). Ecological and sustainable accounting reporting analysis incorporated into strategic planning and control aimed to address environmental factors and to manage and mitigate investments associated with financial risks.

Sustainability accounting focusing on the market includes process improvements, planning and control decisions, organizational growth and development, management and accounting costs in sustainable development, performance measures, etc. Ecological anthropology approach supports the economic and technological sustainability, the development dimensions of market and social components to protect natural resources and the environment. Long term sustainability interests require calculations for investments, production, and preservation of ecological and natural resources (Hopwood, 2009).

Ecocultures in cultural, environmental communication and psychology link ecology and culture and advocating sociocultural identity inseparable of ecology and recognizing local knowledge and memories in a dynamic lynk between the landscapes and ecocultural identities that promote resilience (Pretty, 2011; Berry, 2004; Nsamenang, 2015; Chen, et al. 2012; Daryl Slack, 2008; Milstein & Castro-Sotomayor, 2020; Hoffmann, 2020; Dahake, 2020; Zedler, & Stevens, 2018).

The eco-cultural perspective advocates sociocultural identity inseparable from ecology based on local memories and knowledge linked to landscapes and human culture shaping ecocultural identities and promoting resilience (Daryl Slack, 2008). Younger generations from villages and indigenous communities go away for opportunities of study and employment losing their best people. Migration can be explained by multiple issues, but the most recurrent point to issues of security, poverty, human rights violations, and climate change. Among the main consequences of migration is the loss of population, a situation that can reduce the productive potential of the communities of origin by generating a shortage of labor in certain sectors or specific industries and therefore tends to hinder economic growth. This issue is related to the conceptual framework in terms of cultural ecology and anthropology (Scudder & Colson, 1982; Scudder, 1973; Mongomery, Bennett, & Scudder, 1973).

Organizational ecological anthropology enhances sustainability and environmental resources management linked to production, service, quality, and managerial systems and promotes organizational learning on environmental and natural resources conservation (Cohen-Rosenthal, 2000; Ehrenfeld, 2000). The organizational abilities to respond to competitive environmental changes are dependent on the availability of ecological resources. Alignment of organizational ecological resources based on knowledge and learning systems development is related to sustainable and environmental management, resources conservation integrated into the organizational practices and activities aimed to improve operational performance.

Ecological anthropology addresses social and cultural forces that shape sustainability development. The ecological anthropological perspective on sustainability implies the joint ownership of resources claimed by stakeholders, performers, and community.

The application of social science approaches, sociology, and anthropology in organizational anthropological ecology. The anthropological ecology perspective of technology tends to solve specific problems in socio-ecological and organizational environments. Culture and ecology are concepts in organizational communication theory, and organizational anthropology theory and analysis, management sciences, and anthropological ecology (Everett, 1985).

Theoretical approaches, sustainable practices and belief systems of ecological populations lead to the generation of sustainability models with implicit ethics of the natural environmental care and particular ways of living. Sustainability accounting reporting systems are part of the ecological population systems that increase competition and survival to use as strategic resources for organizational performance measures associated with growth, survival, and death. Ecology and ethnoecology study the relationships between organisms and the physical, biological, and social factors they come into contact with, based on a political ecology principle that the contemporary human society and natural environment are not under control of exploitation and deterioration processes (Toledo, 1997).

Development of sustainable relationships with the natural environment focuses on sustainability models leading to some approaches in interdependence with human beings in their communities. The term Political ecology was used by Eric Wolf (1972), an anthropologist who described and analyzed the interactive relationship between human environment, territory, and space without an explicit connection to biological sciences.

The existing models of sustainability based on ethnoecology are already threatening to maintain the long-term sustainability of natural environments as the livelihoods of communities (Toledo, 1997). The ethno-ecology sustainable development at the community requires the natural and cultural endowments of the traditional ecological knowledge. The ecodevelopment has the objective defined as the strategy to produce and apply knowledge and techniques for the sustainable management of ecosystems and their struggles in communities for their social wealth and appropriation of natural resources (Leff, 1995).

The ethno-ecological knowledge kept by indigenous communities of people and increasingly used for natural history and anthropological studies (Heyd, 1995; Gragson & Blount, 1999). Ethno-ecology makes relevant the kind of knowledge in which humanity and their natural environments are integrated in sustainability. Many ecological populations are at the crossroads between the unsustainable and the traditional sustainable environments which resist change forces of sustainable development.

The ecosystem models the scientific and conventional logical habits among the ecological relations. The social ecological model is proposed by Golden & JoEarp, (2012), McLeroy et al., (1988), Stokols, (1992) and Stokols, (1996). Application of Eco semiotics considers humans and other species to co-constitute ecological phenomena (Maran & Kull 2014). Local technoscientific ecological models of the damage-centered environment with individual suffering related to the empirical ecological relations of human-environments (Mc-Clintock, 2014). The objective model of local ecology must make visible the spiritual connections to place, land, and the environment to generate the meaning. Thus, a comprehensive, systematic and naturalistic vision of development is generated, understood as a complex process, which responds to the influence of multiple factors closely related to the ecological environment.

Technoscientific models of relationality, such as radioecology, enable us to visualize the cross-boundary movements. An ecological relationality framework brings relational arrangements by interrelated chance, supernatural force, and extra scientific logic, besides through blood, marriage, and fictive kinship (Hashimoto, 2013; Jensen et al. 2016; Goldfarb, 2016). The relational model proposed by Nozawa (2015) is different from the decontamination technoscientific policy and radioecology across the space and time linkages between humans, nonhumans, and the environment (Creager, 2013).

The radioecological framework isolates humans from contaminants forcing locals to coproduce nuclear waste. The radioecological across the multiple human relations to local accounts of connectivity. Locals consider that radioecology offers more than limited human relations and delimits an Eco semiotic or ineffable interrelated of living, decaying, and dying things.

The anthropocentric delimitation of human-environment rationality leads to socio ecological policy. The anthropocentric assumption about human separability from the environment to justify harming lives, values, historicity, relationships, things, and futurity (Morimoto, 2022) is complemented by a more functionalist approach to local forager culture guided by ecological anthropological principles and genetic determinism is adaptive to some animals, such as the elephants Rappaport, 2000; Reich, 2018). A functionalist approach to local forager culture guided by ecological anthropological principles and genetic determinism is adaptive to the elephants Rappaport, 2000; Reich, 2018).

Wild boars are emblematic of the ecological upheaval (Walker, 2005) that residents experience in finding pre-disaster residence habituated by animals bided by anthropocentric division between wilderness and home (Cram, 2016). The dominance of biomedical and ecological orientation against the anthropocentric narratives illuminates the multiscale semiotic decontamination efforts.

The efforts of the state to remove and contain contaminants transform local ecology through decontamination presupposing the residents connected to the land, ancestors, nonhumans, and the environment. State and technoscientific decontamination rely on a radioecological model focusing on the environment to do entanglements of humans and contaminants (Masco, 2006).

Radioecology uses specific radioisotopes to investigate tracing and mapping connections of radiological contaminants and their transboundary movements between the earth and the atmosphere (Odum, 1959). The resultant production of accumulative nuclear waste brings ecology to collective recovery. Nuclearism is the ecological and technopolitical distribution of nuclear elements across time, space, human and non-human (Hecht, 2012).

Appearance and disappearance of radioisotopes and ecological diagrams among humans, nonhumans and abiotic factors leading to constitute models of ecological relationship in the post fallout environment. Liberation ecology is based on the idea that the time comes for the liberation of humanity and the natural environment (Marcuse, 1972; Gómez Hinojosa, 1990). Liberation ecology movements are more concerned for the environmental integrity for livelihood, entitlements, and social justice (Peet & Watts, 1996).

Traditional technology is part of the organizational space in relationship with organizational anthropology perspective in the articulation with modern technology in organizational productive developments for example, in rural organizations and business. The movements reveal the limits of the state to the post fallout ecology. Theoretical approach to fallout links human behaviors and actions, technological capabilities, atmospheres, environments, and ecologies in a new formation of contamination (Masco, 2015). The state`s policy approach to ecological redress post fallout impacts needs a local framework of relationality.

Achieving radiation safety implementing a strategy of decontamination produces ecological harm rendering wild boars, local food chains and land complicit in production of nuclear waste. The decontamination policies enable the gradual return of evacuees across the land with the opportunistic incursions of animals in asymmetrical redistribution of contaminants in the local ecology. Wild boars unconstrained move contaminants across the evacuation zones frustrating attempts at containment (Morimoto, 2022). Anthroponotic diseases are caused by global warming and changes in anthropological ecology (Desjeux, 2001) caused by the causative agent "L" tropica.

Scientific problematization of the post fallout environment and state usage of an objective and factual model of local ecology, ruptures, and redress. Post fallout ecology tends to threaten the local model of relationality among animate and inanimate things, animals and plants connected to the environment (Goldfarb, 2016; Nozawa, 2015). The ecological fallout in a planetary scope is the process of regional contamination manifested in local struggles with ecological upheaval. The ethnography of fallout ecology aims to localize the ecological relationality of the radiation-centered model framed by co-occurring scientific theorization of Eco semiotics and Eco semiotic concepts and dynamic representations of the environment Eco semiotics by various local actors and residents (Nöth, 1998; Kull, 1998; Maran, 2018; Maran & Kull, 2014).

Social ecology, natural ecosystems, cultural and anthropological ecology are relevant subjects to approach sustainable organizational, management and network ecology issues. Social ecology incorporates the biological orientation of human and anthropology ecologies to integrate the human agency socially embedded with natural environmental contexts. Social ecology embodies certain social movements with practical consequences for human wellbeing in natural sustainability movements such as the rescue of cultural diversity, relationships of human beings inserted in the environment and the social dimension of environmental problems.

SOCIO-ECOLOGICAL SUSTAINABLE DEVELOPMENT

In 1987, the Brundtland Report introduced the term sustainable development enabling humanity to continue the economic growth and expansion ensuring ecological viability in the commitment to growth in which sustainability is to degrowth (Hickel, 2020; Paulson, 2020). The Brundtland commission proposed Our Common Future (United Nations, 1987) concerned with a balance between ecological sustainability, global justice, and growth to propose the concept of sustainable development. The concept of sustainable development has been established in the United Nations report to reconcile this concept with economic growth.

According to the report, sustainable development meets the needs of the present without compromising the ability of future generations to meet their own needs based on alliance between present and future generations. (United Nations, 1987; The World Commission on Environment and Development, 1987; Mao & Robinson, 2019). In other words sustainable development is the process to preserve, conserve and protect the planet's natural resources for the benefit of the benefit of current and future generations.

The sustainable development notion elaborated in sustainable development goals is a global vision of anthropology presupposing economic growth and cultural diversity. The concept of environment is essential to sustainable development. Later formulation of ecological sustainability leads to the sustainable development goals with an emphasis on global inequality but ignores cultural diversity. The 17 sustainable development goals presented by the United Nations in 2015 guide the efforts of socio ecological challenges facing climate action, sustainable agriculture, sustainable industrialization, resilient and sustainable cities, sustainable energy, etc. It has been argued that fulfillment of the 17 sustainable development goals.

The sustainability concept is divested on connection to the growth and development defined as the ability of the system to reproduce the conditions of existence as a societal challenge for humanity.

The concept of sustainable development is concerned with ecologically sustainable practices which are relevant to the study of societies framed by anthropology (Hendry, 2014). Sustainable development focuses on the continued generation of goods and services for their consumption by human beings, while sustainability is the condition for human and non-human natural beings, for a sustainable community. Community sustainable development brings about sustainability. The new sustainable development focuses on ecological solutions in natural, anthropological, social, cultural senses considered preservation values from both sustainability development and research investments (Zan & Lusiani, 2011).

Organizational and anthropological ecological practices in cultural adaptations, competition and strategy are the foundations for socio-ecological sustainable development. Anthropological and sociological ecologies provide the theoretical framework for the ecology of sustainability integration in accounting reporting (Hopwood, 2009, 2010) in specific conceptual areas such as the financial accounting, managerial accounting, and auditing.

Sustainability development includes corporate financial and accounting reporting as a differentiated competitive strategy among organizations. Sustainability reporting is a recent development in financial and accounting reporting. Sustainability accounting reporting integrates economic, social and environmental development for community growth. Setting boards include guidelines for the conduct and development of sustainability reports assuring audit services co-evolving to secure legitimacy.

Socio-ecological sustainable development and environmental management are components based on ecological anthropology to establish anthropological, ecological, and organizational relationships. Social soundness analysis is related to socio-ecological sustainable development, culturally appropriate, ecologically sensitive, and self-regenerating change (Kottack, 1999). Creation of sustainable development implies a sustainable society with human beings and natural environments together, which are already suffering a severe crisis due to the failure to recognize human nature as the one to care (Boff, 1999).

The acts of socio ecological sustainable development are intentional, planned and designed to sustain ecological value considering the approaches and processes to the application of concepts and practices in sustainability and resilience. Sustainable development practices have implications in complex organizations. Sustainable development is not always tied to bureaucracy as the organizational form of modernity related to the human agency modes (du Gay, 1994, 2000; Kallinikos, 2001). There is a remarkable growth in the coverage of sustainable development practices in complex greening organizations. Complex societies are recent developments in human history with the tendency to fall to some chaos leaving the alternative the return to normal human condition of lower complexity and sustainable societies (Tainter, 2008).

Stable local communities and societies favored by anthropology with cosmologies and ethics dictating sustainable practices but in absence of indigenous concepts of societal development and change (Lévi-Strauss, 1962). Organizations involved in local communities practice the anthropological perspective of sustainability and ownership, sponsoring public culture, and public recreational events, etc., always involved in local sustainability and social development programs (Esty and Winston, 2006). Nongovernmental organizations (NGOs) including the social sector organizations address local needs in sustainable development.

Ecology promotes development sustainability management embedded in the natural selection of the Darwinian theory, individual actions based on economic choices that make stability and maintenance of social systems. Environmental and social data in development sustainability is related to co-existing ecological and natural resources management in geographical systems to ensure sustainable relationships and governance of individuals, groups and community behaviors, values, mores, and cultures of sustainability.

Cultural matrices are for sustainability, guiding everyday life, integrating the natural environment and human beings in feasible models for sustainable community development and appropriate ethics of care (Plumwood, 1995). Sustainable cultural matrices integrate nature and human beings in conditions of sustainable communities to guide the way of life in individuals which may point towards feasible models of sustainable development based on appropriate environmental ethics of care.

Historical, anthropological, and ethnographic sources support the analysis of the scale and the effects of human relationships in socio-ecology systems (Armstrong et al., 2017; Jackson et al., 2001; Kittinger et al., 2015; Pandolfi et al., 2003; Roberts, 2007; Tushingham et al., 2020). Historical ecology fosters sustainable relationships and interactions between human communities with ecosystems to sustain the environment aiming to human wellbeing focused on international policy to improve socio-ecosystems and develop sustainable economies (European Commission, 2017; Food and Agriculture Organization, 2017; United Nations Environment Program, 2012; United Nations General Assembly, 2017).

The historical ecology sources of analysis used in human interactions and integrations with the socio-ecosystems dynamics to foster sustainable environmental relationships. Historical, ecological and environmental history analyzes the forms and functions of socio-ecosystems and socio-ecological changes aimed to foster the interactions of environmental sustainability and the good practices of sustainable communities (Caswell et al., 2020; McClenachan & Kittinger, 2013). Environmental sustainability is a difficult social problem to find solutions that conflict with market capitalism producing ecological precarity.

The resource-based ecological view of an organization has heterogeneity in ecological physical, economic, financial, and natural resources. The resource-based ecological approaches of sociology and anthropology to integrate the co-evolution of organizational sustainability influencing corporate financial and accounting reporting. The resource-ecological view of organizational approaches to the development of sustainability financial and accounting reporting as the strategic management process. Internal legitimacy needs to be enforced and audited by external oversight to control the reporting quality of auditing including the organizational sustainability programs integrated into the strategic planning processes.

Urban political ecology is engaged in ecological imaginaries beyond the eco-criticism as the cultural articulation and counterpart to Anthropocene of alternative environmental sceneries (Gabriel, 2014; Millington, 2013). Urban political ecology contributes to critical analysis implicit on the Anthropocene and historical conception of urban space framework. The imaginary place related to the politics of the Anthropocene contribution by urban political ecology (Braun, 2015) Ecological imaginary is in the context of urban environmental sustainability. Urban political ecology is a concept gaining intellectual reach in the resilience field of the adaptive Anthropocene of social sciences. The urban political ecology takes a lead from history to distinguish between different forms of agency of nature in relation to anthropogenic environmental disturbance.

Sustainability planning evolves into ecological and natural resources providing ecosystem endowments to operate in competitive environmental resources conservation. Integration of sustainability as a by-product of organizational ecological and management of natural environmental resources embedded in development and conservation aimed to balance the economic, social, environmental, and ecological objectives of societies, communities, individuals, and organizations.

Based on the land development sustainability approach, contributions of urban ecological planning and design, sustainable urbanism, natural and green urban areas for protection and low impact development, green infrastructure, brownfield redevelopment, etc. (Arendt, 1999; Barnett, 2009; Benedict & McMahon, 2006; Farr, 2008; Palazzo & Steiner, 2011; Wang et al., 2011). Ecological planning and design apply bioecology and human ecology theoretical and conceptual frameworks to ecological urban development.

Sustainable urban land use and development policies must carry various capacities rather than concentrate on economic growth (Pfaffenbichler, Emberger, Shepherd, 2010; Jim, 1999; Postel, 1994). Urban sustainable and development policies for decision making processes are concerned with city planning and land use management based on system thinking of the phenomena resulting from the unlimited developable land and city sprawl. The system thinking of urban sustainability and city development identifies characteristics of dynamic interactions among the system structures and elements (Pfaffenbichler, Emberger, Shepherd, 2010; Department of Statistics, the Ministry of the Interior, 2014). Unlimited developable land leads to the loss of city growth with positive and negative effects for sustainability and development.

Research is exploring ecology of urban design and development and ecological urbanism (Lehmann, 2010; Mostafavi & Doherty, 2010; Spirn, 2011; Hill, 2007; Palazzo & Steiner, 2011) that are not using sound ecological principles in their practice and implementation.

Sustainable development and environmental management as components based on ecological anthropology to establish anthropological, ecological, and organizational relationships. Socio-ecological sustainability is integrated with natural resources and environmental management forming the core foundation of ecological ethics. The sustainability embedded in ecological and environmental ethics concerns natural resources conservation and ethics of land use. Transformations of land uses must consider past and present contributions of generations to shape the development without compromising the future needs of generations. Organizational sustainability programs support economic development programs more compatible with cultural practices (Bozzoli, 2000; Stone, 2003).

Long term socio-ecological sustainability interests require calculations for investments, production, and preservation of ecological and natural resources (Hopwood, 2009). The economic value-added measures increase the development of profitable investments with more responsible environmental policies (Epstein & Young, 1999). Sustainability enhances the value of ownership and sharing organizational resources used to formulate and implement strategic plans for long-term sustainable development promoting green innovation and organizational performance.

Structuring and mobilizing mechanisms are necessary to achieve the objectives of technological innovation capacities development to benefit the society. Indirect stimuli forms support creation of environments for innovation and competitiveness in regional development supported by venture capital.

CONCLUSION

This study aimed to analyze anthropological ecology and ecological anthropology which are then used as the framework approach for the analysis of socio-ecological sustainable development, from the assumption that sustainable development requires a socio-ecological approach sustained by anthropology and ecology. The study concludes that anthropology and ecology are sciences that combine conceptual, theoretical, and empirical elements to develop the framework to sustain the anthropological ecology and ecological anthropology approaches leading to the analysis of a socio-ecological sustainable development.

Ecological anthropology addresses social and cultural forces that shape sustainability development. The co-evolution of ecological anthropological and organizational ecological perspectives of sustainable development framed by the resource-based approach for the integration of sustainability accounting reporting. The adaptive Anthropocene supports the radical ecology critique combining neo-Marxian analysis of environmental change and critical race study. The historical ecology leverages the opportunities to foster sustainable relationships leading to reconnecting socio-ecological systems with human communities related to achieve sustainable human interactions. By the development of new sustainable economic, social, and environmental activities, political ecology is a powerful tool in cultivating a socially just and sustainable future

The consumption theory is expanding leading to the development and economic anthropology behavior.

The threats of state-sponsored corporations to sustainable community development require taking control of the processes that arise. Long-term ecological, environmental, and sustainability concerns in shaping new and emerging market strategies among organizations. Making it necessary for both individuals and companies to take into account aspects such as diversity (biological, genetic, ecological, landscape, productive, etc.), self-sufficiency, integration (of productive practices, natural cycles, etc.), equity (of resources, participation, productive, etc), economic justice, among other key aspects when it comes to operating in any economic environment. Regarding the sustainability reports within the ecological framework, they are internal and external reports used by management and the necessary parties, necessary to have a broader picture of the current situation and the challenges that organizations face.

REFERENCES

Alland, A. (1966). Jr. Medical Anthropology and the Study of Biological and Cultural Adaptation. *American Anthropologist*, *68*, 40–51. doi:10.1525/aa.1966.68.1.02a00040

Arendt, R. (1999). *Growing greener: putting conservation into local plans and ordinances*. Island Press.

Armstrong, C. G., Shoemaker, A. C., McKechnie, I., Ekblom, A., Szabó, P., Lane, P. J., McAlvay, A. C., Boles, O. J., Walshaw, S., Petek, N., Gibbons, K. S., Quintana Morales, E., Anderson, E. N., Ibragimow, A., Podruczny, G., Vamosi, J. C., Marks-Block, T., LeCompte, J. K., Awâsis, S., & Crumley, C. L. (2017). Anthropological contributions to historical ecology: 50 questions, infinite prospects. *PLoS One*, *12*(2), e0171883. doi:10.1371/journal.pone.0171883 PMID:28235093

Barnett, J. (2009). The way we were, the way we are the theory and practice of designing cities since 1956. A. Krieger, W.S. Saunders (Eds.), *Urban design*, University of Minnesota Press (2009), pp. 101-110 NED—New edition Retrieved from: https://www.jstor.org/stable/10.5749/j.ctttspsh.9View Record in ScopusGoogle Scholar

Barnett, J., & Adger, W. N. (2003). Climate dangers and atoll countries. *Climatic Change*, *61*(3), 321–337. doi:10.1023/B:CLIM.0000004559.08755.88

Belz, F.-M., & Peattie, K. (2010). Sustainability marketing: An innovative conception of marketing. *Marketing Review St. Gallen*, *27*(5), 8–15. doi:10.100711621-010-0085-7

Benedict, M., & McMahon, E. T. (2006). *Green infrastructure: linking landscape and communities*. Island Press.

Berry, J. W. (2004). An Ecocultural Perspective on the Development of Competence. In R. Sternberg & E. Grigorenko (Eds.), *Culture and Competence: Contexts of Life Success* (pp. 3–22). American Psychological Association. doi:10.1037/10681-001

Bliege Bird, R., & Codding, B. F. (2022). Promise and peril of ecological and evolutionary modelling using cross-cultural datasets. *Nature Ecology & Evolution*, *6*(1), 6–8. doi:10.103841559-021-01579-w PMID:34697456

Boff, L. (1999). *Saber Cuidar: Ética do humano – compaixão pela terra*. Editora Vozes.

Borland, H., & Lindgreen, A. (2013). Sustainability, epistemology, ecocentric business, and marketing strategy: Ideology, reality, and vision. *Journal of Business Ethics*, *117*(September), 173–187. doi:10.100710551-012-1519-8

Bozzoli, M. E. (2000). A role for anthropology in sustainable development in Costa Rica. *Human Organization*, *59*(3), 275–279. doi:10.17730/humo.59.3.eu5h42p81wk26578

Braun, B. (2014). A new urban dispositive? Governing life in an age of climate change. *Environment and Planning. D, Society & Space*, *32*(1), 49–64. doi:10.1068/d4313

Cajee, L. (2014). Eco-Cultural Tourism: A Tool for Environmental, Cultural and Economic Sustainability (A Case Study of Darap Village, West Sikkim). *SHS Web Conf.*, 12, 01029. 10.1051hsconf/20141201029

Caswell, B., Klein, E. S., Alleway, H. K., Ball, J., Cardinale, M., Eero, M., & Thurstan, R. H. (2020). Something old, something new: 200 years of a blue growth agenda. *Fish and Fisheries*, *21*, 774–796. doi:10.1111/faf.12460

Chen, Y.-W., Milstein, T., Anguiano, C., Sandoval, J., & Knudsen, L. (2012). Challenges and Benefits of Community-Based Participatory Research for Environmental Justice: A Case of Collaboratively Examining Ecocultural Struggles. *Environ. Commun*, *6*(3), 403–421. doi:10.1080/17524032.2012.698291

Cohen-Rosenthal, E. (2000). A walk on the human side of industrial ecology. *The American Behavioral Scientist*, *44*(4), 245–264. doi:10.1177/00027642000044002007

Cram, S. (2016). Wild and Scenic Wasteland: Conservation Politics in the Nuclear Wilderness. *Environmental Humanities*, *7*(1), 89–105. doi:10.1215/22011919-3616344

Dahake, S. (2020). The making of fluid ecocultural identities in urban India. In T. Milstein & J. Castro-Sotomayor (Eds.), *Routledge Handbook of Ecocultural Identity* (pp. 333–350). Routledge. doi:10.4324/9781351068840-20

Daryl Slack, J. (2008). Resisting ecocultural studies. *Cultural Studies*, *2008*(22), 477–497. doi:10.1080/09502380802012575

Davis, L. J., & Morris, D. B. (2007). Biocultures Manifesto. *New Literary History*, *38*(3), 411–418. doi:10.1353/nlh.2007.0046

Dayton, P. K., Tenger, M. J., Edwards, P. B., & Riser, K. L. (1998). Sliding Baselines, Ghosts and Reduced Expectations in Kelp Forest Communities. *Ecological Applications*, *8*(2), 309–322. doi:10.1890/1051-0761(1998)008[0309:SBGARE]2.0.CO;2

Department of Statistics. (2014). *Statistical Yearbook of Interior*. DOS. http://sowf.moi.gov.tw/stat/year/list.htm

Desjeux, P. (2001) *Trans. of the Royal Society of Trop. Med. and Hygiene 95*(3) 239–43. NIH.

du Gay, P. (1994). Colossal immodesties and hopeful monsters. *Organization*, *1*(1), 125–148. doi:10.1177/135050849400100114 du Gay, P. (2000) In praise of bureaucracy: Weber, organization, ethics. London: Sage. doi:10.4135/9781446217580

(2015). Ecocultures: Towards sustainable ways of living. InBöhm, S., Bharucha, Z. P., & Pretty, J. (Eds.), *Ecocultures: Blueprints for Sustainable Communities* (pp. 3–26). Routledge.

Ehrenfeld, J. R. (2000). Industrial ecology: Paradigm shift or normal science? *The American Behavioral Scientist*, *44*(2), 229–244. doi:10.1177/00027642000044002006

Elith, J. (2006). *Ecography*, *292*, 129–151. doi:10.1111/j.2006.0906-7590.04596.x

Epstein, M. J., & Young, S. D. (1999). Greening' with EVA. *Management Accounting*, *80*(1), 45–49.

Esty, D. C., & Winston, A. S. (2006). *Green to Gold*. Yale University Press.

European Commission. (2017). *Report on the blue growth strategy towards more sustainable growth and jobs in the blue economy*. European Commission.

Everett, J. L. (1985). *Culture and ecology in the analysis of organizations*. [PhD Thesis, University of Colorado at Boulder].

Farr, D. (2008). *Sustainable urbanism—urban design with nature*. John Wiley & Sons.

Food and Agriculture Organization. (2017). *Food and agriculture organization blue growth initiative: Partnering with countries to achieve the sustainable development goals*. United Nations.

Gabriel, N. (2014). Urban political ecology: Environmental imaginary, governance, and the non-human. *Geography Compass*, *8*(1), 38–48. doi:10.1111/gec3.12110

Ghatee, M. A., Taylor, W. R., & Karamian, M. (2020). The Geographical Distribution of Cutaneous Leishmaniasis Causative Agents in Iran and Its Neighboring Countries, A Review. *Frontiers in Public Health*, *8*, 111–113. doi:10.3389/fpubh.2020.00011 PMID:32391301

Giblett, R. (2012). Nature is ordinary too: Raymond Williams as the founder of ecocultural studies. *Cultural Studies*, *26*(6), 922–933. doi:10.1080/09502386.2012.707221

Golden, S. D., & Earp, J. A. L. (2012). Social Ecological Approaches to Individuals and Their Contexts: Twenty Years of Health Education & Behavior Health Promotion Interventions. *Health Education & Behavior*, *39*(3), 364–372. doi:10.1177/1090198111418634 PMID:22267868

Goldfarb, K. E. (2016). 'Coming to Look Alike': Materializing Affinity in Japanese Foster and Adoptive Care. *Social Analysis*, *60*(2), 47–64. doi:10.3167a.2016.600204

Gómez Hinojosa, J. F. (1990). De la ecología a la ecofilía: Apuntes para una ecología liberadora'. *Pasos (El Sauzal)*, *30*(July–August).

Gragson, T. L., & Blount Ben, G. (Eds.). (1999). *Introduction Ethnoecology: Knowledge, Resources, and Rights*. University of Georgia.

Hashimoto, K. (2013). *En no Shakaigaku: Fukushi Shakaigaku no Shitenkara*. Harvest-sha.

Hendry, J. (2014). *Science and Sustainability: Learning from Indigenous Wisdom*. Palgrave Macmillan. doi:10.1057/9781137430069

Heyd, T. (1995). Indigenous knowledge, emancipation, and alienation. *Knowledge and Policy*, *8*(1), 63–73. doi:10.1007/BF02698557

Hickel, J. (2020). *Less is More: How Degrowth Will Save The World*. Windmill.

Hill, K. (2007). Urban ecological design and urban ecology: an assessment of the state of current knowledge and a suggested research agenda. V. Novotny, P. Brown (Eds.), Cities of the future: towards integrated sustainable water and landscape management. IWA Publishing, London (2007), pp. 251-266

Hoffmann, J. A. (2020). Memory, Waterways, and Ecocultural Identity. In T. Milstein & J. Castro-Sotomayor (Eds.), *The Routledge Handbook of Ecocultural Identity*. Routledge. doi:10.4324/9781351068840-9

Hoke, M. K., & Schell, L. M. (2020). Doing biocultural anthropology: Continuity and change. *American Journal of Human Biology*, *2020*(32), e23471. PMID:32681558

Hoke, M. K., & Schell, L. M. (2020). Doing biocultural anthropology: Continuity and change. *American Journal of Human Biology*, *2020*(32), e23471. PMID:32681558

Hopwood, A. G. (2009). Accounting and the environment. *Accounting, Organizations and Society*, *34*(3-4), 433–439. doi:10.1016/j.aos.2009.03.002

Hopwood, A. G. (2010). In memoriam, Anthony G. Hopwood, 1944-2010. *Accounting, Organizations and Society*, *35*(4), 496–497. doi:10.1016/j.aos.2010.05.002

(2019). Introduction: Biocultures. InEhlers, N., & Krupar, S. (Eds.), *Deadly Biocultures: The Ethics of Life-Making*. The University of Minnesota Press.

Jackson, J. B. C., Kirby, M. X., Berger, W. H., Bjorndal, K. A., Botsford, L. W., Bourque, B. J., Bradbury, R. H., Cooke, R., Erlandson, J., Estes, J. A., Hughes, T. P., Kidwell, S., Lange, C. B., Lenihan, H. S., Pandolfi, J. M., Peterson, C. H., Steneck, R. S., Tegner, M. J., & Warner, R. R. (2001). Historical overfishing and the recent collapse of coastal ecosystems. *Science*, *293*(5530), 629–638. doi:10.1126cience.1059199 PMID:11474098

Jensen, C. B., & Miho, I. (2016). Attuning to the Webs of En: Ontography, Japanese Spirit Worlds, and the 'Tact' of Minakata Kumagusu. *HAU*, *6*(2), 149–172. doi:10.14318/hau6.2.012

Jim, C. Y. (1999). A planning strategy to augment the diversity and biomass of roadside trees in urban Hong Kong. *Landscape and Urban Planning*, *44*(1), 13–32. doi:10.1016/S0169-2046(98)00113-3

Kallinikos, J. (2001). 'bureaucracy: Exploring organization forms in the age of contingency. Paper presented at the 17th EGOS Colloquium, The Odyssey of Organizing, 5–7 July, Lyon. (Organization, special issue on Bureaucracy, 2003). 616. *Organization Studies*, *24*(4).

Kempera, J. A., & Ballantine, P. W. (2019). What do we mean by sustainability marketing? *Journal of Marketing Management*, *35*(3–4), 277–309. doi:10.1080/0267257X.2019.1573845

Kilbourne, W., McDonagh, P., & Prothero, A. (1997). Sustainable consumption and the quality of life: A macromarketing challenge to the dominant social paradigm. *Journal of Macromarketing*, *17*(1), 4–24. doi:10.1177/027614679701700103

Kittinger, J. N., McClenachan, L., Gedan, K. B., & Blight, L. K. (2015). *Marine historical ecology in conservation: Applying the past to manage for the future*. University of California Press.

Kottack, C. P. (1999). The new ecological anthropology. *American Anthropologist*, *101*(1), 23–35. doi:10.1525/aa.1999.101.1.23

Krupar, S., & Ehlers, N. (2020). Biocultures: A critical approach to mundane biomedical governance. *Culture, Theory & Critique*, *61*(4), 440–456. doi:10.1080/14735784.2020.1857810

Kull, K. (1998). Semiotic Ecology: Different Natures in the Semiosphere. *Sign Systems Studies*, *26*(1), 344–371. doi:10.12697/SSS.1998.26.15

Leff, E. (1995). *Green Production*. Guilford Press.

Lehmann, S. (2010). *The principles of green urbanism: transforming the city for sustainability*. Routledge.

Leonard, W. R. (2020). Re-examining Biocultural Approaches in Human Biology. *American Journal of Human Biology*, *32*(4), e23475. doi:10.1002/ajhb.23475 PMID:32885558

Lévi-Strauss, C. (1962). *La Pensée Sauvage*. Plon.

Lyle, J. T. (1985). *Design for human ecosystems: landscape, land use, and natural resources*. Van Nostrand.

Mao, Y., & Robinson, D. (2019). Three pillars of sustainability: In search of conceptual origins. *Sustainability Science*, *14*(3), 681–695. doi:10.100711625-018-0627-5

Maran, T. (2018). Two Decades of Ecosemiotics in Tartu. *Sign Systems Studies*, *46*(4), 630–639. doi:10.12697/SSS.2018.46.4.11

Maran, T., & Kull, K. (2014). Ecosemiotics: Main Principles and Current Developments. *Geografiska Annaler. Series B, Human Geography*, *96*(1), 41–50. doi:10.1111/geob.12035

Marcuse, H. (1972). *Counterrevolution and Revolt*. Boston Beacon Press.

Masco, J. (2006). *The Nuclear Borderlands: The Manhattan Project in Post–Cold War New Mexico*. Princeton University Press. doi:10.1515/9781400849680

McClenachan, L., & Kittinger, J. N. (2013). Multicentury trends and the sustainability of coral reef fisheries in Hawai'i and Florida. *Fish and Fisheries*, *14*(3), 239–255. doi:10.1111/j.1467-2979.2012.00465.x

McClintock, P. (2014, March). *Box office milestone: 'Frozen' becomes No. 1 animated film of all time*. Hollywood Reporter. https://www.hollywoodreporter.com/news/box-office-milestone-frozen-becomes-692156

McCool, W. C., Vernon, K. B., Yaworsky, P. M., & Codding, B. F. (2022). Subsistence strategy mediates ecological drivers of human violence. *PLoS One*, *17*(5), e0268257. doi:10.1371/journal.pone.0268257 PMID:35604917

McElroy, A. (1990). Biocultural Models in Studies of Human Health and Adaptation. *Medical Anthropology Quarterly*, *4*(3), 243–265. doi:10.1525/maq.1990.4.3.02a00010

McHarg, I. (1996). *Design with nature*. The Natural History Press.

McLeroy, K. R., Bibeau, D., Steckler, A., & Glanz, K. (1988, Winter). An ecological perspective on health promotion programs. *Review Health Educ Q*, *15*(4), 351–377. doi:10.1177/109019818801500401 PMID:3068205

Merçon, J., Vetter, S., Tengö, M., Cocks, M., Balvanera, P., Rosell, J. A., & Ayala-Orozco, B. (2019). From local landscapes to international policy: Contributions of the biocultural paradigm to global sustainability. *Global Sustainability*, *2*(e7), 1–11. doi:10.1017us.2019.4

Millington, N. (2013). Post-industrial imaginaries: Nature, representation and ruin in Detroit, Michigan. *International Journal of Urban and Regional Research*, *37*(1), 279–296. doi:10.1111/j.1468-2427.2012.01206.x

Milstein, T., & Castro-Sotomayor, J. (Eds.). (2020). *Routledge Handbook of Ecocultural Identity*. Routledge. doi:10.4324/9781351068840

Montgomery, E., Bennett, J. W., & Scudder, T. (1973). The impact of human activities on the physical and social environments: New directions in anthropological ecology. *Annual Review of Anthropology*, *2*(1), 27–61. doi:10.1146/annurev.an.02.100173.000331

Morimoto, R. (2022). A wild boar chase: Ecology of Harm and Half-Life Politics in Coastal Fukushima. *Cultural Anthropology*, *37*(1), 69–98. doi:10.14506/ca37.1.08

Mostafavi, M., & Doherty, G. (Eds.), *Ecological urbanism*. Lars Müller Publisher.

Ndubisi, F. (2002). *Ecological planning: a historical and comparative synthesis*. The Johns Hopkins University Press.

Ndubisi, F. (2014). *The ecological design and planning reader*. Island Press. doi:10.5822/978-1-61091-491-8

Netting, R. M. (1974). Agrarian ecology. *Annual Review of Anthropology*, *3*(1), 21–56. doi:10.1146/annurev.an.03.100174.000321

Nöth, W. (1998). Ecosemiotics. *Sign Systems Studies*, *26*(1), 332–343. doi:10.12697/SSS.1998.26.14

Nozawa, S. (2015). Phatic Traces: Sociality in Contemporary Japan. *Anthropological Quarterly*, *88*(2), 373–400. https://muse.jhu.edu/article/582266. doi:10.1353/anq.2015.0014

Nsamenang, A. B. (2015). Ecocultural Theories of Development. In J. Wright (Ed.), *International Encyclopedia of the Social & Behavioral Sciences* (Vol. 6, pp. 838–844). Elsevier. doi:10.1016/B978-0-08-097086-8.23205-4

O'Neil, D. (2018, September 16). The EU needs a stability and wellbeing pact, not more growth. *The Guardian*. https://www.theguardian.com/politics/2018/sep/16/the-eu-needs-a-stability-and-wellbeing-pact-not-more-growth

Odum, E. P. (1959). *Fundamentals of Ecology* (2nd ed.). W. B. Saunders.

Palazzo, D. (1997). Sulle spalle di giganti. (On the Shoulders of Giants) Franco Angeli, Milano.

Palazzo, D., & Steiner, F. R. (2011). *Urban ecological design—a process for regenerative places*. Island Press.

Pandolfi, J. M., Bradbury, R. H., Sala, E., Hughes, T. P., Bjorndal, K. A., Cooke, R. G., McArdle, D., McClenachan, L., Newman, M. J. H., Paredes, G., Warner, R. R., & Jackson, J. B. C. (2003). Global trajectories of the long-term decline of coral reef ecosystems. *Science*, *301*(5635), 955–958. doi:10.1126cience.1085706 PMID:12920296

Paulson, S., D'Alisa, G., Demaria, F., & Kallis, G. (2020). *The Case for Degrowth*. Polity.

Pauly, D. (1995). Anecdotes and the Shifting Baseline Syndrome of Fisheries. *Trends in Ecology & Evolution*, *10*(10), 430. doi:10.1016/S0169-5347(00)89171-5 PMID:21237093

Peet, R., & Watts, M. (1996) Liberation ecology: development, sustainability, and environment in an age of market triumphalism in: Richard Peet & Michael Watts (Eds) Liberation Ecologies: Environment, Development, Social Movements. Routledge.

Petterson, M., Kensek, K., & Noble, D. (2017). Supple Skins: Considering the Relevance, Scalability, and Design Strategies for Façade System Resilience. *Journal of Architectural Education*, *71*(1), 34–45. doi:10.1080/10464883.2017.1260919

Pfaffenbichler, P., Emberger, G., & Shepherd, S. A. (2010). System dynamics approach to land use transport interaction modelling: The strategic model MARS and its application. *System Dynamics Review*, *26*(3), 262–282. doi:10.1002dr.451

Plumwood, V. (1995). Nature, self and gender: feminism, environmental philosophy, and the critique of rationalism in: Christine Pierce & Donald VanDeVeer (Eds) People, Penguins and Plastic Trees. Belmond Wadsworth.

Postel, S. (1994). Carrying capacity: Earth's bottom line. In L. R. Brown, A. T. Durning, C. Flavin, H. F. French, N. Lenssen, M. D. Lowe, A. Misch, S. Postel, M. Renner, P. Weber, & ... (Eds.), *State of the World* (pp. 3–21). W.W. Norton.

Pretty, J. (2011). Interdisciplinary progress in approaches to address social-ecological and ecocultural *systems. Environmental Conservation*, *38*(2), 127–139. doi:10.1017/S0376892910000937

Prothero, A., Dobscha, S., Freund, J., Kilbourne, W. E., Luchs, M. G., Ozanne, L. K., & Thøgersen, J. (2011). Sustainable consumption: Opportunities for consumer research and public policy. *Journal of Public Policy & Marketing*, *30*(1), 31–38. doi:10.1509/jppm.30.1.31

Rappaport, R. A. (2000). *Pigs for the Ancestors: Ritual in the Ecology of a New Guinea People*. Waveland Press.

Raworth, K. (2012). A safe and just space for humanity: Can we live within the doughnut? Oxfam Policy and Practice. *Climate Change and Resilience*, *8*, 1–26.

Reich, D. (2018). *Who We Are and How We Got Here: Ancient DNA and the New Science of the Human Past*. Oxford University Press.

Roberts, C. M. (2007). *The unnatural history of the sea*. Island Press.

Schnarch, B. (2004). Ownership, control, access, and possession (OCAP) or self-determination applied to research: A critical analysis of contemporary First Nations research and some options for First Nations communities. *Journal of Aboriginal Health*, *1*, 80–97.

Scudder, T. (1973). The Human Ecology of Big Projects: River Basin Development and Resettlement. [Section 3 in Montgomery, Bennett, and Scudder (1973)] In B. J. Siegel, A. R. Beals, & S. A. Tyler (Eds.), *Annual Review of Anthropology*. Annual Reviews Inc.

Scudder, T., & Colson, E. (1982). From Welfare to Development: A Conceptual Framework for the Analysis of Dislocated People in Involuntary. In A. Hansen & A. Oliver-Smith (Eds.), *Migration and Resettlement: The Problems and Responses of Dislocated People* (pp. 267–287). Westview Press, Westview Special Study.

Simberloff, D. (2018). Nature, Culture, and Natureculture: The Role of Nonnative Species in Biocultures. In R. Rozzi, R. H. May Jr, F. S. Chapin III, F. Massardo, M. C. Gavin, I. J. Klaver, A. Pauchard, M. A. Nunez, & D. Simberloff (Eds.), *From Biocultural Homogenization to Biocultural Conservation* (pp. 207–218). Nature. doi:10.1007/978-3-319-99513-7_12

Slater, D., & Tonkiss, F. (2001). *Market society: Markets and modern social theory*. Polity Press.

Spirn, A. W. (2011). *Ecological urbanism: a framework for the design of resilient cities*. Anne Whistonspirn. https://annewhistonspirn.com/pdf/spirn_ecological_urbanism-2011.pdf

Steiner, F. R. (1991). *The living landscape: an ecological approach to landscape planning*. McGraw-Hill.

Steiner, F. R. (2001). *Human ecology: following nature's lead*. Island Press.

Steiner, F. R. (2016). *Human ecology: how nature and culture shape our world*. The Island Press.

Stiglitz, J. (2015). *Globalization and its discontents*. Penguin.

Stokols, D. (1992). Establishing and maintaining healthy environments: Toward a social ecology of health promotion. *The American Psychologist*, *47*(1), 6–22. doi:10.1037/0003-066X.47.1.6 PMID:1539925

Stokols, D. (1996). Translating social ecological theory into guidelines for community health promotion *American Journal of Health Promotion* Mar-Apr;10(4):282-98. doi:10.4278/0890-1171-10.4.282

Stone, M. (2003). Is sustainability for development anthropologists? *Human Organization*, *62*(2), 93–99. doi:10.17730/humo.62.2.9cfam6hd6e04yac8

Tainter, J. A. (2008). Collapse and Sustainability: Rome, the Maya, and the Modern World. *Archeological Papers of the American Anthropological Association*, *24*(1), 201–214. doi:10.1111/apaa.12038

Temesgen, A., Storsletten, V., & Jakobsen, O. (2021). Circular economy – reducing symptoms or radical change? *Philosophy of Management*, *20*(March), 37–56. doi:10.100740926-019-00112-1

Thompson, G. F., & Steiner, F. R. (Eds.). (1997). *Ecological design and planning*. John Wiley & Sons, Inc.

Toledo, V. M. (1997) Sustainable development at the village community level: a Third World perspective in: Fraser Smith (Ed.) Environmental Sustainability Boca Raton St. Lucie Press pp. 233–250 doi:10.1201/9781420048742.ch11

Tushingham, S., Hopt, J., Christiansen, C., Bommelyn, M. L., Green, J., Peterson, M. R., Steinruck, S., & Stewart, C. (2020). In the footsteps of Amelia Brown: Collaborative historical ecology at Shin-yvslh-sri~, a Tolowa village on the north coast of California. *Journal of Island & Coastal Archaeology*, *15*(1), 3–27. doi:10.1080/15564894.2018.1539789

United Nations. (1987). *Our Common Future. Report of the World Commission on Environment and Development*. Oxford University Press.

United Nations Environment Programme. (2012). *Green economy in a blue world: Synthesis report*. United Nations.

United Nations General Assembly. (2017). Resolution 71/312 Our ocean, our future: Call for action. In *Resolution adopted by the general assembly on 6 July 2017*. United Nations.

Van der Ryn, S., & Cowan, S. (2007). *Ecological design: tenth anniversary edition*. Island Press.

Walker, P. (2005). Political ecology: Where is the ecology? *Progress in Human Geography*, *29*(1), 73–82. doi:10.1191/0309132505ph530pr

Wallace-Wells, D. (2019). *The uninhabitable earth: Life after warming*. Tim Duggan Books.

Wang, X., Shuster, W., Pal, C., Buchberger, S., Bonta, J., & Avadhanula, K. (2011). Low impact development design—Integrating suitability analysis and site planning for reduction of post-development stormwater quantity. *Sustainability*, *2*(8), 2467–2482. doi:10.3390u2082467

Weick, K. E. (1969). *The Social Psychology of Organizing*. McGraw Hill.

Weston, A. (2009). *The incompleat eco-philosopher: essays from the edges of environmental ethics*. State University of New York Press.

Wiley, A. S., & Cullin, J. M. (2016). What Do Anthropologists Mean When They Use the Term Biocultural? *American Anthropologist*, *2016*(118), 554–569. doi:10.1111/aman.12608

Willermet, C. (2016). Biological Anthropology in 2015: Open Access, Biocultural Interactions, and Social Change. *American Anthropologist*, *118*(2), 118. doi:10.1111/aman.12529

Wolf, E. (1972). Ownership and political ecology. *Anthropological Quarterly*, *45*(3), 201–205. doi:10.2307/3316532

World Commission on Environment and Development. (1987). *Our common future*. Oxford University Press.

Yongming, Z. (2010). How Our Village Becomes "Ecocultural". In W. Ascher, & J. Heffron (eds.) Cultural Change and Persistence, Press, Washington, D.C. doi:10.1057/9780230117334_7

Zan, L., & Lusiani, M. (2011). Managing Change and Master Plans: Machu Picchu Between Conservation and Exploitation. *Arch*, *7*(2), 329–371. doi:10.100711759-011-9167-7

Zedler, J. B., & Stevens, M. L. (2018). Western and Traditional Ecological Knowledge in Ecocultural Restoration. *San Francisco Estuary and Watershed Science*, *16*(3), 1–18. doi:10.15447fews.2018v16iss3art2

Chapter 2
Anthropological Perspective of the Implications Between the Environment and Sustainability

José G. Vargas-Hernandez
Instituto Tecnológico Mario Molina, Mexico

Jorge H. Zamudio-Abdala
Universidad Cristobal Colon, Mexico

Omar C. Vargas-González
https://orcid.org/0000-0002-6089-956X
Tecnológico Nacional de México, Ciudad Guzmán, Mexico

ABSTRACT

This study aims to analyze some of the theoretical, conceptual, and methodological implications between anthropology and the environment and sustainability. Departing from the assumption that anthropological and ethnographic analysis and interpretive research on organizational anthropology has an emergent and symbolic role rooted in social processes and with no a priori assumptions, with explanations and categories defined by the organizational actors, which had an impact on sustainability and the environment through the green marketing practices. The method employed is based on an analytical and descriptive issues from the theoretical and empirical literature review leading to reflective analysis. It is concluded that the ethnographic and anthropological methodology is pertinent to be used in the analysis of its interactions between anthropology, the environment and sustainability as a new specialty in organizational studies. Also, the study proposes the implementation of green marketing habits and practices on sustainability drawing from the organizational anthropology.

DOI: 10.4018/978-1-6684-6924-8.ch002

INTRODUCTION

Organizational environmental sustainability is critical in its practice in the ecology of the organizational population (Salimath & Jones, 2011). Innovation as organizational change is a learning process through organization to develop innovation capabilities aimed to enhance the organizational performance (Chin & Chuang, 2015; Shahadan & Oliver, 2016). When green environmental performance support is high, technological innovation adapts to improve the sustainable competitive advantage. Green technology innovation increases environmental performance. Green technology innovation support shows moderate organizational innovation and environmental performance (Xing, Wang, & Tou, 2019; Porter & van der Linde, 1995). That is, when global environmental solutions are at a higher level, innovation is more willingly adapted to the improvement of sustainable competitive advantage.

The growing interest for sustainable environmental socio-ecosystem services is a result of the social dimension that reinforces the socio-ecosystem management legitimation and contributes to enhance constructive conflict resolution. Organizations can manage their capabilities and processes to be able to innovate and compete in the global landscape (Barney, 1991; Teece et al. 1997; and Santos et al. 2009). In theory, every organization implement programs of innovation in organizational models of corporate social responsibility and customer relationship managements as the result of organizational transformations and restructuration.

Economic growth and efficiency contribute to sustainable environmental governance and affecting green sustainable development. Environmental regulations have an impact on the innovative behaviors and is not a perfect theoretical system. Environmental regulation theory linkage international environmental governance. The appropriate regulatory intensity, firms control the opportunistic behaviors to achieve environmental governance. The technology governance capabilities should be improved through environmental regulations.

Technological innovation is a factor affecting green development efficiency. The stronger the technological innovation capability is, it is more conducive to enhance green sustainable development (Chen & Golley, 2014; Guo et al., 2017; Chen et al., 2020; Wang et al., 2021). Technological innovation features and characteristics are perceived as causes of green technology innovation for sustainable competitive advantage. Green environmentally sustainable support moderates' green technology innovation and sustainable competitive advantage relationship.

Green technology innovation is a complex technological behavior and the effects of environmental sustainability regulations on green behavior are still not well known (Huang et al., 2022). Green technology innovation is a strategic contributor to advance organizational knowledge capacities and gaining a sustainable competitive advantage (Alavi & Leidner, 2001). Green technology innovation is related positively to environmental sustainability performance leading to sustainable competitive advantage in environmental sustainability (Seebode, Jeanrenaud, & Bessant, 2012; Zhang, Sun, Yang, & Li, 2018; Huang & Li, 2017; Ge et al., 2018; Chiou, Chan, Lettice, & Chung, 2011; Chang, 2011).

Organizational green technology innovation approach has the potential to protect the environment, develop competitive market leadership, become more efficient, etc. Technological innovation characteristics may lead to organizational sustainable competitive advantage.

To analyze the implications of the organizational environmental sustainability business model in green technology innovation, first it is analyzed the organizational environmental sustainability continuing with the organizational business model innovation leading to the analysis of green technology innovation, Finally, some conclusions are presented suggesting future research.

THEORETICAL BACKGROUND

Environmental Sustainability

In the organizational and environmental sustainability fit the organization performs better routines more valued by the environment. Theories on the effects of organizational aging on organizational process are competing to contrast claiming on the effects on the fit between the environment and organizations, growth, and survival and do not provide evidence of the different mechanisms (Ranger-Moore,1997). The environmental sustainability effects have some negative effects. Enhancing and sustaining ecosystem resilience is a function of ecosystem management and social capacity responding to environmental sustainability feedback over time as well as space (Berkes & Folke, 1998).

Environmental protection is a path to sustainable development. Technical and environmental sustainability protection and emissions standards are naturally different for various firms. This deterioration is expected to be transitory by reducing the CO2 emissions and requiring more environmental protection measures to achieve environmental sustainability. The environmental sustainability regulations are divided in the elements of command-based, incentive-based, and voluntary environmental sustainability regulations. Command-based regulations, incentive-based, and voluntary environmental sustainability regulations can be implemented (Shi, 2019).

Incentive-based environmental sustainability regulations improve efficiency and policy flexibility. Voluntary environmental sustainability regulation motivates firms. Incentive-based environmental sustainability regulations and voluntary environmental sustainability regulations do not promote technology governance capabilities. Voluntary environmental sustainability regulations have an active participation on meeting the environmental sustainability goals. In other hand the implementation of voluntary environmental sustainability regulations is weaker than command-based and incentive-based environmental sustainability regulations and must be improved. Finally, the improvement of voluntary environmental sustainability regulations needs the supportive participation of government.

According to the Porter Hypothesis, environmental regulations induce firms to make up for compliance costs to promote the competitiveness (Porter & Van der Linde, 1995), confirmed by (Dechezlepr^etre et al., 2015; Wang et al., 2019; Weiss & Anisimova, 2019). Access to resources within the communities for socio-ecosystem management projects fulfilling nonmonetary goals of education, socio-economic development, and environmental sustainability protection. An adaptive socio-ecosystem approach is advocated by governance processes and activities of tradeoffs and a sustainability vision and direction operationalized by management and monitoring (Boyle et al., 2001).

Organization-level and firms at the same industry-level facing the same external environmental sustainability context have different responses as a function of differences in ages. Industry in developing countries can maintain an environmental sustainability sustainable socio-ecosystem and overcome dependence on commoditized products. Manufacturing may overcome their dependence on commoditized products and maintain an environmental sustainability sustainable socio-ecosystem.

Management in moderating the relationship between innovation and age, is related to inertia as a powerful force in high-technology firms. Some relevant elements for innovation development in high-technology oriented firms have not relevant relationship. The impact of external factors on capital price mechanisms may hinder the improvement of energy-saving technology and affects the efficiency of environmentally sustainable development (Sun et al. 2020).

Technological advance in organizations force them to change their business models and become more responsive to the dynamics of the environment (Chesbrough, 2010). Stakeholders ensure the adoption of voluntary environmental sustainability regulations beyond the mandatory regulations to generate benefits while incentive-based environmental sustainability regulations bridge the loss caused by mandatory regulation

Developing countries need achieving sustainable development to alleviate the environmental sustainability crisis. Environmental sustainability regulations make use of credibility of government to ensure implementation. International communities are more concerned with an environmental sustainability governance model to control environmental sustainability pollution and improve its environmental sustainability regulation system.

Formulation and implementation of strategies to optimize environmental sustainability regulation are required. Environmental sustainability regulations should be straightened in the face of uncertain economic and environmental sustainability to ensure the implementation of government policies (Işık et al., 2019b). Environmental sustainability regulations based on the force of government damage the market development. Promotion of environmental sustainability regulation strategies according to the characteristics and interest of firms in local conditions of the different industries aimed to achieve the environmental sustainability governance. Normative and coercive pressures from external constituencies prompt the commitment of firms to environmental protection policies (Hyatt & Berente, 2017; Truong et al., 2021).

Organizational Business Model Innovation

Innovation as the new processing technology, new product, or service new management system and structure or a new plan (Patel et al. 2015). Organizational innovation is the creation of new business process, products, and services (Chen et al. 2015). New technology, management, and strategy in organizational innovation (Marwan et al. 2016) stresses in new products and services, new markets and promotes customer satisfaction. Innovation in organizations has elements of vision, innovation intention, leadership organizational structure, efficient teamwork, multidimensional communication, continuous devotion, creative culture, involvement, and support, etc. (Titrek, 2015).

Innovation has the learning organization as a primary task (Chen et al. 2017). Organizational innovation is the learning process to cope with environmental changes (Alanoğlu and Demirtaş, 2016). Organizational innovation is an outcome of organizational learning that facilitates the sources of competitive advantage and organizational performance. The Knowledge-based view is a management concept of organizational learning that refers to knowledge as a resource, cause and antecedent for strategic sustainable competitive advantage firm innovativeness, and performance (Kogut & Zander, 1992; Darroch, 2005). Organizational learning enhances innovation capabilities to being able to do new things (Daft, 2016). A learning organization stresses on organizational innovative learning to strengthen the organizational capabilities (Schuurman et al. 2016).

Learning organization has positive effects on organizational innovation. The learning organization is positively related to organizational innovation with both positive effects on organizational performance (Chen, Wang, Lin, Chang, 2018). Continuous organizational innovation leads to organizational learning and performance. Innovation differentiates the value between competitors striving in a homogeneous market and enhancement of organizational performance (Chen et al. 2015). Organizational innovation has positive effects on organizational performance.

Organizational learning and organizational change are core concepts encourage the organizations and individuals to combine development objectives for a learning culture, creating thinking abilities, create a common vision through team learning, systemic thinking and innovation (Ahmad & Zabri, 2016; Wales, 2016; Daft, 2016). Organizational learning and work are continuous processes that combined result in changes of knowledge, beliefs, behaviors, enhance innovation and growth capabilities.

Propensity, posture and performance are elements of an organizational framework to become competitive by changing positions within the organizational socio-ecosystem, adopting and adapting innovation culture and routines for the improvement of innovation development, performance and environmental sustainability impact, enhanced by cross-functional and cross-organizational collaborations (Carayannis & Provance, 2008; De Waal, 2006). Organizational structure, culture and strategy are factors influencing innovation to improve synergetic performance (Xu et al. 2007).

Innovation proceeds from organizational posture and position within the business ecosystem, propensity of processes and routines, capabilities in organizational culture and financial, products, patents, and environmental sustainability performance. The framework of sustainability innovations increase the economic, social and environmental sustainability capital stock of organizations with ethics and culture (Hansen et al. 2009).

Organizational management innovation refers to education, training and forming new ideas, processes, systems, etc. The development of organizational management innovation requires flexible organizational design, innovation and ambidexterity to enable sustainability (O'Reilly & Tushman, 2004). Organizational management innovation applies governance and organizational design competencies to incorporate resources and capabilities aimed to develop competitive advantages and entrepreneurship to exploit new opportunities and achieve organizational sustainability.

Organizations are forced to innovate its organizational model due to changing environmental sustainability and market conditions. Organizational model innovation aligns to economic, financial, social, and environmental sustainability goals. The concept of business model innovation has foundations in corporate strategic management and practices, industrial economics and across its business ecosystem. The concept of business model innovation is based on the principle that organizations innovate by leveraging their use of resources and capabilities (Zott & Amit, 2010a) leading to the formulation and implementation of innovation strategies (Reinmoeller & van Baardwijk, 2005) such as in knowledge management, entrepreneurship, exploration, and cooperation.

The conceptualization of business innovation model and value proposition provides benefits to the organizations in terms of flexibility and opportunity to remain innovative. Business model innovation in the organization is a method of lean innovation with resources and capabilities inherent and minimum investments. The business model framework change development and innovation driven by transformations related to interactions. A framework for innovation based on sustainable development provides business expansion through regulatory push and vision pull model leading to business growth (Day, 1998; Hockerts, 2007; Preuss, 2007).

Business model innovation embedded in the core business with capitalization of capabilities or dealing with disruptive innovation with the integration into a new organization (Lindgardt et al. 2009; Christensen, (1997). Organizations that have more than one business model innovation have greater chances of being successful (Clausen & Rasmussen, 2012).

The innovation of a business model cannot be predicted by examining the current organization business model. According to George & Bock (2011) business models reflect upon the organizational design, resources-based view of the firm, narrative and sense making, nature of innovation and opportunity, and transactive structures. Business model innovation leads to disruptions that needs redesign of the organization while established firms tend to be successful with sustainable innovations and less successful in business model innovation.

Ambidexterity is required by the organizational model of innovation positioned at the core of organizational strategy, information and communication technology and organization, illustrating the influence of organizational design. Organizational design is critical for the emergence of an ambidextrous organizational form with the capability to optimize explorative and exploitative innovation aimed to enhance sustainability and performance (He and Wong, 2004). Organizational design and business model innovation support organizational sustainability. Organizational design and governance have influence on business model innovation. American and European schools of business models distinguish and designing and modelling approaches, classifications and use of open innovation (De Reuver et al. 2013).

Most of the business models reinforce innovation, but not all of them, leading to higher level of innovativeness. The doubt of Porter (2000) about the business model concept who provide a concise framework that explains how the organizations create and capture value, and the means to monetize their innovations (De Reuver et al. 2013). Stakeholders of large organizations are potentially responsible for the business model innovation, although the responsibility is assigned to mid-level management with leadership gaps (Chesbrough, 2007; Santos et al. 2009).

The implementation process of an innovative business model is driven by actions on the external and internal threats and opportunities (Bucherer et al. 2012). Organizations adopting business models to combine and distribute research-based innovations to other different market segments have impacts on technology transfer agents (Clausen & Rasmussen, 2012). Technology transfer agents transform scientific and technological knowledge into marketable innovative products. Organizational technology innovation increases the functions of products and services to enhance the attraction. The business model innovation has effects on organizational sustainability, design, governance and the role of the different stakeholders, partners, and customers in innovation process towards organizational sustainability.

An institutional environment encourage innovation and experimentation, facilitates individuals and organizations to improve the solution of complex problems (Imperial, 1999). Government environmental sustainability regulations are forcibly implemented; organizations must allocate innovation funds to meet the environmental sustainability regulations. When the coercive force is weak, the speculation hinders the implementation of green technology innovation. The effectiveness of government environmental sustainability regulations is a means to achieve sustainable development.

Government formulates technical specifications and standards for environmental sustainability protection for green production performance. Government environmental sustainability regulations promote the development of green technology innovation and the ecological protection aimed to transform firms and reduce environmental sustainability pollution. Pollution discharge permit system must meet the environmental sustainability protection standards. Government environmental sustainability regulations have abnormal characteristics and command-based environmental sustainability regulations stands out to promote green technological innovation. Strong government environmental sustainability regulations stimulate firms to engage in green technology innovation (Cainelli et al., 2020; Chen et al., 2021; Nie et al., 2021).

The indicators of command-based environmental sustainability regulation are the technical regulation, clean technology standards, requirements for wastewater and gas discharge, and standards for waste residue discharge. Command-based environmental sustainability regulations inhibit green economic and industrial growth, (Liu et al. 2021). Command-based government environmental sustainability regulations set technical specifications and standards for pollutant emissions of firms.

Command-based environmental sustainability regulation has effects on green technology innovation of the firm through formulation and implementation of green technology standards and emissions, as the strict mandates from the government that firms must comply to avoid penalizations. Command-based environmental sustainability regulation enhances manufacturing green product innovation capabilities, green process innovation capabilities and technology governance capabilities. Command-based environmental sustainability regulations give support to the green product innovation capability, green process innovation capability, and governance technology capabilities of firms.

The indicators of incentive-based environmental sustainability regulation are the appropriate allocation of clean production support funds, the appropriate allocation of technological special funds, the standards collection of environmental sustainability protection taxes, and the appropriate transaction permit. Incentive-based environmental sustainability regulations have not a remarkable role in green technology requirements leading to reducing polluted firms (Zhang, 2022).

Incentive-based environmental sustainability regulations leading to the implementation of green technology innovation are realized through green taxes, green emission permit trading, government green subsidies, etc. Firms improve green production processes, environmental sustainability protection, and reduce emissions to meet the government environmental sustainability protection (Deng and Chen, 2020). Incentive-based environmental sustainability regulations have effects on green product innovation capability and green process innovation capabilities.

Voluntary environmental sustainability regulations are motivated restrictions to uncontrolled environmental sustainability behaviors by actions such as disclosing environmental sustainability information, certification on competitive environment of the firm (Li et al., 2018). Voluntary environmental sustainability regulation promotes the green product innovation capabilities of firms

Environmental sustainability regulations have an impact on innovation intensity, although the impact of innovation quality with different motivations (Hu et al., 2020; Chen et al., 2021; Ma & Li, 2021). The firm must examine perceived quality and efficiency of command-based regulations, incentive-based, and voluntary environmental sustainability regulations.

Environmental sustainability regulations have a decreasing impact on technological innovation affected by the incentives and government subsidies. Research has shown that incentive-based environmental sustainability regulation has not significant impact on technology governance capability. Voluntary environmental sustainability regulation has not significant impact on green process innovation capability.

Green Technology Innovation

Firm innovation is a strategic behavior aimed to technological progress and competitive advantage, catering stakeholders and government regulation with quality of innovation (Tong et al., 2014; Truong et al., 2021). The government is the initiator of environmental sustainability regulations and is responsible of supervision and taking measures to control external effects, reduce the risks and uncertainties inherent on innovation (Wu, 2017).

Firms take the opportunity to adjust their technical structure, cultivate green technology innovation competitiveness and achieve the goal of environmental sustainability protection. Green technology innovation cannot be separated from technological innovation, although it is unknown if the Porter hypothesis of green technology innovation is still valid. Some studies could not verify the Porter hypothesis and cannot distinguish green and non-green technology innovation. Data on environmental sustainability regulation must be separated from data on green technology innovation to analyze the positive impact on the green technology innovation of firms.

The green technology innovation of firms can be divided into substantive green technology innovation and symbolic green technology innovation caused by the differences in regulatory captures, environmental sustainability regulations, and government subsidies from motivation to analyze the impact of environmental sustainability regulations. Government subsidies constrained by environmental sustainability regulations promote green technology innovation of firms although policymaking support with different intensity levels with different impacts on firms depending on the motivations for green technology innovation (Klette et al., 2000; Hud & Hussinger, 2015). Driving effects and results orientation government provides subsidies to firms engaged in green technology innovation activities.

In the context of strict environmental sustainability regulation to achieve green sustainability development and reduce carbon emissions, government must allocate subsidies to encourage the introduction of green technologies, environmental sustainability-friendly equipment, encourage and have an impact on green technology innovation. Environmental sustainability subsidies signal to investors that government legitimizes firms, according to the signal theory (Wei & Zuo, 2018; Ren et al., 2021). Robust environmental sustainability regulations with more strict enforcement but rising costs, firms gain competitive advantage through independent innovation (Xu et al., 2019; Jiang et al., 2020).

The dimensions of green technology innovation from the motivation perspective have different objectives leading to different levels of investments and energy constraints, improvements of green technology innovation of the firms and enhancing environmental sustainability and social responsibility performance. One of two dimensions may require more resources and organizational changes to improve the environmental sustainability performance at the cost of disrupting the internal flexibility (Hawn, 2012). Based on the perspective of motivation, green technology innovation is divided in green technology innovation behavior aimed to the advancement of corporate green technology and innovation strategy catering to environmental sustainability regulations ensuring that the firms meet social expectations of green technology innovation.

Green technology innovation behavior can be substantive and symbolic which varies with motivations and the perspective of innovation effects (Bronzini & Piselli, 2016; Li & Zheng, 2016; Hu et al., 2020). A behavior model created with characteristics of green technology innovation and government-enterprise, the government subsidies and regulatory capture lead to transmission mechanisms. Green technology innovation and green utility model patents are applied by firms (Huang, 2016).

Green technology innovation and environmental sustainability regulation in firms have an impact on technological innovation depending on the balance between compliance costs and innovation compensation (Ma & Li, 2021). Low-level and minor innovation is a low innovation cost, with less time, and a likelihood of obtaining government subsidies where regulatory capture outweighs the loss. Firms explore and develop new knowledge and technology out of the existing technology innovation paradigms, although some experience longer period without technological innovation results. Selected participants have a deep knowledge on organizational innovation and entrepreneurial activities. Innovation and growth processes are conditioned by entrepreneurship and systematic accumulation of knowledge and manpower skills.

Organizational ambidexterity in exploratory innovation generates and develops new knowledge and promotes radical innovation while exploitative innovation while exploitative innovation is based on current knowledge aimed at incremental innovation to achieve competitive advantage and enhance performance (Atuahene-Gima 2005; Benner & Tushman, 2003; Gibson & Birkinshaw, 2004). Ambidextrous organizations are sustainable and achieve high performance by implementing explorative innovation strategies and exploitative innovation strategies.

The market power supports firms to allocate ecological resources conducive to technological innovation. Environmental sustainability regulation has different types to cultivate micro mechanisms of green technology innovation in the of manufacturing industry. Laying a theoretical framework for policy proposal. The micro level structure of mechanism on environmental sustainability regulation of the elements of green technology innovation of manufacturing firms.

Environmental sustainability regulations have different effects on green technology innovation of firms. The relationship between technology innovation and environmental sustainability regulation is uncertain with and may be not a linear relationship or a threshold effect (Yang & Zeng, 2018; Cao et al., 2019). Government environmental sustainability regulations in technological innovation of firms is being clarified involving measures to ensure sustainable economic development in symbiosis with ecological economy (Du et al., 2021). Responding to environmental sustainability regulations, some firms are more inclined toward green technology innovation than to carry out non-green technology innovation (Nesta et al., 2014; Feng et al., 2017).

A research focusing on the adoption of characteristics of innovative technological characteristics using a model developed by Issa & Jabbouri, (2022) on the knowledge-based theoretical perspective for the adoption of green technological innovation in the health care industry in the region of MENA consisting of technological innovation characteristics such as the relative advantage, complexity, compatibility, observability, triability as antecedents, green technology innovation as a mediator, and sustainable competitive advantage as an outcome with government environmental support as a moderator. Trialability is a characteristic determinant of the adoption of green technology innovation (Le, Hollenhorst, Harris, McLaughlin, & Shook, 2006). Trialability is perceived positively related to green technology innovation.

Green technology innovation can be separated from technological innovation to evaluate the impact of environmental sustainability behavior on green firms. Environmental sustainability regulations have behavioral constraints driving firms to provide benefits to regulators seeking to soften the regulatory requirements leading to destroy the potential incentives for green technology innovation activities. Green technology innovation has attracted the attention (Kunapatarawong & Martínez-Ros, 2016; Sun et al., 2017; Ilg, 2019; Xie et al., 2022) to promote a low-carbon economy and neutrality (Popp, 2019; Zhang et al., 2021). The impact of green policy on green technology innovation attracts widespread attention, among the carbon emitters (Qi et al., 2021). The mechanism of environmental sustainability regulation policies influences the promotion of green low-carbon transformation and the green technology innovation of firms.

Green technology innovation is characterized by double externalities (Bi et al., 2016; Bai et al., 2019). A positive externality of green technology innovation without the support of government lead to market invalidation and poor motivation for the firm. Green technology innovation in firms is a quasi-public good with a positive externality. The quantity and speed of green technology innovation pursued by firms signals the environmental sustainability compliance to the stakeholders without compromising economic interests. Governments and stakeholders pressure organizations to achieve sustainable competitive advantage by adopting organizational green technologies innovations to remain competitive in the market (Brooks, Hedman, Henningsson, Sarker, & Wang, 2018).

Firms that have invested in green technology innovation resources, the benefits are not always exclusive leading to the free-riding in competition (Malen & Marcus, 2019; Xiang et al., 2022). A negative externality is the pollutant emissions. The pollution characteristics is used in research of environmental sustainability economics to build a model of environmental sustainability research policy on firm green technology innovation. High-quality green technology innovations are preferred by governments to increase financial support because can reduce adverse effects and maximize eco-environmental sustainability dividends (Lin et al., 2021).

The moderating effect of government subsidies and regulatory capture most be tested on the relationship between environmental sustainability regulation and the firm' green technology innovation. The model to be tested must include the fixed effects of the firm, industry, and time. Government subsidies and regulatory capture subject to environmental sustainability regulatory constraints have moderating effects with motivations on firms' green technology innovation. The regulatory capture as a supply of financial resources is linked to environmental sustainability regulations with effects on the support of green technology innovation resources (Murphy et al., 1993; Xue et al., 2021). Regulatory capture has a negative effect on environmental sustainability regulations process to promote the green technology innovation of firms.

The regulatory capture may negatively moderate the promotion of environmental sustainability regulations which may be the reason for differences between green technology innovation behaviors. Lack of resources for high-quality independent innovation ability, firms cannot respond to environmental sustainability regulations and laws only by imitating and low quality innovation. Firms that imitate lacks independent high quality innovation capabilities which requires capital investment in long-term technology innovation accumulation.

Green process innovation capability directs to process design meeting the requirements for environmental sustainability protection. Organizational design for innovation aligned to the organizational business model creates an environment for organizational performance. Environmental sustainability regulations are a policy variable to investigate the impact on improving the green technology innovation capabilities of firms (Liu et al., 2021; Cui et al., 2022).

The green product innovation capability is related to the healthy products that are beneficial to consumers and environmental sustainability protection.

Green terminal technology innovation governance capability is related firms meeting the environmental sustainability protection through the waste's treatment (Song et al., 2020). Funds for environmentally sustainable governance led to efficient supply of environmental services and public services (Bai et al., 2019). Regional sustainable environmental quality caused by environmental governance improves development efficiency.

Firm green technology innovation is top management strategy. Measurement of corporate green technology innovation with patent is strategic behavior (Hall & Harhoff, 2012; Tong et al., 2014). The firm green technology innovation methods are not unified and standardized, they belong to different perspectives. A research method developed by (Wurlod and Noailly, 2018) identifies green invention patent applications as the measure of green technology innovation ability.

Organizations coping with environmental sustainability changes, must adopt new ideas, behaviors, and forms, including incremental and radical innovation activities, management systems innovation, new culture, equipment and techniques, services, and ideas, etc. (Demirtaş, 2016). The innovation compensation effect exceeding the compliance cost effect, using green factor productivity, indicates that environmental sustainability regulation leads to green technological innovation (Xie et al., 2017; Wang et al., 2019).

Challenges and threats of a changing environment of organizations in global competition require constantly to learn, innovate, and reengineer. Some of the challenges that corporations meet are the cost-pressures, differentiation, and threats of substitution in environments where the culture and imitation are over innovation and sustainable development.

RESEARCH METHODOLOGY

To carry out this bibliometric review, electronic literary, and scientific sources were used as the basis for on ecological innovation, organizational aging, organizational ecology, patents, and its impact on the organizational ecology innovation. The study was conducted in the main scientific search engines. The research has been in English and are related to the publications and consulting reports.

RESULTS AND DISCUSSION

An environmental sustainability positive attitude and organizational members must innovate the environmental sustainability concept, formulate, and implement green strategies to improve the green technology innovation capabilities. Environmental sustainability regulation is correlated to green technology innovation and is positively related to sustainable competitive advantage. Environmental sustainability regulations have a direct impact on green technology innovation ability of firms despite the differences on the implementation effect caused by different variables. Environmental sustainability regulations improve the green technology innovation capabilities of firms.

The structure of environmental sustainability regulations must be simultaneously implemented. The internal structure of environmental sustainability regulations improves the organic integration of internal elements crucial for the development. The environmental sustainability regulations need to cultivate technology governance capabilities to improve incentive-based environmental sustainability regulations and voluntary environmental sustainability regulations. Environmental sustainability regulations must mobilize the green technology innovation capabilities of firms. Incentive-based environmental sustainability regulations support green technological innovation capabilities. Voluntary environmental sustainability regulations accommodate green economic development.

Policymaking must focus on reducing environmental pollution, encourage environmental technological innovations, and raise awareness of environmental culture to achieve sustainable development goals. Organizations must pursue innovation and changes to maintain flexible responses to customer needs and continuous product and service innovation. Organizational management must implement an innovation capability for research and development of technology to create organizational competitiveness and sustainable management. Stakeholders, policymakers, government officials, and organizations must be aware of the environmental impact on enhancing the development of green technological innovations aimed to promote clean and sustainable environment.

CONCLUSION

Local governments may improve the environmentally sustainable governance systems. Local governments are active in introducing technological innovation to build a resource-saving and sustainable environmental production and protection system. Local governments must increase the resources establishing a dynamic environmental monitoring system, disclose the environmental information, have strict environmental sustainability supervision and enforcement mechanisms to urge firms to abide by the environmental regulations and promote the environmental performance evaluation.

The adoption of green technology innovations supports the transition to a sustainable environment easing the consequences of climate change. Increase of energy consumption leads to strain on the environment. Green technological innovation tends to reduce carbon emissions in the long run. Transitions from fossil fuels to sustainable development shifting to renewable energies enhances environmental quality. Green technological innovation shifting to sustainable energy sources for example, reduce environmental pollution.

Future research is needed in the analysis of the environmental sustainability regulations. Future research must focus on the involvement of government and the dual effects and consider the effect intermediary.

Further research must be conducted to explore, define, and analyze the contributions to organizational transformation and the applicability of technology transfer to the organizational management innovation aimed to the innovativeness, competitiveness, and sustainability of organizations.

REFERENCES

Ahmad, K., & Zabri, S. M. (2016). The Effect of Non-financial Performance Measurement System on Firm Performance. *International Journal of Economics and Financial Issues*, *6*(6S), 50–54.

Alanoğlu, M., & Demirtaş, Z. (2016). The Relationships between Organizational Learning Level, School Effectiveness and Organizational Citizenship Behavior. *Journal of Education and Training Studies*, *4*(4), 35–44. doi:10.11114/jets.v4i4.1262

Alavi, M., & Leidner, D. E. (2001). Review: Knowledge management and knowledge management systems. *Management Information Systems Quarterly*, *25*(1), 107–136. doi:10.2307/3250961

Atuahene-Gima, K. (2005). Resolving the capability: Rigidity paradox in new product innovation. *Journal of Marketing*, *69*(4), 61–83. doi:10.1509/jmkg.2005.69.4.61

Bai, J., Lu, J., & Lu, S. (2019). The influence of capital market distortion on environmental pollution: Based on the analysis of provincial spatial dynamic panel data. *J Nanjing Audit Univ*, *16*(1), 37–47.

Bai, Y., Song, S., Jiao, J., & Yang, R. (2019). The impacts of government R&D subsidies on green innovation: Evidence from Chinese energy-intensive firms. *Journal of Cleaner Production*, *233*, 819–829. doi:10.1016/j.jclepro.2019.06.107

Barney, J. (1991). Firm resources and sustained competitive advantage. Journal of Management, 17(1), 99–120.

Benner, M. J., & Tushman, M. L. (2003). Exploitation, exploration, and process management: The productivity dilemma revisited. *Academy of Management Review*, *28*(2), 238–256. doi:10.2307/30040711

Berkes, F., & Folke, C. (Eds.). (1998). *Linking Social and Ecological Systems: Management Practices and Social Mechanisms for Building Resilience*. Cambridge University Press.

Bi, K., Huang, P., & Wang, X. (2016). Innovation performance and influencing factors of low-carbon technological innovation under the global value chain: A case of Chinese manufacturing industry. *Technological Forecasting and Social Change, 111*, 275–284. doi:10.1016/j.techfore.2016.07.024

Boyle, M., Kay, J., & Pond, B. (2001). Monitoring in support of policy: an adaptive ecosystem approach. In T. Munn (Ed.), *Encyclopedia of Global Environmental Change* (Vol. 4, pp. 116–137). Wiley and Son.

Bronzini, R., & Piselli, P. (2016). The impact of R&D subsidies on firm innovation. *Research Policy, 45*(2), 442–457. doi:10.1016/j.respol.2015.10.008

Brooks, S., Hedman, J., Henningsson, S., Sarker, S., & Wang, X. (2018). Antecedents and effects of green IS adoptions: Insights from Nordea. *Journal of Cases on Information Technology, 20*(4), 32–52. doi:10.4018/JCIT.2018100103

Bucherer, E., Eisert, U., & Gassmann, O. (2012). Towards systematic business model innovation: Lessons from product innovation management. *Creativity and Innovation Management, 21*(2), 183–198. doi:10.1111/j.1467-8691.2012.00637.x

Cainelli, G., D'Amato, A., & Mazzanti, M. (2020). Resource efficient eco-innovations for a circular economy: Evidence from EU firms. *Research Policy, 49*(1), 103827. doi:10.1016/j.respol.2019.103827

Cao, H., & Cao, W. (2019). Study on the Slow-Release Effect of Social Responsibility on Financing under the Node of Enterprise Life Cycle. *Procedia Manufacturing, 30*, 619–626. doi:10.1016/j.promfg.2019.02.087

Carayannis, E. G., & Provance, M. (2008). Managing firm innovativeness: Towards a composite index built on firm innovative posture, propensity and performance attributes. *International Journal of Innovative Research and Development, 1*(1), 90–107. doi:10.1504/IJIRD.2008.016861

Chang, C. (2011). The influence of corporate environmental ethics on competitive advantage: The mediation role of green innovation. *Journal of Business Ethics, 104*(3), 361–370. doi:10.100710551-011-0914-x

Chen, H., Lin, H., & Zou, W. (2020). Research on the regional differences and influencing factors of the innovation efficiency of China's high-tech industries: Based on a shared inputs two-stage network DEA. *Sustainability, 12*(8), 3284. doi:10.3390u12083284

Chen, K.-H., Wang, J.-S., Lin, M.-H., & Chang, W.-Y. (2018). The Influence of Learning Organization on Organizational Innovation and Organizational Performance Relationship: The Case of Ecology Industry. *Ekoloji, 27*(106), 329–335.

Chen, S., & Golley, J. (2014). 'Green' productivity growth in China's industrial economy. *Energy Econ, 44*, 89–98. doi:10.1016/j.eneco.2014.04.002

Chen, Y.-G., Cheng, J.-N., & Sato, M. (2017). Effects of school principals' leadership behaviors: A comparison between Taiwan and Japan. *Educational Sciences: Theory and Practice, 17*(1), 145–173.

Chen, Y. W., Saggi, N., Benitez-Amado, J., & Gang, K. (2015). IT Capabilities and Product Innovation Performance: The Roles of Corporate Entrepreneurship and Competitive Intensity. *Information & Management, 52*(6), 643–657. doi:10.1016/j.im.2015.05.003

Chen, Z., Zhang, X., & Chen, F. (2021). Do carbon emission trading schemes stimulate green innovation in enterprises? Evidence from China. *Technological Forecasting and Social Change*, *168*, 120744. doi:10.1016/j.techfore.2021.120744

Chesbrough, H. (2007). Business model innovation: It's not just about technology anymore. *Strategy and Leadership*, *35*(6), 12–17. doi:10.1108/10878570710833714

Chesbrough, H. (2010). Business model innovation: Opportunities and barriers. *Long Range Planning*, *43*(2–3), 354–363. doi:10.1016/j.lrp.2009.07.010

Chin, J. M., & Chuang, C. P. (2015). The Relationships among School-Based Budgeting, Innovative Management, and School Effectiveness: A Study on Specialist Schools in Taiwan. *The Asia-Pacific Education Researcher*, *24*(4), 679–693. doi:10.100740299-014-0220-3

Chiou, T., Chan, H. K., Lettice, F., & Chung, S. H. (2011). The influence of greening the suppliers and green innovation on environmental performance and competitive advantage in Taiwan. *Transportation Research: E-Logistics & Transportation*, *47*(6), 822–836. doi:10.1016/j.tre.2011.05.016

Christensen, C. M. (1997). *The innovator's dilemma: When new technologies cause great firms to fail.* Harvard Business School Press.

Clausen, T. H., & Rasmussen, E. (2012). Parallel business models and the innovativeness of research-based spin-off ventures. *The Journal of Technology Transfer*, *38*(6), 836–849. doi:10.100710961-012-9294-3

Cui, J., Dai, J., Wang, Z., & Zhao, X. (2022). Does environmental regulation induce green innovation? A panel study of chinese listed firms. *Technological Forecasting and Social Change*, *176*, 121492. doi:10.1016/j.techfore.2022.121492

Daft, R. L. (2016) Organization theory and design (10th ed.), South-Western College Publishing. Göksoy S (2015) Distributed Leadership in Educational Institutions. Journal of Education and Training Studies, 3(4): 110-118. doi:10.11114/jets.v3i4.851

Darroch, J. (2005). Knowledge management, innovation, and firm performance. *Journal of Knowledge Management*, *9*(3), 101–115. doi:10.1108/13673270510602809

Day, R. M. (1998). *Beyond eco-efficiency: Sustainability as a driver for innovation.* Washington: World Resources Institute Sustainable Enterprise Initiative. Dechezlepr^etre, A., Neumayer, E., & Perkins, R. (2015). Environmental regulation and the cross-border diffusion of new technology: Evidence from automobile patents. *Research Policy*, *44*(1), 244–257. doi:10.1016/j.respol.2014.07.017

De Reuver, M., Bouwman, H., & Haaker, T. (2013). Business model roadmapping: A practical approach to come from an existing to a desired business model. *International Journal of Innovation Management*, *17*(01), 1340006. doi:10.1142/S1363919613400069

De WaalA. A. (2006). The characteristics of high performance organization. https://ssrn.com/abstract=931873

Demirtaş, A. M. Z. (2016). The Relationships between Organizational Learning Level, School Effectiveness and Organizational Citizenship Behavior. *Journal of Education and Training Studies*, *4*(4), 35–44. doi:10.11114/jets.v4i4.1262

Deng, F., & Chen, C. H. (2020). R&D Input Intensity and Green Innovation Efficiency in China - a Threshold Study Based on Environmental Regulation. *Indust. Technol. Econ.*, *2*, 30–36. doi:10.3969/j.issn.1004-910X.2020.02.004

Du, K., Cheng, Y., & Yao, X. (2021). Environmental Regulation, Green Technology Innovation, and Industrial Structure Upgrading: The Road to the Green Transformation of Chinese Cities. *Energy Econ*, *98*, 105247. doi:10.1016/j.eneco.2021.105247

Feng, C., Shi, B., & Kang, R. (2017). Does Environmental Policy Reduce Enterprise Innovation?—Evidence from China. *Sustainability*, *9*(6), 872. Advance online publication. doi:10.3390u9060872

Ge, B., Yang, Y., Jiang, D., Gao, Y., Du, X., & Zhou, T. (2018). An empirical study on green innovation strategy and sustainable competitive advantage: Path and boundary. *Sustainability*, *10*(10), 3631. doi:10.3390u10103631

George, G., & Bock, A. J. (2011). The business model in practice and its implications for entrepreneurship research. *Entrepreneurship Theory and Practice*, *35*(1), 83–111. doi:10.1111/j.1540-6520.2010.00424.x

Gibson, C. B., & Birkinshaw, J. (2004). The antecedents, consequences, and mediating role of organizational ambidexterity. *Academy of Management Journal*, *47*(2), 209–226. doi:10.2307/20159573

Guo, L. L., Qu, Y., & Tseng, M. L. (2017). The interaction effects of environmental regulation and technological innovation on regional green growth performance. *Journal of Cleaner Production*, *162*, 894–902. doi:10.1016/j.jclepro.2017.05.210

Hall, B., & Harhoff, D. (2012). Recent research on the economics of patents. In K. Arrow, & T. Bresnahan (Eds.), Annual review of economics, pp. 541–565. doi:10.3386/w17773

Hawn, O. V. (2012). Do actions speak louder than words? *The case of corporate social responsibility (CSR)*, *2012*(1), 14137.

He, Z. L., & Wong, P. K. (2004). Exploration vs. exploitation: An empirical test of the ambidexterity hypothesis. *Organization Science*, *15*(4), 481–494. doi:10.1287/orsc.1040.0078

Hockerts, K. (2007). *Managerial perceptions of the business case for corporate social responsibility*. CBS Center for Corporate Social Responsibility.

Hu, J., Pan, X., & Huang, Q. (2020). Quantity or quality? The impacts of environmental regulation on firms' innovation–Quasi-natural experiment based on China's carbon emissions trading pilot. *Technological Forecasting and Social Change*, *158*, 120122. doi:10.1016/j.techfore.2020.120122

Huang, C. (2016). *Estimates of the value of patent rights in China. Innovation and IPRs in China and India*. Springer.

Huang, J., & Li, Y. (2017). Green innovation and performance: The view of organizational capability and social reciprocity. *Journal of Business Ethics*, *145*(2), 309–324. doi:10.100710551-015-2903-y

Huang, L., Wang, C., Chin, T., Huang, J., & Cheng, X. (2022). Technological knowledge coupling and green innovation in manufacturing firms: Moderating roles of mimetic pressure and environmental identity. *International Journal of Production Economics*, *248*, 108482. doi:10.1016/j.ijpe.2022.108482

Hud, M., & Hussinger, K. (2015). The impact of R&D subsidies during the crisis. *Research Policy*, *44*(10), 1844–1855. doi:10.1016/j.respol.2015.06.003

Hyatt, D. G., & Berente, N. (2017). Substantive or Symbolic Environmental Strategies? Effects of External and Internal Normative Stakeholder Pressures. *Business Strategy and the Environment*, *26*(8), 1212–1234. doi:10.1002/bse.1979

Ilg, P. (2019). How to foster green product innovation in an inert sector. *Journal of Innovation & Knowledge*, *4*(2), 129–138. doi:10.1016/j.jik.2017.12.009

Imperial, M. T. (1999). Institutional Analysis and Ecosystem-based Management: The Institutional Analysis and Development Framework. *Environmental Management*, *24*(4), 449–465. doi:10.1007002679900246 PMID:10501859

Işık, C., Sirakaya-Turk, E., & Ongan, S. (2019b). Testing the Efficacy of the Economic Policy Uncertainty Index on Tourism Demand in USMCA: Theory and Evidence. *Tourism Economics*, *26*(8), 1344–1357. doi:10.1177/1354816619888346

Issa, H., & Jabbouri, R. (2022). Green Innovation in the MENA Healthcare Industry: A Knowledge-Based View. [IJTHI]. *International Journal of Technology and Human Interaction*, *18*(1), 1–26. doi:10.4018/IJTHI.299072

Jiang, W., Wang, A. X., Zhou, K. Z., & Zhang, C. (2020). Stakeholder relationship capability and firm innovation: A contingent analysis. *Journal of Business Ethics*, *167*(1), 111–125. doi:10.100710551-019-04161-4

Klette, T. J., Møen, J., & Griliches, Z. (2000). Do subsidies to commercial R&D reduce market failures? Microeconometric evaluation studies. *Research Policy*, *29*(4–5), 471–495. doi:10.1016/S0048-7333(99)00086-4

Kogut, B., & Zander, U. (1992). Knowledge of the firm, combinative capabilities, and the replication of technology. *Organization Science*, *3*(3), 383–397. doi:10.1287/orsc.3.3.383

Kunapatarawong, R., & Martínez-Ros, E. (2016). Towards green growth: How does green innovation affect employment? *Research Policy*, *45*(6), 1218–1232. doi:10.1016/j.respol.2016.03.013

Le, Y., Hollenhorst, S., Harris, C., McLaughlin, W., & Shook, S. (2006). Environmental management: A study of Vietnamese hotels. *Annals of Tourism Research*, *33*(2), 545–567. doi:10.1016/j.annals.2006.01.002

Li, W., & Zheng, M. (2016). Is it substantive innovation or strategic innovation? Impact of macroeconomic policies on micro-enterprises' innovation. *Economic Research Journal*, *4*, 60–73.

Li, Z., Liao, G., Wang, Z., & Huang, Z. (2018). Green loan and subsidy for promoting clean production innovation. *Journal of Cleaner Production*, *187*, 421–431. doi:10.1016/j.jclepro.2018.03.066

Lin, J., Wu, H.-M., & Wu, H. (2021). Could government lead the way? Evaluation of Chi na's patent subsidy policy on patent quality. *China Economic Review*, *69*, 101663. doi:10.1016/j.chieco.2021.101663

Lindgardt, Z., Reeves, M., Stalk, G., & Deimler, M. S. (2009). *Business model innovation: When the game gets tough, change the game*. The Boston Consulting Group.

Liu, L., Jiang, J., Bian, J., Liu, Y., Lin, G., & Yin, Y. (2021). Are Environmental Regulations Holding Back Industrial Growth? Evidence from China. *Journal of Cleaner Production*, *306*, 127007. doi:10.1016/j.jclepro.2021.127007

Liu, Y., Wang, A., & Wu, Y. (2021). Environmental regulation and green innovation: Evi-dence from China's new environmental protection law. *Journal of Cleaner Production*, *297*, 126698. doi:10.1016/j.jclepro.2021.126698

Ma, H., & Li, L. (2021). Could environmental regulation promote the technological innovation of China's emerging marine enterprises? Based on the moderating effect ofgovernment grants. *Environmental Research*, *202*, 111682. doi:10.1016/j.envres.2021.111682 PMID:34270994

Malen, J., & Marcus, A. A. (2019). Environmental externalities and weak appropriability: Influences on firm pollution reduction technology development. *Business & Society*, *58*(8), 1599–1633. doi:10.1177/0007650317701679

Marwan, Z., & Abdul, H. (2016). Effect of organizational culture, leadership behavior, achievement motivation, and job satisfaction on performance of lecturer at Private university in the Province of Aceh. *IOSR Journal of Humanities and Social Science*, *21*(4), 33–45.

Murphy, K. M., Shleifer, A., & Vishny, R. W. (1993). Why is rent-seeking so costly to growth? *The American Economic Review*, *83*(2), 409–414.

Nesta, L., Vona, F., & Nicolli, F. (2014). Environmental policies, competition and innovation in renewable energy. *Journal of Environmental Economics and Management*, *67*(3), 396–411. doi:10.1016/j.jeem.2014.01.001

O'Reilly, C., & Tushman, M. (2004). The ambidextrous organization. *Harvard Business Review*, *82*, 74–83. PMID:15077368

Patel, P. C., Kohtamäki, M., Parida, V., & Wincent, J. (2015). Entrepreneurial orientation-as-experimentation and firm performance: The enabling role of absorptive capacity. *Strategic Management Journal*, *36*(11), 1739–1749. doi:10.1002mj.2310

Popp, D. (2019). Environmental Policy and Innovation: A Decade of Research. *International Review of Environmental and Resource Economics*, *13*(3–4), 265–337. doi:10.1561/101.00000111

Porter, M. E. (2000). Strategy and the internet. *Harvard Business Review*, *79*(3), 62–78. PMID:11246925

Porter, M. E., & Van der Linde, C. (1995). Toward a new conception of the environment-competitiveness relationship. *The Journal of Economic Perspectives*, *9*(4), 97–118. doi:10.1257/jep.9.4.97

Preuss, L. (2007). Contribution of purchasing and supply management to ecological innovation. *International Journal of Innovation Management*, *11*(4), 515–537. doi:10.1142/S1363919607001850

Qi, S., Zhou, C., Li, K., & Tang, S. (2021). The impact of a carbon trading pilot policy on the low-carbon international competitiveness of industry in China: An empirical analysis based on a DDD model. *Journal of Cleaner Production*, *281*, 125361. doi:10.1016/j.jclepro.2020.125361

Ranger-Moore, J. (1997). Bigger may be better, but is older wiser? Organizational age and size in the New York life insurance industry. *American Sociological Review*, *62*(6), 903–921. doi:10.2307/2657346

Reinmoeller, P., & Van Baardwijk, N. (2005). The link between diversity and resilience. *MIT Sloan Management Review*, *46*(4), 61–64.

Ren, S., Sun, H., & Zhang, T. (2021). Do environmental subsidies spur environmental? innovation? Empirical evidence from Chinese listed firms. *Technological Forecasting and Social Change*, *173*, 121123. doi:10.1016/j.techfore.2021.121123

Salimath, M. S. & Jones, R. (2011). *Population ecology theory: implications for sustainability.* Emerald Group Publishing Limited.

Santos, J., Spector, B., & Van der Heyden, L. (2009). *Toward a theory of business model innovation within incumbent firms*. INSEAD. doi:10.2139srn.1362515

Schuurman, D., Marez, L. D., & Ballon, P. (2016). The impact of living lab methodology on open innovation contributions and outcomes. *Technology Innovation Management Review*, *6*(1), 7–16. doi:10.22215/timreview/956

Seebode, D., Jeanrenaud, S., & Bessant, J. (2012). Managing innovation for sustainability. *R & D Management*, *42*(3), 195–206. doi:10.1111/j.1467-9310.2012.00678.x

Shahadan, A., & Oliver, R. (2016). Elementary School Leaders' Perceptions of Their Roles in Managing School Curriculum: A Case Study. *Educational Research Review*, *11*(18), 1785–1789.

Shi, C. K. (2019). Exploring the Evolutionary Trajectory of Corporate Green Technology Innovation under Environmental Regulatory Constraints. *J. Econ. Res.*, *13*, 15–16. doi:10.3969/j.issn.1673-291X.2019.13.007

Sun, L., Miao, C., & Yang, L. (2017). Ecological-economic efficiency evaluation of green technology innovation in strategic emerging industries based on entropy weighted G. Lian, A. Xu and Y. Zhu *Journal of Innovation & Knowledge, 7.*

Sun, X., Chen, Z., & Huang, L. (2020). Effects of factor price distortion on industrial environmental efficiency: Evidence from environmental pollution in China. *Polish Journal of Environmental Studies*, *29*(5), 3803–3812. doi:10.15244/pjoes/116104

Teece, D. J., Pisano, G., & Shuen, A. (1997). Dynamic capabilities and strategic management. *Strategic Management Journal*, *18*(7), 509–533. doi:10.1002/(SICI)1097-0266(199708)18:7<509::AID-SMJ882>3.0.CO;2-Z

Titrek, O. (2015). The Level of Innovation Management of School Principals' in Turkey. *Anthropologist*, *19*(2), 449–456. doi:10.1080/09720073.2015.11891679

Tong, T. W., He, W., He, Z. L., & Lu, J. (2014). Patent regime shift and firm innovation: Evidence from the second amendment to China's Patent Law. *Academy of Management Annual Meeting Proceedings*, *2014*(1) 14174–14174.

Truong, Y., Mazloomi, H., & Berrone, P. (2021). Understanding the impact of symbolic and substantive environmental actions on organizational reputation. *Industrial Marketing Management, 92*, 307–320. doi:10.1016/j.indmarman.2020.05.006

Wales, W. J. (2016). Entrepreneurial orientation: A review and synthesis of promising research directions. *International Small Business Journal, 34*(1), 3–15. doi:10.1177/0266242615613840

Wang, K. H., Umar, M., Akram, R., & Caglar, E. (2021). Is technological innovation making world "Greener"? An evidence from changing growth story of China. *Technological Forecasting and Social Change, 165*, 120516. doi:10.1016/j.techfore.2020.120516

Wang, Y., Sun, X., & Guo, X. (2019). Environmental regulation and green productivity growth: Empirical evidence on the Porter Hypothesis from OECD industrial sectors. *Energy Policy, 132*, 611–619. doi:10.1016/j.enpol.2019.06.016

Wei, J., & Zuo, Y. (2018). The certification effect of R&D subsidies from the central and local governments: Evidence from China. *R & D Management, 48*(5), 615–626. doi:10.1111/radm.12333

Weiss, J. F., & Anisimova, T. (2019). The innovation and performance effects of well- designed environmental regulation: Evidence from Sweden. *Industry and Innovation, 26*(5), 534–567. doi:10.1080/13662716.2018.1468240

Wu, A. (2017). The signal effect of Government R&D subsidies in China: Does ownership matter? *Technological Forecasting and Social Change, 117*, 339–345. doi:10.1016/j.techfore.2016.08.033

Xiang, X., Liu, C., & Yang, M. (2022). Who is financing corporate green innovation? *International Review of Economics & Finance, 78*, 321–337. doi:10.1016/j.iref.2021.12.011

Xie, R., Yuan, Y., & Huang, J. (2017). Different Types of environmental regulations and heterogeneous influence on "Green" productivity: Evidence from China. *Ecological Economics, 132*, 104–112. doi:10.1016/j.ecolecon.2016.10.019

Xie, X., Hoang, T. T., & Zhu, Q. (2022). Green process innovation and financial performance: The role of green social capital and customers' tacit green needs. *Journal of Innovation & Knowledge, 7*(1), 100165. doi:10.1016/j.jik.2022.100165

Xing, X., Wang, J., & Tou, L. (2019). The relationship between green organization identity and corporate environmental performance: The mediating role of sustainability exploration and exploitation innovation. *International Journal of Environmental Research and Public Health, 16*(6), 921. doi:10.3390/ijerph16060921 PMID:30875787

Xu, D., Zhou, K. Z., & Du, F. (2019). Deviant versus aspirational risk taking: The effects of performance feedback on bribery expenditure and R&D intensity. *Academy of Management Journal, 62*(4), 1226–1251. doi:10.5465/amj.2016.0749

Xu, Q., Zhu, L., Zheng, G., & Wang, F. (2007). Haier's Tao of innovation: A case study of the emerging total innovation management model. *The Journal of Technology Transfer, 32*(1–2), 27–47.

Xue, F., Chen, Q., Chan, K. C., & Yi, Z. (2021). Is corporate social responsibility value relevant? Evidence from a quasi-natural experiment of anti-corruption campaign. *Journal of Business Research*. Advance online publication. doi:10.1016/j.jbusres.2021.11.020

Yang, S. & Zeng, G. (2018) The ecological innovation effect of environmental regulation: From the perspective of regional differences. *Ecological Economy*, *34*(9), 41-49.

Zhang, D. (2022). Environmental Regulation and Firm Product Quality Improvement: How Does the Green Washing Response? *International Review of Financial Analysis*, *80*, 102058. doi:10.1016/j.irfa.2022.102058

Zhang, J., Zhang, N., & Bai, S. (2021). Assessing the carbon emission changing for sus- tainability and high-quality economic development. *Environmental Technology & Innovation*, *22*, 101464. doi:10.1016/j.eti.2021.101464

Zhang, W., He, L., & Yuan, H. (2021). Enterprises' decisions on adopting low-carbon technology by considering consumer perception disparity. *Technovation*, *102238*. doi:10.1016/j.technovation.2021.102238

Zhang, Y., Sun, J., Yang, Z., & Li, S. (2018). Organizational learning and Green innovation: Does environmental proactivity matter? *Sustainability*, *10*(10), 3737. doi:10.3390u10103737

Zott, C., & Amit, R. (2010a). Business model innovation: Creating value in times of change (No. D/870). IESE Business School

Chapter 3
Designing a Futuristic Solar Smart Bench for Smart Cities:
Towards Developing the Futuristic Urban Infrastructure

Rodney Takudzwa Chakwesha
Namibia University of Science and Technology, Namibia

K. S. Sastry Musti
https://orcid.org/0000-0003-4384-7933
Namibia University of Science and Technology, Nambia

ABSTRACT

Several smart cities have been established all over the world and versatile infrastructure is being developed to enhance the resident experience. Environmentally friendly urban infrastructure development is critical for societal health and overall development. Solar smart benches are now gaining popularity in smart cities and indeed considered as part of essential infrastructure for futuristic smart cities. They produce electricity during the daytime and provide various services to users. This chapter presents engineering design and analysis of solar smart benches. Contemporary smart features have been considered and design alternatives have been developed. Technical specifications for the designs have been provided. Suitable information and communication technologies have been identified for putting the infrastructure to use. Solar smart benches have the potential to revolutionize the smart city ecosystem.

INTRODUCTION

Over the last 10 years, the smart cities have witnessed phenomenal growth and have become the leading urban development paradigm all over the world (Schaffers, 2011; Vallianatos, 2015; Musti, 2020a). Most nations have now keen on adding innovative, smart and environmentally friendly technologies and furniture to every aspect of city ecosystems to transform them into smart cities (Grace et. al., 2021). In several cities such as London and Amsterdam, municipalities are trying to find smart ways to use new

DOI: 10.4018/978-1-6684-6924-8.ch003

technologies to make frictionless and automated future cities. The crossover to this new technology is quite understandable as it comes along with several benefits. Smart cities are considered to be a concept of the future. Quite a number of them are already active all thanks to the rise of industry 4.0 and awareness about clean environment. However, at the street level there are several futuristic furniture and installations, specifically for those that are still starting or yet to start. Solar smart benches and other street furniture are some of the simple entry points to a world of smart cities (Riklan et. al, 2021; Musti, 2020b; Saber et. al, 2017).

Generally urban spaces tend to suffer from poor air quality and higher pollution levels due to increased industrialization, relatively higher use of fossil fuels based vehicular transportation and higher energy consumptions., etc. Crowded and poorly designed interiors of the urban buildings result in poor air quality even inside the buildings (Fernandez-Antolin et.al, 2022). Thus urban health is effected in different ways and in different spaces. Several strategies for mitigating the impact of pollution in urban spaces were reported. Among them, increased usage of renewable energy technologies (RETs) is very popular due to its lower production costs and environmentally friendly nature. Urban health and solar energy are two important topics that are increasingly interconnected in today's world. The quality of life in urban areas is affected by a variety of environmental factors, including air pollution, noise pollution, and access to clean water and energy. Solar energy is a clean and renewable source of energy that can help improve the health and well-being of urban residents in several ways (Matheus and Musti, 2023; Fernandez-Antolin et. al., 2022). Policymakers strongly recommend renewable energy technologies (RETs) particularly for smart cities. A few reasons exist behind this. Firstly, solar energy can help reduce air pollution in cities. Fossil fuels are a major contributor to air pollution due to greenhouse gas emissions. Thus, renewable energies, specifically the solar energy is a clean alternative to fossil fuels. Secondly, the levelized costs of solar energy are now very less compared to other RETs and also non-RETs. Thus, solar energy can provide reliable and affordable electricity, which can impact their health and quality of life. Thirdly, solar energy can help improve access to clean water in urban areas. Solar-powered water pumps and purification systems can help provide clean and safe drinking water to urban residents, reducing the risk of water-borne diseases. Overall, the use of solar energy in urban areas can have a positive impact on the health and well-being of residents by reducing air pollution, providing reliable and affordable energy, and improving access to clean water. In addition to these aspects; renewable energy based smart city furniture is gaining popularity. Premier et. al (2022) illustrated various forms of solar powered furniture for futuristic smart cities that include solar trees, solar car ports, pergolas, canopies, solar bus stops and solar smart benches etc. Typically, such furniture is provided in urban areas with the intention of meeting the electricity needs in the immediate surroundings, while utilizing minimum amount of land. Most of such furniture items are not only innovative in nature, but also provide cleaner energy and at the same time they provide additional functionality such as monitoring the pollutants, air quality. Modern smart benches have all such attributes and in addition, they provide free Wi-Fi service and interesting information through attractive dashboards. Thus, it is clear that the terms - urban health, solar energy, smart cities and solar smart benches are strongly related to one another (Riklan et. al, 2021).

Smart urban street furniture is gaining popularity as numerous real-life projects are coming up all around the world and a good number of companies are now developing infrastructure integrated with photovoltaic technologies. Specifically, smart bus stops, carports, solar trees are now being re-purposed or re-shaped to provide an aesthetic look that is pleasing to the citizens and also useful in terms of providing some basic services. For instance, charging facilities for mobiles, laptops, e-bikes, e-scooters, Wi-Fi based internet services and also information services through dashboards (Hardt et. al., 2019;

Musti, 2020b). Smart urban furniture comes along with so many benefits such as having self-powered rechargeable outlets for electronic devices and interestingly, they produce the energy using solar PV panels on top of them. Which means, smart benches are designed in such way that they produce cleaner energy and provide services in urban spaces. They can also be used to gather contextual data that can be used to analyze a particular area (Smartnet, 2019). Smart solar benches are the new pieces in urban furniture that will assist parks, universities, retail or even business centres to make a user-friendly, better, and safer environment using renewable energy. Installing these innovative pieces of tech furniture will definitely have an impact on the improvement of visitor's frequency and satisfaction. Smart cities are no longer a concept of the past, they are now reality, a smart city bench that is smart in technology, will help introduce the public to the idea of smart renewable cities. Regular benches that are normally seen every day in the neighbourhoods are old fashioned and static, offering nothing else but a place just to sit, wait and/relax. Smart Solar Benches will not just be regular benches, in addition they are smart in technology and they will provide users with facilities that most humans need in public urban areas (Hoffman, 2020). Though the concept of solar smart benches seems to be obvious or simple, there can be several factors that can make the actual, real-world deployment somewhat complex. Literature did not deal with several issues pertaining to solar smart benches such as design options, engineering analysis of design alternatives, ownership issues, land use, operational costs, service models, safety for the apparatus itself from the nature and miscreants, ownership of data collected, surveillance and monitoring costs etc. (Vallianatos, 2015; Smartnet, 2019). Therefore, this chapter aims to address this very gap of lack of details about engineering design. For this, the chapter first considers design criteria, and a few versatile designs. A thorough design analysis is taken up on the design alternatives to study their effectiveness and also to test the effectiveness of overall design process and strategy. The content in this chapter is divided into different sections. Foundation to the discussion is provided through a thorough a through literature review and then objectives are identified. Then design criteria and design alternatives are presented. Discussion and conclusions are provided in the later sections.

LITERATURE REVIEW

The whole idea of a smart city refers to the cumulative extent to which urban places are composed of 'Everyware' (Greenfield, 2010); which means the state of technological development in which information processing has been integrated into the very fabric of urban environments. Examples of Everyware include fixed and wireless telecom networks, digitally controlled utility services and transport infrastructure, sensor and camera networks, building management systems, and so on and these are typically used for monitoring, managing and regulating city flows and processes, often in real-time. In a way, mobile computing through smart phones is now used in urban areas to engage with and navigate the city which themselves give off data about their location and activity. Connecting up, integrating and analyzing the information produced by these various forms of Everyware, it is argued, gives a more cohesive and smart understanding of the city that improves efficiency and sustainability (Hancke et al. 2012; Nathali et. al, 2018; Townsend 2013) and gives useful data that can be utilized to better depict, model and predict urban processes and re-enact the likely outcomes of future urban advancement (Schaffers, 2011; Smartnet, 2019).

Over the last two decades, urban analysts and scholars have been monitoring and plotting the advancement of cities amid a period where information and communication technologies (ICTs) have been applying a developing and inescapable impact on the nature, structure, and enactment of urban infrastructure, management, economic activity, and everyday life (Musti, 2020b). Cities that have understood the importance of ICT as an advancement methodology, being at the forefront in installing computerized infrastructure and systems into their urban environment and making use of them for entrepreneurial and administrative impact, are generally called with terms such as 'wired cities', 'cyber cities', 'digital cities', 'intelligent cities' (Musti, 2020a; Nathali et. al, 2018), 'smart cities' (Hollands 2008; Saber et. al, 2017) or 'sentient cities' (Hancke et. al, 2012). Each of these labels is used in a specific way to form a concept or idea of the link between ICT and contemporary urbanism, they share a center on the impacts of ICT on urban form, processes, and modes of living, and lately have been subsumed within the term 'Smart cities', a label which has picked up traction in governments, business world, and in other published articles (Kitchin, 2014; Musti, 2020a)

The very first study on smart cities was carried out in the nineteen seventies after the Community Analysis Bureau of Los Angeles used cluster analysis and infrared aerial photography to produce data reports on demographics and housing quality (Vallianatos, 2015; Musti, 2020a). The next breakthrough was in 1994 when Amsterdam introduced to the world the virtual digital city—internet access became available to a larger group of citizens for the first time (Hamilton, 2001). In the mid-2000s things began speeding up when IBM and Cisco launched separate initiatives. Here are the major milestones in the smart cities theme, extracted from the Smart cities – Thematic Research report produced by Global Data. In 2005 Cisco put up $25m project for research into smart cities. In 2008 IBM Smarter Planet project investigated applying sensors, networks and analytics to urban issues. In the following year IBM also unveiled $50m Smarter Cities campaign to help cities run more efficiently, the American Recovery and Reinvestment Act (ARRA) provided funding for US smart grid projects, and EU Electricity Directive required EU states to roll out smart meters to 80% of consumers by 2020. In the year 2010 the Japanese government named Yokohama as a smart city demonstrator project and in 2011 IBM named 24 cities as Smart City winners from 200 applicants, 6000 visitors from over 50 countries also attended the first Smart City Expo World Congress in Barcelona in the same year. In 2012, Barcelona deployed data-drive urban systems, including public transit, parking, and street lighting and in 2013, China announced first batch of pilot smart cities, comprising 90 cities, districts and towns in the same year the mayor of London created Smart London Board to shape London's digital technology strategy. During power outages, whether scheduled or unexpected, the residents need to be provided with detailed information as electricity is an essential commodity in the smart cities. For this utilities deploy a comprehensive outage management system to provide timely information (Sastry, 2007; Sastry and Sahadeo, 2015). It is possible to use the solar smart benches to provide the outage information as well, however this aspect needs to be fully developed. Geographical Information Systems need to be used for location identification studies that can combine users of smart benches and electricity users in the vicinity (Sastry and Sahadeo, 2015).

In 2014 China launched second batch of 103 pilot smart cities and Vienna City Council launched Smart City Wien Framework Strategy until 2025. In 2015 China announced third batch of 84 smart cities, comprising 277 in all and India's Prime Minister Narendra Modi launched "Smart Cities Mission" for 100 Indian cities. In the year 2016 Columbus won US Dept. of Transportation's $50m Smart Cities Challenge. In 2017, UK government launched 5G testbeds and trials program and Hong Kong launched smart city blueprint. In the following year, Toronto and Google offshoot Sidewalk Labs announced plan to develop smart waterfront area, London updated 2013 plans with launch of 'Smarter London Together' roadmap, IESE Business School Cities in Motion Index ranked New York, London and Paris as its top 3 cities and Singapore won Smart City of 2018 award at the Smart City Expo World Congress. In 2019,

Ford committed to support Cellular Vehicle to Everything (C-V2X) standard, Sidewalk Labs' Toronto planning document fiercely criticized over data privacy implications, G20 nations picked World Economic Forum as secretariat for a G20 Global Smart Cities Alliance, US Federal Communications Commission picked New York and Salt Lake City as 5G testbeds. In the year 2020, Vietnam to start work on new $4.2bn smart city close to Hanoi, with completion target of 2028. By 2030, the number of cities in the world with a population of more than 10 million will grow to 43, and by 2050, up to 70% of the world's population is expected to live in cities. Due to the existence of several possibilities for versatile designs, adding smart features in providing information and charging services to the public; prospects of reducing greenhouse gases etc., the research on smart benches can be naturally interdisciplinary. Though solar smart benches are not likely to make a negative impact on the power grids, energy production, power consumption patterns and power quality studies need to be undertaken.

Smart benches are typically designed and operated to charge smart phones, laptops and also e-bikes and electric vehicles etc. However, the ability of smart benches in providing such service depends on their energy capacity for which they are designed for (Hardt et. al, 2019). Though it is possible to design smart benches with batteries, functionality of such smart benches can be limited during night or even outside the solar shine hours (Acharya et al, 2020). Since solar smart benches are energy producers during the daytime, they may further augment the existing duck curve phenomenon (Pitra and Musti, 2022). This results in excess generation conditions; however, it should be noted that smart benches do not initiate the duck curve phenomenon by themselves, but they further compound the existing problem, especially if the smart benches are installed in more numbers. It is for this reason, locations for the smart benches need to be identified carefully depending on the demand side management (DSM) data (Musti et. al, 2020). Solar smart benches as reported in literature appear in versatile design. However, technical specifications and their limitations are also not provided in every case.

From the above, it can be seen that there is a significant interest in smart benches. However, a majority of the earlier authors have presented the general usage experience and look and feel of the structures. Engineering design and/or design alternatives are not very well treated thus far. To address this gap, this chapter presents a few interesting conceptual designs for solar smart benches on the basis of how solar energy can be used to provide people in outdoor areas with facilities that they need when sitting down in a public urban area, (facilities such as charging outlets, Wi-Fi, night time lighting, interactive LCD screen for general public information: advertisements). In the process, the chapter also discusses aspects related to providing adequate electric charging infrastructure, and allows the bench to collect contextual data, process the data, upload, and display on a cloud-based dashboard. This data can be incredibly useful to governing authorities, urban planners, and park managers.

PROPOSED DESIGN FRAMEWORK

Given the nature of engineering complexities, applications, financial and societal aspects, several parameters have been considered in this work. Detailed discussion and in-depth treatment of design parameters are out of scope of this work and thus avoided. The key aspects that influenced the proposed design are 1. Public safety 2. Digital Connectivity 3. Solar panel configuration 4. Materials required 5. Charging station 6. Aesthetics 7. Data collection 8. Marketing. A few design alternatives have been developed and all of them are carefully analyzed. The design concept included two categories – a) physical design b) technical design.

Different software design tools are considered, as the smart benches are required to be modelled, designed and simulated in three-dimensional space. Google Sketch-Up software is used as it proved to be a very user friendly and efficient tool to for three-dimensional drawing and building remodeling (Fernandez-Antolin et. al., 2022). All the designs are drawn on uniform scaling to ensure realistic comparison and to enhance the prospects of real-world deployment, after rigorous verification.

DESIGN ALTERNATIVES

Though several design alternatives are considered, two different designs are presented to provide insights into the engineering design approach.

Design Alternative 1

Figure 1 shows the first alternative for the solar smart bench. The typical dimensions of this alternative are Length: 3.5 meters, width: 0.8 meter, height: 2 meters and the overall weight of the structure is about: 320 kg. The weight estimates are done based on the choice of the materials used (Grabiec et. al, 2022). Table 1 provides various design features.

The technical design part covers the details of various parameters of the alternative, which are shown in table 2.

Figure 1. 3D representation of first design alternative
(Chakwesha and Musti, 2023)

Table 1. Features for first design alternative

Public safety The design integrates SOS button and a camera that will help the citizens communicate with city services in emergency situations and also provide 24/7 monitoring for increased public safety.	**Aesthetics** With its curved design, stainless steel for longevity and special wood cover for seating. Having a cover over the users is also crucial when using the charging services or internet access during bad weather. Blue, white, black and metallic colors are chosen for enhancing the ambience
Digital Connectivity Complimentary internet access is available within the immediate vicinity of each solar leaf Free W-Fi zone providing internet access within 15 meters around the bench. The innovative Smart Wi-Fi digital platform enhances the user experience and offers valuable marketing insights for private and public operators on consumers' needs and preferences.	**Data Collection** Capabilities to collect important environment data through special hardware - sensors and software – cloud platform solutions to help engineers with urban planning and pollution reduction measures.
Solar Panel Specification and Configuration Reaches 20% efficiency; Pure silicon monocrystalline panels are chosen, Panels appear black in color; Temperature coefficient of -03%/C to -0.5%/C; Expected life span of about 25 years	**Marketing** Each solar bench has a dedicated space for placing ads and public information to support marketing and public services and deliver the information at an appropriate pace.
Charging Station Emergency recharge points are available for all types of devices; Powered by the sun; Several built in USB ports provide charging for all types of all types of smart devices; wireless charging technology is integrated, so that users can place devices on the marked spot and wait for until charging is completed.	**Materials used** Stainless Steel Aluminum Wood

The solar panel specifications are more of the interest since; they provide the energy to the structure. Relevant specifications and details are provided in the table 3.

Since the claim regarding the use of solar smart bench is about lower air pollution and improved urban health; it is necessary to evaluate the benefit. Based on the above information, it is possible to determine the coal avoided and also avoided release of carbon dioxide into the atmosphere. Since, the nominal power of the panel is 130W at 12V, annual energy produced (assuming no losses and 5 sunshine hours per day) will be 130*12 * 5* 365, which is about 2847 kWh. This is equivalent to an equivalent of carbon dioxide of 663 kg. Now, to produce 2847kWh of energy, 350kg of coal is required. This is a simple calculation based on solar energy production at full capacity. In reality, solar panel will not be able to produce all the that nominal energy due to intermittency, weather changes and other issues. At the same time this computation is for only a single smart solar bench; and thus urban health can be enhanced definitely when more solar benches are used.

Design Alternative 2

Figure 2 shows the second alternative for the solar smart bench. The typical dimensions of this alternative are Length: 4.5 meters, width: 3.2 meters, height: 2.5 meters and the overall weight of the structure is about: 470 kg. The weight estimates are done based on the choice of the materials used (Grabiec et. al, 2022). This configuration presents a versatile and different look and feel to the users and also serves as a parking and charging station for bicycles and electric scooters. The module contains sockets for charging for charging electric scooters and bicycles. An interactive information kiosk is separately provided for enhanced user experience. Night camera capabilities are added as part of the design. Table 4 provides various design features.

Table 2. Technical specifications of first design alternative

Smart solar bench general specifications	
Light source	LED Bar Light + LED strip light
Solar Power	1x135Wp, Monocrystalline
Battery System	Lithium Battery 12v 1x55Ah
Dimensions	2030 x 686 x 30 mm
Materials that are likely to be used	Stainless steel, WPC Wood, Tempered Glass
Bench Features	USB Charging Ports, Wireless Charger Wi-Fi Router, Advertising Display, Environmental sensors
LED bar light parameters	
power	20W
Input Voltage	12V DC
Light source	LED Chip
Beam Angle	180 degrees
color	Cool white
Life span	30 000 hours
Battery Main characteristics	
type	Lithium Battery
Rated voltage	12.8V
Rated capacity	55Ah
Dimensions	295 x 170 x 65 mm
weight	9 kg
Charge voltage	14.2 V
Float voltage	10.8 V
Solar Panel Mechanical Characteristics	
Solar Cell Type	Monocrystalline 125 mm
Dimensions of Module	1870 x 992 x 32 mm
Structure	Front: 3.2mm high transmittance tempered glass sealing Back: PET/TPT
Environmental Conditions	Outdoor use without shading in the sun

The technical design part covers the details of various parameters of the alternative, which are shown in table 5.

The solar panel specifications are more of the interest since; they provide the energy to the structure. Relevant specifications and details are provided in the table 6.

Though the concept of Solar smart benches may look simple and straight forward, engineering design to manufacture can be a quite exhaustive and even complex. Though this section illustrated two different design models, there can be several variations and even other innovative models can be designed for obvious reasons. For each of such design alternative, overall space for different components such as the solar panels, electronic components, users to sit/ stand while waiting, dashboards and storage batteries etc., need to carefully factored. Then such design alternatives need to be carefully evaluated based on a set criterion. Thus, engineering design and analysis assumes prominent role from the conception of (specific)

Table 3. Solar energy system specifications of first design alternative

Solar Panel Main Characteristics	
Maximum Output Power (Pmpp)	135 Wp
Power Tolerance	+/-5%
Solar Cell Efficiency	21.6
Voltage at Pmpp (Vmpp)	22.5 V
Current at Pmpp (Impp)	6 A
Open Circuit Voltage (Voc)	27 V
Short Circuit Current (Isc)	6.33 A
Maximum System Voltage	600 V
Maximum Series Fuse Rating	10 A
Charger Controller Model Characteristics	
model	Tracer 2606BP
Battery Voltage (auto select)	12 V DC
Rated Charge Current	10 A
Nominal PV Power	130W / 12 V
Max. PV Open Circuit Voltage	60v max
Charge Voltage 'Absorption'	14.5 V
Charge Voltage 'Float	12.8 V

Figure 2. 3D representation of second design alternative
(Chakwesha and Musti, 2023)

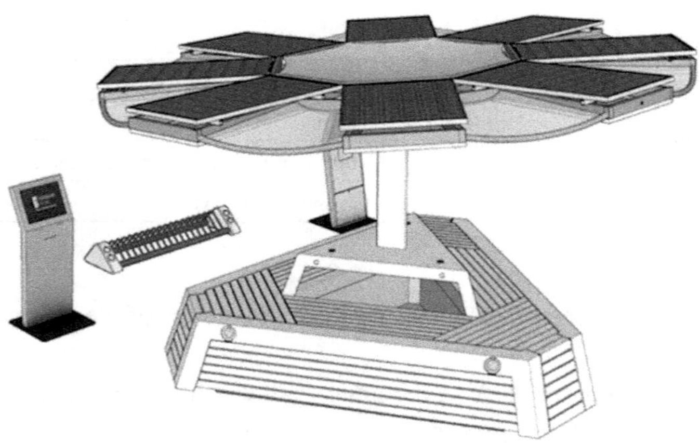

a model to energy production and its end use. Another point is that not all models may support roof or space for solar panels. In such a case, solar panels can be kept somewhere closely; like on top of a car port or a gas station or any public kiosk etc., and the required wiring can be done to transfer the energy.

Engineering design and analysis does not end with the physical structure of the solar smart bench itself. Solar panels typically produce DC power and thus the same requires to be converted to AC power

Table 4. Features for second design alternative

Public safety The design integrates SOS button and a camera that will help the citizens communicate with city services in emergency situations and also provide 24/7 monitoring for increased public safety. The designs uses solar panels that will be manufactured from homogenous polycarbonate, guaranteeing them protection from weather conditions and vandalism.	**Aesthetics** With its top umbrella type dome design, stainless steel for longevity and special wood cover for seating. Dome provides an excellent cover for users during bad weather, without service interruption. All surfaces covered with basic colors - front and back, as well as the sides, can be used for this purpose, while the inner (hollow) part of the bench can be in one color at the request of the client.
Digital Connectivity Complimentary W-Fi zone providing internet access within 15 meters around the bench. The innovative Smart Wi-Fi digital platform enhances the user experience and offers valuable marketing insights for private and public operators on consumers' needs and preferences.	**Data Collection** Capabilities to collect important environment data through special hardware - sensors and software – cloud platform solutions to help the engineers with urban planning and pollution reduction measures.
Solar Panel Specification and Configuration Photovoltaic modules Monocrystalline / Total power: 200W each, reaches 20% efficiency, Pure silicon monocrystalline panels are chosen, Appear black in color, Temperature coefficient of -03%/C to -0.5%/C, Expected life span of about 25 years	**Marketing** Design has a dedicated space for placing ads and public information to support marketing and public services and deliver the information at an appropriate pace. Clients who want to send their marketing messages through City Gecko solutions could use the advertising space that is provided.
Charging Station Emergency recharge points are available for all types of devices; Powered by the sun; Several built in USB ports provide charging for all types of all types of smart devices; wireless charging technology is integrated, so that users can place devices on the marked spot and wait for until charging is completed.	**Materials used** Stainless Steel Aluminum Wood

Table 5. Technical specifications of second design alternative

Smart solar bench general specifications	
Light source	LED Bar Light + LED strip light
Solar Power	Monocrystalline / Total power: 110W
Battery System	Type: AGM / Capacity: 72Ah
Dimensions	1227 x 445 x 32 mm
Material	Stainless steel Tempered Glass
Bench Features	USB Charging Ports, Wireless Charger Wi-Fi Router, Advertising Display, Environmental sensors
Battery Main characteristics	
type	Type: AGM
Rated voltage	12.8V
Rated capacity	400 Ah
Dimensions	295 x 170 x 65 mm
Solar Panel Mechanical Characteristics	
Solar Cell Type	Monocrystalline 125 mm
Dimensions of Module	1776 x 445 x 512 mm
Structure	Front: 3.2mm high transmittance tempered glass sealing Back: PET/TPT
Environmental Conditions	Outdoor use without shading in the sun

Table 6. Solar energy system specifications of second design alternative

Solar Panel Main Characteristics	
Maximum Output Power (Pmpp)	110 Wp
Power Tolerance	+/-5%
Solar Cell Efficiency	21.6
Voltage at Pmpp (Vmpp)	22.5 V
Current at Pmpp (Impp)	6 A
Open Circuit Voltage (Voc)	27 V
Short Circuit Current (Isc)	6.33 A
Maximum System Voltage	600 V
Maximum Series Fuse Rating	10 A
Charger Controller Model Characteristics	
model	Tracer 2606BP
Battery Voltage (auto select)	12 V DC
Rated Charge Current	10 A
Nominal PV Power	130W / 12 V
Max. PV Open Circuit Voltage	60v max
Charge Voltage 'Absorption'	14.5 V
Charge Voltage 'Float	12.8 V

for the consumers to use. There can be several views and arguments such as – it is efficient or better to use DC power directly for some applications such as charging electric vehicles etc. In reality, charging cables / inlets of all the devices and the modern electric vehicles usually are designed to function on AC power. At the same time, it is important to note that DC charging requirements for devices and vehicles vary from model to model. For instance, a typical USB port operates at 5V DC (Hoffman, 2020). Therefore, a properly designed ecosystem is required for meeting the general or most commonly anticipated charging requirements. On a careful observation, the energy conversion system of any solar power production facility has its own design requirements and criteria, as it consists of different components within itself. Sizing each component and connecting with another requires careful analysis, sizing and design in realizing a properly functioning energy conversion system. The design for electrical circuitry and wiring is also of significant importance for modularity and replication purposes. This allows the service providers to mass produce the smart solar benches. The schematic of the electrical circuitry and the wiring is provided in figure 3.

As can be seen from the figure 3, energy conversion system has several components. The apparatus for end-use, such as the USB charging ports, wireless charging facilities, routers, street lights and the dashboard etc. Design analysis is important in the sense, space available for solar panels is a major constraint in deciding the power capacity of the system. Charge controller and inverters need to be designed based on the power capacity. Due to various energy losses, energy conversion efficiencies and economic factors, inverter capacity is always chosen less than the kilo-watt-peak rating of the panels. Further, energy conversion system has the ability to feed the energy into the grid whenever possible. In other words, excess energy (after supplying the connected users and devices in the facility) can be

Figure 3. Schematic of the energy conversion system for the second design alternative
(Chakwesha and Musti, 2023)

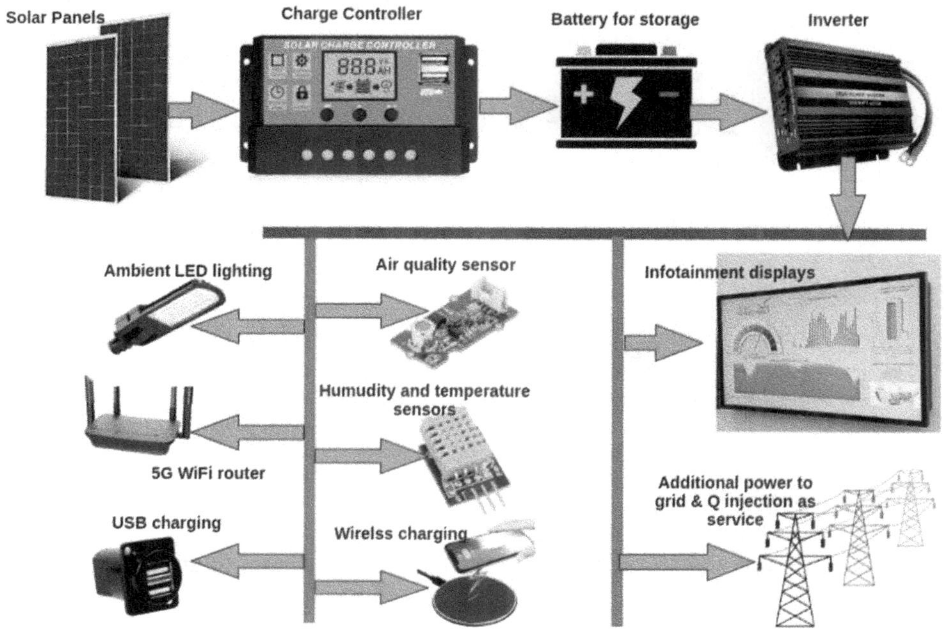

pumped into the grid. However, such energy in-take into the grid is subjected to a set of standards and specifications. Voltage and frequency need to be constant at a specific level and such energy should be free from unwanted harmonics. Detailed discussion on such design aspects and calculations can be lengthy and complex and thus is avoided in this chapter. As shown in figure 3, the components are located in different parts of the physical structure for obvious reasons and thus wiring connections also require some degree of design and thinking.

Wide rating designs are reviewed for designing the information dashboard. Just as other parts of the structure and overall services, the dashboard needs to be versatile to capture attention of the users. Figure 4 shows the design of the dashboard that is added to all the design alternatives. This uniform nature of the dashboard with more or less same controls and sequence for information presentation are important to reduce complexity in understanding the dashboard itself.

Design of the dashboard assumes a lot of importance as this is the component that provides a visual interface to the end user. Typically, users will be provided infographics related to WiFi status, WiFi username/ password, status of charging ports in terms of usage, status of batteries. Importantly, the system can also display weather information and carbon dioxide content in the immediate surroundings if the appropriate sensors are added to the ecosystem. Though most of the information that is displayed is typically about the solar smart bench ecosystem itself, the space can also be used to display commercial advertisements. This aspect assumes another dimension to the solar smart benches, as this brings revenues that can be used for upkeep and maintenance activities of the bench.

Figure 4. Information dashboard for smart solar bench
(Chakwesha and Musti, 2023)

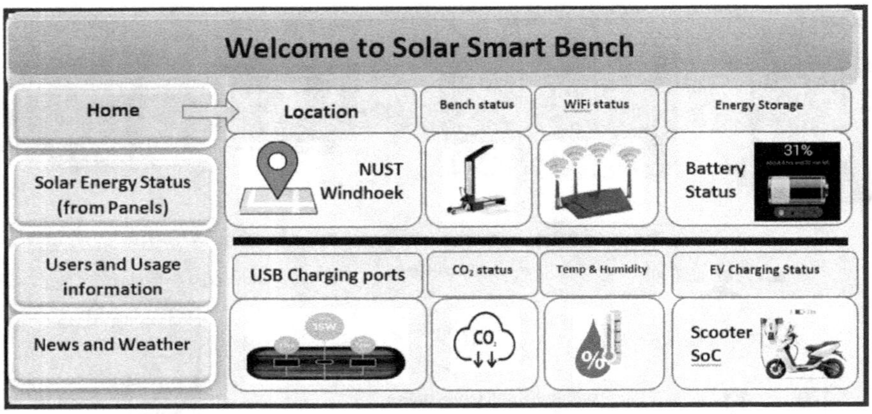

DISCUSSION

Since solar smart benches are niche apparatus, they attract a lot of attention and thus design alternatives invite interesting aspects/ questions that need to be addressed. Some of those include – physical design, charging times, materials used, charging and discharging times, consequences of loss of energy, and choice of communication technologies. Some of the aspects are considered here for discussion here in this section.

- Physical design and materials: Solar smart benches can be designed in several different configurations. Some can be simply flat without roof and some can have large roof and as part of building etc. Thus, seating facilities for the users differ from model to model. Interestingly, some authors pointed to the fact that providing a back rest would disrupt that concept and potentially create problems with charging due to forming a shadow over PV modules. For the safety of users and sturdiness, smart bench needs to be installed on a solid surface such as the concrete, or asphalt or stone and that the surface needs to be at least 10 cm deep (Grabiec et. al, 2022).
- Charging and Discharge durations: Most users anticipate this information the moment they connect their device(s) to the ecosystem. Though charging times depend on charging type and model of the device and its existing state of charge; the solar smart bench needs to be designed in such a way that it can determine the required information and provide it to the users on the dashboard. Typical charging times range from 90 minutes and beyod in wireless charging segment with most smartphones and cable based, USB ports need between 1 and 1.8% of battery per 1 minute (Hoffman, 2020). Charging speed will also depend on whether the users are using their smartphone while it is charging, or the phone is in stand-by mode. Thus sensors and dashboards (generally designed on top of Android operating systems) need to be programmed carefully to provide relevant and reasonably accurate information to the users. Users also may want to know the current status of the smart bench itself in terms of stored energy. In typical summer days, the smart benches may be able to charge its battery system within a single day, while during winter it may take up to three days, though there can be exceptions. This is why it is recommended that the smart benches should mostly operate in standby mode during most of the day in winter and the users need to be aware of this aspect. Thus design of development of the dashboard also is important.

SCOPE FOR FURTHER WORK

From the above sections, it can be seen that research related to solar smart benches is niche in nature and involves interdisciplinary research. Thus, this topic provides excellent opportunities for further work. Since solar smart benches stay in urban spaces, generate clean energy and serve wider public; it is imperative to investigate the ownership and licensing issues. Though it is possible for the state authorities to encourage enthusiastic investors to establish these facilities, studies need to conducted to examine the benefits if the state-owned power utility itself establishes under its ownership (Grace et. al., 2021). This might help them in obtaining the information about local demand response and energy usage patterns (Musti, 2020b; Musti et. al., 2020b). On the other hand, urban residents generally come out and walk around public places during power outages. If the outage is not expected, then there is a possibility for the residents to visit solar smart benches and try to seek information about the power outage itself. This naturally can feed the information about the nature of outage to the utility and thus enabling them to do the needful. Then issues related to operational and maintenance costs of solar smart benches need to be studied. However, such studies are possible only after establishing a working system and then collecting the data. In-depth analysis of manufacturing costs and overall cost-benefit studies need to be undertaken. Lastly, ownership of the user data, information collected and further use of user data need to be studied as well.

CONCLUSION

The objective of presenting the engineering design and analysis of solar smart benches has been achieved in this chapter. Various design alternatives and design evaluation criteria are presented as well. The overall approach for the design and analysis presented in this chapter has the potential to provide a system model that can be used to brainstorm innovative ideas for smart street furniture and serve as a start point for future research designs and smart city development projects. The designs are based on harnessing solar energy to provide public urban areas with different user facilities. Importantly, this chapter highlights the role of solar smart benches in transforming the surroundings as futuristic and eco-friendly; enhancing the urban health through providing clean energy; and also helping the users with news and important information.

REFERENCES

Acharya, P., & Aithal, P. S. (2020). A Comparative Study of MPPT and PWM Solar Charge Controllers and their Integrated System. *Journal of Physics: Conference Series*, *1712*(1), 012023. doi:10.1088/1742-6596/1712/1/012023

Allwinkle, S., & Cruickshank, P. (2011). Creating Smart-er Cities: An Overview. *Journal of Urban Technology*, *18*(2), 1–16. doi:10.1080/10630732.2011.601103

Fernandez-Antolin, M.-M., Manuel del Río, J., & González-Lezcano, R. A. (2022). Building Performance Simulations and Architects against Climate Change and Energy Resource Scarcity. *Earth (Waukesha, Wis.)*, *3*(1), 31–44. doi:10.3390/earth3010003

Grabiec, A. M., Łacka, A., & Wiza, W. (2022). Material, Functional, and Aesthetic Solutions for Urban Furniture in Public Spaces. *Sustainability*, *14*(23), 16211. doi:10.3390u142316211

Grace, M., Scott, A. J., Sadler, J. P., Proverbs, D. G., & Grayson, N. (2021). Exploring the smart-natural city interface; re-imagining and re-integrating urban planning and governance. *Emerald Open Res*, *2*(7), 7. Advance online publication. doi:10.35241/emeraldopenres.13226.2

Greenfield, A. (2010). *Everyware: The dawning age of ubiquitous computing*. New Riders, public lecture, MIT. http://web.mit.edu/uricchio/Public/television/documentary/Greenfield_Everyware.pdf

Hancke, G., Silva, B., & Hancke, G. Jr. (2012). The Role of Advanced Sensing in Smart Cities. *Sensors (Basel)*, *13*(1), 393–425. doi:10.3390130100393 PMID:23271603

Hardt, C., & Bogenberger, K. (2019). Usage of e-Scooters in Urban Environments. *Transportation Research Procedia, 37*(November), 155–162. doi:10.1016/j.trpro.2018.12.178

Hoffman, C. (2020). USB Type A Connector. Everything You Need to Know. *How To Geek*. https://www.howtogeek.com/690160/usb-type-a-connector-everything-you-need-to-know

Hollands, R. (2008). Will the real smart city please stand up? *Will the Real Smart City Please Stand Up*, *12*(3), 303–320. doi:10.1080/13604810802479126

Kango, R., Hadiyanto, E. H. P., & Pongtuluran, E. H. (2021). Design and Implementation of Smart Bench Integrated Solar Cell for Public Space Electricity Saving. *International Journal Papier Advance and Scientific Review*, *2*(2), 72–81. doi:10.47667/ijpasr.v2i2.121

Kitchin, R. (2014). The real-time city? Big data and smart urbanism. *GeoJournal*, *79*(1), 1–14. doi:10.100710708-013-9516-8

Matheus, N. M. & Sastry, M. (2023). Design and Simulation of a Floating Solar Power Plant for Goreagab Dam, Namibia. In *Human Agro-Energy Optimization for Business and Industry*. IGI-Global. doi:10.4018/978-1-6684-4118-3.ch001

Musti, K. S. S. (2020a). *Circular Economy in Energizing Smart Cities*. Book Chapter in Handbook of Research on Entrepreneurship Development and Opportunities in Circular Economy., doi:10.4018/978-1-7998-5116-5.ch013

Musti, K. S. S. (2020b). Quantification of Demand Response in Smart Grids. *IEEE Int. Conf. INDISCON*, pp. 278-282. 10.1109/INDISCON50162.2020.00063

Musti, K. S. S., Iileka, H., & Shidhika, F. (2020). *Industry 4.0-Based Enterprise Information System for Demand-Side Management and Energy Efficiency*. Book Chapter in Novel Approaches to Information Systems Design. doi:10.4018/978-1-7998-2975-1.ch007

Nathali, B., Khan, M., & Han, K. (2018). Towards sustainable smart cities: A review of trends, architectures, components, and open challenges in smart cities. *Sustainable Cities and Society*, *38*, 697–713. doi:10.1016/j.scs.2018.01.053

Pitra, G. M., & Musti, K. S. S. (2021). Duck Curve with Renewable Energies and Storage Technologies. *13th International Conference on Computational Intelligence and Communication Networks (CICN)*, (pp. 66-71). IEEE. 10.1109/CICN51697.2021.9574671

Premier, A., GhaffarianHoseini, A., & GhaffarianHoseini, A. (2022). Solar-powered smart urban furniture: Preliminary investigation on limits and potentials of current designs. *Smart and Sustainable Built Environment*, *11*(2), 334–345. doi:10.1108/SASBE-09-2021-0152

Raza, U., Kulkarni, P., & Sooriyabandara, M. (2017). Low Power Wide Area Networks: An Overview. *IEEE Communications Surveys and Tutorials*, *19*(2), 855–873. doi:10.1109/COMST.2017.2652320

Sastry, M. K. S. (2007). Integrated Outage Management System: An effective solution for power utilities to address customer grievances. *International Journal of Electronic Customer Relationship Management*, *1*(1), 30–40. doi:10.1504/IJECRM.2007.014424

Sastry, M. K. S., & Sahadeo, A. (2015). Distributed Cloud Computing Based GIS Solution for Electrical Power Utility Asset Management. *Int. Conf. on Computational Intelligence and Communication Networks,* (pp. 832-838). IEEE. 10.1109/CICN.2015.169

Schaffers, H., Komninos, N., Pallot, M., Trousse, B., Nilsson, M., & Oliveira, A. (2011). Lecture Notes in Computer Science: Vol. 6656. *Smart Cities and the Future Internet: Towards Cooperation Frameworks for Open Innovation*. Springer. doi:10.1007/978-3-642-20898-0_31

Smartnet. (2019). DataSmart Cities: Empowering Cities through Data. *SmmartNet.* https://smartnet.niua.org/data-smart-cities

Talari, S., Shafie-khah, M., Siano, P., Loia, V., Tommasetti, A., & Catalão, J. (2017). A Review of Smart Cities Based on the Internet of Things Concept. *Energies*, *10*(4), 1–23. doi:10.3390/en10040421

Vallianatos, M. (2015). Uncovering the early history of Big Data and the "Smart City". Los Angeles. *Boom: A Journal of California*. https://boomcalifornia.org/2015/06/16/uncovering-the-early-history-of-big-data-and-the-smart-city-in-la/

KEY TERMS AND DEFINITIONS

Smart City: This is a modern form of a city or an urban space that provides smart living experience. Smart cities are supposed to produce most of the energy required within their own ecosystems and thus are supposed to be eco-friendlier than their legacy versions. They operate more on digital platforms that are powered by niche technologies such as the IIoT.

Solar Smart Bench: This is a futuristic bench that comes in different designs and shapes and is normally installed in public places. It generally has the capability to provide charging a range of facilities such as ports for charging smartphones and e-bikes.

Urban health: This is the term that represents the general health of humans living in modern and urban spaces. Urban health depends on air quality, level of pollution, greenhouse gas emissions in the immediate surroundings.

APPENDIX

A few interesting aspects related to solar smart benches are discussed in terms of questions and answers here in this annexure.

What happens if the battery runs out of power?

The bench will have indicators on it to show the status of the battery, and these should be able to notify the user when the battery is low. The smart bench should have an AC grid connector to connect onto the grid in the case that the battery power has depleted, users can use power from the grid (Acharya et al, 2020). But in the case that the solar smart bench is located in an area where it cannot be connected to the grid, it will have an indicator to let the user know that the battery is recharging. This is also the important reason why data collected by sensors is uploaded onto an online dashboard. The users are able to view the status of the battery, how many devices have been charged on that day and how much power is left in the battery to charge before they get to the bench.

How many days can solar smart bench work without sunlight?

This depends on several factors – such as the number of bench users, share of cloudy hours compared to sunny hours in a day etc (Acharya et al, 2020). The solar smart bench should function normally up to 5 days without direct sun exposure, before the first features start to shut down to save the battery. The last thing that shuts down are USB charging ports.

How to choose networking technologies?

Technical and safety issues related to the use of communication networks can be too wide and exhaustive (Sherif et. Al, 2015). A few, contemporary ICTs have been considered here for solar smart benches. Long Range (LoRa) and Low-Power, Wide-Area Networks (LPWAN) make use of sensors that run on small, low-cost batteries that can be used for years in an operating range that is usually 5 kilometres in urban settings (Raza et. al., 2017). For sending and receiving small amounts of data in a dense location (cities or large buildings) that require long-term monitoring LPWANS are best suited. LoRa LPWAN sensors connect to gateway devices without any connectivity fees (similar to the way that devices might connect to a WiFi network). Cellular: Cellular networks require contracted service agreements, with fees per sensor. In addition to the expense, cellular sensors also struggle with battery life, gaps in coverage and technology sun setting. Sun setting is when a technology is intentionally phased out: there are currently more than 30 million 2G endpoints in the US that no longer work due to sun setting. Cellular networks are best suited for sending larger amounts of data and in cases where short battery life is not a concern. Hardware is typically more expensive. Cellular-based IoT solutions are generally utilized by larger corporations or for smaller sensor deployment numbers.

Chapter 4
Hamburg at the Forefront of the Active Cities

Carlos F. Lahoz
https://orcid.org/0000-0002-8126-5101
Escuela Politécnica Superior. Universidad CEU San Pablo, Spain

José Antonio Blasco
Taller de Ideas – Urban Networks, Spain

ABSTRACT

A sedentary lifestyle is a global and complex problem that, nevertheless, finds a very natural solution: movement. However, promoting physical activity among the population is not a simple task. It requires great efforts from individuals, society, and, particularly, from the urban environment. The concept of an active city arises as a response to make more livable and healthier cities. An increasing number of cities are committing to the active cities model. One of the most advanced is Hamburg. The Hanseatic city counts on a comprehensive strategy involving its entire territory. In this research, the main characteristics of the active city model of Hamburg will be presented and discussed, and the case of two urban interventions that show how the model can be applied to different urban settings: HafenCity and Oberbillwerder. The object of investigating the Hamburg case is to build evidence and references so that other cities can direct their urban policies and actions.

INTRODUCTION

Sedentary lifestyle and physical inactivity have become two of the biggest public health challenges of the 21st century. Already considered pandemics, they are global and complex problems that, nevertheless, find a very natural solution: movement. However, promoting physical activity among the population is not a simple task. It requires great efforts from individuals, society and, particularly, from the urban environment. The severity of this global threat demonstrates, once again, the importance of the role of cities in the maintenance of the health of their inhabitants.

DOI: 10.4018/978-1-6684-6924-8.ch004

To cope with this situation, a new model of managing, planning, and designing cities is being discussed. This model gives priority to health in all its actions, creating opportunities in the built and social environments so that citizens can be physically active in their daily lives. This new model is starting to be known as the *Active City.*

Due to the recentness of this situation and the slowness with which urban processes take place, even though currently an increasing number of cities are committing to the Philosophy of the Active Cities, the reality is that there are very few comprehensive examples of good practice globally. Although several cities have achieved very considerable accomplishments, the case of the German city of Hamburg is particularly relevant. The Hanseatic city is unique because it has an integral strategy involving its entire territory with two large–scale urban development projects of diverse nature that show how the model can be applied to different urban settings. This is the reason why it has been decided to study the Free and Hanseatic City.

Therefore, the object of the research is to present the case of Hamburg and how it is implementing the Model of Active Cities in its territory with the intention of building evidence and references so that other cities can direct their urban actions in the same direction.

To accomplish this end, the argument scheme will be developed structuring its content after the following steps. First, in the background will be discussed: the relevance of inactivity and sedentary behavior and how they are becoming some of the most important public health problems in global terms; the role that built environment can play to tackle this challenge and to promote active behavior; and finally, the Active Cities Model will be presented and defined. Later, on the discussion, the research will delve into the main characteristics of the *Active City Model* of Hamburg (Active City Master Plan) and how the city is implementing it. For doing so, the research will center its focus on the case of two urban interventions that show how the model can be applied to two different urban settings: HafenCity and Oberbillwerder.

Finally, it is important to note that the methodology used to approach the application of the Active City model in the case of the two urban development projects, particularly Oberbillwerder, follows the approach set out in the book *Hacia la Ciudad Activa. Estrategias urbanas para hacer las ciudades más vivibles y saludables* (Blasco Abad, Lahoz Palacio, & Martínez-Arrarás Caro, 2022; Lahoz & Blasco, 2023). The book develops a guide for the analysis and design of the Active City Model which proposes 15 criteria for its evaluation.

BACKGROUND: HEALTHY CITIES IN THE 21ST CENTURY, TOWARDS THE ACTIVE CITY

Inactivity and Sedentary Behavior: An Emerging Pandemic

Cities are like people who, at certain times in their lives, tend to face situations that require a far-reaching decision for their evolution. They come to a crossroad and must determine the most appropriate way forward.

The frenetic urban development of the last decades (Oginga-Martins & Sharifi, 2022) has generated a varied set of problems with harmful consequences for the human health: from the poor environmental quality due to air pollution, to the increasing diagnosis of diseases related to excessive sedentary behavior (Frank, Andresen, & Schmid, 2004; Swinburn et al., 2019) or the lack of social interaction, which has a very negative impact on the mental well-being of the citizens.

However, modern society is seeking health with determination, even obsessively. But, although in general terms, adequate habits are adopted to preserve health, contradictory customs are often maintained, such as smoking or drinking alcohol in excess, among others. They are, of course, individual decisions, but as it is stated by the World Health Organization (WHO, 2022), they also have very direct links to community affairs such as the management of public health and social security systems.

Of particular concern is the direct influence of physical inactivity on the appearance and development of many non-communicable diseases and chronic disorders such as obesity, diabetes, heart disease, high blood pressure, depression or different types of cancer, as well as on premature mortality (Lee et al., 2012). Proof of the veracity and significance of this relationship is the publication by the World Health Organization of various resolutions: WHA51.18 (World Health Organization Assembly, WHOA, 1998), EB109/1 (109 Executive Board, World Health Organization, WHOEB, 2002), WHA55.23 (WHOA, 2002), for its prevention and control. In the case of Spain, as it is stated by the Fundación España Activa in its Sedentary lifestyle thermometer in Spain, 2017, 13.4 percent of all deaths are attributable to physical inactivity, representing more than 52,000 deaths per year (Mayo, Del Villar, & Jiménez, 2017). This figure is similar to the number of deaths from COVID-19 in the country during the first year of the pandemic (Centro de Coordinación de Alertas y Emergencias Sanitarias, 2021) and 50 times higher when compared to the number of deaths from traffic accidents in the same territory as it is stated by the Dirección General de Tráfico (DGT, 2021), the Traffic Authority of the Spanish Government. In addition, on an economic level, the impact of physical inactivity on health entails an annual burden for the country which has been estimated at EUR 1,560 million (Mayo et al., 2017).

The trend towards inactivity and sedentary behavior has accelerated in recent decades (MacCallum, Howson, & Gopu, 2016). Moreover, it is a global problem, which does not affect only developed societies. Emerging economies also seem to follow this dynamic, even more rapidly (MacCallum et al., 2016). This acceleration and globalization of sedentary behavior in recent years is the perverse result of the profound changes in the forms of production and entertainment, as well as of the processes of global urbanization and motorization (Blasco Abad et al., 2022; Frank et al., 2004).

The phenomenon is very complex. However, medical research points towards simple and natural solutions: the motion of the individuals and the interaction between them (WHO, 2010). This new behavior means reconsidering the way citizens move, the way they relate, the day-to-day decisions they make, etc. The city, the physical environment, is decisive for this (Edwards & Tsouros, 2006). Thus, in the 21st century, health has come into play by pointing the way: the active behavior of citizens.

The Role of The Physical Environment on The Promotion of Active Behavior

Cities, as the main scene of human life, have a great responsibility on the promotion of physical exercise. Consequently, architecture and urban spaces have a substantial impact on the health status of their inhabitants (Edwards & Tsouros, 2008; Active Well-being Initiative, 2017). This maxim is verified to the extent that it can be stated that urban planning and health are two concepts inextricably linked together. This statement has generated intense debates that have marked the evolution of buildings, city structures and urban spaces (Colomina, 2021). In addition, cities have once again gained prominence as the main centers of the battle against epidemics. Not only COVID-19, but also regarding one the most harmful pandemics in recent years: sedentary behavior.

As it already happened in the 19th century with the consequences derived from the Industrial Revolution (Engels, 2020; Johnson, 2007), the city can play a crucial role in combating the epidemics associated with this time. It is important to highlight obesity or other chronic related diseases, that have already been mentioned, are the result of unhealthy habits. On the other hand, many scientific studies (Mayo et al., 2017) point out the importance of appropriate architectural and urban design to promote regular physical activity or healthy eating (Eitler, McMahon, & Thoerig, 2013). Consequently, to ensure the health of citizens, it is once again that society is looking towards physical exercise and sport as a remedy. And, it is also again, that cities take on a major responsibility. The current advantage is that these types of practices have already been assumed by society. However, the aim this time is to transform the way people carry them out. Active practices must stop being something specific and linked mainly to leisure time to become a regular activity, fully integrated in people's lives.

As a result, there is no question about the fact that cities can help overcome these unprecedented health problems by favoring the active behavior of the population. As a positive reaction, aware of the role they are called to play in improving the quality of life of the present and future generations, many cities are beginning to promote a dynamic and healthy culture in their urban spaces.

These cities are starting to be known as Active Cities: a new model for achieving healthier cities with greater quality of life (Edwards & Tsouros, 2008).

The Active Cities Model

An Active City could be defined as the one that decides to give real priority to health in all its actions, creating opportunities in the built and social environments so that citizenship can be physically active in its daily life (Blasco Abad et al., 2022).

Any city can become active. It only must commit itself to the real promotion of healthy living habits, to provide a structure to work in that direction and to implement a transversal process in the design and management of the city. This is the way to achieve more livable, healthier, and more sustainable cities.

The challenge of transforming a city into an Active City requires the participation of the entire community. Promoting physical activity in the population is not a simple task and requires individual, social, and environmental efforts. Of course, the behavior of people, who must adopt active customs as a new way of life, is essential, but this decision should be facilitated by the characteristics of the physical environment, because the design of the city determines how citizens use it.

Active behavior does not only affect formal sports practice or other structured physical activities but includes many other practices such as strolling or active transport, walking or by bicycle, that are very effective for maintaining or improving the health, and for which the characteristics of the environment are crucial. The aim is to integrate physical activity into daily life, enabling it to be developed in as many areas as possible, with particular attention to those places where most of the daily life takes place, such as workspace or school, squares and parks or streets (Lahoz & Blasco, 2023).

An increasing number of towns are committing to the concept of Active City ("Global Active City Label," n.d.). Some have achieved very considerable accomplishments and are at the forefront of the application of the model. They are cities that stand out above others because of the ambition of their programs and the degree of fulfillment with the model. Hamburg is at the forefront of this group (Beacher, 2018; hamburg.de, 2018). The German city stands out for the extension and depth of its vision of the Active City Model (Beckereit et al., 2022). This vision combines policies and general proposals applicable throughout its territory with specific interventions, both for existing areas, but also for the new, with recent developments being designed according to the model guidelines.

HAMBURG AT THE FOREFRONT OF THE ACTIVE CITIES

The recent history of Hamburg has a very significant date: 1989. The Fall of the Berlin Wall precipitated the disappearance of the Iron Curtain, leading to the German Reunification. This enabled Hamburg to restore its privileged strategic location. Since then, the city would tackle major urban transformations to take on a leading role in the new Germany.

The urban renewal undertaken would meet that fundamental objective, but other complementary goals would also be engaged, such as achieving a more humane, attractive, sustainable, and healthy city. Many of the interventions focused on environmental issues, which led to the designation of Hamburg as European Green Capital in 2011 (European Commission, 2011). Various initiatives were promoted in this direction, highlighting, for example, the *Green Network Plan* (F Landschaftsarchitekten, 2018) designed to ensure all green areas of the city would be connected by pedestrian and cycle paths, or the construction of a 3.5 km park over the A-7 Highway with the aim of reconnecting the surrounding neighborhoods that had been segregated since the construction of the large traffic infrastructure 30 years before.

Sport would emerge as the other major driver of the urban strategy. Hamburg firmly believed that sport and exercise would play an increasingly important role in ensuring a healthy and happy population.

In 2011, a number of institutions related to the world of sports and the economic sectors launched together a declaration called *Sportgeist Hamburg* (Beckereit et al., 2011), in which they encouraged to enhance the sporting spirit of the city. The statement was assumed by the Hamburg Senate, initiating a strategy that would be developed in the following years. This strategy, named *HAMBURGmachtSPORT* (Beckereit et al., 2011), translatable as Hamburg Practices Sport, would orientate to the transformation of the Hanseatic City to a place especially linked to sports and active life. Since then, the whole city has been involved in its evolution towards the Active City Model. This is initially apparent from the fact that, although Hamburg has a considerable number of sports facilities (hamburg.de, n.d.), it aims to further strengthen that infrastructure and, moreover, to extend the opportunity for doing physical exercise to the whole city. In order to achieve this objective, the authorities approved the *Active City Master Plan* (Der Freien und Hansestadt Hamburg, 2016) which, with the theme *Für mehr Bewegung in Hamburg* (For More Exercise in Hamburg), sets out the guidelines and projects to be carried out until 2024.

In addition to this general programming, it is worth highlighting two recent cases, which may represent Hamburg's commitment to the Active City Model and how the city applies it to different urban circumstances. The first case is somewhat particular because it was designed before the concept of Active City was consolidated. This is HafenCity, one of the most recognized large scale urban development projects in recent times (Lobo, 2014), whose design anticipates many of the model's requirements by suggesting ways of adapting pre-existing spaces. The second case is especially paradigmatic because it involves the creation of a new district which aspires to become an example of good practice of the Active City Model: Oberbillwerder. Its design represents a qualitative jump in Urban Planning because, for one of the first times, physical exercise and health are incorporated as priority requirements from the outset (IBA Hamburg GmbH, 2017). Its willingness to become a healthy and active life reference determines both its innovative conception and its development.

Both examples are revealing because of their innovative proposals, many of which will be treated in more depth later. Many of the common features and fundamental objectives that have been addressed in these outstanding urban interventions coincide with the main strategies that characterize and guide the action of cities that want to evolve towards the Active City Model (Blasco Abad et al., 2022). These strategies are:

1. Intensification, with gradual density and compactness.

The Active City claims the presence of citizens in public space. For ensuring that, it is important to foster high population densities (increasing the number of dwellings as much as it is desirable and possible) and reaching certain spatial compacity.

2. Diversification, with an intense mix of varied uses.

The Active City requires diversity. The mix of uses is essential for this purpose, so that the multiplication of activities in the same place propels the vitality of space, social interaction, and the reduction of distant commuting.

3. Distribution, making everyday needs easily reachable.

The Active City aims at service distribution that tends to homogeneously distribute throughout its territory. The closer it approaches that hypothetical perfection; the closer supply will be to demands of all kinds. For the Active City it is essential that the citizens can meet their daily needs in their close by environment.

4. Systematization, integrating nature and urban areas into the network.

The Active City demands a new relationship with nature, both external and internal, and proposes the creation of a system that relates all elements to a purpose. The Active City seeks to link spaces to allow fluidity in contrast to the discontinuity that produces leaps. Systematizing involves connecting the city with its territory to create an integrated compound.

5. Approximation, because public spaces "come out" to meet the citizen.

The Active City proposes squares and parks to take part in the daily lives of people. The Active City pursues the proximity of the citizen to a variety of distributed uses, but also to the gathering places that reactivate social life, that allow physical exercise and offer free and quality air.

6. Experimentation, thanks to its programming to allow multiple activities.

The Active City aims to provide its citizens with attractive and varied activities in their public places, being this one of the most effective ways for their use and occupation. Programming is to think about users and to provide them with a sampler of activities that will meet their interests.

7. Universalization, due to its integrative and inclusive nature, covering all ages and circumstances.

The Active City is the city of all citizens and one of the main features of that principle is the design of an inclusive, accessible, secure, that is, universal space.

8. Connectivity, with physical and emotional links to the environment.

The urban network of the Active City should be a grid that allows the possibility of alternative journeys, that guarantees the creation of routes, that ultimately offers multiple ways of being traveled through with a varied and free set of options.

9. Stimulation, because they are neighborhoods designed to stroll and enjoy space.

The Active City aims to make urban spaces more viable, e.g., to animate them by incorporating incentives to attract citizens to move around them. The expected result is to enhance the walkability as the starting point of a process that feedbacks itself because people are the best claim for people.

10. Prioritization of public transport with attractive and efficient stations.

The Active City therefore aims to increase the importance of public transport in the city. Mass transportation provides sustainability, efficiency and economy, basic criteria that are complemented by the performance of physical exercise on the way to access it.

11. Modulation of road traffic, making the car almost unnecessary.

To modulate is to establish grades as harmoniously as possible. The Active City wants to adjust the intensity of the relationship between different modes of traffic by regulating their presence according to new criteria, such as the calming of the private vehicle mobility.

12. Toning up the residents, thanks to the proposed mobility dynamics that help their physical condition.

Toning up is to give strength or invigorate the body or a part of it. This has a direct relationship with the physical form that the Active City aspires to induce in citizens. One of the best ways to achieve this is to walk and pedal, e.g., fulfilling the purposes for alternative mobility.

13. Hybridization, for example, by seeking to merge sport facilities with daily life.

A hybrid is the product of the fusion of elements of different nature. Physical exercise should become part of the lifestyle of the citizens, either as an activity on its own or by filling the gaps between other daily actions. To promote this, the Active City encourages the hybridization of sports centers with many other functions.

14. Citizen application and interaction.

To apply oneself is to do something conscientiously, to make efforts to achieve a goal, to put the maximum interest in executing something. The Active City Schools aim to become the nucleus of neighborhood life, to transform themselves into centers around which residents orbit, integrating learning with social interaction, leisure, culture and intergenerational sporting practice.

15. Balancing, helping to make work compatible with physical exercise.

To balance is to find an equilibrium between things or issues that appear to be contradictory or very different. The word has been successful as a reference to the necessarily fair relation between personal and work life. The Active City moves one step forward by proposing the compatibility of professional activities with the exercise. The working environment, in particular the buildings, should facilitate this aspiration.

The Hamburg Active City Master Plan

Hamburg's commitment to sport has been intense for many years. Both citizens and policymakers have historically driven this involvement. Proof to this has been the *HAMBURGmachtSPORT* strategy (Beckereit, Holstein, Unkelbach, Mantell, & Beine, 2016; Beckereit et al., 2011). Its implementation led the city to submit its nomination in 2015 to organize the 2024 Olympic Games (Projektgruppe „Olympia für Hamburg", 2014). The results of the surveys and studies carried out that year seemed to endorse the aspirations (Planungsmanagement & Projektberatung GmbH, PROPROJEKT & Albert Speer & Partner GmbH, AS&P, 2016):

- 80% of Hamburg residents practiced sport, with the same degree of participation in all genders.
- 600,000 people, almost one third of the population, were members of sports clubs or belonged to sports associations.
- More than 1,000 gifted and talented children were being trained to compete in the Olympic Games.
- There were nearly 1,600 sports facilities, including 240 sports fields and 120 tennis courts.

Nevertheless, despite these favorable indicators, the city ended up withdrawing the nomination that same year when 51,6% of the population rejected the proposal in a referendum (Behörde für Inneres und Sport. Freien und Hansestadt Hamburg, 2016). Economic concerns seemed to have been critical to the decision.

However, the city had taken important steps in the preparation of the Olympic bid, so the authorities considered studying how to take advantage of the progress made by setting new objectives to guide its strategy for the future. The Senate of Hamburg was aware of the close link between sports and urban planning policies. So, as a result, the City of Hamburg got prepared to become the experimental laboratory of a strong idea: Hamburg would be a reference to the *Sport for All Philosophy* (Beacher, 2018) which aimed to form an active urban society that would show the strengths of physical exercise and healthy living to achieve well-being and a good quality of life. By taking that decision, Hamburg took the definitive steps to walk towards the Active Cities Model.

Different lines of action were then opened. It is worth mentioning the great momentum for children's and youth sports in clubs, educational and social institutions, for high-performance sport and for the promotion of major sporting events, as well as for the support for professional leagues. Although the main objective was not forgotten: the promotion of health, leisure, sport and physical exercise for the general public. This purpose was evidenced on the support to the work of sports clubs and private institutions.

Hamburg's Active City Master Plan conceived by Planungsmanagement & Projektberatung GmbH (PROPROJEKT) & Albert Speer & Partner GmbH (AS&P) (2016) was created with the main objective of encouraging Hamburg citizens, regardless of their age, to increase their physical activity. It was initially organized into five areas. Three covered interventions for the general population and amateur sport with sports fields in schools and sports clubs, the promotion of physical activity and sport practice in public spaces and sports for all programs. Two were directed towards competition in sports by supporting young and high-performance athletes.

Complementarily, the failed Olympic bid forced a review of the *HAMBURGmachtPORT* strategy in 2016 (Beckereit et al., 2016). Ten lines of action were then established which included most of the original objectives, but focused on the general population, as detailed below. The renewed Master Plan is an example of institutional coordination between the different departments involved such as the Sports Department, Urban Development and Housing, Environment and Energy, Economy, Transport, as well as the Finance Department along with the Chamber of Commerce. Its time horizon ends in 2024, although the tool has been conceived with a certain degree of flexibility in its objectives, so the monitoring and evaluation of achievements are constantly reviewed. The *Active City Master Plan* (PROPROJEKT & AS&P, 2016) is based on some basic assumptions: Sport is considered the basis of health and social life. Therefore, adequate facilities should be readily available throughout the city and, finally, people should be properly motivated and activated to practice sports. The Master plan contemplates measures that involve all forms of physical activity, from physical education for children or exercise therapy for the elderly to the support of professional athletes.

The ten main guidelines are:

1. ***SPORTmachtSTADT.*** Sport makes a city. With this statement, sport (also physical exercise) becomes a guiding vector of the urban development, structuring growth (as it will be seen in the case of Oberbillwerder) and providing criteria for the renewal of existing urban spaces.
2. ***PLATZmachtSPORT.*** Investments in sports facilities, which are essential to achieving the main objective. The plan proposes significant expenditure in an already well-equipped urban infrastructure.
3. ***HAMBURGmachtLEISTUNG.*** With the theme: From kindergarten to Olympic Champion, the Master Plan encourages children and young people to begin a life linked to sport or, at least, to regular physical activity. In the end, the training of champs is a secondary objective compared to the basic purpose of making physical exercise an inseparable part of the lives of children, youngsters and, ultimately, of everyone.
4. ***EVENTmachtHAMBURG.*** The city as a venue for sporting events. In parallel to the more urban-oriented measures, such as the first two listed before, Hamburg does not neglect the power of high-performance sport as a driver for physical activity. Other aspects, essentially regarding economic and identity considerations, also favor cities that serve as venues for major sporting events.
5. ***SPORTmachtUMWELT.*** Sport as support of the environment. Hamburg, openly declared in favor of sustainability and the environment, as it was confirmed by its nomination as European Green Capital in 2011 (Klocke, Kastens, & Buhr, 2012), insists on the influence of sport and physical activity for the improvement of the environment. To back up this claim, the city proposed measures to transform mobility, with strong support for walkability and cycling.
6. ***SPORTmachtGESUND.*** Sport as support of health. This guideline is the main foundation of the Active City. Hamburg is therefore committed to encouraging citizens to acquire active habits through campaigns and other strategies.
7. ***HAMBURGmachtSERVICE.*** Another important aspect concerns the public administration in charge of providing sport services. Despite some legislative acts for promoting physical activity and sport, or the ease of the use of public facilities, Hamburg conducts information campaigns as well as surveys and workshops to involve citizens and public administration officials.

8. ***SPORTmachtHAMBURG.*** The image of the city is linked to sports. The influence of high-performance sports to encourage the population to start their practice is very high. Moreover, it also contributes to forging an identity that, correctly channeled by the power of media, can be very beneficial for the economy of the city. Hosting sport events brings together these two drivers of motivation and projection.
9. ***HAMBURGmachtSTARK.*** Based on the *Sport for All* Program, Hamburg strongly supports the physical activities of all its residents, no matter their circumstances. Regardless of age, gender, origin, or difficulties that they may suffer, everyone, with their own possibilities, will be included in the sports offer of the city.
10. ***SPORTmachtPOLITIK.*** Sport as a conditioning factor of politics. The program concludes with a directive that expresses the commitment of the political leaders to the Active City Model. An active citizenship will ensure that the continuous work implied by the acceptance of the Active City Model does not decline at any time. In this sense, the attitude of the population becomes a critical factor to guarantee the continuity and coherence of politicians, who are regularly evaluated through elections.

Based on these categories, the Active City Master Plan proposes specific projects, programs, events, and various initiatives of different kinds. Among these, interventions in the public space which aim to promote outdoor sport practice, such as the installation of sports infrastructure in parks, running routes and the city's cycling network, are particularly noteworthy. It is also worth mentioning the "Sport for All" campaign, with fitness initiatives for senior citizens, or the increase of inclusive sports offers, both public and private, to improve the integration of immigrants and refugees. In parallel to the new initiatives, a program has also been launched to improve facilities in schools or sports clubs, as well as those linked to high-performance sports. This is the case with the cycling and ice-skating track in Stellingen, the tennis courts in Rotherbaum, the equestrian park in Klein Flottbek or rowing in Dove-Elbe.

In addition to the above, Hamburg sums its own App to promote physical activity among its citizens, Active City Hamburg (Active City Hamburg, n.d.; Freie und Hansestadt Hamburg, n.d.). It is a free mobile app that provides information on events, courses, and other sports-related activities. It also offers suitable places for carrying out specific sports and routes throughout the city. Complementary, the app finds and connects people with an affinity according to their favorite sport disciplines, their schedules, locations, etc. with the aim of integrating groups, or simply to help find partners to avoid lonely practicing. Among the app's very diverse utilities it is also included the collection of data about the journeys followed by different users or the intensity of their training to allow comparisons to improve performance or to accomplish health related goals. Although there are various applications on the market that offer these possibilities, the particularity of the one developed in Hamburg is that it focuses on the possibilities of the city, reaching a level of urban detail much higher than that of the more generic applications.

Hafencity, An Active City Before the Active City

HafenCity is one of the most recognized urban renewals of recent times and, although it was designed before the consolidation of the concept of Active Cities, the design meets the requirements of the model in many aspects. The circumstances involved with the birth of this project were linked to the availability of the old port facilities on the north bank of the Elbe next to the urban center, and to the fall of the Iron Curtain, which allowed Hamburg to regain its central location in Germany and more so, in Europe. This privileged position made the location particularly attractive for large multinational companies, driving demand for new facilities and spaces for both the executives and the many workers arriving from the former German Democratic Republic. In 1991, the regeneration of all the old port began, anticipating a high quality new urban space that became the soul of the whole urban renewal project. Its location made it possible to expand the city center with a mix-use urban program that brought together new business areas, public facilities, leisure spaces and good design. While the first proposals were made public in 1997, the complete Master Plan was finally presented in 2000 (Ministry of Urban Development and Environment and Ministry of Labour and Economic Affairs. Free and Hanseatic City of Hamburg, 2006). The team responsible for the design, as the result of winning the First Price in an International Competicion, comprised ASTOC Architects & Planners, KCAP (Kees Christiaanse Architects & Planners) and Hamburgplan AG.

Figure 1. HafenCity Masterplan; Designed by ASTOC, KCAP and Hamburgplan AG for: HafenCity Hamburg GmbH and Freie und Hansestadt Hamburg; Lic. ©ASTOC/KCAP Architects and Planners/ Hamburgplan AG

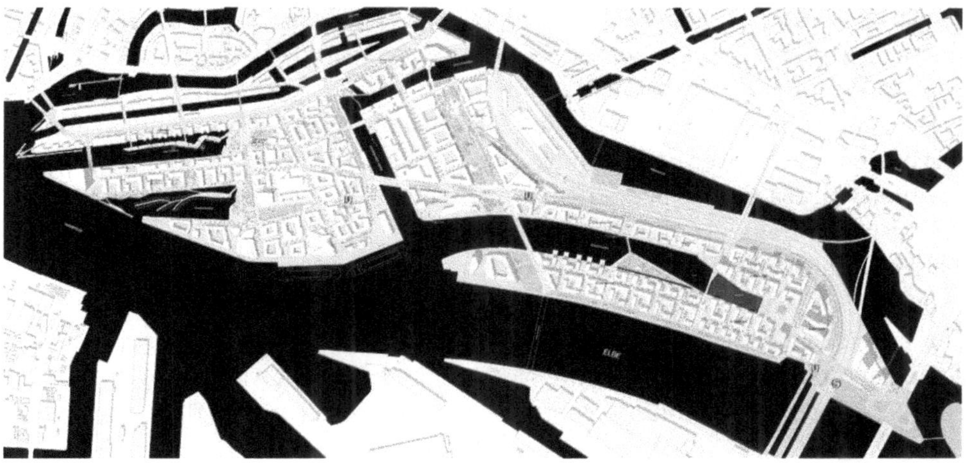

As it is stated in the final version of HafenCity Hamburg Masterplan, the 157 hectares area of intervention (30 of which are water) holds 7,000 dwellings, space for productive activities capable of generating 45,000 jobs (35,000 office employments), 200,000 m^2 of retail space, 300,000 m^2 of public facilities and nearly 28 hectares of public space, as well as 10 kilometers of river fronts.

The construction work started in 2002. The following year, the first commercial building was opened, while the initial residents arrived in 2006. The project conclusion is estimated in 2030.

HafenCity as Active City

Although HafenCity is a new neighborhood, its configuration has been conditioned by several preexisting buildings and infrastructures that were maintained. The complex is organized in ten areas that hold a specific character but without falling into the traditional zoning conceptions. The idiosyncrasy of each one of them, achieved by a thorough work on the proposed uses, enhances the value of the whole. This makes HafenCity perceived as a unit, with a continuous spatial narrative, although structured into individual chapters with their own identity. To be precise, the way in which the mix of uses has been articulated in the compound is one of the main reasons that brings it closer to the philosophy of the Active City. In HafenCity, the residential, commercial, office, public or tourist uses are mixed not only in plan, but also three-dimensionally, in the buildings themselves, both at the street level and above (Bruns-Berentelg, Jürgen, 2017). A physical repercussion of this will is reflected, for example, on the fact that the ground floors of the buildings, even the residential ones, are 5 meters high (Freire Silva, 2014). This dimension, which is much larger than the most frequently measurements used for dwellings, prepares the buildings to accommodate uses with special spatial needs related to cultural or commercial programs. In addition, they are more suitable for refurbishment and transformation, thus providing added flexibility in the long-term use.

Besides the three-dimensional mix of uses, another feature that brings HafenCity closer to the requirements of the Active City is its mobility strategy. Firstly, because the arrangement of some of the proposed main facilities are located at distant points. This effect introduces an urban tension that centers the focus on these points, setting destinations and generating acceptable internal routes to stimulate walking or cycling journeys. A policy of gradual replacement of private automobiles with other alternative mobility options, such as car sharing, has also been adopted. On this line, it should be noted that a station has been installed with almost 400 vehicles available to be shared. Electric mobility is also being promoted through a solid infrastructure of charging stations.

The design of the public space of HafenCity is also aligned with the intentions of the Active City Philosophy even before the appearance of the actual model. Streets, squares and parks offer a wide variety of recreational places and the pedestrian areas predominate over the roads (Praticò, 2015), giving preference to the public transport over private.

A peculiarity of HafenCity´s urban space is the way it responds to one of Hamburg's traditional problems, the rising of the water levels of the Elbe. The water level rises two or three times a year, between three and four meters, both due to the influence of the tides (even though the North Sea is far away) and the flow increments collected in the Hamburg basin. Although dikes, walls and ground level rises have been implemented to ensure the protection of the area and to avoid periodic flooding, in some areas, the possibility of river overflows has been considered as part of the design of public spaces.

HafenCity seeks urban intensity, density of people and interactions. Therefore, it is committed to the functional complexity of a compact program with a mixture of varied uses. The balance between urban activities, the unique configuration of public spaces or the strategy for the use of its pre-existences, make the new district of Hamburg a good model for other urban centers of European cities in the 21st century.

Oberbillwerder, An Active-From-The-Start District

Oberbillwerder represents a qualitative jump in Urban Planning because, for the first time, physical exercise and health are incorporated as priority requirements from the outset. Its willingness to become a healthy and active life reference determines both its innovative conception and its development.

The creation of the new neighborhood follows two different strategies: *Mehr Stadt in der Stadt* (More City in the City), which proposes increases in the density of the central areas; and *Mehr Stadt an Neuen Orten* (More city in New Places), which enables new developments.

As it is stated in *The Connected City. Masterplan Oberbillwerder* (IBA Hamburg GmbH, 2019), the process began in 2016, with an ambitious participation process aimed to learn about the aspirations of citizens. The results obtained allowed it to set the general objectives as well as its cost and financing plan. In 2018, the Senate created a specific company for the implementation of the new district: IBA Projektentwicklongs GmbH & Co. KG and an international competition for the urban planning of the area was launched. The winning proposal was the Masterplan designed by the team ADEPT APS from Copenhagen (ADEPT, 2019), KARRES + BRANDS from Holland (KARRES + BRANDS, n.d.) and Transsolar Energietechnik GmbH from Stuttgart (Transsolar Energietechnik GmbH, 2019). The first construction works are planned to begin in 2023, while the housing units will start construction by 2026.

The main figures of the urban program point to the construction of 7,000 affordable housing units of different typologies; the creation of some 5,000 jobs, complemented by various educational centers (university, schools, and nurseries), as well as several social, cultural and leisure institutions. The district will have about 28 hectares of open and green public spaces with numerous play and sports areas.

Figure 2. Oberbillwerder masterplan; © IBA Hamburg GmbH, © ADEPT ApS, © KARRES + BRANDS

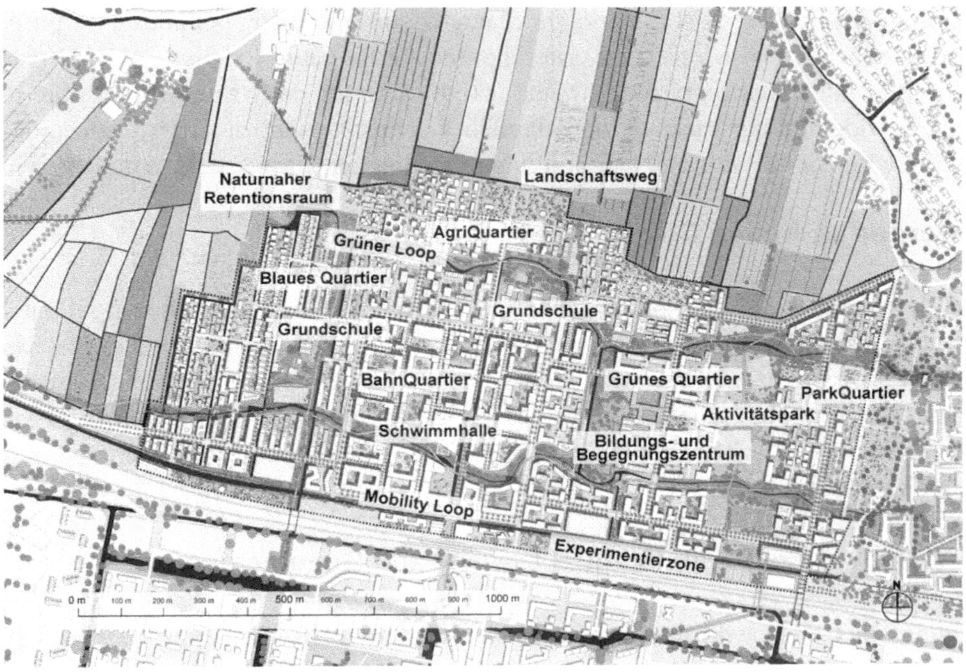

Oberbillwerder is organized in five different districts. The central position is occupied by *Bahn-Quartier* (Neighborhood Station), the most "urban" and equipped of all, which is distinguished by its closed-block morphology. To the west is *Blaue Quartier* (Blue District), characterized by the presence of water in its drainage canals. In the north, the *AgriQuartier* (Agricultural Neighborhood or Garden) makes the transition with the adjacent cultivated landscapes and, on to the east, it is possible to find the *Grüne Quartier* (Green District) which links with a large activity park that includes a great sporting offer. Finally, at the eastern end, it is the *ParkQuartier* (Neighborhood Park) articulating the new district with neighboring Bergedorf-West.

The coexistence of very different typologies of urban tissues is also characteristic. It is possible to distinguish conventional streets with different sections according to the traffic they host, or streets sided by water canals. But, above all, the rich network of public spaces, a green and blue grid (vegetation and water), which is deployed intertwining all parts of the new urban core while being the main feature of the district: *The Grüner Loop* (Green Loop).

Finally, the various visual relations established both internally and towards the outside are also unique. In the north-south direction, the streets are mostly straight and continuous, allowing distant prospects of the surrounding landscape in both directions. On the other hand, in the east-west direction, the straight street guidelines are truncated so that there is no visual continuity. This is also the case with the Grüner Loop due to its winding route.

The main idea of the project is that of a *Connected City*, which was the leitmotif used by the winning team of the competition. This is explained both by the physical connections with the exterior and in the interior design thanks to the *Grüner Loop*. It is also expressed by the "spiritual" links that integrate the way of life of its citizens with the environment and with themselves. Oberbillwerder was also born as a sustainable city, proposing a complete ecosystem in which water and nature, energy or resource treatment are substantial. But the most remarkable characteristic of the compound for the purpose of this investigation is the way it has adopted the criteria of the Active City Model.

Oberbillwerder integrates sport and physical activity into the daily lives of its future residents. It does not only provide running tracks or football pitches. It ensures that all citizens can enjoy a dynamic community life with comfortable and safe walking or cycling and easy access to daily services.

Oberbillwerder as Active City

The methodology applied for the evaluation of Oberbillwerder follows the approach set out in the book *Hacia la Ciudad Activa. Estrategias urbanas para hacer las ciudades más vivibles y saludables* (Towards the Active City. Urban strategies to make cities more livable and healthier) (Blasco Abad et al., 2022; Lahoz & Blasco, 2023). The book develops a guide for the analysis and design of the Active City Model which proposes 15 criteria for its evaluation. The following comments on Oberbillwerder are structured upon those guidelines.

Intensification: A District With Gradual Density and Compactness

As it is stated in The Connected City Masterplan Oberbillwerder (IBA Hamburg GmbH, 2019), the new district, which will be Hamburg's 105th, covers 123.7 hectares and is expected to house 15,000 residents. The gross density is 121 persons per hectare (12,096 people/km^2) or 56.6 dwellings per hectare (7,000 planned units). It needs to be noticed that all these figures are gross and present differences by area due to an intelligent approach for the distribution of the compacities and densities in the formal model. The district has a gradually increasing density towards the center. Out of the five entities that make up the complete district, the central one offers the highest parameters, while the other four that surround the center and articulate the transition of the urban areas with the periphery (agricultural land in the north and west, urban land to the south and east) present lower ratios. Thus *BahnQuartier* (Neighborhood Station) is the densest of all, holding 200 people per hectare (nearly 100 housing units per hectare). These values decrease fifty percent for the remaining areas.

Given that half of the area is not buildable, it can be assumed that the net density values are proportionally higher. Moreover, Oberbillwerder will offer 1,020,000 m^2 built-in units, providing a compactness ratio (buildability index) of 0.82 m^2/m^2.

Diversification: A District With an Intense Mix of Very Varied Uses

The mix of uses is a priority objective in the planning approach of Oberbillwerder, which aims to be a diverse and lively place. To achieve this, an intense functional combination is presented, allowing a wide range of options for living, working, education, culture, and leisure. The functional structure of the district is articulated by the distribution of a set of small-scale facilities. This preference for the proposal of small facilities distributed throughout the area, compared to the traditional concentrations in a single location, is one of the most distinctive signs of identity and character of the district.

The basic principle is to distribute elements with great flexibility, in the expectation that time and circumstances may force changes, especially those related to the economic situation. Regarding this concern, the distribution of uses mixes very diverse functions: daily supplies and services; small retail, preferably located close to the railway station; coworking spaces and offices, both integrated within apartment blocks or in complete buildings; start-ups and other specific spaces labeled as tiny innovation campus; premises for the provision of health, education and social services; and, even, dedicated land for craft and soft industries, essentially located in the *Experimental Area*.

The variety of functions presented on the ground floors of the constructions is reinforced with that of the higher levels in some buildings, so the final diversification of uses is both horizontal and vertical.

Distribution: A District Where Everything Is "At Hand"

The dimensions of the district make it very walkable. This helps to ensure the proximity of the main services, but their distribution is also decisive for guaranteeing that proximity. The distribution of uses, reinforced by the general organization structured in five areas, results in an urban environment aligned as well with the 15 Minutes City Model (Allam, Moreno, Chabaud, & Pratlong, 2022).

Systematization: A District in Which the Natural and the Urban Are Integrated Into a Network

The integration of the natural and urban environments is outstanding thanks to the symbiosis created by the mixture of the characteristics of the landscape with the functional requirements of the inhabited places. It is also remarkable how water has been integrated as a design resource (the blue network). The water table in Oberbillwerder is almost at the surface level, making drainage an essential topic. The old irrigation ditches, in which water concentrates for extraction, have inspired the urban structure of the new district whose channels continue to fulfill that mission. In addition, there is the meandering *Grüner Loop*, the green network of about 15 hectares, that overflows the internal space of the district linking its five neighborhoods with a system of green spaces.

Approximation: A District Where Public Spaces Go Out to Meet the Citizen

The proximity of the public spaces is optimal. The dimensions of the new district, some 1,700 meters in the east-west direction and 750 meters in average on the north-south, favors this proximity. Although the main factor is the high proportion of public spaces with respect to the total area. Only the green and blue networks account for 27.2% of the whole area.

Experimentation: A District Programmed With Multiple Activities

The public space offers different alternatives for free or programmed use. It has been designed to allow diverse types of sports modalities (practiced individually or in groups but also informally or in specific spaces such as tracks or pitches), as well as collective activities for social interaction.

Moreover, it is worth mentioning the planned horticultural parcellations, totaling six hectares of land and divided into some 200 lots of approximately 300 m^2. Gardening and horticulture provide multiple benefits. The physical exercise involved in their maintenance is crucial, but the actual production of food (although in some cases it can be considered merely cosmetic) and the satisfaction of the cultivator for the accomplishment of the work done, are also very important.

It is also particularly interesting the so-called Experimental Area, the southern strip separating the district from the railway line. It will hold temporary buildings and interventions for events, while offering opportunities for large areas for play and sports, orchards, and other related uses.

Universalization: An Inclusive District for all Ages and Circumstances

Oberbillwerder will be a socially diverse city. It is estimated that the population will comprise people of different income levels, as well as of different ages, professions, and origins. It will be an inclusive city thanks to the design of its public space, which addresses gender requirements, like women's safety, intergenerational requirements, with a special focus on children and elderly, and, more widely, the needs of the different social groups of residents. In addition, the public space is designed with universal accessibility criteria, offering adapted routes and short distances between destinations. This will promote walking as the main transport mean for every layer of society.

Connectivity: A District Whose Theme is The Connected City

The theme of the winning proposal of the international competition for Master Plans was *The Connected City*. This is reflected both in the physical connections with the neighboring districts, as in its internal ramifications thanks to the *Grüner Loop* and the network formed by all the other open spaces that link every part of the new urban core.

Stimulation: A District Designed to Walk Around and Enjoy Public Space

To make the city walkable, it is not enough for the space to be within walking distance. It should also hold the adequate quantity of stimuli to motivate the transit. The design of Oberbillwerder aims to provide an inspiring urban scene for daily activities to be carried out walking. To this end, architecture contributes with its formal and functional diversity, while the public space design facilitates the task by totally freeing the streets, squares, and parks of architectural barriers and by incorporating a significant level of greenery.

Intensification (Public Transport): A District With a Metro Station as a Reference

The district is limited to the south by the railway line that links Hamburg to Berlin. This route was the structural support for the parallel layout of the city's metro line, which has a station next to Oberbillwerder.

The existence of this point of access to public transport is very important. Indeed, it is particularly relevant for the productive sector. Some 5,000 jobs are expected to be created in the compound. However, it is probable that many people will continue to travel to other areas of Hamburg or that external residents will come to Oberbillwerder to work. Public transport is the priority option, which is evidenced by the creation of Mobility Hubs, spaces that fulfill different functions, including that of the exchange of transport systems.

Modulate (Road Traffic): A District Where the Car is Almost Unnecessary

Oberbillwerder does not eliminate cars, although it makes them practically unnecessary. The space has been designed for favoring alternative mobility in the internal journeys, which allows the removal of motor vehicles. However, cars may be unavoidable because they are often needed when travelling outwards, a fact that implies the need for parking space for the people living in the site. Considering the difficulty of underground building and the aspiration to ensure that outdoor space is as free as possible from the presence of vehicles, parking spaces for residents and visitors are concentrated in the Mobility Hubs. These people may leave there their own cars and change their mode of transport by choosing out of a variety of mobility of options: individual transports such as conventional o electric bicycles or public transport including, in the near future, small autonomous shuttle buses. With this approach, the streets are free of car parking and enhanced in terms of citizen use. The Mobility Hubs also incorporate other uses such as small retail stores or cultural and social amenities, with the aim of becoming small neighborhood centers and meeting places.

Toning Up (Residents): A District Whose Mobility Dynamics Help the Physical Shape of its Citizens

Oberbillwerder is designed for walking and cycling, a fact that will make the district a symbol of future mobility. The urban structure has been conceived to make sport and physical exercise an essential part of daily life. This dynamism will help to maintain the tone and physical shape of the residents.

Hybrid: A District Where Sports Facilities Are Fused With the Daily Life

When considering the functional distribution of Oberbillwerder, it is worth noting that in, the core, the *Bahn Quartet*, the central position is occupied by a large Sports Center. This decision renders character to the entire district. The situation of the Sports Center makes it easy to access for the students in the nearby schools as well as for residents. Even, given its proximity to the *S-Bahn Station*, it will also be very accessible for users coming from outside the neighborhood. The building will have a constructed area of about 10,000 square meters.

In addition to this, it is important to highlight the role of the sports fields located along one of the main green areas of the compound, located on the east side. This *Activity Park*, with an area of 4.5 hectares located between *Grüne Quartier* and *ParkQuartier*, includes two large sports fields and several smaller ones, as well as minor courts open for a wide variety of uses (including a large children's park). During the day, the Activity Park will also host school students whose facilities are within a short distance. Moreover, the Activity Park will be available at night and at weekends. These two large facilities are the most representative of a numerous set of areas planned for sporting practice distributed throughout the district next to the residences. And, of course, not to forget the multi-purpose *Grüner Loop*.

Application: A District to Learn and Practice "Life Sciences"

Oberbillwerder is born with an important teaching engine, due both for its potential of attraction and its theme. This is the Faculty of Life Sciences (*Fakultät Life Science*) of the University of Applied Sciences of Hamburg (*HAW Hamburg, Hochschule für angwandte Wissenschaften*) (Behörde für Wissenschaft, Forschung, Gleichstellung und Bezirke. Freie und Hansestadt Hamburg, 2019). The criteria selected for placing this educational infrastructure in the new district don´t differ from the spirit that has encouraged its creation. However, appreciating the value of this proposal, the Active City has other objectives. It is remarkable the implementation of 14 day-care centers distributed throughout the neighborhood along the main roads, especially, in the vicinity of the *Grüner Loop*. Primary and secondary education also count with two notable centers (two primary schools of 1.6 hectares each and two secondary schools of approximately double that size) that are in strategic sites, along the main communication axis, creating safe and green pedestrian and bicycle routes.

The location of the schools near the homes of the students provides the youngsters with the opportunity to reach them on foot or by bicycle. Since these facilities have a wide sport and leisure program: fitness center, sports hall, playgrounds, etc., it is expected that the school district and the city or private organizations may reach agreements for sharing their use. This will allow the community use of the facilities outside of the opening hours, which may significantly extend the community's options for physical activity.

Balance: A District That Makes Working Compatible With Practicing Physical Exercise

The Oberbillwerder project estimates the creation of up to 5,000 jobs. The option of living and working in the same place will allow for a considerable reduction in external journeys, favoring the mobility criteria of the Active City Model. The implementation of these productive uses in the district has taken place in several areas. Although private entrepreneurship will have the ultimate responsibility for the design of the workspace, it is expected to comply with the standards suggested by the Active City and the Healthy Offices Model.

CONCLUSION

The Active City is the necessary direction to achieve more livable, more sustainable, and healthier cities. To fulfill this end, real priority should be given to health in all actions, creating opportunities in the built and social environments so that citizens can be physically active in their daily lives. Any city can become active. It must only commit to the real promotion of healthy living habits, to provide itself with a structure to work in that direction and to implement a cross-cutting process in the design and management of the city.

There is an increasing number of cities that are committing to the Active Cities Model. Some have made considerable progress. Among them, certain cities stand out above the rest for having placed themselves at the vanguard of the application of the model thanks to the ambition of their Active City Programs and the degree of compliance with them. Hamburg is within these leading positions. The German city stands out for the breadth and depth of its vision of the Active City, which combines general policies and proposals applicable throughout the city, with specific interventions both for existing areas and, above all, for new growths, which are being designed following the guidelines of the Active City Model.

The Hamburg Active City Master Plan has become an international reference of good practices. The specific projects that it proposes, as well as the programs, events and different actions are examples for many cities to follow. In a similar way, urban developments such as Hafen City act as prototypes, especially due to their special attention to interventions in public space. And, in a unique way, Hamburg acts as a guiding light with its proposal for the new Oberbillwerder district. Although the construction of this neighborhood is still far from realization, and only when it will become an inhabited realty in it will be possible to judge whether it accomplished its mission of becoming the first active-from-the-start district, the project has been born pointing out the horizon to which cities should aspire to become more livable and healthy places. Up to now, everything indicates so. Hopefully its proposals and decisions will exert a great influence on future developments in other parts of the world.

Therefore, after studying the case of Hamburg, it can be stated that is a reference for many other cities that are initiating the process of becoming Active Cities.

REFERENCES

Active City Hamburg. (n.d.). *Active City Hamburg*. Active City Hamburg. https://activecity.hamburg.de/

Active Well-being Initiative. (2017). *The 2017 Active Well-being Initiative White Paper on urbanisation, non-communicable diseases and the potential for cities to enhance the individual and collective well-being of their population.* Active Well-being Initiative. http://activewellbeing.org/wp-content/uploads/2017/09/AWI-White-Paper-2017.pdf

ADEPT. (2019). *Oberbillwerder*. ADEPT. https://www.adept.dk/project/oberbillwerder-the-connected-city

Allam, Z., Moreno, C., Chabaud, D., & Pratlong, F. (2022). Proximity-Based Planning and the "15-Minute City": A Sustainable Model for the City of the Future. In *The Palgrave Handbook of Global Sustainability* (pp. 1–20). Springer International Publishing. doi:10.1007/978-3-030-38948-2_178-1

Beacher, R. (2018, July). Hamburgo. El Legado sigue vivo. *Olympic Review*, (107), 68–71.

Beckereit, M., Holstein, C., Unkelbach, I., Mantell, J., & Beine, C. (2016). HAMBURGmachtSPORT: Kommentierung 2016. Eine Dekadenstrategie für den Hamburger Sport erstellt von der "Zukunftskommission Sport." *Hamburger Senat. Freie und Hansestadt Hamburg.* https://www.hamburg.de/contentblob/5924192/7b238ce5fd6ba7fb4487a33aa05eec4d/data/2016-04-29-dl-dekadenstrategie.pdf

Beckereit, M., Holstein, C., Unkelbach, I., Mantell, J., Kodolitsch, K., Troeder, M., & Hellberg, A. (2022). *Hamburger Sportbericht. Im Rahmen der Dekadenstrategie für den Hamburger Sport.* Hamburg: Zukunftskommission Sport. https://www.hamburg.de/contentblob/16314304/d1927b14bd5433d314e13c5c8dbd2023/data/2022-06-30-d-hamburger-sportbericht-2022.pdf

Beckereit, M., Unkelbach, I., Ploß, G., Wolf, R., Beyer, T., & Hinzpeter, C. (2011). HAMBURGmachtSPORT. Eine Dekadenstrategie für den Hamburger Sport ukunftskommission Sport. Hamburg: Der Hamburger Senat. https://www.hamburg.de/contentblob/3115782/3368559d735158cfe3237b3398651d11/data/2011-09-29-bis-bt-zukunftskommission-sport.pdf

Behörde für Inneres und Sport. Freien und Hansestadt Hamburg. (2016). *Erfahrungsbericht des Landesabstimmungsleiters, der Bezirksabstimmungsleitungen und des Statistischen Amts für Hamburg und Schleswig-Holstein.*Hamburg: Behörde für Inneres und Sport. Freien und Hansestadt Hamburg. https://www.hamburg.de/contentblob/5456574/4798e7c85a74fd64feaed2b03368069f/data/erfahrungsbericht-olympia-referendum-dl.pdf

Behörde für Wissenschaft, Forschung, Gleichstellung und Bezirke. Freie und Hansestadt Hamburg. (2019, August 12). *Fakultät der HAW Hamburg zieht nach Oberbillwerder. Neuer Campus in Bergedorf für die Life Sciences.* Freie und Hansestadt Hamburg. https://www.hamburg.de/pressearchiv-fhh/12787776/haw-hamburg-oberbillwerder/

Blasco Abad, J. A., Lahoz Palacio, C. F., & Martínez-Arrarás Caro, C. (2022). *Hacia la ciudad activa: Estrategias urbanas para hacer las ciudades más vivibles y saludables.* Dykinson. doi:10.2307/j.ctv2zp4v16

Bruns-Berentelg, J. (2017, May). HafenCity, 21st Century, Urban Development, Continuity & Transformation. Presented at *the UPSI – BVS / REALTY 2017*, Brussels. Brussels.

Centro de Coordinación de Alertas y Emergencias Sanitarias. (2021). *Enfermedad por el coronavirus (COVID-19). 04.01.2021* (No. 283). Dirección General de Salud Pública. Secretaria de Estado de Sanidad. Ministerio de Sanidad. Gobierno de España. https://www.lamoncloa.gob.es/serviciosdeprensa/notasprensa/sanidad14/Paginas/2021/04012021_datoscovid19.aspx

Colomina, B. (2021). *Arquitectura de rayos X.* Puente Editores.

Der Freien und Hansestadt Hamburg. (2016). *Mitteilung des Senats an die Bürgerschaft Masterplan ActiveCity (MPAC) – Für mehr Bewegung in Hamburg Haushaltsplan 2016* (No. 21/6800). Hamburg: Senat. Freie und Hansestadt Hamburg. https://www.hamburg.de/contentblob/7472822/ab9b4fa02dbf-dad4540e1b27eaa3a230/data/mitteilung-senat.pdf

Dirección General de Tráfico. (2021, August 21). *En 2020 fallecieron 1.370 personas en accidentes de tráfico.* [Nota de prensa]. https://www.dgt.es/comunicacion/notas-de-prensa/en-2020-fallecieron-1.370-personas-en-accidentes-de-trafico/

Edwards, P., & Tsouros, A. D. (2006). *Promoting Physical Activity and Active Living in Urban Environments: The Role of Local Governments.* World Health Organization. Regional Office Europe.

Edwards, P., & Tsouros, A. D. (2008). *A healthy city is an active city: A physical activity planning guide.* World Health Organization.

Eitler, T. W., McMahon, E., & Thoerig, T. (2013). *Ten principles for building healthy places.* Urban Land Institute.

Engels, F. (2020). *La situación de la clase obrera en Inglaterra.* Akal.

European Commission. (2011). *Hamburg, winner 2011: European Green Capital, an initiative of the European Commission: Green cities – Fit for life*. LU: Publications Office of the European Union. https://data.europa.eu/doi/10.2779/64936

Executive Board, World Health Organization, WHOEB. (2002). *EB 109/14. Executive Board 109th session, Geneva, 14-21 January 2002: Summary records* (No. EB109/2002/REC/2; pp. 78–83). Geneva: World Health Organization, WHO. https://apps.who.int/iris/handle/10665/259565

Frank, L. D., Andresen, M. A., & Schmid, T. L. (2004). Obesity relationships with community design, physical activity, and time spent in cars. *American Journal of Preventive Medicine*, *27*(2), 87–96. doi:10.1016/j.amepre.2004.04.011 PMID:15261894

Freie und Hansestadt Hamburg. (n.d.). *Active City Hamburg. Sport & Aktivitäten in Hamburg*. Apple. https://apps.apple.com/de/app/active-city-hamburg/id1481226913

Freire Silva, M. J. (2014). Permeabilidad, mixtura y escala: Tres “Cosas Urbanas” en HafenCity. *VI Seminario Internacional de Investigación en Urbanismo, Barcelona-Bogotá,* Pontificia Universidad Javeriana de Bogotá. 10.5821iiu.6093

Global Active City Label. (n.d.). Active Well-being Initiative. http://activewellbeing.org/global-active-city/

hamburg.de. (2018). *Hamburg ist Global Active City.* Offizielles Stadtportal für die Hansestadt Hamburg. https://www.hamburg.de/active-city/11684660/hamburg-ist-global-active-city/

hamburg.de. (n.d.). Active City Map. *Geoportal.* https://geoportal-hamburg.de/activecity-maps/index.html?filter=[%22name%22:%22Sportst%C3%A4tten%22,%22isSelected%22:true,%22rules%22:[]]

IBA Hamburg GmbH. (2017). *Oberbillwerder. Wettbewerblicher Dialog. Vergabeunterlagen mit Aufgabenstellung und Verfahrensablauf.* Hamburg: IBA Hamburg GmbH. https://www.oberbillwerder-hamburg.de/wp-content/uploads/OBW_Aufgabenstellung_Wettbewerblicher_Dialog.pdf

IBA Hamburg GmbH. (2019). *The Connected City. Oberbillwerder—Hamburgs Neuer Stadtteil.* IBA Hamburg GmbH. https://www.oberbillwerder-hamburg.de/wp-content/files/Oberbillwerder_Folder.pdf

Johnson, S. (2007). The ghost map: The story of London’s most terrifying epidemic and how it changed science, cities, and the modern world. New York: Riverhead.

KARRES + BRANDS. (n.d.). *Oberbillwerder: Europe’s most sustainable urban masterplan.* Karres and Brands. https://www.karresenbrands.com/news/oberbillwerder-europes-most-sustainable-urban-masterplan

Klocke, E., Kastens, B., & de Buhr, K. (2012). *Hamburg – European Green Capital 2011. Final Report.* Hamburg: Behörde für Stadtentwicklung und Umwelt. https://ec.europa.eu/environment/europeangreencapital/wp-content/uploads/2011/04/Doku-Umwelthauptstadt-engl-web.pdf

Lahoz, C. F., & Blasco, J. A. (2023). Healthy Cities in the 21st Century: Toward the Active City. In Green Research, Developments, and Programs. Sustainable and Healthy Building Environments (Roberto Alonso González Lezcano, pp. 75–98). New York: Nova Science Publishers. doi:10.52305/TKOH1520

Landschaftsarchitekten, F. (2018). *Grün Vernetzen. Fachkarte für das Landschaftsprogramm—Erläuterungen -*. Behörde für Umwelt und Energie, Amt für Naturschutz, Grünplanung und Energie. Freie und Hansestadt Hamburg. https://www.hamburg.de/contentblob/12763874/85efe919b45682d9d973d70ee378af0e/data/d-fachkarte-gruen-vernetzen-erlaeuterungen.pdf

Lee, I.-M., Shiroma, E. J., Lobelo, F., Puska, P., Blair, S. N., & Katzmarzyk, P. T. (2012). Effect of physical inactivity on major non-communicable diseases worldwide: An analysis of burden of disease and life expectancy. *Lancet*, *380*(9838), 219–229. doi:10.1016/S0140-6736(12)61031-9 PMID:22818936

Lobo, D. (2014, January 21). ULI Global Awards for Excellence: Hafen City, Hamburg, Germany. *Urban Land Magazine*. https://urbanland.uli.org/planning-design/hafen-city-hamburg-germany/

MacCallum, L., Howson, N., & Gopu, N. (2016). *Design to move. A Physical Activity Action Agenda. A Guide for City Leaders*. The American College of Sports Medicine (ACSM). NIKE, Inc. The International Council of Sport Science and Physical Education (ICSSPE).

Mayo, X., Del Villar, F., & Jiménez, A. (2017). *X Termometro del Sedentarismo en Espana: Informe sobre la inactividad física y el sedentarismo en la población adulta española* (*Vol. 1*). Madrid, Spain: Observatorio de la Vida Activa y Saludable de la Fundación España Activa. Centro de Estudios del Deporte, Universidad Rey Juan Carlos, CSIC.

Ministry of Urban Development and Environment and Ministry of Labour and Economic Affairs. (2006). *HafenCity Hamburg—The Masterplan*. HafenCity Hamburg GmbH in co-operation with the Ministry of Urban Development and Environment of the Free and Hanseatic City of Hamburg. https://edisciplinas.usp.br/pluginfile.php/5130780/mod_resource/content/0/Hafen%20City%20Hamburg_ASTOC.pdf

Oginga-Martins, J., & Sharifi, A. (2022). *World Cities Report 2022: Envisaging the Future of Cities*. United Nations Human Settlements Programme (UN-Habitat)

Praticò, A. (2015). *The analysis of the new strategic area of Hamburg: The redevelopment project of the Hafencity's waterfront*. Research Gate. doi:10.13140/RG.2.2.36784.56322

Swinburn, B. A., Kraak, V. I., Allender, S., Atkins, V. J., Baker, P. I., Bogard, J. R., Brinsden, H., Calvillo, A., De Schutter, O., Devarajan, R., Ezzati, M., Friel, S., Goenka, S., Hammond, R. A., Hastings, G., Hawkes, C., Herrero, M., Hovmand, P. S., Howden, M., & Dietz, W. H. (2019). The Global Syndemic of Obesity, Undernutrition, and Climate Change: The Lancet Commission report. *Lancet*, *393*(10173), 791–846. doi:10.1016/S0140-6736(18)32822-8 PMID:30700377

Transsolar Energietechnik Gmb, H. (2019). Oberbillwerder Masterplan, Hamburg, Deutschland. *Transsolar.* Www.transsolar.com https://transsolar.com/de/projects/hamburg-oberbillwerder-masterplan

World Health Organization, (2010). Global recommendations on physical activity for health. WHO.

World Health Organization. (2022). *Global status report on physical activity 2022*. Geneva: World Health Organization. https://apps.who.int/iris/bitstream/handle/10665/363607/9789240059153-eng.pdf?sequence=1&isAllowed=y

World Health Organization Assembly. (1998). *WHA51.18: Noncommunicable disease prevention and control. Resolution.* (No. Agenda item 13.18). Fifty-fifth World Health Assembly. Geneva: World Health Organization, WHO. https://apps.who.int/gb/ebwha/pdf_files/WHA55/ewha5523.pdf

World Health Organization Assembly. WHO. (2002). *WHA55.23: Diet, physical activity and health. Resolution.* (No. Agenda item 13.11). Fifty-fifth World Health Assembly. Geneva: World Health Organization. https://apps.who.int/gb/ebwha/pdf_files/WHA55/ewha5523.pdf

ADDITIONAL READING

A Healthy City Is an Active City: A Physical Activity Planning Guide. Peggy Edwards & D. Tsouros Agis. (2008). World Health Organization.

Building Healthy Places Toolkit. (2015). *Strategies for Enhancing Health in the Built Environment. Urban Land Institute.* Urban Land Institute.

Guidelines, A. D. (2010). *Promoting Physical Activity and Health in Design.* City of New York. City of New York., https://www1.nyc.gov/assets/planning/download/pdf/plans-studies/active-design-guidelines/adguidelines.pdf

Movilidad Urbana Sostenible. (2010). *Un reto energético y ambiental.* Carmen Mataix González. Obra Social Caja Madrid. Argumentos para la Cultura.

Planning and Design for Sustainable Urban Mobility: Global Report on Human Settlements 2013. (2013). Un-Habitat. New York: Routledge. https://unhabitat.org/sites/default/files/download-manager-files/Planning%20and%20Design%20for%20Sustainable%20Urban%20Mobility.pdf

Promoting Physical Activity and Active Living in Urban Environments: The Role of Local Governments. Peggy Edwards & D. Tsouros Agis. World Health Organization. Regional Office Europe, 2006.

The 2017 Active Well-Being Initiative White Paper on Urbanisation, Non-Communicable Diseases and the Potential for Cities to Enhance the Individual and Collective Well-Being of Their Population. Active Well-being Initiative. (2017). Active Well-being Initiative. http://activewellbeing.org/wp-content/uploads/2017/09/AWI-White-Paper-2017.pdf

KEY TERMS AND DEFINITIONS

Active Behavior: Physical activities that require the expenditure of energy and result in movement of the body. Active behavior does not only affect formal sports practice or other structured physical activities but includes many other practices such as strolling or active transport, walking or by bicycle, that are very effective for maintaining or improving the health.

Active City: A City that decides to give real priority to health in all its actions, creating opportunities in the built and social environments so that citizenship can be physically active in its daily life.

Active City Model: A new urban model for achieving healthier cities with greater quality of life by integrating physical activity into daily life.

Active Transport: Transportation modes which are wholly or primarily powered by human energy such as walking, running, and bicycling.

Built environment: Human-made structures, spaces and facilities that are created to support human activities and provide the infrastructure for everyday life. The term encompasses a plethora of elements such as buildings, public spaces, transportation networks and other public infrastructure, cities, etc.

Healthy Offices: Office Buildings that promote the physical, psychological, and social health and well-being of their users.

Mixed use: Urban spaces where diverse functions are physically and functionally integrated.

Physical inactivity: Lack of regular moderate-to-vigorous physical activity. Physical inactivity can be a result of a sedentary lifestyle, but it can also result from other factors, such as a lack of access to safe and convenient places to be physically active.

Sedentary lifestyle: Pattern of behavior characterized by sitting or lying down for extended periods of time. A sedentary lifestyle is associated with a lack of physical activity and a low energy expenditure.

Urban Development Project: Planned initiative aimed at improving and transforming a specific area within a city or town. It involves the construction of new buildings, infrastructure, and public spaces, as well as the redevelopment or revitalization of existing structures and spaces.

Walkability: The measure of how conducive an area is to walking as a means of transportation. It considers various factors such as the availability of sidewalks and streetlights, the proximity of destinations to access daily needs, the presence of street activity, and the overall physical and visual comfort of the environment.

Chapter 5
Organizational Socio-Ecology and Green Technological Innovation

José G. Vargas-Hernandez
Instituto Tecnológico Mario Molina, Mexico

María Fernanda Higuera-Cota
https://orcid.org/0000-0001-8285-1076
Universidad Autónoma de Sinaloa, Mexico

Omar C. Vargas-González
https://orcid.org/0000-0002-6089-956X
Instituto Tecnológico Nacional de México, Ciudad Guzmán, Mexico

ABSTRACT

This study intends to analyze the impact of environmental regulation and incentives in socio-ecological and green technological innovation. It departs from the assumption that environmental regulation affects the performance of socio-ecological and green technological innovation in organizations. The method employed is critical analytical and reflective based on the theoretical, conceptual, and methodological literature. It is concluded that the analysis confirms that there is a direct relationship between the incentives of environmental regulation and the socio-ecological and green technological innovation in organizations.

INTRODUCTION

The rapid global diffusion of innovative technologies has modernized the various economic sectors (primary, secondary, and tertiary) that contribute to environmental pollution and other health hazards, in turn limiting the development of green solutions. For Amburgey & Rao (1996) the progress of organizational sociology represents a key element to understand the relational nature of aspects such as culture and

DOI: 10.4018/978-1-6684-6924-8.ch005

organizational change, two fundamental aspects to understand the interdependence established between the organization and society.

In the words of Salimath & Jones (2011) the solution points to the study of the relationship between sustainability and the socio-ecology of the population. In other words, the theoretical proposal is built on the theories of organizational choice, the resource dependency theory (Pfeffer & Salancik, 1978) until arriving at the ecological theory of organizations focusing on the specificities of the sector as exercises of elections.

Thus, from the theoretical framework of organizational socio-ecology and sociological theory, ecological principles are applied to organizational study. Starting from the notion that both organizational sociology and socio-ecological theory serve as tools to formulate and implement socio-ecological principles through organizational strategies with the aim of strengthening those organizations that present low performance, resulting in new economic and social environments. characterized by a non-linear development.

In addition, organizational socio-ecology theory assumes that there is a convergence between the organizational socio-ecology paradigm and the sociological perspectives that drive organizational research. For the foundation of socio-ecology rests on the differentiation of organizational populations. At the same time, it addresses contemporary issues such as climate change, environmental responsibility, planetary balance, etc., and links them with other disciplines of organizational thought. The link in question arises from the incorporation of methodological innovations such as strategic simulation models.

And although the study of socio-ecology has been widely accepted in recent decades, it has been strongly criticized because it is based on the assumption that organizational destiny is a controllable variable. However, from practice it has been shown that organizational socio-ecology is dynamic and is based on the methodology of the analysis of temporary events, which help to extract and interpret representative situations on the underlying relationships between the data and allow to a different extent with different confidence extrapolate or interpolate the data and thus forecast possible scenarios.

On the other hand, the theory of the socio-ecology of the population is considered as the instrument for the theoretical and empirical analysis of organizational phenomena, constituting a perspective of convergent intersection with sustainability that integrates dimensions, levels and analysis of results. Birnholtz, Cohen & Hoch (2007) define the socio-ecology of routines as the ability to regenerate a socio-ecology of action patterns.

Research in socio-ecology is relevant for its contribution to the analysis of the interactions of organizational populations and for its contribution to sustainable development. This contribution arises from the application of principles and assumptions of socio-ecology to the study of the sustainability of organizations. Dimaggio & Powell (1983) describe the theory of organizational socio-ecology as an analysis of the alterations, difficulties and restrictions of organizational populations in the conditions of application based on social Darwinism, that is, based on competition between individuals. Specifically, the fight for survival.

Regarding the research in the ecological theory of the population, this is consolidated in the theory of socio-ecology of the population in coordination and convergence with organizational sustainability, considering that there are several areas carried out with the sustainability of populations that potentially contribute to their sustainability (Salimath & Jones, 2011). In particular, variables such as the control of greenhouse gas emissions, the reduction of energy consumption, innovation in green technology, institutional quality, economic growth, and the benefits from urbanization are all considered interdependent and co-integrated. That is, they are considered as part of the process by which society can meet its needs and improve its quality of life without jeopardizing the ability of future generations to meet their own needs.

This demonstrates the close relationship that exists between environmental regulation and green innovation. What makes it necessary to assign values to environmental regulations as these lead to the performance of green innovation. An archetype contrary to what is indicated here occurs when the environmental regulation system is weak, with a tendency to maximize company profits. Where, as compensation, governments apply environmental taxes to try to balance the cost of the lack of regulation.

Regarding the research on green innovation, this focuses on the creation and commercialization of improved technologies from the environmental point of view, as well as the diffusion and adoption of these technologies. At the same time, it addresses learning about environmental management systems, the development of technological systems adopted by organizations and the adoption of innovative technologies related to the integration of environmentally friendly practices. It should be stressed that green innovation is supported by normative and regulatory institutions, science and technological development.

Other fundamental aspects are 1) exploration of the impact of environmental regulation, as it is an instrument of environmental policy that has the objective of preventing, mitigating and restoring damage to the environment, as well as regulating activities to mitigate the negative effects in the environment and human health, 2) incentives in socio-ecological and green technological innovation, by conditioning or inducing behaviors towards organizational, technological and productive innovation activities.

Next, some implications of organizational socio-ecology will be addressed with the aim of developing a framework to understand the relational nature of aspects such as leadership, culture and organizational change and the interdependence established between the organization and society. Organizational green technological innovation will also be analyzed to determine the impact of environmental regulation policies and incentives.

ORGANIZATIONAL SOCIOECOLOGY

Organizational socio-ecology proposes the study of the behavior of individuals in interaction with their environmental systems. Hence, its implications for organizational theories. It promotes the appearance of models that value resources and external influences. Authors such as Hu et al. (2020) and Chen et al. (2021) state that organizations are restricted by internal factors, such as capital, investment in R&D, and inclusion factors such as interest groups and bureaucratic advances in terms of environmental regulation policies. However, the above situation is not the case of SMEs, since in the vast majority of cases strict environmental policies make them inclined to invest in improving pollution control instead of betting on the development of green technologies, since the latter imply larger investments.

From the organizational socio-ecological theory, organizational size is studied, arguing that SMEs are immersed in a greater number of problems to obtain investments or credits and thus capitalize, so they are more likely to dissolve.

It is through organizational socio-ecology that the organization-environment assumption is broken, since the analysis focuses on aggregate propositions at the population level and not on the individual organization. As in the theory of socio-ecology, the classical approach to the environment and the contingency theory seek to evaluate existing scenarios through objective data and thus create plans to adapt to the needs of the organization. So, the contingency theory states that there is no single way to solve problems, but that organizational change must be based on the capacity for adaptability and aligned adjustment between the organization and the internal and external environment of the organization.

Organizational socio-ecology suggests that organizations tend to compete for resources and positioning against their competitors. The previous situation is explained from the niche width theory, understood as a category of the general theory, that is, of organizational socio-ecology. Regarding the niche width theory, it is based on organizations' chances of survival from environmental changes (Hannan and Freeman, 1977). It is thus that, from the organizational socio-ecology, the plans originating from the ecological contingencies imposed from the demands of the environment are necessary.

Aldrich & Auster (1986) affirm that organizational socio-ecology examines the characteristics of the vital manifestations of organizational populations, such as disappearance, considering individual situations such as their size and age, two elements associated with survival. Thus, the socio-ecology of the population reflects on the changes suffered by populations over time.

As a social demand, organizational socio-ecology exceeds the internal limits and affects the influence on the human being and the natural environment. Consequently, corporate social responsibility is integrated into the fields of organizational socio-ecology, together with the establishment of socio-ecological and environmental measures (Oller, 2021).

In relation to the construction of an organizational socio-ecology to learn the professional development management model, the latter must be based mainly on orientation and not on control as is thought (Le Boterf, 1999). Also, the Organizational socio-ecological framework uses its knowledge to formulate and implement organizational strategies for change, which requires consensus for the cumulative generation of knowledge.

Regarding routines at the company level, as well as the notion of organizational character from organizational socio-ecology, these make up the capacities of the participants to regenerate a coherent socio-ecology of action patterns (Birnholtz, Cohen & Hoch, 2007). For Pentland (2004) organizational routines are synonymous with ecologies. Since organizational routines are characterized by being organizational habits that arise from past experiences of the organization itself and make up the so-called organizational memory, thus conditioning future actions. While, ecologies make up the relationships of living beings with each other with the environment in which they live, from which they constantly learn.

The interdependence between routines challenges scholars to find the interactions in a socio-ecology between routines considering that routines never work in a vacuum (Howard-Grenville et al. 2016) but are ubiquitous in organizations (Becker, 2008), configured interdependently as a network (Feldman et al., 2016; Pentland, 2011; Sele& Gran, 2016; Spee, Jarzabkowski & Smets, 2016). According to Howard-Grenville et al. (2016) routines meet intertwined by actions, artifacts and people linked to other routines. And they are located at a particular level of the macro and micro analysis of actors and activities.

From the above, authors such as Dietz et al. (2003), Eckerberg & Joas (2004), Folke et al. (2005) and Ostrom (2005) affirm that the adaptive governance of ecosystems and socio-ecological systems serves as a gear in the search for change in the stability properties of ecological interactions. Where the implications of chaos-induced dispersal in continuous time models for socio-ecology are important (Sole & Bascompte, 1995). For example, removal of affected species by habitual loss and fragmentation of spatial ecological patterns provides a direct criterion (Hannan, 2005).

Regarding sustainability practices, these converge with the socio-ecology of the population, by composing a tool for the analysis of macro-organizational phenomena that tracks the use in theoretical and empirical research aimed at studying actions that help reduce the negative impact at the global level. that derive from productive practices (Salimath, & Jones, 2011).

As an archetype of the above are the industrial structure as it has effects on regional economic growth and ecological well-being (Zhao et al., 2020; Huang et al., 2021) and the technological innovation infrastructure system by improving the efficiency of innovation by protecting property rights.

The opposite of sustainability practices could be the culture that most developing countries have around the pursuit of rapid economic growth based on dependence on non-renewable energy consumption, which results in significant carbon dioxide emissions. of carbon with adverse effects on the quality of the environment. It is factual, that currently economic growth is promoted through the substantial consumption of fossil fuels with harmful influence on the environment. And that companies seek to increase their production above environmental concerns. For this reason, in recent decades multiple methods have emerged to assess environmental performance (Zhou et al., 2008; Sueyoshi & Goto 2012; Wu et al., 2019).

The environmental performance is characterized by a lack of green development, where polluting emissions are present in most geographic spaces.

ORGANIZATIONAL GREEN TECHNOLOGICAL INNOVATION

Over the last three decades, the concept of green ergonomics has gained relevance in the context of green technological innovation, including the development of products and services aimed at achieving ecological benefits and reducing organizational environmental impacts (Bernroider, 2002; Damanpour, 1992). Said ergonomics focuses on the study of environmental factors, which constitute the environment of the system formed by a connection between the human being and nature taking, and reducing the environmental impact, by linking the design of innovative products and services aimed at reducing the emissions and pollution with other pro-nature benefits (Mandavilli, Rys & Russell, 2008; Sanquist, 2008; Hilliard & Jamieson, 2008).

In the opinion of Sneideriene & Rugine (2019), Kousar et al. (2017), Weng & Lin (2011) and Lin & Ho (2011) organizations seek to create and commercialize better technologies from the environmental point of view, since the use of technological innovations can affect the diffusion and adoption of these technologies. Likewise, the government encourages organizations to adopt and develop green technological technology, and contributes to this objective through technical assistance services, financing or training for its adoption.

However, efforts by the government and organizations are not always necessary, since in the vast majority of cases organizations tend to adopt technological innovation with high levels of environmental uncertainty, since they do not always develop taking technological innovation as a banner. green (Zailani, Iranmanesh, Nikbin & Jumadi, 2014). Even when the adoption of said innovation reduces the negative organizational impacts of the processing of technological systems and internal administrative processing. In some cases, attempts to adopt this type of innovation are repeated, even before final adoption, which implies that they are expensive and unattractive to organizations (Baines, Brown, Benedettini & Ball, 2012).

In addition, the green innovation of organizations is related to life cycles by constituting a set of practices related to technology that focus on sustainability. Well, it leads to offering ecological and reliable products and services, friendly to the environment at competitive prices delivered on time (Thatte, 2007).

Elements such as the company's ownership structure, life cycle, size, etc., affect environmental regulations that in turn affect green innovation. And these, by having a direct positive relationship with green technological innovation, can hinder or prolong the processes of reducing pollutants or patenting (Amore & Bennedsen, 2016; Fujii & Managi 2016). As Rogers (2003) states, organizational innovation is characterized by traceability, which forms a stage of creativity based on real information collected, and a series of tests before the use and implementation of the innovation in question due to the degree of uncertainty.

The research finds that the relative advantage is related to the adoption of green innovation. The relative advantage is the perception of the characteristic of the organizational technological innovation in terms of price, quality, satisfaction, use and useful life over its costs. Authors such as Lin & Ho (2011), Rogers (2003), Kousar et al. (2017) and Grandon & Pearson (2004) agree with the fact that if the organizational perception of the relative advantage of the innovation is greater than the cost and better than the current technology, the organization can adopt the innovation.

On the other hand, innovation management is related to internal and external practices. Regarding the externalities of innovation Bi et al. (2006), Li et al. (2018) and Liu et al. (2020), state that these are addressed through government subsidies for research and development. R&D, as well as human capital and gross domestic product per capita, have effects on the development of green innovation, which in turn has an influence on human capital and gross domestic product and on the development of green innovation. The previous situation shows the latent need for high investments in R&D, human capital and gross domestic product by organizations for the consolidation of a better performance of green innovation.

Investments in R&D are essential to improve the technological innovation capabilities of the organization. However, for these to go hand in hand with sustainable development, they must be allocated to initiatives that prioritize energy conservation and environmental protection. The latter is the responsibility of governments (Li et al., 2015; Jiang et al., 2020; Wang & Jiang, 2021). Well, it is the governments that are in charge of deploying policies focused on the development of a more sustainable economy.

Grossman & Krueger (1995) argue that regional economic development is an operation related to the level of investment in innovation. Well, it is understood as the process of socioeconomic and environmental change whose central objective is to improve the well-being of the population of the territory where it is circumscribed. In other words, local governments are in charge of investing in organizations with the aim of promoting the development of innovative activities through the technological benefits of foreign investment and incentives for competition.

Regarding the complexity of innovation, it falls on the degree of organizational perception of technological innovation in terms of use. In other words, if the complexity of the innovation increases due to the difficulties of innovation diffusion and knowledge exchange, adoption decreases.

Thus, the perception of organizational complexity is negatively related to green innovation. Otherwise, when innovation is disseminated and knowledge is shared, where the organization tends to adopt technological innovation. It should be noted that Kousar et al (2017), Etzion (2007), Rogers (2003), Tornatzky & Klein (1982), Deng & Ji (2015) and Bradford & Florin (2003) state that innovation requires skills and efforts that increase complexity while the level of adoption decreases. Furthermore, Li, Pan, Kim, Linn, and Chiang (2015) clarify that there is a lack of green technological innovations in developing countries compared to developed nations.

Technological innovation is adopted after observing the impacts (Shahrul & Normah, 2015; Tan & Eze, 2008). Therefore, it is considered visible for potential adoption, reflecting the result of the expected observation or the perception of observability (Rogers, 2003). Thus, it is considered that the perception of observability is positively related to green innovation, as stated by Hatimtai & Hassan (2018) and Rogers

(2003), considering it a significant characteristic of green innovation because it allows organizations to identify the benefits of green innovation. innovation with high chances of being adopted by organizations.

Chen, Shih, Shyur & Wu (2012) and Chen & Hsu (2009) classify green innovation as green management, green process and green product.

Companies are promoting enterprises' green technology innovation capabilities, green product innovation capabilities followed by green process innovation capabilities, and governance technology capabilities. Wang et al. (2019) argue that green innovation capabilities, green product innovation, green process innovation, and governance technology capabilities should be implemented based on firms' green technology innovation capabilities. Thus, organizational innovations compatible with the organization's capabilities have positive effects on the environment (Etzion, 2007). So, the perception of organizational compatibility is positively related to green technological innovation.

Antonioli, Mancinelli & Mazzanti (2013) state that, green process innovation is related to updates in systems, methods and processes, and process innovation aims to produce green goods and services to meet ecological concerns and environmental objectives. As for the innovation capabilities of a green process, these are measured through indicators such as strengthening the transformation and improving protection design processes, eliminating contamination, and reviewing the green process. While, government environmental regulation actions have effects on pollution removal investments.

Definitively, the innovation capacities in green technology of companies are related to the elements of green product innovation, process innovation and technological governance. Consequently, Li (2019), Wang et al. (2018) and Saud et al. (2019) affirm that organizations should intensify innovation in green technology to meet the technical specifications and green emission standards established by governments, improve the governance capacities of technology through waste and the innovation capacities of green products and processes, and develop innovation in green technology.

Organizational learning represents an alternative capable of transforming information into knowledge, but, like innovation, it thrives in informal environments (Gunderson, 1999). Likewise, Teece (2016) argues that the internal fit of a learning organization has a positive relationship with organizational innovation, and this with organizational performance. Therefore, the organizational learning intention has effects on the innovation capacity and this on organizational performance.

Thus, organizational learning guides organizational innovation in knowledge-intensive organizations. For Rahim, Eldwiah & Rahman (2013), the knowledge-based vision extends the resource-based vision and is being used in various studies on stakeholder theory, open innovation, microdata, subcontracting and offshoring (Hoskisson, Gambeta, Green, & Li, 2018; Santoro, Vrontis, Thrassou & Dezi, 2018; Xu, Frankwick & Ramirez, 2016 and Pereira, Munjal & Ishizaka, 2019). Specifically, individual and organizational learning leads to innovation that improves organizational performance. Organizational learning guides organizational innovation (Visser & Togt, 2016).

Authors such as Toffler (1970) and Mintzberg (1979) propose the adhocratic organization structure to promote creativity and innovation. Since the adhocratic model is flexible, organic, innovative and collaborative. Furthermore, you can merge different disciplines into a project team avoiding the pitfalls of bureaucratic structures such as division of labor and coordination is the result of interactions.

From the perspective of motivation, green innovation must be worked in a disjointed way with technological innovation. Well, it is considered that organizational behaviors are classified according to their motivations in symbolic strategic environmental actions of cooperation and substantive environmental actions, or substantive strategies and cooperation (Delmas & Montes Sancho, 2010; Neumann, 2021; Truong et al., 2021).

ENVIRONMENTAL REGULATION POLICIES AND INCENTIVES

The mechanism of environmental regulation policy influences the motivation of green innovation companies to differentiate between green innovation behaviors in regulation and the regulated objects of the government company. In other words, government environmental support increases the adoption of green innovation through the implementation of environmental production methods (Lin & Ho, 2010; Gadenne, Kennedy & McKeiver, 2009). Government environmental support shapes systems that take the form of environmental regulations, policies, standards and interventions that tend to reduce environmental impact and encourage companies to engage in environmental technological innovation (Eiadat, Kelly, Roche & Eyadat, 2008).

The mechanisms of environmental regulation policies affect organizational green innovation in different green innovation behaviors. By promoting conservation and rational use of goods and services that reduce the environmental impact in the world. Zhou et al. (2017) and Bai et al (2019) in a study on state ownership and business innovation in China, found that state-owned enterprises assume responsibilities that non-state enterprises do not in implementing green innovation development under the constraints of environmental regulations. Consequently, SOEs do better after the implementation of environmental regulations since, due to the policy of restricted environmental regulations,

In the case of small companies, regulatory policies imply an improvement in pollution control, while, for growing companies, they mean access to abundant funds for investments in R&D in green innovation to improve environmentally friendly production. the environment and green technology (Cao & Cao, 2019). For this reason, the formulation of environmental policies must consider specific measures for the pollution control capabilities of companies according to their ownership structure, size, life cycle, etc.

The policy on environmental regulations is of great importance, considering the commercial value of carbon, as it has a strong incentive effect to improve the green innovation of organizations. Although, the opening does not have a significant impact on green innovation because the effect is indirect. Dauda et al. (2021) and Ko et al. (2021) value technological innovation in organizations as a process capable of reducing carbon emissions and improving environmental quality. Since from practice it has been proven that green innovation significantly reduces energy consumption and as a result CO2 gas emission.

The carbon emissions trading market should be liberalized by positioning the organizations' emissions in pricing mechanisms to stimulate green technological innovation activities. In other words, a higher level of CO2 emissions and environmental pollution as causal links requires the establishment of effective institutional quality for green innovation. That is, the causal link is established between energy consumption and institutional quality. Thus, there is a relationship between green innovation and institutional quality.

Research has found causal relationships between variables that range from CO2 emissions to economic growth, CO2 emissions to green innovation and institutional quality, urbanization and energy consumption to economic growth and institutional quality. In turn, the research points to the existence of a two-way link between economic growth and gas emissions. Thus, institutional quality and urbanization in developing countries can increase CO2 emissions.

The influence of environmental regulations on green technology innovation by mature and growing companies achieves the greatest impact, while green technology innovation by start-ups has severe financial constraints, struggles to meet capital needs, and faces a high level of risk taking leading to the lowest impact (Shahzad et al., 2019).

The mechanism between the good allocation of capital, green development and technological innovation leads to a more efficient socio-ecological environment. The incorporation of the capital allocation in technological innovation in an analytical framework promotes the efficiency of regional green development. Regarding heterogeneity, the effect of capital allocation is significant (Schmidt et al., 2020; Gao et al., 2019). Since, the allocation of capital has a positive relationship with technological innovation that improves the contribution of companies with an impact on the efficiency of green development.

Government intervention on misallocated capital can lead to environmental degradation. In the words of Zhang & Lu (2017), if there is price distortion in the market, the capital allocation cannot be optimized. Firms find it difficult to raise the necessary capital for technological innovation from the firm, which weakens the motivation to conduct research and development (Gao et al., 2019). If the price of capital is controlled by the government, firms tend to seek rents for low-cost factors that attract research and development funds and reduce the efficiency of innovation (Murphy et al., 1993). The intervention of external factors can destroy the capital price mechanism, lowering the costs of production factors for polluting industries. Technological innovation has a mediating role with the allocation of capital in the efficiency of green development.

Technological innovation increases the use of clean processes by reducing environmental pollution (Hua et al. 2018). At the same time, it stimulates companies to use efficient resources, adopt equipment and promote the improvement of industries (Sun et al. 2020b). And it tends to facilitate the development of the green economy and has a mediating role in the allocation of capital on green economic efficiency, while the allocation of capital improves the efficiency of green development. For these reasons, technological innovation has a mediating role with the allocation of capital and improves the efficiency of green development.

Another element that contributes to the development of green innovation in organizations is green finance (Luo et al., 2021). They motivate organizations to invest in green technological innovation and are the driving force for the green transformation of contaminated companies through participation in green innovation activities. Whereas, environmental regulation enhances the effects of green finance on green innovation.

It is thought that companies tend to adopt conservative strategies to invest in green technological projects with intense environmental regulations and low risk (Boubakri et al. 2013; Chiu & Lee 2020). This is where green finance and environmental regulations have positive effects on green innovation. The moderating effects of environmental regulation advance the effects of green finance on this type of innovation, as low levels of environmental regulations lead to increased innovation performance as green finance performance increases.

An emphasis on green innovation results by companies requires more efficient green financing to produce green innovation. And the results of this innovation can be achieved by incentivizing organizations to use green finance and investments and avoiding time-consuming projects. This type of finance is subject to the implementation of environmental regulations, since they improve the effects of green finance on green innovation.

Large companies have more resources and tend to improve the quality of green technological innovation. At the same time, they have a more mature development of organizational systems, achieving high innovation management (Yu et al., 2022b). Well, they have access to abundant innovation resources such as capital, R&D, patents, technological talents (Gupeng & Xiangdong, 2012; Hu et al., 2017). Of the aforementioned resources, the green patent application is a measure that has green finance effects on boosting green technological innovation. And the use of these patents is used to measure innovative behavior is not exhaustive for the different motivations in the green innovation options.

Both large companies and small companies are limited to promote green technological innovation. Large companies face complex scenarios as a result of environmental regulations, while small companies are more restricted by capital, technology, talent, etc., they have more difficulties in promoting green innovation. And although the behavior of companies must be limited by environmental regulations to develop green technological innovation. The implementation of intense environmental regulations improves green innovation considering that the limitations of companies may not lead to the transformation of technologically innovative production.

Green innovation as a dependent variable can be measured by the number of patent applications associated with energy intensity (Wurlod & Noailly, 2018). Green patent applications indicate the advancement of green innovation (Tolliver et al. 2021) and are leading to innovation activities without institutional preferences or time lags, which are used as indicators to assess green innovation (Fujii & Managi 2016; Cho & Sohn, 2018; Fuji 2016).

Environmental regulation has a positive impact on green innovation patents and green utility model patents, although from an influence perspective, the impact of environmental regulation on green innovation may decrease if companies have not phased out the innovation strategic green. For Westwood & Low (2003) green technology innovation strategies must be formulated and implemented sensitively considering cultural differences that have an impact on innovation processes.

Environmental regulations influence government subsidies to eliminate compliance costs by improving green innovation with minimal impact on green innovation behaviors. And the latter must be classified into the various types to determine the effect on the choices of innovative behaviors with different motivations. That is why, government innovation subsidy policies should be more specific and flexible according to the qualifications of the companies that need them and the suitability of the subsidies, coinciding with the development stage in the life cycle to improve core competitiveness and achieve positive effects on green technological innovation.

Regulatory capture and government subsidies are moderating variables. Grants allow organizations to conduct green innovation aligned with government technology innovation goals (Boeing, 2016; Bai et al., 2019). Although they promote green innovation; Regulatory capture has a negative role in the regulatory process of environmental regulation that promotes green innovation by companies. Even so, the increase in green subsidies leads companies to have more resources and funds to invest in the development of green technologies, improving the capacities of technological governance, process innovation and green products (Saud et al., 2019; Lin et al., 2020). Consequently, regulatory capture behavior requires more precise indicators to provide verification of results on the impact of green innovation effects.

And while regulatory capture leads to different green innovation behaviors, it has a distorting effect on substantive high-quality incentives that lead to economic consequences of environmental regulations. That is, it has a negative effect on environmental regulation in the promotion of companies as an explanation of the different behaviors of green innovation. Since, they can expire due to regulatory rigor as the main cause of environmental accidents that intentionally balance profits (Graham et al., 2011; Steinzor, 2012). Thus, firms that take a profit-maximizing orientation may have more potential benefits from regulatory capture behavior than those that have strong motivational behavior for regulatory capture (Li et al., 2021; Zhang et al., 2021).

Environmental regulations tend to influence green innovation by mature and growing companies at the highest level, while the startup stage has the lowest impact due to available resources in capital, technology, and talent.

CONCLUSION

In general terms, this analysis concludes that there is a direct relationship between the incentives of environmental regulation and socio-ecological and green technological innovation in organizations. And that the socio-ecology of the organizational population has implications for sustainability. Besides that, institutional reforms are essential to reduce green emissions and achieve climate change targets.

It was also found that companies perform high-quality green innovation behavior to promote green technology to gain competitive advantage. And that green innovation firms are highest during periods of growth and maturity when they enhance green technological innovation and develop a keen sense of social responsibility for more active innovation activities.

Regarding environmental regulation, this affects the company's green innovation through innovation compensation mechanisms and compliance costs. That is why companies that bear excessive environmental costs should lean towards regulatory capture rather than improve green technology environmental protection, which can destroy the incentive mechanism with a long time and higher costs. In addition, the institutional environment is relevant in the allocation of factors and environmental performance.

Regarding business differences in ownership, life cycle, size, etc., they have a significant impact on the incentives for green innovation of environmental regulation. Both environmental regulations and green finance have effects on green technological innovation.

On the other hand, the levels of green financing of green innovation have heterogeneous impacts with a moderating effect on environmental regulations. On the other hand, environmental regulation is a moderator that is used to examine the effects of green innovation, through the level of contribution of green finance and the application of green patents.

In sum, green finance, green innovation, and environmental regulations tend to be stable with fixed effects.

Finally, the research results suggest that subsidies do not explain the gap between green technology innovation behaviors.

RECOMMENDATIONS

The role of technological innovation should be strengthened to improve the efficiency of green development. That is, the organization should implement and review the implementation of green product innovation capabilities, green process innovation capabilities, and technology governance capabilities.

Regarding environmental regulation, the scientific design of environmental regulation policy tools should be strengthened to monitor emission reductions and carry out green innovation. The intensity of environmental regulation should be increased according to the specific situations of companies.

Governments in policy making and stakeholders should facilitate organizational green strategies to invest in technological innovation projects aimed at reducing environmental pollution. Policy making must strengthen institutional quality and enact more effective policies to address environmental challenges. The different impacts of institutional settings must assume the research model.

Finally, regarding green financing, governments must support the development of innovative companies with tax incentives and financial subsidies that encourage more capital flows towards green technological innovations and clean processes.

SCOPE FOR FURTHER WORK

The critical exercise carried out here leads to considering the role of the principles and assumptions of the socio-ecology of the population to examine organizational sustainability in organizations. As well as the evaluation of the individual effects of government subsidy mechanisms and regulatory capture on the behavior of green innovation with different motivations.

REFERENCES

Aldrich, H., & Auster, E. R. (1986). Even dwarfs started small: Liabilities of age and size and their strategic implications. In B. M. Staw & L. L. Cummings (Eds.), *Research in Organizational Behavior* (Vol. 8, pp. 165–198). JAI Press.

Amburgey, T., & Rao, H. (1996). Organizational ecology: Past, present, and future directions. *Academy of Management Journal*, *39*(5), 1265–1286. doi:10.2307/256999

Amore, M. D., & Bennedsen, M. (2016). Corporate governance and green innovation. *Journal of Environmental Economics and Management*, *75*, 54–72. doi:10.1016/j.jeem.2015.11.003

Antonioli, D., Mancinelli, S., & Mazzanti, M. (2013). Is environmental innovation embedded within high- performance organizational changes? The role of human resource management and complementarity in green business strategies. *Research Policy*, *42*(4), 975–988. doi:10.1016/j.respol.2012.12.005

Bai, Y., Song, S., Jiao, J., & Yang, R. (2019). The impacts of government R&D subsidies on green innovation: Evidence from Chinese energy-intensive firms. *Journal of Cleaner.*, *233*(9), 819–829. doi:10.1016/j.jclepro.2019.06.107

Baines, T., Brown, S., Benedettini, O., & Ball, P. (2012). Examining green production and its role within the competitive strategy of manufacturers. *Journal of Industrial Engineering and Management*, *5*(1), 53–87. doi:10.3926/jiem.405

Becker, M. C. (Ed.). (2008). Handbook of organizational routines. Cheltenham, UK: Edward Elgar Publishing Becker, M. C. (Ed.). (2008). Handbook of organizational routines. Cheltenham, UK: Edward Elgar Publishing. doi:10.4337/9781848442702

Bernroider, E. (2002). Factors in SWOT analysis applied to micro, small-to-medium, and large software enterprises: An Austrian study. *European Management Journal*, *20*(5), 562–573. doi:10.1016/S0263-2373(02)00095-6

Bi, K., Huang, P., & Wang, X. (2016). Innovation performance and influencing factors of low-carbon technological innovation under the global value chain: A case of Chinese manufacturing industry. *Technological Forecasting and Social Change*, *111*, 275–284. doi:10.1016/j.techfore.2016.07.024

Birnholtz, J. P., Cohen, M. D., & Hoch, S. V. (2007). Organizational character: On the regeneration of Camp Poplar Grove. *Organization Science*, *18*(2), 315–332. doi:10.1287/orsc.1070.0248

Boeing, P. (2016). The allocation and effectiveness of China's R&D subsidies—Evidence from listed firms. *Research Policy*, *45*(9), 1774–1789. doi:10.1016/j.respol.2016.05.007

Boubakri, N., Cosset, J. C., & Saffar, W. (2013). The role of state and foreign owners in corporate risk-taking: Evidence from privatization. *Journal of Financial Economics*, *108*(3), 641–658. doi:10.1016/j.jfineco.2012.12.007

Bradford, M., & Florin, J. (2003). Examining the role of innovation diffusion factors on the implementation success of enterprise resource planning systems. *International Journal of Accounting Information Systems*, *4*(3), 205–225. doi:10.1016/S1467-0895(03)00026-5

Cao, X., Deng, M., Song, F., Zhong, S., & Zhu, J. (2019). Direct and moderating effects of environmental regulation intensity on enterprise technological innovation: The case of China. *PLoS One*, *14*(10), e0223175. doi:10.1371/journal.pone.0223175 PMID:31589643

Chen, C. C., Shih, H. S., Shyur, H. J., & Wu, K. S. (2012). A business strategy selection of green supply chain management via an analytic network process. *Computers & Mathematics with Applications (Oxford, England)*, *64*(8), 2544–2557. doi:10.1016/j.camwa.2012.06.013

Chen, H. L., & Hsu, W. T. (2009). Family ownership, board independence, and R&D investment. *Family Business Review*, *22*(4), 347–362. doi:10.1177/0894486509341062

Chen, Z., Zhang, X., & Chen, F. (2021). Do carbon emission trading schemes stimulate green innovation in enterprises? Evidence from China. *Technological Forecasting and Social Change*, *168*, 120744. doi:10.1016/j.techfore.2021.120744

Chiu, Y. B., & Lee, C. C. (2020). Effects of financial development on energy consumption: The role of country risks. *Energy Econ*, *90*, 104833. doi:10.1016/j.eneco.2020.104833

Cho, J. H., & Sohn, S. Y. (2018). A novel decomposition analysis of green patent applications for the evaluation of R&D efforts to reduce CO2 emissions from fossil fuel energy consumption. *Journal of Cleaner Production*, *193*, 290–299. doi:10.1016/j.jclepro.2018.05.060

Damanpour, F. (1992). Organizational size and innovation. *Organization Studies*, *13*(3), 375–402. doi:10.1177/017084069201300304

Dauda, L., Long, X., Mensah, C. N., Salman, M., Boamah, K. B., Ampon-Wireko, S., & Dogbe, C. S. K. (2021). Innovation, trade openness and CO2 emissions in selected countries in Africa. *Journal of Cleaner Production*, *281*, 125143. doi:10.1016/j.jclepro.2020.125143

Delmas, M. A., & Montes-Sancho, M. J. (2010). Voluntary agreements to improve environmental quality: Symbolic and substantive cooperation. *Strategic Management Journal*, *31*(6), 575–601.

Deng, Q., & Ji, S. (2015). Organizational green IT adoption: *Concept and evidence. Sustainability*, *7*(12), 16737–16755. doi:10.3390u71215843

Dietz, T., Ostrom, E., & Stern, P. L. (2003). The Struggle to Govern the Commons. *Science*, *302*(5652), 1907–1912. doi:10.1126cience.1091015 PMID:14671286

DiMaggio, P., & Powell, W. W. (1983). The iron cage revisited: Collective rationality and institutional isomorphism in organizational fields. *American Sociological Review*, *48*(2), 147–160. doi:10.2307/2095101

Eckerberg, K., & Joas, M. (2004). Multi-level Environmental Governance: A Concept under Stress? *Local Environment*, *9*(5), 405–412. doi:10.1080/1354983042000255315

Eiadat, Y., Kelly, A., Roche, F., & Eyadat, H. (2008). Green and competitive? An empirical test of the mediating role of environmental innovation strategy. *Journal of World Business*, *43*(2), 131–145. doi:. jwb.2007.11.012 doi:10.1016/j

Etzion, D. (2007). Research on organizations and the natural environment, 1992-present: A review. *Journal of Management*, *33*(4), 637–664. doi:10.1177/0149206307302553

Feldman, M. S. (2016). Past, Present, and future. In J. Howard-Grenville, C., Rerup, A., Langley, & H., Tsoukas (Eds.). Organizational Routines: How They are Created, Maintained, and Changed (pp. 23-46) Oxford: Oxford University Press

Folke, C., Hahn, T., Olsson, P., and Norberg, J. (2005). Adaptive Governance of Social–ecological Systems. *Annual Review of Environment and Resources*, in press (will be published in October 2005).

Fujii, H. (2016). Decomposition analysis of green chemical technology inventions from 1971 to 2010 in Japan. *Journal of Cleaner Production*, *112*, 4835–4843. doi:10.1016/j.jclepro.2015.07.123

Fujii, H., & Managi, S. (2016). Research and development strategy for environmental technology in Japan: A comparative study of the private and public sectors. *Technological Forecasting and Social Change*, *112*, 293–302. doi:10.1016/j.techfore.2016.02.012

Gadenne, D. L., Kennedy, J., & McKeiver, C. (2009). An empirical study of environmental awareness and practices in SMEs. *Journal of Business Ethics*, *84*(1), 45–63. doi:10.100710551-008-9672-9

Gao, X., Lyu, Y., Shi, F., Zeng, J., & Liu, C. (2019). The impact of financial fac-tor market distortion on green innovation efficiency of high-tech industry. *Ekoloji*, *28*(107), 3449–3461.

Graham, B., Reilly, W., Beinecke, F., Boesch, D., Garcia, T., Murray, C., & Ulmer, F. (2011). *Deep water: The Gulf oil disaster and the future of offshore drilling. Report to the President*. National Commission on the BP Deepwater Horizon Oil Spill and Offshore Drilling.

Grossman, G. M., & Krueger, A. B. (1995). Economic growth and the environment. *The Quarterly Journal of Economics*, *110*(2), 353–377. doi:10.2307/2118443

Gunderson, L. (1999). Resilience, Flexibility and Adaptive Management: Antidotes for Spurious Certitude? *Conservation Ecology*, *3*(1), 7. http://www.consecol.org/vol3/iss1/art7. doi:10.5751/ES-00089-030107

Gupeng, Z., & Xiangdong, C. (2012). The value of invention patents in China: Country origin and technology field differences. *China Economic Review*, *23*(2), 357–370. doi:10.1016/j.chieco.2012.02.002

Hannan, M. (2005). Ecologies of Organizations: Diversity and Identity. *The Journal of Economic Perspectives*, *19*(1), 51–70. doi:10.1257/0895330053147985

Hannan, M. T., & Freeman, J. (1989). *Organizational Ecology*. Harvard University Press. doi:10.4159/9780674038288

Hannan, M. T., & Freeman, J. H. (1977). The Population Ecology of Organizations. *American Journal of Sociology*, *82*(5), 929–963. doi:10.1086/226424

Hatimtai, M. H., & Hassan, H. (2018). The relationship between the characteristics of innovation towards the effectiveness of ICT in Malaysia productivity corporation. *Malaysian Journal of Communication*, *34*(1), 253–269. doi:10.17576/JKMJC-2018-3401-15

Hilliard, A., & Jamieson, G. A. (2008). Winning solar races with interface design. *Ergonomics in Design*, *16*(2), 6–11. doi:10.1518/106480407X312374

Hoskisson, R. E., Gambeta, E., Green, C. D., & Li, T. X. (2018). Is my firm-specific investment protected? Overcoming the stakeholder investment dilemma in the resource-based view. *Academy of Management Review*, *43*(2), 284–306. doi:10.5465/amr.2015.0411

Howard-Grenville, J., Rerup, C., Langley, A., & Tsoukas, H. (2016). Introduction: Advancing a process perspective on routines by zooming out and zooming in. In J. Howard-Grenville, C., Rerup, A., Langley, & H., Tsoukas (Eds.). Organizational routines: how they are created, maintained, and changed (pp.1-22.) Oxford: Oxford University Press.

Hu, A. G. Z., Zhang, P., & Zhao, L. (2017). China as number one? Evidence from China's most recent patenting surge. *Journal of Development Economics*, *124*, 107–119. doi:10.1016/j.jdeveco.2016.09.004

Hua, Y., Xie, R., & Su, Y. (2018). Fiscal spending and air pollution in Chinese cities: Identifying composition and technique effects. *China Economic Review*, *47*, 156–169. doi:10.1016/j.chieco.2017.09.007

Huang, M., Ding, R., & Xin, C. (2021). Impact of technological innovation and industrial-structure upgrades on ecological efficiency in China in terms of spatial spillover and the threshold effect. *Integrated Environmental Assessment and Management*, *17*(4), 852–865. doi:10.1002/ieam.4381 PMID:33325155

Jiang, Z., Wang, Z., and Lan, X. (2021). How Environmental Regulations Affect Corporate Innovation? the Coupling Mechanism of Mandatory Rules and Voluntary Management. *Technol. Soc.*, *65*, 101575. doi:. 2021.101575 doi:10.1016/j.techsoc

Ko, Y.-C., Zigan, K., & Liu, Y.-L. (2021). Carbon capture and storage in South Africa: A technological innovation system with a political economy focus. *Technological Forecasting and Social Change*, *166*, 120633. . techfore. 2021. 120633 doi:10.1016/j

Kousar, S., Sabri, P. S. U., Zafar, M., & Akhtar, A. (2017). Technological factors and adoption of green innovation- moderating role of government intervention: A case of SMEs in Pakistan. *Pakistan Journal of Commerce and Social Sciences*, *11*(3), 833–861.

Le Boterf, G. (1999). *L'ingénierie des compétences*. Éditions d'Organisation.

Li, J., Pan, S. Y., Kim, H., Linn, J. H., & Chiang, P. C. (2015). Building green supply chains in eco-industrial parks towards a green economy: Barriers and strategies. *Journal of Environmental Management, 162*, 158–170. doi:10.1016/j.jenvman.2015.07.030 PMID:26241931

Li, N. B. (2019). Environmental Regulation and Corporate Green Technology Innovation - a Conditional Process Analysis. *Inn. Mong. Soc. Sci. Chin. Ed, 40*(6), 109–115. doi:10.14137/j.cnki.issn1003-5281.2019.06.016

Li, S., Song, X., & Wu, H. (2015). Political connection, ownership structure, and corporate philanthropy in China: A strategic-political perspective. *Journal of Business Ethics, 129*(2), 399–411. doi:10.100710551-014-2167-y

Li, Z., Liao, G., Wang, Z., & Huang, Z. (2018). Green loan and subsidy for promoting clean production innovation. *Journal of Cleaner Production, 187*, 421–431. doi:10.1016/j.jclepro.2018.03.066

Lin, C. Y., & Ho, Y. H. (2010). The influences of environmental uncertainty on corporate green behavior: An empirical study with small and medium-size enterprises. *Social Behavior and Personality, 38*(5), 691–696. doi:10.2224bp.2010.38.5.691

Lin, Y. X., Sha, K. C., & Wang, J. (2020). Practical Experience and Inspiration of Foreign Emission Permit System. *Environ. Impact. Assess., 42*(1), 14–16. CNKI: SUN:SXHS.0.2020-01-004.

Liu, J., Zhao, M., & Wang, Y. (2020). Impacts of government subsidies and environmental regulations on green process innovation: A nonlinear approach. *Technology in Society, 63*, 101417. doi:10.1016/j.techsoc.2020.101417

Liu, Y., Wang, A., & Wu, Y. (2021). Environmental regulation and green innovation: Evi-dence from China's new environmental protection law. *Journal of Cleaner Production, 297*, 126698. doi:10.1016/j.jclepro.2021.126698

Luo, Y., Salman, M., & Lu, Z. (2021). Heterogeneous impacts of environmental regulations and foreign direct investment on green innovation across different regions in China. *The Science of the Total Environment, 759*, 143744. doi:10.1016/j.scitotenv.2020.143744 PMID:33341514

Mandavilli, S., Rys, M. J., & Russell, E. R. (2008). Environmental impact of modern roundabouts. *International Journal of Industrial Ergonomics, 38*(2), 135–142. doi:10.1016/j.ergon.2006.11.003

Mintzberg, H. (1979). *The structuring of organizations: A synthesis of the research.* Prentice Hall.

Murphy, K. M., Shleifer, A., & Vishny, R. W. (1993). Why is rent-seeking so costly to growth? *The American Economic Review, 83*(2), 409–414. https://www.jstor.org/stable/2117699

Neumann, T. (2021). Does it pay for new firms to be green? An empirical analysis of when and how different greening strategies affect the performance of new firms. *Journal of Cleaner Production, 317*, 128403. doi:10.1016/j.jclepro.2021.128403

Oller Alonso, M. (2021). *La Responsabilidad Social Corporativa de las empresas del mármol en la comarca del Almanzora, Almería (2019-2021): análisis de sus estrategias de comunicación integral.* Doctorado en Gestión de la Información y de la Comunicación en las Organizaciones Universidad de Murcia Escuela Internacional de Doctorado.

Ostrom, E. (2005). Understanding Institutional Diversity, Princeton University Press, Princeton New Jersey, USA. Ovesson, P. (2003). Markhävdkartering 2002, Hävdtillståndet på betesmarker och slåtterängar inom Nedre Helgeåns våtmarksområde i Kristianstads Vattenrike. Länsstyrelsen i Skåne län, Kristianstads kommun, Högskolan i Kristianstad.

Pentland, A. (2004, October). *Social Dynamics: Signals and Behavior. International Conference on Developmental Learning*, Salk Institute, San Diego, CA

Pentland, B. T., Hærem, T., & Hillison, D. (2011). The (N)Ever-Changing World: Stability and Change in Organizational Routines. *Organization Science*, *22*(6), 1369–1383. doi:10.1287/orsc.1110.0624

Pereira, V., Munjal, S., & Ishizaka, A. (2019, October). Outsourcing and offshoring decision making and its implications for businesses- A synthesis of research pursuing five pertinent questions. *Journal of Business Research*, *103*, 348–355. doi:10.1016/j.jbusres.2019.07.009

Pfeffer, J., & Salancik, G. (1978). *The External Control of Organizations: A Resource Dependence Perspective*. Harper & Row.

Rahim, A., Eladwiah, R., & Abdul Rahman, A. (2013). Resource-based framework of green IT capability toward firms 'competitive advantage. *Resource (Saint Joseph, Mich.)*, *6*, 18–2013.

Rogers, E. M. (2003). Elements of diffusion. *Diffusion of Innovations*, *5*, 1–38.

Salimath, M., & Jones, R. III. (2011). Population ecology theory: Implications for sustainability. *Management Decision*, *49*(6), 874–910. doi:10.1108/00251741111143595

Sanquist, T. F. (2008). Human factors and energy use. *HFES Bulletin*, *51*(11), 1–3.

Santoro, G., Vrontis, D., Thrassou, A., & Dezi, L. (2018). The Internet of Things: Building a knowledge management system for open innovation and knowledge management capacity. *Technological Forecasting and Social Change*, *136*, 347–354. doi:10.1016/j.techfore.2017.02.034

Saud, S., Chen, S., Haseeb, A., Khan, K., & Imran, M. (2019). The Nexus between Financial Development, Income Level, and Environment in Central and Eastern European Countries: A Perspective on Belt and Road Initiative. *Environmental Science and Pollution Research International*, *26*(16), 16053–16075. doi:10.100711356-019-05004-5 PMID:30968296

SchmidtC.SchneiderY.SteffenS.StreitzD. (2020). Capital misal-location and innovation. *Available at* SSRN 3489801. doi:10.2139/ssrn.3489801

Sele, K., & Grand, S. (2016). Unpacking the dynamics of ecologies of routines: Mediators and their generative effects in routine interactions. *Organization Science*, *27*(3), 722–738. doi:10.1287/orsc.2015.1031

Shahrul, N. S., & Normah, M. (2015). Digital version newspaper: Implication towards printed newspaper circulation in Malaysia. *Malaysian Journal of Communication*, *31*(2), 687–701.

Shahzad, F., Lu, J., & Fareed, Z. (2019). Does firm life cycle impact corporate risk taking and performance? *Journal of Multinational Financial Management*, *51*, 23–44. doi:10.1016/j.mulfin.2019.05.001

Sneideriene, A., & Rugine, H. (2019). Theoretical approach on the green technologies development. *Regional Formation and Development Studies*, *2*(28), 124–134.

Sole, R. V., & Bascompte, J. (1995). Spatial Self Organization Self-Organization in complex Ecosystems Princeton University Press. Pág. 84 – 125

Spee, P., Jarzabkowski, P., & Smets, M. (2016). The influence of routine interdependence and skillful accomplishment on the coordination of standardizing and customizing. *Organization Science*, *27*(3), 759–781. doi:10.1287/orsc.2016.1050

Steinzor, R. (2012). The case for abolishing centralized white house regulatory review. *Michigan Journal of Environmental & Administrative Law*, *1*(1.1), 209. doi:10.36640/mjeal.1.1.case

Sueyoshi, T., & Goto, M. (2012). Efficiency-based rank assessment for electric power industry: A combined use of data envelopment analysis (DEA) and DEA-discriminant analysis (DA). *Energy Economics*, *34*(3), 634–644. doi:10.1016/j.eneco.2011.04.001

Sun, X., Zhou, X., Chen, Z., & Yang, Y. (2020b). Environmental efficiency of electric power industry, market segmentation and technologi-cal innovation: Empirical evidence from China. *The Science of the Total Environment*, *706*, 135749. doi:10.1016/j.scitotenv.2019.135749 PMID:31940733

Tan, K. S., & Eze, U. C. (2008). An empirical study of internet-based ICT adoption among Malaysian SMEs. *Communications of the IBIMA*, *1*, 1–12.

Teece, D. J. (2016). Dynamic capabilities and entrepreneurial management in large organizations: Toward a theory of the (entrepreneurial) firm. *European Economic Review*, *86*, 202–216. doi:10.1016/j.euroecorev.2015.11.006

Thatte, A. A. (2007). *Competitive advantage of a firm through supply chain responsiveness and SCM practices* [Doctoral dissertation, The University of Toledo].

Toffler, A. (1970). *Future shock*. Random House.

Tolliver, C., Fujii, H., Keeley, A. R., & Managi, S. (2021). Green innovation and finance in Asia. *Asian Economic Policy Review*, *16*(1), 67–87. doi:10.1111/aepr.12320

Tornatzky, L. G., & Klein, K. J. (1982). Innovation characteristics and innovation adoption-implementation: A meta-analysis of findings. *IEEE Transactions on Engineering Management*, *29*(1), 28–45. doi:10.1109/TEM.1982.6447463

Truong, Y., Mazloomi, H., & Berrone, P. (2021). Understanding the impact of symbolic and substantive environmental actions on organizational reputation. *Industrial Marketing Management*, *92*, 307–320. doi:10.1016/j.indmarman.2020.05.006

Visser, M., & Togt, K. (2016). Learning in Public Sector Organizations: A Theory of Action, Approach. *Public Organization Review*, *16*(2), 235–249. doi:10.100711115-015-0303-5

Wang, F. Z., Jiang, T., & Guo, X. C. (2018). Government Quality, Environmental Regulation and Corporate Green Technology Innovation. *Sci. Res. Manage, 39* (1), 26–33.

Wang, K., & Jiang, W. (2021). State ownership and green innovation in China: The con-tingent roles of environmental and organizational factors. *Journal of Cleaner Production*, *314*, 128029. doi:10.1016/j.jclepro.2021.128029

Wang, Y., Sun, X., & Guo, X. (2019). Environmental regulation and green productivity growth: Empirical evidence on the Porter Hypothesis from OECD industrial sectors. *Energy Policy*, *132*, 611–619. doi:10.1016/j.enpol.2019.06.016

Weng, M. H., & Lin, C. Y. (2011). Determinants of green innovation adoption for small and medium-size enterprises (SMES). *African Journal of Business Management*, *5*(22), 9154–9163.

Westwood, R., & Low, D. R. (2003). The multicultural muse: Culture, creativity, and innovation. *International Journal of Cross Cultural Management*, *3*(2), 235–259. doi:10.1177/14705958030032006

Wu, H. Y., Tsai, A., & Wu, H. S. (2019). A Hybrid Multi-Criteria Decision Analysis Approach For Environmental Performance Evaluation: An Example Of The Tft-Lcd Manufacturers In Taiwan. [EEMJ]. *Environmental Engineering and Management Journal*, *18*(3), 597–616. doi:10.30638/eemj.2019.056

Wurlod, J. D., & Noailly, J. (2018). The impact of green innovation on energy intensity: An empirical analysis for 14 industrial sectors in OECD countries. *Energy Econ*, *71*, 47–61. doi:10.1016/j.eneco.2017.12.012

Xu, Z., Frankwick, G. L., & Ramirez, E. (2016). Effects of big data analytics and traditional marketing analytics on new product success: A knowledge fusion perspective. *Journal of Business Research*, *69*(5), 1562–1566. doi:10.1016/j.jbusres.2015.10.017

Yu, Z., Khan, S. A. R., Ponce, P., & Jabbour, A. B. L. (2022). Factors affecting carbon emissions in emerging economies in the context of a green recovery: Implications for sustainable development goals. *Technological Forecasting and Social Change*, *176*, 121417. doi:10.1016/j.techfore.2021.121417

Zailani, S., Iranmanesh, M., Nikbin, D., & Jumadi, H. B. (2014). Determinants and environmental outcome of green technology innovation adoption in the transportation industry in Malaysia. *Asian Journal of Technology Innovation*, *22*(2), 286–301. doi:10.1080/19761597.2014.973167

Zhang, D. G., & Lu, Y. Q. (2017). Impact of market segmentation on energy efficiency. *China Popul Resour Environ*, *27*(1), 65–72.

Zhang, W., He, L., & Yuan, H. (2021). Enterprises' decisions on adopting low-carbon technology by considering consumer perception disparity. *Technovation*, *102238*. doi:10.1016/j.technovation.2021.102238

Zhao, X., Shang, Y., & Song, M. (2020). Industrial structure distortion and urban ecological efficiency from the perspective of green entre-preneurial ecosystems. *Socio-Economic Planning Sciences*, *72*, 100757. doi:10.1016/j.seps.2019.100757

Zhou, K. Z., Gao, G. Y., & Zhao, H. (2017). State Ownership and firm innovation in China: An integrated view of institutional and efficiency logics. *Administrative Science Quarterly*, *62*(2), 375–404. doi:10.1177/0001839216674457

Zhou, P., Ang, B. W., & Poh, K. L. (2008). Measuring environmental performance under different environmental DEA technologies. *Energy Economics*, *30*(1), 1–14. doi:10.1016/j.eneco.2006.05.001

Chapter 6
Reuse of Spanish Industrial Architecture From Tobacco Factories to Cultural and Public Spaces

Tamar Awad
https://orcid.org/0000-0001-9119-504X
Comillas Pontificial University, Spain

ABSTRACT

The interest of the buildings analysed lies in the possibility of reusing and adapting them for other uses, as versatile examples that can be transformed into public, social and cultural centres. The time frame in which the study is framed is from the 17th century, with the creation of the first Tobacco Factory in Seville in 1620, to the present day, when the old factories and the urban environments in which they are located continue to be transformed. The enormous versatility of industrial architecture has allowed these factories to survive the passage of time and to adapt to changes in use. The reasons why they have been preserved are due to their dimensional characteristics and the fact that many of them were included in the historic city centres. These buildings can be considered as astute infrastructures because they are useful, sustainable, and functional.

1. INTRODUCTION

The content of this article arises from the analysis of the constructive characteristics of the industrial architecture of tobacco, as it is a typology with sufficient entity and an example of architecture that has managed to adapt to other uses (Awad Parada, 2015).

Industrial architecture should be highlighted within the heritage ensemble, due to its own characteristics that allow it to be differentiated from the rest of the architecture ().

Knowing the productive structure allows us to analyse these constructions correctly, as the initial programme is basic to understanding the organisation of the interior space (Sánchez-Montañés & Castilla, 2020).

DOI: 10.4018/978-1-6684-6924-8.ch006

The interest of these buildings lies in the fact that they contain part of the industrial heritage, which could be considered as industrial archaeology (Leurquin, 2000; Monego et al., 2017; Palmer, 2005).

Production architecture reflects the advances of industrialisation, anticipating the use of materials and types of structures, and condenses the complex relationships between product, people and space into a specific typology (Almasifar et al., 2021; Arkhangelskaya, 2017; Brokāne & Strode, 2018; Dong & Jin, 2021; Somoza-Medina & Monteserín-Abella, 2021).

Figure 1. Facades of Sevilla and Logroño tobacco factories

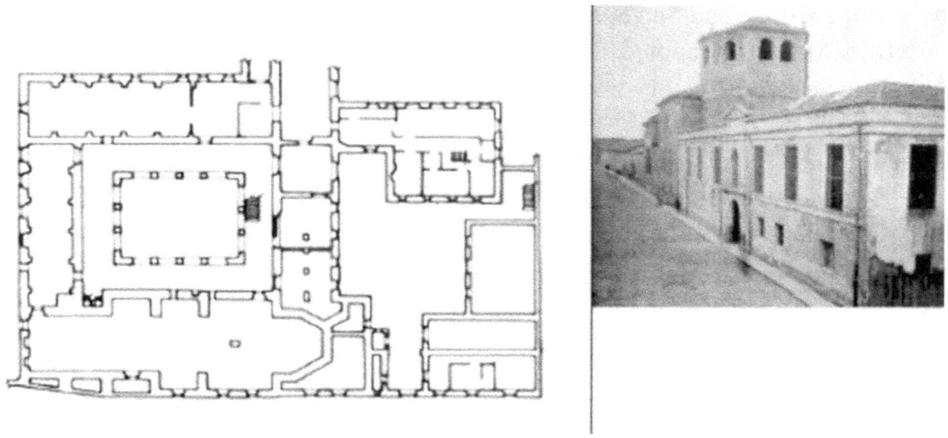

The time frame in which the study is framed is from the 17th century, with the creation of the first Tobacco Factory in Seville in 1620, to the present day, when the old factories and the urban environments in which they are located continue to be transformed (Somoza-Medina & Monteserín-Abella, 2021).

The origin of the royal factories is in France, at the court of Louis XIV, in search of luxury manufactures. In Spain they were founded under the Bourbons, with Philip V.

The first tobacco factory in the world to grind tobacco leaves was the factory in Seville, a city that received products from the Americas, and tobacco leaf was one of them. There is evidence of its activity since 1620. In front of the parish church of San Pedro.

Secondly, in 1741, Philip V ordered the construction of the Royal Tobacco Factory in Cadiz, as a complement to the one in Seville.

In the first decade of the 1800s, the First Generation of Factories was built: Alicante, La Coruña and Madrid.

The Alicante factory, which occupied the Casa de la Misericordia in 1801, was the first factory located in the Mediterranean.

The factory in La Coruña in 1808 reused the Arsenal of La Palloza and constituted a strategic point of communication in the northwest of the Peninsula. The Madrid factory, in Embajadores, was located in the building constructed in 1790 as a factory for all kinds of royal manufactures (eau-de-vie, liqueurs, playing cards, stamped paper and leaden effects). It was the first factory not to be located on a coastal site, which created a radial transport network between the factories.

The second generation of factories developed between 1830 and 1840, and three more were built in: Gijón, Valencia and Santander.

Gijón factory was established in 1823 in the Casa Valdés (an initiative of the Minister Canga Argüelles), and in 1842 it moved to the Convent of the Augustinian Recoletas Nuns.

Valencia factory in 1828 was located in the 17th century Customs building, the second enclave in the Mediterranean.

Santander factory was set up in the Santa Cruz convent in 1835. Together with La Coruña and Gijón factories, it was the third factory in the North of Spain.

With the 1876 law, the tobacco monopoly was extended to the Basque Country during the Restoration, and in 1878 the Bilbao and San Sebastian factories were set up.

In 1878 the Bilbao factory occupied the building used as a barracks, in a walled enclosure of 5 hectares.

In 1878, the San Sebastián factory was installed in the provincial Alhóndiga building. It was the fifth and last factory on the north coast.

In 1890, the Logroño factory occupied the Convent of La Merced. At that time, Amós Salvador Rodrigáñez was the president of the CAT (Compañía Arrendataria de Tabaco: Tobacco Leasing Company) and Práxedes Mateo Sagasta was the president of the Liberal Party, so the decision to move the factory to Logroño was a political one, as both wanted to favour the economic and industrial development of their province.

The last two factories were in Malaga and Tarragona, with the same project, but with a different style.

Malaga factory was built between 1923 and 1928, and although it was designed as a factory, it was used as a Tobacco Cultivation Experimentation Centre.

Tarragona factory was authorised in 1922, but completed in 1932, as Roman remains were discovered during the project, which are preserved in the part dedicated to the Museum.

Finally, some factories were built as: Navalmoral de la Mata factory in 1931, called CETARSA (Compañía Española de Tabaco en Rama S.A.) as an active tobacco processing centre; Sevilla New factory was built in 1954 and closed in 2007; the new one of Logroño was built in 1978 and closed in 2016; Cádiz factory, called C.I.T. Centro Industrial Tabaquero Planta de Productos en Rama was built in 1980 and closed in May 2014; Palazuelo factory called P.P.R. Branch Products Plant was built in 1991 and closed in 2012; Alicante New factory was built in 2002 and the new one of Santander.

2. MATERIALS AND METHODS

The analysis of Spanish tobacco factories is carried out on the basis of different parameters:

1. Current use
2. Year of construction
3. Accessibility for the transport of goods
4. Previous use
5. Classification according to production

The article is based at the doctoral thesis of Awad Parada, Tamar (2015). Arquitectura industrial tabacalera en la España peninsular: secaderos y fábricas. Tesis (Doctoral), E.T.S. Arquitectura (UPM). https://doi.org/10.20868/UPM.thesis.38794.

The materials that have been used to obtain the data of the article have been firstly the consultation of references of: industrial buildings, texts about tobacco, about its production, historical texts about the cities where the factories are located, documentary bases and archives of plans of the buildings. Visits were made to the cities and buildings to see their current state. Interviews were conducted with current and former workers in the factories.

Comparative tables, individual files for each factory, location maps have been made to analyse the accessibility of the goods to the cities and to study the connections between them.

3. RESULTS

3.1. Classification of Factories According to Order of Construction:

Sevilla factory was built in 1620
Cádiz factory was built in 1741
Alicante factory was located in a convent built in 1801
La Coruña factory was built in 1808
Madrid factory was built in 1809
Gijón factory was located in a convent built in 1823
Valencia factory was built in 1828
Santander factory was located in a convent built in 1835
Bilbao factory was built in 1878
San Sebastián factory was built in 1878
Logroño factory was built in 1890
Málaga factory was built in 1923
Tarragona factory was built in 1932

Table 1. Year of start production, and production period of Spanish tobacco factories by Tamar Awad

Year of Start Production	Production Period in the Factory	Short Code	Factory City
1620	1770-1951	S	Sevilla
1741	1829-2003	CA	Cádiz
1801	1752-1951	A	Alicante
1808	1808-2002	CO	La Coruña
1809	1809-2000	M	Madrid
1823	1823-2002	GI	Gijón
1828	1909-2002	V	Valencia
1835	1835-2002	S	Santander
1878	1978-1937	BI	Bilbao
1878	1912-2003	SS	San Sebastián
1890	1890-1978	LO	Logroño
1923	1928-2002	MA	Málaga
1932	1930-2007	T	Tarragona

Figure 2. Plans of Spanish tobacco factories, drawn by Tamar Awad

SEVILLA FACTORY

Figure 3. Sevilla tobacco factory from Tamar Awad thesis

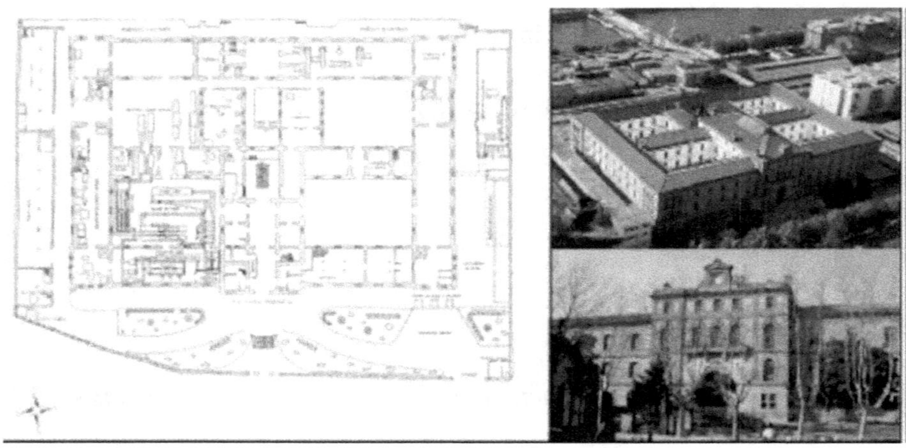

YEAR OF CONSTRUCTION: 1728-1770
PREVIOUS USE: NO
DECLARED B.I.C. (asset of cultural interest.) IN 1959
PROJECT AUTHORS: ENGINEERS: J. Próspero de Verboom, Ignacio Sala, Diego Bordick, and Sebastián Van der Borcht.
SURFACE AREA: 25.897m2
Nº OF FLOORS: 5
Nº OF COURTYARDS: 5+10
CLOSURE: 1951
CURRENT USE: University rectorate
FIRE FIGHTING: No
ELECTRIFICATION: 1897

PRODUCTION: Cigarettes, cigars, and snuff
CONNECTIONS: Train, river, road
NUMBER OF WORKERS: 5,501 in 1895 and 1,658 in 1935

HISTORY: The first tobacco factory in Spain was the factory in Seville, a city that received products from the Americas, and tobacco leaf was one of them. There is evidence of its activity as early as 1620. The ships arrived in the city by sailing up the Guadalquivir.

In 1620, the different tobacco factories in Seville came together, giving rise to the first factory in Seville in a large house opposite the church of San Pedro. They imported ground tobacco from Cuba, which was reworked in Seville.

In 1647, the original factory complex consisted of a workshop with three stone mills, warehouses, stables and several courtyards for the production of powdered tobacco. Extensions to the initial establishment were made between 1669 and 1670.

In 1684, it was the only tobacco-producing centre. With the Bourbon reform of 1701, it became the main tobacco processing centre on the Iberian Peninsula.

In order to meet the growing demand, a new factory was built in Seville, work on which began in 1728 and was not completed until 1770, culminating in the largest civil building in Spain and the largest tobacco factory in the world.

The Hacienda did not manufacture snuff until 1786, with the establishment of a snuff factory within the Seville factory.

It was located near the Tagerete stream, for its water supply, was surrounded by a moat on three sides and a wall on the main front. It had a prison and chapel, a drawbridge and sentry boxes, like a military citadel.

The surface area was 211 x 117 varas castellanas (176.3 x 147.9 m), as a result of the repetition of a module between pillars of 7 varas. The total height is 20 varas.

It was a non-combustible building, vaulted in the factory area. Although its labyrinthine floor plan made surveillance difficult.

Most of the building is laid out in a grid pattern. It was designed by Ignacio Sala.

The façade, the moat, the chapel and the prison are by Van der Borcht.

Materials: plinths, doorways and cornices in limestone, sandstone in the rest and brick paving.

CÁDIZ FACTORY

YEAR OF CONSTRUCTION: 1829
PREVIOUS USE: Yes
DECLARED B.I.C. IN 2011
PROJECT AUTHORS: Architect Federico Gil de los Reyes
AREA: 4.743 m2
Nº OF FLOORS: 3
Nº OF COURTYARDS: 2
EXTENSIONS:1881
CLOSURE: 2003
CURRENT USE: Conference centre

Figure 4. Cádiz tobacco factory from Tamar Awad thesis

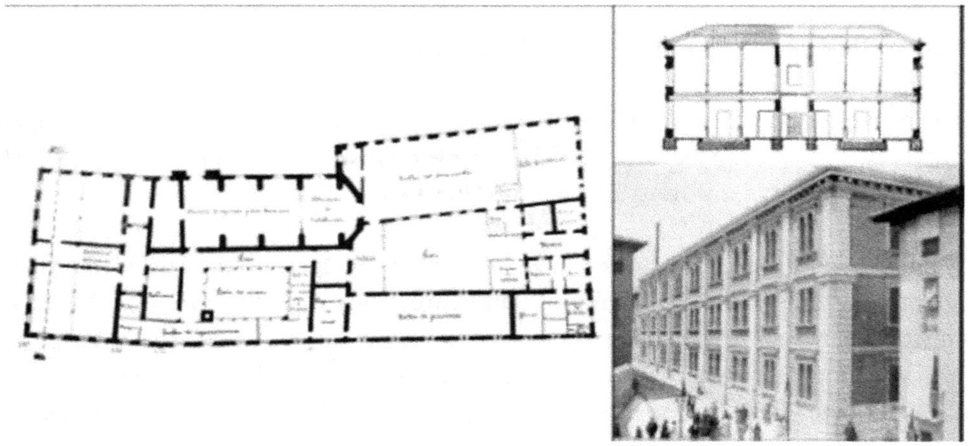

FIRE: NO
ELECTRIFICATION: 1893
PRODUCTION: Cigarettes, and cigars
CONNECTIONS: Maritime and road
NUMBER OF WORKERS:1.989 in 1895 and 969 in 1935

HISTORY: The factory had four different locations:

1. In 1741 The Royal Tobacco Factory of Cadiz was created by Philip V, as a complement to the factory in Seville, in a large house opposite the Puerta de Sevilla, where the Customs building would later be built; it was later moved to Calle del Rosario.
2. In 1829 it was moved to the Alhóndiga, where it remained between 1829 and 1887. The factory building, in neo-Mudejar style, was built in 1829 in Calle Plocia. This building is currently the Palacio de Congresos.
3. A law of 1881 agreed to extend the Cádiz factory and to provide it with equipment suitable for its production; the municipality agreed to build a tobacco factory, which would be handed over to the Treasury for its use. Construction began in 1881 on the site of the old factory, to which some adjoining plots were added.

In 1887 the new factory was inaugurated, a few months after the CAT (Tobacco Leasing Company) was established. While the works were being carried out, the Ministry of Finance granted two large vaults in the Santa Elena Barracks for two years, where the workshops were installed.

Between 1895 and 1897 the adjoining warehouse was built.

4. In 1980 the factory moved to a building on the outskirts of Cádiz: New Industrial Tobacco Centre Building (C.I.T.). With the following uses: Cigar factory, P.P.R. Rama Preparation Plant, Manufacture of expanded tobacco, Manufacture of reconstituted tobacco, Aging and customs warehouses.

Secondly, in 1741, Philip V ordered the construction of the Royal Tobacco Factory in Cadiz, as a complement to the one in Seville, opposite the Puerta de Sevilla.

In the first decade of the 1800s, the first generation of factories was built in Alicante, La Coruña and Madrid, while the factories in Seville and Cadiz were reorganised.

ALICANTE FACTORY

Figure 5. Alicante tobacco factory from Tamar Awad thesis

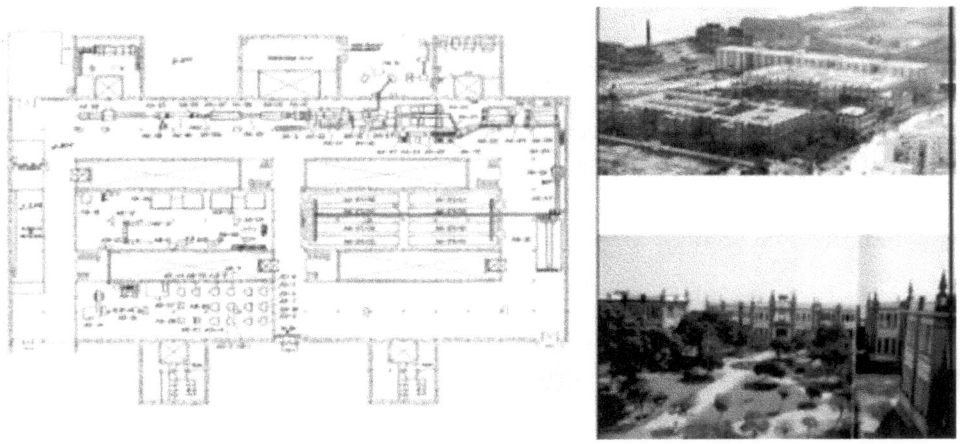

YEAR OF CONSTRUCTION: 1741-1752
PREVIOUS USE: Yes
DECLARED B.I.C. in 2008
PROJECT AUTHORS: Architect Antonio Jover, transformation to a factory.
AREA: 3.166 m2
Nº OF FLOORS: 3
Nº OF COURTYARDS: 1
EXTENSIONS:1828, 1844, 1885 and 1929
CLOSURE: 1951
CURRENT USE: Cultural centre
FIRES: 1844, 1900 AND 1908
ELECTRIFICATION: 1898
PRODUCTION: Cigarettes, cigars and chopped tobacco
CONNECTIONS: Maritime and road
NUMBER OF WORKERS: 4,552 in 1895 and 2,058 in 1935

HISTORY: The Alicante factory occupied the Casa de la Misericordia in 1801. At that time, Alicante enjoyed excellent communications with the rest of Spain, and was the first factory located in the Mediterranean. The connections between Seville, Cadiz and Alicante were made by sea, as it was the cheapest and safest way.

In 1801 the Bishop of Orihuela ceded part of the old palace Asilo y Casa de la Misericordia, located in the San Antón neighbourhood, which ended up occupying it completely, except for the church, in 1838. Antonio Jover directed the work of transforming the building into a factory.

On 20 May 1844, a fire in the diesel engine destroyed part of what Jover had built. At that time, 5,000 people were employed, most of them women.

In 1858 the railway line linked Alicante with Madrid.

In 1869 the factory had 3,997 workers.

There was a riot in 1908 that ended with the burning of several cigar making machines.

1914 the factory had 2,952 workers.

1974 the main courtyard was covered with a glass vault.

During its almost two centuries of existence, the factory produced all types of tobacco: common strong cut tobacco, "caldo de gallina" cigarettes, "ideales", "Celtas sin boquilla", "Ducados" and the famous "Farias de Alicante" cigars.

It is currently being refurbished to become a cultural centre with concert halls, library and Casa de las Ideas, archaeology warehouse, recording rooms, cinema, dance.

The main façade is 51 m. long.

Floors: ground, first and second.

Materials: stone.

LA CORUÑA FACTORY

Figure 6. La Coruña tobacco factory from Tamar Awad thesis

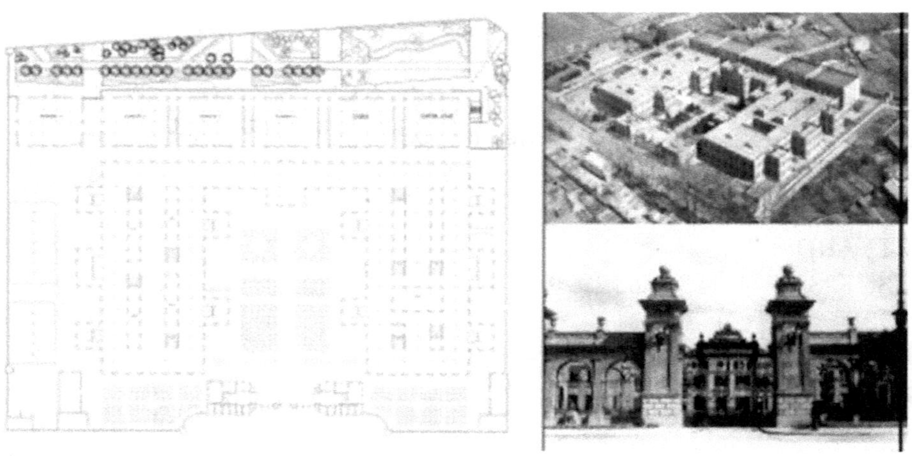

YEAR OF CONSTRUCTION: 1790
PREVIOUS USE: Yes
DECLARED B.I.C. asset of cultural interest. 2013
PROJECT AUTHORS: Antonio de Mesa and Álvarez
SURFACE AREA: 6.890 m2
Nº OF FLOORS: 3

Nº OF COURTYARDS: 4
EXTENSIONS: 1796, 1802, 1828, 1828, 1850, 1850, 1860, 1885, 1899, 1904, 1906, 1910
CLOSURE: 2002
CURRENT USE: Dwellings and public spaces
FIRES 1886 AND 1920
ELECTRIFICATION 1901
PRODUCTION OF Cigarettes and cigars
CONNECTIONS: Maritime, train in 1858 and road 1899
NUMBEROF WORKERS 5,501 in1895 and 1,658 in 1935

HISTORY: The factory in La Coruña in 1808 reused the arsenal of La Palloza and constituted a strategic point of communication between the Cantabrian Sea and the Atlantic Ocean in the northwest of the Peninsula. Communications with the rest of the factories were also made by sea.

In 1808 it was installed in the building that used to be the Arsenal of La Palloza. Renovations were carried out from 1826 onwards. Neoclassical building built in 1790 by Antonio de Mesa y Álvarez to house the Colonies' Maritime Postal Service.

The refurbishment work of 1887 was carried out by F. Domínguez y Romay, who added a floor to the building.

It was very close to the seaport, with its own jetty, and near the mouth of the river Monelos.

1858 La Coruña-Madrid Railway.

1899 the breakwaters were removed and the road was built.

In 1882 E. Pardo Bazán described the factory in La Tribuna.

The complex consisted of:

- The old factory from 1790 with a surface area of 9,269 square feet.
- The new factory of 1827 with a surface area of 10,520 square feet.
- The factory below from 1885 with 4 floors, is the definitive one. The main façade is 90 m. long.

Its production was mixed, cigars and cigarettes were made.

The factory closed in 2002.

Currently in disuse, it is planned its transformation into Judicial Headquarters in 2013, 200 V.P.O. Recovery of 18.000 m2: 9.000m2 public spaces, 10.000m2 road network and 3.400 m2 public parking.

MADRID FACTORY

YEAR OF CONSTRUCTION: 1780-1790
PREVIOUS USE: Yes
DECLARED B.I.C. in 1977
PROJECT AUTHORS: Architect Manuel de la Ballina
AREA: 11.150 m2
Nº OF FLOORS: 4
Nº OF COURTYARDS: 3

Figure 7. Madrid tobacco factory from Tamar Awad thesis

EXTENSIONS:1891, 1901, 1903, 1908 and 1929
CLOSURE: 2000
CURRENT USE: Cultural centre and exhibition hall
FIRES: 1862 AND 1890
ELECTRIFICATION: 1897
PRODUCTION: Cigarettes, cigars
CONNECTIONS: Train and road
NUMBER OF WORKERS: 4,827 in 1895 and 1,927 in 1935

HISTORY: The Madrid factory, Portillo de Embajadores, was located in the building constructed in 1790 as a factory for royal manufactures of all kinds (liqueurs, playing cards, stamped paper and leaden effects). Communication with the other factories had to be by land, using the railway as a means of transport, and the drags as a support. It was the first factory that did not have a coastal location, which generated a diagonal northwest-southeast connection from La Coruña to Alicante, and also connected with the Seville factory through a central-southwest branch. From this point onwards, a radial transport network can be observed between the factories.

This factory was built in 1780 by José de la Ballina, a disciple of Juan de Villanueva, as a factory for the manufacture of eau-de-vie, liqueurs, playing cards, stamped paper and leaden effects.

de Villanueva, as a factory producing eau-de-vie, liqueurs, playing cards, stamped paper and leaded paper.

In 1809 Joseph Bonaparte turned it into a cigar and snuff factory, which it remained until it was closed.

Built on a granite plinth with three upper floors, it is arranged around three courtyards, the central one landscaped.

The trees in the courtyard are protected by the Botanical Gardens.

The factory was in regular operation in 1825. It was first a cigarette and stinging factory and then C. I. D., Research and Development Centre.

In 1897 it was ordered the installation of electric light in the factory in Madrid.

In 1901 it was decided to install steam engines and generators in the factory, with their electrical transmission for the different machines. This meant entering the 20th century, in which steam was used to drive the engines, until it was to drive the engines, until it was replaced by diesel.

In 1921 the electrification of the Madrid factory was approved.

In 2000 the factory closed.

Nowadays it is the Self-managed Social Centre La Tabacalera and part of the building is attached to the Ministry of Culture.

It is the future headquarters of the National Centre for Visual Arts (Nieto and Sobejano, winners of the public competition).

The second generation of factories was developed between 1830 and 1840, and three more were built in the cities of Gijón, Valencia and Santander.

GIJÓN FACTORY

YEAR OF CONSTRUCTION: 1684-1733
PREVIOUS USE: YES

Figure 8. Gijón tobacco factory from Tamar Awad thesis

DECLARED B.I.C. IN 1987
PROJECT AUTHORS: ARCHITECT Ignacio de Palacio and Juan de San Miguel
SURFACE AREA: 3.476 m2
Nº OF FLOORS: 3
Nº OF COURTYARDS: 2
ENLARGEMENTS:1887 and 1907
CLOSURE: 2002
CURRENT USE: Cultural centre
FIRES: 1954
ELECTRIFICATION: 1899
PRODUCTION: Cigarettes, cigars, and snuff
CONNECTIONS: Maritime and road
NUMBER OF WORKERS: 1,828 in 1895 and 964 in 1935

HISTORY: The Gijón factory was established in 1823 in the Palace of the Marquises of Casa Valdés (an initiative of the Minister Canga Argüelles), and in 1842 it moved to the Convent of the Augustinian Recollect Nuns. The connection with the factory in La Coruña was by sea.

During its first years of activity, it was dedicated to the production of cigars until 1874, when the first tobacco grinding machines were installed.

In 1887, the State leased the monopoly to CAT (Tobacco Leasing Company) and a modernisation plan was launched: expansion of the centre and its range of products to include Farias cigars and cigarillos. New machines are installed to make use of residual products and hydroextraction and drying machinery. In 1895, the factory employed 1,828 workers, mostly women.

In 1899 the facilities were electrified.

In 1914 it began to produce cigarettes with cardboard mouthpieces.

Between 1939 and 1957, the factory produced chopped tobacco and Ideal fine cigarettes.

In 2000, the multinational group Altadis decided to close the Gijón factory and transfer the staff and production facilities to Santander factory.

The drafting of the project for the new cultural centre and museum in Gijón is currently postponed. Winning project by Román Villasana.

VALENCIA FACTORY

YEAR OF CONSTRUCTION: 1905-1909
PREVIOUS USE: NO
DECLARED B.I.C. IN 1982
PROJECT AUTHORS: Architect Celestino Aranguren and Ramón Lucini
ING: Federico García, and Mauro Serret.
SURFACE AREA: 15.532 m2
Nº OF FLOORS: 6
Nº OF COURTYARDS: 4
CLOSURE: 2002

Figure 9. Valencia tobacco factory from Tamar Awad thesis

CURRENT USE: Courthouse
FIRES: 1895
ELECTRIFICATION: 1893
PRODUCTION: Cigarettes, cigars, and snuff
CONNECTIONS: Rail, maritime, river, and road
Nº. OF WORKERS: 2,962 in 1895 and 1,487 in 1935

HISTORY: The Valencia factory in 1828 occupied the 17th century Customs building, was the second enclave in the Mediterranean, and was very well connected with Madrid.

Between 1828 and 1914, the factory occupied the Customs Building (in La Glorieta), now the Palace of Justice.

In 1828 it was established in the building that had been built for Customs in 1758. It was designed on the initiative of Joseph de Avilés. Once the building was completed during the reign of Charles III, it was used for various services of the Administration, and was used as a tobacco factory in 1818.

It was finally converted into a tobacco factory in 1828.In 1888, the Nursing Home School was founded.

In 1892 the tram service was inaugurated in Valencia.

In 1893 it was one of the first factories to introduce electricity, together with those of Cádiz and Logroño.

In April 1899, leaf stripping was abolished at the Valencia factory, the only factory that used to use the The operation was replaced by the cutting of the trunk of the vein.

In 1900, electricity production was internalised at the factory for the extension of the lighting system.

In 1904, studies were carried out to build a factory in Valencia.

In 1905 the King laid the first stone of the building, and in 1908 its construction was completed.

In 1909, with the Universal Exhibition in Valencia, the Tobacco Factory in Calle Amadeo de Saboya was built by the architect Celestino Aranguren, and the engineers Federico García and Mauro de Saboya, by the architect Celestino Aranguren, and the engineers Federico García and Mauro Serret.

In 1913, the electrical network was installed in the factory.
In 1914 the new factory in Valencia began to operate, and the old building was returned to the State.
From 1936 to 1937 it was the headquarters of La CAT Republicana.
In 2001 the new factory was closed. The process for its refurbishment began in 2007.
Currently the customs building has been transformed into the courthouse.

SANTANDER FACTORY

Figure 10. Santander tobacco factory from Tamar Awad thesis

YEAR OF CONSTRUCTION: 1641-1656
PREVIOUS USE: Yes
DECLARED B.I.C. in 1982
PROJECT AUTHORS: ARCHITECT Fray Lorenzo de Jorganes, Gregorio de la Roza, José de Calderón, and Juan Gómez de Somomayor.
SURFACE AREA: 3.790 m2
Nº OF FLOORS: 2
Nº OF COURTYARDS: 2
CLOSURE: 2002
CURRENT USE: town hall offices
FIRES: 1916
ELECTRIFICATION: 1899
PRODUCTION: Cigars
CONNECTIONS: Road
Nº OF WORKERS: 1381 in 1895 and 645 in 1935.

HISTORY: The one in Santander in 1835 was located in the convent of Santa Cruz. The goods arrived at the Port of Suances. It was the third factory in the North, together with that of La Coruña and Gijón.

In 1822 a factory was set up in one of the rooms of a civil hospital.

In 1835 it was moved to the convent of the nuns of Santa Cruz del Monte Calvario, built between 1641 and 1656. The building underwent important transformations, as it had previously been used as a barracks.

In 1916 there was a fire

In 1982 it was declared an Asset of Cultural Interest.

It is currently a warehouse for vehicles seized by Customs. 6,250 m2 plot of land with various projects for future housing, car park, and town hall offices.

BILBAO FACTORY

Figure 11. Bilbao tobacco factory from Tamar Awad thesis

PREVIOUS USE: Yes
DECLARED B.I.C. No
Nº OF FLOORS: 4
Nº OF COURTYARDS: 1
CLOSURE: 1937
FIRES: 1916
ELECTRIFICATION: 1899
PRODUCTION: Cigars
CONNECTIONS: Rail and road
NUMBER OF WORKERS: 576 in 1895 and 236 in 1935.

HISTORY: With the law of 21 July 1876, the tobacco monopoly was extended to the Basque Country during the Restoration, and in 1878 the factories in Bilbao and San Sebastian were set up.

In 1828, the factory occupied the building used as a meeting house and barracks, in the Begoña neighbourhood, in a walled area of 5 hectares.

There were ovens where tobacco from Virginia was ground and cooked, Barbados and Kentucky, which arrived on ships flying English, Dutch and French flags.

The Bilbao tobacco factory was founded under the protection of the Royal Decree, on the 1st of July 1878, in what is today the today's Barriada Párroco Unceta, between the Morro mine and Santutxu street, up the slope from Zabalbide to Santutxu, very close to some land belonging to the Marquis of Villarías.

Around 1951, a group of houses was built on the site of the factory.

SAN SEBASTIÁN FACTORY

Figure 12. San Sebastián tobacco factory from Tamar Awad thesis

YEAR OF CONSTRUCTION: 1886-1912
PREVIOUS USE: No
DECLARED B.I.C. No
DESIGNERS: ING: Mauro Serret, José Tarancón and Wenceslao Aguirrebengoa.
SURFACE AREA: 13.277 m2
Nº OF FLOORS: 4
Nº OF COURTYARDS: 5
CLOSURE: 2003
CURRENT USE: International Centre for Contemporary Culture Tabakal
ELECTRIFICATION: 1922

PRODUCTION: Cigarettes
CONNECTIONS: Rail, maritime, and road
Nº OF WORKERS: 778 in 1895 and 1014 in 1935

HISTORY: The San Sebastián factory was set up in 1878 in the provincial Alhóndiga building. It was the fifth and last factory on the north coast. The connections between them were made by sea.

In 1878, the factory occupied a building that had been designed by Antonio de Cortázar, in 1868, for the provincial Alhóndiga in Garibay Street. In 1878, the original factory shared its headquarters with the Provincial Council of Gipuzkoa for six years, until it occupied the entire building in 1885.

The most important task was the production of cigarettes, as the city had a large quantity of Virginia and Kentucky cigarette leaves.

In 1888, the project for the new factory was approved. Mauro Serret was the engineer in charge of drawing up the plans and estimates for the project.

In 1888, José Tarancón was appointed chief engineer and director of the works of the new factory, succeeded by Wenceslao Aguirrebengoa. The land for the new factory was almost 40,000 m2.

In 1890, a new project had to be drawn up for the foundations of the building, using piling and a drainage system in the basement for when the tide came in and out. Loading and unloading docks were built next to the railway tracks.

In 1913, it moved to the new building, which became operational on 18 July.

The following workshops were uthorized to be set up in the factory: one for semi-mechanical cigarettes, one for cigarette stubbing, one for strand cigarettes, one for packing common stubbing, and one for minor repairs.

The factory occupied a 13,277 m2 site.

In 2003 the factory closed after ninety years of activity.

It is now the Tabakal International Centre for Contemporary Culture.

LOGROÑO FACTORY

YEAR OF CONSTRUCTION: 1596
PREVIOUS USE: YES
DECLARED B.I.C. 1983
PROJECT AUTHORS: Architect Luís Barrón
SURFACE: 3.790 m2
Nº OF FLOORS: 4
Nº OF COURTYARDS: 1
CLOSURE: 1978
CURRENT USE: La Rioja government headquarters, exhibition hall and municipal library
ELECTRIFICATION: 1893
PRODUCTION: Cigars
CONNECTIONS: Train and road
Nº OF WORKERS: 412 in 1895 and 705 in 1935.

Figure 13. Logroño tobacco factory from Tamar Awad thesis

HISTORY: In 1890 the Logroño factory occupied the 16th century Convent of La Merced. At that time, Amós Salvador Rodrigáñez was the president of CAT (Compañía Arrendataria de Tabacos: Tobacco Leasing Company) and Práxedes Mateo Sagasta, a native of Logroño, was the President of the Liberal Party; therefore, the decision to move the factory to Logroño was a political one, as both wanted to favour the economic and industrial development of their province.

A warehouse was installed in the Casa de la Beneficiencia.

In 1891, work on the convent was completed. Cigars were made.

In 1944 there was a fire in the nave of the church.

In 1978 the old factory closed and the new factory opened in Logroño, which was initially destined for Madrid.

Today the old factory has been the headquarters of the Government of La Rioja, the Amós Salvador Exhibition Hall and Library since 1984.

The last two factories were in Malaga and Tarragona, with the same project, but with a different style.

MÁLAGA FACTORY

YEAR OF CONSTRUCTION: 1923-1928
PREVIOUS USE: NO
DECLARED B.I.C. NO
PROJECT AUTHORS: Architect Mariano G. Morales and F. González-Estéfani
ING: J. Francisco Delgado, Carlos Dendariena, and Fernando Guerra
AREA: 50.000 m2
Nº OF FLOORS: 3/5
Nº OF PATIOS: 4
CLOSURE: 2002

Figure 14. Málaga tobacco factory from Tamar Awad thesis

CURRENT USE: Experimental centre for tobacco growing.
FIRES: 1993
ELECTRIFICATION: 1923
PRODUCTION: Cigars
CONNECTIONS: Maritime and road

HISTORY: Malaga was built between 1923 and 1928, and although it was designed as a factory, it was used as an Experimentation Centre for the cultivation of tobacco.

In 1922 the CAT (Tobacco Leasing Company) authorises the construction of the factory.

Construction work began in 1923. The authors of the project were the industrial engineers Juan Francisco Delgado and Carlos Dendariena and the civil engineer Fernando Guerra, with the collaboration of the architect Mariano García Morales and the industrial engineer Francisco González Estéfani.

Construction was completed in 1928, and although it was designed as a factory, it was used as a fermentation centre for Spanish tobacco.

In 1930 the building became the Sole Fermentation Centre of Spain, and all the indigenous tobacco was taken to Malaga.

The total area of all the land was 122,275 m2 with eleven buildings occupying around 55,000 m2.

The National Crop Service would have an area of 18,900 m2 (12,852 of land and 6,048 buildings) and Tabacalera 35,000 m2 (23,694 of land and 11,366 buildings).

In 1977, it began work as a cigar factory.

TARRAGONA FACTORY

Figure 15. Tarragona tobacco factory from Tamar Awad thesis

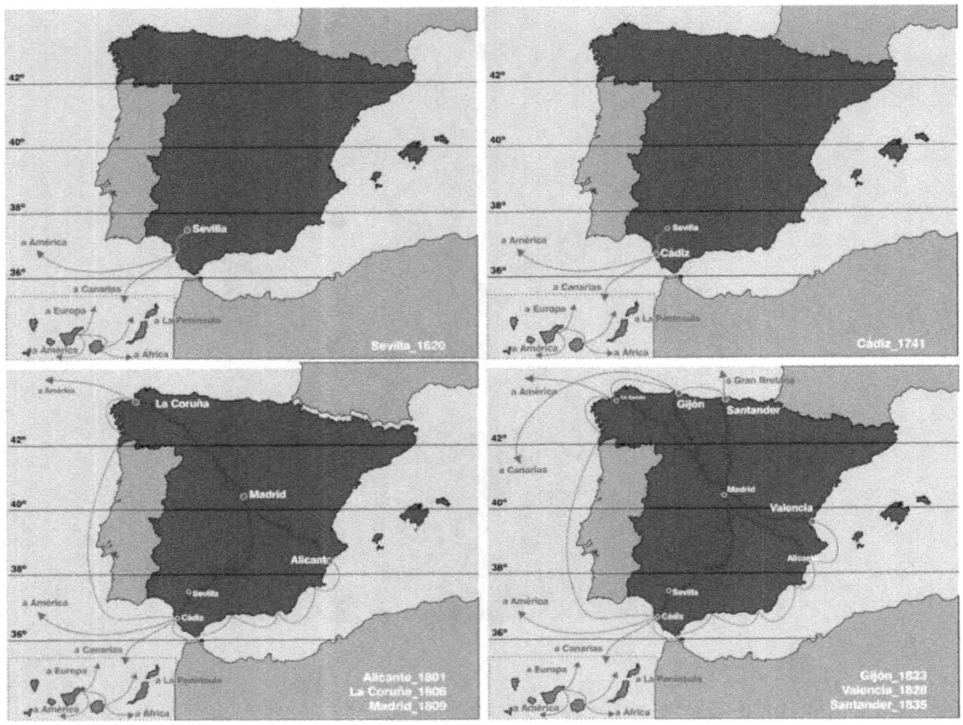

YEAR OF CONSTRUCTION: 1923-1930
PREVIOUS USE: NO
DECLARED B.I.C. NO
PROJECT AUTHORS: Architect Lloreç Rossell and the engineer Josep Tulla Planella
AREA: 37.932 m2
Nº OF FLOORS: 2
Nº OF COURTYARDS: 0
CLOSURE: 2007
CURRENT USE: Municipal archive and national museum of archaeology
ELECTRIFICATION: 1932
PRODUCTION: Cigars and cigarettes
CONNECTIONS: Sea and road
Nº OF WORKERS: 111 in 1935

HISTORY: The Factory project was authorised in 1922, but it was not completed until 1932, as Christian Roman remains were discovered during the project, which are preserved in the part dedicated to the Archaeological Museum.

The Lessee approved the construction of a museum annexed to the factory. The works were carried out between 1929 and

1930, and the Museum project was drawn up by Lloreç Rossell.

In 1932 the building was inaugurated, practically a twin of the one in Malaga.

It had a frontage of 218 metres and a depth of 174 metres.

From the autumn of 1932 to 1937, the factory was dedicated to the chopping of yarn.

It moved to Vic from 16th April 1938 to 11th March 1939.

In 1939, the Tobacco Factory returned to its premises in the city of Tarragona. Seriously damaged at the end of the Civil War, it resumed manufacturing activity in 1943.

In 1941 the building was donated to the State.

From the 1960s onwards, the Tarragona factory was devoted exclusively to the manufacture of cigarettes, mainly dark tobacco. Between 1955 and 1965, Farias and Entrefinos Cortados were also produced.

Between 1955 and 1965, the factory was a warehouse for raw tobacco, basically indigenous, together with the factories in La Coruña, Gijón and Logroño.

In 2007, the factory was ordered to close.

The project for the National Museum of Archaeology of Tarragona is currently approved. Part of the building is the Municipal Archive.

3.2. Analysis in Terms of the Accessibility of Goods to Factories

The location of the factories was determined by very different reasons, the most important of which were: geographical, strategic and political (Aytekin, 2018; Christiernsson et al., 2021; Loures & Panagopoulos, 2007; Xie, 2015). In most of the factories, the choice of the city of location was linked to the reception of raw materials, which was mainly done by sea, or by water (in the case of Seville), and by land, using the railway as a means of transport. The factories occupied cities with ports for the proper maritime transport of goods and to stop smuggling (Jiaping et al., 2020). Only two cases, Madrid and Logroño, had their factories in the interior of the Peninsula. The one in Madrid was built because of its central location, and because it was geographically at the centre of all land communications by road and rail. The Logroño factory, however, was built for political reasons, as the president of CAT was a relative of President Sagasta, and both were from La Rioja.

Production sites were to be close to the distribution area, but there was an imbalance, as half of the factories were on the north coast.

The accessibility of goods to the factories had some constants, such as proximity to seaports and railway stations, but in each case, it depended on the proximity of these infrastructures.

To the Sevilla factory: The goods arrived via the navigable Guadalquivir.

Cádiz factory was in front of the port.

Alicante factory is in the city, it does not have a quay in the port, because the building of an old convent was used, so the goods arrived by road to the factory. Connections between Seville, Cadiz and Alicante were made by sea, as it was the cheapest and safest way.

La Coruña factory is close to the port. Between the Atlantic and the Cantabrian Sea. Communications with the rest of the factories were also by sea.

Madrid: Communication with the other factories had to be by land, using the railway as a means of transport from 1855 onwards, and the drags as a support. This generated a diagonal northwest-southeast

Figure 16. Warehouse of Cádiz
Source: Image from the Tabacalera Archive.

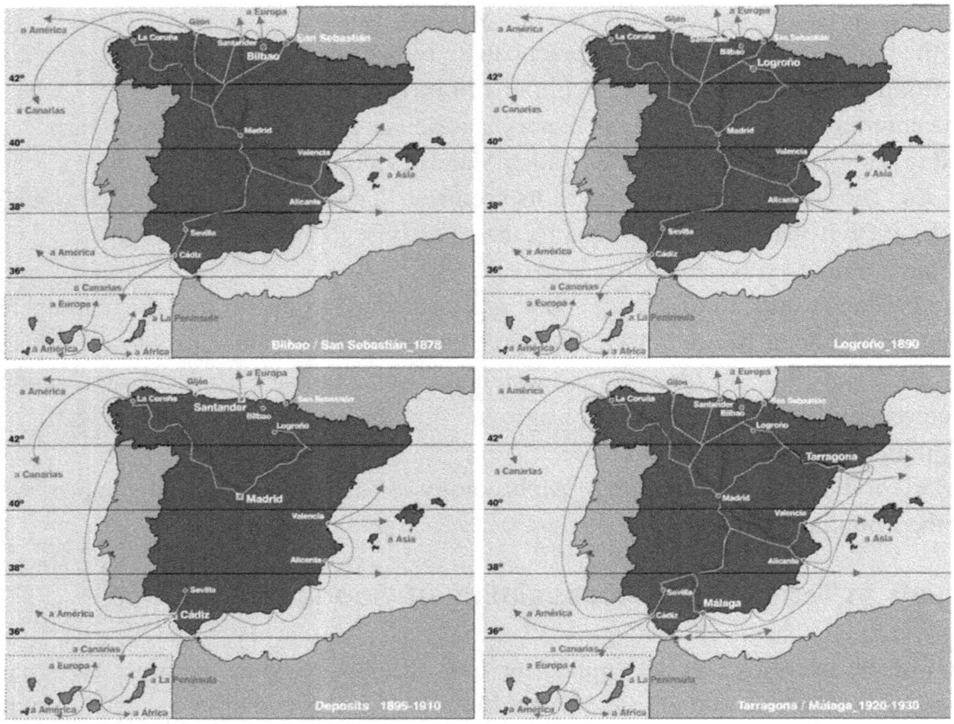

connection from La Coruña to Alicante, also connecting with the Seville factory through a central-southwest branch. From this point onwards, a radial transport network can be observed between the factories.

Gijón factory is in the upper part of the city, it is not at the foot of the port. The port of Musel was very important, it was the arrival area for iron ore from Vizcaya. It was connected to La Coruña by sea.

Valencia factory was on the banks of the Turia, but not near the port. very well connected to Madrid.

Santander factory was not close to the port. The goods arrived at the port of Suances, and from there they were transported by road.

Bilbao: the factory was close to the railway station.

San Sebastián: does not have a goods port, it has a fishing port. The factory was on the banks of the estuary, not in the port, so the goods arrived by lorry from the port of Pasajes.

To Logroño factory, the raw tobacco arrived by lorry. The area where the factory was located is the old town and access was not easy. At first, part of the supply would arrive by rail and then by small lorries from the station to the factory, but there were also arrivals by lorry from nearby warehouses such as Santander.

Málaga factory is near the port.

Tarragona factory is in the port, but the goods were delivered by truck to the factory.

the new factory of Logroño was built with two tracks inside the enclosure, for unloading wagons, with access from the Arrubal station, but the supply by rail was gradually abandoned and now everything is

Figure 17. Cádiz factory façade in 1908
Source: Image from the Tabacalera Archive.

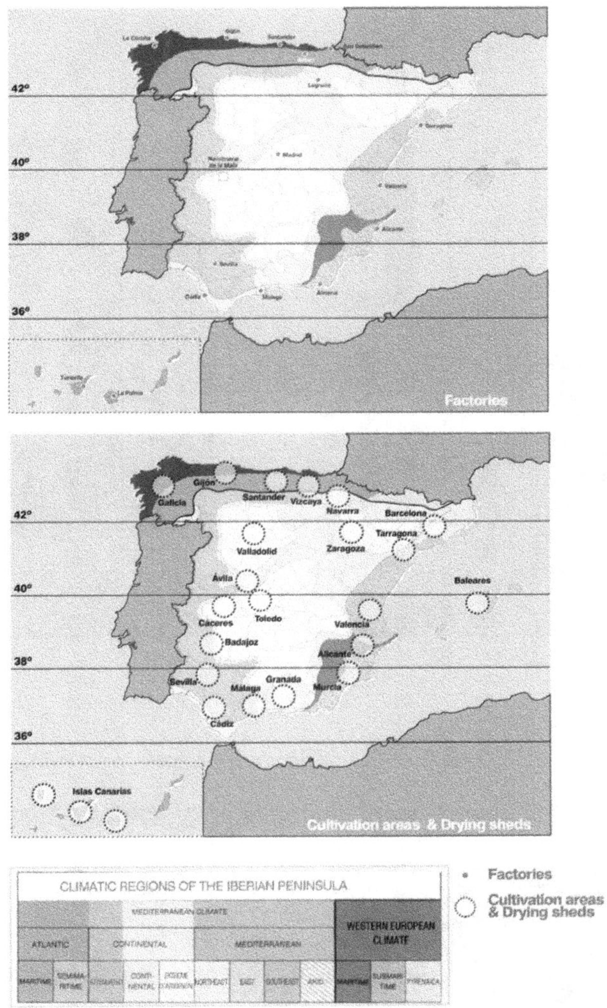

by lorry, whether it be raw materials, semi-finished products, or effects (materials needed for cigarettes and packaging in general).

TOBACCO WAREHOUSES

Three warehouses were authorised, distributed in different areas of the Peninsula.

In 1895, the Central warehouse, in Madrid on Calle General Lacy. It was accessed by rail. It supplied the factories in Madrid and La Coruña.

In 1901 the Norte warehouse in Santander. It supplied the factories in Gijón, Santander, Bilbao and San Sebastián.

Figure 18. Aerial image of La Coruña factory
Source: Image of La Coruña City Hall.

Figure 19. Aerial image of Madrid factory of the Tabacalera self-construction group

In 1910 the South warehouse in Cádiz. It supplied the factories in Seville, Cadiz, Alicante and Valencia.

As one of the conclusions of the study, it can be determined that the factories did not come close to tobacco production, except in two cases: Cádiz and Palazuelo, where drying sheds and tobacco leaf fields do exist in nearby areas.

Figure 20. Aerial view of the Gijón Factory
Source: Image of Gijón Town Hall.

Figure 21. Aerial view of the Valencia Factory
Source: Image of Paisajes Industriales.

Dark tobacco is produced in Palazuelo and tobacco from the surrounding areas was stored in Cádiz.

The main reason for this separation is that the process of obtaining tobacco is a process divided into two main phases: the primary process and the secondary process.

In the primary process, the tobacco leaf is dried in the drying sheds, where the climate is a determining factor, but only in the case of air-drying.

In the secondary process, however, the tobacco arrives pre-treated at the factories, so the climate has no influence on this part of the process.

Figure 22. Aerial view of the San Sebastián Factory
Source: Image of Gárate (2005, p. 136).

Figure 23. Aerial view of the Malaga Factory
Source: Image of Campos Luque, Concepción (2004, p. 33).

Figure 24. Aerial view of the Tarragona Factory
Source: Image of Altadis documentary collection.

Figure 25. Maps showing the location of factories and their means of transporting goods from 1620 to 1835
Source: Drawn by Tamar Awad.

Figure 26. Maps showing the location of factories and their means of transporting goods from 1878 to 1930
Source: Drawn by Tamar Awad.

This reason determines that in the climatic zones where the study is focused, there are areas where there are factories and drying sheds and others where there are only factories, or only drying sheds.

The following classification determines the existence of drying sheds and factories according to climatic zones:

Extreme continental climate zone: Cáceres, Madrid and Toledo. There are drying sheds in Cáceres, in the villages of: Navalmoral de la Mata, Jarandilla de la Vera, Talayuela and the tobacco processing centre in Navalmoral de la Mata. There are also drying sheds in the villages of Toledo: Talavera and Calera y Chozas. The Madrid factory is located in this area.

Climatic zone Iberia parda, attenuated continental: Seville, Malaga and Cadiz. There are also drying sheds in the Andalusia climate zone, and factories in: Seville, Cadiz and Malaga.

Green Iberian maritime region - European climate: San Sebastián. There are factories but no drying sheds.

Continental climate zone, brown Iberia: Logroño. There is a factory but no drying sheds.

3.3. Previous Use of the Building Before It Became a Factory

Tobacco factories in Spain were set up in buildings created for that purpose, or existing buildings were reused.

In 1728, the Seville factory was installed in a building designed and built as the first tobacco factory in the world, after having been in different locations.

In 1829 the Cádiz factory was installed in the Alhóndiga building, which was used for the sale, purchase and storage of grain and other foodstuffs.

The Alicante factory was installed in the House and church of Misericordia, built between 1741 and 1752, to house the town's beggars, at the initiative of the bishop of Orihuela.

The old religious buildings were not in good condition, as they had been used by the army in the wars of Independence and the Carlist Wars, which required repairs and renovations to prepare the workshops

Figure 27. Maps showing the location of factories and tobacco drying sheds in different climatic zones
Source: Drawn by Tamar Awad.

and warehouses. The Cádiz Tobacco Factory had been created in 1741, as a complement to the Seville factory, in a large house opposite the Puerta de Sevilla, where the Customs building would later be built; it was later moved to Calle del Rosario, and in 1829 to the Alhóndiga.

The creation of new factories was a novelty, because tobacco production had been concentrated in Seville, with the exception of Cadiz and other smaller establishments. The new factories were intended to cover the gap between production and consumption and, above all, to produce the new types of tobacco, which required a large workforce.

The government also decided to disperse production in several factories in order to reduce the costs of distributing the work and to prevent workers' riots, which became more frequent the more concentrated the factories were.

In the first decade of the 19th century, factories were set up in Madrid, Alicante and La Coruña and those in Seville and Cadiz were reorganised. In the 1930s, three other tobacco factories began production in Gijón, Santander and Valencia. The factories in Alicante, Santander and Gijón were established in churches and convents.

The factory in La Coruña was set up in 1808 in the building that used to be the Arsenal de la Palloza, which underwent costly renovations from 1826 onwards.

In 1809, the Madrid factory occupied the premises of a factory for eau-de-vie, liqueurs, playing cards, stamped paper and lead effects, which had been built in 1790. Its operation as a tobacco factory was irregular until 1825, due to war and political conflicts.

The Valencia factory was established in 1828, in a large building that had been built for Customs in 1758, and which had been used for civilian functions until it was remodelled for the manufacture of tobacco.

The Santander factory was definitively established in 1835 in the Convent of Santa Cruz de Monte Calvario. The main problem of this factory was the inadequacy of the building, which underwent multiple alterations throughout the century.

The Bilbao factory was located in the town of Begoña, from 1 July 1878, on the site known as Santucho, next to the hermitage of San Francisco. Former shelter and barracks during the Carlist wars.

The San Sebastián factory occupied a recently constructed building, which had been designed by Ramón Antonio de Cortázar, in 1868, as a provincial alhóndiga.

On 10 June 1887, the Bank of Spain awarded the tobacco monopoly to the Compañía Arrendataria de Tabacos (C.A.T.), which would keep it until the Spanish Civil War.

At the beginning of the Restoration, when the tobacco stamp was extended to the Basque Country, factories were set up in Bilbao and San Sebastián. Thus, when CAT was created in 1887, there were ten tobacco factories in Spain. However, their facilities were not optimal for factory production, as became evident when the machines began to be installed. The Treasury located the factories in large buildings that were available, as it could not finance new constructions; most of them were disentailed religious buildings, which ended up in the hands of the municipalities or the Treasury. Among their advantages was the spaciousness of the buildings, which allowed for the transfer and storage of raw materials and finished products, as well as the installation of large workshops to accommodate the increasing number of female workers.

In Logroño and San Sebastián, two other factories began to be built and construction progressed slowly. Although the Logroño factory was also old, the Council asked the Ministry of Finance to admit it as one of the new factories to be built.

After having established a first factory in Gijón in 1823, whose life was limited to 40 days, in 1837 it was established again in the stately Casa de Valdés, from where six years later it moved to the convent of the Augustinian Recollect nuns.

In 1912, the budgets for the completion of the new factory building in San Sebastián were approved.

In 1922 the Treasury authorised the construction of the factories in Malaga and Tarragona and bought the land to build them. The budget and plans were the same for both factories. Work began in July 1923 in both capitals.

Table 2. Table with previous use of factory buildings by Tamar Awad

Starting Year	City of the Factory	Use of the Building
1728	Sevilla	Factory
1828	Cádiz	Wheat market
1741	Alicante	Convent
1790	La Coruña	Arsenal/ Barracks
1809	Madrid	Royal Manufacturing Factory
1684	Gijón	Convent
1905	Valencia	Factory
1641	Santander	Convent
1878	Bilbao	Barracks
1888	San Sebastián	Factory
1596	Logroño	Convent
1923	Málaga	Factory
1932	Tarragona	Factory

3.4. Classification According to Production

Another way of classifying the factories is according to their production, although initially they were all cigar and picadura factories, and Seville as well as snuff factories, they were later divided into: cigar factories, cigarette factories and mixed factories.

The consumption of powdered tobacco, which was introduced into the Peninsula in the 16th century and was ground by hand in mortars. This product was obtained in factories with animal-driven stone mills.

To make a cigar, the first step was to grind the tobacco, as it had to be completely dry before it could be transported. The best leaves were used for the wrapper and the worst for the filler. All the leaves were deveined and then the cigars were rolled. In order to obtain the tobacco, the tobacco was first cut with blades and then sieved.

The raw material of the cigarette is the picadura or chopped tobacco, which could be of two kinds: squared (or Spanish-style) and in strands.

- **Mixed:** Cigars and cigarettes. La Coruña and Madrid
- **Cigars:** Gijón, Santander, old Logroño, Bilbao, Málaga, old Cádiz.
- **Cigarettes:** San Sebastián, Logroño Nueva, Tarragona, Valencia, Alicante and Seville.

The new factory in Cádiz is a Preparation Plant (Ligature Preparation Plant (L.P.P.) for blond, expanded and reconstituted tobacco. Aging warehouse.

The Palazuelo factory is a Ligature Preparation Plant (L.P.P.) for dark tobacco, a Rama Preparation Plant (P.P.R.) and warehouses.

City of the factory: SE= Sevilla, CA=Cádiz, A=Alicante, CO= La Coruña, M=Madrid, GI= Gijón, V= Valencia, S=Santander, BI= Bilbao, SS= San Sebastián, LO= Logroño, MA=Málaga, and T= Tarragona.

Table 3. Table with main and secondary production of factories

	SE	CA	A	CO	M	GI	V	S	BI	SS	LO	MA	T
Snuff	○												
Cigars	○	●	○	●	●	●	○	●	●		●	●	○
Cigarrettes	●	○	●	●	●	○	●			●	○		●
stings		○	○		○	○	○						

● Principal production
○ Secondary production

Future research directions could be:

- Analysis of the processes of change in the urban environments near the buildings that were once tobacco factories (Crane et al., 2021).

- Evolution of the means of transport and accessibility to these buildings and their proximity to railway stations and seaports (Yang et al., 2019).
- Study of the invariant characteristics of tobacco factory buildings and their comparison with those of other countries (Barišić Marenić & Vukojevic, 2019; Cioni et al., 2019).

3.5. Current Use

Factories that were built as factories from the beginning have adapted better to changes in use than those that were not initially created as factories. (Awad Parada, 2013; Awad Parada, 2015; Awad Parada, 2017).

Industrial architecture offers an enormous capacity for adaptation, which has allowed these factories to survive the passage of time and changes in use. The reasons why they have been preserved include their dimensional characteristics and the fact that many of them were included within historic city centres. These buildings are useful, sustainable and functional. These buildings have gone from being tobacco factories to cultural and public spaces. (Alonso et al., 2006; Awad Parada, 2021; Comín & Martín Aceña, 1991).

The Royal Tobacco Factory of Seville: Nowadays it is the University, Library and Rectorate.

The Royal Tobacco Factory of Seville ofCádiz has been transformed into a conference centre.

Figure 28. Cádiz factory
Source: Image from Cristóbal Santos Corrales (2009).

Alicante factory is being refurbished to become a cultural centre with concert halls, a library and Ideas House, an archaeology warehouse, recording rooms, cinema and dance.

For the factory in La Coruña, called La Palloza, it became a court headquarters with a 2014 project.

The Royal Tobacco Factory of Madrid it was a liquor and playing card factory, then a cigarette and cigarette factory, before becoming a Research and Development Centre and Pilot Plant. It is currently divided into an Exhibition Hall and a self-managed Social Centre. It was declared BIC (Asset of Cultural Interest and is awaiting transformation into the headquarters of the National Centre of Visual Arts.

Figure 29. The tobacco warehouse of the factory in Cádiz
Source: Image from Cristóbal Santos Corrales (2009).

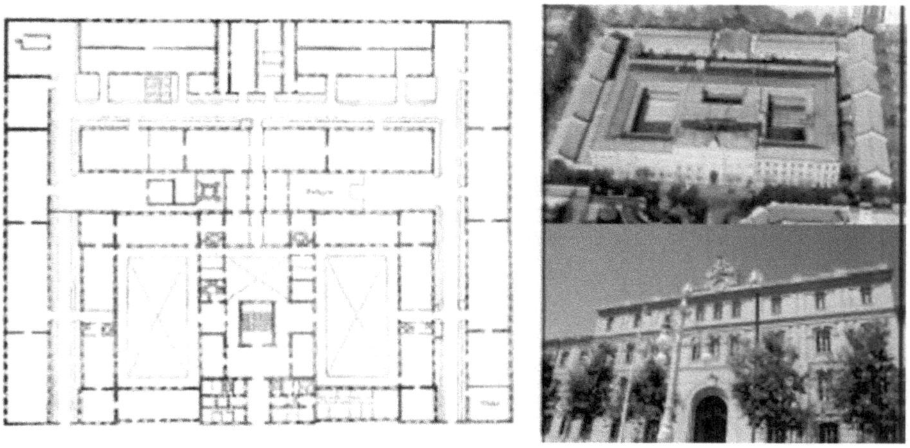

Figure 30. Cádiz conference centre
Source: Image from Cristóbal Santos Corrales (2009).

Figure 31. La Coruña factory
Source: Image from the A Coruña City Council Archive.

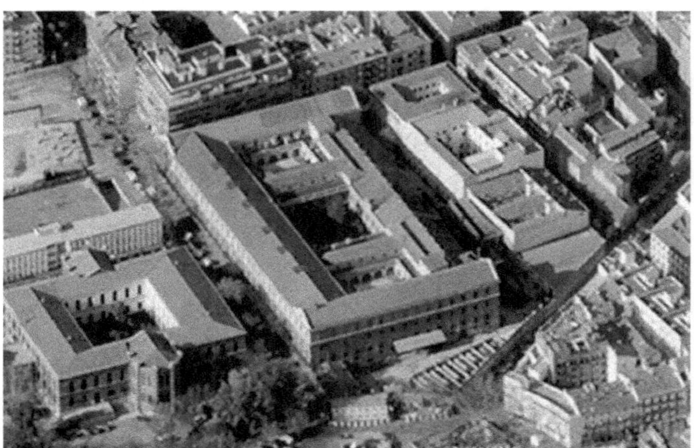

Figure 32. Madrid Exhibition Hall
Source: Image by Tamar Awad.

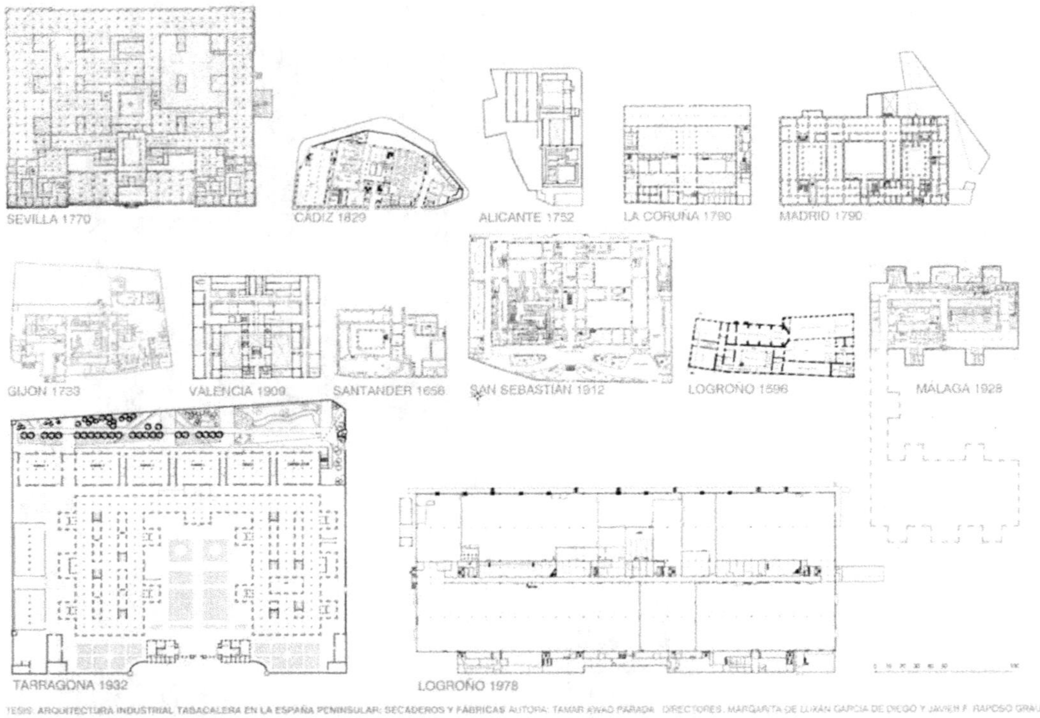

Figure 33. Tabacalera Cultural Centre Madrid
Source: Image by Tamar Awad.

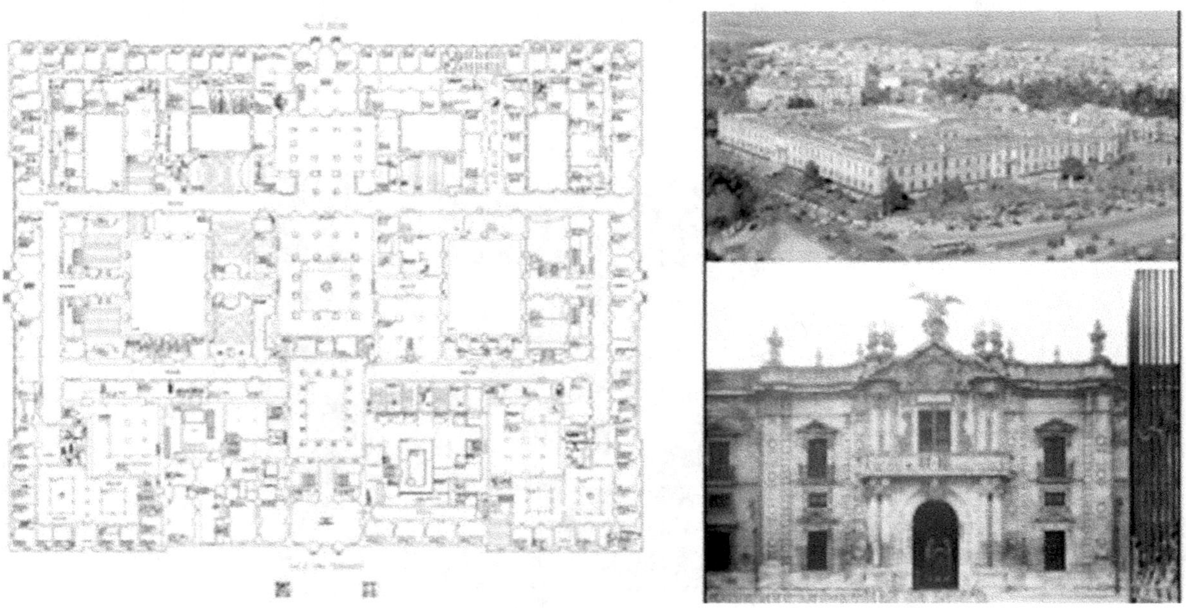

Gijón factory is currently a cultural centre and the project to house the Gijón museum has been approved.

The Royal Tobacco Factory of Valencia is today's Town Hall.

The one in Santander, a former convent, began its activity in 1835 until 2002, when production was moved to the more modern facilities in Entrambasaguas. The old building, which was also declared BIC, has been the subject of several failed projects since then, although it seems that it will finally be used to unify the judicial headquarters in a single space. However, in 2009, work was completed on the remodelling of the former General Tobacco Warehouse in Rama, which became the headquarters of the Provincial Historical Archive and Public Library of Santander.

Figure 34. Santander factory was a former convent
Source: Image from the Santander City Council Archive.

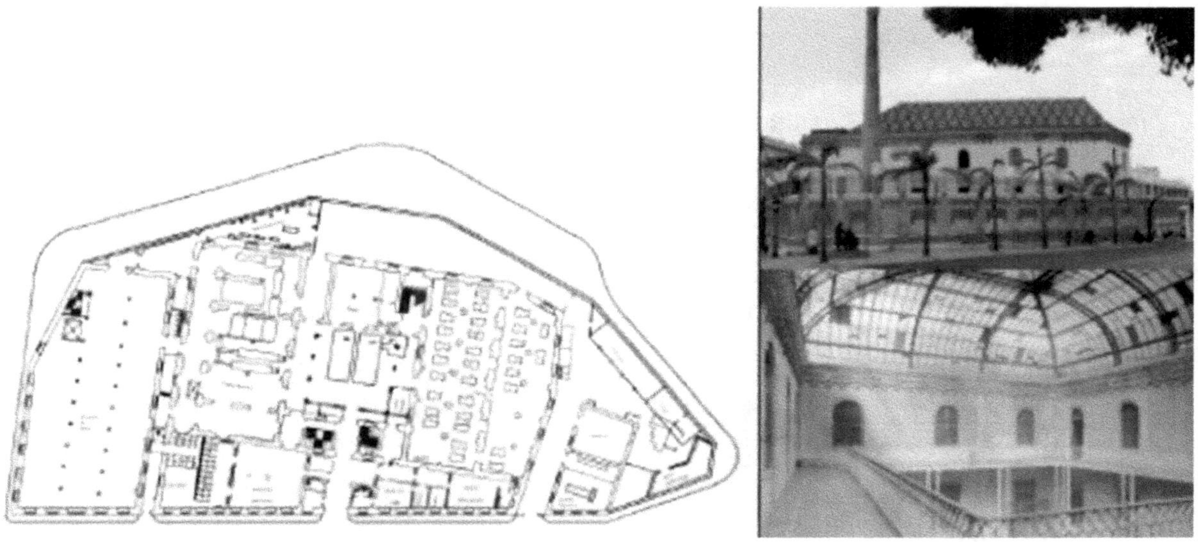

The Bilbao factory was closed in 1937 and is the only one of the factories that has not been preserved.

The San Sebastian factory is the Tabakalera International Centre for Contemporary Culture.

Logroño factory has become: the Parliament of La Rioja, Municipal Library and Exhibition Hall.

The Malaga factory is the Cultivation Experimentation Centre.

The building was reopened in 2007 with different uses. since 2010, it houses the city's Automobile Museum and the Fashion Museum. since 2015, the collection of the Russian Museum of St. Petersburg. In addition to housing the Polo Digital, it is also occupied by different municipal offices such as the Public Tax Management Agency or the municipal IT centre, as well as the Malaga Business School.

Of the Tarragona factory, the main building is abandoned and two warehouses have been restored and converted into the Municipal Archive and the national archaeology museum, a historical museum with an interpretation centre so as not to forget the factory's history, a part for companies, an archaeological area, self-management spaces for residents' associations and other entities, as well as areas for commercial activities related to culture, the provincial library, study rooms and a cafeteria.

New factories built in buildings for that use from the beginning.

Figure 35. Interior of San Sebastián factory
Source: Image of the San Sebastian City Hall Archive.

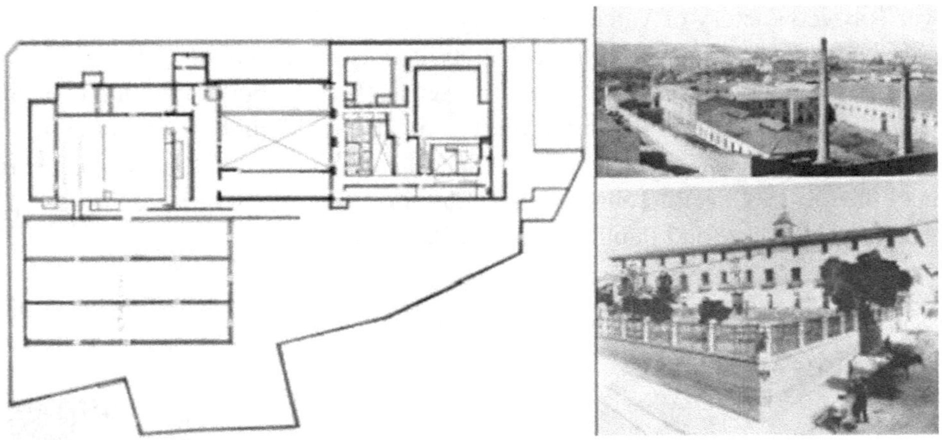

Figure 36. Façade of the old Logroño factory, now a library
Image by Tamar Awad.

- The new factory in Santander produced cigars.
- The new factory in Logroño produced cigarettes was closed in 2016.
- Palazuelo factory R.P.P. Raw products plant (tobacco leaf) was closed in 2012.
- The new factory of Cádiz: R.P.P. Raw tobacco products plant (tobacco leaf) was closed in 2014.
- Talayuela factory: (CETARSA) a modern factory, it is the only place where growers take their production. The head office is in Navalmoral de la Mata (Cáceres).

A comparative table of all common characteristics and parameters of the factories is made. It has been necessary to divide it into two tables in order to increase its readability, these are tables 4 and 5. (Gárate Ojanguren, 1994; García de Paredes Andujar, 2008; García París, 1991; González Enciso, 2007; González Enciso & Torres Sánchez, 1999; Jordan, 1994).

Figure 37. The old Logroño factory, now a library
Source: Image by Tamar Awad.

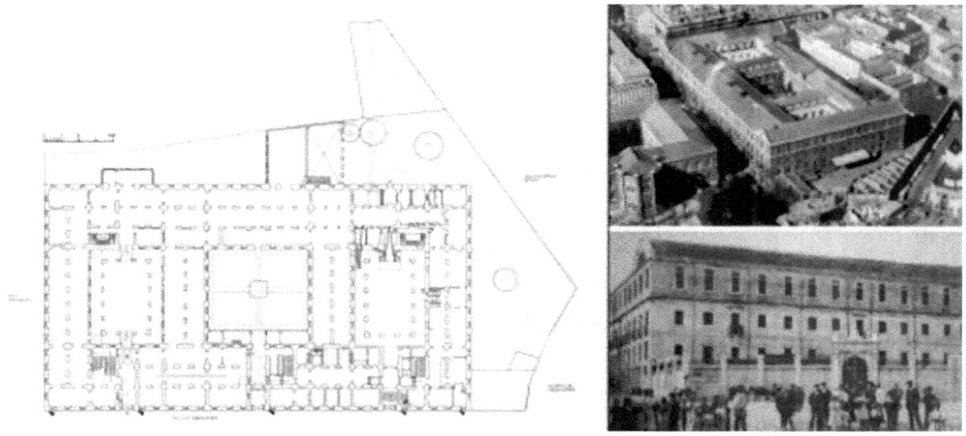

Figure 38. Interior of the Tarragona Tobacco Factory
Source: Image from the Tabacalera Archive.

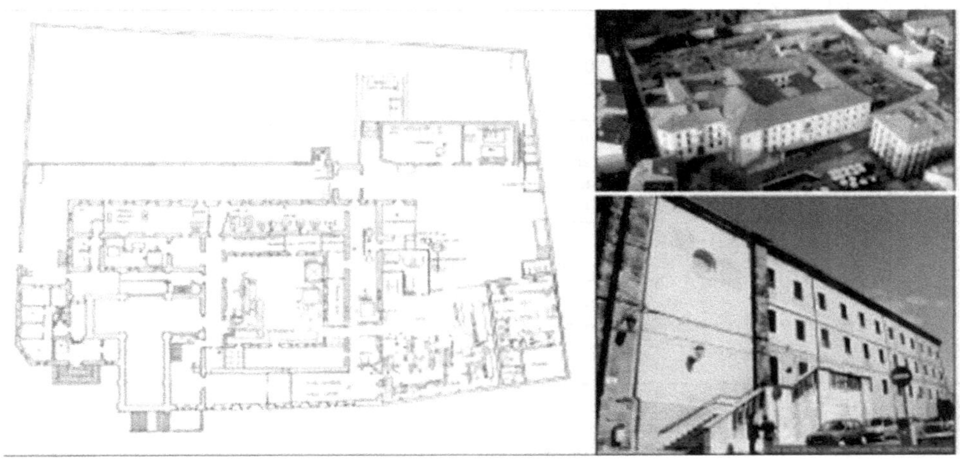

4. CONCLUSION

The tobacco factories do not respond to bioclimatic criteria, but their location is due to aspects of reception of goods and political criteria.

The location of the factories was based on geographical, strategic, political and raw material reception reasons.

The following conclusions can be drawn from the study of the maps showing the location of the factories and the transport of goods:

In most of the factories, the choice of the city of location was linked to the reception of raw materials, which was mainly done by sea, or by water (in the case of Seville), and by land, using the railway as a means of transport. The factories occupied cities with a port for the adequate maritime transport of

Table 4. Comparison between Spanish tobacco factories I

FACTORY OF	Sevilla	Cadiz	Alicante	La Coruña	Madrid	Gijón	Valencia
YEAR OF CONSTRUCTION OF THE BUILDING	1728-1770	1828	1741-1752	1790	1780-1790	1684-1733	1905-1909
PREVIOUS USE	NO	Wheat market	Convent	Arsenal/ Barracks	Royal Manufacturing Factory	Convent	NO
PRODUCTION START	1620	1741	1801	1808	1809	1823	1828
B.I.C.	1959	2011	2008	2013	1977	1987	1982
AUTHORS	Verboom, Bordick, & Van der Borcht	Gil de los Reyes	Antonio Jover	Mesa and Álvarez	De la Ballina	De Palacio and De San Miguel	Aranguren, Lucini, García, and Serret.
AREA m2	25.897	4.743	3.166	6.890	11.150	3.476	15.532
FLOORS	5	3	3	3	4	3	6
COURTYARDS	5 + 10	2	1	4	3	2	4
CLOSURE	1951	2003	1951	2002	2000	2002	2002
CURRENT USE	University rectorate	Conference centre	Cultural centre	Dwellings and public spaces	Cultural centre and exhibition hall	Cultural centre	Courthouse
FIRES	No	No	1844, 1900, and 1908	1886 and 1920	1862 and 1890	1954	1895
ELECTRIFICATION	1897	1893	1898	1901	1897	1899	1893
PRODUCTION	Cigarettes, cigars, and snuff	Cigarettes, and cigars	Cigarettes, cigars, and chopped tobacco	Cigarettes, and cigars	Cigarettes, and cigars	Cigarettes, cigars, and snuff	Cigarettes, cigars, and snuff
CONNECTIONS	Train, river, road	Maritime and road	Maritime and road	Maritime, train in 1858 and road 1899	Train and road	Maritime and road	Rail, maritime, river, and road
Nº OF WORKERS IN 1895	5501	1989	4552	5501	4827	1828	2962
Nº OF WORKERS IN 1935	1658	969	2058	1658	1927	964	1487

goods. Only two cases, Madrid and Logroño, had their factories in the interior of the Peninsula. The one in Madrid was built because of its central location and because it was geographically at the centre of all land communications by road and rail. The Logroño factory, however, was built for political reasons, as the president of the CAT was a relative of President Sagasta, and both were from La Rioja.

From the historical table showing the evolution of the factories, it can be deduced that similar events and processes took place in all of them, although not simultaneously, in terms of fires, mechanisation, adaptation of workshops, reforms, extensions, relocations and changes of use.

Fires occurred in all the factories, because tobacco burned easily and because machinery accidents were common, as there were many mechanical elements with gears and micro-switches.

The factories that were factories from the beginning have had a better adaptation than those that were transformed from an earlier use.

Table 5. Comparison between Spanish tobacco factories II

FACTORY OF	Santander	Bilbao	San Sebastián	Logroño	Málaga	Tarragona
YEAR OF CONSTRUCTION OF THE BUILDING	1641-1656	1828	1886-1912	1596	1923-1928	1923-1930
PREVIOUS USE	Convent	Barracks	NO	Convent	No	No
PRODUCTION START	1835	1878	1878	1890	1923	1932
B.I.C.	1982	No	No	1983	No	No
AUTHORS	De Jorganes, De la Roza, Calderón, and G. De Somomayor		Serret, Tarancón and Aguirrebengoa	Barrón	Morales and González-Estéfani	Rossell and Tulla Planella
AREA m2	3.790	50.000	13.277	3.790	50.000	37.932
FLOORS	2	4	4	4	3/5	2
COURTYARDS	2	1	5	1	4	0
CLOSURE	2002	1936	2003	1978	2002	2007
CURRENT USE	Town hall offices	Demolished building	Cultural centre	Government headquarters, exhibition hall and municipal library	Experimental centre for tobacco growing	Municipal archive and national museum of archaeology
FIRES	1916	1916		1886 AND 1920	1993	
ELECTRIFICATION	1899	1899	1922	1901	1923	1932
PRODUCTION	Cigars	Cigars	Cigarettes	Cigarettes, and cigars	Cigars	Cigarettes, and cigars
CONNECTIONS	Road	Rail and road	Rail, maritime, and road	Maritime, train in 1858 and road 1899	Maritime, and road	Maritime and road
Nº OF WORKERS IN 1895	1381	576	778	5501		
Nº OF WORKERS IN 1935	645	236	1014	1658		111

A clear differentiation can be made between factories that were made when the production process was handmade or mixed, and those of the mechanised process. When the production process was manual, the building has a more human scale, and when the process is mechanised and carried out by machines, the factory is less adaptable to uses such as (libraries, cultural centres, parliaments, etc.).

We can conclude that architecture is more adaptable the more handcrafted the activity carried out in it.

Those of manual production have a more human scale, as opposed to those of mechanised processes, in which the scale is determined by the size of the machines and is mainly concerned with the production process, the factory is less adaptable to human activities (libraries, cultural centres, parliaments, etc.).

It is essential that industrial buildings are designed by a team of engineers and architects, even if they are factories, taking into account the people who will work inside them, and not only considering the production process. When the growth of cities catches up with the new factories, these buildings can be used for non-industrial purposes. Thus, the new factory in Logroño is designed for a mechanised production process, without natural light, closed to the outside, while the old factories, in which manual or mixed tasks were carried out, have been able to be transformed into other uses, as they were designed for artisan processes, with a more human scale.

Factory buildings have evolved differently, depending on their state of conservation, their location within the historic city centres, and for economic and political reasons where they are located.

It would be good for these buildings to enjoy heritage protection and to be part of the history of Spanish industrial architecture.

The study carried out in Tamar Awad's thesis (Awad Parada, 2015) is the first complete architectural study of Spanish tobacco factories.

It is important to note that Spanish island factories have not been included in this study.

Most of the former factories have been converted into cultural spaces, so these buildings have the capacity for transformation and adaptation to other uses. This condition is remarkable and should be considered at the urban planning level as it allows for the use and sustainability of industrial architecture.

Author Contributions: Conceptualization, T.A.P. and R.A.G.-L.; methodology, T.A.P; software, T.A.P and R.A.G.-L; validation, T.A.P, and R.A.G.-L; formal analysis, T.A.P; investigation, T.A.P; resources, T.A.P; data curation, T.A.P; writing—original draft preparation, T.A.P; writing—review and editing, T.A.P and R.A.G.-L; visualization, T.A.P; supervision, T.A.P and R.A.G.-L.; project administration, T.A.P; funding acquisition, R.AG.-L All authors have read and agreed to the published version of the manuscript.

Funding: This research received no external funding.

Conflicts of Interest: The authors declare no conflict of interest. The funders had no role in the design of the study; in the collection, analyses, or interpretation of data; in the writing of the manuscript, or in the decision to publish the results.

REFERENCES

Almasifar, N., Canbolat, T. Ö., Akhavan, M., & González-Lezcano, R. A. (2021, December 1). Proposing a new methodology for monument conservation "scope management" by the use of an analytic hierarchy process project management institute system and the ico-mos burra charter. *Sustainability (Switzerland)*. doi:10.3390/su132313174

Alonso, L., Gálvez, L., & de Luxán, S. (2006). Tabaco e Historia Económica. Estudios sobre fiscalidad, consumo y empresa (siglos XVII-XX), Fundación Altadis, Los libros de Altadis, nº 7, Madrid.

Arkhangelskaya, I. V. (2017). The Principles Shaped The Perception Of Objects Of Industrial Heritage In Urban Space. *Vestnik Tomskogo Gosudarstvennogo Universiteta. Kul'turologiya i Iskusstvovedenie*, (26), 126–130. doi:10.17223/22220836/26/13

Awad Parada, T. (2013). *Patrones y permeabilidad en los secaderos cacereños*. Accesit.

Awad Parada, T. (2015). *Arquitectura industrial tabacalera en la España peninsular: secaderos y fábricas*. [Tesis Doctoral, E.T.S. Arquitectura (UPM)]. doi:10.20868/UPM.thesis.38794

Awad Parada, T. (2015). *Arquitectura industrial tabacalera española: secaderos y fábricas*.

Awad Parada, T. (2017). *Celosías de ladrillo en los Secaderos de tabaco*

Awad Parada, T. (2021). *Permeability in bioclimatic modular facades Spanish sheds.*

Aytekin, A. (2018). Using hybrid method in selecting timber factory location. *Drvna Industrija*, *69*(3), 273–281. doi:10.5552/drind.2018.1736

Barišić Marenić, Z., & Vukojevic, I. (2019). Adaptive reuse of zagreb tobacco factory buildings in the context of contemporary Urban regeneration. *Architektura a Urbanizmus*, *53*(1–2), 103–113.

Brokāne, N., & Strode, A. (2018). Heritage of industrial architecture in nowadays' cultural environment. *Arts and Music in Cultural Discourse. Proceedings of the International Scientific and Practical Conference.* 10.17770/amcd2017.2823

Christiernsson, A., Geijer, M., & Malafry, M. (2021). Legal aspects on cultural values and energy efficiency in the built environment—A sustainable balance of public interests? *Heritage*, *4*(4), 3507–3522. doi:10.3390/heritage4040194

Cioni, C., Di Sivo, M., & Ladiana, D. (2019). Use of bim technology as a safety tool in the restoration phase of buildings: Case study of the faÇade of the "royal tobacco factory" in seville, spain. In WIT Transactions on the Built Environment, 192, 291–303 WITPress. doi:10.2495/BIM190251

Comín, F., & Martín Aceña, P. (1991). *Historia de la empresa pública en España*. Espasa-Calpe.

. Crane, M., Lloyd, S., Haines, A., Ding, D., Hutchinson, E., Belesova, K., & Turcu, C. (2021, February 1). Transforming cities for sustainability: A health perspective. *Environment International.* Elsevier Ltd. doi:10.1016/j.envint.2020.106366

Dong, M., & Jin, G. (2021). Analysis on the Protection and Reuse of Urban Industrial Architecture Heritage. In IOP Conference Series: Earth and Environmental Science (Vol. 787). IOP Publishing Ltd. doi:10.1088/1755-1315/787/1/012175

Gárate Ojanguren, M. (1994). *Comercio ultramarino e Ilustración.* La Real Compañía de La Habana. Colección La Ilustración Vasca.

García de Paredes Andujar, J. (2008). *El cultivo del tabaco Virginia en España*. CETARSA.

García París, J. (1991). Intercambio y difusión de plantas de consumo entre el Nuevo y el Viejo Mundo. Ministerio de Agricultura, Pesca y Alimentación.

González Enciso, A. (2007). *Política económica y gestión de la Renta de tabaco en el s. SVIII.* ALTADIS.

González Enciso, A., & Torres Sánchez, R. (1999). *Tabaco y economía en el siglo XVIII.* Eunsa.

Jordan, G. (1994). *Tobacco in History: The cultures of dependence*. Paperback.

Jiaping, C., Jing, L., & Yaohong, W. (2020). Supplying space for innovation from the old factory from the perspective of land rent residual: Comparison between Guangzhou and Shenzhen. *Tropical Geography*, *40*(5), 795–807. doi:10.13284/j.cnki.rddl.003273

Leurquin, J. (2000). Hunter J. et Ralston I. (éd.) : The Archaelogy of Britain. An Introduction from the Upper Palaeolithic to the Industrial Revolution (L'archéologie en Grande-Bretagne depuis le Paléolithique supérieur jusqu'à la révolution industrielle). L'Anthropologie, 104(1), 176. doi:10.1016/S0003-5521(00)90017-7

Loures, L., & Panagopoulos, T. (2007). Sustainable reclamation of industrial areas in urban landscapes. *WIT Transactions on Ecology and the Environment*, *102*, 791–800. doi:10.2495/SDP070752

Monego, M., Fabris, M., Menin, A., & Achilli, V. (2017). 3-D Survey applied to industrial archaeology by tls methodology. In International Archives of the Photogrammetry, Remote Sensing and Spatial Information Sciences - ISPRS Archives (Vol. 42, pp. 449–454). International Society for Photogrammetry and Remote Sensing. doi:10.5194/isprs-archives-XLII-5-W1-449-2017

Palmer, M. (2005). Understanding the workplace: A research framework for industrial archaelogy in Britain. *Industrial Archaeology Review*, *27*(1), 9–17. doi:10.1179/030907205X50441

Pardo Abad, C. J. (2020). Valuation of industrial heritage in terms of sustainability: Some cases of tourist reference in spain. *Sustainability (Switzerland)*, *12*(21), 1–23. doi:10.3390u12219216

Preite, M. (2021). Recovered factories: Industrial heritage reuse in Italy. *Ural'skij Istoriceskij Vestnik*, *71*(2), 55–64. doi:10.30759/1728-9718-2021-2(71)-55-64

Sánchez-Montañés, B., & Castilla, M. V. (2020). Resilience factories. An opportunity for industrial heritage: La trinidad case study. *Architecture. City and Environment*, *15*(43), 1–18. doi:10.5821/ace.15.43.9192

Somoza-Medina, X., & Monteserín-Abella, O. (2021). The sustainability of industrial heritage tourism far from the axes of economic development in Europe: Two case studies. *Sustainability (Switzerland)*, *13*(3), 1–27. doi:10.3390u13031077

Xie, P. F. (2015). A life cycle model of industrial heritage development. *Annals of Tourism Research*, *55*, 141–154. doi:10.1016/j.annals.2015.09.012

Yang, R., Liu, Y., Liu, Y., Liu, H., & Gan, W. (2019). Comprehensive public transport service accessibility index-a new approach based on degree centrality and gravity model. *Sustainability (Switzerland)*, *11*(20), 5634. doi:10.3390u11205634

Zhang, J., Cenci, J., Becue, V., & Koutra, S. (2021, January 1). The overview of the conservation and renewal of the industrial belgian heritage as a vector for cultural regeneration. *Information (Switzerland). MDPI AG*. doi:10.3390/info12010027

Zhang, J., Cenci, J., Becue, V., Koutra, S., & Ioakimidis, C. S. (2020). Recent evolution of research on industrial heritage in Western Europe and China based on bibliometric analysis. *Sustainability (Switzerland)*, *12*(13), 5348. doi:10.3390u12135348

Chapter 7
Sound and Light Waves in Healthy Environments:
Architecture and the Health of People Through the Stages of Life

Daniel Arranz-Paraiso
https://orcid.org/0000-0002-0277-5462
Universidad CEU San Pablo, Spain

David Baeza-Moyano
Universidad CEU San Pablo, Spain

Roberto Alonso González-Lezcano
https://orcid.org/0000-0002-6185-4929
Universidad CEU San Pablo, Spain

ABSTRACT

Architects need the freedom to design their projects with the assurance that they will be inspiring aesthetic as well as healthy places, i.e., buildings, streets, parks, avenues, and squares that offer a complete living experience in an environment that takes into account light, sound, vibration, climate, and all those aspects that can disturb people's well-being. We know that prolonged exposure to noise can cause discomfort and sleep disorders, which affect the quality of life. This noise is not the only pollutant as there are other sound waves such as infrasound and ultrasound that are not perceptible but potentially harmful to health. Not forgetting electromagnetic waves, the light that reaches our bodies and which has regulated our lives throughout the existence of the species. The invention of electric lighting had the consequence that people spend practically all day indoors. Days are poorly illuminated, and the nights have too much light. On the other hand, the intensity of artificial light is a fraction of that of daylight and the spectral composition is also different.

DOI: 10.4018/978-1-6684-6924-8.ch007

1. INTRODUCTION

In the modern world, there are more and more equipment and instruments in homes and around us that generate vibration from household appliances, air conditioners, and car engines. This generates vibration in the range of ultrasound and infrasound of which little is known and it is necessary to develop regulations to know what is received, the amount that affects our body if it is harmful or not. It is essential to generate regulations to control how much reach our homes. On the other hand, since the discovery 25 years ago of the non-visual effects of light, we have realized or know that not receiving natural light during the waking state has undesirable effects. That gives rise to the need to develop a new luminaire from the studies that are being developed.

All acoustic and non-acoustic waves (ultrasound and infrasound) are transmitted through the medium by the collision generated between the particles that compose it (Powles et al., 2018). Depending on the medium through which they are transmitted, they can have a different propagation speed, for example, sounds in aqueous media reach speeds of about 1500 m/s while in the air it is maintained at about 340 m/s (Muller, 2021). There are also changes in their intensities as they are transmitted through the media, as well as when they cross-media interfaces. The detriments in the intensity are due to several phenomena that the waves undergo and they are reflection, refraction, scattering, and absorption (Larsen & Radford, 2018; Powles et al., 2018; Su et al., 2022; Trikootam & Hornikx, 2019). It is these physical properties that are used to generate ultrasound imaging systems for medical purposes (Pham et al., 2022; Tai et al., 2019; Xia et al., 2018) and in geolocation systems such as the Echo-sonar (Neupane & Seok, 2020; Shang et al., 2019) which uses frequencies between 10 kHz and 50 kHz. Through the use and combination of the aforementioned phenomena, it is possible to achieve the construction of new architectural works where total comfort can be generated for users by eliminating both acoustic waves that are potentially harmful to organic physiology and those that are disturbing to the senses of human beings.

Continuous exposure to perceptible or imperceptible sound waves has harmful effects (Baeza Moyano & González Lezcano, 2022; Moyano et al., 2022) such as increased irritability, neuronal excitability, concentration difficulties, decreased alertness, poor visual acuity, and memory problems (Bilski, 2017a; Smagowska & Pawlaczyk-Łuszczyńska, 2013). These effects have been used to make weapons or population control systems without employing more harmful or less invasive strategies such as water cannons, rubber ball rifles, or live ammunition (Golea & Ştefan Cozma, 2021; Little, 2015). In addition to being able to control acts of terrorism or vandalism through the use of ultrasound capable of shooting down objects that are not allowed to fly, such as drones, by disabling their gyroscopes (Son et al., 2015).

The discovery of the non-visual effects of light absorbed through our eyes opens up a new way of understanding lighting for interior designers and architects. Human and animal biology has adapted over the centuries to achieve the best possible synchrony and use of available natural resources. One example is the production of functional vitamin D through the skin's reception of solar ultraviolet radiation.

The objective of this article is to review the literature describing the possible undesirable effects of inadequate reception of light and infrasonic, audible and ultrasonic noise.

2. ACOUSTIC WAVES

2.1. Ultrasound

Ultrasound is considered to be acoustic waves whose frequency is higher than 20 kHz. The value of 20 kHz is not static or absolute since, according to different authors, low-intensity ultrasound levels are considered to be those between 10 kHz and 60 kHz (Pham et al., 2022; Rokhina et al., 2009a; Tai et al., 2019).

The physics of ultrasound is the same as all other sound waves due to wave motions propagating through the media. A very important characteristic of ultrasound that helps to make it less harmful is that it is a short but high-frequency wave. This peculiarity makes them waves with little transmission power in terms of distance through the air because they are absorbed and neutralized by this medium (Mazurek, 2018; Moyano et al., 2022). This phenomenon is even used as a distance measurement system. Knowing the intensity detriments of ultrasound and using mathematical procedures, measurements can be determined without the need for synchronization between emitters and receivers. This is important in architecture, as small, versatile, energy-saving, and easy-to-handle devices are essential when it is difficult to take measurements in rooms (Carotenuto et al., 2021).

HIFU generates when they come into contact with living tissue, an increase in temperature in the area where they affect. This increase in temperature can burn and destroy the cells that make up the tissue on which they act (Elhelf et al., 2018; Izadifar et al., 2020). The focused temperature can reach 60º C - 100º C in the area of incidence. These temperatures are fatal for the cells as the water inside evaporates, generating bubbles, after which cavitation is generated with the consequent cell death. The main problem is the adjustment of the focus of the attack, as well as contact with the skin. In the treatment of pancreatic and hepatic tumors, burns of varying degrees have been reported in about 24% of treated patients (Diana et al., 2016). These problems are solved by forced cooling of the skin in the treated area with water at about 15°C (Marinova et al., 2021).

In the case of Low-Intensity Pulsed Ultrasound (LIPUS), it has been shown that it does not significantly raise the temperature of the tissues where it is used (Tufail et al., 2010; Tyler et al., 2008). This is important because LIPUS is used for bone tissue regeneration with an increase in cell proliferation and viability, as well as an increase in the levels of osteogenic hormones such as osteocalcin and alkaline phosphatase (Maung et al., 2021). Activity has also been demonstrated with neurodegenerative diseases inducing neuroprotection and neuromodulatory effects (Xiaoxue Jiang et al., 2019).

2.2. Sound

Exposure to acoustic waves is continuous throughout an individual's lifetime at all frequencies emitted by living or non-living things around us. Waves that are in the range of what is perceptible to humans are easier to detect because of tacit knowledge of their presence. In humans, the average normal values for sound detection are considered to be waves between 0.02 kHz and 20 kHz (Lin et al., 2022)depending on the idiosyncrasies of each individual. These variations are mainly caused by age-related neural impairment, as well as by noise conditions (Herrmann & Butler, 2021; Rogers et al., 2020)as well as the noisy conditions to which we are exposed throughout life (Fink & Mayes, 2021; Zaw et al., 2020). We are continuously exposed to sound waves, whether of greater or lesser intensity. These sounds are generated by artificial systems (household appliances, vehicles, engines, etc.) and by nature itself (e.g. weather phenomena, locations where people, animals, and water currents are usually concentrated).

Noise pollution, commonly known as noise, in large cities is higher than that generated in rural areas due to 24-hour activities. There is a relationship between the generation of mental disorders such as anxiety and depression, leading to suicide due to increased stress (Díaz et al., 2020; Morillas et al., 2018; Veber et al., 2022). The attack of this pollutant generates states of stress that can be considered as an initial level where a hypothalamic excitation is generated and a deeper level which is the one that generates organic disorders. The physiological alteration is generated by a release of hormones and neurotransmitters from the hypothalamic-pituitary axis that increases the excitation of the sympathetic nervous system. This increased activity generates an increase in circulating hormones of the catecholamine group by the sympathetic-adrenal-medullary axis (Mendoza-Castejon et al., 2020; Recio et al., 2016). The cascades that are initiated are the same as those that have developed naturally

With modern architecture and with the technological advances available, cities can monitor the worst noise pollution hotspots. This is done through fixed and mobile structures that transmit the pollution values in real-time (Alías & Alsina-Pagès, 2019; Lebrusán & Toutouh, 2020; López et al., 2020). This makes it possible to plan the internal structure of the city for the future, e.g. by reorganizing railway systems and road traffic with the construction of tunnels or noise-blocking walls on the slopes of roadside verges (Fiorini, 2022).

The reduction and control of noise pollution levels also depend on builders and engineers. They are challenged to find systems, components, and compounds that reduce the sonic levels emitted by elements such as wheels of wheeled vehicles, and railway tracks that eliminate noise and reduce noise levels (Wehr et al., 2021)rail tracks that eliminate the rattling and screeching of metal braking systems (Ivanov et al., 2017; Talotte et al., 2003; Zvolenský et al., 2017).

To understand the complexity and multidisciplinarity involved in improving noise reduction, noise reduction in road traffic tires is studied. Noise studies can be done in situ and with laboratory tests. The methods are described and test conditions are stipulated including ISO certifications (ISO 11819-1, ISO/DIS 11819-2). The control of the sound emitted by the rubber grip of tires on the ground is essential in big cities as it is one of the limiting points in terms of loudness. It does not matter what fuel is used as all vehicles require tires to move. Noise reduction can be tackled at several points:

1. Noise control by simulation and direct measurements. Sound waves are generated by friction between the tire surface and the road surface. Changes in the morphologies of both surfaces can generate different sounds both in quantity and emission interval. There are models where only algorithms are used (Edwards et al., 2020) and others where they are combined to generate three-dimensional designs with descriptive texture parameters (Wehr et al., 2021). There are other developments where there is a combined system of sound level meter and pressure sensor inside the tire chamber. This system can provide real-time data to improve wear or bumpy sections and even predict areas with poor tire grip by analyzing the noise generated by the rubber when sliding (Masino et al., 2017).
2. Re-engineering of the tire and tire-tire system. Noise elimination can be addressed by implementing new tire and rim construction architectures. One of the strategies that have been devised focuses on improving the elasticity of the usual monobloc systems. Wheels with continuous and point damping systems with new highly elastic tires with concentric rings (Deng et al., 2022). Tires are being developed to include structures inside the tires that can absorb and block the sounds that

are generated. This includes for example Helmholtz resonators which can reduce sound by 15 dB (O'Boy, 2020; Zhao et al., 2021).

3. Road paving. Regardless of dirt or gravel roads, roads, and especially expressways have traditionally been paved with a multilayer system. This system combines layers of sand and gravel of various diameters and on top of this a layer of non-porous or low-porosity asphalt (Balaguera et al., 2018). The new asphalts are intended to achieve porosity combinations that improve rain and stormwater drainage, increase vehicle grip, reduce tire wear, enhance material recycling and reduce environmental noise. The use of construction materials derived from demolition and crumb rubber mixtures (M. Chen et al., 2011) and mixtures with crumb rubber (Lou et al., 2022). The use of these recycled rubbers improves the fatigue and thermal breakdown resistance of the pavement with an increase in material recycling and a reduction in raw material consumption (Picado-Santos et al., 2020; Q.-Z. Wang et al., 2020). Blends can also be made with unvulcanized or devulcanized rubbers. Unvulcanized mixes allow the production of asphalts with a lower density that requires lower manufacturing temperatures and is more stable in hot storage with better compatibility with bitumen (Bressi et al., 2019; Yu et al., 2011). In the case of porous roads, raveling phenomena can occur with loss of material and spillage of material, which is one of the reasons why it has not been developed and implemented more extensively in road pavements (D. Wang et al., 2017).
4. Tire composition and surface morphology. To reduce tire rolling noise, it is known that tires can be made with one or more of the following layers. The outermost layer should preferably be soft, with low stiffness to make the wheel-asphalt contact smooth. There may be a porous inner layer with a large number of air-containing alveoli, similar to a sponge. Another layer that reduces sound emission is a soft layer consisting of aggregates of small particles (Hanson et al., 2004). It must be taken into account that in a single wheel there are up to 12 different components with 10 different parts that form the sidewall, the tread, and the reinforced band that connects to the rim. Besides considering that the manufacturing is a balance between durability, grip, wear, crystallization of the components, safety, braking distance, use in various weather conditions, increases and decreases of the internal pressure due to the heating of the tire, use with and without load, speed index and resistance to external conditions and agents that can damage the structure such as potholes, irregularities, potentially sharp surfaces, among others (Koštial et al., 2012; Saemann, 2008).

The exposures that have been described so far can reach the most damaging ranges on a continuous and sustained basis, with intensities above 85 dBA. The perceived noise is a combination of rolling noise combined with the sounds of vehicle horns, door openings and closings, engine accelerations, malfunctioning or modified engine silencing systems, exhaust sounds, as well as heavy braking and emergency braking (Phan et al., 2010; Saremi, 2020).

2.3. Infrasound

Infrasound, like ultrasound, is an acoustic wave that is undetectable by the human ear. This is also known as a black sound and derives from all the elements that we have in continuous use in the home, from fans to freezers or refrigerators, vehicles, and machines in the workplace.

In the case of road vehicles and more specifically in trucks, there is evidence that after exposing people who do not drive trucks to the infrasound inside the cab, they end up developing a symptomatology of mental discomfort or disturbance (Genell et al., 2006). This infrasound is also generated in buses and can disturb both the driver and passengers. By studying 15 different buses, it was estimated that infrasound exposure is between 103.8 dBG and 111.2 dBG. This value is higher than the established limit (100 dBG) and can therefore be detrimental to the psycho-physical state of passengers and drivers (Ming et al., 2014). An important point to note is that infrasound is transmitted by the bending vibration of the springs. In Japan, it has been studied that rear-drive trucks generate a vibration of 3.0 Hz in addition to the spring vibration between 10 Hz and 20 Hz, which is transmitted to houses adjacent to the track (Fukada et al., 2016). This transmission is pollution that must be eliminated in today's urban architecture. Exposure must be reduced because it is so harmful that it can even cause hearing loss in e.g. tractor drivers together with drowsiness, fatigue, and reduced work efficiency (Bilski, 2017b).

Currently, there is a major source of emissions that is increasing almost exponentially year by year, namely wind turbines for electricity generation (Nielsen, 2022; Sens et al., 2022). This new source of pollution affects rural areas to a greater extent than urban areas due to the extensions of land required for the installation of turbines and all the associated equipment required. The turbines generate infrasound levels of approximately 1 Hz to 2 Hz and between 90 dB and 100 dB 15/16 (Howe, 2010). A consideration that has not been made throughout this document is that animals are configured to assimilate noise as a hazard. Some claims describe increases in the activity of the sympathetic system, i.e. activation of the alert system that serves to escape from dangerous situations. This system increases blood pressure, generates corticosteroid release, and increases blood glucose levels, heart rate, alertness, and other processes (Jeffery & Brett Horner BA, 2014). Despite all this, the noise levels that reach homes near wind farms have been estimated as not harmful by studies and by the French Agency for Food, Environmental and Occupational Safety (Agence Française de Sécurité Alimentaire, Environnementale et du Travail) (Mathieu-Huart et al., 2014). It is also indicated that there is a possible auto-suggestion syndrome resulting from the information received by the inhabitants near the wind turbines (Crichton et al., 2014; Ingielewicz et al., 2014; Schomer, 2013; Tonin et al., 2016).

Other important emitters due to their wide distribution are hydraulic systems used in heavy machinery such as excavators, lifts, workshop lifts, water pipes, as well as cooling systems. All these systems emit low-frequency sounds between 20 Hz and 100 Hz, and infrasound below 20 Hz (Koszarny & Jankowska, 1998). In the case of infrasound analyzed in dwellings, it is observed that it is difficult to dampen by the structures that make up the homes. Therefore, problems have been described with nausea, drowsiness, headaches and even vibrational sensation processes have been identified (Møller & Lydolf, 2002).

There is a correlation between the overproduction of collagen and elastin without inflammation and exposure to infrasound. This disorder is known as vibroacoustic disease which is significantly generated in the aeronautical sector (Alves-Pereira & Castelo Branco, 2007). Abnormal growths of essential organic structures such as blood capillaries or the trachea are observed (Harding et al., 2007).

3. ELECTROMAGNETIC WAVES

The largest source of electromagnetic waves that we naturally receive is the sun. These radiations derive from nuclear fusion reactions that are generated inside the star. They are produced by the sun's extreme conditions of high pressures and temperatures (Haider, 2019). These conditions have not yet been reproduced in a stable way to generate almost infinite energy at the laboratory level, but great progress has been made in recent years to try to mitigate climate change (Harding et al., 2007; Ming et al., 2014). Depending on the time of year in which we find ourselves, there are variable radiations derived both from the proximity or remoteness of the earth to the sun and from the natural tilt of the planet. The tilt is what determines which of the poles has the greatest incidence of solar radiation (van der Geest et al., 2015; Weinstein, 2013).

The use and abuse of solar radiation filtering systems, as well as changes in lifestyle habits, are currently having their consequences in the appearance of diseases such as myopia in children, as well as chronodisruption with alteration of the circadian rhythm.

Concerning the myopia pandemic, it should be pointed out in the first instance that the natural light we receive is insufficient. A high-risk group is children who spend a large part of the day at school, enter at night or dawn and sometimes leave at dusk or after dark. Little natural light enters the classroom and light sources are used that are insufficient in comparison to the luminance they should receive from the sun (Baeza Moyano & González Lezcano, 2021). This has been associated with risks of damage to children's vision due to poor lighting and light distribution (Ho et al., 2008; Nocera et al., 2018; Piderit Moreno & Labarca, 2015; Winterbottom & Wilkins, 2009). There is evidence to confirm that higher natural radiation is associated with a lower incidence of myopia, for example, Chinese children living in Sydney have an estimated incidence of myopia ten percentage points lower than children in Singapore (Lanca et al., 2019). On the other hand, violet (360-400 nm) is known to be protective against myopia by suppressing axial elongation of the eye. This light is abundant in solar radiation but is eliminated when it passes through windows and glass so that actual exposure is very moderate (Xiaoyan Jiang et al., 2018; Torii et al., 2017).

In addition to the above, the fact that in today's life working with near vision points (paper and screens) may be a risk factor that increases the prevalence of myopia (Lanca et al., 2019; Saw, 2002). This implies that school age may be a risk factor for continuous reading and writing where the more hours of study, the higher the risk of myopia (Mountjoy et al., 2018).

Chronodisruption, continuous nocturnal awakenings, and circadian rhythm disturbance are a pathology that is generated more intensely in patients of advanced age (Y. Chen et al., 2017). This is accentuated by increased lens thickening that induces greater filtering of incident light (Turner & Mainster, 2008). In addition to the narrowing or reduction of pupillary size (M. G. Figueiro et al., 2020). Lighting deficits may also play a role in degenerative processes such as the development of Alzheimer's disease. Exposing patients to deep darkness at night supplemented by high-intensity daytime lighting is known to improve the progression or stage of Alzheimer's disease (M. G. Figueiro et al., 2020; Konis et al., 2018; van Someren et al., 1997). Reductions in the amount of perceived light are wavelength-dependent due to the yellowish opacification of the crystalline lens so that wavelengths of between 0.5 and 0.5 wavelengths are reduced (Giménez et al., 2016) Thus, wavelengths between 500 nm and 600 nm require 11% exposure to achieve the physiological effect when comparing 65-year-old and 11-year-old observers (Moyano & González Lezcano, 2021). Despite the existing evidence, it should be noted that no legislation establishes how indoor installations should be carried out to meet physiological needs (Dai et al., 2017; M. G. Figueiro et al., 2020)

As there are two types of effects, visual and non-visual, new measurement systems have to be described in which biological activation levels are taken into account. The illuminance is calculated from the photopic sensitivity curve of the eye-returning values in lux (Dai et al., 2016). These fluxes do not provide biological value, so a new measurement system is beginning to be developed to take into account this relationship with the sensitivity of melatonin suppression.

Lighting metrics remain contingent on visual task performance (horizontal work plane illuminance and illuminance uniformity) (Dai et al., 2017; M. Figueiro et al., 2020; ISO 8995/CIE S 008: 2003.

Lighting of Indoor Work Places. International Commission on Illumination. Austria, n.d.), energy saving and visual discomfort.

There is strong scientific evidence that light is not only essential for vision but also elicits important biological, non-image-forming effects, and emotional effects that are highly relevant to human performance and well-being. Current lighting practice and the demand for energy saving tends to reduce indoor illumination levels. This can create lighting conditions that are sub-optimal for human well-being and functioning. The emotional and biological effects of light have a direct impact on human performance and well-being with large implications for architecture, interior design, and lighting as well as for social and work schedules (*UNE-EN 12464-1:2022 Luz e Iluminación. Iluminación de Los Lugares de Trabajo. Parte 1: Lugares de Trabajo En Interiores.*, 2022).

There is a measurement system endorsed by the International Commission on Illumination (CIE) (CIE, 2018) that relates illumination to the effective impact on the five opsins that constitute the three types of cones, rods, and ipRGCs. These are known as α-topic irradiances. From this point, a new metrology system has been defined in which the relevance of the equivalent melanotic daytime illuminance (EDI) is enhanced. For the calculation, the reference of the average natural daylight (D65) is considered the gold standard.

4. DISCUSSION

Extensive literature on the possible negative effects of the absorption of inadequate doses of acoustic waves by the human body. Inadequate light reception both during the day and at night can significantly affect health.

The complexity of managing all potentially harmful acoustic and luminous sources for both humans and the environment, in general, the control must be a priority to reduce the risks to which we are exposed. Modern and future architecture must be able to eliminate as far as possible all potentially harmful agents for the users of the various spaces in cities and towns such as dwellings, offices, parks, roads, avenues, and streets.

One of the most important pollutants is acoustic noise because it can be perceived consciously. Among the agents that induce this pollutant to a greater extent is road traffic that generates infrasound and audible sounds with levels that vary according to speed, load, vehicle aerodynamics, as well as airflow (Grafkina et al., 2019; Rybnov et al., 2018). It is necessary to generate structures that block and dampen this intrinsic pollution, especially in highly populated areas (Cai et al., 2019). Some meta-analyses support a correlation between this constant exposure and the generation of cardiovascular problems such as hypertension and sleep disturbance (Cai et al., 2019; Kim et al., 2012).

On the other hand, within sound pollutants, there is HIFU due to the organic effects it generates. This pollutant should be blocked as effectively as possible because continuous or intermittent exposure can induce increases in body temperature. Increases in temperature at the molecular level cause, among other effects, protein destructuring due to the loss of quaternary to secondary folding of proteins. This is especially relevant in the process of blood coagulation since an increase in body temperature from 37.6ºC to 39.4ºC induces an alteration of the thrombin-fibrinolysis equilibrium, increasing the risk of thrombus generation and disseminated intravascular coagulopathy with an incidence of 48%. (Brenner & Lisman, 2018; He et al., 2022; Iba et al., 2022; Levi, 2018). A nearby example is a coagulopathy caused by infections such as SARs-CoV2, it attacks organ capillaries simultaneously in distant and varied areas of the organism and can cause multi-organ failure (Bayrak & Çadirci, 2021; Chang, 2020; Herpertz et al., 2022; Walborn et al., 2019).

European noise directives define limits and permissible audible noise doses. Equivalent regulations need to be developed in both the infrasound and ultrasound ranges. For audible noise there is a European directive that limits the level of audible sound that people can receive in their working environment (Directive 89/391/EC) and another in non-working environments (DIRECTIVE 2002/49/EC).

Architects need the freedom to design their projects with the assurance that they will be inspiring and aesthetically pleasing as well as healthy places, i.e. buildings that provide a complete living experience in an environment that takes into account light, sound, vibration, climate, and all those aspects that can disturb people's well-being. We know that prolonged exposure to noise can cause discomfort and sleep disturbances, which affect the quality of life. 50% of the population is regularly exposed to noise levels that are harmful to health and the WHO, as early as March 2011, identified environmental noise as the second most important environmental health risk in Western Europe. This is why one solution widely used today is rock wool, which becomes a solution that gives architects the necessary freedom to design inspiring and aesthetically pleasing environments with the guarantee of creating a healthy environment. For example, rock wool panels are featured in the Cogeco Amphitheatre, Trois-Rivières, Quebec 2016, The House at Cornell Tech, New York, 2017, Olympic Park Stadium, London, 2014, Port House, Antwerp, Belgium 2016, Philharmonie de Paris, 2015 and Stockholm Metro, Sweden, 2016 to name but a few emblematic projects.

New luminaires are being developed based on a new understanding of interior lighting so that it does not disturb our internal biorhythms. In the future, lux meters that measure melanotic lux will be used to choose the intensity and proportion of light colors.

5. CONCLUSION

1. Architects need to be aware of the possible undesirable effects of the reception of acoustic waves and visible light when choosing the materials from which houses are to be built and the type of luminaires to be installed.
2. The eradication or control of pollution in all its forms must be a priority objective for all professionals. There must be coordination in the action plan by setting up multidisciplinary working groups to plan the way and manner of attacking polluting sources.
3. Regarding low-frequency ultrasound, it should be noted that beneficial effects have been described when applied in a localized and controlled manner to induce organ regeneration or restructuring. However, continuous exposure without professional control may lead to the scenario of a possible generation of cystic or tumor cell masses. At the moment no literature has been found where this possibility has been demonstrated or studied.
4. Authorities must control and monitor the emission sources of all auditory and non-auditory sound waves. All of them generate or induce harm if continuous and intermittent exposures are made when they have intensities above the maximum toxicity thresholds.
5. The interior lighting of the spaces where we spend a significant amount of our time must be adequate to be able to cover and make up for the deficits in exposure to natural radiation that we present due to the filters that surround us.

REFERENCES

Alías, F., & Alsina-Pagès, R. (2019). Ma. (2019). Review of Wireless Acoustic Sensor Networks for Environmental Noise Monitoring in Smart Cities. *Journal of Sensors*, *2019*, 1–13. doi:10.1155/2019/7634860

Alves-Pereira, M., & Castelo Branco, N. A. A. (2007). Vibroacoustic disease: Biological effects of infrasound and low-frequency noise explained by mechanotransduction cellular signalling. *Progress in Biophysics and Molecular Biology*, *93*(1–3), 256–279. doi:10.1016/j.pbiomolbio.2006.07.011 PMID:17014895

Baeza Moyano, D., & González Lezcano, R. A. (2021). *The Importance of Light in Our Lives.*, doi:10.4018/978-1-7998-7023-4.ch011

Baeza Moyano, D., & González Lezcano, R. A. (2022). Effects of infrasound on health: Looking for improvements in housing conditions. *International Journal of Occupational Safety and Ergonomics*, *28*(2), 809–823. doi:10.1080/10803548.2020.1831787 PMID:33019907

Balaguera, A., Carvajal, G. I., Albertí, J., & Fullana-i-Palmer, P. (2018). Life cycle assessment of road construction alternative materials: A literature review. *Resources, Conservation and Recycling*, *132*, 37–48. doi:10.1016/j.resconrec.2018.01.003

Bayrak, M., & Çadirci, K.BAYRAK. (2021). Mortal disseminated intravascular coagulopathy and cutaneous involvement in a COVID-19 positive patient; case report. *Anatolian Current Medical Journal*, *3*(3), 259–261. doi:10.38053/acmj.930047

Bilski, B. (2017a). Exposure to infrasonic noise in agriculture. *Annals of Agricultural and Environmental Medicine*, *24*(1), 86–89. doi:10.5604/12321966.1233897 PMID:28378979

Bilski, B. (2017b). Exposure to infrasonic noise in agriculture. *Annals of Agricultural and Environmental Medicine*, *24*(1), 86–89. doi:10.5604/12321966.1233897 PMID:28378979

Brenner, B., & Lisman, T. (2018). Hemostasis and Thrombosis in Extreme Physiological and Pathological Conditions. *Seminars in Thrombosis and Hemostasis*, *44*(07), 615–616. doi:10.1055-0038-1666826 PMID:30253425

Bressi, S., Fiorentini, N., Huang, J., & Losa, M. (2019). Crumb Rubber Modifier in Road Asphalt Pavements: State of the Art and Statistics. *Coatings*, *9*(6), 384. doi:10.3390/coatings9060384

Cai, M., Lan, Z., Zhang, Z., & Wang, H. (2019). Evaluation of road traffic noise exposure based on high-resolution population distribution and grid-level noise data. *Building and Environment*, *147*, 211–220. doi:10.1016/j.buildenv.2018.08.037

Carotenuto, R., Pezzimenti, F., della Corte, F. G., Iero, D., & Merenda, M. (2021). Ranging with Frequency Dependent Ultrasound Air Attenuation. *Sensors (Basel)*, *21*(15), 4963. doi:10.339021154963 PMID:34372207

Chang, J. C. (2020). Disseminated intravascular coagulation: New identity as endotheliopathy-associated vascular microthrombotic disease based on in vivo hemostasis and endothelial molecular pathogenesis. *Thrombosis Journal*, *18*(1), 25. doi:10.118612959-020-00231-0 PMID:33061857

Chen, M., Lin, J., & Wu, S. (2011). Potential of recycled fine aggregates powder as filler in asphalt mixture. *Construction & Building Materials*, *25*(10), 3909–3914. doi:10.1016/j.conbuildmat.2011.04.022

Chen, Y., Nondahl, D. M., Schubert, C. R., Klein, B. E. K., Klein, R., & Cruickshanks, K. J. (2017). The Relation between Sleep Disruption and Cataract in a Large Population-Based Study. *Ophthalmic Epidemiology*, *24*(2), 111–115. doi:10.1080/09286586.2016.1259640 PMID:28139160

CIE. (2018). *CIE S 026/E:2018 CIE System for Metrology of Optical Radiation for ipRGC-Influenced Responses to Light*. CIE. doi:10.25039/S026.2018

Crichton, F., Chapman, S., Cundy, T., & Petrie, K. J. (2014). The Link between Health Complaints and Wind Turbines: Support for the Nocebo Expectations Hypothesis. *Frontiers in Public Health*, *2*. Advance online publication. doi:10.3389/fpubh.2014.00220 PMID:25426482

Dai, Q., Cai, W., Shi, W., Hao, L., & Wei, M. (2017). A proposed lighting-design space: Circadian effect versus visual illuminance. *Building and Environment*, *122*, 287–293. doi:10.1016/j.buildenv.2017.06.025

Dai, Q., Hao, L., Lin, Y., & Cui, Z. (2016). Spectral optimization simulation of white light based on the photopic eye-sensitivity curve. *Journal of Applied Physics*, *119*(5), 053103. doi:10.1063/1.4941396

Deng, Y., Zhao, Y., Lin, F., & Zang, L. (2022). Influence of structure and material on the vibration modal characteristics of novel combined flexible road wheel. *Defence Technology*, *18*(7), 1179–1189. doi:10.1016/j.dt.2021.05.016

Diana, M., Schiraldi, L., Liu, Y.-Y., Memeo, R., Mutter, D., Pessaux, P., & Marescaux, J. (2016). High intensity focused ultrasound (HIFU) applied to hepato-bilio-pancreatic and the digestive system—Current state of the art and future perspectives. *Hepatobiliary Surgery and Nutrition*, *5*(4), 329–344. doi:10.21037/hbsn.2015.11.03 PMID:27500145

Díaz, J., López-Bueno, J. A., López-Ossorio, J. J., Gónzález, J. L., Sánchez, F., & Linares, C. (2020). Short-term effects of traffic noise on suicides and emergency hospital admissions due to anxiety and depression in Madrid (Spain). *The Science of the Total Environment*, *710*, 136315. doi:10.1016/j.scitotenv.2019.136315 PMID:31923678

Edwards, M., Chevillotte, F., Bécot, F.-X., Jaouen, L., & Totaro, N. (2020). Polynomial relations for cylindrical wheel stiffness characterization for use in a rolling noise prediction model. *Acta Acustica (Les Ulis)*, *4*(2), 4. doi:10.1051/aacus/2020003

Elhelf, I. A. S., Albahar, H., Shah, U., Oto, A., Cressman, E., & Almekkawy, M. (2018). High intensity focused ultrasound: The fundamentals, clinical applications and research trends. *Diagnostic and Interventional Imaging*, *99*(6), 349–359. doi:10.1016/j.diii.2018.03.001 PMID:29778401

Figueiro, M., Steverson, B., Heerwagen, J., Yucel, R., Roohan, C., Sahin, L., Kampschroer, K., & Rea, M. (2020). Light, entrainment and alertness: A case study in offices. *Lighting Research & Technology*, *52*(6), 736–750. doi:10.1177/1477153519885157

Figueiro, M. G., Sahin, L., Kalsher, M., Plitnick, B., & Rea, M. S. (2020). Long-Term, All-Day Exposure to Circadian-Effective Light Improves Sleep, Mood, and Behavior in Persons with Dementia. *Journal of Alzheimer's Disease Reports*, *4*(1), 297–312. doi:10.3233/ADR-200212 PMID:33024938

Fink, D., & Mayes, J. (2021). *Too loud! Non-occupational noise exposure causes hearing loss. 040002.* ASA. doi:10.1121/2.0001436

Fiorini, C. V. (2022). Railway noise in urban areas: Assessment and prediction on infrastructure improvement combined with settlement development and regeneration in central Italy. *Applied Acoustics*, *185*, 108413. doi:10.1016/j.apacoust.2021.108413

Fukada, S., Osafune, T., Sano, Y., Matsumoto, Y., Shimura, M., Kamiakito, N., Hama, H., & Hayashi, K. (2016). Characteristics of Bridge Vibration and Infrasound due to Moving Different Types of Trucks. *INTER-NOISE and NOISE-CON Congress and Conference Proceedings, 253*(2), 6016–6023.

Genell, A., Västfjäll, D., Kleiner, M., & Hedlund, A. (2006). Components in Evaluation of cOmplex Interior Truck Sounds. *Journal of Low Frequency Noise, Vibration and Active Control*, *25*(4), 227–237. doi:10.1260/026309206779884865

Giménez, M., Beersma, D., Daan, S., Pol, B., Kanis, M., van Norren, D., & Gordijn, M. (2016). Melatonin and Sleep-Wake Rhythms before and after Ocular Lens Replacement in Elderly Humans. *Biology (Basel)*, *5*(1), 12. doi:10.3390/biology5010012 PMID:26891336

Golea, D. G., & Ştefan Cozma, L. (2021). The Use of Piezoelectric Materials for the Purpose of Creating Infrasound and Ultrasound Sources for Terrorist Acts. SSRN Electronic Journal. doi:10.2139/ssrn.3852014

Grafkina, M., Nyunin, B., & Sviridova, E. (2019). Environmental Monitoring and Simulation of Infrasound Generating Mechanism of Traffic Flow. *Journal of Ecological Engineering*, *20*(7), 90–97. doi:10.12911/22998993/109877

Haider, Q. (2019). Nuclear fusion: holy grail of energy. In *Nuclear Fusion-One Noble Goal and a Variety of Scientific and Technological Challenges*. IntechOpen. doi:10.5772/intechopen.82335

Hanson, D. I., James, R. S., & NeSmith, C. (2004). *Tire/pavement noise study.*

Harding, G. W., Bohne, B. A., Lee, S. C., & Salt, A. N. (2007). Effect of infrasound on cochlear damage from exposure to a 4kHz octave band of noise. *Hearing Research*, *225*(1–2), 128–138. doi:10.1016/j.heares.2007.01.016 PMID:17300889

He, L., Lin, Q., Zhong, L., Zeng, Q., & Song, J. (2022). Thromboelastography maximum amplitude as an early predictor of disseminated intravascular coagulation in patients with heatstroke. *International Journal of Hyperthermia*, *39*(1), 605–610. doi:10.1080/02656736.2022.2066206 PMID:35465816

Herpertz, G. U., Nykamp, L., & Radke, O. C. (2022). Letaler Hitzeschock mit disseminierter intravasaler Koagulopathie. *AINS - Anästhesiologie · Intensivmedizin · Notfallmedizin · Schmerztherapie, 57*(01), 68–78. doi:10.1055/a-1508-0726

Herrmann, B., & Butler, B. E. (2021). Aging auditory cortex. In Assessments, Treatments and Modeling in Aging and Neurological Disease (pp. 183–192). Elsevier. doi:10.1016/B978-0-12-818000-6.00017-2

Ho, M.-C., Chiang, C.-M., Chou, P.-C., Chang, K.-F., & Lee, C.-Y. (2008). Optimal sun-shading design for enhanced daylight illumination of subtropical classrooms. *Energy and Building*, *40*(10), 1844–1855. doi:10.1016/j.enbuild.2008.04.012

Howe, B. (2010). *Low frequency noise and infrasound associated with wind turbine generator systems: a literature review.*

Iba, T., Connors, J. M., Levi, M., & Levy, J. H. (2022). Heatstroke-induced coagulopathy: Biomarkers, mechanistic insights, and patient management. *EClinicalMedicine*, *44*, 101276. doi:10.1016/j.eclinm.2022.101276 PMID:35128366

Ingielewicz, R., Zagubień, A., & ... (2014). Infrasound noise of natural sources in environment and infrasound noise of wind turbines. *Polish Journal of Environmental Studies*, *23*(4), 1323–1327.

ISO 8995/CIE S 008: 2003. Lighting of Indoor Work Places. International Commission on Illumination. Austria. (n.d.).

Ivanov, N. I., Boiko, I. S., & Shashurin, A. E. (2017). The Problem of High-Speed Railway Noise Prediction and Reduction. *Procedia Engineering*, *189*, 539–546. doi:10.1016/j.proeng.2017.05.086

Izadifar, Z., Izadifar, Z., Chapman, D., & Babyn, P. (2020). An Introduction to High Intensity Focused Ultrasound: Systematic Review on Principles, Devices, and Clinical Applications. *Journal of Clinical Medicine*, *9*(2), 460. doi:10.3390/jcm9020460 PMID:32046072

Jeffery, R. D., & Brett Horner, BA, C. M. A. (2014). Industrial wind turbines and adverse health effects. *Canadian Journal of Rural Medicine*, *19*(1), 21. PMID:24398354

Jiang, X., Kurihara, T., Torii, H., & Tsubota, K. (2018). Progress and Control of Myopia by Light Environments. Eye & Contact Lens: Science &. *Clinics and Practice*, *44*(5), 273–278. doi:10.1097/ICL.0000000000000548 PMID:30048342

Jiang, X., Savchenko, O., Li, Y., Qi, S., Yang, T., Zhang, W., & Chen, J. (2019). A Review of Low-Intensity Pulsed Ultrasound for Therapeutic Applications. *IEEE Transactions on Biomedical Engineering*, *66*(10), 2704–2718. doi:10.1109/TBME.2018.2889669 PMID:30596564

Kim, M., Chang, S. I., Seong, J. C., Holt, J. B., Park, T. H., Ko, J. H., & Croft, J. B. (2012). Road Traffic Noise. *American Journal of Preventive Medicine*, *43*(4), 353–360. doi:10.1016/j.amepre.2012.06.014 PMID:22992352

Konis, K., Mack, W. J., & Schneider, E. L. (2018). Pilot study to examine the effects of indoor daylight exposure on depression and other neuropsychiatric symptoms in people living with dementia in long-term care communities. *Clinical Interventions in Aging*, *13*, 1071–1077. doi:10.2147/CIA.S165224 PMID:29881263

Koštial, P., & Krmela, J., Frydr\`yšek, K., & Ružiak, I. (2012). The chosen aspects of materials and construction influence on the tire safety. *Composites and Their Properties*, *13*, 265–298.

Koszarny, Z., & Jankowska, D. (1998). Wystepowanie i ocena halasow niskiej czestotliwosci w budynkach mieszkalnych. *Roczniki Panstwowego Zakladu Higieny*, *3*(49), 347–363. PMID:9930028

Lanca, C., Teo, A., Vivagandan, A., Htoon, H. M., Najjar, R. P., Spiegel, D. P., Pu, S.-H., & Saw, S.-M. (2019). The Effects of Different Outdoor Environments, Sunglasses and Hats on Light Levels: Implications for Myopia Prevention. *Translational Vision Science & Technology*, *8*(4), 7. doi:10.1167/tvst.8.4.7 PMID:31360613

Larsen, O. N., & Radford, C. (2018). *Acoustic Conditions Affecting Sound Communication in Air and Underwater.*, doi:10.1007/978-1-4939-8574-6_5

Lebrusán, I., & Toutouh, J. (2020). Using Smart City Tools to Evaluate the Effectiveness of a Low Emissions Zone in Spain: Madrid Central. *Smart Cities*, *3*(2), 456–478. doi:10.3390martcities3020025

Levi, M. (2018). Hemostasis and Thrombosis in Extreme Temperatures (Hypo- and Hyperthermia). *Seminars in Thrombosis and Hemostasis*, *44*(07), 651–655. doi:10.1055-0038-1648231 PMID:29920620

Lin, Z., Zhang, G., Xiao, X., Au, C., Zhou, Y., Sun, C., Zhou, Z., Yan, R., Fan, E., Si, S., Weng, L., Mathur, S., Yang, J., & Chen, J. (2022). A Personalized Acoustic Interface for Wearable Human–Machine Interaction. *Advanced Functional Materials*, *32*(9), 2109430. doi:10.1002/adfm.202109430

Little, C. (2015). The 'Mosquito' and the transformation of British public space. *Journal of Youth Studies*, *18*(2), 167–182. doi:10.1080/13676261.2014.944119

López, J. M., Alonso, J., Asensio, C., Pavón, I., Gascó, L., & de Arcas, G. (2020). A Digital Signal Processor Based Acoustic Sensor for Outdoor Noise Monitoring in Smart Cities. *Sensors (Basel)*, *20*(3), 605. doi:10.339020030605 PMID:31979005

Lou, K., Xiao, P., Kang, A., Wu, Z., & Dong, X. (2022). Effects of asphalt pavement characteristics on traffic noise reduction in different frequencies. *Transportation Research Part D, Transport and Environment*, *106*, 103259. doi:10.1016/j.trd.2022.103259

Marinova, M., Feradova, H., Gonzalez-Carmona, M. A., Conrad, R., Tonguc, T., Thudium, M., Becher, M. U., Kun, Z., Gorchev, G., Tomov, S., Strassburg, C. P., Attenberger, U., Schild, H. H., Dimitrov, D., & Strunk, H. M. (2021). Improving quality of life in pancreatic cancer patients following high-intensity focused ultrasound (HIFU) in two European centers. *European Radiology*, *31*(8), 5818–5829. doi:10.100700330-020-07682-z PMID:33486605

Masino, J., Pinay, J., Reischl, M., & Gauterin, F. (2017). Road surface prediction from acoustical measurements in the tire cavity using support vector machine. *Applied Acoustics*, *125*, 41–48. doi:10.1016/j.apacoust.2017.03.018

Mathieu-Huart, A., de Lentdecker, C., Riviere, G., Sissoke, F., & Rousselle, C. (2014). French Agency for Food, Environmental and Occupational Health and Safety (ANSES) health reference values (RV). *Archives des Maladies Professionnelles et de l'Environnement*, *75*(3), 292–301. doi:10.1016/j.admp.2014.01.008

Maung, W. M., Nakata, H., Miura, M., Miyasaka, M., Kim, Y.-K., Kasugai, S., & Kuroda, S. (2021). Low-Intensity Pulsed Ultrasound Stimulates Osteogenic Differentiation of Periosteal Cells In Vitro. *Tissue Engineering. Part A*, *27*(1–2), 63–73. doi:10.1089/ten.tea.2019.0331 PMID:32164486

Mazurek, G. (2018). Basic channel parameters of ultrasound transmission in air. *2018 22nd International Microwave and Radar Conference (MIKON),* 607–609. 10.23919/MIKON.2018.8405300

Mendoza-Castejon, D., Fraile-García, J., Diaz-Manzano, M., Fuentes-Garcia, J. P., & Clemente-Suárez, V. J. (2020). Differences in the autonomic nervous system stress status of urban and rural school teachers. *Physiology & Behavior*, *222*, 112925. doi:10.1016/j.physbeh.2020.112925 PMID:32417231

Ming, Z., Desuo, C., Pangao, W., & Yongxiang, Z. (2014). Research on the Infrasound Generated by Busses. *Journal of Low Frequency Noise, Vibration and Active Control*, *33*(1), 1–11. doi:10.1260/0263-0923.33.1.1

Møller, H., & Lydolf, M. (2002). A Questionnaire Survey of Complaints of Infrasound and Low-Frequency Noise. *Journal of Low Frequency Noise, Vibration and Active Control*, *21*(2), 53–63. doi:10.1260/026309202761019507

Morillas, J. M. B., Gozalo, G. R., González, D. M., Moraga, P. A., & Vílchez-Gómez, R. (2018). Noise Pollution and Urban Planning. *Current Pollution Reports*, *4*(3), 208–219. doi:10.100740726-018-0095-7

Mountjoy, E., Davies, N. M., Plotnikov, D., Smith, G. D., Rodriguez, S., Williams, C. E., Guggenheim, J. A., & Atan, D. (2018). Education and myopia: assessing the direction of causality by mendelian randomisation. BMJ, k2022. doi:10.1136/bmj.k2022

Moyano, D. B., & González Lezcano, R. A. (2021). *Indoor Lighting Workplaces*. doi:10.4018/978-1-7998-7279-5.ch012

Moyano, D. B., Paraiso, D. A., & González-Lezcano, R. A. (2022). Possible Effects on Health of Ultrasound Exposure, Risk Factors in the Work Environment and Occupational Safety Review. *Health Care*, *10*(3), 423. doi:10.3390/healthcare10030423 PMID:35326901

Muller, M. (2021). Can We Use Ultrasound to Monitor and Diagnose Lung Diseases? *Acoustics Today*, *17*(4), 29. doi:10.1121/AT.2021.17.4.29

Neupane, D., & Seok, J. (2020). A Review on Deep Learning-Based Approaches for Automatic Sonar Target Recognition. *Electronics (Basel)*, *9*(11), 1972. doi:10.3390/electronics9111972

Nielsen, F. G. (2022). Perspectives and Challenges Related Offshore Wind Turbines in Deep Water. *Energies*, *15*(8), 2844. doi:10.3390/en15082844

Nocera, F., lo Faro, A., Costanzo, V., & Raciti, C. (2018). Daylight Performance of Classrooms in a Mediterranean School Heritage Building. *Sustainability*, *10*(10), 3705. doi:10.3390u10103705

O'Boy, D. J. (2020). Automotive wheel and tyre design for suppression of acoustic cavity noise through the incorporation of passive resonators. *Journal of Sound and Vibration*, *467*, 115037. doi:10.1016/j.jsv.2019.115037

Pham, V. H., Nguyen, V. T., Ly, C. D., Choi, J., Park, S., Mondal, S., Vo, T. H., Lim, H. G., & Oh, J. (2022). Development of fast photoacoustic and ultrasound imaging system based on slider-crank scanner for small animals and humans study. *Expert Systems with Applications*, *206*, 117939. doi:10.1016/j.eswa.2022.117939

Phan, H. Y. T., Yano, T., Sato, T., & Nishimura, T. (2010). Characteristics of road traffic noise in Hanoi and Ho Chi Minh City, Vietnam. *Applied Acoustics*, *71*(5), 479–485. doi:10.1016/j.apacoust.2009.11.008

Picado-Santos, L. G., Capitão, S. D., & Neves, J. M. C. (2020). Crumb rubber asphalt mixtures: A literature review. *Construction & Building Materials*, *247*, 118577. doi:10.1016/j.conbuildmat.2020.118577

Piderit Moreno, M., & Labarca, C. (2015). Methodology for Assessing Daylighting Design Strategies in Classroom with a Climate-Based Method. *Sustainability, 7*(1), 880–897. doi:10.3390u7010880

Powles, A. E. J., Martin, D. J., Wells, I. T. P., & Goodwin, C. R. (2018). Physics of ultrasound. *Anaesthesia and Intensive Care Medicine, 19*(4), 202–205. doi:10.1016/j.mpaic.2018.01.005

Recio, A., Linares, C., Banegas, J. R., & Díaz, J. (2016). Road traffic noise effects on cardiovascular, respiratory, and metabolic health: An integrative model of biological mechanisms. *Environmental Research, 146*, 359–370. doi:10.1016/j.envres.2015.12.036 PMID:26803214

Rogers, C. S., Jones, M. S., McConkey, S., Spehar, B., van Engen, K. J., Sommers, M. S., & Peelle, J. E. (2020). Age-Related Differences in Auditory Cortex Activity During Spoken Word Recognition. *Neurobiology of Language, 1*(4), 452–473. doi:10.1162/nol_a_00021 PMID:34327333

Rokhina, E., Lens, P., & Virkutyte, J. (2009). Low-frequency ultrasound in biotechnology: State of the art. *Trends in Biotechnology, 27*(5), 298–306. doi:10.1016/j.tibtech.2009.02.001 PMID:19324441

Rybnov, Y., Spivak, A. A., Kharlamov, V. A., & Soloviev, A. v. (2018). Infrasound noises of megapolis. In O. A. Romanovskii, & G. G. Matvienko (Eds.), *24th International Symposium on Atmospheric and Ocean Optics: Atmospheric Physics* (p. 26). SPIE. 10.1117/12.2502335

Saemann, E.-U. (2008). Contribution of the tyre to further lowering tyre-road noise. *Acoustics (Basel, Switzerland)*, 5429–5434.

Saremi, P. (2020). Environmental Pollution and ways to Reduce Contamination with use of Environmental Engineering Techniques in Metropolises of Developing Countries. International Journal of Environment. *Agricultural Biotechnology, 5*(3), 566–581. doi:10.22161/ijeab.53.9

Saw, S.-M. (2002). Near-Work Activity, Night-lights, and Myopia in the Singapore-China Study. *Archives of Ophthalmology, 120*(5), 620. doi:10.1001/archopht.120.5.620 PMID:12003612

Schomer, P. D. (2013). Comments on Recently Published Article, "Concerns about Infrasound from Wind Turbines. *Acoustics Today, 9*(4), 7. doi:10.1121/1.4827009

Sens, L., Neuling, U., & Kaltschmitt, M. (2022). Capital expenditure and levelized cost of electricity of photovoltaic plants and wind turbines – Development by 2050. *Renewable Energy, 185*, 525–537. doi:10.1016/j.renene.2021.12.042

Shang, Z., Zhao, & Zhang. (2019). Obtaining High-Resolution Seabed Topography and Surface Details by Co-Registration of Side-Scan Sonar and Multibeam Echo Sounder Images. *Remote Sensing, 11*(12), 1496. doi:10.3390/rs11121496

Smagowska, B., & Pawlaczyk-Łuszczyńska, M. (2013). Effects of Ultrasonic Noise on the Human Body—A Bibliographic Review. *International Journal of Occupational Safety and Ergonomics, 19*(2), 195–202. doi:10.1080/10803548.2013.11076978 PMID:23759188

Son, Y., Shin, H., Kim, D., Park, Y., Noh, J., Choi, K., Choi, J., & Kim, Y. (2015). *Rocking Drones with Intentional Sound Noise on Gyroscopic Sensors.* 24th USENIX Security Symposium (USENIX Security 15). USENIX. https://www.usenix.org/conference/usenixsecurity15/technical-sessions/presentation/son

Su, Q., Deng, X., Liu, Z., Tan, C., & Dong, F. (2022). Phase fraction measurement of oil–gas–water three-phase flow with stratified gas by ultrasound technique. *Measurement Science & Technology*, *33*(7), 075302. doi:10.1088/1361-6501/ac60f6

Tai, H., Khairalseed, M., & Hoyt, K. (2019). 3D H-scan ultrasound imaging system and method for acoustic scatterer size estimation: Preliminary studies using phantom materials. 2019 IEEE International Ultrasonics Symposium (IUS), (pp. 1515–1518). IEEE.. 10.1109/ULTSYM.2019.8926174

Talotte, C., Gautier, P.-E., Thompson, D. J., & Hanson, C. (2003). Identification, modelling and reduction potential of railway noise sources: A critical survey. *Journal of Sound and Vibration*, *267*(3), 447–468. doi:10.1016/S0022-460X(03)00707-7

Tonin, R., Brett, J., & Colagiuri, B. (2016). The effect of infrasound and negative expectations to adverse pathological symptoms from wind farms. *Journal of Low Frequency Noise, Vibration and Active Control*, *35*(1), 77–90. doi:10.1177/0263092316628257

Torii, H., Kurihara, T., Seko, Y., Negishi, K., Ohnuma, K., Inaba, T., Kawashima, M., Jiang, X., Kondo, S., Miyauchi, M., Miwa, Y., Katada, Y., Mori, K., Kato, K., Tsubota, K., Goto, H., Oda, M., Hatori, M., & Tsubota, K. (2017). Violet Light Exposure Can Be a Preventive Strategy Against Myopia Progression. *EBioMedicine*, *15*, 210–219. doi:10.1016/j.ebiom.2016.12.007 PMID:28063778

Trikootam, S. C., & Hornikx, M. (2019). The wind effect on sound propagation over urban areas: Experimental approach with an uncontrolled sound source. *Building and Environment*, *149*, 561–570. doi:10.1016/j.buildenv.2018.11.037

Tufail, Y., Matyushov, A., Baldwin, N., Tauchmann, M. L., Georges, J., Yoshihiro, A., Tillery, S. I. H., & Tyler, W. J. (2010). Transcranial Pulsed Ultrasound Stimulates Intact Brain Circuits. *Neuron*, *66*(5), 681–694. doi:10.1016/j.neuron.2010.05.008 PMID:20547127

Turner, P. L., & Mainster, M. A. (2008). Circadian photoreception: Ageing and the eye's important role in systemic health. *The British Journal of Ophthalmology*, *92*(11), 1439–1444. doi:10.1136/bjo.2008.141747 PMID:18757473

Tyler, W. J., Tufail, Y., Finsterwald, M., Tauchmann, M. L., Olson, E. J., & Majestic, C. (2008). Remote Excitation of Neuronal Circuits Using Low-Intensity, Low-Frequency Ultrasound. *PLoS One*, *3*(10), e3511. doi:10.1371/journal.pone.0003511 PMID:18958151

van der Geest, L. G. M., Lam-Boer, J., Koopman, M., Verhoef, C., Elferink, M. A. G., & de Wilt, J. H. W. (2015). Nationwide trends in incidence, treatment and survival of colorectal cancer patients with synchronous metastases. *Clinical & Experimental Metastasis*, *32*(5), 457–465. doi:10.100710585-015-9719-0 PMID:25899064

van Someren, E. J. W., Kessler, A., Mirmiran, M., & Swaab, D. F. (1997). Indirect bright light improves circadian rest-activity rhythm disturbances in demented patients. *Biological Psychiatry*, *41*(9), 955–963. doi:10.1016/S0006-3223(97)89928-3 PMID:9110101

Veber, T., Tamm, T., Ründva, M., Kriit, H. K., Pyko, A., & Orru, H. (2022). Health impact assessment of transportation noise in two Estonian cities. *Environmental Research*, *204*, 112319. doi:10.1016/j.envres.2021.112319 PMID:34740439

Walborn, A., Rondina, M., Mosier, M., Fareed, J., & Hoppensteadt, D. (2019). Endothelial Dysfunction Is Associated with Mortality and Severity of Coagulopathy in Patients with Sepsis and Disseminated Intravascular Coagulation. *Clinical and Applied Thrombosis/Hemostasis*, *25*, 107602961985216. doi:10.1177/1076029619852163 PMID:31140293

Wang, D., Schacht, A., Leng, Z., Leng, C., Kollmann, J., & Oeser, M. (2017). Effects of material composition on mechanical and acoustic performance of poroelastic road surface (PERS). *Construction & Building Materials*, *135*, 352–360. doi:10.1016/j.conbuildmat.2016.12.207

Wang, Q.-Z., Wang, N.-N., Tseng, M.-L., Huang, Y.-M., & Li, N.-L. (2020). Waste tire recycling assessment: Road application potential and carbon emissions reduction analysis of crumb rubber modified asphalt in China. *Journal of Cleaner Production*, *249*, 119411. doi:10.1016/j.jclepro.2019.119411

Wehr, R., Fuchs, A., & Breuss, S. (2021). Statistical tyre/road noise modelling based on continuous 3D texture data. *Acta Acustica (Les Ulis)*, *5*, 52. doi:10.1051/aacus/2021040

WeinsteinG. (2013). The 1905 Relativity Paper and the "Light Quantum" https://arxiv.org/abs/1307.2132

Winterbottom, M., & Wilkins, A. (2009). Lighting and discomfort in the classroom. *Journal of Environmental Psychology*, *29*(1), 63–75. doi:10.1016/j.jenvp.2008.11.007

Xia, W., Kuniyil Ajith Singh, M., Maneas, E., Sato, N., Shigeta, Y., Agano, T., & Ourselin, S., J. West, S., & E. Desjardins, A. (. (2018). Handheld Real-Time LED-Based Photoacoustic and Ultrasound Imaging System for Accurate Visualization of Clinical Metal Needles and Superficial Vasculature to Guide Minimally Invasive Procedures. *Sensors (Basel)*, *18*(5), 1394. doi:10.339018051394 PMID:29724014

Yu, G.-X., Li, Z.-M., Zhou, X.-L., & Li, C.-L. (2011). Crumb Rubber–Modified Asphalt: Microwave Treatment Effects. *Petroleum Science and Technology*, *29*(4), 411–417. doi:10.1080/10916460903394102

Zaw, A. K., Myat, A. M., Thandar, M., Htun, Y. M., Aung, T. H., Tun, K. M., & Han, Z. M. (2020). Assessment of Noise Exposure and Hearing Loss Among Workers in Textile Mill (Thamine), Myanmar: A Cross-Sectional Study. *Safety and Health at Work*, *11*(2), 199–206. doi:10.1016/j.shaw.2020.04.002 PMID:32596016

Zhao, W., Liu, X., Shan, Y., & He, T. (2021). Design and simulation of Helmholtz resonator assembly used to attenuate tire acoustic cavity resonance noise. *INTER-NOISE and NOISE-CON Congress and Conference Proceedings, 263*(6), 942–953. 10.3397/IN-2021-1706

Zvolenský, P., Grenčík, J., Pultznerová, A., & Kašiar, Ľ. (2017). Research of noise emission sources in railway transport and effective ways of their reduction. *MATEC Web of Conferences, 107*, 00073. 10.1051/matecconf/201710700073

Chapter 8
Sustainability in Construction, Housing, and the City

Tamar Awad
https://orcid.org/0000-0001-9119-504X
Comillas Pontificial University, Spain

Jesús Guardiola
Comillas University, Madrid, Spain

Mariano Jiménez
Comillas University, Madrid, Spain

Roberto Alonso González-Lezcano
https://orcid.org/0000-0002-6185-4929
Universidad CEU San Pablo, Spain

ABSTRACT

Since the 1960s, a more rational and modern construction has been sought in line with industrialisation. In addition, due to the shortage of housing, professionals in the construction sector have been looking for solutions. The industrialisation of construction was first attempted after the Second World War through prefabrication. Today, it is moving towards more open concepts, making the industrial development of its products compatible with a construction that is still archaic and in need of updating. On the other hand, architects have reviewed the programmes and needs of users and citizens, in housing, workplaces, commerce, leisure and cities, and have proposed more contemporary solutions, with greater flexibility. Sustainability can be seen in a techno-biological environment, where artificial activity is integrated with the life and resources of the environment, in a new balanced ecological system. The methodology implemented is based on systems theory, according to tools specifically developed in construction, for proposals and designs around the industrialisation of housing.

DOI: 10.4018/978-1-6684-6924-8.ch008

INTRODUCTION

The first oil crisis, around the 1960s, led to the first awareness that resources were not unlimited, the official stance was to improve energy efficiency, and wastefulness was frowned upon, even administrative regulations specified and limited energy consumption: IT.IC regulation standards.

Later, and more recently, with the emissions of gases into the atmosphere, alternative sources of energy were sought, in addition to the fact that Western countries, without natural resources of oil, sought to reduce political dependence on this fuel, and from all this we have the new official regulations on building, formalised in the Technical Code, whose derivation to the use of energy is the CT-HE.

Much earlier, other concerns were developing in building; on the one hand, a more rational and modern construction was being sought, in line with industrialisation, and on the other, the shortage and scarcity of housing, a problem that had been dragging on since the First World War, meant that professionals in the sector, architects, engineers and building technicians, were looking for solutions.

On the one hand, the industrialisation of construction, which was first tried out after the Second Great War: prefabrication, and which is now moving towards more open concepts, making the industrial development of its products compatible with an integration with a construction that is still archaic and awaiting updating.

On the second, architects who have reviewed the programmes and needs of users, families and citizens, in housing, workplaces, commerce, leisure and cities, and who have been proposing more contemporary and current solutions, among options that seek flexibility in the housing programme.

This is converging in a generalist orientation, in what we are currently hearing about sustainability, and that if for the problem of technological development in an environment of finite resources, it does not contemplate new solutions, it does so in a systemic and integral way.

Sustainability can be seen in a techno-biological environment, where artificial activity is integrated with the life and resources of the natural environment, in a new balanced ecological system.

The framework of this design exercise can be understood as the interaction between two areas, the internal environment, referring to the "artificial" thing, an entity with defined functional characteristics, where we influence, as a matter or issue of the problem to be solved, and the external environment, the environment of the entity that supplies, communicates, relates, pours, the frame of reference and external conditions of its operation.

The methodology to be implemented in this study is based on the Systems Theory, (Bertalanffy, 1968): according to concepts and tools developed specifically for this case, used in issues related to building, for proposals and designs around the industrialisation of housing.

One of these developments was previously presented in the INVISO project, sponsored by the Instituto de Ciencias de la Construcción Eduardo Torroja, and which was awarded the first prize in the annual call of May 2008: Project for the Industrialisation of Housing, by C. Tartas, R. Guridi, and J. Guardiola.

BACKGROUND

Sustainability Objectives of House Building

The objectives define the parameters to be achieved in the framework configured in this case, and the environment within the design.

The objectives of this work will be to obtain a modular and flexible building, to minimise the impact on the site, to optimise the design of installations and to review the needs of the habitat, in harmony with the surroundings and integrated with the environment.

A. Considering building in the framework of sustainable development, the following key concepts are key:
   - Flexibility versus rigidity
   - Recycling versus demolition
   - Open versus closed construction
   - Renewable versus permanente

Entering into the environment of systems thinking, contemplating the activity of building: design, construction and habitat, as a system:

- Open and dynamic systems versus inert, hermetic groupings

The building is an open system between the functionality of the habitat and its surroundings, where the infrastructure of the services provided and connected accesses interact.

Habitat: uses and activities of the family group.

Infrastructure: support of energies and services, communications, accesses as well as the supporting constructive container.

And the environment is the border, the open boundary between the internal, artificial environment and the external, natural environment.

B. In order to meet this new framework, the following conditions, specifications of the "sustainable" framework, are set out

Facilitate the fluid and energy supply system:

- exchange
- accessibility
- replacement
- repair.

Recycling of effluents: waste and inputs

- input and discharge cycle
- combination of remote and nearby resources

Habitat flexibility

- ease of use
- modification of activities
- and changing needs

C. Impact of the building components on the construction and functional system, specifications for the architecture, its programme and construction:

Habitat design:

- privacy-communication
- filters and insulation
- barriers against aggressions
- surroundings and environments

Construction versus assembly:

- simplification of elements
- assembly materials
- autonomous systems

Maintenance and operation:

- consumption and performance
- records and accessibility for repairs and overhaul changes and modifications

Mission Statement

Considering building in the framework of sustainable development, the following key concepts, highlighted from those stated above, are focused on in reference to building concepts:

- Flexibility versus rigidity: ease of change
- Recycling versus demolition: making the most of what exists at the time
- Open versus closed construction: integrating surrounding industrial systems
- Renewable versus permanent: possibility of upgrades to the future
- Integration versus isolation: tuning in to the environment

The following objectives are specified:

- To obtain a modular and flexible building
- To optimise the design of installations
- To recover natural resources within reach.
- Revise the habitat, in harmony with the surroundings and integrated with the environment.

And in reference to functional concepts, the building is an open system between the functionality of the habitat and its environment, where the infrastructure of the services provided and the connected accesses interact.

- Optimisation versus waste: obtaining maximum performance
- Zero waste
- Self-consumption: use of direct natural resources.
- Diversification versus centralisation

Figure 1. Housing unit, with the following functional elements highlighted

A housing unit design is developed, which contemplates the above objectives, which are grouped into two classes:

- Of a constructive nature, on how to design, build and exploit the housing unit, with the first two.
- Functional references, referring to the use, services and consumptions, included in the habitable programme, with the last two.

MAIN FOCUS OF THE CHAPTER

Attributes to the Sustainability of Residential Construction

The attributes will define the specifications that, based on regulations and standards, will provide criteria to be applied to the design, within the environment defined by the objectives.

The proposed design method allows, within the discipline of design, to integrate contemporary building into the current industrial environment, following the framework of "sustainable development".

Sustainability Norms, Standards and Benchmarks

There are three application references in the industrial environment of residential building, for sustainable activity, and one application standard.

1. The international standard ISO 14001-2015, (Cuatrecasas, 2017) establishes among its environmental management objectives to contribute to sustainable development, "control or influence the way in which the organisation designs, manufactures, distributes, consumes and carries out the final disposal of products or services, using a life cycle perspective that can prevent environmental impacts from being unintentionally transferred to another point in the life cycle".
2. At the same time, on 25 September 2015, world leaders adopted a set of global goals to eradicate poverty, protect the planet and ensure prosperity for all as part of a new sustainable development agenda. Each goal has specific targets to be achieved over the next 15 years. To achieve these goals, everyone has to do their part: governments, the private sector, civil society and each of us (United Nations, 2021).
3. The industrial environment of building is an unavoidable and continuous trend, and is therefore the basis of this project study, where traditional construction is considered to have been superseded, and passed into the nostalgic field of its history. It will be in this field of industrial activity where we propose the necessary premises for its sustainable development.

The methodologies developed under the Lean concept (Jiménez et al., 2021) seek to maximise the competitiveness of facilities through optimised processes that achieve cost reductions and consolidate continuous improvement. A wide variety of methodologies are available and applied in different stages and areas to optimise the entire system. The main requirement is a long-term strategy, which allows the analysis and modification of some elements of the organisational system (Charron et al., 2014), (Cuatrecasas, 2017) (Brau, 2016). Its integration involves an intensive process in which "the weaknesses of the system are analysed in order to determine the areas of possible lean application" (Zhou, 2016).

During the development of an industrial construction different formats of waste arise that can appear during the whole construction process. These generated wastes are called Muda, Mura and Muri. With the initial study of these three constraints most of the activities can be optimised. These three words were first used in the industrial environment by Toyota using the prefix "mu" which reflects the intention to improve a system. The identification of these wastes allows the establishment of an action plan for their elimination and optimisation of the construction activity.

Lean methodology not only affects the physical processes of an activity, but also influences the management of construction and the relationships between entities. In this way, it is possible to obtain quick responses within the construction processes, while eliminating surpluses, expenses and time losses (Navarro, 2017). Therefore, in order to talk about the Lean methodology, it is first necessary to know the five basic principles, which were defined by (Womack & Jones, 2005):

- Establish the quality requested by the client, in order to build exactly what is requested without waste. In other words, the aim is to achieve zero defects in the construction processes, in order to achieve this quality while increasing productivity.
- Identify the activities that add the required value. This can eliminate these tasks, which do not add value to the construction activities, but do add extra cost; and at the same time reduce the amount of material required.
- Create a continuous flow that adds value to construction, so that a system of continuous process improvement can be applied. This allows to increase the productivity of the activity and to improve times whenever possible.

- Employ a system to build what the client demands, as this will allow for quick changes in construction activities and adapt to real needs.
- Generate permanent relationships with suppliers through different agreements to ensure a mutually beneficial future.
- These principles, although defined in different ways, have the same objectives and origins. The implementation of Lean methodologies (Awad et al., 2021) must be carried out through a disciplined process, and to this end, a method of order and control must be used to ensure that the different stages are carried out correctly. This orderly sequencing, linked to increased resource efficiency, ensures that the final objective is underpinned by the principles of Quality - Cost - Delivery time (QCD).

This methodology is based on a design system that facilitates these principles of constructive suitability, which from the Lean philosophy also achieves the QDC quality principles.

At present, an international standard for design in construction refers to the "disassembly and adaptability of buildings in engineering": DfD/A: DESIGN FOR DISASSEMBLY AND ADAPTABILITY, ISO 20887, and is structured as follows, contemplating these two groups with various categories each:

-Adaptability, which in turn comprises three categories related to flexibility of use.

-Versatility, by its possibility of several simultaneous uses, convertibility; changing the use, expansion, which allows its enlargement.

-Disassemblability, which includes: accessibility: ease of registration of components; durability of longer period of use; exposed and reversible connections: ease of interchangeability of components, elements or parts; independence: autonomy of functions between components; recycling: possibility of return to the reuse of materials. (ISO, 2020).

In other words, it is a question of considering the flexibility of uses and the change of the components, one referring to habitability, the other to construction.

Therefore, in this section, we want to approach the central issue of the study, proposing a design system oriented towards a rational execution, where the industrial criteria of optimisation, economy and performance, within a framework of sustainable progress, lead this process.

The following design elements are identified, within an industrial environment, which respect the principles of sustainability, but in an advanced proposal.

Design System: Sustainability of Housing Construction

These design elements are grouped into two groups, those that deal with the nature of the construction, following the principles and methodologies of current industrial technology, and those referring to its activity, characterised by the dynamics of energies and fluids, which refer to the regime of its operation.

Construction Methodology

The construction elements allow for an open and flexible building, which facilitates changes, repairs and modifications, as well as growth or shrinkage, without resorting to the destruction or demolition of the building.

Autonomous Systems: self-sufficient set of components

Open Components: free selection of parts

Rigging Systems: methods of coupling between parts, reversible and detachable.

Autonomous systems, understood as independent in their design, carried out in parallel, by different specialities.

The way of building with free components, not fixed by the execution system, which allows solving a design premise by means of a range of possible alternatives of components on the market, available by the industry. (Guardiola & Reyes, 2019).

Finally, a way of connecting the materials and elements, which is flexible and returnable, which facilitates the maintenance or flexibility of the habitat, and which facilitates the changes or modifications of the assembled components (Guerrero et al., 2009).

Three categories of elements to be developed as components of the constructive system of the proposed industrial design are analysed: Autonomous Components, Open Elements and Connectivity.

Autonomous Components

The building contemplates several sets of components that can be grouped as systems, fulfilling the properties that characterise them.

These systems must behave autonomously in their design, which facilitates their specialised conception and subsequent assembly.

Figure 2. Self-contained, replaceable service module

Each of these systems shall be characterised by its technical functional speciality, corresponding to a design function:

Insulation: networks
Filter: energy
Stability: fluids

These systems are specialised, which implies that they will not serve more functions than those initially foreseen, so that each of them is optimal in its usefulness.

An order condition is applied, assigning levels, according to the category of integration that has been assigned.

Each component, due to its free and unconditioned character, in its conception and assembly, is carried out autonomously. Its function, likewise, is independent, assigned exclusively by differentiated components.

The subsystems can be grouped into: construction parts, enclosure, roof, equipment, etc.

Which, in turn, can again be grouped into room modules: bedroom, toilets, kitchen, work studio, etc.

Open Elements

These are the elements of each system, grouped within the general construction system, but external and incorporated from the industrial environment of the construction market, with the following characteristics.

Released couplings: Their mode of assembly, by means of assembly, will be exclusive and specialised for their characteristics as a product, but they will be integrated without difficulty in their location within the construction set, without interfering with other neighbouring components, as part of the general system of the building.

Flexibility of solutions: different proposals that solve the required function are tolerated, according to the range available on the market.

Like the systems to which they belong, each component is autonomous, i.e. both its conception and assembly are carried out independently, and therefore, it is not conditioned by other components.

The components are experts, i.e. their technical progress, being free from the rest of the components, is left to the initiative of the industrial companies that develop them. The improvement is left to the industry, according to the expectations detected in each case, by the available technology, the experience gained, or the optimised performance, but with the guaranteed autonomy, in the design environment, it will never encounter barriers that are alien to the problems of its own product.

Reversible Connections

Open connectivity system between components of the systems, grouped through the general integration operation, which will allow assemblies: assemblies and even disassemblies, throughout the useful life of the building, without repercussions on the normal foreseen activity.

This composition of parts with simpler elements requires a union solution that allows them to be assembled, forming the required mechanical unit with attached, non-glued elements, which is called a dry joint.

Figure 3. Bolted structural node

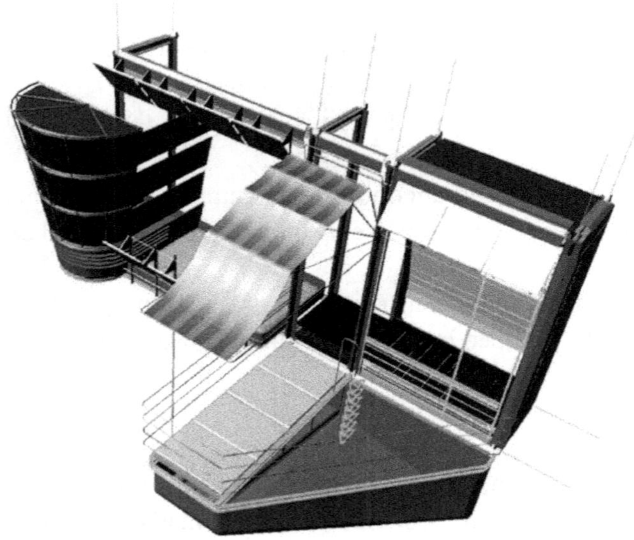

Reverse Deconstruction

- This deconstruction facilitates the flexibility of the use of the building, by changing the position of the structural elements required in the rooms and rooms that need to be modified.
- On the other hand, the maintenance for the repair is more affordable, in the need to replace, clean, paint... for deterioration elements, which for their access it is necessary to dismantle other parts.

Margin/Slot/Tolerance

The components are not stacked together, they are supported independently, so margins of clearance must be provided between different components, to avoid interferences. The continuity between components is achieved by overlapping parts designed for this purpose.

Operating Dynamics

Within the operation of the system, attributes of sustainable engineering can be identified, within the parameters of imported consumption and extracted flows.

Understanding the building as a whole as a system with internal conditions, internal environment, which operate under external constraints, external environment, we will seek a balance between input variables (energy, fluids, electricity, water, etc.) and output variables (waste and disturbances, noise, fumes, etc.).

Three strategies are proposed, defined as follows:

Cycling: Consumption is reincorporated before final discharge to cover other needs, and the use of these cycles is optimised.

"Soft Programming". The activity programme must also be sufficiently flexible to adapt to the changing needs of families, who modify its uses with the development of their family life

Combined Cycle: Between the artificial resources, of remote origin and transport, and those of the natural environment itself, which are closer, but of low reliability, we must integrate their availability in order to improve the exchange savings

Three categories are also analysed, among those of a functional nature, on the activity of the systems: habitat and infrastructure.

Combined Cycle

Supply systems of different species are integrated:

- Artificial" systems: of remote origin, with guaranteed access,...
- Natural" systems: of proximate origin, of uncertain operation,...

Both systems must be integrated into a coordinated installation, for access according to availability and continuity and scope or degree of use: magnitude of power.

These "parallel" systems, one complementary to the other, supply the required consumption on the basis of the savings from the "natural" collection, within reach.

The systems are combined in the continuity and degree of availability with "parallel" connections, although the natural resource is "cheap", it is very difficult to predict its availability, so the "artificial" system, of greater reliability, will be the resource of basic provision, completing the former with the latter.

- Zero discharge

Likewise, disposal systems are provided, with recycling options, for use according to decreasing quality levels...

The "outward" discharges are also integrated with "inward" consumption, combining surpluses with input requirements of the same level, thus reducing the total amount of outward discharge and increasing other consumption savings.

- Natural Supplies

Supplies are obtained from the natural environment:

- Thermal: heat pump: cold-heat of the environment.
- Water: rain, condensation
- Light: photovoltaic with favourable sun orientations

Soft Programming

The design shall allow for flexible and open use, facilitating different options for use or operation.

It shall facilitate the possibility of different habitat programmes, according to the changing needs, due to the variability of family composition, over time.

Likewise, flexible technological systems shall be provided to meet the needs of the changing housing programme.

"Cycling".

Consumption and inputs have different levels of use, water, for example, is used both for drinking and for washing: washing or helping evacuation, which gives it up to three different levels of use, or degrees of quality.

Consumption and inputs alternate, for maximum use, from the highest quality level to the lowest usable level.

Discharges, which have a certain degree of utilisation, are reintegrated into the unit to compensate for consumption. In this way, consumption and discharge are combined in parallel levels of usefulness, thus saving on new consumption. See figure 4.

Figure 4. Fluid recycling flows: "black", "dirty" water, "clean" wáter and rain

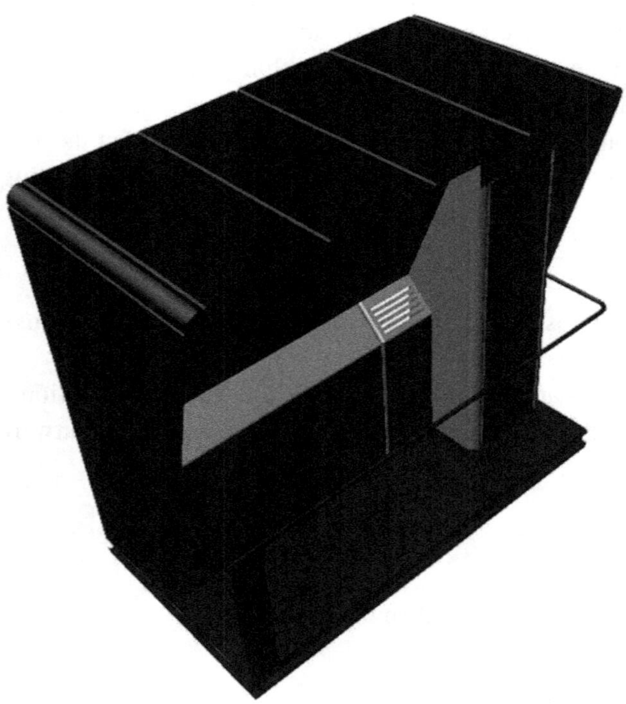

System Generation: Sustainability Features in Residential Buildings

In this chapter we will develop a proposal for the design of a housing unit, in the environment of "sustainable development", under "systemic" criteria and conceptions, detailing its characteristics.

A housing unit model is proposed, designed using the concepts and tools of Systems Engineering, different from the typical methodology of traditional construction and its means in architecture.

The industrial environment of building is an unavoidable and continuous trend, and is therefore the basis of this project methodology, where traditional construction is considered to be surpassed and it will be in this field of industrial activity where we propose the necessary premises for its sustainable design.

The implications and repercussions on the external environment, the "natural" surroundings, are also unavoidable in the context of sustainable building.

Description of the Proposal

The proposal is developed, based on the above design principles, in a housing cluster, where flexibility, participation of all agents, including users, can make their decisions with new rules.

This project is the result of the presentation to the call made by the Instituto de Ciencias de la Construcción IETcc, within the project initiated for the industrialisation of Housing. It won First Prize in the INVISO (Industrialisation of Sustainable Housing) ideas competition held in 2007 for the EMVs (Empresa Municipal de la Vivienda y Suelo, Madrid City Council) to implement the system in some of its developments, but shortly after the "real estate bubble" burst in Spain at that time and the project was not developed. The architects who developed this project at the competition level were: Guridi, R., Tartás, C., Guardiola, J. and García, A.

This proposal arose from the INVISO research group's call for an ideas competition. The aim of the competition was to improve the construction techniques and procedures for the quality of the final product, as well as the functionality and maintenance of the house. And the answer given by the winning team is to be guided by the principles of "open industrialisation", and thus create a System of construction by compatible components (S.3c) capable of generating a grouping of dwellings which, being standardised, can also be adapted to certain particular needs of their inhabitants (through variations and possibilities that the system itself provides automatically): flexible. The solution requested is necessarily very generic and indeterminate initially, given that the competition brief does not establish a real urban situation, nor a building typology or regulations to be adhered to.

With these premises, the proposal is for a grouping of dwellings developed as a linear block in height with dwellings open directly to the two opposite exterior orientations. Given the energy sustainability required in the competition rules, one of the orientations is more favoured with respect to solar gain, as opposed to the opposite one, which is more protected (closed) as it is preferably the northern one, as there are no regulations or plot (plot) that would condition this.

With these previous determinations, the general plan of the grouping is distributed as a "spatial topology in comb, with two longitudinal bands (B1 and B2) and a central zone (Zc) between them with two expansion zones (Ze), in North and South orientations. *Figure 5.*

In this kind of topological scheme, one of the two strips is highly specialised with respect to the other, and in this case, B2 houses all the spaces associated with facilities and wet areas, while B1 is left free and as a complementary space to its corresponding space in B2 (direct relationship between server space and served space). Between B1 and B2 a Zc is determined that functions as a transition zone between

Figure 5. Floor plan of the complex

the two, which is occupied by circulations or spaces complementary to the strips, and which serve for the dwellings to function without any conflict (spaces that are compatible with each other and with the adjoining ones). The North Ze is used to locate the access galleries and the general supply networks, and the South Ze to hang balconies, awnings, solar collectors or water tanks, wherever these components are necessary (spatial filters / energy regulators).

Once this general distribution of the grouping has been decided, and its dimensions and modulation have been refined, the building typology that complies with these conditioning factors is obtained, and the material components of the system that serve to build the proposal can be inserted into it without any conflict.

- Structure: a steel lattice structure is used, based on beams and pillars with bolted nodes, with a maximum span of 4.50 m. The floors are made of wooden boards reinforced with metal profiles based on bottom purlins or curled panels. The material quality of all these components makes the Meccano very easy to dismantle and modify (dry construction), being able to extend where needed, or to generate double heights where desired (two-storey dwellings are produced).
- South enclosure: based on light sandwich panels, and metal carpentry for insulating glass.

The structural steel grid serves as a BUS to hang the continuous skin wherever it is needed, and also allows all kinds of spatial complements to be connected to it to achieve an expansion zone (Ze) that functions as an energy regulating filter (balcony, awnings, tanks, PV panels, etc.).

- North enclosure: this side is reserved for hanging the 3D-compact units that contain the "mechanisms and wet appliances" necessary for the B1 band to be correctly served according to the housing variation to which they correspond. With these 3D units, plus the entrance bridge to the dwellings from the access gallery, the entire enclosure of this slope is covered and watertight. A vertical lifting system guided from the roof allows the 3D-comp units to be easily moved or re-

Figure 6. Detachability of the "service" modules: 3rd-component

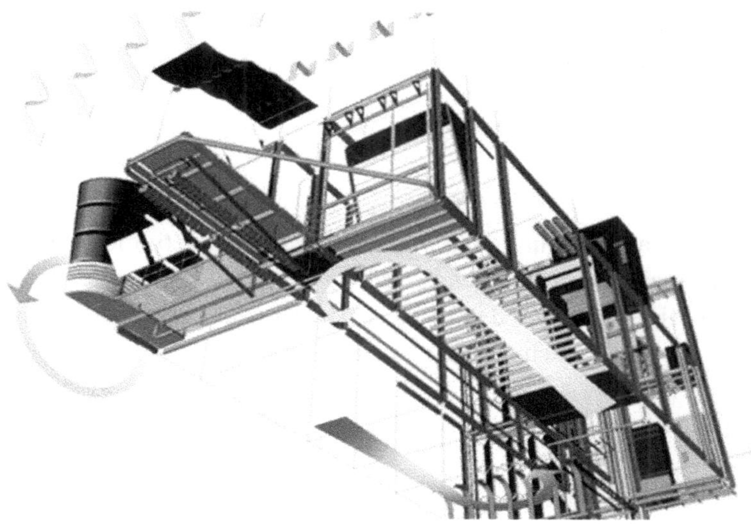

placed (their weight varies between 0.7 and 1.5 tonnes, and their largest dimension is 3 metres). The enclosure of the units is a metal monocoque, which can be opened and closed, acting as both a structure and an insulating shell.

- Installations: their layout and organisation are fundamental to the proper functioning of the proposal. The entire north face is reserved for the passage of the installations, which pass between the access gallery and the structural steel grid, and once hung from the structure, and always in view, serve as a BUS system to which any of the 3D units that the catalogue makes available to users can be applied at their connection points. With three types of bathroom and three types of kitchen, all the variations that appear in the general floor plan are achieved (figure 5).

Elements of Design in Housing Projects

This correlation is what the related *hierarchical systems* (Simon, 1968) allow us to do, and so we identify the systems by their functions, correlated with the needs to be fulfilled, and grouping and identifying the following components.

Some of these, as modules, formally configure a series of "boxes", which are added in layers, like "onion peels", around the spaces to be enabled for their activity and use within the assigned architectural design.

The architecture is a "container", on the one hand, which integrates everything; and on the other, it is redesigned so that it can be personalised, by means of these layers associated with levels, according to degrees of freedom, which allow it to be adapted to each of the users, according to their needs at any given moment.

The building reorganises a relatively fixed infrastructure, a stable but replaceable skeleton, the cladding is easily modified, with the equipment incorporated and the interior partitions easily moved.

On the other hand, the installations are grouped together, from their connections, and developing through the building, they serve the technical components that require it.

Finally, the building is located in an environment, with which it must be integrated, in its relationship as an "internal environment" on an "external environment".

In order of their flexibility within the building as a whole, all these building components can be distinguished, on a scale of autonomy, from the smallest to the largest:

- Fixed
- Autonomous

On the other hand, from a functional point of view, the habitat activities are also organised, which are integrated into the formal configuration defined above.

And two orders are defined, the one due to its structural character, and the functional one, by the order of the supported activities, which are developed below.

Elements of Design

There are three design elements that make up the housing unit.

1. Natural resource capture components:

Water and oxygen are transferred to transfer elements by means of cisterns, plant terraces, greenhouses, which treat or store them and prepare them for later consumption.

With these elements, natural resources are recovered within reach of the external environment. See figure 7.

2. Autonomous components of the housing programme

Functional elements within the housing programme: toilet, kitchen and bedroom are arranged as separate units. See Figure 8.

These "modules" will facilitate the flexible functioning of the dwelling, which, due to their interchangeability, make their use more flexible.

3. Technology patch panel.

Figure 7. Outdoor cisterns for water collection

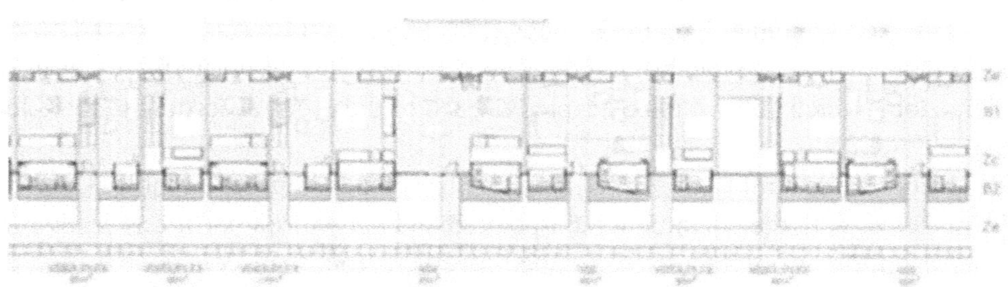

Figure 8. Service Module

The set of technological resources, energy and fluid supplies, remotely generated, at a distance from the housing unit, are grouped in a vertical panel, separate and independent from the housing programme, leaving a margin of security and access for better registration. See Figure 9.

Maintenance is facilitated by the independent access they have, and safety is improved by the distance to users outside the living space.

Figure 9. Energies panel

This "energy" panel will be located on the side closest to the consumption points inside the dwelling, located by the toilets, kitchens and workstations.

This design of the technical systems optimises their operation by their maintainability and their proximity to the consumption points.

Configuración de Programa

Firstly, the different functional elements are defined, which are distributed throughout the building, and which, responding to the habitat needs, configure the dwelling.

Inside a rigid container: Structure and Basic Installation or INFRASTRUCTURE, (Guerrero et al., 2011) the previous modules are arranged, ordered from least to most flexible, in the penetration towards the habitable space.

The energy plane is placed on the structural "box", which will facilitate the supply of water, electricity, gas, telephone, TV, to the housing unit, configuring an autonomous plane and separated from the habitable building.

These supplies enter the building from the outside, through the "artificial" system of energies and fluids that provide them, by means of remote transport from their generation.

Next to this plane of "energies", the accesses and transits are developed through a system of walkways that leave openings for transporting and lifting the work modules: kitchens, toilets, etc., to facilitate their exchange along the length of the building.

to facilitate their exchange throughout the life of the building.

Attached to the structure of the living space are these modules, which, like equipment "backpacks", are connected to the housing units.

Their connections to the infrastructure systems are very close, their registration for maintenance is immediate, even without access to the living space of the dwelling, and their exchange is feasible.

Inside the housing unit, its external connection with the environment is at the opposite end to the plane of "energies" and "work modules" described above.

At this end is the relationship with the "natural" external environment, from which it obtains its natural tributaries: light, air and water.

These other inputs are obtained in an immediate, close and direct way, due to their proximity, but they are not controlled, so they need to be stored and controlled by means of filters.

Finally, in order to define the interior space of the habitat, by functional divisions of the programme: bedrooms, living room, dining room, leisure, etc., the ergonomic definition is left for the level of greater autonomy, concretised in screens, ceilings, floors and arranged for "DIY".

Constructive Order

The components are divided into the following groups, according to their degree of autonomy, because of their flexibility in the construction as a whole:

- Fixed: the most rigid, subject to the terrain and its connection to the technological networks of the "artificial" environment: with the city.
- Free: manufactured components, available on the market, ready to be mounted on the planned structural system.

In between, components are identified that allow changes in their internal elements: Removable.

Fixed

The first module is the STRUCTURAL system, with stability functions. As it is the first level, its design, in addition to stability, must guarantee the integration of the second level systems: Enclosure, Divisions, Floor-Ceilings and Interior Installation.

With the same characteristic of support, the INSTALLATION is included, in its level of connection and main uprights for piping and wiring derivations of the housing units.

Structure and Installation configure the connection with the External Environment of the complete Housing System, the land and the urban supply networks, so we define this grouping by INFRASTRUCTURE, which is the most rigid, fixed and stable level.

Free

Next, the second module corresponds to the equipment SERVICE module: cookers, sanitary appliances and interior connections. They allow modifications by changing the complete unit.

Although it has not yet reached the market, there is already some development in the line of components for kitchen and toilet modules.

The next module remains for the living space where the social and personal activities of the family and the individual take place. This system includes the interior finishes that spatially configure the habitat.

Removibles

This module is shared equally by DIVISIONS and PAVING and ROOFS, which are removable elements of continuous consumption and available on the market, within the reach of any user.

The last module connects the habitat with the outside environment, and includes constructive elements of closure and protection, such as the façade and roofs, which, although interchangeable, require a higher technological condition.

Functional Order

The previous groups of the habitable programme, in turn, are defined within another more abstract order, in reference to their level of activity.

Three main groups of activities can be distinguished:

- Activity I: tasks that are oriented towards the satisfaction of the most basic needs (see Marslow's pyramid), and that refer to food, hygiene, work, etc.

These activities require the highest degree of technification, due to their consumption of energy resources, and therefore have a greater technological repercussion, with the assistance of installations and artificial systems.

At this level, the technological systems are connected, which from the "artificial" outside, and from a remote origin, supply fluids and energy, through a grouping in the so-called technological systems panel.

Figure 10. Rear plan view: access platform technologies, between the facilities on the left and the stand-alone service modules on the right

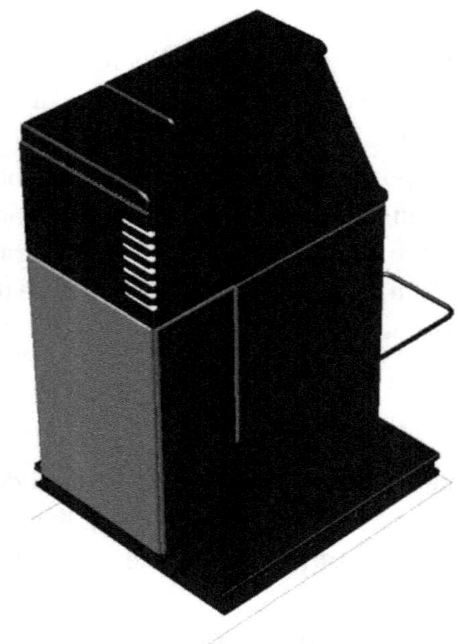

- Activity II: occupations inside the dwelling oriented towards social activity, both family, social and even personal. These tasks include relaxation, communication and leisure activities.

These activities do not require a level of technical assistance, so they are developed in an environment "clean" of technology, more open to the natural environment, with which they relate to the next step of habitat design.

Between groups I and II we can differentiate a step of functional transfer, which transforms the product of group I into the more "friendly" product of group II.

- Activity III: Activities in relation to the natural environment. This next step involves direct contact with the surroundings, the natural environment of the habitat, and its uses are those typical of "green": orchard, garden, cistern, solarium, etc.

These are recreational activities, in a natural environment that take place in contact with air, water, light, etc. in the outdoor environment.

CONCLUSION

There is a need for a reference on what we should understand by a sustainable building, and although there are currently various standards, norms and canons available, there is still a need for greater concreteness and detail, including solutions to contrast results.

Figure 11. Natural connection with the outside environment: cistern, vegetable garden, and greenhouse

The proposals for sustainable building must be included in a broad framework, ranging from the necessary revision of the habitat, to the design of a more flexible and efficient construction, which combines both natural resources within reach with technological service systems, such as the recycling of waste at the level of use.

By applying Lean criteria in construction, it is possible to optimise building processes and reduce costs. Modulation and systematisation are key to the successful industrialisation of the processes that make up the city and the habitat.

All this in a design applied in new proposals for Housing Units, for which we have applied a systemic point of view, and aided by the techniques of Systems Engineering, we contemplate the housing unit as an artificial system in a multiple and wider environment, with which it must be integrated.

On the basis of a project proposal, the INVISO project, an available example has been given as a reference to provide a solution to the broad concepts of sustainable building, a concept that requires ever greater analysis and detail.

All the previous study has been formalised in a methodology, design elements have been enunciated, and applied in building projects for a sustainable environment and advanced construction in the framework of industrialisation.

As a final result, a solution has been provided, where the concepts of this sustainable building can be analysed and referenced.

REFERENCES

Awad T, Guardiola J. and Fraíz D. (2021). *Sustainable Construction: Improving Productivity through Lean Construction.*

Bertalanffy, Ludwig von (1968): Teoría general de los sistemas. (1976). Fondo de Cultura Económica.

Brau S.J. (2016). Lean Manufacturing 4.0: La Evolución Tecnológica del Lean. *Guía Práctica sobre la Correcta Utilización de Tecnología en Proyectos Lean.*

Charron, R., Wiggin, H., Voehl, F., & Harrington, H. J. (2014). *The Lean Management Systems Handbook*. Productivity Press, Taylor & Francis. doi:10.1201/b17201

Cuatrecasas, L. (2017). *Ingeniería de Procesos y de Planta: Ingeniería Lean*. Bresca.

Guardiola, J., & Reyes, J. M. (2019). Del Sistema al Prototipo y viceversa, revista Torroja. *Informes de la Construcción, 71*, 555.

Guerrero, A. L., García, C., Pérez Laorga, F., & Guardiola, J. (2009) El Ingeniero del ICAI y el desarrollo Sostenible. Chapter 21: Edificación y Urbanismo, sistemas, métodos & tecnologías.

Jiménez M, Espinosa Mª M., Domínguez M., Romero M. and Awad T.(2021) Adaptation of the Lean 6S Methodology in an Industrial Environment under Sustainability and Industry 4.0 Criteria.

Navarro, F. J. (2017). *Implementación de herramientas Lean Manufacturing en la planta de producción de un proveedor del sector automoción* [Master's thesis, Universitat Politècnica de Catalunya].

Simon H.A., (1968) The Science of the artificial.

United Nations. (2021). *Sustainable Development Goals*. UN. https://www.un.org/sustainabledevelopment/es/objetivos-de-desarrollo-sostenible/

Womack, J. P., & Jones, D. T. (2005). *Lean thinking: cómo utilizar el pensamiento Lean para eliminar los despilfarros y crear valor en la empresa*. Grupo Planeta GBS.

Zhou, B. (2016). Lean principles, practices, and impacts: A study on small and medium-sized enterprises SMEs. *Annals of Operations Research, 241*(1-2), 1–2, 457–474. doi:10.100710479-012-1177-3

Chapter 9
Sustainable Acoustics for Better Livability and Wellbeing

Laura de Azcárate
Architectural Association School of Architecture, UK

ABSTRACT

Acoustics is being addressed as a part of the LCA methodologies in construction, hence research in new acoustic materials is being developed on the benefit of natural materials that can be an alternative to traditional materials. It´s important to consider its acoustic performance as a key parameter in the choice of sustainable building materials. The impact of applying sustainable acoustic materials for a particular space function and typology can be measured, defined, and quantified when creating healthy and comfortable spaces for a better acoustic comfort and wellbeing. The use of environmentally friendly acoustic materials in architecture, as well as the rest of the aspects that combined define a sustainable practice for a business, contribute to merge health and livability in urban environments. Human health and wellbeing are a consequence of a designer's intention, where acoustics play an important role. Applying sustainable acoustic strategies embedded in the rest of the disciplines is a key factor to deliver holistic and appropriate architectural environments.

INTRODUCTION

Since health and livability involve many aspects of human comfort in buildings, sustainable design implies addressing the three key areas – social, economical and environmental- without compromising the ability of future generations to meet their own needs in order to deliver appropriate indoor and outdoor environments. Human comfort, leads to a particular behavior and use of the space, which is crucial for a designer to respond to a particular design brief taking into account that architectural projects should be conceived from a circular point of view.

Sustainability is the balance between environment, equity and economy (Heywood, 2015). It's a complex topic that is at the same time easy to summarize: sustainability means a productive balance with nature. The construction industry is responsible of approximately 40% of CO2 emissions, 40% of natural resource consumption and 40% of waste generation (Gonçalves de Lassio & Naked Haddad, 2016).

DOI: 10.4018/978-1-6684-6924-8.ch009

The construction sector has become one of the most significant sectors that cause real environmental impacts by emitting a large amount of emissions into the atmosphere (G. Horvath, 2006) The goal of World Green Building Council (World GBC) is to reduce the buildings and construction sector's CO2 emissions and achieve net zero emissions building by 2050, supporting the 17 Sustainable Development Goals (SDGs). (World Green Building Council, 2016-2022):

Table 1. Sustainable Development Goals (SDGs) adopted by the United Nations in 2015 as an universal call to action to end poverty, protect the planet and ensure that by 2030 all people enjoy peace and prosperity (United Nations Development Programme, 2023)

1. No poverty	2. Reduced inequalities
3. Zero hunger	4. Sustainable cities and communities
5. Good Health and Well-being	6. Responsible consumption and production
7. Quality education	8. Climate action
9. Gender equality	10. Life below water
11. Clean water and sanitation	12. Life on land
13. Affordable and clean energy	14. Peace, justice and strong institutions
15. Decent work and economic growth	16. Partnerships for the goals
17. Industry, innovation and infrastructure	

These goals, adopted by the United Nations Member States in 2015, were part of the 2030 agenda for a Sustainable Development. (United Nations.Department of Economic and Social Affairs, s.f.) They lead green construction towards a resilient design, infrastructures, renewable energy, health and wellbeing, fewer emissions, circular principles, etc.

A Life Cycle Assessment (LCA) or analysis is a methodology that, even if it does not address social or economical aspects, enables to bring on board all aspects of the construction process that are chained and affect each other on a symbiotic manner. Every product, service or process has a life cycle which impacts on the environment and should be assessed for sustainable purposes (to achieve carbon footprint goals). This analysis help designers and police makers on taking informed decisions, identifying opportunities to improve the environmental performance, and circulating necessary information (marketing, labels, product declarations…).

There exists many types of Life Cycle Assessment (LCA), from internal revisions to external (PRE-Sustainability, s.f.) which enable to compare products (Environmental Product Declarations- EPD), to comply with a particular standard (Product Environmental Footprint – PEF-, Organizational Environmental Footprint – OEF) or long term monitoring studies.

According to the International Organization for Standardization ISO (International Organization for Standarisation, s.f.) LCA addresses the environmental aspects and potential environmental impacts (e.g. use of resources and environmental consequences of releases) throughout a product's life cycle from raw material acquisition through production, use, end-of-life treatment, recycling and final disposal (i.e. cradle-to-grave"

Two standards describe and define this methodology:

- ISO 14040: 2006- Environmental Management, Life Cycle Assessment, principles and framework (ISO, Environmental management.Life cycle assessment.Principles and framework, 2006)
- ISO 14044:2006: Environmental Management, Life Cycle Assessment, requirements and guidelines (for conducting an LCA) (ISO, Environmental management.Life cycle assessment . Requirements and guidelines, 2006)
- These standards cover two types of studies (Life Cycle Assessment-LCA- studies and Life Cycle Inventory -LCI- studies) and specify different phases of an LCA:
  - Goal and scope: It ensures the analysis is performed consistently (From the scope to the final goals, the analysis should not be very different from reality)
  - Inventory analysis: Analysing environmental inputs and outputs associated with the product, service or process, helps to build the Life Cycle Inventory (LCI) to collect and model relevant data
  - Impact assessment: The Life Cycle Impact Assessment (LCIA) draw the conclusions.
  - Interpretation: The ISO 14044 standard helps confirming the conclusions obtained

What a sustainable material is, is not simple to define: considering its environmental impact, energy consumption, generated waste, durability, transportation, toxicity, maintenance, disposal, preparation and assembly…all these aspects play an important role to dismiss or accept material options for a particular design. Sustainable materials are gaining popularity in construction projects, also being called "environmentally friendly building materials or "eco-materials", they can even change completely the aesthetics and the project concept design. Architects give new opportunities to local materials, look at vernacular architecture and traditional construction techniques, even mixing components and forms, to obtain and re-think how sustainability can help on single decisions in order to comply with global warming limitations. The same way computational design contribute to "see" new forms, arrangements, and to conceive spaces, a sustainable approach can be the driver of an idea.

Health and livability in Architecture si not only affected by sustainability. Architecture has progressed along with the rest of events at each moment in history, trying to adapt to new unexpected conditions, necessities and resources.

Rules that drove architectural trends during the XIX and XX century, as well as other stages, were driven by socioeconomics, aesthetics, functionality and other aspect such as "comfort" understood by "ergonomics". Material supply was also important due to political reasons, as well as economy. From Frank Lloyd Wright, Alvar Aalto, le Corbusier, to Antoni Gaudi, Architectural movements did not take into account any life cycle assessment of building materials nor circular economy.

During the XIX century economic growth and socio-political transformations lead to an Architecture that used to deal with perception, experimentation, and new materials (steel and glass). Eclecticism and historicism as well as the use of these mentioned new materials and structural methods, were the two main factors that described this period which was greatly influenced by earlier architectural movements and the Industrial Revolution. The magnificent progress in science and technology made easier to have a positive approach to new trends, and to be able to "manipulate" pre-existing elements (the Neoclassicism). Designer's interest was in finding a new style "Art nouveau" as the first modern architectural movement. However, industrialization was also one of the historical events that contributed to accelerate climate change. According to the World Economic Forum (World Economic Forum, s.f.) "from 1880, the Earth's average surface temperature has risen by 0.07ºC every decade. From 1851-1935 and overlapping with the Second Industrial Revolution, the global temperature increased form -0.4° to +0.6°, and from 1936-2020 overlapping with the Third Industrial Revolution it increased from +0.6° to 1.5° and up". It took several decades for the scientists to realize that the industrial improvements came at the cost of burning fossil fuels and hence accumulating carbon dioxide in the atmosphere, which had a very negative impact on the planet.

The XX century was driven by a number of architectural styles and trends that looked at functionality and interior space arrangements. It was the century of rationalism, where "the five points in Architecture" published by Le Corbusier in 1927 (Corbusier, 2013 -18th edition) were put in practice, thanks to application of reinforced concrete:

1) "pilotis" supported the building and separated them from the ground, in order to connect private and public space at ground floor
2) "the roof garden" was possible, allowing to connect with nature also on the top of the building
3) The "plan libre" (free plan) enabled new space arrangements, reducing structural sections thanks to the steel. Load-bearing walls were removed, allowing for new space indoor distributions
4) "La façade libre" (free facade) allowed architects to place long windows, as they placed the structure back from it.
5) "la fenetre en longueur" (ribbon window), was also possible because of the reinforced concrete. This connected the building with nature from the inside to the outside (perimeter) allowing for the views and natural light to get in.

Civil architecture and urban planning were the main focus of society on applying these new design concepts. The avant-garde movements did not organize social life on the basis of burgeois conventions, but around creativity of every artist.

Design rules at XXI century have changed dramatically in order to accomplish very restrictive energy performance goals to address an unstoppable climate change .globalization makes material supply easier at every corner of the planet, which has turned the situation increasingly difficult to measure in terms of footprint. International organizations, educators, designers, as well as other institutions and the rest of the construction industry has had the need of re-adapting design criteria and prioritizing carbon reduction in order to reach net-zero greenhouse emissions by 2050.The Intergovernmental Panel on Climate Change (IPCC), the United Nations body for assessing the science related to climate change, prepared a "Special Report in 2018 on the impacts of global warming of 1.5° above pre-industrial levels and related global greenhouse gas emission pathways". This took part of the 21st Conference of Parties of the United Nations Framework Convention on Climate Change to adopt the Paris Agreement (The intergovernmental Panel on Climate Change, 2022)

Designers at this point need to focus on prioritizing climate concerns, making a constant effort in defending the benefits of long-terms results in construction. This is translated in transforming their minds when conceiving spaces, choosing materials in order not only to respond to client preferences, but to their needs as a end user, as well as evaluating the life cycle of the project. Besides aesthetics and functionality, comfort in Architecture needs to go together with sustainable goals in order to fulfill a common purpose: creating a sustainable built environment from now on. Researchers are working together to find necessary steps for economic growth to ensure a sustainable development.

SUSTAINABLE ACOUSTIC PRODUCTS AS A PART OF LCA

Raw materials are the materials used in the manufacturing process of goods (Banton y otros, 2022) They are being bought and sold on commodities exchanges worldwide (a commodity usually refers to a raw material used to manufacture finished goods; a product, on the other hand, is the finished good sold to costumers) Due to the increasing high demand on raw materials, the world has committed on reducing and recycling the use to minimize greenhouse gas emissions.

Circularity of resources is hence needed in order to reduce the environmental impact of production systems and consumption patterns which are driven by circular economy (Brandstrom & Saidani, 15 October 2022) Circularity is mostly associated with material efficiency strategies, however little effort has been made to quantitatively assess the connection between circularity, material efficiency and environmental sustainability. Material-based circularity metrics can be valuable for circular economy as they do not require methodological expertise, and can align the results with a Life Cycle Assessments at some specific situations.

According to the Ellen Macarthur Foundation (Ellen Macarthur Foundation, s.f.) The circular economy is a systems solution framework that tackles global challenges like climate change, biodiversity loss, waste and pollution. Circular economy is based on three principles, driven by design:

1) Eliminate waste and pollution

In a circular economy the materials need to re-enter the economy at the end of their use. Doing this we change a linear system by a circular system. Many products can be circulated by being repaired, renovated, refurbished, redesigned, and at the last instance, recycled.

Many companies contribute to this by creating acoustic panels such as *Liko-acoustics-* using PET bottles. (Likos International, s.f.) PET bottles (Polyethylene Terephalate) are non-toxic, recyclable bottles used for most of the containers we use in everyday life (food, beverage…). The starting products of PET are derived from natural gas or crude oil. As a thermoplastic resin PET can be moulded when exposed to heat, which is usually processed at the bottling company (as the small PET preforms are small and easy to handle, it is better for transportation) Once the bottles have come to an end of use, they end up as waste even in the ocean (80% of the ocean debris is waste plastics) By manufacturing this into acoustic products, circularity of resources is achieved successfully, reducing the environmental impact and helping species of marine life around the world that are injured by ingesting them. (Forum PET, 2021)

These resulting acoustic panels have an excellent sound absorption and noise reduction properties, they are easy to clean and water resistant. Both a wide range of possible design solutions and their valuable functionality described above, are positioning the product on a high level of increasing demand.

2) Circulate products and materials (at their highest value)

This second principle means keeping materials in use as long as possible, maintaining their product capacities or transforming them in components or raw materials so they don't become waste. There are two fundamental cycles that promote that products and materials keep circulating.

- The technical cycle.

By extending the original use of the product as long as possible (e.g.a phone used as a phone) we extend the value. It is more valuable as a phone than by its separate components). This involves processes like repairing or re-saling the product. Once the product cannot longer be used, the components can be remanufactured or recycled. Even if recycling is the last resort, its important to do it to keep the material in a circular process, and not linear.

- The biological cycle.

Some materials cannot be reused, hence they need to be recirculated by the biological cycle. Biodegradable materials can contribute to fill the land and produce other renewable materials such as cotton, wood or natural fibres.

Products made out of natural materials (e.g wooden furniture) can be returned by both the technical cycle and the biological cycle. Research in new acoustic materials is being developed on the benefit of natural materials as an alternative to traditional ones, which will grow and develop in the next few years.

Some companies contribute to this process according to the second principle such as *Geopannel* (Geopannel, s.f.) by using an 85% of their raw materials (100% cotton) from recycled textiles (clothes) to create construction products. These products are used for acoustic solutions (sound insulation or room acoustics). In the process of manufacturing the panels, denim fabrics are classified, and technical pieces like zips or buttons are separated from fibers Clothes are frayed and shredded looking for a specific fiber diameter and length, an air system separates all the fibers to be mixed later with other materials depending on needs. Finally the material goes through an oven at low temperature (250ºC) which is the manufacturing temperature difference with other types of insulations that makes the lowest carbon footprint of the market

Designers are responsible of a product being able to fit in both of these cycles: the technical cycle and the biological cycle. It is crucial that designers have circularity in mind, so they foresee separation of technical parts from biological parts, or don't mix synthetic with natural materials to allow an easy separation.

3) Regenerate nature

The third principle of circular economy is to regenerate nature: the key to success is to actively improve the environment. By changing the approach from linear to circular, we shift extraction by regeneration (e.g improving soil or ocean health) aiming to imitate natural systems which regenerate themselves.

Regenerative farming practices allow restoring soils which hold water, reducing the risk of flooding (Agroecology, conservation agriculture and agroforestry). This results on a more biodiverse land, that increase and improve natural ecosystems

An example of a sustainable product that supports this principle is *Rockfon Grodan* (Rockfon Grodan, s.f.) an horticultural stone wool- an inert medium discovered near volcanoes in the 1800's and later created in factories by *Grodan* to facilitate growing plants with sustainable stone wool substrate, no soil (hydroponic growing).

By recycling thousands of tons of stone wool every year (achieving 45% of recycling rate, and aiming to achieve 65% in the next 3 years), this helps growers to reach the goal of producing more with less resources, to grow more healthy products. This also helps feeding urban generations through vertical farming which plays a crucial role in our future global food production.

Also by keeping materials in circulation after use, we decouple economic activity with material extraction. The more we circulate products and materials at their highest value and we eliminate waste and production, the more land can be returned to nature (reducing extraction of virgin raw materials).

Acoustics is addressed as a part of the Life Cycle Assessment (LCA) methodologies in construction. The embodied environmental impact of building construction can be evaluated from the point of view of separate materials itself, however decisions taken by designers from an early stage are crucial to define environmental inputs and outputs associated with the process (LCI-Life Cycle Inventory) These decisions involve consequences for different construction methods, transportation, assembly, re-use, etc.

As a holistic approach to design, acoustic needs understanding implies designer involvement with its combined properties for other construction requirements or demands. Nothing is more sustainable than "avoiding construction". The same way an architectural project can reduce material quantities according to the structural system chosen, an optimal acoustic strategy undertaken at an appropriate stage is crucial to reduce costs, combine material techniques and processes (e.g vibrational energy caused by a structure selection depending if it is wood, steel or concrete could change sound insulation between rooms)

Spatial arrangements early review could help the designer focusing the intention on a particular direction: material selection involve limitations and advantages for space isolation, perception, activities, etc. The same way the discovery of new industrial materials in the XIX century (industrial revolution) changed building heights, occupation, and hence fire regulations as a consequence, new design techniques such as parametric rules could involve structural and acoustic decisions taken at early stages.

Passive strategies that isolate the building from the outdoors, as well as new open plan and arrangements lead to evaluate "comfort" conceived inside the building, looking at "comfort areas" according to a building as a "whole". Space versatility and multifunctionality lead to an intelligent architecture which adapts to conditions at every moment.

Careful attention also need to be paid to local architecture, traditions and user habits. Sustainability and circularity do not only account for local products (and actions involved) but passive design techniques should be carried out accounting for user's understanding of the space (mechanical ventilation is implemented in Mediterranean countries even if natural ventilation is very important for the users up to the point where they don´t activate it once installed) Cultures play a key role in the way people use buildings, hence the way to address sustainability requirements should adapt to the rapid change addressing global warming. Strict criteria expressed in legislation is presently being translated from cold-indoor northern cultures to warm-outdoor southern countries as a "global strategy", which is opposite to what "sustainable" means in terms of local needs.

But what is comfort and wellbeing? Is a white empty room with perfect conditions of temperature, air velocity, light and acoustics a comfortable space? Research is being carried out about human's indoor comfort conditions, especially after the COVID19 lockdowns in 2020. (Jackson y otros, 2021) For instance, the wellbeing benefits of natural ventilation -the process, akin to a building "breathing" that draws in fresh air and expels stale air. Further research should be carried out on how human perception is affected by variable conditions within a natural environment such as a forest or a beach against an artificial environment designed and built (an office).

ACOUSTIC PERFORMANCE ASSESSMENT OF SUSTAINABLE BUILDING MATERIALS

When selecting a material for construction purposes, there are many considerations to take into account (Adams, 2016): cleanability, resistance to abrasion, mechanical strength, weight, resistance to impacts, cost, installation, durability, visual appearance…

Acoustic performance is assessed in terms of sound absorption and sound insulation, which are opposite properties. When a material is a poor sound absorber is usually good blocking sound and conversely. Due to this, some acoustic materials are the result of a combination that together form a composite which both blocks and absorb sound (e.g. dense vinyl layer combined with a porous absorber)

Light reflectance can have a significant impact in the interior if the material accumulates dirt and is installed over a large interior surface (e.g. a ceiling). Hence cleanability or the capacity to be painted can be very important when selecting an acoustic material. A high light reflectance will be very efficient when for both daylight and artificial lighting reducing the luminance ratio

Considering fire resistance which is one of the most important requirements, there are different tests carried out to certify that is suitable for the space functionality due to the flame spread, smoke production, heat release and occurrence of flaming droplets of particles. Material flammability requirements will vary according to the country and project typology.

Sustainability is one of the newest and most important requirements for an acoustic material. It is usually evaluated through independent rating systems (LEED, BREEAM, WELL…) which look at their Life Cycle Assessment (LCA) (from the extraction of raw materials to the end of their life as a product. The product content is analyzed in terms of their ability to be recycled, toxicity (paints, coatings and binders), energy used in the production process, distance to transport the material to the construction site sourcing of raw materials from sustainable sources, etc.

In recent years sustainable acoustic materials and natural materials have been evaluated in terms of performance,_also being compared with traditional materials such as rock wool and glass wool. It´s important to consider its acoustic properties as a key parameter in the choice of sustainable building materials. Both non- acoustic and acoustic properties (i.g as a thermal insulators) make a material suitable for an integrated approach to a holistic design. Careful analysis should be carried out under comparison as often synthetic materials have less of an impact than those derived from natural resources.

Presenting a set of acoustic materials as an example such as mineral wool, sheep's wool and cellulose fiber, we could analyze and compare different factors in terms of performance and sustainability. (e.g Although mineral wool is a better insulator, it has potential human health problems such as skin irritation and others)

As a first case study stone wool (Rockwool, 2022): is one of the most commonly used acoustic material in construction, used for sound absorption (improving sound insulation if used inside partitions). Stone wool consist in 5% solid material in the form of stone fibers (the remaining 95% is made up of pores). The basic materials are basalt and limestone which are melted to form lava in an oven with a temperature of 1500 ºC and processed into fibers. They are compressed to form a sturdy mass from which the slabs and blocks are then cut.

As a second case sheep's wool is an animal fiber conceived as an Eco-material alternative to traditional mineral wools. (Sheep whool insulation, s.f.)To make sheep's wool suitable as an insulation material it must be processed. The first process requires the farmer to sort the wool according to colour, then is pressed into bales. At the scouring plant, the wool is washed with warm water several times until there is only the raw fiber remaining. The wool is then fully protected using ionic protect as the wool insulation is being produced. Once dried the wool is carded and given a desired thickness to produce a roll of insulation

The third example is cellulose fiber (Makron, 2022)a plant fiber also conceived as an alternative eco-material. It is a green material manufactured from recycled paper which is transported to a cellulose fiber insulation production plant. The manufacturing process goes from receiving the raw material to

Figure 1. Acoustic performance data sheet for a commercial mineral wool-based acoustical and thermal panels (Cool "n" comfort series of products) by Rockwool Asia

Sound absorption coefficient at different Octave Band (50mm thickness)

Product	125 Hz	250 Hz	500 Hz	1000 Hz	2000 Hz	4000 Hz	NRC	α_w
Cool 'n' Comfort RL920	0.20	0.60	1.00	1.00	1.00	1.00	1.00	0.90
Cool 'n' Comfort RL940	0.20	0.70	1.00	1.00	1.00	1.00	1.05	1.00
Cool 'n' Comfort SL920	0.20	0.60	1.00	1.00	1.00	1.00	1.00	0.90
Cool 'n' Comfort SL940	0.20	0.70	1.00	1.00	1.00	1.00	1.05	1.00
Cool 'n' Comfort SL950	0.20	0.75	1.00	1.00	1.00	1.00	1.05	1.00
Cool 'n' Comfort SL960	0.30	0.85	1.00	1.00	1.00	1.00	1.05	1.00

Technical Parameters

Product Name	Cool 'n' Comfort RL920	Cool 'n' Comfort RL940	Cool 'n' Comfort SL920	Cool 'n' Comfort SL940	Cool 'n' Comfort SL950	Cool 'n' Comfort SL960	Standard
R-value at 50mm thickness (m^2K/W)	1.39	1.47	1.39	1.47	1.47	1.47	
Thermal Conductivity 20°C λ Value (W/mk)	0.036	0.034	0.036	0.034	0.034	0.034	ASTM C518
Water Absorption (partial immersion (kg/m^2)	1.0	1.0	0.5	0.5	0.5	0.5	EN1609.97
Water Vapor Absorption	Less than 0.04 Vol %	Less than 0.04 Vol %	Less than 0.04 Vol %	Less than 0.04 Vol %	Less than 0.04 Vol %	Less than 0.04 Vol %	ASTM C1104 C1104M
Fire Performance Non Combustibility	A1 Non-combustible						EN 13501-1 BS EN 1182
Melting Point	More than 1000°C						ASTM E794
Form Factor	Blanket	Blanket	Slab	Slab	Slab	Slab	
Thickness (mm)	50, 75, 100						EN 822
Width x Length (mm)	1200 x 5000		600 x 1200				EN 822
Recommended for these common applications	Single skin metal roof for food centre or canteen, usually non air-condition, without walls and highly ventilated environment. Also commonly used in walkways and common pavilion in residential estates	Single skin metal roof for high end residential, to provide a better thermal performance and long term savings on energy bill	Double skin metal roof for residential & commercial buildings for general thermal performance	Double skin metal roof for industrial, warehouse and factory where higher insulation thickness is designed to be slightly compressed for acoustic damping of the metal roof	Double skin metal roof for exhibition hall, school & educational institute for versatile roof design and high durability	Double skin metal roof for concert hall & airport where high acouctic performance on low sound frequencies are required	

Figure 2. Acoustic performance data sheet for a commercial sheep's wool-based acoustical and thermal panels (Thermafleece cosywool panels) by Eden Renewable Innovations Ltd

Specification

- 70 mm Softwood timber studs @ 600mm centres.
- One layer 12.5 mm plasterboard (8 kg/m^2) each side.
- 75mm Thermafleece CosyWool between studs.
- Nominal thickness = 95 mm

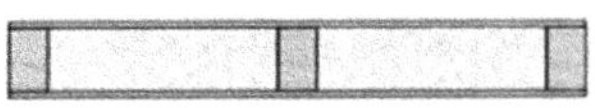

Weighted Sound Reduction Index (R_wdB) = 40dB

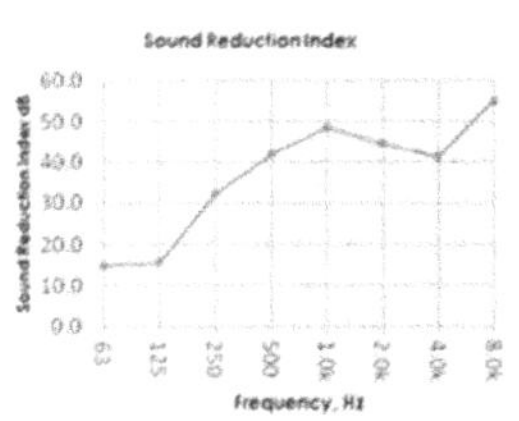

Frequency, Hz	Sound Reduction Index (dB)
63	14.8
125	15.6
250	32.3
500	41.9
1.0k	48.5
2.0k	44.5
4.0k	41.3
8.0k	55.1

Practical Absorption Coefficients

Frequency, Hz	PRACTICAL ABSORPTION COEFFICIENT			
	50 mm	75mm	100mm	140mm
125	0.20	0.25	0.45	0.60
250	0.40	0.60	0.85	0.90
500	0.65	0.85	1.00	0.95
1.0k	0.75	0.90	1.00	1.00
2.0k	0.85	0.95	1.00	1.00
4.0k	0.95	1.00	1.00	1.00
EN ISO 11654 1997	Class C	Class B	Class A	Class A
NRC to ASTM C 423-01	0.70	0.85	1.05	1.00

crushing it, to adding the chemicals and processing the material at different stages, and finally packing the finished product. The recycled cellulose fiber is then used as a thermal and acoustic insulation.

Figure 3. Acoustic performance data sheet for a commercial cellulose-based acoustical and thermal panels (CFAB cellulose panels) by Acoustical Surfaces Inc

CFAB Cellulose Panels – Acoustical Testing Data

Thickness	Absorption Coefficients @ Octave Band Frequencies (Hz)						NRC
	125	250	500	1,000	2,000	4,000	
½"	0.05	0.09	0.33	0.64	0.87	1.01	0.50
1"	0.09	0.26	0.84	1.05	1.05	1.05	0.80
2"	0.39	0.63	1.18	1.11	1.06	1.09	1.00

CFAB Cellulose Panels – Physical Property Data

Property	Test Method	Value
Surface Burning Characteristics	ASTM E-84, UL 723	Flame Spread: 15 Smoke Developed: <450 (Class A)
Critical Radiant Flux	ASTM E-970	>0.12 w/cm²
Corrosiveness	ASTM C-739	Acceptable
Fungal Growth	ASTM C-1338	Acceptable
Thermal Resistance	ASTM C-518	3.6 – 3.7 R per Inch
Moisture Absorption	ASTM C-739	Acceptable
Odor Emission	ASTM C-1304	Acceptable

Comparing different factors between these three examples, we could classify its properties as follows:

1) Acoustic performance.

Sound absorption happens when an acoustic wave encounters a material and vibrational energy is converted into heat inside it. Density and thickness are a key parameter when considering acoustic absorption properties, especially at low frequency ranges, however the most sensitive frequency range of the human hearing is between 500 and 4000 Hz (mid-high frequency range).

It has been demonstrated (del Rey y otros, 2017) that sheep's wool is a good sound absorbing material at medium and high frequencies. It is also shown that sheep wool has comparable sound absorption performance to that of mineral wool or recycles polyurethane foams. Mineral wool is an excellent acoustic and thermal insulator due to its high density and porosity. The performance varies depending on featuring in acoustic systems (as an absorptive material as opposed to a dense and heavy material). Acoustic performance of cellulose fibre is also good and depends on thickness as the rest of porous absorbers.

2) Sustainability factors associated with the material and quantification when comparing with alternative materials

Sheep wool insulation requires less than 15% of the energy required for production than a traditional material such as glass fiber insulation. Wool is a sustainable and renewable source as it is being made from natural (animal) fibers. It has zero ozone depletion potential and at the end of its life it can be remanufactured or biodegraded It can absorb indoor air pollutants such as formaldehyde, nitrogen dioxide and sulphur dioxide. It requires only a fraction of the energy to produce compared to that of a manmade counterparts (installing sheep wool insulation will pay back its energy costs more than 5 times sooner (only 15kW of energy are used to produce 1m^3). The material is treated with Borax to prevent insects and fungi growth, which is not harmful for humans but for animals on a large doses.

Mineral wool (Homelogic-:solutions for better homes, 2019) can be recycled and comes from a natural resource that is ready available (it does not require manufacturing). However, it is extremely energy-intensive to produce and has high embodied energy (production emissions include carbon monoxide, formaldehyde and phenol). The manufacturing process involves on-site fuel combustion and it is not biodegradable. The quarrying of material can result in land-degradation.

Cellulose fiber (ISOCELL, 2022) requires much less energy to be processed than other raw materials. (it amounts to only 30% of glass wool and only 15% of polystyrene). It can be processed as a plant fertilizer (if the trees grow again the cycle closes). Most boards are completely recyclable and no scrap is produced during manufacturing, thus it helps to reduce waste

3) Non- acoustic properties of the materials relevant to their use as acoustic absorbers

Sheep wool insulation is safe (Sheep whool insulation, s.f.): it does not require protective clothing or special breathing apparatus to stall it, as it does not cause irritation to the eyes, skin or lungs (wool fibers are not harmful) In terms of fire performance, it has higher fire resistance than cellulose and cellular plastic insulation. It does not burn (wool has a very high inflammation point of 560 ºC due to its nitrogen content) and extinguishes itself (because of its high Limiting Oxygen Index LOI 25.2) which means to completely burn wool an oxygen content of 25.2% is necessary whereas air only has 21%). Wool fiber is hygroscopic by nature (it can absorb up to 35% of their own weight from the surroundings, helping to preserve surrounding timbers. While absorbing this moisture it releases heat thus raising the temperature around (in warmer seasons, wool creates a cooling effect). Sheep wool insulation does not settle due to the high elasticity of the wool fibers ensuring no loss of performance over time. As a thermal insulator it as a heat conductivity of U. 0.039 W/m ºC)

Mineral wool has a very good thermal performance as it holds warm air within the air pockets (stone wool U=0.32-0046 W/m ºC, fiberglass wool (U:0.038-0.046 W/m ºC) (Rockwool, 2022). In terms of fire resistance, it is non-combustible (it can withstand temperatures of up to 1000 ºC). it is safe for health if installed in buildings according to the tests carried out by the WHO. Mineral wool is one of the cheapest types of insulation, and it is rarely affected by rodents.

Cellulose fiber is a good thermal insulator with a particularly low heat conductivity (U:0.0038 W/m K) (ISOCELL, 2022). It exists as an insulator since 30 years, and so far there is no evidence that the cellulose insulation is altered by ageing. It has a moisture-regulating effect being water vapour permeable and transporting moisture in the fiber (cellulose has a capillary conductivity which means it absorbs any moisture that forms and thus it avoids diffusion). Cellulose performs better than other traditional insulators on a passive role: it increases air tightness by 74% (compared to 41%) regardless of material density

4) Limitations of the alternative materials and further research to improve their quality and suitability

Sheep wool has a limited stock, as it is available once per year. Logistics and availability increase the cost of the insulation, if compared with other available materials. Also cleaning and preparing the sheep wool involves harsh chemicals to disinfect the material which can leave organophosphates behind the wool that are proven to cause neuropsychological health issues.

Mineral wool is irritating to the skin and lungs if breathed in (tiny fibers are made from glass and stone which can be embedded in the skin), hence gloves and mask are necessary for installation. In terms of effectiveness, mineral wool insulation will start to compress and fall as it ages: air gaps, especially when laid into a ceiling or vertical wall, reduce the performance. If mineral wool becomes wet des not dry easily and need to be replaced. Mineral wool can create condensation, as it holds warm air that cools rapidly and causes condensation.

Cellulose fiber is processed with a few chemicals that are fire retardants and carcinogens (boric acid) Ammonium sulfate can decompose over time from moisture and heat releasing sulfuric acid that is corrosive. After a point, cellulose fiber loses fire retardant abilities and become a combustion hazard since its original material is highly combustible (quite unstable insulator material)

As a conclusion of the comparison above it could be generalized that most of the natural materials are suitable as an alternative to traditionally used commercial products because of their low toxicity, sustainability, and renewability. They are harmless and biodegradable, however there exist many negative inputs to take into account that make the eco-material not suitable nor possible to choose, such as availability and cost. Synthetic materials have a higher environmental impact than natural fibers due to higher energy consumption, however and as described above, careful analysis should be carried out under comparison as often synthetic materials have less of an impact than those derived from natural resources

Table 2. Summary of acoustic performance assessment of sustainable building materials. Performance comparison for mineral wool, sheep wool and cellulose fiber

	ACOUSTIC PERFORMANCE	SUSTAINABILITY	NON-ACOUSTIC PROPERTIES	LIMITATIONS
MINERAL WOOL	Good (as a porous absorber)	Can be recycled High energy demand Embodied carbon Not biodegradable Land degradation	Thermal insulator Fire resistance Safe for health Low cost	Skin irritation-health hazards Performance reduced Can create condensation
SHEEPS WOOL	Good (as a porous absorber)	Renewable source Low energy required Chemicals for protection	Does not require protective clothing Fire resistance Hygroscopic Keeps performance Thermal insulator	Limited stock High cost Chemicals to disinfect
CELLULOSE FIBER	Good (as a porous absorber)	Low energy demand Recyclable Reduces waste	Thermal insulator Moisture regulator Improves air tightness	Chemicals Fire resistance reduced Unstable material

Does acoustic performance need to be prioritized when compared with other building requirements? This depends on many aspects and on space typology. We are never able to respond to all queries in a project due to economic reasons or timeframes. The same way we cannot respond to all needs, we could prioritize and combine solutions to deliver the best possible design when following space function. Basic principles of acoustics can be applied to all interior spaces, however a particular function of a space require a specific aural environment. When an appropriate design follows function acoustics enhance the purpose and improves comfort and wellbeing. (Bosnyak y otros)

In learning environments where students and teachers interact, the ability to hear, understand and be able to focus is critical for the learning process. Acoustics should be prioritized as it is crucial to fulfill the need for what the space was designed for. Mid and high frequencies (speech) are the specific range to solve in this case, which is relatively easy to undertake with porous absorption evenly distributed in the room. There are many sustainable options to fulfill this requirement at present.

In healthcare projects and food preparation areas, acoustics is also important to provide stress reduction. Needs usually come before regulations which could be a problem due to other related issues: materials need to be easy to clean with high-pressure washing and disinfectants and they don't have to have porosity as it accumulates dirt (being also fire retardant). In hospital environments the cleanability is always prioritized, hence acoustics is sometimes lost in specifications (depending on country and its regulations). In restaurants, cleanability is more important in food preparation areas where acoustics can be avoided for marketing purposes (despite noise exposure problems to staff), which don't have an impact on business.

In Sport facilities, acoustics is not crucial to carry out the activities, however the environment and comfort improves enormously when acoustic treatment is in place. In this case materials need to withstand high temperatures or moisture, as well as impacts (balls, sport tools, players, objects impacting against walls or ceilings)

IMPACT OF SUSTAINABLE ACOUSTIC MATERIALS WHEN CREATING HEALTHY AND COMFORTABLE SPACES

Investment in sustainability is translated in better conditions for the user in terms of health, comfort and aesthetics. The selection of a particular material leads to assess the balance between impacts and benefits across its Life Cycle Assessment, including both acoustics and cost. The Impact that applying sustainable acoustic materials has for a particular space function and typology can be measured, defined and quantified when creating healthy and comfortable spaces for a better acoustic comfort and wellbeing.

Moving forward more sustainable practices some companies are looking at green building standards or rating systems such as BREEAM, LEED or WELL. In contrast to the rest of certifications which primarily focus on environmental impact, the WELL building standard certification is the world's first building standard to focus on enhancing people's health and wellbeing through the built environment (focusing on the occupants of a building). It includes a set of strategies that aim to support human health and wellness through design interventions and operational policies. According to this certification (International WELL Building Institute, 2022)" the acoustical comfort of a space can be quantified by the overall level of satisfaction of an occupant in a given environment". These guidelines establish a criteria to achieve comfortable spaces, through fortification of façade elements to reduces noise ingress, replacing areas of hard surfaces with porous absorption to improve privacy etc. In combination with the WELL Materials concept that aims to reduce human exposure to chemicals that may impact health during the construction, remodeling, furnishing and operation of buildings requirements, this certification facilitates the way to quantify and control unwanted effects of uninformed design decisions.

Depending on the activities, sustainable construction becomes crucial as a solution to address problems derived from space function:

In learning environments acoustics is critical for the learning process. Classrooms with poor acoustics affects negatively the ability of the students to comprehend the speech, read, concentrate and behave appropriately, which is intensified for foreigners and students with hearing impairments (Astolfi y otros, 2019). Teachers also suffer vocal damage from lack of acoustic treatments, as they tend to talk over classroom noise. Long term noise exposure can also cause hearing damage and consequences from prolonged stress. On the contrary successful acoustics help student engagement and improve learning outcomes. In one study student behavior improved by 17%, in another study teacher absence decreased from 15% to 2% post treatment. Sustainable applications for learning centers are key as a solution, especially for "eco-schools" where learning involve recycling and re-using, having to address immediate refurbishments to reduce energy demands on old buildings.

In healthcare projects the main goal for a successful design is to provide an environment suitable for recovery, sleep and healing. According to (DH, 2013) *"Good acoustic conditions improve patient privacy and dignity, and promote essential sleep patterns. Such conditions are key to healing. Good acoustic design brings other benefits in terms of patient and staff comfort and morale, as well as improved efficiency and usability of equipment"* The ability to relax and recuperate are just as important as speech confidentiality and to have an appropriate work environment for doctors, nurses and other staff members. In a hospital noise include footsteps in the corridor, conversations, banging doors and beeping medical equipment. Research carried out demonstrate that more than annoyance, noise causes sleep disturbance, elevated blood pressure, increased heart and respiration rate, higher medication needs post-surgery and negative impacts on wound healing. Conversely, good acoustics has improved satisfaction on a hospital care: incidences of re-hospitalization decreased and other positive impacts appeared. Applying sustainable construction techniques or, for instance, introducing biophilic design complying the requirement WELL M02.1, better acoustics and wellbeing can be addressed introducing greenery in the room, sounds, or reducing reverberation through patterns, and shapes.

Besides Psychoacoustics, the branch of acoustics that involve how humans perceive sounds, further research has been done to measure this impact has in terms of health (i.e Lack of productivity, stress and worse mental well-being can be consequences of inappropriate and uninformed design decisions. The WHO defines health as a "state of complete physical, mental and social well-being and not merely the absence of disease or infirmity" The WHO Environmental Noise Guidelines for the European Region (Europe, 2018) provide criteria to protect human health from harmful exposure to environmental noise, coming from five relevant noise sources: road traffic noise, railway noise, aircraft noise, wind turbine noise and leisure noise. These guidelines are public health-oriented recommendations, based on scientific reports that put in relationship health effects and noise levels, and are carried out to serve as a basis for policy-making processes. They study the effectiveness of interventions in reducing noise exposure at health, being underpinned by eight systematic reviews based on several health outcomes:

Table 3. Health outcomes as a consequence of noise levels defined by The WHO Environmental Noise Guidelines for the European Region

Cardiovascular and metabolic effects	Hearing impairment and tinnitus
Annoyance	Adverse birth outcomes
Effects on sleep	Quality of life
Cognitive impairment	Mental health and well-being

The architectural response to adverse effect of environmental noise results in improving sound insulation and on the building envelope and also inside to protect functionalities. Room acoustics plays a key role on improving acoustic comfort conditions once the noise has entered inside the building. As described above, architectural trends need to adapt to new materials and socio-economic conditions in order to give a holistic response to comfort. Road traffic noise will decrease with electric vehicles, and building installations will become more silent along time. New comfort zones and holistic passive strategies will have to take into account modified sources of noise and how they propagate through the new building designs.

Research has been carried out for a better understanding of the specific impact that green building creates on individuals (Zitars y otros, 2021). In order to promote health, wellbeing and productivity, there must be a relationship between green building features and its occupants. In terms of acoustics, protection against elements such as surrounding sounds is important for psychological security and privacy (protection from overstimulation): the fact of including private rooms in open plan arrangements has a positive impact on occupants. Increasing social contact in a building is found to be positive for the users, however acoustic comfort plays a crucial role on how this should be carried out: private meeting rooms, proximity to coworkers, small workstations are multiple possibilities on how to address design options by, for instance, giving the user the option to regulate their own social contact. Communicating with others is necessary for an individual to conduct their work, which involves interaction, meeting and sharing. This sometimes affects negatively mental activities for individuals that require concentration and focusing. Also the fact of promoting biophilic design has a positive impact on health and affecting acoustic perception (living walls reduce reverberation in a room).

SUSTAINABLE DESIGN INTENTIONALITY VS PRACTICAL APPLICATION

Ideal architectural comfort environments are the result of a combination of aesthetics, costs, function and material performance. Concept design starts at considering space perception goals, site implications, orientation, climate…designer's responsibility at costs, health issues, comfort, etc begin from stage 0 of the design process.

Prioritizing sustainability in the first line of design intentionality should be taken into account when delivering projects in cost, purposes and time. Rather than focusing only on generating profit (financial performance), companies should commit to the called "Triple Bottom Line" This is a business concept where firms address also a social and environmental impact (Miller, 2022)

Table 4. Components of the Triple Bottom Line where firms should commit to a social and environmental positive impact

1	Profit- Profits are maximized for shareholders while reducing costs and minimizing risks, but it has been proved that adopting sustainable initiatives has lead also to a business success.
2	People- Every business has a social impact. By embracing sustainability, every business can impact positively their related stakeholders (costumers, employees etc). Many organizations have created a partnership with a non-profit organization to share a common- sustainable goal, to drive a social change.
3	Planet- Business are the main contributors of climate change, hence they are responsible to drive a positive change on reducing carbon footprint (streamline transportation, reducing energy consumption or use ethically sourced materials)

A Carbon Majors Database shows than 100 companies are responsible of one trillion tonnes of greenhouse gas emissions, over 70% of emissions since 1988 (Griffin, July 2017) Carbon dioxide and methane emissions deriving from fossil fuel producers have contributed to the global warming by being emitted mostly by 25 corporate and state producers in 28 years as in the 237 years since industrial revolution. These "Carbon majors" along with investors need to take urgent climate action in order to reduce carbon emissions. Many oil and gas majors are already developing scenarios to take a new role on the incoming energy system.

Most often the designer's intention in terms of sustainability gets cut off by budget, unless legislation requires to achieve a particular design criteria, or unless the client gets a Return On Sustainability Investment (ROSI) (Atz y otros, 2022) According to a study carried out on *How to quantify sustainability's impact on the bottom line on a case study with Brazil's beef industry* (Whelan y otros, 2017) embedded sustainability improve financial performance through mediating factors such as innovation, operational efficiency, risk reduction, customer and supplier loyalty etc. Applying that five step methodology that quantifies sustainable actions from an economical point of view, the conclusion was that "sustainable agriculture practices create financial opportunity for all value chain actors" Hence the study concluded that the described methodology (ROSI) there is a positive financial return. This can be adapted for any industry by analyzing the drivers of improved performance, identifying key benefits and quantifying the benefits in financial terms. In summary, financial improvements could be quantified being a powerful tool with business decision makers.

However during the design stage the question is, what are the real opportunities for a designer to carry out sustainable solutions if they are not the most cost-effective ones? Architects are the main responsible of delivering a holistic sustainable design despite client objections. Considering actions that designers are taking in practice to do so (Architectural Association School of Architecture Public Programme, 2022) we could describe some successful approaches (see table5)

Table 5. Actions and successful approaches to be considered by architects for design purposes

1	Selecting the right team: if the entire design team focus on decisions on a particular direction, the proposal will be supported by a majority and hence will be pushed to a success (Collaborative design has always a positive impact)
2	Embedding sustainability and performance into design, will convert the sustainable outcomes on a necessity.
3	Communicating complex concepts clearly will enhance the need of a sustainable option on a long-term basis (e.g thermal losses if there is not enough insulation nor appropriate passive construction details within the building envelope)
4	Deciding performance requirements internally, will set a technical and professional criteria for a proposal at a particular site, which should not be questioned externally
5	Despite economic reasons, other variables to consider exist on the design process that could drive to a more sustainable option (e.g a retrofit instead of a new build)
6	Considering cost, we should also consider execution time as a strong argument (most of timber structures are installed on a shorter time if compared with steel and concrete)
7	Persuading developers with sustainable outcomes can become a challenge, but it will bring better results on a mid and long-term basis.

CONCLUSION

In summary, the use of environmentally-friendly acoustic materials in architecture, as well as the rest of the aspects that combined define a sustainable practice, contribute to a better livability and wellbeing. Human health and wellbeing is a consequence of a designer's intention as a first instance, where acoustics plays an important role. A performance assessment of acoustic materials is key for a correct selection of building materials for a holistic approach to design brief.

Circularity of resources is hence needed in order to reduce the environmental impact of production systems and consumption patterns. Designers at this point need to focus on prioritizing climate concerns, making a constant effort in defending the benefits of long-terms results in construction. When an appropriate design follows function acoustics enhance the purpose and improves comfort and wellbeing.

Depending on the activities, sustainable construction becomes crucial as a solution to address problems derived from space function. Space versatility and multifunctionality lead to an intelligent architecture which adapts to conditions at every moment. New comfort zones and holistic passive strategies will have to take into account modified sources of noise and how they propagate through the new building designs.

REFERENCES

Adams, T. (2016). *Sound Materials: a compendium of Sound Absorbing Materials for Architecture and Design*. Frame Publishers.

Architectural Association School of Architecture Public Programme. (2022). AA School. https://www.aaschool.ac.uk/publicprogramme/whatson/so-farpractice-in-times-of-climate-crisis

Astolfi, A., Puglisi, G., Murgia, S., Minelli, G., Pellerey, F., Prato, A., & Sacco, T. (2019). Influence of Classroom Acoustics on Noise Disturbance and Well-Being for First Graders. *Frontier in psychology*. doi:10.3389/fpsyg.2019.02736

Atz, U., Van Holt, T., & Douglas & Tensie, E. (2022). The Return on Sustainability Investment (ROSI): Monetizing Financial Benefits of Sustainability Actions in Companies. In *Sustainable Consumption and Production Volume II -Circular economy and beyond* (pp 303–354). Ranjula Bali Swain, Susanne Sweet.

Banton, C., Potters, C., & Kvilhaug, S. (2022, 09 13). *Investopedia*. (D. Meredith, Editor) Investiopedia. https://www.investopedia.com/terms/r/rawmaterials.asp

Bosnyak, D., Aziz Mahmoud, N., Wagenmann, T., Carballeira, A., & Gomez-Agustina, L. (n.d.). *The book of acoustics:vmaking people happy at work*. BAUX AB.

Brandstrom, J., & Saidani, M. (2022, October 15). Comparison between circularity metrics and LCA: A case study on circular economy strategies. *Journal of Cleaner Production*, *371*, 33537. doi:10.1016/j.jclepro.2022.133537

Corbusier, L. (2013 -18th edition). Œuvre complète - Les 5 points d'une architecture nouvelle. In W. B. Stonorov (Ed.). Birkhäuser. 1 doi:0.1515/97830356

del Rey, R., Uris, A., Alba Fernández, J., & Candelas, P. (2017). Characterization of Sheep Wool as a Sustainable Material for Acoustic Applications. *Materials (Basel)*, *10*(11), 1277. doi:10.3390/ma10111277 PMID:29112133

DH. (2013). *Health Technical Memorandum 08-01. Acoustics.* Department of Health and Social Care.

Ellen Macarthur Foundation. (n.d.). Circular economy introduction: https://ellenmacarthurfoundation.org/topics/circular-economy-introduction/overview

Europe, W. H. (2018). *Environmental noise guidelines for the European region*. WHO. https://www.who.int/europe/activities/providing-environmental-noise-guidelines-for-the-european-region

Fraval, S. E., van Middelaar, C. G., Ridoutt, B., & Opio, C. (2019). Life Cycle Assessment of Food Products. In Encyclopedia of food security and sustainability (Vol. 3, pp. 488-496). doi:10.1016/B978-0-08-100596-5.22221-X

Gonçalves de Lassio, J., & Naked Haddad, A. (2016). Life cycle assessment of building construction materials: Case study for a housing complex. *Revista de la Construcción*, *15*(2), 69–77. Advance online publication. doi:10.4067/S0718-915X2016000200007

Griffin, P. (July 2017). *The Carbon Majors Database CDP Carbon Majors report 2017*. CMD.

Heywood, H. (2015). *101 Rules of Thumb for Sustainable Buildings and Cities*. RIBA publishing. https://www.homelogic.co.uk/wool-insulation-pros-and-cons-the-great-debate

Horvath, G., A. (2006). Decision-support tool for assessing the environmental effects of constructing commercial buildings. *Journal of Architectural Engineering*.

Jackson, A., Humber, S., Idzikowski, I., & Kyle, T. (2021). Environmental Wellbeing: Engineering healthier spaces post Covid-19. *Plus journal-Foster and partners*.

Likos International. (n.d.). Likos International. https://www.liko-acoustics.com/en/acoustic-panels

Makron. (2022, 12 02). Recycled Cellulose Fiber Insulation Production brochure. https://makron.com/en/industries/industrial-circular-economy-solutions/recycled-cellulose-insulation-technology/

Miller, K. (2022, 09 28). *The triple bottom line: what it is & why it's important*. Harvard Buisness School Online https://online.hbs.edu/blog/post/what-is-the-triple-bottom-line

PRE-Sustainability. (n.d.). Life Cycle Assessment. https://pre-sustainability.com/articles/life-cycle-assessment-lca-basics/

Rockfon Grodan. (n.d.). Grodan 101. https://www.grodan101.com/about-grodan/

Sheep wool insulation. (n.d.). Sheep Wool. https://www.sheepwoolinsulation.com/

The intergovernmental Panel on Climate Change. (2022). IPCC. https://www.ipcc.ch/

United Nations Development Programme. (2023). UNDP. https://www.undp.org/

United Nations.Department of Economic and Social Affairs. (n.d.). Sustainable Development. https://sdgs.un.org/goals

Whelan, T., Zappa, B., Zeidan, R., & Fishbein, G. (2022). (2017, 10 13). *Harvard Business Review*. [from How to Quantify Sustainability's Impact on Your Bottom Line.]. *Retrieved*, *11*, 2.

Yang, T., Hu, L., Xiong, X., Petru, M., Tayyab Noman, M., Mishra, R., & Militký, J. (2020). Sound Absorption Properties of Natural Fibers. *Sustainability*, *12*(20), 8477. doi:10.3390u12208477

Zitars, J., Spadafore, B., Coulombe, S., Riemer, M., Dreyer, B., & Whitney, S. (2021). Understanding the psycho-environmental potential functions of a green building to promote employee health, wellbeing and productivity: A theoretical perspective. *Building and Environment, 205*, 108268. doi:10.1016/j.buildenv.2021.108268

KEY TERMS AND DEFINITIONS

Acoustic performance: This is the assessment that can be done for a material in terms of sound absorption and sound insulation, which are opposite properties. Some acoustic materials are the result of a combination that together form a composite which both blocks and absorb sound.

Circularity: This describes economic, technical, and environmental systems that aim to eliminate waste and maximise the reuse of resources. Circularity is mostly associated with material efficiency strategies, however little effort has been made to quantitatively assess the connection between circularity, material efficiency and environmental sustainability.

Commodity: This is a basic good used in commerce that is interchangeable with other goods of the same type. Commodities usually refers to a raw material used to manufacture finished goods.

A life cycle assessment (LCA): This is a systematic analysis of the potential environmental impacts of products or services during their entire life cycle. Even if it does not address social or economical aspects, it enables to bring on board all aspects of the construction process that are chained and affect each other on a symbiotic manner.

A life cycle inventory (LCI): This is a phase of an LCA that involves the compilation of data to quantify resource use and emissions for each process in the defined system. A life Cycle Inventory can be compiled in a spreadsheet, statistical package, dedicated LCA software and is often designed to allow for a sensitivity analysis to be carried out in the Life Cycle Impact Assessment (LCIA) stage (Fraval y otros, 2019)**Product:** This is the finished good, service or idea that can be offered in a market to satisfy customer needs.

Raw materials: These are the materials used in the manufacturing process of goods. They are being bought and sold on commodities exchanges worldwide.

Return On Sustainability Investment (ROSI): This is a methodology for guiding managers to better value sustainability's financial benefits. Ultimately, monetizing sustainability can lead to a competitive advantage and shared value for multiple stakeholders.

Sustainability: This is the balance between environment, equity and economy: a productive balance with nature. It is usually evaluated through independent rating systems (LEED, BREEAM, WELL…) which look at their Life Cycle Assessment (LCA) (from the extraction of raw materials to the end of their life as a product. The product content is analyzed in terms of their ability to be recycled, toxicity (paints, coatings and binders), energy used in the production process, distance to transport the material to the construction site sourcing of raw materials from sustainable sources, etc.

Sustainable design: This is the philosophy of design carried out to comply with the principles of sustainability and also aimed at improving the health and comfortability of occupants in a building. Sustainable design seeks to reduce negative impacts on the environment, the health and well-being of building occupants, thereby improving building performance. The basic objectives of sustainability are to reduce the consumption of non-renewable resources, minimize waste, and create healthy, productive environments.

Sustainable material: This is a material used throughout our consumer and industrial economy that can be produced in required volumes without depleting non-renewable resources and without disrupting the established steady-state equilibrium of the environment and key natural resource systems.

Triple Bottom Line: This is a business concept that posits firms should commit to measuring their social and environmental impact—in addition to their financial performance—rather than solely focusing on generating profit, or the standard "bottom line." It can be broken down into "three Ps": profit, people, and the planet.

Chapter 10
Sustainable Cities With Gamification:
How Gamification Can Help Improve Citizen Health and Reduce the Carbon Footprint

Vinod Anand Bijlani
https://orcid.org/0000-0003-3442-5077
Independent Researcher, Australia

ABSTRACT

This chapter talks about multi-dimensional sustainability by emphasizing the importance of people-participation through behavioral change and persuasive design via gamification technology to bring about a change for good. It describes the criticality of a sustainability performance information platform that brings together all the aspects of a sustainable cities, social, economic, and environmental qualities through intelligent management and operations. This chapter is an attempt for a framework that will lead to greater collaborative efforts towards more intelligent, sustainable cities with improved citizen health.

INTRODUCTION

The world is going green. Everyone, from governments and industries to commercial public enterprises and private businesses, are proceeding with purpose, looking to Smart sustainable infrastructure to pay off big and champion the environment. A lot of thinking has been going into protecting the planet and safeguarding against worsening climate change.

However, what we need to remember is that the plans of today are as transient as our surroundings. The world is evolving as fast as the technology that is driving it. The infrastructural design that works today to near-perfection may only become a burden to bear tomorrow. Consider reputed architect Norman Foster's design for Apple Inc's headquarters in Cupertino, California (Technacy Solutions, 2017). The eight-year project with a glassy open-to-nature façade features a massive underground carpark that can

DOI: 10.4018/978-1-6684-6924-8.ch010

hold 11,000 vehicles – an impressive amenity that may soon seem defunct with changing trends towards green transportation infrastructure. What this and similar examples point to is the fact that the future of urban design needs to be flexible. Flexible designs not only save long-term operational costs, they can also be altered to match dynamic changes in occupancy, energy consumption patterns, and infrastructural trends. Foster believes that the best designs are those that can be adapted to the way humans and society change (Stinson, 2017) to make spaces more livable.

Workspaces and commercial buildings are not just about work or business. They are about lifestyles and living. They are a confluence of the people who occupy them, making it all the more necessary to plan energy conservation and sustainability around occupants. Businesses and large corporations housed in commercial buildings are looking for a new genetic code (Keller, 2015) that will help them survive and thrive in a state of permanent disruption. Interestingly, organization-led purpose may be able to redefine sustainability values at a business level. However, for a marked change that is both effective and sustainable, the purpose has to be defined at an individual level.

Studies show occupant behavior in buildings to be among the top influencers of energy-specific building performance (EEA, 2013), along with building maintenance, operations, equipment, and indoor environment. With building occupants spending more than 90% (BPIE, 2011) of their time indoors, and employees clocking more than a third (McCormick, 2018) of their waking time at work, occupants' expectations and behaviors can influence energy consumption patterns significantly.

Individual occupants of Smart commercial buildings, driven both by purpose and their responsibility towards the planet, must be motivated to stay on the sustainability course. Energy savings may be the chief driver in Smart sustainable buildings, what with building operations contributing to 37% (UNEP, 2021) of global greenhouse gas emissions and 55% (UNEP, 2020) of electricity consumption. Incidentally, going by the current global energy consumption trends, energy consumption from buildings is expected to rise 32% (US EIA, 2017) by 2040. In fact, extant research also reveals that energy consumption can go 40% above expected levels (Yu et al., 2011) if occupants demonstrate inefficient usage behavior. This is because buildings do not use energy; occupants do (Janda, 2011). Evidently, modelling occupant behavior in buildings is critical to achieving a significant reduction in energy usage while also persuasively engaging in long-term behavioral change. Therefore, it is cross-scale behavioral change among occupants that can set the high energy consumption drive on reverse gear.

Rules and regulations may guide the behavior of people in commercial buildings, but it is both external stimulus and inherent motivation that stem from social, health, and cost benefits (NSF, n.d.) that undergird long-term change. A strong motivational push comes from game mechanics and gamification. Gamification led by the internet of things (IoT) and artificial intelligence (AI) can literally be the game changer for the climate concerns of the century. Prodding building occupants to transition from their old habits to cultivate environmentally-responsible behavior, gamification can play a largely significant role in transforming planetary health.

THEORY AND LITERATURE REVIEW

Climate change that is anthropogenic is a stinging reality. There are studies and reports (Jachimowicz et al., 2018; Proestakis et al., 2018; Yokum et al., 2018) that establish that governmental interventions and imposed legislations alone cannot achieve as much by themselves as sustainable behavioral changes can.

Scholars propose structural and non-structural approaches (Chui & Wai, 2017) to curb high energy consumption. The structural approach spotlights the use of technology and associated tools, while the non-structural model focuses on behavioral change. While the structural approach is what several Smart sustainable buildings have been embracing, the non-structural approach is also finding its footing in both commercial and community built-spaces. Research since the beginning of the millennium (Wai, 2009; Abrahamse et al., 2005; Ting et al., 2011; Kok et al., 2011; Ouyang et al., 2009; Herring, 2006) has supported the non-structural approach, with evidence that high energy consumption concerns are anthropogenic and can be brought under check through behavioral change.

But then, bringing about a marked and lasting change in behavior is not easy, especially as occupants of commercial buildings are adults with well-formed opinions and beliefs. Markman (2018) points out that despite humans being inherently motivated to avoid threats, they are not so driven when it comes to acting on climate change and energy conservation. There are several theories that support Markman's reasoning, which explain the challenges of urging individuals to more climate-responsible behavior.

One theory is that of temporal discounting (Loewenstein & Prelec, 1992) where long-term benefits are undervalued compared to the more immediate returns. Individuals do not want to make changes to their mode of commute, the products they buy, or the appliances they use, because the impact on carbon emission is not immediately evident (Markman, 2018). Besides the slow returns from climate conscious actions, the fact that high carbon emissions and energy consumption are a nonlinear problem fuel the challenge further. Individuals are better at linear judgements (DeLosh et al., 1997) which show immediate cause and effect. It has taken decades for the impact of irresponsible energy usage and environmental disregard to snowball into the climate crisis that we are dealing with today. The consequences from unobvious threats that build up over time are difficult for people to extrapolate from.

Further, studies about the construal level theory (Trope & Liberman, 2010) show that concepts that are psychologically or proximally distant are usually construed abstract, little motivating individuals to act on them with force or determination. This could include natural disasters that have occurred in another country or the impact of carbon emissions that seems a distant truth. Besides, the behavioral tendency to discount an uncertain future (Gollier, 2002) is another reason several climate change skeptics believe that the bruhaha about planetary health, sustainability, and livability is neither dire nor certain. This is seen in what is commonly known as the shifting baseline syndrome. The syndrome has been explained as "the persistent downgrading of perceived 'normal' environmental conditions with every sequential generation, leading to under-estimation of the true magnitude of long-term environmental change on a global scale" (Jones et al., 2020). The condition makes believers feel that the climate change debate is a far-fetched truth.

With multiple individual behavioral theories at play, the challenge on hand could be larger than envisaged. Jachimowicz et al. (2018) argue that most behavioral interventions, such as informing people about the environmental impact of their behavior, are futile. Traditional policy approaches pursue energy efficiency using economic incentives, information dispersal, or mandated regulations. Economic incentives could be pricing based on duration of energy use or subsidies on energy efficient usage. Information dispersal could include energy efficiency labelling or distributing flyers on efficient energy consumption. Mandated regulations are those that set minimum energy performance standards. And yet, traditional approaches fall short due to the complex mechanisms that affect the way individuals interpret and act on the information available to them. Behavioral economics applies psychological insights to comprehend how people make real-life decision and act on information. Accordingly, scholars (Kahneman, 2012; Dolan et al., 2012) have been able to identify strategies to counter sub-optimal decision making.

Research shows that an alternative approach of showing individuals what others around them do can help. Labelled 'descriptive norms' (Jachimowicz et al., 2018), they vary from traditional approaches, and can prove effective in various contexts of energy conservation. These alternative behavioral policy interventions (IEA, n.d.), which are policy impositions that encourage behavioral changes, can contribute significantly by exploiting several behavioral levers in tandem. These levers could be energy-saving competitions, games, social comparisons of energy utility levels, achievable milestones, targets, instantaneous feedback, and incentives. The main idea behind such an approach is to make use of the building blocks of games (Werbach & Hunter, 2012) and game mechanics, and implement them in a variety of innovative, non-gaming contexts (Zichermann & Linder, 2013).

Gamification has been defined as the use of game design elements within non-game contexts (Deterding et al., 2011a). It is a blanket term that includes employing gaming elements to engage and motivate people through behavioral change interventions using Smart technology, such as smartphones and mobile devices (Deterding et al., 2011b) supported by IoT, AI, and data analytics. While gamification as a concept has been studied in several scenarios, little scholarly attention had been paid to its motivational and engagement components linked to behavioral change, until recently (Harris, 2019). Figure 1 lists the characteristics of game mechanics for behavioral change.

When gamification is applied to group and personal interactions, studies show that it encourages the intrinsic human need for competition through comparison, resulting in engaging participants in either competitive or collaborative challenges (Bamidis et al., 2016). These could be steps walked as a team or as an individual at the workplace, mode of transport for the commute to and from work, or an augmented reality (AR) experience to elicit an expected target response. When used most effectively, in almost idealistic settings, the line that sets a gamified experience apart from an actual game may even be 'academic' (Behavior Institute, n.d.).

Gamification can be a powerful transformation tool (Dulskaia et al., 2017). It not only provides an explanation of the change, it supports it, forms habits and drives engagement (Gartner, 2012). The competition element of gamification incentivizes individual participants to act towards the final goal, while group dynamics in a larger setting has a significant impact on the dynamics of the competition itself, determined by factors such as pre-competition activity levels, past experience of participants in such settings, chances of winning, and group constitution, among others (Shameli et al., 2017).

A review of extant literature (Looyestyn et al., 2017; Sailer et al., 2017; Burguillo, 2010) reveals that the design elements make a difference to its success, with leaderboards proving more effective than badges, ranks, points, and rewards. The scholars also establish that leaderboards and badges have a positive impact on satisfaction from competence needs and task meaningfulness perceptions. The competition from leaderboards contribute to the social pressure that is required to enhance player engagement, resulting in a positive and constructive effect on participation (Burguillo), learning, and action. They state that meaningful stories in the games, avatars, and teammates have a significant relation to experiences of social relatedness (Sailer et al.).

Game mechanics can be used towards fulfilling environmental protection goals (Gustafsson et al., 2009), fostering behavioral change that is target-oriented, goal-directed, and continual (Schunk et al., 2014). In the specific context of energy conservation, gamification can promote and motivate energy conservation behavior in a fun and engaging way (Chui & Wai, 2017). In turn, this also results in heightened awareness about energy issues and the importance of carbon control. With the main goal of

Figure 1. Characteristics of game mechanics for behavioral change
Image by the author

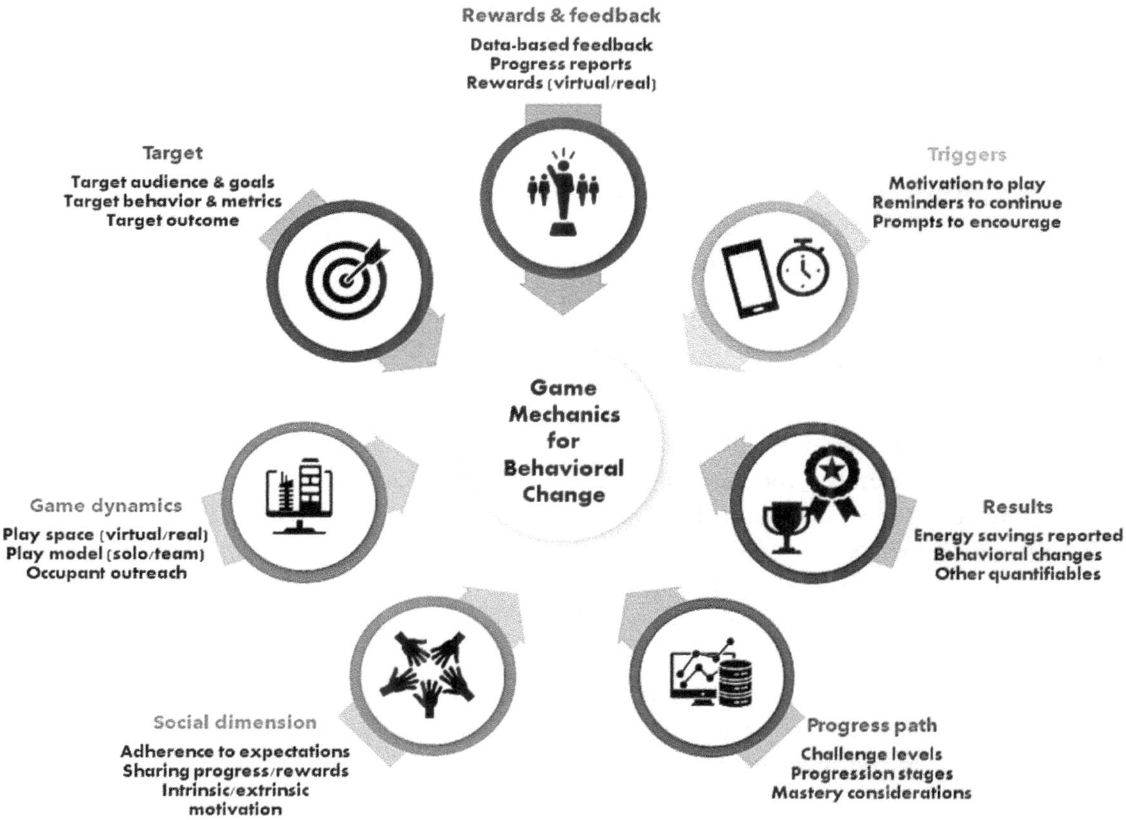

using gamification in commercial spaces being enhancing employee motivation to obtain the targeted behavior, the combination of the task and game engagement can make occupants excited (McCormick, 2013; Wu, 2018) about achieving the final outcome. Several gamification apps under development that foster environment-friendly behavior pit participants' performance against one another or between teams (Johnston, 2019), helping track and compare energy conservation performance, and inspiring competitive spirit.

Gamification and game-based business strategies towards sustainable goals have made their way into the energy and carbon market. Achieving meaningful, planetary goals through well-conceived serious games has seen an upturn in the last few years. Gartner's (2014) prediction from more than a decade ago about gamification having tremendous potential to digitally motivate people while overcoming the barriers of scale, time, cost, and connectivity is finally unravelling itself globally across industries, owing to the sustainability revolution to creating more livable spaces. In the rest of this chapter, we will look at how gamification can be implemented in commercial and public Smart buildings to bring down the carbon and environmental footprint through energy-conscious behavioral changes. The chapter will also provide real-world implementations and examples of sustainability-focused gamification for more livable spaces.

BEHAVIORAL CHANGE TOWARDS ENERGY-SAVING USING GAMIFICATION

Large businesses are housed in huge urban towers, and realize they are not only the prime influencers of environmental, social, and governance (ESG) objectives but also the leading contributors to environmental disarray. Additionally, the livability of their cities, their people, and the communities around them are a significant aspect of concern. The responsibility that large commercial buildings have towards the environment not only through creating a green image (Alam & Islam, 2021) but also contributing to the net zero cause has seen much research and study in the last couple of decades.

Industries are in dire straits with their carbon emissions skyrocketing. Chasing ESG targets and incorporating the United Nations' Sustainable Development Goals (UN SDGs) into their green strategies often comes to naught if they are not backed by employee engagement in their business policies.

Why Individual Social Responsibility Matters

A fifth of the enterprises across the globe have pledged their commitment to net zero targets (Martella, 2022) to reduce their overall carbon emissions and their reliance on fossil fuels for energy generation. More and more commercial and public building owners are embracing sustainability as a requisite part of their built environment and operations to promote more livable conditions in the cities they owe their businesses and existence to. While this may be a critical part of their corporate social responsibility, sustainability and climate-consciousness are as much individual social responsibility as they are corporate and governmental.

Insufficient building performance, impractical expectations of occupant behavior, lack of incentives to conform to targets and design assumptions can lead to incongruity in the intended objective and real usage of the intelligent and sustainable building (Gill et al, 2010; Silva & Ghisi, 2014), often rendering the sustainable design efforts futile. Game mechanics and gamification, which come with rewards and incentivization, form the prime motivator (Donato & Link, 2013) in an organization's sustainability strategies for individual engagement and behavioral change (Pasini et al., 2017). Additionally, precise mensuration of occupant impact on the built environment, along with the contribution of each occupant in energy savings, can help create a more sustainable building (Ferreira et al., 2018).

A green culture adopted at an individual level can go a longer way to creating a greener living space as individuals are extensions of the society and communities that they live in. Green habits and energy-conscious behavior adopted in commercial buildings as part of their workplace requirements can then be relayed to their living and community spaces as well. The environment-related attitudinal aspects, norms, and values that the individual occupants cultivate can then bring about a noticeable improvement in sustainability-driven inventiveness (Ogiemwonyi et al., 2020) in all areas of their lives.

Intelligent Energy Management and Gamification in Buildings

Commercial buildings have been shown to have greater challenges in maintaining lower energy consumption levels. This is primarily attributed to the lack of occupant motivation and individual responsibility (Papaioannou et al., 2017). Research conducted on game mechanics and gamification approaches in over 70 case studies in commercial buildings and workspaces have shown positive results in energy conservation, with between 6% and 10% savings in narrow- to large-participant sustainability programs (Grossberg et al., 2015). However, this is possible through continual and instantaneous, real-time monitoring of energy consumption. The measurement of energy usage must be correlational, in that it must measure the consumption by both occupants as well as building operations, in order to help with savings in operational costs and bring down carbon emissions (Wilson, 2016).

Enterprise Energy Management System

Research (EDF, 2019) shows data analytics in Smart buildings to have the greatest potential impact on sustainability – 35%. In a Smart building, it is the Enterprise Energy Management System (EEMS) that secures data for predictive and preventive analytics. The EEMS goes through constant data monitoring and measuring sequences, deriving inputs from already-installed IoT sensors and devices that serve as energy trackers. These could be near-field communication (NFC), Bluetooth low energy (BLE), indoor and outdoor sensors, computer vision and intelligent video analytics (IVA), and other devices already installed within the Smart building. Building occupants are connected to each other and to the IoT gateway through these devices, and through their smartphones and wearables. These devices either track occupant actions or record them based on occupant inputs, sending this data to the backend engines, including the occupancy calculator and the energy analyzer.

In short, the EEMS comprises the entire gamut of data-collection devices and an AI-based system. The devices and the AI system gather, examine, and display information and analytics on building energy consumption patterns (Motegi et al., 2020) on a single dashboard. This allows for quicker diagnostics and faster data integration and disaggregation from a centralized platform. Based on this analysis, the EEMS intelligently identifies opportunities to increase the energy efficiency of the built environment through optimally suited measures.

The EEMS integrates with the Building Management System (BMS), which is the energy control center of the building. The BMS monitors and controls the structure's energy requirements and operational elements, by gathering operational data from the environment. It uses this data to gauge lighting usage, water consumption, waste accumulation, temperature fluctuations, humidity variations, ventilation conditions, among others. Figure 2 depicts the framework for an intelligent sustainability performance measurement platform in a commercial Smart building.

IoT-Enabled Gamification

Interestingly, gamification that is supported by IoT results in more interactive, and at times immersive, experiences, higher participation rates, greater engagement among occupants and participants. IoT-enabled gamification ensures deeper and quicker analysis of sensory inputs, while also showing a more dynamic outcome. Rather than deploying pure gamification, the hybrid and converged model of IoT with gamification harnesses the strategy of game mechanics and the context-awareness of IoT devices to create a more effective amalgamation towards motivating behavioral change (Xiao et al., 2021). Participants demonstrate longer engagement, motivated from multisensory feedback and game-related enjoyment.

Characterized by the game elements of social collaboration, comparisons, competition, feedback, and inventiveness, IoT-enabled gamification also provides for more effective rewards for energy-saving actions as data collection affords greater accuracy in recording behavioral motivation. Simple mobile apps that engage occupants through various activities (Oppong-Tawiah et al., 2020) can also translate into clearly observable results when the set objectives are achieved through accurately measured outcomes.

Figure 2. Representative framework for an intelligent sustainability performance measurement platform in a commercial Smart building
Image by the author.

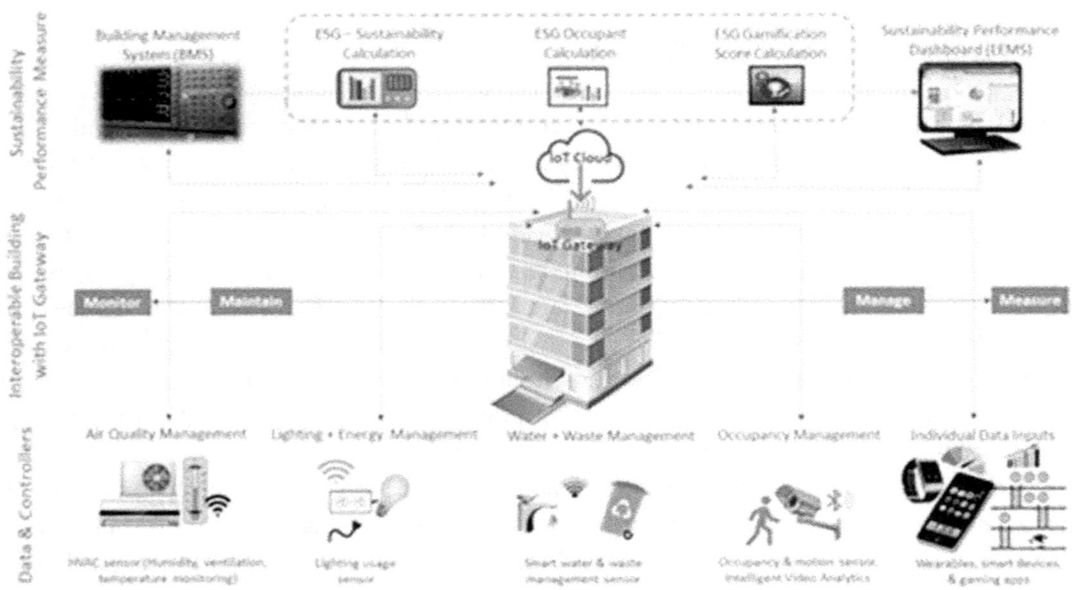

Super-app Ecosystem to Motivate Behavioral Change

An IoT-enabled gamification platform in a commercial built-environment can incorporate an ESG super-app system. The super-app ecosystem can consist of multiple micro-apps that integrate into a single user interface. Each micro-app records and monitors a singular aspect of sustainable behavior within or outside the building. These could be electricity, water or waste management, lighting, mode of commute to work, steps walked, etc. The game logic behind each micro-app is incorporated into the ESG super-app, with the micro tasks accomplished and scores secured being written back to the super-app. They allow participants' in-game behaviors to be continually measured (Sailer et al., 2013) so they receive immediate feedback as a reward or penalty. Figure 3 represents a super-app ecosystem that can be used in a commercial built-environment.

When the target behavior based on the micro tasks is achieved, participants are awarded points, badges, ranks, and rewards. These could be experience points, redeemable points, or reputation points. Badges could depend on points earned (Werbach & Hunter, 2012), and also serve as virtual reputation symbols, putting peers or team members under friendly competitive pressure to work harder (Antin & Churchill, 2011). Leaderboards are a consolidation of the points and badges, ranking participants based on their overall performance, measuring them against the benchmarked criteria (Costa et al., 2013), making them indicators of progress both with regard to individual performance and comparable performance. The super-app provides the leaderboard with the winning trends by communicating with the micro-aps via API (Pereira, 2019). While team members can promote cooperation and collaboration when there is a shared objective (Kapp, 2012), team-based game mechanics also help foster quicker learning and reinforcement.

Figure 3. Example of a super-app ecosystem that can be used in the context of a commercial Smart building. Image by the author

Table 1 depicts a summary of the proposition put forth by Sailer et al. (2017) about the different behavioral and psychological needs that can be addressed via various game design elements.

Integrating the Super-app with the EEMS

The super-app ecosystem that comprises the micro-apps brings together data from smartphones, wearables and other individual devices as well as from the sensors and IoT controllers. It also combines analytics from the backend engines to offer a birds'-eye view of the sustainability practices within the building

Table 1. Psychological needs mapped to feedback mechanism and game design elements

Psychological need	Mechanism	Game design element
Need for competence	Granular feedback	Points
	Sustained feedback	Performance graphs
	Cumulative feedback	Badges
	Cumulative feedback	Leaderboards
Need for autonomy (decision freedom)	Choices	Avatars
Need for autonomy (task meaningfulness)	Volitional engagement	Meaningful stories
Need for social relatedness	Sense of relevance	Teammates
	Shared goal	Meaningful stories

Source: Sailer et al. (2017).

through the EEMS dashboard. This intelligent energy management platform helps in energy disaggregation. What this means is that it provides data on energy wastage and usage at the individual, device, equipment, floor, department, team, and building levels. Such a break-up of energy consumption assists building owners in understanding usage patterns, plug wastages, optimize sustainability performance, and devise continual operational efficiencies. Figure 4 shows an example of how data disaggregation can work in an office environment in a Smart building.

Data Disaggregation for Platform Integration

Those circuits from where data needs to be captured, such as the lights, computers, printers, water systems, air conditioners, elevators, among others, have power meters fitted. The meters capture readings from these devices and send them to the central database in the cloud. Meanwhile, occupants use their personal NFC-enabled devices to swipe equipment, switches, etc., that are tagged with RFID to record their energy consumption. BLE technology is used to determine occupancy and proximity within occupied spaces and with other connected sensors and devices (Papaioannou et al., 2018). With each swipe, data from all these sources are recorded through the micro-apps and finally sent to the super-app to be disaggregated. This data disaggregation helps understand energy consumption at individual and equipment level, or floor and department level as well. It assists in identifying those equipment and devices that gross the highest energy usage, and those that result in steepest energy costs. Most importantly, it identifies individuals who are neglecting sustainable and energy-conscious practices. The low scoring and ranking from such consumption leads to a penalty, thereby motivating such individuals to do better to earn points and rewards in the energy saving game.

Figure 4. Example of the data disaggregation process in a routine day in an office environment in a Smart building
Image by the author

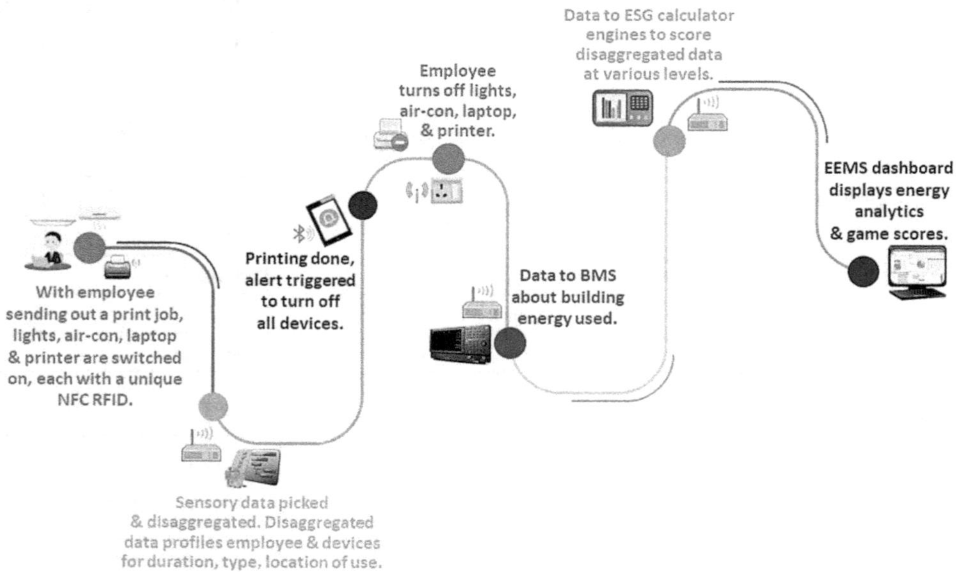

In a deeper analysis of the design, data disaggregation also supports the concept of responsible and explainable AI, where the data is at once interpretable and clear. Explainable AI plays a critical role in gamification for sustainability as it involves evaluation and transformation of human behavior at scale (Fulton et al., 2020). Therefore, it is essential in ensuring fairness in the dynamic nature of game mechanics and score design.

Real-World Examples IoT-Enabled Gamification Platforms

An IoT-enabled gamification configuration was piloted in the CleAnweb Gamified Energy Disaggregation (ChArGED, n.d.) project, a good example of introducing and reinforcing behavioral change by educating occupants of their energy consumption patterns. Implemented in public buildings in Luxembourg, Spain, and Greece, the social and behavior-driven gamification app targets energy wastage. It tracks and triggers personalized real-time alerts and recommendations to individuals on an event-driven basis (Papaioannou et al., 2017). The app reinforces participants' commitments to sustainability through several rewards and incentives, such as accomplishments points, ranks, virtual trophies, and leadership-designate titles.

A research group (Iria et al., 2020) from Australia, Portugal, and Turkey piloted IoT-based 'Grid Responsive Society through Building Automation Systems (GReSBAS).' The mobile app demonstrated 20% savings on electricity usage, with real-time contests, immediate insights, and peer comparisons, signifying notable behavioral changes in the pilot group. Similarly, the Context-Aware Framework for Collaborative Learning Activities (CAFCLA) presents occupants with checklists of energy-saving actions (García et al., 2017). Occupants with high energy-conservation habits are awarded virtual coins; those who don't make the mark are penalized. Clustering techniques are used for game scores for serious competition through peer pressure.

Research from the recent past (Oppong-Tawiah et al., 2020) shows that simple stand-alone micro-apps without an elaborate ecosystem of a super-app can also engage occupants and show sustainable behavioral change towards energy conservation. This is demonstrated in how workspaces encourage their employees to walk more or use the stairs – all activities that are part of their daily routine, tracked through wearables or a workplace app installed on their mobile devices. Citibank's Step-Up initiative (Bates, 2021) has employees logging the flights of stairs they climbed or the steps they walked, comparing data between branches worldwide. Similar strategies of combining competition, sustainability, and employee wellbeing have been adopted by several enterprises.

Toyota and SAP motivate their employees to car-pool to work to reduce carbon emissions and reduce traffic. Another successful gamification app called My Backyard Garden (Oppong-Tawiah et al., 2020) managed to lower electricity consumption in the building with occupants encouraged to adopt sustainable habits.

An IoT-enabled framework proposed by scholars (Cowley et al., 2011) entails a triple vertical framework involving Behavlets, comprising an action-resource-outcome model. The framework includes games, quizzes, and information nuggets on energy conservation, coupled with real-time feedback and insights. Climate Race (Simon et al., 2012) is another gamified app that correlates energy usage to occupant activities and behavior. Providing energy-saving recommendations to occupants based on sensor data and occupant behavior is GreenSoul, another successful game-based app (Zhang et al., 2016).

Extending Gamification to Communities and Homes

Behavioral interventions outside of commercial built-spaces are urgent if planetary health and livability challenges in cities have to reach near-resolution. Such interpositions are critical to expanding the scope of energy conservation and making cities more livable. Feedback mechanisms that track household energy consumption patterns, alerts that are triggered when energy usage peaks, reminders to save more through using less (OECD, 2017), are some of the ways that can facilitate conservation outside of commercial spaces. Simplifying and effectively disseminating information on energy conservation, offering real-time feedback, encouraging sportive social comparisons, setting objectives and competitive goals, introducing reward schemes, and constantly making changes to gamification design for keeping up participant interest levels are some of the other ways to harness behavioral levers to bring about energy-conscious transition in communities (IEA & UTCP, 2020).

Along with these levers, an adaptive framework (Kiang & Malone-Lee, 2017) can help create more sustainable communities within resilient, livable cities by setting achievable and practical targets for sustainability, triggering change where and when needed through continual assessment, and creating a fertile common ground for action that could double up as platform for self-assessment, comparative analysis, collective learning, and benchmarking progress (Kiang &Malone-Lee). Gamification in the context of homes and communities also provides a similar platform. After all, energy conservation is not a one-time event; it requires repeated behavioral attention and effort.

Research in the field has demonstrated that customized programs have the potential to significantly reduce household electricity consumption (Ayres et al., 2013; Delmas & Lessem, 2014), especially when designed using social comparisons and behavioral normative appeals that are typical of gamification. Energy conservation behavior in households is habitual and often calls for timely and effective feedback on monetary and social costs (Gilbert and Graff-Zivin, 2014). While monetary feedback may come in the form of monthly bills, the social price of high usage goes unnoticed. Therefore, gamification of household energy consumption can prove significantly effective by providing comparative insights from other households as well as through incentivized outcomes from savings.

Gamification at Play in Household and Community Energy Usage Reduction

Consider the app in-development called 'The Neighbourhood Effect' in Canberra that uses behavioral psychology to make it convenient, fun, and rewarding for Australian households to save energy and reduce environmental impact (Johnston, 2019). Or Brisbane's gamified 'Reduce You Juice' mobile app-based behavior change program, which resulted in substantial cut in household electricity bills, with residents saving up to AUD 2000 a year. Recording a 12.3% savings in energy, it has helped build the motivation to change through community involvement and social encouragement (Jewell, 2016).

Volkswagon's Piano Stairs (Dankov, 2021) at a subway exit in Stockholm aims to change human behavior through fun, taking a banal task and transforming it to attract attention and modify habits. Each step in the musical stairs is a key that plays a note. Everyone going up the stairs creates their own music. This has resulted in 66% more people preferring stairs over the escalator, saving on continual energy consumption as well as improving health.

Large and small corporations alike are spending more time and resources year after year to come up with newer strategies that can influence energy conservation and health behaviors. The collective aim of such efforts is to develop digital, gamified experiences that can integrate software design with game mechanics, along with public health theory and behavioral insights (King et al., 2013). Several software developers, data analysts, and behavioral scientists get together each month at the Google campus in London to discuss and strategize behavioral levers than can transform cities to become more livable. Driving behavioral change, therefore, is a collective effort, but the real changemakers are essentially individuals.

LIMITATIONS OF GAMIFICATION

In the context of energy saving in commercial spaces, gamification can be used as a tool for behavioral change to obtain the desired attitudes and achieve energy conservation targets. However, when the approach is applied at scale, building occupants from different backgrounds are seen to be influenced in different ways. Therefore, it is important when designing the gamified approach to keep cultural influences in mind to be able to better achieve desired results (AlMarshedi et al., 2016). This implies that gamification is a diverse concept – as diverse in its approach as the spaces and target group it is applied to.

Most existing research treats gamification and game mechanics as a universal concept that is uniformly applied to various settings. Practically, though, game design and implementation are unique (Sailer et al., 2017), taking as many forms as the many factors that influence them. Designers of gamification, as well as scholars of game mechanics, must restrain from treating gamification as a general concept, especially in a workplace environment, as it could then lead to apprehensive employees and management, with a low rate of uptake of the gamified solution (Lounis et al., n.d.) Further, they must also not fall prey to the widely-acknowledged psychological phenomenon of the shifting baseline syndrome explained earlier in this chapter, as there is a high possibility that the shifting baseline might keep some occupants from participating in energy-conscious behavior.

Dentifying energy wastage, particularly in a workplace environment, may therefore lead to dismay by employees and higher management, and therefore decreased usage of the gamified solution.

FUTURE RESEARCH DIRECTION

Scholars who have variously studied the effect on gamification and sustainability on conserving energy in residential premises (Fraternali & Gonzalez, 2019; Launonen et al., 2019) as well as within office spaces (Fraternali et al., 2018; Iria et al., 2020), have not considered the combined aspects of net zero transformations, occupant engagement, clean technology, and sustainability in their research. Future studies must focus on a more holistic solution to expand the limited extant research and the depth of information on the subject.

The Anthropocene epoch, which marks the evidence as well as extent of human action that has impacted the environment and the planet's natural ecosystems (Crane et al., 2021) calls for greater individual accountability to make an impact on the planet and drive economic growth. Dismissing the value of individual responsibility is only a call for impending doom. Encouraging more responsibility and answerability to human action can expand our perspectives on climate consciousness and open up more avenues to a more sustainable, livable world. Therefore, a focus on individual behavior cannot be neglected.

Along with individual behavior, research must spotlight the characteristics and context of the individuals as these determine the motivation behind behavioral change. Lasting change can be challenging to achieve at scale as what works in one context or location may not be applicable to another (Yokum et al., 2018; Proestakis et al., 2018). Therefore, dedicated effort should be put into arriving at the appropriate game design that would motivate participants and keep them inspired in each context. The success of the gamified platform would then depend on the experience of the game designers conceiving the game, and their ability to keep participants as hooked as they would be to fun and entertainment (King et al., 2013).

What is also vital is that behavioral levers focus on cross-infrastructural change. While this would make the game design more intricate and complex, it would essentially add depth and context to the gamified platform, with a shift from single objective outcomes to multiple targets. With such an approach the motivation to conserving energy would also lead to the drive to save water and responsibly manage waste.

Gamification activism and effective climate change policies, built on the pillars of public support and governmental regulations can give the necessary push for gamifying the journey to carbon-consciousness, energy conservation, and planet health on a larger scale. The change needs to start early, and target young individuals. Old habits die hard, and those that are learnt in childhood stay for life. If children can be involved in gamified platforms that are aimed at energy conservation, the long-term impact would be phenomenal. Consider the example of Australia's Healthy Active School Travel program that encourages families to cycle or walk their children to school when and where possible. Children receive incentives, such as stickers and trinkets, that motivate them to score better on their 0%-carbon-100%-health commute to school. The gamified approach has gained quick popularity with more than 35% single-family car trips (AHKGA, 2018) to and from school converting into net zero outcomes.

CONCLUSION

Sustainability and livability are interwoven concepts. They can benefit planetary health and livability in cities if they are both approached in an integrated, gamified way (Haines et al., 2009). If current and future challenges to health and livability in cities have to be addressed, a transformative change towards sustainable living is the need of the hour. Sustainable living is as critical to the planet as it is to public health and the economy. Elkington's triple bottom line of people, planet, and profits (Elkington, 2018) clearly forms the foundation of sustainability and resilience in today's disrupted world. Employee satisfaction, health, and productivity are as important in the larger scheme of things as are kilowatt savings and carbon control.

The slowly-growing realization of the potential of the combination of behavioral change and sustainability to make cities more livable has led to the drive to gamify daily carbon-heavy activities. In the context of commercial buildings in large cities, the threat to planetary health is rapid and real. Behavioral change at the individual level needs to occur at an unprecedented pace and scale. Gamification can help us get there with behavioral levers acting as the catalysts of change.

REFERENCES

Abrahamse, W., Steg, L., Vlek, C., & Rothengatter, T. (2005). A review of Intervention Studies aimed at household energy conservation. *Journal of Environmental Psychology*, *25*(3), 273–291. doi:10.1016/j.jenvp.2005.08.002

AHKGA. (2018). *Australia active healthy kids global alliance.* Active Healthy Kids Global Alliance. Retrieved November 30, 2022, from https://www.activehealthykids.org/australia/

Alam, S. M., & Islam, K. M. (2021). Examining the role of Environmental Corporate Social Responsibility in building Green Corporate Image and green competitive advantage. *International Journal of Corporate Social Responsibility*, *6*(1), 8. Advance online publication. doi:10.118640991-021-00062-w

AlMarshedi, A., Wanick, V., Wills, G. B., & Ranchhod, A. (2016). Gamification and behaviour. *Progress in IS*, 19–29. doi:10.1007/978-3-319-45557-0_2

Antin, J., & Churchill, E. F. (2011). Badges in social media: A social psychological perspective. *Paper presented at the CHI 2011*, Vancouver.

Ayres, I., Raseman, S., & Shih, A. (2009). *Evidence from two large field experiments that peer comparison feedback can reduce residential energy usage*. NBER. doi:10.3386/w15386

Bamidis, P. D., Gabarron, E., Hors-Fraile, S., Konstantinidis, E., Konstantinidis, S., & Rivera, O. (2016). Gamification and behavioral change. *Participatory Health Through Social Media*, 112–135. doi:10.1016/B978-0-12-809269-9.00007-4

Bates, H. (2021). *5 Businesses Using Green Gamification to Save the World*. GivingForce. https://www.givingforce.com/blog/5-businesses-using-green-gamification-to-save-the-world

Behavior Institute. (n.d.). *Gamification for behavior change - Studies, products, and examples*. Behavior Change Tactic. https://www.besci.org/tactics/gamification

BPIE. (2011). *Europe's buildings under the microscope - A country-by-country review of the* July 28, 2022, from https://bpie.eu/wp-content/uploads/2015/10/HR_EU_B_under_microscope_study.pdf

Burguillo, J. C. (2010). Using game theory and competition-based learning to stimulate student motivation and performance. *Computers & Education*, *55*(2), 566–575. doi:10.1016/j.compedu.2010.02.018

ChArGED. (n.d.). Check.energy μ spare Einfach Energiekosten Ein. checkenergy. *Charged*. http://www.charged-project.eu/

Chui, W. S., & Wai, C. W. (2017). Gamification: Motivating Users' Energy Conservation Behaviour. *International Journal of Real Estate Studies*, *11*(1), 37–42.

Costa, J. P., Wehbe, R. R., Robb, J., & Nacke, L. E. (2013). Time's up. *Proceedings of the First International Conference on Gameful Design, Research, and Applications*. ACM. 10.1145/2583008.2583012

Cowley, B., Moutinho, J. L., Bateman, C., & Oliveira, A. (2011). Learning principles and interaction design for 'green my place': A massively multiplayer serious game. *Entertainment Computing*, *2*(2), 103–113. doi:10.1016/j.entcom.2011.01.001

Crane, M., Lloyd, S., Haines, A., Ding, D., Hutchinson, E., Belesova, K., Davies, M., Osrin, D., Zimmermann, N., Capon, A., Wilkinson, P., & Turcu, C. (2021). Transforming Cities for Sustainability: A Health Perspective. *Environment International*, *147*, 106366. doi:10.1016/j.envint.2020.106366 PMID:33422969

Dankov, K. (2021). *5 businesses using green gamification to save the world.* GivingForce. Retrieved September 5, 2022, from https://www.givingforce.com/blog/5-businesses-using-green-gamification-to-save-the-world

Delmas, M. A., & Lessem, N. (2014). Saving power to conserve your reputation? the effectiveness of private versus public information. *Journal of Environmental Economics and Management, 67*(3), 353–370. doi:10.1016/j.jeem.2013.12.009

DeLosh, E. L., Busemeyer, J. R., & McDaniel, M. A. (1997). Extrapolation: The sine qua non for abstraction in function learning. *Journal of Experimental Psychology. Learning, Memory, and Cognition, 23*(4), 968–986. doi:10.1037/0278-7393.23.4.968 PMID:9231439

Deterding, S., Dixon, D., Khaled, R., & Nacke, L. (2011). From game design elements to gamefulness. *Proceedings of the 15th International Academic MindTrek Conference on Envisioning Future Media Environments - MindTrek '11.* ACM.10.1145/2181037.2181040

Deterding, S., Sicart, M., Nacke, L., O'Hara, K., & Dixon, D. (2011). Gamification. using game-design elements in non-gaming contexts. *Proceedings of the 2011 Annual Conference Extended Abstracts on Human Factors in Computing Systems - CHI EA '11.* ACM.10.1145/1979742.1979575

Dolan, P., Hallsworth, M., Halpern, D., King, D., Metcalfe, R., & Vlaev, I. (2012). Influencing behaviour: The mindspace way. *Journal of Economic Psychology, 33*(1), 264–277. doi:10.1016/j.joep.2011.10.009

Donato, P., & Link, M. W. (2013). AMA Marketing Research: The Gamification of Marketing Research

Dulskaia, I., Bellini, F., Zabal, R., Garcia Pañella, O., & D'Ascenzo, F. (2017). Gamification as an instrument for organizational behaviour change during the meeting: Case study «ROBATIEMPOS». *Proceedings of the International Conference on Business Excellence, 11*(1), 359–367. 10.1515/picbe-2017-0039

EDF. (2019). *Business and the fourth wave of environmentalism.* Environmental Defense Fund. https://www.edf.org/sites/default/files/Business-and-the-Fourth-Wave-of-Environmentalism_2019.pdf

EEA. (2013). *Achieving energy efficiency through behaviour change: What does it take?* European Environment Agency. https://www.eea.europa.eu/publications/achieving-energy-efficiency-through-behaviour

Elkington, J. (2018, June 25). *25 Years Ago I Coined the Phrase "Triple Bottom Line." Here's Why It's Time to Rethink It.* HBR. https://hbr.org/2018/06/25-years-ago-i-coined-the-phrase-triple-bottom-line-heres-why-im-giving-up-on-it

Ferreira, J., Afonso, J., Monteiro, V., & Afonso, J. (2018). An Energy Management Platform for Public Buildings. *Electronics (Basel), 7*(11), 294. doi:10.3390/electronics7110294

Fraternali, P., Cellina, F., Herrera, S., Krinidis, S., Pasini, C., Rizzoli, A. E., Rottondi, C., & Tzovaras, D. (2018). A socio-technical system based on gamification towards Energy Savings. *2018 IEEE International Conference on Pervasive Computing and Communications Workshops (PerCom Workshops).* IEEE. doi10.1109/PERCOMW.2018.8480405

Fraternali, P., & Gonzalez, S. L. (2019). An augmented reality game for Energy Awareness. *Lecture Notes in Computer Science, 11754*, 629–638. doi:10.1007/978-3-030-34995-0_57

Fulton, L. B., Lee, J. Y., Wang, Q., Yuan, Z., Hammer, J., & Perer, A. (2020). Getting playful with explainable AI: Games with a purpose to improve human understanding of AI. *Extended Abstracts of the 2020 CHI Conference on Human Factors in Computing Systems*. 10.1145/3334480.3382831

García, Ó., Alonso, R., Prieto, J., & Corchado, J. (2017). Energy efficiency in public buildings through context-aware social computing. *Sensors (Basel)*, *17*(4), 826. doi:10.339017040826 PMID:28398237

Gartner. (2012, November 12). *Gamification: Engagement strategies for business and IT*. Gartner. Retrieved November 28, 2022, from https://www.gartner.com/en/documents/2246217

Gartner. (2014). *Gartner reveals how Gamification Drives Digital Business*. Gartner. https://www.gartner.com/en/newsroom/press-releases/2014-04-08-gartner-reveals-how-gamification-drives-digital-business

Gilbert, B., & Graff Zivin, J. (2014). Dynamic salience with intermittent billing: Evidence from Smart Electricity Meters. *Journal of Economic Behavior & Organization*, *107*, 176–190. doi:10.1016/j.jebo.2014.03.011

Gill, Z. M., Tierney, M. J., Pegg, I. M., & Allan, N. (2010). Low-energy dwellings: The contribution of behaviours to actual performance. *Building Research and Information*, *38*(5), 491–508. doi:10.1080/09613218.2010.505371

Gollier, C. (2002). Discounting an uncertain future. *Journal of Public Economics*, *85*(2), 149–166. doi:10.1016/S0047-2727(01)00079-2

Grossberg, F., Wolfson, M., Mazur-Stommen, S., Farley, K., & Nadel, S. (2015). *Gamified Energy Efficiency Programs*. ACEEE. https://www.aceee.org/sites/default/files/publications/researchreports/b1501.pdf

Gustafsson, A., Katzeff, C., & Bang, M. (2009). Evaluation of a pervasive game for domestic energy engagement among teenagers. *Computers in Entertainment*, *7*(4), 1–19. doi:10.1145/1658866.1658873

Haines, A., McMichael, A. J., Smith, K. R., Roberts, I., Woodcock, J., Markandya, A., Armstrong, B. G., Campbell-Lendrum, D., Dangour, A. D., Davies, M., Bruce, N., Tonne, C., Barrett, M., & Wilkinson, P. (2009). Public health benefits of strategies to reduce greenhouse-gas emissions: Overview and implications for policy makers. *Lancet*, *374*(9707), 2104–2114. doi:10.1016/S0140-6736(09)61759-1 PMID:19942281

Harris, M. A. (2019). Maintenance of behaviour change following a community-wide gamification based Physical Activity Intervention. *Preventive Medicine Reports*, *13*, 37–40. doi:10.1016/j.pmedr.2018.11.009 PMID:30510892

Herring, H. (2006). Energy efficiency—A critical view. *Energy*, *31*(1), 10–20. doi:10.1016/j.energy.2004.04.055

IEA. (n.d.). *The potential of behavioural interventions for optimising energy use at home*. IEA. https://www.iea.org/articles/the-potential-of-behavioural-interventions-for-optimising-energy-use-at-home

IEA & UTCP. (2020). *Users TCP*. UsersTCP. https://userstcp.org/news/behavioural-insights-for-demand-side-energy-policy-and-programmes-report-published

Iria, J., Fonseca, N., Cassola, F., Barbosa, A., Soares, F., Coelho, A., & Ozdemir, A. (2020). A gamification platform to foster energy efficiency in office buildings. *Energy and Building*, *222*, 110101. doi:10.1016/j.enbuild.2020.110101

Jachimowicz, J. M., Hauser, O. P., O'Brien, J. D., Sherman, E., & Galinsky, A. D. (2018). The critical role of second-order normative beliefs in predicting energy conservation. *Nature Human Behaviour*, *2*(10), 757–764. doi:10.103841562-018-0434-0 PMID:31406290

Janda, K. B. (2011). Buildings don't use energy: People do. *Architectural Science Review*, *54*(1), 15–22. doi:10.3763/asre.2009.0050

Jewell, C. (2016). *How gamification is saving Brisbane renters thousands on energy bills*. The Fifth Estate. https://thefifthestate.com.au/home-and-lifestyle/how-gamification-is-saving-brisbane-renters-thousands-on-energy-bills/

Johnston, P. (2019, July 30). *How gamification can influence environmental behaviour*. The Fifth Estate. https://thefifthestate.com.au/urbanism/environment/how-gamification-can-influence-environmental-behaviour/

Jones, L. P., Turvey, S. T., Massimino, D., & Papworth, S. K. (2020). Investigating the implications of shifting baseline syndrome on conservation. *People and Nature*, *2*(4), 1131–1144. doi:10.1002/pan3.10140

Kapp, K. M. (2012). *The gamification of learning and instruction: Game-based methods and strategies for training and Education*. Pfeiffer.

Kiang, H. C., & Malone-Lee, L. C. (2017). *An assessment framework for monitoring cities' sustainability*. CENTRE FOR SUSTAINABLE ASIAN CITIES NATIONAL UNIVERSITY OF SINGAPORE. https://cde.nus.edu.sg/csac/wp-content/uploads/sites/29/2019/11/Full-template-for-Benchmark-Booklet.pdf

King, D., Greaves, F., Exeter, C., & Darzi, A. (2013). 'Gamification': Influencing health behaviours with games. *Journal of the Royal Society of Medicine*, *106*(3), 76–78. doi:10.1177/0141076813480996 PMID:23481424

Kok, G., Lo, S. H., Peters, G.-J. Y., & Ruiter, R. A. C. (2011). Changing energy-related behavior: An intervention mapping approach. *Energy Policy*, *39*(9), 5280–5286. doi:10.1016/j.enpol.2011.05.036

Launonen, H., Tisov, A., Germini, A. M., Olivadese, R., Koroleva, K., Lukasik, M., Malamou, A., Arabsolgar, D., Zacharis, E., & Garbi, A. (2019). Exploitation of the European research projects aiming to achieve a behavior change for energy saving through innovative IT solutions. *Sustainable Places*, *2019*, 13. Advance online publication. doi:10.3390/proceedings2019020013

Loewenstein, G., & Prelec, D. (1992). Anomalies in intertemporal choice: Evidence and an interpretation. *The Quarterly Journal of Economics*, *107*(2), 573–597. doi:10.2307/2118482

Looyestyn, J., Kernot, J., Boshoff, K., Ryan, J., Edney, S., & Maher, C. (2017). Does gamification increase engagement with online programs? A systematic review. *PLoS One*, *12*(3), e0173403. Advance online publication. doi:10.1371/journal.pone.0173403 PMID:28362821

Lounis, S., Kotsopoulos, D., Bardaki, C., Papaioannou, T. G., & Pramatari, K. (n.d.). 1st International GamiFIN Conference. In *CEUR Workshop Proceedings* (2017th ed., Vol. 1857, pp. 129–134). Pori, Finland; Elsevier.

Markman, A. (2018, October 11). *Why people aren't motivated to address climate change*. Harvard Business Review. https://hbr.org/2018/10/why-people-arent-motivated-to-address-climate-change

Martella, R. (2022). *Now is the time for businesses to act on Global Sustainability*. World Economic Forum. https://www.weforum.org/agenda/2022/05/global-sustainability-corporations-lead-net-zero/

McCormick, K. (2018). *The business case for Healthy Buildings: Insights from Early Adopters*. Urban Land Institute. https://www.buildup.eu/en/practices/publications/business-case-healthy-buildings-insights-early-adopters

McCormick, T. (2013). ANTHROPOLOGY OF AN IDEA GAMIFICATION. *Foreign Policy*, *201*, 26–27.

Motegi, N., Watson, D. S., & McKane, A. T. (2020). Enterprise Energy Management System Installation Case Study at a food processing plant. *Web Based Enterprise Energy and Building Automation Systems*, 101–108. doi:10.1201/9781003151234-13

NSF. (n.d.). *Behaviour Change - Research Overview*. Sustainable Healthy Cities Network. https://www.sustainablehealthycities.org/behaviour-change/

OECD. (2017). *Tackling environmental problems with the help of behavioural insights*. OECD. doi:10.1787/9789264273887-en

Ogiemwonyi, O., Harun, A. B., Alam, M. N., & Othman, B. A. (2020). Do we care about going green? measuring the effect of green environmental awareness, green product value and environmental attitude on green culture. an Insight from Nigeria. *Environmental and Climate Technologies*, *24*(1), 254–274. doi:10.2478/rtuect-2020-0015

Oppong-Tawiah, D., Webster, J., Staples, S., Cameron, A.-F., Ortiz de Guinea, A., & Hung, T. Y. (2020). Developing a gamified mobile application to encourage sustainable energy use in the Office. *Journal of Business Research*, *106*, 388–405. doi:10.1016/j.jbusres.2018.10.051

Ouyang, J., Gao, L., Yan, Y., Hokao, K., & Ge, J. (2009). Effects of improved consumer behavior on energy conservation in the urban residential sector of Hangzhou, China. *Journal of Asian Architecture and Building Engineering*, *8*(1), 243–249. doi:10.3130/jaabe.8.243

Papaioannou, T., Dimitriou, N., Vasilakis, K., Schoofs, A., Nikiforakis, M., Pursche, F., Deliyski, N., Taha, A., Kotsopoulos, D., Bardaki, C., Kotsilitis, S., & Garbi, A. (2018). An IOT-based gamified approach for reducing occupants' energy wastage in public buildings. *Sensors (Basel)*, *18*(2), 537. doi:10.339018020537 PMID:29439414

Papaioannou, T. G., Kotsopoulos, D., Bardaki, C., Lounis, S., Dimitriou, N., Boultadakis, G., Garbi, A., & Schoofs, A. (2017). IOT-enabled gamification for energy conservation in public buildings. *2017 Global Internet of Things Summit (GIoTS)*. doi:10.1109/GIOTS.2017.8016269

Pasini, D., Reda, F., & Häkkinen, T. (2017). User engaging practices for energy saving in buildings: Critical Review and new enhanced procedure. *Energy and Building*, *148*, 74–88. doi:10.1016/j.enbuild.2017.05.010

Pereira, J. P. A. M. (2019). *Gamification in building automation - the Human in the loop in a Cyber-Physical System* [Dissertation, Universidad Nova de Lisboa]

Proestakis, A., di Sorrentino, E. P., Brown, H. E., van Sluijs, E., Mani, A., Caldeira, S., & Herrmann, B. (2018). Network interventions for changing physical activity behaviour in Preadolescents. *Nature Human Behaviour*, *2*(10), 778–787. doi:10.103841562-018-0436-y PMID:30886902

Sailer, M., Hense, J. U., Mayr, S. K., & Mandl, H. (2017). How gamification motivates: An experimental study of the effects of specific game design elements on psychological need satisfaction. *Computers in Human Behavior*, *69*, 371–380. doi:10.1016/j.chb.2016.12.033

Shameli, A., Althoff, T., Saberi, A., & Leskovec, J. (2017). How gamification affects physical activity. *Proceedings of the 26th International Conference on World Wide Web Companion - WWW '17 Companion*. IEEE. 10.1145/3041021.3054172

Silva, A. S., & Ghisi, E. (2014). Uncertainty analysis of user behaviour and physical parameters in residential building performance simulation. *Energy and Building*, *76*, 381–391. doi:10.1016/j.enbuild.2014.03.001

Simon, J., Jahn, M., & Al-Akkad, A. (2012). Saving energy at work. *Proceedings of the 11th International Conference on Mobile and Ubiquitous Multimedia - MUM '12*. ACM. d10.1145/2406367.2406379

Stinson, L. (2017, June 8). Apple's architect says the future of offices must be flexible. *Wired*. https://www.wired.com/2017/06/apples-architect-says-future-offices-must-flexible/

Technacy Solutions. (2017, August 24). *Apple's architect says the future of offices must be flexible*. Technacy Solutions. https://www.technacysolutions.com/apples-architect-says-the-future-of-offices-must-be-flexible/

Ting, L. S. bin Mohammed, A. H., & Wai, C. W. (2011). 2011 International Conference on Social Science and Humanity. In *Promoting Energy Conservation Behaviour: A Plausible Solution to Energy Sustainability Threats* (*Vol. 5*). Singapore; IACSIT Press.

Trope, Y., & Liberman, N. (2010). Construal-level theory of psychological distance. *Psychological Review*, *117*(2), 440–463. doi:10.1037/a0018963 PMID:20438233

UNEP. (2020). *2020 Global Status Report for Buildings and Construction*. Global Alliance for Buildings and Construction. https://wedocs.unep.org/bitstream/handle/20.500.11822/34572/GSR_ES.pdf?sequence=3

UNEP. (2021). *Global Status Report for Buildings and Construction: Towards a Zero emission, Efficient and Resilient Buildings and Construction Sector*. Global ABC. https://globalabc.org/sites/default/files/2021-10/GABC_Buildings-GSR-2021_BOOK.pdf

US EIA. (2017, September 14). *International Energy Outlook 2017*. https://www.eia.gov/. https://www.eia.gov/outlooks/ieo/pdf/0484(2017).pdf

Wai, C. W. (2009). The conceptual model of Energy Awareness Development Process: The Transferor segment. *2009 3rd International Conference on Energy and Environment (ICEE)*. ICEEE. 10.1109/ICEENVIRON.2009.5398630

Wilson, A. (2016). Making the case for Green Building. *BuildingGreen*. https://www.buildinggreen.com/feature/making-case-green-building

Wu, M. (2018, March 8). *Gamification from a company of pro gamers*. LinkedIn. https://www.linkedin.com/pulse/20140923144022-66703918-gamification-from-a-company-of-pro-gamers

Xiao, R., Wu, Z., & Hamari, J. (2021). Internet-of-gamification: A review of literature on IOT-enabled gamification for user engagement. *International Journal of Human-Computer Interaction*, *38*(12), 1113–1137. doi:10.1080/10447318.2021.1990517

Yokum, D., Lauffenburger, J. C., Ghazinouri, R., & Choudhry, N. K. (2018). Letters designed with Behavioural Science Increase Influenza Vaccination in Medicare beneficiaries. *Nature Human Behaviour*, *2*(10), 743–749. doi:10.103841562-018-0432-2 PMID:31406294

Yu, Z., Fung, B. C. M., Haghighat, F., Yoshino, H., & Morofsky, E. (2011). A systematic procedure to study the influence of occupant behavior on building energy consumption. *Energy and Building*, *43*(6), 1409–1417. doi:10.1016/j.enbuild.2011.02.002

Zhang, H., Jovcic, D., Lin, W., & Far, A. J. (2016). Average value MMC model with accurate blocked state and cell charging/discharging dynamics. *2016 4th International Symposium on Environmental Friendly Energies and Applications (EFEA)*. IEEE. 10.1109/EFEA.2016.7748768

ADDITIONAL READING

Kahneman, D. (2012). *Thinking, fast and slow*. Penguin.

Keller, V. (2015). (*rep.*). The Business Case for Purpose.

Schunk, D. H., Meece, J. L., & R., P. P. (2014). *Motivation in education: Theory, research, and applications*. Pearson.

Stieglitz, S., Lattemann, C., Bissantz, S. R., Zarnekow, R., & Brockmann, T. (2018). *Gamification: Using game elements in serious contexts*. Springer.

Werbach, K., & Hunter, D. (2012). *For the Win: How game thinking can revolutionize your business*. Wharton Digital Press.

Zichermann, G., & Linder, J. (2013). *Gamification revolution: How leaders leverage game mechanics to crush the competition*. McGraw-Hill Education.

KEY TERMS AND DEFINITIONS

Anthropocene: The evidence as well as extent of human action that has impacted the environment and the planet's natural ecosystems.

Data disaggregation: The separation of large compilations of data into smaller units.

Enterprise Energy Management System: The entire gamut of data-collection devices and an AI-based system in the building that secures data for predictive and preventive analysis.

Gamification: The use of game design elements within non-game contexts.

Chapter 11
The Application of Serviqual Tool to Improve Client Satisfaction in a Health Facility:
Service Quality in a Health Center

Skhumbuzo Gcabashe
Durban University of Technology, South Africa

Noluthando Shirley Matsiliza
https://orcid.org/0000-0002-9472-9294
University of Fort Hare, South Africa

ABSTRACT

The use of SERVQUAL as a tool to measure service quality in healthcare facilities is a giant step towards effectiveness and efficiency in health management and in public affairs. The purpose of this chapter is to assess the extent to which service standards in a health facility like Rietvlei Hospital are applied to improve service provision and the quality of lives of the customers. Although government adopted health policies in South Africa, there are still gaps in quality of services rendered by public healthcare institutions. The implementation of healthcare policies can demonstrate that they are fragmented. The key dimensions of service quality were investigated at Rietvlei and SERVQUAL was used as a tool to measure the effectiveness of service quality using a mixed methodology. Data was drawn from a probabilistic sample using mainly questionnaires and interviews.

INTRODUCTION

Vulnerable group of people living in urban and rural areas in South Africa lack proper health facilities. Scholars alluded on the key issues of managing quality to satisfy clients as evolving around responsiveness, tangibility, reliability, assurance, and apathy. Health services in the post-apartheid South Africa are plagued with service gaps that needs proper attention from the government. There are organisations such

DOI: 10.4018/978-1-6684-6924-8.ch011

as Gift of the Givers that assist vulnerable people with health problems, by providing them support by providing public goods when they are needed in areas when government failed them and during disasters. In some areas government collaborated with the other service providers to address the discrepancies and attend to community needs.

The focal point of this chapter is to examine carefully the interval between service delivery and healthcare services provided by rural healthcare facilities to their customers. This chapter also analyses the level of patients satisfaction based on the data collected from the participants through an empirical research. This study uses the case of Rietvlei Hospital application of service quality (SERVQUAL) to measure the satisfaction of patients. This empirical investigation seeks to determine how customers/ patients in rural communities feel about the quality of service delivery to them at the healthcare center. Furthermore, to scrutinize patients perception about service delivery and healthcare services that is furnished by Rietvlei Hospital to its patients.

BACKGROUND TO THE PROBLEM

In the current decades after democratic elections in South Africa, government introduced healthcare policy reforms to improve the performance of healthcare services in South Africa. In some of the policy gaps, it has been indicated that government did not focus more on quality of service delivery provided by healthcare institutions to its customers. The legacy of apartheid in South Africa left healthcare facilities with fragmented healthcare service delivery in terms of race, gender, political affiliation as well as socioeconomics status. South African communities were complaining about the quality of service delivery and healthcare services which was provided to them by public healthcare institutions. Javed *et al.* (2019) argued that healthcare sector is vulnerable to many challenges and that resulted to poor services offered in some health facilities. Ballim (2017) posited that policies such as the group areas Act of 1940 which was implemented by apartheid government in South Africa to its citizens, did not only moved black people to rural and remote areas, but it also fragmented service delivery and healthcare services to South Africans. This group areas Act of 1940 also perpetuated discrimination against black people living in rural and remote areas. Due to this Act, Rietvlei Hospital is still facing legacy obstacles that inhibit adequate service delivery in the healthcare facilities where patients are being taken care of. Andre de la (2016) also attest that the apartheid government in South Africa allocated resources unequally to its society according to race and political affiliation.

Day, Cornell and Malherbe (2019) indicated that people that are engulfed by poverty and hunger are black people in South Africa, especially those who live in rural and remote areas. These communities from rural areas are still having limited access to basic services delivery and healthcare services. Liu *et al.* (2016) mentioned that South African democratic government must ensure that all resources are dole out equally to all South African citizens, irrespective of their race or skin colour in order to refine service delivery as well as healthcare services that is provided by rural healthcare institutions to its communities. Meyer *et al.* (2017) are of the view that over the past two and half decades after the election of democratic government in South Africa, there is an increase of resources allocated from Gross Domestic Product (GDP) which are allocated to service delivery in order to the aforementioned inequalities. The democratic government which was elected in 1994 has an obligation eradicate inadequacies which was created by apartheid government. Anderson *et al.* (2015) stated that poor allocation of resources to service delivery and healthcare services to rural areas has created a huge challenge to government in order to address healthcare related issues that affect rural communities.

INTERSECT OF HEALTH, LIVELIHOOD, AND HUMAN BEHAVIOR IN SOUTH AFRICA

There is a complex and dynamic intersection of health, human behaviour and livelihoods relationships in South Africa. The persons health status can affect the way that person behaves and the ability to live and earn a living can also impact their health. In addition, human behaviour plays a critical role in determining both health decisions and livelihood outcomes. In this equation, the government is a provider to basic health needs, by providing the services to the people through health clinics/ hospitals and other health care centres.

The Impact of Poor Health Conditions

The other interesting account on the gaps in health care system is the poor administration, lack of resources and proper infrastructure to deliver services. Service quality is new in public affairs and is underpinned by the partnering, and collaboration of private sector and non-governmental organisations with government. The private and public projects (PPP) in the health system have made a difference in intersecting the health care with the community livelihood. This also instigated a comparison between the private healthcare with public healthcare performance which resulted to demands for more improvement on the public sector health care side. In the case of municipal areas, service quality is observed when there is dissimilarity among perceived expectations and performance services that is furnished by rural healthcare facilities. There are gaps in literatures of the rural health service quality in public health facilities in South Africa, and poor health environment. There is growing need to look for the society to understand service quality also regarding public healthcare service quality. The society is demanding better service delivery and healthcare services from public healthcare institutions to enhance their health status. The integration of health care systems of disadvantaged areas to modernised previously advantaged centres was partially successful. Some rural hospitals still suffer from limited capacity, and poor crowded infrastructure to offer services. The government also invited foreign doctors like Cubans to fill the gap and work in rural health canters are where South African doctors are not able to go.

The Impact of Poor Economic Conditions

The government uses Hospitals and clinics, to offer health care services to all citizens in South Africa. As more people from South Africa are crowding health care centres, the government cannot meet their demands due to inflation and the rising costs of health care resources and the advanced technology needed to offer best practice. Health care in private hospitals is more competent in-service delivery more than public health care that is funded by government. African countries in achieving Millennium Development Goals (MDG), need to provide basic healthcare services that is improved, and be able to reduce their mortality rates. There is a connection between health care service provision and the quality of life. Therefore, when there are shortages of health care services and poor infrastructure, people move to live to other areas where they can access health care services. According to Liu *et al.* (2015) the migration of health professionals from African continent occur mostly in rural areas of Africa, and is a source of contention that created shortage of healthcare workers in rural and remote areas that are under-developed for young doctors to live. These challenges are barriers towards South African healthcare institutions to achieve the Universal Health Coverage (UHC). Gilson *et al.* (2014) are of the view that the democratic government elected in 1994 implemented new policies and tried to allocate more resources to enhance healthcare services but human needs are endless. James and Miza (2015) suggested the healthcare challenges has been aggravated by senior and experienced healthcare workers who resign from public healthcare institutions in South Africa due to low wages. van Rensburg (2014) alluded to the shortages in health care system, as emanating from the fact that healthcare workers from rural areas are migrating to urban areas, and also to other developed nations where there are greener pastures, and where better wages are paid to health workers.

Impact on Human Behaviour

There's an impact on the behaviour of people due to their social and cultural affiliation. Culture and norms pursued people to make decisions about their lives and behave in a certain manner by displaying attitudes towards seeking healthcare and medicines. Some cultures and religions forbids people to get blood infusion and some operations and removal of body parts.

Factors such as lifestyle such as diet, food consumption and exercise can have a positive impact on ones' health. When there is poor health, one will seek health care from the facility and clinics due to poor health due to circumstances and also self-destruction. Human behaviour can be observed to be changing when they are not satisfied more than when they are satisfied, when they show how happy they are as clients and customers about the services they have received according to their expectations. In the context of this chapter, the government in a public hospital is required to bring forth only basic health services to the community even though patients' expectations might exceed what the government can provide since the cost of saving people's lives can be immeasurable. Information regarding customer satisfaction can be collected through surveys and ratings; hence SERVQUAL can be used as a tool to rate determinants of customer satisfaction in health service quality.

This term customer contentment explains more about the quality of service provided by the organisation and how customers perceive that service. In line with the adoption of the New Public Management (NPM), governments interlinked the principles of the NPM adopted few private sector practices to improve performance in various departments Tabrizi *et al.* (2018). Customer satisfaction is observed when customers' needs and demands are not met. The public health sector adopted from the private sector practices to improve quality of life of their citizens but they can't cope with the standards needed to improve the health sector. Private health sector is concerned about the bottom line, hence they are keen to change the lives of their patents as long as they are paid to make profit. In the public sector, customer satisfaction is adopted to improve service delivery and to enhance the general welfare.

There are several policies and legislation by governments to improve the standards of health to improve human behaviour. It is also important to look at the impact of individual behaviour on health.

Managers and supervisors that oversee the provision of services in a health facility are obliged to comply with principles like 'Batho Pele' which also imply that quality must be maintained in service provision when principles like, curtesy, access to services, responsiveness, value for money, transparency, and redress are observed. Public hospitals are expected to engage with stakeholders and employees in assuring and managing quality and the operations of the organisation especially during the COVID 19 epidemic Mazibuko (2019). Employee engagement is conducted to ensure that employees are involvement in decision making process of the organisation, especially in issues affecting them. Involving employees will ensure the effective implementation of the strategy of the organisation. Provision of quality service delivery includes effective implementation of organisation strategy, process as well as management systems Rani (2019). All these strategies and process will help the organisation to achieve its mission and vision.

It is therefore important to understand intersection of health, livelihood and human behaviour because that is critical for a developing country like South Africa to know when finding interventions to improve health outcomes and to promote sustainable livelihoods. This does not require to improve only the health quality standards, but it needs an multi-disciplinary approach that considers the interplay between socio-economic factors, individual behaviour, and the broader social context. This chapter focus more on the standards that are adhered to at the health service centres to improve the services provided to patients, thereby improving their quality of lives. The following section will indulge on the conceptualisation and the application of service quality which is also known as SERVIQUAL.

MODELS AND APPROACHES SUPPORTING SERVICE QUALITY

Diverse scholars alluded on various theories, models and approaches that support service quality in health affairs. The Nordic Model was introduced by Ghotbabadi, Feiz and Baharun (2015) as a first model to measure service quality in organisations in the early 1980s. In the context of the Nordic Model, organisations must understand the perceptions of customers to be successful in implementing service quality model. On the same line, Parasuraman, Zeithaml and Berry (1985) produced SERVQUAL model to measure service quality provided by organisations and meet customer's needs. This model also determines the satisfaction and expectation of the customers. Furthermore, the SERVQUAL model has been used worldwide to assess quality of healthcare service that is provided by public healthcare institutions to its patients and to determine if the healthcare services meet the expectations of the patients.

Manulik, Rosińczuk and Karniej (2016) highlighted that quality of service that is administered by organisations to its customers is very important in healthcare institutions to secure competitive privilege against their contenders. Javed *et al.* (2019) stated that initial the SERVQUAL model had five dimensions and 22- item scale. However, as the time went by the researchers enhanced the SERVQUAL model based on the bases of the society needs. It can be deemed that SERVQUAL model has been successfully in assessing the service quality provided by different organisations to their customers. The SERVQUAL model has been used by different literatures to determine the quality of services provided by organisations to its customers.

Kim *et al.* (2017) are of the view that service quality challenges which are encountered need to be addressed through the notion of SERVQUAL model. However, SERVQUAL model is a common tool used to assess service quality provided by organisations and to categories service quality based to five value systems that oversee the outcomes. Dabestani *et al.* (2017) mentioned that customers are classified into two categories, the first category is the group of customers who are satisfied easily (ordinary customers), the second categories are those who are difficult to satisfy or to please (Fastidious customers). Furthermore, these customers they measure the quality of service differently based to their levels of satisfaction levels and to their needs.

Figure 1. Conceptual model of services
Source: Johann (2015)

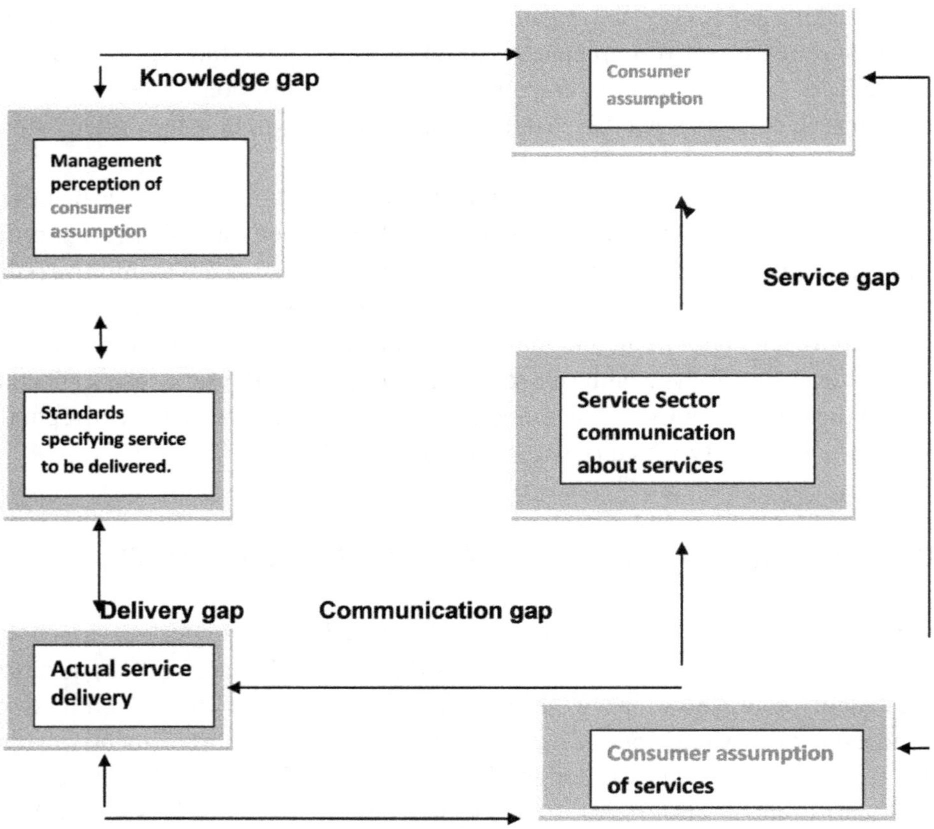

Johann (2015) mentioned that the 22 item scale of SERVQUAL model consist of two sections, the first section indicate customer expectations of an excellent firm at a specific industry. The second section indicate customer perception about the service provided by the organisations. Furthermore, Johann (2015) stated that the level of customer expectations and their expectations about the service provided by the organisations are determined through the seven point scale. Moreover, the result of the measurement of both sections are compared to the gap of service delivery have been identified. Manulik, Rosińczuk and Karniej (2016) stated that there are elements which are commonly used for quality management such as structural outline, deliriousness, pareto chart, Eisenhower box, punishment analysis, rewards as well as critical incidents techniques.

The figure 1 above lay out a comprehensive understanding of gaps between quality service provided and the perceived service quality by the customers, identified through using SERVQUAL model. Furthermore, this figure also imply the use of remedies to mitigate the challenges of providing quality services delivery by organisations to its customers as they perceived to meet their ever-changing needs. According to Johann (2015) there are gaps which occurs outside of the organisation amongst customers and service providers, such as knowledge gap, perception gap, as well as service quality gap. The following section will look at gaps in service quality.

Gaps in Service Quality

There are gaps that occur inside the organisation between its departments and sections which are coursed by the policies such as delivery gaps and communication gaps.

Gap 1: Customer Assumption Management Perception Gap (the Knowledge Gap)

Johann (2015) asserts that knowledge gap refers to dissimilarities amongst management perceptions and customer perceptions of the organisation about service delivery. However, there are many factors which determine the size of the knowledge gap such as organisation orientation about customers, communication of the first-line employees, management is customer orientated as well as the complexity of organisational structure. Moreover, knowledge gap will decrease if the organisation is aware of customers' needs on regular basis and ensure that customer needs are cascaded down to all organisational levels. In the context of health intersection, knowledge about good diet and good behaviour of clients must be available to them before they get unwell so that they can make choices in fife and avoid toxic food and other food and lifestyle that can create diseases and bad health.

Gap 2: Management Feelings Service Quality Requirements Gap (Standards Gap)

Mosadeghrad (2014: 77) stated that different firms have experience different challenges in their attempt to meet or to achieve customer needs and desired quality service. The management of the organisations are of the view that there are many issues which hinder the organisation to meet the customer needs. Furthermore, executives of the organisations experience gaps when there is a breakdown when consumers want a quick response for them to view the service as the best service. Also, managers need to use various approaches when they prepare service infrastructure and identify the needs of stakeholders in the value chain of service delivery.

Mosadeghrad (2014: 78) specified that many organisations have challenges to develop remedies by providing quick response to challenges, instead of offering long lasting solutions. In some instances, the hospital personnel are not well trained because of fluctuation of the customer's demands and lack of resources in the health public facilities. However, besides constraints in resource and marketing there are many variables that create gaps between customer expectations and actual service provided. These variables include poor commitment of management to quality of the service provided. However, all these discrepancies are the major challenges which have affected service quality provided by organisations to meet the standard of service quality that is perceived by customers.

Gap 3: The Specification of Service Quality Gap

The specification of the service quality gap must be known to that the managers are aware of the type of a gap they are dealing with. Gaps can emanate from infrastructure, personnel skills shortage and misplacement of staff in positions, and lack of resources and assets to provide services to the clients. According to Johann (2015: 92) service delivery gaps occurs when there is a noticeable difference between a promised standard of service with standard that is provided by the organisation. Hence, service delivery gaps depend to the ability and desire of employees of the organisation to provide a particular service delivery according standard set by management of the organisation. However, the quality-of-service delivery interweave with policies of employees employed by the organisation. If organisation recruitment section selects genuine candidates, provide good training, appraise employees, and have a control procedure which is well implemented, the organisation can lower service delivery challenges.

Gap 4: External Environment Imparting of Service Delivery (Communication Gap)

Parasuraman, Zeithaml and Berry (1985) mentioned that consumer expectations can be affected by media advertising and other communication means that speculate on the economic outlook and affordability of clients. However, organisations need to update their mission to meet what they can offer to clients to avoid empty promises. Hence, if organisations promise consumers more it will raise their expectations, and if they don't receive what they have been promised it will then reduce consumers trust about the organisation and they will feel that they have been betrayed by the organisation. Johann (2015: 92) attested that messages which is sent by the organisation through its communication channels can influence the consumers' expectations. However, if the organisation provides differ service quality than the one which have been narrated to external communication that contradict the actual quality of services delivered can course a communication gaps. Public health organisations can also improve their technology, benchmark, do quality circles and collaborate with other health centres to improve their performance.

Gap 5: Anticipation of Service-Discern Service (Service Gap)

Johann (2015: 92) suggested that service gap is a result of other gaps that are experienced by consumers. Service delivery gap is a contrast between the services quality expected by customers to the service quality provided by organisations to customers. Parasuraman, Zeithaml and Berry (1985) stated that the key to address service gap is to provide quality service delivery to customers which meet and exceeds their expectations about the quality of the service.

SERVQUAL CHALLENGES IN PUBLIC HEALTHCARE INSTITUTIONS

Shahin and Samea (2010) assert that to implement SERVQUAL model correctly, organisations must ensure that it is implemented in all levels of the organisation in a uniform way. Seviqual needs people who don't only understand service delivery alone, but all other components to satisfy the clients. Sumaedi, Yarmen and Yuda Bakti (2016), cited in Nagata *et al.* (2004) mentioned that SERVQUAL model is a well-known phrase which is used worldwide prominent and progressive organisations to evaluate service which is provided by organisations to its customers. Cronin Jr and Taylor (1992) asserts that challenges of effectiveness of SERVQUAL model in assessing service quality can be changed. Furthermore, they then considered performance as the only measurement which can measure the service quality provided by the organisation. Hence, they suggested that there must be a new model to measure service quality which will be derived from performance called SERPERF, which will be a suitable model to measure service quality.

Shafieisabet, Doostisabzi and Azharianfar (2017) stated that SERVQUAL model have been criticised by many researchers because it only measures the satisfaction levels of the end user of the service, if service provided by the organisations meet their expectations and perceive quality of the service. Hence, SERVQUAL model cannot be used to access the quality of service provided by the organisations. However, SERQUAL model is a most popular and common instrument which is used to determine the quality of the service delivery provided by the organisation, if it meet the ever changing needs of customers. Shafei, Walburg and Taher (2019) claimed that SERVQUAL and SERVPERF must be used together to determine service quality of the organisation, since both have a high score of validity and reliability which they produce.

LEGISLATIONS SUPPORTING SERVICE STANDARDS AND QUALITY MANAGEMENT IN PUBLIC INSTITUTIONS

The legislations that govern the healthcare institutions and provision of service delivery and healthcare services in South Africa are derived from the South African Constitution Act 108 Of 1996, since the South African Constitution is a supreme law of the country. According to South Africa Constitution Act 108 of 1996, section 27(1), all South African citizens are entitled to obtain quality service delivery and quality healthcare services from the government.

The South Africa Constitution Act 108 of 1996

South African Constitution Act 108 of 1996, Section 24(a), states that everyone has a right to access quality healthcare services, including reproductive and no one may be refused to access medical treatment. Furthermore, the South African Constitution Act 108 of 1996 section 195 states that all public institutions and administration need to ensure professionalism and high-quality standard, ensure quality and fair in-service delivery, need to ensure to be impartial, address society's needs, and ensure the provision of precise information to society.

National Health Act no. 61 of 2003

National Health Act no. 61 of 2003 ensure that all healthcare institutions in South Africa practice uniform healthcare standards and it is responsible for ensuring that all healthcare facilities provide equal and quality service delivery to all citizens, this Act also ensure the prioritisations of vulnerable groups of people such as woman, children, people living with disabilities as well as elderly people. This Act also provides responsibility of the end user of healthcare services that they need to treat healthcare workers with respect and humanity. Furthermore, the Act indicate that that if the end user refuse treatment they must sign the release of liability to show that they have refuse to be treated. Moreover, The Act provide for the establishment of District Health Care System which will be determined by the size of population that will be served by that healthcare institution.

Occupational Health and safety Act 85 of 1993

Occupational Health and Safety Act no. 85 of 1993 ensure health and safety of people at workplaces, and it also provide for health and safety of employees using plants and machinery at their workplaces.

This Act also protects employees at their workplaces against hazards to health and safety which can arise while performing their daily duties at workplaces. The Act also provide for the establishment of advisory council for occupational health and safety which will attend to matters connected therewith. The Act also provide for the appointment of health and safety raps who will be responsible for overseeing safety measures within working environment and who will critique the effectiveness of all record keeping pertaining safety measure at the workplace.

Labour Relation Act 66 of 1995

The Labour Relations Act no 66 of 1995 this Act regulates the formation of trade unions at workplaces, and it gives rights to employees join trade union of their choice. It also allows employees to participate or engage to trade unions activities during work times. It also promotes the facilitation of collective bargaining at workplaces, forums and to dispute resolution. It provides for strikes and lockouts within workplaces. The Act also promotes fair labour practices at workplaces, it also encourages employee's participation in decision making process and ensure effective resolution of any disputes. When the dispute arises at the working environment managers need to adhere to labour relations act to address that dispute. This Act also provide for the establishment of CCMA, Labour Court as well as Appeal Court which will be superior courts with exclusive jurisdiction to decide on matters arise from Labour Relations Act 66 of 1995.

The preface of the National Health Act 61 of 2003 intends to provide framework for the regulation, development and management of national health system and set standards for rendering health services in the federation as well as related matters. This Act ensures the promotion and adherence of National Health act principles, norms, and standard of providing quality service delivery and quality healthcare services to society. This Act also ensures the healthcare practitioners are capacitated with knowledge and skills to enforce and ensure the effective implementation of the Act.

Batho Pele Principles and Service Standards

The first democratic government was elected in 1994 in South Africa. In 1997 the democratic government introduced a white paper to transform service delivery as Batho Pele principles. The aim of Batho Pele principles was to ensure the effective implementation of Constitutional mandate of providing effective and efficient service delivery to society. The gist of Batho Pele principle was to enhance service delivery which is rendered by public servants to society. Batho Pele Handbook (2005: 8) indicated that South African citizens can use Batho Pele principle to hold public servants accountable and responsible about service delivery. The significance of Batho Pele principles is to enhance service delivery provided by government.

In 1997 the Department of Public Service and Administration (DPSA) adopted Batho Pele principles as a policy framework to advocate eight principles which will assist public servants to provide effective service delivery society. The eight Batho Pele principles include consultation, curtesy, value for money, transparency and access to information, service standards and redress in handling service clients.

National Core Standards (NCS)

According to Whittaker *et al.* (2011) South African government has plans to provide quality healthcare services to all communities which emanate from South African Constitution, Batho Pele principles,

Patients' Rights, and National Core Standards (NCS). Furthermore, South Africa healthcare is still faced by burden of infectious diseases and other discrepancy that still exist in the post-COVID 19 era, which burdens the system in providing quality healthcare services to achieve the National Development Plan's (NDP) vision for 2030. Even though government goals are legit, they are broad and are not easy to be implemented without all needed resources. Steenkamp (1995) cited that South African Constitution, Act 108 of 1996 section 27, supports the right of citizens to quality healthcare services, including reproductive healthcare services. Brauns and Wallis (2014) they attested that healthcare system in South Africa is still faced with challenges which were created by apartheid government by fragmenting service delivery according to racial groups.

Mayosi and Benatar (2014) believe that due to poor allocation of resources to public healthcare institutions makes it to be difficult for healthcare institutions to render quality healthcare services to the society, which makes society to be still plagued to infectious and communicable disease. However, due to large number of refugees and economic migrants who are coming to South Africa exacerbate the demands of health resource, which compromised the health care system. This makes it difficult for healthcare institutions to render quality healthcare services to society. Gilson *et al.* (2014) mentioned that in the past two decades and half democratic government in South Africa is still trying to enhance healthcare services in order to address the needs of its citizens. Ataguba, Day and McIntyre (2014) mentioned that in South Africa healthcare issues were created by colonialism and apartheid.

Ramson, Govender and Naidoo (2016) mentioned that healthcare challenges in African countries are added by healthcare workers who migrate from African countries to developed countries looking for greener pastures. Furthermore, this migration of health professionals from African countries to developed countries creates a shortage of health professionals and it impacts the service provision and hospital operations.

Furthermore, these government plans identify the most significant areas which are considered from the first three domains of (NCS).

- Value and attitude of staff toward patients, this will ensure patients are treated with courtesy and respect.
- Reduction of waiting times and queues, this will reduce waiting times for administration or assessment.
- Cleanliness of facilities, it includes buildings, equipment, and staff.
- Welfare of patients and provision of authentic care by decreasing unfavourable events which result from poor healthcare provision and the failures of the system and workers through ignorance.
- Prevention of infections within the hospital or clinics, especially hospital acquired more infections.
- Availability of medicine, supplies, and equipment, this will assist in ensuring that patients get their medication on the same date of prescription.

It can be argued that suggested healthcare institutions need to focus more into these significant areas to improve the provision of quality healthcare services to its patients. According to Senkubuge, Modisenyane and Bishaw (2014) government need to improve their attempts on healthcare reform in public healthcare institutions, and provide sustainable and long lasting changes which will improve efficiency and equity. Kim *et al.* (20173) indicated that healthcare institution must ensure that they practice Patients Right when they are dealing with patients, because patient treatment have a huge impact in the relationship between patients and healthcare facility. Furthermore, treating patients bad can result in patients taking legal actions against the healthcare institution for malpractice.

Table 1. Domains and sub-domains of the NCS

Domain	Sub-domain
Domain 1: Patient Rights The domain of Patient Rights which sets out what hospital or clinic must do to make sure that patients are respected and have their rights upheld. This domain ensures that patients have access to quality healthcare services, it also encourages that patients are addressed in a respectful manner, obtain a dignified attention, and encourage that patients are treated in a hygienic environment in accordance with Bath Pele principles and Patients Right.	Respect and dignity Information to patients Physical access Continuity of care Reducing delays in care Emergency care Access to package of services Complaints management
Domain 2: Patient Safety, Clinical Governance, and Care The Patient Safety, Clinical Governance and Clinical Care domain covers how the healthcare institution can ensure nursing quality, clinical care as well as ethical practices. This domain also ensures the reduction of unintended harm to patients and identifies cases of clinical risk. Furthermore, this domain manages problems or adverse events of healthcare which is associated with infections and to support affected patients or staff.	Patient care Clinical management for improved health outcomes Clinical leadership Clinical risk Adverse events infection prevention and control
Domain 3: Clinical Support Services The Clinical Support Services domain covers specific services which are important in providing clinical care to patients. This includes timely availability of medicines, efficient provision of diagnostic therapeutic, clinical support services, necessary medical technologies as well as systems to monitor the efficiency of the care provided to patients.	Pharmaceutical services Diagnostic services Therapeutic and support services Health technology services Sterilisation services Mortuary services Efficiency management
Domain 4: Public Health The Public Health domain indicates how healthcare institutions should work with NGO's, private healthcare institutions, communities as well as other relevant health sectors to promote health, prevent illness, and reduce further complications. This coalition will ensure that integrated and quality care is provided to the whole society including during times of disasters.	Population based service planning and delivery. Health promotion and disease prevention Disaster preparedness Environment control
Domain 5: Leadership and Corporate Governance The Leadership and Corporate Governance domain covers the strategic direction provided by senior management through proactive leadership planning and risk management, supported by the hospital board clinic committee as well the relevant supervisory support structures, which include strategic functions of communication and quality improvement.	Oversight and accountability Strategic management Risk management Quality management Effective leadership Communications and public relations
Domain 6: Operational Management The Operational Management domain covers the day-to-day responsibilities which involve the support and ensuring the delivery of safe and effective patient care. Furthermore, this domain includes the management of human resources, finances assets, consumables, information, and records.	Human resource management and development Employee wellness Supply chain management Transport and fleet management Information management Medical records
Domain 7: Facilities and Infrastructure The Facilities and infrastructure domain is based on cleanliness, safety and secure of physical infrastructure (buildings, plant, and machinery equipment) and functional, well managed hotel services; and effective waste disposal.	Buildings and grounds Machinery and utilities Safety and security Hygiene and cleanliness Linen and laundry Food services

Source: Whittaker *et al.* (2011: 63)

Furthermore, if healthcare institutions can strive to improve service delivery and healthcare services that they provide to its patients, it will automatically change the negative perception of community about public healthcare services in South Africa. Sung and Lee (2019) stated that healthcare facilities need to have a Usual Source of Care (USC) which will provide an increase in patients accessing quality healthcare services and improve preventative measures that will decrease the number of patients who will visit emergency rooms. Furthermore, it will enhance healthcare status and increase the satisfaction levels of patients about healthcare services. Hence, this Usual Source of Care (USC) refers to an alternative place which can be consulted by patients when they sick medical attention or medical advice.

According to Mosadeghrad (2014) minister of health in South Africa need to prioritise the free provision of Primary Health Care service (PHC) to unprivileged group of people, especially for those who leave in rural and remote areas. Gustafsdottir *et al.* (2017) indicated that if healthcare institutions can reform their healthcare system and implement healthcare service in a modern healthcare system, it can have a huge influence in life expectation, morbidity as well as to traditionally disadvantage group of society. National Department of Health (2012) indicated that the media and community reports which were revealed in 2009 which indicated that South African healthcare institutions are failing to meet the set standard of providing quality healthcare services to society and, they have challenges in meeting and satisfying the needs of patients. Hence, the South African government has put measures in place to achieve the set commendable goals of enhance service deliver and healthcare services.

THE APPLICATION OF SERVICE QUALITY AT RIETVLEI PUBLIC HEALTH CARE

Research Methodology

The study adopted a mixed research methodology that uses both qualitative and quantitative research methods for collecting and analysis data. Creswell (2014) attested that mixed-methodology is a research design which uses both qualitative and quantitative research methods, since it provide a specific direction for the procedure in a research design. This study has used a simple random technique which made any member of the population to stand an equal chance to be included in the sampling. The researcher has selected to use this technique because the hospital had lot of medical staff who works different shift pattern. The researcher also has to draw data from different patients who visited the hospital seeking medical attention in different days, and also the hospital had patients who are admitted in the hospital. The researcher decided to use this technique because it was feasible and suitable since every population member stands a possibility to be included in the survey.

The researcher piloted questionnaires to ten (10) study participants, which include Rietvlei Hospital health professionals, admitted patients and walk-in patients. Pre-testing was conducted to determine if questionnaires will be the suitable and reliable to obtain data from participants. Letter of informed consent was included in all questionnaires stating that participating to the study is voluntary and participants can withdraw at any time providing reasons for his or her withdrawal. The target population of this study healthcare professionals, inpatients and outpatients as well as society around Rietvlei Hospital. The total of one hundred and fifty questionnaires was issued to all survey participants, but the research only received hundred and twenty-six (126) questionnaires which was brought back by participants.

Qualitative data was collected through interviews to other study participants, including Rietvlei Hospital management, healthcare professionals as well as other managers at Rietvlei hospital. The questions for interviews was designed as open-ended questions. The data which was collected through interviews was collected from six Rietvlei employees. The interviews were all recoded and later transcribed into written text in English. Noble and Smith (2015) indicated that to promote validity the researcher must not include his or her personal experience and his or her viewpoint of the situation, because if the researcher include his or her point of view it can result in methodological bias which can lead not accurately portraying the perspective of the participants. The data which was collected through qualitative method of structured interviews was analyse using the *Nvivo* Version 10.

DATA ANALYSIS AND INTEPRETATION

The District Hospital was surveyed with semi-structured questionnaires to obtain data from 126participants. In the sample of 126 participants, 30 were inpatients, and 30 were outpatients and 66 were health professionals. Another data was collected through interviews from 6 health professionals. When conducting data analysis, the statistical characteristics are very significant and the biographic ones were composed of gender, race as well as age were an important factor in assessing patient perception about quality-of-service delivery and healthcare services which is rendered by public healthcare institutions. It also assisted in evaluating the patient's satisfaction level about the healthcare services provided by Rietvlei hospital. The collected data was analysed and converted into percentage form based on aims and objectives of the survey. Analysis of the respondent profile is shown in Table 2.

Based on the above table, the sum of 60% participants were females, while males were 40% of the composition. Furthermore, since the study was conducted in a rural healthcare institution, the sum of 96,7% participants were black. However, there were only 3.3% of study participants who were coloured people. From the participants, a 41.7% of participants were in between the ages of 36-55 years, up to 26, 7% were between the age group less than 25 years, 25% were at the age group of 26-35 and 4% were above the age of 55 years. This figure had a significant impact on how participants view the service delivery and healthcare service provided at Rietvlei hospital.

As indicated in the above table, data revealed that females were more dominant than males. The female healthcare professionals who participated in the study were 75.8% and the male's healthcare professionals who participated in the survey were 24.2%. Furthermore, since the study was conducted at a rural health facility, the health professionals who were the most are black people with a 97%. However, only

Table 2. Patients distribution according to gender, race, and age

Predictor variable	No. Of patients	Percentage (%)
Gender of patient's participants		
Male	24	40%
Female	36	60%
Race of patient's participants		
Black	58	96.7%
Coloured	2	3.3%
Age of patient's participants		
Less than 25 years	16	26.7%
26-35 years	15	25%
36-55 years	25	41.7%
Over 55 years	4	6.7%

Table 3. Distribution of health professionals according to gender, race, and age

Predictor variable	No. Of health professionals	Percentage (%)
Gender of health professionals' participants		
Male	16	24.2%
Female	50	75.8%
Race of health professionals' participants		
Black	64	97%
Coloured	1	1.5%
Asian	1	1.5%
Age of health professionals' participants		
Less than 25 years	5	7.6%
26-35 years	9	13.6%
36-55 years	42	63.6%
Over 55 years	10	15.2%

1.5% Coloured healthcare professionals who participated in the study as well as1.5% of Asian health professionals who participated in the survey. The healthcare professionals who participated mostly in the study were between the ages of 36-55 years with 63.6%, other health professionals were above the age of 55 years with 15.2%, 13.6% of health professionals were between the ages of 26-35. Lastly 7.6% of health professionals were below 25 years of age.

Table 4 presents the responses on the perceptions of service quality at Rietvlei hospital as follows:

1. The perception about the waiting period.

Most of the participants indicated that the waiting period for receiving treatment was not reasonable. Participants who were patients also alluded on the fact that they were not satisfied with lack of supervision which was provided by healthcare workers to end user of the service. There is also a relation between lack of supervision and lack of skills needed to provide good quality service to patients, due to the fact that participants were dissatisfied about the skills and knowledge which was possessed by health professionals at the rural healthcare institutions. Hence there was low response rate on reliance as a principle for service quality. Health professionals were perceived to lack skills and knowledge have a tendency to provide low quality production and services to their clients. When the participants were probed to rate the services at the Rietvlei hospital, they revealed that majority of patients was dissatisfied about way in which health professionals understand their problems. This imply that all these factors contribute to poor quality services rendered at Rietvlei hospital. This observation on poor response rate and waiting period imply poor responsiveness as a principle for service quality. Also, the absence of knowledge and skills about most of service provision matters imply shortages in meeting the Assurance principle in as far as service standards are concerned. When the employees don't care and also don't understand the problems of the patients, they don't meet the expectations on Assurance as a principle for service quality.

2. Patients perceptions about the health professionals' methods of communication

Table 4. Patients perspective about their satisfaction levels on health services

		Strongly Agree	Agree	Neutral	Disagree	Strongly Disagree	Total (%)
	Patient's perception about waiting times before getting medical attention						
1	The waiting period is reasonable	31.7%	16.7%	25%	11.7%	15%	100%
2	There is regular supervision by healthcare workers	0	3.3%	16.7%	18.3%	61.7%	100%
3	The healthcare professionals understand patients' problems	11.7%	0	8.3%	25%	65%	100%
4	The hospital uses advanced and modern equipment's	0	1.7%	1.7%	20%	76.7%	100%
5	Health professionals can provide quick diagnoses of patient's diseases	0	0	20%	28.3%	51.7%	100%
6	Responses from patients' treatment	0	5%	11.7%	20%	63.3%	100%
	Patient's perception about the way in which health professional communicate with patients						
7	There are good communication lines between patients and health professionals	11.7%	3.3%	3.3%	20%	71.7%	100%
	Patient's perception about the availability of health professionals at the hospital						
8	Health professionals are mostly available to work at the hospital during their core-time	1.7%	0	16.7%	8.3%	73.3%	100%
	Patient's perception about the availability of beds at the hospital						
9	The hospital beds are available when there are needed for patients use.	1.7%	1.7%	13.3%	10%	73.3%	100%

The study revealed that the majority of the participants were not satisfied about the methods of communication adopted by the health centre while patients are receiving their treatment. The participants expected better and reasonable conversations with health worker but all was not practical as the health officials were working under pressure and had not been exposed in various communication skills enough to impress the patients.

3. Perceptions about the availability of health professionals at Rietvlei hospital

Participants were probed on the availability of health professionals at Rietvlei hospital during their core-time/ working hours. The sum of 73%, which was the majority, was not satisfied with the availability of health officials at the hospital during their core-time. The shortage of staff during their working hours has become a norm to most of non-performing hospitals in South Africa. This leads to poor service quality. This observation of lack of staff and physical infrastructure relates to poor ratings on tangibility as a principle for service quality.

4. Perceptions about the availability of beds at the hospital

The study revealed that beds were not always available to admit patients in the hospital; 73.3 study participants revealed the shortage of beds for admission. The responses suggest discrepancy in the service delivery by healthcare officers and staff in public healthcare institutions. This table shows a gap between healthcare services provided by public healthcare institutions, with the expectations of the end user of healthcare services. The observation on the shortage of beds relates to poor ratings on tangibility as a principle for service quality.

IMPLICATIONS FOR SERVICE QUALITY

The management of the Hospital needs to beef-up the hospital performance in relations to the five dimensions for service quality that were observed in this study. These dimensions will assist the hospital to enhance service delivery and healthcare services to its customers, and later improve the citizens lives. These dimensions are tangible, reliability, satisfaction, responsibility as well as empathy. These dimensions are significant because they are used by patients to measure the quality-of-service delivery and healthcare service which is provided by healthcare institution to them. If these dimensions were implemented correctly, they could have enhanced the satisfaction level of the hospital customers. The organisation must ensure that they encourage health professionals to perform to the best of their abilities by implementing performance appraisal. It can be deduced that the service standards that are not met at Rietvlei can hurt the patients' lives and that of Umzimkhulu area.

CONCLUSION

Service delivery and healthcare service is significant to satisfy the hospital customers as it may affect the lives of the citizens. Patients who receive their medical attention from public healthcare institutions expect to get quality service delivery and quality healthcare service from public healthcare institutions. Findings from this chapter demonstrate that there is a gap in service delivery and healthcare service which provided by rural healthcare institutions to its customers. Using the case of Rietvlei hospital, some other health centres can learn lessons on how service quality can be used to assess the provision of services in a public health facility. The majority of the study's respondents were dissatisfied about the quality service delivered at the healthcare service center, which cannot be generalised to all other rural healthcare institutions.

The reason for community expectation is that they also contribute to tax and revenue which government allocate to public healthcare institutions. This chapter revealed that proper services must be delivered in order to improve the quality of lives of the patients and that of the health workers. It is significant for a developing nation like South Africa to continue training the citizens on how they can alter their life styles in order to limit their crowding in health facilities where there is limited state resources.

The Management have minimum interference in most of these items, hence this chapter can suggest a training and refresher training to all health professionals employed at Rietvlei hospital. Management must ensure that all health professionals adhere to Batho Pele principles, service standards and patients right when they provide services during their core-time. The management must develop proper communication strategy, to improve their methods and channels of communicating with patients. They must research continuously to investigate on how patient feels about the service delivery and the healthcare service which they provide. The hospital needs to ensure that they attend to all complain rose by the patients.

REFERENCES

Abbas, M., Gao, Y., & Sayyed Sadaqat Hussain, S. (2018). CSR and Customer Outcomes: The Mediating Role of Customer Engagement. *Sustainability, 10*(11), 4243. doi:10.3390u10114243

Adeniji, A. A., & Mash, B. (2016). Patients' perceptions of the triage system in a primary healthcare facility, Cape Town, South Africa. *African Journal of Primary Health Care & Family Medicine, 8*(1), e1–e9. doi:10.4102/phcfm.v8i1.1148 PMID:27380788

Anderson, T. J., Saman, D. M., Lipsky, M. S., & Lutfiyya, M. N. (2015). A cross-sectional study on health differences between rural and non-rural U.S. counties using the County Health Rankings. *BMC Health Services Research, 15*(1), 441. doi:10.118612913-015-1053-3 PMID:26423746

Andre de la, P. (2016). Spirituality and healthcare: Towards holistic people-centred healthcare in South Africa. *Hervormde Teologiese Studies, 72*(4), e1–e9.

Ataguba, J. E., Day, C., & McIntyre, D. (2014). Monitoring and evaluating progress towards Universal Health Coverage in South Africa. *PLoS Medicine, 11*(9), e1001686. doi:10.1371/journal.pmed.1001686 PMID:25243462

Atuoye, K. N., Dixon, J., Rishworth, A., Galaa, S. Z., Boamah, S. A., & Luginaah, I. (2015). Can she make it? Transportation barriers to accessing maternal and child health care services in rural Ghana. *BMC Health Services Research, 15*(1), 333. doi:10.118612913-015-1005-y PMID:26290436

Ballim, F. (2017). The Un-making of the Group Areas Act: Local Resistance and Commercial Power in the Small Town of Mokopane. *South African Historical Journal, 69*(4), 568–582. doi:10.1080/02582473.2017.1377760

Barron, P., Padarath, A., Ranchod, S., Adams, C., Burger, R., Carvounesi, A., Stewart, J., Dreyer, K., Smith, A., & van Biljon, C. (2017). Twenty years of the South African Health Review; South Africa's hospital sector: old divisions and new developments. *Health Systems Trust, Durban.*

Blecher, M., Pillay, A., Patcharanarumol, W., Panichkriangkrai, W., Tangcharoensathien, V., Teerawattananon, Y., Pannarunothai, S., & Davén, J. (2016). Guest Editorial: Health financing lessons from Thailand for South Africa on the path towards universal health coverage. *South African Medical Journal, 106*(6), 533–534.

Brauns, M. & Wallis, M. (2014). Performance management and public policy: the case of the health sector in South Africa. *Administratio publica, 22*(1), 149-170.

Buechel, B., Emrich, E., & Pohlkamp, S. (2016). Nobody's Innocent: The Role of Customers in the Doping Dilemma. *Journal of Sports Economics, 17*(8), 767–789. doi:10.1177/1527002514551475

Chang, C.-W., Tseng, T.-H., & Woodside, A. G. (2013). Configural algorithms of patient satisfaction, participation in diagnostics, and treatment decisions' influences on hospital loyalty. *Journal of Services Marketing, 27*(2), 91–103. doi:10.1108/08876041311309225

Cole, M. B., Wright, B., Wilson, I. B., Galárraga, O., & Trivedi, A. N. (2018). Medicaid expansion and community health centers: Care quality and service use increased for rural patients. *Health Affairs, 37*(6), 900–907. doi:10.1377/hlthaff.2017.1542 PMID:29863920

Creswell, J. W. (2014). *A concise introduction to mixed methods research.* SAGE publications.

Cronin, J. J. Jr, & Taylor, S. A. (1992). Measuring service quality: A reexamination and extension. *Journal of Marketing*, *56*(3), 55–68. doi:10.1177/002224299205600304

Dabestani, R., Shahin, A., Shirouyehzad, H., & Saljoughian, M. (2017). A comparative study of ordinary and fastidious customers' priorities in service quality dimensions. *Total Quality Management & Business Excellence*, *28*(3-4), 331–350. doi:10.1080/14783363.2015.1082420

Dávideková, M., & Greguš ml, M. (2017). Concept of Dynamic Advertisement Composition Model Tailored to Customers´ Needs Based on Interactive Customer Input. *Procedia Computer Science*, *109*, 1016–1021. doi:10.1016/j.procs.2017.05.449

Day, S., Cornell, J., & Malherbe, N. (2019). Discourses of 'service delivery protests' in South Africa: An analysis of talk radio. *Critical Discourse Studies*, 1–18.

De Juan, A., & Wegner, E. (2019). Social Inequality, State-centered Grievances, and Protest: Evidence from South Africa. *The Journal of Conflict Resolution*, *63*(1), 31–58. doi:10.1177/0022002717723136

De la Porte, A. (2016). Spirituality and healthcare: Towards holistic people-centred healthcare in South Africa. *Hervormde Teologiese Studies*, *72*(4), 1–19. doi:10.4102/hts.v72i4.3127

Doherty, J., Kirigia, D., Okoli, C., Chuma, J., Ezumah, N., Ichoku, H., Hanson, K., & McIntyre, D. (2018). Does expanding fiscal space lead to improved funding of the health sector in developing countries?: Lessons from Kenya, Lagos State (Nigeria) and South Africa. *Global Health Action*, *11*(1), 1461338–1461311. doi:10.1080/16549716.2018.1461338 PMID:29768107

Fan, L.-H., Gao, L., Liu, X., Zhao, S.-H., Mu, H.-T., Li, Z., Shi, L., Wang, L.-L., Jia, X.-L., Ha, M., & Lou, F.-G. (2017). Patients' perceptions of service quality in China: An investigation using the SERVQUAL model. *PLoS One*, *12*(12), e0190123. doi:10.1371/journal.pone.0190123 PMID:29272312

Fatima, T., Malik, S. A., & Shabbir, A. (2018). Hospital healthcare service quality, patient satisfaction and loyalty: An investigation in context of private healthcare systems. *International Journal of Quality & Reliability Management*, *35*(6), 1195–1214. doi:10.1108/IJQRM-02-2017-0031

Foko, T. T., Legare, L., & Maremi, K. (2017). Addressing Service Delivery in Rural Areas through Deployment of Information and Communication Technology Platforms. n 2017 IST-Africa Week Conference (IST-Africa), (pp. 1-9). IEEE.

Fusheini, A., & Eyles, J. (2016). Achieving universal health coverage in South Africa through a district health system approach: Conflicting ideologies of health care provision. *BMC Health Services Research*, *16*(1), 558. doi:10.118612913-016-1797-4 PMID:27717353

Ghotbabadi, A. R., Feiz, S., & Baharun, R. (2015). Service quality measurements: A review. *International Journal of Academic Research in Business & Social Sciences*, *5*(2), 267. doi:10.6007/IJARBSS/v5-i2/1484

Gilson, L., Elloker, S., Olckers, P., & Lehmann, U. (2014). Advancing the application of systems thinking in health: South African examples of a leadership of sensemaking for primary health care. *Health Research Policy and Systems*, *12*(1), 30. doi:10.1186/1478-4505-12-30 PMID:24935658

González, I. B., Pedraza Melo, N. A., Lavín Verástegui, J., & Monforte García, G. (2017). Service quality and users satisfaction assessment in the health context in Mexico. [Universidad del Valle]. *Cuadernos Americanos*, *33*, 36–47.

Gustafsdottir, S. S., Fenger, K., Halldorsdottir, S., & Bjarnason, T. (2017). Social justice, access and quality of healthcare in an age of austerity: Users' perspective from rural Iceland. *International Journal of Circumpolar Health*, *76*(1), 1347476–1347479. doi:10.1080/22423982.2017.1347476 PMID:28762300

Hendricks, S. J., Buch, E., Seekoei, E., Bossert, T., & Roberts, M. (2014). Decentralisation in South Africa: Options for district health authorities in South Africa. *South African Health Review*, *2014*(1), 59–72.

Hüttel, B. A., Ates, Z., Schumann, J. H., Büttgen, M., Haager, S., Komor, M., & Volz, J. (2019). The influence of customer characteristics on frontline employees' customer need knowledge. *Journal of Services Marketing*, *33*(2), 220–232. doi:10.1108/JSM-11-2017-0367

Jacobsen, K. H., & Hasumi, T. (2014). Satisfaction with healthcare services in South Africa: Results of the national 2010 General Household Survey. *The Pan African Medical Journal*, *18*, 172. doi:10.11604/pamj.2014.18.172.4084 PMID:25422690

James, S., & Miza, T. M. (2015). Perceptions of professional nurses regarding introduction of the Batho Pele principles in State hospitals. *Curationis*, *38*(1), 1–e9. doi:10.4102/curationis.v38i1.1128 PMID:26016696

James, T. L., Villacis Calderon, E. D., & Cook, D. F. (2017). Exploring patient perceptions of healthcare service quality through analysis of unstructured feedback. *Expert Systems with Applications*, *71*, 479–492. doi:10.1016/j.eswa.2016.11.004

Jang, S. H., Kim, R. H., & Lee, C. W. (2016). Effect of u-healthcare service quality on usage intention in a healthcare service. *Technological Forecasting and Social Change*, *113*, 396–403. doi:10.1016/j.techfore.2016.07.030

Javed, S. A., Liu, S., Mahmoudi, A., & Nawaz, M. (2019). Patients' satisfaction and public and private sectors' health care service quality in Pakistan: Application of grey decision analysis approaches. *The International Journal of Health Planning and Management*, *34*(1), e168–e182. doi:10.1002/hpm.2629 PMID:30160783

Johann, M. (2015). *Services Marketing*. [Thesis, Warsaw School of Economics]. https://scholarworks.wmich.edu/honors_theses/2741

Kamimura, A., Ashby, J., Myers, K., Nourian, M. M., & Christensen, N. (2015). Satisfaction with healthcare services among free clinic patients. *Journal of Community Health*, *40*(1), 62–72. doi:10.100710900-014-9897-8 PMID:24912587

Kim, C. E., Shin, J.-S., Lee, J., Lee, Y. J., Kim, M., Choi, A., Park, K. B., Lee, H.-J., & Ha, I.-H. (2017). Quality of medical service, patient satisfaction and loyalty with a focus on interpersonal-based medical service encounters and treatment effectiveness: A cross-sectional multicenter study of complementary and alternative medicine (CAM) hospitals. *BMC Complementary and Alternative Medicine*, *17*(1), 174–112. doi:10.118612906-017-1691-6 PMID:28351389

Kinfack, E. C., & Akinboade, O. A. (2015). Financial development, economic growth and millennium development goals in South Africa: Is there a link? *International Journal of Social Economics*, *42*(5), 459–479. doi:10.1108/IJSE-01-2013-0006

Kruk, M. E., Kelley, E., Syed, S. B., Tarp, F., Addison, T., & Akachi, Y. (2017). Measuring quality of health-care services: What is known and where are the gaps? *Bulletin of the World Health Organization*, *95*(6), 390–390. doi:10.2471/BLT.17.195099 PMID:28603302

Kumar, R. (2018). The Delhi declaration 2018:"Healthcare for all rural people"–Alma Ata revisited. *Journal of Family Medicine and Primary Care*, *7*(4), 649. doi:10.4103/jfmpc.jfmpc_217_18 PMID:30234032

Liu, W., Liu, Y., Twum, P., & Li, S. (2016). National equity of health resource allocation in China: Data from 2009 to 2013. *International Journal for Equity in Health*, *15*(1), 68. doi:10.118612939-016-0357-1 PMID:27093960

Liu, X., Dou, L., Zhang, H., Sun, Y., & Yuan, B. (2015). Analysis of context factors in compulsory and incentive strategies for improving attraction and retention of health workers in rural and remote areas: A systematic review. *Human Resources for Health*, *13*(1), 61. doi:10.118612960-015-0059-6 PMID:26194003

Lourens, G. (2012). The National Core Standards and evidence-based nursing: Professional practice. *Professional Nursing Today*, *16*(1), 3–4.

Mahmoud, A. B., Ekwere, T., Fuxman, L., & Meero, A. A. (2019). Assessing Patients' Perception of Health Care Service Quality Offered by COHSASA-Accredited Hospitals in Nigeria. *SAGE Open*, *9*(2), 215824401985248. doi:10.1177/2158244019852480

Manulik, S., Rosińczuk, J., & Karniej, P. (2016). Evaluation of health care service quality in Poland with the use of SERVQUAL method at the specialist ambulatory health care center. *Patient Preference and Adherence*, *10*, 1435–1442. doi:10.2147/PPA.S108252 PMID:27536075

Mayosi, B. M., & Benatar, S. R. (2014). Health and Health Care in South Africa— 20 Years after Mandela. *The New England Journal of Medicine*, *371*(14), 1344–1353. doi:10.1056/NEJMsr1405012 PMID:25265493

Mazibuko. (2019). *Epidemic and the health of African Nations*. Pretoria: Published by the Mapungubwe Institute for Strategic Reflection (MISTRA).

Meyer, J. C., Schellack, N., Stokes, J., Lancaster, R., Zeeman, H., Defty, D., Godman, B., & Steel, G. (2017). Ongoing initiatives to improve the quality and efficiency of medicine use within the public healthcare system in South Africa; a preliminary study. *Frontiers in Pharmacology*, *8*, 751. doi:10.3389/fphar.2017.00751 PMID:29163151

Mosadeghrad, A. M. (2014). Factors influencing healthcare service quality. *International Journal of Health Policy and Management*, *3*(2), 77–89. doi:10.15171/ijhpm.2014.65 PMID:25114946

Nagata, H., Satoh, Y., Gerrard, S., & Kytömäki, P. (2004). The dimensions that construct the evaluation of service quality in academic libraries. *Performance Measurement and Metrics*, Naidoo, S. (2012). The South African national health insurance: A revolution in health-care delivery! *Journal of Public Health*, *34*(1), 149–150.

Nicol, E., & Hanmer, L. A. (2015). Routine Health Information Systems in South Africa—Opportunities for Improvement. *Studies in Health Technology and Informatics, 216*, 993. PMID:26262295

Noble, H., & Smith, J. (2015). Issues of validity and reliability in qualitative research. *Evidence-Based Nursing, 18*(2), 34–35. doi:10.1136/eb-2015-102054 PMID:25653237

Olorunfemi, S. (2016). Rural Road Infrastructural Challenges: An Impediment to Health Care Service Delivery in Kabba-Bunu Local Government Area of Kogi State, Nigeria. *Academic Journal of Interdisciplinary Studies, MCSER Publishing, Rome-Italy, 5*(2), 35–44.

Ostrom, Q. T., Gittleman, H., Fulop, J., Liu, M., Blanda, R., Kromer, C., Wolinsky, Y., Kruchko, C., & Barnholtz-Sloan, J. S. (2015). CBTRUS statistical report: Primary brain and central nervous system tumors diagnosed in the United States in 2008-2012. *Neuro-Oncology, 17*(suppl_4), iv1–iv62. doi:10.1093/neuonc/nov189 PMID:26511214

Otalora, M. L., Rosenbaum, M. S., & Orejula, A. R. (2018). Understanding health care service quality in developing Latin America. *Health Marketing Quarterly, 35*(3), 167–185. doi:10.1080/07359683.2018.1514733 PMID:30588870

Parasuraman, A., Zeithaml, V. A., & Berry, L. L. (1985). A Conceptual Model of Service Quality and Its Implications for Future Research. *Journal of Marketing, 49*(4), 41–50. doi:10.1177/002224298504900403

Pineo, R. (2019). Preface to the 2019 Special Issue on Public Healthcare in the Developing World. *Journal of Developing Societies, 35*(1), 1–15. doi:10.1177/0169796X19826774

Pomey, M.-P., Hihat, H., Khalifa, M., Lebel, P., Néron, A., & Dumez, V. (2015). Patient partnership in quality improvement of healthcare services: Patients' inputs and challenges faced. *Patient Experience Journal, 2*(1), 29–42. doi:10.35680/2372-0247.1064

Ramson, P., Govender, P., & Naidoo, K. (2016). Recruitment and retention strategies for public sector optometrists in KwaZulu-Natal Province, South Africa. *African Vision and Eye Health, 75*(1), e1–e10. doi:10.4102/aveh.v75i1.349

Rani, P. (2019). Strategy Implementation in Organizations: A Conceptual Overview pushpa rani. *Management, 14*(3), 205–218. doi:10.26493/1854-4231.14.205-218

Reichstein, C., & Härting, R.-C. (2018). Potentials of changing customer needs in a digital world – a conceptual model and recommendations for action in tourism. *Procedia Computer Science, 126*, 1484–1494. doi:10.1016/j.procs.2018.08.120

Ross, C. K., Frommelt, G., Hazelwood, L., & Chang, R. W. (1987). The role of expectations in patient satisfaction with medical care. *Journal of Health Care Marketing, 7*(4). PMID:10302171

Senkubuge, F., Modisenyane, M., & Bishaw, T. (2014). Strengthening health systems by health sector reforms. *Global Health Action, 7*(1), 1–7. doi:10.3402/gha.v7.23568 PMID:24560261

Shafei, I., Walburg, J., & Taher, A. (2019). Verifying alternative measures of healthcare service quality. *International Journal of Health Care Quality Assurance, 32*(2), 516–533. doi:10.1108/IJHC-QA-05-2016-0069 PMID:31017062

Shafieisabet, N., Doostisabzi, B., & Azharianfar, S. (2017). An Assessment of Villagers' Satisfaction with the Quality of Construction-Related Services Based on the SERVQUAL Model. *Current Urban Studies*, *5*(01), 20–34. doi:10.4236/cus.2017.51002

Shafiq, M., Naeem, M. A., Munawar, Z., & Fatima, I. (2017). Service Quality Assessment of Hospitals in Asian Context: An Empirical Evidence From Pakistan. *INQUIRY: The Journal of Health Care Organization, Provision, and Financing*, *54*, 46958017714664. PMID:28660771

Shahin, A., & Samea, M. (2010). Developing the Models of Service Quality Gaps: A Critical Discussion. *Business Manaagement and Strategy*, *1*(1), 1–11. doi:10.5296/bms.v1i1.395

Sidze, E. M., Beekink, E., & Maina, B. W. (2015). Challenges associated with tracking resources allocation for reproductive health in sub-Saharan African countries: The UNFPA/NIDI resource flows project experience. *Reproductive Health*, *12*(1), 39. doi:10.118612978-015-0033-8 PMID:26012472

Steenkamp, A. J. (1995). The South African Constitution of 1993 and the Bill of Rights: An Evaluation in Light of International Human Rights Norms. *Human Rights Quarterly*, *17*(1), 101–126. doi:10.1353/hrq.1995.0010

Stewart, T. A., & O'Connell, P. (2017). (201)7. HOW TO MEET YOUR CUSTOMER'S NEEDS—AND YOUR OWN: UNDERSTANDING SERVICE DESIGN ARCHETYPES. *Leader to Leader*, *2017*(84), 48–54. doi:10.1002/ltl.20291

Sumaedi, S., Yarmen, M., & Yuda Bakti, I. G. M. (2016). Healthcare service quality model. *International Journal of Productivity and Performance Management*, *65*(8), 1007–1024. doi:10.1108/IJPPM-08-2014-0126

Sung, N.-J., & Lee, J.-H. (2019). Association between Types of Usual Source of Care and User Perception of Overall Health Care Service Quality in Korea. *Korean Journal of Family Medicine*, *40*(3), 143–150. doi:10.4082/kjfm.17.0093 PMID:30419631

Tabrizi JS, Goshayie EH, Doshmangir L, Yousefi M. (2018)The Barriers to Implementation of New Public Management Strategies in Iran's Primary Health Care: A Qualitative Study. *J Liaquat Uni Med Health Sci. 17*(01), 08-17. . doi:10.22442/jlumhs.181710542

Taherdoost, H. (2016). Validity and reliability of the research instrument; how to test the validation of a questionnaire/survey in research. *International Journal of Academic Research in Management (IJARM)* *5*(3), 28-36.

Teshnizi, S. H., Aghamolaei, T., Kahnouji, K., Teshnizi, S. M. H., & Ghani, J. (2018). Assessing quality of health services with the SERVQUAL model in Iran. A systematic review and meta-analysis. *International Journal for Quality in Health Care*, *30*(2), 82–89. doi:10.1093/intqhc/mzx200 PMID:29408970

van Rensburg, H. C. J. (2014). South Africa's protracted struggle for equal distribution and equitable access - still not there. *Human Resources for Health*, *12*(1), 26–26. doi:10.1186/1478-4491-12-26 PMID:24885691

Von Pressentin, K. B., Mash, B. J., & Esterhuizen, T. M. (2017). Examining the influence of family physician supply on district health system performance in South Africa: An ecological analysis of key health indicators. *African Journal of Primary Health Care & Family Medicine*, *9*(1), e1–e10. doi:10.4102/phcfm.v9i1.1298 PMID:28470076

Wasserman, H., Chuma, W., & Bosch, T. (2018). Print media coverage of service delivery protests in South Africa: A content analysis. *African Studies*, *77*(1), 145–156. doi:10.1080/00020184.2018.1426312

Whittaker, S., Linegar, A., Shaw, C., & Spieker, N. (2011). Quality standards for healthcare establishments in South Africa. *South African Health Review*, *2011*(1), 59–67.

Winchester, M. S., & King, B. (2018). Decentralization, healthcare access, and inequality in Mpumalanga, South Africa. *Health & Place*, *51*, 200–207. doi:10.1016/j.healthplace.2018.02.009 PMID:29709650

Young, M. (2016). Private vs. public healthcare in South Africa. Honors Theses. 2741. https://scholarworks.wmich.edu/honors_theses/2741

Young, T., Garner, P., Clarke, M., & Volmink, J. (2016). Series: Clinical Epidemiology in South Africa. Paper 1: Evidence-based health care and policy in Africa: past, present, and future. *Journal of Clinical Epidemiology*, *83*, 24–30. doi:10.1016/j.jclinepi.2016.06.006 PMID:27349186

Chapter 12
The Extent of New Technologies in Urban Environments:
Virtual Reality, Lighting, and Accessibility

Sandra Arranz-Paraíso
Complutense University of Madrid, Spain

Daniel Arranz-Paraíso
https://orcid.org/0000-0002-0277-5462
Universidad CEU San Pablo, Spain

ABSTRACT

The United Nations estimated in 2018 that 68% of the population would live in urban areas in 2050. At the time of the estimate, the percentage was 55%, which would mean an increase of 13% in 32 years. Furthermore, according to their calculations, there will be 43 megacities with more than 10 million citizens by 2030. To ensure that the development of city dwellers takes place in the best possible conditions, the United Nations is committed to a sustainable urban design that guarantees the quality of life of city dwellers. The use of new technologies comes into play in the design of the urban environment to guarantee access to decent housing, employment, the inclusion of people with disabilities, transportation, energy systems, lighting, and other types of infrastructure, as well as essential services such as health, culture, and education. Considering all these challenges and their complexity of resolution, modern architecture must be constituted, planned, and made up of multidisciplinary groups that embrace the interrelationships between human beings and the environment as a whole.

1. INTRODUCTION

From the origin of the first cities in the years between approximately 9000-7500 BC until the period between approximately 3000-2500 BC, cities developed a sophisticated and complex structure, already in Egypt with perfect grid planning, sophisticated housing constructions, temples or pyramids, as well as walls that acted as defence systems. Another important civilization is the Romans, where the impor-

DOI: 10.4018/978-1-6684-6924-8.ch012

tance of water management as an advance in social welfare should be highlighted. Access to drinking water was managed in such a way that they built artificial cisterns to retain rainwater (Chiocchini, 2019) which was redistributed through aqueduct channeling, perforating mountains, crossing valleys, and always maintaining the necessary inclination for the free circulation of water that could be distributed, giving sufficient flow capacity to supply canals, gardens, homes, and public baths (Deming, 2020). All this was complemented by a drainage system that at the time could redirect dirty water through the Cloaca Maxima, which was built around the 6th century BC (Nederveen Pieterse, 2021). Evidently, in the period between 2500 BC and 2022 AD, numerous events took place, which is reflected in the urban environment design of today's cities.

One of the most important milestones was the First Industrial Revolution which began at the end of the 18th century. Since that time, numerous changes have taken place, as reported by (Xu et al., 2018), who distinguish between four periods of the industrial revolution. They date the First Industrial Revolution between 1760 and 1900 and point to the use of coal as a source of energy, the invention of the steam locomotive, and the development of the textile and steel industries as major milestones. Between 1900 and 1960 the Second Industrial Revolution occurred, with the use of oil electricity as an energy resource, the design of internal combustion engines, and the development of the automobile industry, metallurgy, and machine building. The Third Industrial Revolution would come with the use of nuclear energy, the development of computers and robots, the use of airplanes, and the development of the chemical and automobile industries between 1960 and 2000. From the year 2000 onwards, these authors mark the origin of the Fourth Industrial Revolution, with renewable energies, high industries, the use of electric cars and high-speed trains, the development of the internet, 3D printers, and genetic engineering, and the development of high-tech industries. However, some indicate that we are already living through the Fifth Industrial Revolution, marked, among other aspects, by the development of nanotechnology, human-machine interfaces, sophisticated robots, the use of big data and artificial intelligence, the Internet of Things and attempts to reduce the waste of resources to achieve the desired zero waste production (Ali et al., 2022; Pathak et al., 2019; Xu et al., 2018).

It is important to understand the major historical changes in order to understand the process that has led to the origin and successive changes in urban design, enabling better urban environment designs in the future.

The use of new technologies comes into play in designing the urban environment to ensure access to decent housing, employment, the inclusion of people living with disabilities, transport, energy systems, lighting, and other kinds of infrastructure, as well as basic services such as health care, culture or education. These mega-cities must be able to absorb the impact of the mobility required by their citizens to carry out their work and leisure activities. The planning must consider the supply of public and private mobility with the possibility of transporting a large number of citizens in a short period of time.

Public mobility is the most important, as it is the one that is accessed by the greatest number of citizens and must therefore be the best adapted. On the one hand, it is essential to use existing technology to be able to synchronise as closely as possible to meet arrival times on trains or buses and to facilitate access to these means of transport for citizens with special needs. One example is mobile applications that allow blind people to know the time remaining before the arrival of the specific means of transport with route indications to reach the desired destination in the best way possible (Adams et al., 2021).

On the other hand, public means of transport must be able to adapt to each user with special needs through the use of audiovisual and physical resources (ramps, lifts, lights, platforms) with the adaptation of possible uncomfortable internal movements that can destabilize the natural posture of users by adjusting the speed of acceleration and braking (Grisé et al., 2019; Park & Chowdhury, 2018).

Security is also crucial for this type of transport. The possibility of being sabotaged by terrorist networks, lone wolves, or people with psychological problems must be considered a high-level risk. To control all these points, it is essential to interconnect with the internet of things (IoT) using cameras, vector network analyzers (Gao et al., 2021), artificial vision and artificial intelligence (Flammini et al., 2022), continuity sensors, and infrared sensors that allow us to know, for example, the real state of the train tracks in real-time (Kauppi et al., 2006), with algorithms (Corman & Meng, 2015; Pencheva et al., 2022).

2. THE ROLE OF VIRTUAL REALITY IN URBAN ENVIRONMENTS

The development of new technologies in general, and computer science in particular, has been possible due to the knowledge generated until the year 2000 by the research and contributions of different disciplines which, on most occasions, have worked in a multidisciplinary way.

The emergence of virtual reality and its multiple applications in different fields (Tarr & Warren, 2002) are generating advances in the broad field of research formed by the cognitive sciences. Virtual reality, which is within the group of the most used new technologies, needs basic research from different disciplines, being an example of this the need to know how we perceive. According to Burdea et al. (1996), virtual reality can be defined as "multimodal interactions with computer-simulated worlds through visual, auditory, and haptic feedback" (Burdea et al., 1996). In other words, virtual reality can be understood as an application of basic cognitive science and, in turn, as a tool for unraveling and studying the most basic psychological aspects. An example of this is the use of virtual reality as a tool in studies on perception, attention, or memory (Kit et al., 2014; Kokkinara et al., 2015).

Sutherland (1965) was a pioneer in the field of virtual reality, although it was not yet named as such because he created interactive 3D worlds by using head orientation sensors and stereoscopic glasses. He predicted that physical immersion involving all senses could be generated in the future. In terms of immersive virtual reality, as early as 1984, it began to be used in the VIEW system at NASA, which employed voice recognition, stereoscopic vision glasses, 3D sound, instrumented gloves, and orientation and position sensors. A definition of the term virtual reality can be found in Lanier (1992). He defines it as a technology that allows the creation of three-dimensional spaces using a computer; that is, it allows the simulation of reality, with the great advantage that the elements and events that are considered useful can be introduced into the virtual environment, according to the objective that we set ourselves. In other words, we can generate spaces with the characteristics we want, within the limits allowed by the technologies, so that people feel that they are inside that space and can interact with the elements in that world (Lanier, 1992).

In accordance with Wilson & Soranzo (2015), the advantages of virtual reality include allowing greater control over stimulus presentation, a variety of response options, the possibility of presenting stimuli in three dimensions, the capability to create complex scenarios, the potential to generate multimodal sensory input, allowing experience through audio, touch, smell and movement simultaneously, as well as greater ecological validity, the possibility of precise and independent manipulation of geometric and photometric relationships between objects, the possibility of examining sophisticated and complex behaviors and, finally, the design of unreal situations that may be dangerous, or ethically questionable to create in real life (Wilson & Soranzo, 2015).

Following these advantages, and specifically, the possibility to generate more natural study contexts (see for example Scarfe & Glennerster, 2015; Soranzo & Wilson, 2014), virtual reality allows for better designs of urban environments, including the city, outskirts, and commercial districts, by studying different aspects such as the lighting design for both public spaces and dwellings (Krupiński, 2020; Scorpio et al., 2020); the aesthetic preferences, for example, the preference of architectural spaces with curved boundaries (Elver Boz et al., 2022; Carreiro et al., 2017); or the influence of soundscape and landscape perception on satisfaction with the urban environment (Jeon & Jo, 2020).

Regarding lighting design, virtual reality simulates realistic scenarios (Abd-Alhamid et al., 2019; Chamilothori et al., 2019; T. Hong et al., 2019; Krupiński, 2020), being able to evaluate lighting scenarios, compare different lighting systems, and assess environmental safety and energy expenditure (Amirkhani et al., 2018; Carneiro et al., 2019; Chamilothori et al., 2019; Heydarian, Carneiro, Gerber, & Becerik-Gerber, 2015; Heydarian, Carneiro, Gerber, Becerik-Gerber, et al., 2015; Heydarian et al., 2017; T. Hong et al., 2019; Y. Hong & Michalatos, 2016; Krupiński, 2020; Lee et al., 2017; Li et al., 2022; Mahmoudzadeh et al., 2021; Nasar & Bokharaei, 2017; Natapov & Fisher-Gewirtzman, 2016; Natephra et al., 2017; Rockcastle et al., 2017; Rodriguez et al., 2021; Tabrizian et al., 2018; Vittori et al., 2021; Wong et al., 2019; see Bellazzi et al., 2021; Scorpio et al., 2020, for a further review). It is a useful tool for both consumers and designers (Hong & Michalatos, 2016; Lee et al., 2017). However, despite participants noting a strong sense of presence (Abd-Alhamid et al., 2019; Chamilothori et al., 2019; Chen et al., 2019; Heydarian, Carneiro, Gerber, & Becerik-Gerber, 2015; Heydarian et al., 2014; T. Hong et al., 2019), further research and technological development are required to get the simulated light distribution in virtual reality to be identical to that in real scenarios (see Chamilothori et al., 2019; Scorpio et al., 2020). Even with some doubts about whether or not the light distribution simulated in virtual reality is identical to that in real scenarios, virtual reality allows better lighting visualization than using videos or photographs (Chen et al., 2019).

As indicated above, virtual reality also serves to conduct studies on other aspects of the design of urban environments. Several articles employ this technology to study aesthetic preferences, showing a preference for spaces with curvature (Hobbs et al., 2015; Shemesh et al., 2017) or at least for moderated curvature (Carreiro et al., 2017), but not in autism (Palumbo et al., 2020). Furthermore, people seem to prefer symmetrical and ornamented spaces (Mouratidis & Hassan, 2020). Other studies have investigated how spacious different interior spaces are perceived as a function of different architectural elements (see, for example, Bokharaei & Nasar, 2016; Simpson et al., 2018; Stamps III, 2011; Stamps III & Krishnan, 2006; von Castell et al., 2014; Wang et al., 2020).

Virtual reality can also be used by the landscape gardening industry (Atwa et al., 2019; R. Li & Xu, 2020). Good planning of green spaces in the environment, through vertical greenery on city buildings or natural elements in offices or at home, can improve resilience against stressors (Chan et al., 2021; Huang et al., 2020; Yin et al., 2020). The interaction between the landscape and the soundscape, and the effects of external noise on indoor spaces have also been studied through virtual reality (Cao & Hsu, 2021; Jeon & Jo, 2019, 2020; L. Jiang et al., 2018; Jo et al., 2019; Jo & Jeon, 2021; Lu et al., 2022). This area of study is very promising, and more research focused on the development of standardized soundscape and landscape assessment protocols is needed (Xu et al., 2020).

It is important that, even though the number of citizens will be very high in the cities of the future, citizens must feel that they are part of the design of the cities they inhabit. This can be done using virtual reality (van Leeuwen et al., 2018), using, for example, a collaborative design platform similar to the one proposed by Imottesjo & Kain (2022).

3. INCLUSIVE URBAN ENVIRONMENTS THROUGH NEW TECHNOLOGIES

According to the World Health Organization, approximately 15% of the world's population lives with some form of disability. All urban environments must be adapted for people with disabilities (Organization & Bank, 2011). As population density increases in urban environments, they become much more complex and sophisticated in structure. To ensure a good quality of life for all the citizens who are part of it, these urban environments must be adapted to the reality of all the inhabitants who live in them. Imagine, for example, being a blind person and having to cross several streets full of people, with redevelopment works and no audible signals at traffic lights. Now imagine you have reduced mobility and you must travel on a train whose track is announced one or two minutes in advance in a station with twenty different tracks spread over several floors of the station. It would be quite a challenge, wouldn't it? That is why when designing and redesigning new urban environments, multiple realities in the population must be considered. Fortunately, the advances in new technologies are making life easier for people living with disabilities and making urban environments more accessible to all, improving health and liveability.

It is important to design inclusive urban environments because mental distress is higher in people living with disabilities (Cree et al., 2020). In particular, these authors indicate that in 2018 at least 17.4 million adults with disabilities exhibit frequent mental distress, defined as more than 14 days of sustained mental distress in the past 30 days, 4.6 times more frequently than people not living with disabilities. Reducing mental distress leads to good health behaviours, reduced mental disorders, reduced limitations in daily life, chronic disease, and reduced use of health services, thereby reducing public and/or private expenditure.

Following the previous examples, suppose a person living with a disability or a blind person goes to a crowded train station or airport. It is essential that the person can avoid the obstacles that are moving around them (in this particular example it would be the other people). To achieve this, there is research that uses new technology, such as Szemes, et al. (2003). Particularly, design an intelligent space that allows the user to avoid collision with other people using a mobile haptic interface. These smart spaces would be configured with mobile robots that guide through the space; computers, screens, or tablets that enable information search; smart cameras and microphones; haptic devices; and loudspeakers. The main objective is to guide people by predicting their future movements based on their past movements, allowing them to avoid collisions with static or moving objects in the smart space. The authors propose a very interesting mathematical model, which allows collision-free guidance of people even if objects within the smart space are moving (Szemes et al., 2003).

There is also basic research on the design of haptic interfaces (for example a haptic vest, see Garcia-Valle et al., 2021; Kapppers & Plaisier, 2022) that could be used for the guidance of people living with disabilities. Such interfaces are particularly useful for people with disabilities, but any user can enjoy their advantages. For example, Prasad, Taele, Olubeko, et al., (2014), who designed the HaptiGo device, indicate that it can be useful for getting from one crowded place to another while being aware of the environment, based on the tactile guidance information provided by the vest, while performing other tasks such as typing text (Prasad, Taele, Olubeko, et al., 2014). Another software is HaptiMoto, which was created to improve the safety of motorbike riding. Motorcycles are a major problem, for example in the USA they account for 2% of road vehicles but 5% of road traffic fatalities. The program uses changing variables such as turns and distance to predict, through algorithms, the risk points in driving (Prasad, Taele, Goldberg, et al., 2014).

A vest with vibrotactile patterns over the torso could be useful for guidance (Elliott et al., 2010; García-Valle et al., 2016; Israr & Poupyrev, 2011; Pielot & Boll, 2010; Prasad, Taele, Olubeko, et al., 2014), generating vibration patterns of varying intensity to identify the proximity of different parts of the body to an object, thus avoiding collisions. They found, using vibration patterns on a vest, that participants performed 100% of the turns correctly by being guided in a Virtual Reality environment using the vibration patterns on the vest. Using it as a GPS through the incorporation of a GPS of position sensing, allows, for example, the person who needs to turn right to reach a point of interest feels a vibration on the right side of the vest, signalling this right turn. The usefulness to incorporate GPS for position sensing was already pointed out by (Ertan et al., 1998). Also, García-Valle et al. (2016) suggested that it would be interesting to develop more elaborate vibration patterns, as well as to incorporate a gyroscope or an accelerometer (Ertan et al., 1998; García-Valle et al., 2016). Such devices are very useful in a megacity as they could signal when to descend a staircase, or a ramp or negotiate uneven terrain. For example, haptic belts have been used for blind guidance and have also proved useful in noisy environments, such as urban environments (Bharadwaj et al., 2019). This is not only useful for guidance within urban environments but also to support social and recreational activities. For example, haptic stimulation, whether implemented in a vest or other clothing or footwear, can be used for postural control, enabling people to perform activities such as golf, violin playing, rock climbing, or making riding a motorbike safer (Feeken et al., 2016; Prasad, Taele, Goldberg, et al., 2014; Prasad, Taele, Olubeko, et al., 2014; van der Linden et al., 2011; Woźniak et al., 2020).

Obviously, the inclusion of this type of device in the everyday life of the residents of the new urban environments also requires them to be affordable, so it is a priority to carry out research using the cheapest but most suitable materials. Following this idea, Garcia-Valle et al. (2021) employed cylindrical-shaped eccentric rotating mass (ERM) motors, which were very useful because provide a greater stimulation range to create patterns and they are affordable, making this type of device more accessible (Garcia-Valle et al., 2021). It is important that new research on this type of device takes this into account and that more research is carried out using inexpensive devices, allowing comparison between the results, and contributing to their generalisation.

Guidance over short distances is important, but it is also important to ensure that people with disabilities can travel long distances, especially in very large urban environments, such as the cities of the future. Autonomous cars have an important role to play in providing mobility without human intervention, facilitating the mobility of people with disabilities, and contributing to an improvement in their quality of life. Studies such as Cordts et al. (2021) or Hwang et al. (2021) show that people with disabilities generally already spend a lot of money on transport and are willing to use autonomous cars even if the cost of autonomous cars is equal to their existing transport or more expensive. Autonomous cars allow them to plan their trips less and are more convenient to use. Obviously, autonomous cars must ensure the safety of the people travelling in them and they must be accessible. Studies so far on how to ensure accessibility in autonomous vehicles for people with disabilities are scarce and have methodological limitations (Dicianno et al., 2021). Moreover, both the autonomous vehicle and everything concerning the travel journey should be adapted to the preferences, circumstances, and needs of each type of disability, as each type of disability has a different set of needs. This is why this field of study needs much more research to find the best accessibility solution for each disability.

Finally, new housing in the urban environments of the future should be adapted for people with disabilities, contributing to their independence and comfort (Elçi et al., 2021). There are smart homes whose system is designed to allow deaf-mute people to control devices by gestures (Iqbal et al., 2016) and other systems developed for people with physical disabilities that can be controlled by voice or mobile phone (see Basanta et al., 2017; Obaid et al., 2014; Parameshachari et al., 2013; Rashid et al., 2017; Sunehra & Tejaswi, 2016; Vamshi et al., 2017). Interestingly, Megalingam et al., (2011) developed a voice recognition system that allowed wheelchair users to move from one point to another automatically, avoiding possible obstacles, after saying the instruction. Also, there are proposals for smart homes using an Alexa or Google Home device connected to smart plugs, lights, video surveillance cameras, etc (Mtshali & Khubisa, 2019; Yue & Ping, 2017). In these cases, the devices could be controlled by voice without the need to use a mobile phone. As indicated by (Mtshali & Khubisa, 2019) it could be implemented to be controlled by sign language. Although this is currently not possible, a gesture recognition system similar to the one proposed by (Basanta et al., 2017) could be implemented in Alexa or Google Home. Controlling these devices other than by voice is also beneficial for older people, as they seem to have problems with voice control (Jakob, 2022). An alternative to voice control could be the control of the house, appliances, energy consumption, and temperature setting via a website (Islam et al., 2021); smartphone APP (Feng et al., 2022), or brain signals (Babu & Vardhini, 2020). The most essential is to adapt the control mode of the systems to the person's disability (Vigouroux et al., 2022).

Fortunately, much research is emerging on the subject, such as Li's (2022) which aims to find out whether it is possible to improve the quality of life of people with disabilities or the elderly through smart home gadgets. They propose the use of sensors that report on the quality of the air in the home, sensors that alert people when they have forgotten to turn off the tap or about possible fainting, the incorporation of robots that keep people company to avoid the feeling of loneliness, devices that allow voice control of electronic devices, video surveillance cameras to act quickly in case of accidents, facial or voice recognition to access homes and prevent access to intruders and the addition of robotic arms on wheelchairs so that users can drink, eat or pick up objects independently. With these sensors implemented in a smart home laboratory, the aim is to study the behaviour and reaction of volunteers with disabilities and elderly people to the smart home.

In short, major improvements in the quality of life of people with disabilities and older people are possible with new technologies. In particular, it has been shown how existing new technologies can contribute to improving the quality of life in large urban environments by being incorporated into short and long journeys, as well as in housing.

4. NEXT ILLUMINATION LEVEL IN FUTURE SMART CITY

a. Next indoor illumination.

In the architectural design of future cities, as described above, consideration should be given to their adaptability for better accessibility and habitability, but also to their capacity to enhance and improve people's health. Correct, sharp, and precise vision is one of the most important skills for carrying out certain work activities that require this sense in order to be performed. The annual global health costs for visual impairment alone in 2011 were estimated at $3 trillion (Gordois et al., 2012). Moreover, an estimated $408.5 billion is lost in GDP worldwide due to the 160.7 million people with severe vision impairment (Marques et al., 2021).

There is currently a great fear or respect for the incidence of the sun's natural radiation on our bodies, skin, and eyes. This fear is mainly due to the arrival of large amounts of ultraviolet radiation due to the damage caused to the ozone layer by the emission of gases such as chlorofluorocarbons. There is an almost abusive use of filters that are even incorporated in intraocular lenses used to treat cataract problems. Furthermore, in the last 150 to 200 years, humans have introduced changes in social and economic life habits that are having consequences for the appearance of visual diseases such as the pandemic of childhood myopia and sleep/wake cycle problems.

As is evident, not everything depends on the architecture of the new cities because blue light filters are imposed on internal lenses, contact lenses, or spectacle lenses. It is of little use to increase the amount of physiological blue light for inhabitants who use or have such filters. However, blue light filtering is also generated naturally by pupil shrinkage (Figueiro et al., 2020) and by the yellowing of the crystalline lens with increasing age due to the precipitation of its constituent proteins (Chen et al., 2017; Turner & Mainster, 2008). For these inhabitants, an increase in the amount of incident light does improve their level of health by favoring the development of a correct cyclic cycle.

Regarding the myopia pandemic, it should be pointed out in the first instance that the natural light we receive is insufficient. A high-risk group is children who spend a large part of the day at school, enter at night or at dawn and sometimes leave at dusk or after dark. Little natural light enters the classroom and light sources are used that are insufficient compared to the luminance they should receive from the sun (Moyano & González Lezcano, 2021). This has been associated with risks of damage to children's vision due to poor lighting and light distribution (Ho et al., 2008; Nocera et al., 2018; Piderit Moreno & Labarca, 2015; Winterbottom & Wilkins, 2009). There is evidence confirming that higher natural radiation is associated with a lower incidence of myopia, for example, Chinese children living in Sydney have an estimated incidence of myopia ten percentage points lower than children in Singapore (Lanca et al., 2019). On the other hand, violet (360-400 nm) is known to be protective against myopia by suppressing axial elongation of the eye. This light is abundant in solar radiation but is eliminated when it passes through windows and glass so that actual exposure is very moderate (X. Jiang et al., 2018; Torii et al., 2017).

In addition to the above, working with near vision points (paper and screens) in today's life may be a risk factor that increases the prevalence of myopia (Lanca et al., 2019; Saw, 2002). This implies that school age may be a risk factor for continuous reading and writing where the longer the hours of study, the higher the risk of myopia (Mountjoy et al., 2018).

Another example of the importance of illumination on the skin and more specifically on the inner ocular epithelium, the retina, is that infrared radiation on the retina at 670 nm is beneficial for the regeneration of retinal tissues by increasing cellular ATP and decreasing ROS (Albarracin et al., 2011; Eells et al., 2008; Kaynezhad et al., 2016; Pope & Denton, 2020; Qu et al., 2010; Shinhmar et al., 2021).

With the expansion of LED lighting in work, home, and healthcare environments, there are deficiencies in the amount of light arriving at wavelengths below 420-430nm. At this wavelength, there is an increase in emission with a peak in blue at 460nm, with a significant peak in yellow at 550nm. The cuts in the wavelength peaks eliminate both violet and blue (360 nm to 400 nm). This is a risk factor for the development of myopia in children (Baeza-Moyano et al., 2022; X. Jiang et al., 2018; Torii et al., 2017). Ultraviolet light acts on the myopia suppressor gene EGR1 more effectively than blue light in chick chorioretinal tissues (Baeza-Moyano et al., 2022; Torii et al., 2017). This wavelength, which reaches us naturally, is attenuated strongly simply by shining solar radiation through a window. This advantage acts as a possibly detrimental filter as it may be a risk factor that is driving the current myopia pandemic.

From the above, the need arises to develop new, more complete light sources that can even imitate sunlight depending on the time of day. Buildings must provide what they themselves, by their constitution and construction, eliminate from natural sources. There are newly registered utility models that can generate the distribution of specific peaks of solar radiation. For example, utility model ES1274209-U incorporates blue and violet and is also capable of modulating the emission levels according to the time of day (Baeza Moyano & González Lezcano, 2021). Another model is ES1257950-U. It was registered in which a complete spectral distribution of the solar range is achieved, but neither violet nor blue is enhanced, which are the wavelengths that can act as a protector against the generation of myopia (Jordana Casamitjana, 2021). The implementation of these systems is important to bear in mind that as beings who have lived under natural light for thousands and thousands of years, we have to be aware of the fact that we have been living in the sun for thousands and thousands of years.

b. Next Street control illumination.

Lighting is as important for health as it is for guiding people through large cities. Traffic lighting is crucial to maintain the organisational rhythms of mobility for private vehicles, public vehicles and pedestrians. There are sometimes such complex cross-structures in urban centres that mix rail networks with roads and pedestrian walkways (Carpintero et al., 2010; de Oña et al., 2010) and even shared roadways with lift bridges and airports (Garcia, 2021). Traditionally and currently most traffic light networks are controlled by basic timing systems with basic programming where the traffic lights controlling the junctions are made dependent on each other but with no real relation to the specific needs generated throughout the day on the roads. (Kumar et al., 2021). This traditional system has been improved by the incorporation of pushbuttons that only close the traffic when pedestrians cross. This avoids CO2 emissions due to increased traffic congestion and saves travel time.

The interrelationships between vehicles, control systems, and pedestrians is are essential for mega-cities, and to improve this, various methods of communication, cross-checking, and linking are under development:

1. Algorithm integration: There are several strategies for using algorithms to generate and ensure dynamic control of city rhythms. The multi-agent reinforcement system (MARL) is based on cluster learning, i.e. learning is performed for street junctions, but without taking into account the overall traffic computation. Despite the drawbacks, it has been used to generate better systems with better communication such as the integrated adaptive traffic signal controller (MARLIN-ATSC) (El-Tantawy et al., 2013; Mannion et al., 2016) or the multi-agent self-communication (MAAC) (Wu et al., 2020).
2. Global IoT communication: Communication between vehicles and urban control structures is becoming a necessity in the new megacities. The transfer of information to drivers about dangers resulting from e.g. vehicle breakdowns on the road can prevent traffic jams and secondary accidents. In addition to helping accident victims by autonomously communicating the exact location of the accident to the rescue and medical services (Bonyar et al., 2017; Narayanan et al., 2021; Shaik et al., 2018). In order to be functional, there must be structures and computer supports with universal communication and protocols that allow for the interconnection of instantaneous data of all the variables that are present at any given moment. To this end, network systems have been developed for the control of urban traffic lights, such as the IoT Urban Traffic-Light Control (IoT-UTLC) network. The aim of this network is the communication between wireless sensors with the telemetry transport protocol Message Queue Server (MQTT), which serves as quality control support. This system has been prototyped after passing the relevant quality controls (Zitouni et al., 2019).

5. DISCUSSION AND CONCLUSION

The designs and projects of future megacities must be conscious of the environment that will surround the inhabitants who will live in them. The promotion of accessibility for people with disabilities must be one of the keys and fundamental pillars for construction. Social integration is the biggest and most important advance, leaving no one behind, always based on the principle of solidarity and accompaniment. Guidance systems, smart homes, and autonomous cars will play an important role in ensuring accessibility for people with disabilities in the megacities of the future.

In terms of architectural, landscape, soundscape, and lighting design, virtual reality is a powerful tool that allows citizens to collaborate in building the megacity of which they are a part, and assists designers in its creation and subsequent modifications.

As described above, small changes and contributions such as the implementation of connectivity of virtual assistants with cameras or simple robotic systems of accompaniment. They can alleviate the pandemic of loneliness in which modern society is immersed. The lack of attention, conversations, and human or humanoid relationships lead to the emergence of serious psychosocial problems. Technology cannot eliminate social and individual human actions, such as receiving a kiss, a hug, or encouragement in the form of pride from another human being. Likewise, it cannot eliminate actions such as going for a walk or going to the countryside to disconnect from the city and technology. But it can be a powerful tool to eliminate that feeling of loneliness. Loneliness should not be understood not as being alone without a partner, friends or close family members, but as feeling lonely. A feeling that can be generated even when surrounded by people. Not having conversations with anyone, simply being alone in a house sitting and receiving stimuli from televisions, radios or computer systems with which you cannot interact and that only return information is the point that could be eliminated with the new technologies that have been proposed. An important example is the Open Source Chat GPT-3 program with which people can have conversations relatively similar to human ones. This artificial intelligence is a tool that continuously learns through neural networks with a deep learning model called Transformer. The important thing is that the AI can respond and maintain relatively natural conversations, in 5 or 10 years there will surely be home automation systems that identically treat us, psychologically speaking, to a person with whom we could be living at that moment.

On the other hand, it has also been argued that there is a need to generate indirect health by regulating interior lighting systems to allow inhabitants more natural and healthy lighting. Mimicking or mimicking solar radiation across the visual spectrum is seen as a tool to alleviate other pandemics such as myopia and insomnia. And what derives from these, are agitation, irritability, lack of concentration, lack of visual definition, stress, anxiety, and drowsiness, among others.

In addition, it is essential that transport and communication systems are in harmony to allow fluidity of movement of both disabled and non-disabled persons. This has an impact on citizens, as improved mobility avoids traffic jams on the roads, shortening daily commuting times. This allows citizens more time for leisure and rest. It also indirectly benefits health, as this time can be spent exercising, sleeping, unwinding, and walking in natural sunlight.

There may be a reluctance to implement new technologies due to potential vulnerabilities and system failures at the software level. This is an entirely feasible reality that can occur with any object or system connected to the internet, from a blender to an electric car, the power plant that controls the water in a dam, or the traffic lights in a city. In addition, these agencies must have the power to ensure that the masses are not under control and adequate treatment of personal data.

On the other hand, it is relevant that these agencies, which may be similar to the European Medicines Agency (EMA) or the US Food and Drug Administration (FDA), ensure the safe use of equipment. Manufacturers should be obliged to offer solutions in case of control failure of the main system to provide the user with an access route other than the main one. For example, a system that works with fingerprint or voice recognition should have another security system, ensuring their usage in case of burnt hands or loss of speech. In addition, manufacturers should add checkpoints to the systems capable of indicating the remaining charge and the estimated life of the batteries that power the equipment, preventing the equipment from shutting down due to a lack of power.

5.1 Final Remarks

This chapter summarises relevant empirical findings on the use of new technologies to improve health, livability, and human behaviour in urban environments, but is not a systematic review of the topic.

REFERENCES

Abd-Alhamid, F., Kent, M., Bennett, C., Calautit, J., & Wu, Y. (2019). Developing an innovative method for visual perception evaluation in a physical-based virtual environment. *Building and Environment*, *162*, 106278. doi:10.1016/j.buildenv.2019.106278

Adams, D., Novak, A., Kliestik, T., & Potcovaru, A.-M. (2021). Sensor-based Big Data Applications and Environmentally Sustainable Urban Development in Internet of Things-enabled Smart Cities. *Geopolitics, History, and International Relations*, *13*, 108.

Albarracin, R., Eells, J., & Valter, K. (2011). Photobiomodulation protects the retina from light-induced photoreceptor degeneration. *Investigative Ophthalmology & Visual Science*, *52*(6), 3582–3592. doi:10.1167/iovs.10-6664 PMID:21421867

Ali, S. H., Al-Sultan, H. A., & al Rubaie, M. T. (2022). Fifth Industrial Revolution. International Journal of Business. *Management and Economics*, *3*(3), 196–212. doi:10.47747/ijbme.v3i3.694

Amirkhani, M., Garcia-Hansen, V., Isoardi, G., & Allan, A. (2018). Innovative window design strategy to reduce negative lighting interventions in office buildings. *Energy and Building*, *179*, 253–263. doi:10.1016/j.enbuild.2018.09.006

Atwa, S. M. H., Ibrahim, M. G., Saleh, A. M., & Murata, R. (2019). Development of sustainable landscape design guidelines for a green business park using virtual reality. *Sustainable Cities and Society*, *48*, 101543. doi:10.1016/j.scs.2019.101543

Babu, K. M. C., & Vardhini, P. A. H. (2020). Brain Computer Interface based Arduino Home Automation System for Physically Challenged. *2020 3rd International Conference on Intelligent Sustainable Systems (ICISS),* (pp. 125–130). IEEE.

Baeza-Moyano, D., Arranz-Paraíso, D., Sola, Y., & González-Lezcano, R. A. (2022). Suitability of blue light filters for eye care. *The European Physical Journal Plus*, *137*(7), 817. doi:10.1140/epjp13360-022-03045-3

Baeza Moyano, D., & González Lezcano, R. A. (2021). *Indor LED luminarie emittering the full visible spectrum of light* (Patent No. ES1274209U).

Basanta, H., Huang, Y.-P., & Lee, T.-T. (2017). Assistive design for elderly living ambient using voice and gesture recognition system. *2017 IEEE International Conference on Systems, Man, and Cybernetics (SMC)*, (pp. 840–845). IEEE. 10.1109/SMC.2017.8122714

Bellazzi, A., Bellia, L., Chinazzo, G., Corbisiero, F., D'Agostino, P., Devitofrancesco, A., Fragliasso, F., Ghellere, M., Megale, V., & Salamone, F. (2021). Virtual reality for assessing visual quality and lighting perception: A systematic review. *Building and Environment*, 108674.

Bharadwaj, A., Shaw, S. B., & Goldreich, D. (2019). Comparing Tactile to Auditory Guidance for Blind Individuals. *Frontiers in Human Neuroscience*, *13*, 443. doi:10.3389/fnhum.2019.00443 PMID:31920601

Bokharaei, S., & Nasar, J. L. (2016). Perceived spaciousness and preference in sequential experience. *Human Factors*, *58*(7), 1069–1081. doi:10.1177/0018720816650068 PMID:27230490

Bonyar, A., Geczy, A., Krammer, O., Santha, H., Illes, B., Kaman, J., Szalay, Z., Hanak, P., & Harsanyi, G. (2017). A review on current eCall systems for autonomous car accident detection. *2017 40th International Spring Seminar on Electronics Technology (ISSE)*, (pp. 1–8). IEEE. 10.1109/ISSE.2017.8000985

Burdea, G., Richard, P., & Coiffet, P. (1996). Multimodal virtual reality: Input-output devices, system integration, and human factors. *International Journal of Human-Computer Interaction*, *8*(1), 5–24. doi:10.1080/10447319609526138

Cao, X., & Hsu, Y. (2021). The Effects of Soundscapes in Relieving Stress in an Urban Park. *Land (Basel)*, *10*(12), 1323. doi:10.3390/land10121323

Carneiro, J. P., Aryal, A., & Becerik-Gerber, B. (2019). Influencing occupant's choices by using spatiotemporal information visualization in Immersive Virtual Environments. *Building and Environment*, *150*, 330–338. doi:10.1016/j.buildenv.2019.01.024

Carpintero, S., Maraña, V., & Barcham, R. (2010). Benefits of urban light rail trains: A perspective from Spain. *WIT Transactions on the Built Environment*, *111*, 239–248. doi:10.2495/UT100221

Carreiro, M., Andrade, M. A. P., & Dias, M. S. (2017). Cognition and evaluation of architecture environments based on geometric contour references and aesthetic judgements. *22nd International Conference of the Association for Computer-Aided Architectural Design Research in Asia*, (pp. 581–591). IEEE. 10.52842/conf.caadria.2017.581

Chamilothori, K., Wienold, J., & Andersen, M. (2019). Adequacy of immersive virtual reality for the perception of daylit spaces: Comparison of real and virtual environments. *Leukos*, *15*(2–3), 203–226. doi:10.1080/15502724.2017.1404918

Chan, S. H. M., Qiu, L., Esposito, G., & Mai, K. P. (2021). Vertical greenery buffers against stress: Evidence from psychophysiological responses in virtual reality. *Landscape and Urban Planning*, *213*, 104127. doi:10.1016/j.landurbplan.2021.104127

Chen, Y., Cui, Z., & Hao, L. (2019). Virtual reality in lighting research: Comparing physical and virtual lighting environments. *Lighting Research & Technology*, *51*(6), 820–837. doi:10.1177/1477153518825387

Chen, Y., Nondahl, D. M., Schubert, C. R., Klein, B. E. K., Klein, R., & Cruickshanks, K. J. (2017). The Relation between Sleep Disruption and Cataract in a Large Population-Based Study. *Ophthalmic Epidemiology*, *24*(2), 111–115. doi:10.1080/09286586.2016.1259640 PMID:28139160

Chiocchini, U. (2019). The Roman cistern of road Cristoforo Colombo, Rome, Italy: Operating mode and connection with the old Appian Way. *Archaeological and Anthropological Sciences*, *11*(1), 321–336. doi:10.100712520-018-0606-x

Cordts, P., Cotten, S. R., Qu, T., & Bush, T. R. (2021). Mobility challenges and perceptions of autonomous vehicles for individuals with physical disabilities. *Disability and Health Journal*, *14*(4), 101131. doi:10.1016/j.dhjo.2021.101131 PMID:34147414

Corman, F., & Meng, L. (2015). A Review of Online Dynamic Models and Algorithms for Railway Traffic Management. *IEEE Transactions on Intelligent Transportation Systems*, *16*(3), 1274–1284. doi:10.1109/TITS.2014.2358392

Cree, R. A., Okoro, C. A., Zack, M. M., & Carbone, E. (2020). Frequent Mental Distress Among Adults, by Disability Status, Disability Type, and Selected Characteristics— United States, 2018. *MMWR. Morbidity and Mortality Weekly Report*, *69*(36), 1238–1243. doi:10.15585/mmwr.mm6936a2 PMID:32914770

de Oña, J., Calvo, F. J., Garach, L., de Oña, R., & López, G. (2010). How to Expand Subway and Urban Railway Networks: Light Rail Extensions in Madrid, Spain. *Transportation Research Record: Journal of the Transportation Research Board*, *2146*(1), 10–17. doi:10.3141/2146-02

Deming, D. (2020). The Aqueducts and Water Supply of Ancient Rome. *Ground Water*, *58*(1), 152–161. doi:10.1111/gwat.12958 PMID:31667822

Dicianno, B. E., Sivakanthan, S., Sundaram, S. A., Satpute, S., Kulich, H., Powers, E., Deepak, N., Russell, R., Cooper, R., & Cooper, R. A. (2021). Systematic review: Automated vehicles and services for people with disabilities. *Neuroscience Letters*, *761*, 136103. doi:10.1016/j.neulet.2021.136103 PMID:34237416

Eells, J. T., DeSmet, K. D., Kirk, D. K., Wong-Riley, M., Whelan, H. T., ver Hoeve, J., Nork, T. M., Stone, J., & Valter, K. (2008). *Photobiomodulation for the Treatment of Retinal Injury and Retinal Degenerative Diseases*., doi:10.1007/978-0-387-71809-5_5

El-Tantawy, S., Abdulhai, B., & Abdelgawad, H. (2013). Multiagent Reinforcement Learning for Integrated Network of Adaptive Traffic Signal Controllers (MARLIN-ATSC): Methodology and Large-Scale Application on Downtown Toronto. *IEEE Transactions on Intelligent Transportation Systems*, *14*(3), 1140–1150. doi:10.1109/TITS.2013.2255286

Elçi, E., Yalçın, N., & Ünaldı, S. (2021). Internet of Things based Smart Home System Design for Individuals with Disabilities. *2021 6th International Conference on Computer Science and Engineering (UBMK),* (pp. 619–622).

Elliott, L. R., van Erp, J. B. F., Redden, E. S., & Duistermaat, M. (2010). Field-Based Validation of a Tactile Navigation Device. *IEEE Transactions on Haptics*, *3*(2), 78–87. doi:10.1109/TOH.2010.3 PMID:27788115

Elver Boz, T., Demirkan, H., & Urgen, B. A. (2022). Visual perception of the built environment in virtual reality: A systematic characterization of human aesthetic experience in spaces with curved boundaries. *Psychology of Aesthetics, Creativity, and the Arts*. doi:10.1037/aca0000504

Ertan, S., Lee, C., Willets, A., Tan, H., & Pentland, A. (1998). A wearable haptic navigation guidance system. Digest of Papers. *Second International Symposium on Wearable Computers (Cat. No. 98EX215),* (pp. 164–165). IEEE. 10.1109/ISWC.1998.729547

Feeken, C., Wasmann, M., Heuten, W., Ennenga, D., Müller, H., & Boll, S. (2016). ClimbingAssist. *Proceedings of the 2016 ACM International Joint Conference on Pervasive and Ubiquitous Computing: Adjunct*, (pp. 57–60). ACM. 10.1145/2968219.2971417

Feng, C., Zeng, H., Sun, Y., Tao, L., Ji, H., & Cai, Z. (2022). Design of Monitoring and Controlling System for Smart Home. *Journal of Physics: Conference Series*, *2160*(1), 012001. doi:10.1088/1742-6596/2160/1/012001

Figueiro, M. G., Sahin, L., Kalsher, M., Plitnick, B., & Rea, M. S. (2020). Long-Term, All-Day Exposure to Circadian-Effective Light Improves Sleep, Mood, and Behavior in Persons with Dementia. *Journal of Alzheimer's Disease Reports*, *4*(1), 297–312. doi:10.3233/ADR-200212 PMID:33024938

Flammini, F., de Donato, L., Fantechi, A., & Vittorini, V. (2022). *A Vision of Intelligent Train Control.*, doi:10.1007/978-3-031-05814-1_14

Gao, Z., Jia, Y., Liu, S., & Zhang, X. (2021). Micro-displacement Measurement of High-Speed Railway Bridge Based on Vector Network Analyzer. *2021 IEEE 15th International Conference on Electronic Measurement & Instruments (ICEMI),* (pp. 420–425). IEEE. 10.1109/ICEMI52946.2021.9679535

Garcia, J. (2021). Gibraltar and the European Union: In and out. *The Round Table*, *110*(3), 384–394. doi:10.1080/00358533.2021.1933728

Garcia-Valle, G., Arranz-Paraiso, S., Serrano-Pedraza, I., & Ferre, M. (2021). Estimation of Torso Vibrotactile Thresholds Using Eccentric Rotating Mass Motors. *IEEE Transactions on Haptics*, *14*(3), 538–550. doi:10.1109/TOH.2020.3048290 PMID:33378262

García-Valle, G., Ferre, M., Breñosa, J., Aracil, R., Sebastian, J. M., & Giachritsis, C. (2016). *Design and Development of a Multimodal Vest for Virtual Immersion and Guidance.*, doi:10.1007/978-3-319-42324-1_25

Gordois, A., Cutler, H., Pezzullo, L., Gordon, K., Cruess, A., Winyard, S., Hamilton, W., & Chua, K. (2012). An estimation of the worldwide economic and health burden of visual impairment. *Global Public Health: An International Journal for Research, Policy and Practice*, *7*(5), 465–481. doi:10.1080/17441692.2011.634815 PMID:22136197

Grisé, E., Boisjoly, G., Maguire, M., & El-Geneidy, A. (2019). Elevating access: Comparing accessibility to jobs by public transport for individuals with and without a physical disability. *Transportation Research Part A, Policy and Practice*, *125*, 280–293. doi:10.1016/j.tra.2018.02.017

Heydarian, A., Carneiro, J. P., Gerber, D., & Becerik-Gerber, B. (2015). Immersive virtual environments, understanding the impact of design features and occupant choice upon lighting for building performance. *Building and Environment*, *89*, 217–228. doi:10.1016/j.buildenv.2015.02.038

Heydarian, A., Carneiro, J. P., Gerber, D., Becerik-Gerber, B., Hayes, T., & Wood, W. (2014). *Immersive virtual environments: experiments on impacting design and human building interaction.*

Heydarian, A., Carneiro, J. P., Gerber, D., Becerik-Gerber, B., Hayes, T., & Wood, W. (2015). Immersive virtual environments versus physical built environments: A benchmarking study for building design and user-built environment explorations. *Automation in Construction*, *54*, 116–126. doi:10.1016/j.autcon.2015.03.020

Heydarian, A., Pantazis, E., Wang, A., Gerber, D., & Becerik-Gerber, B. (2017). Towards user centered building design: Identifying end-user lighting preferences via immersive virtual environments. *Automation in Construction*, *81*, 56–66. doi:10.1016/j.autcon.2017.05.003

Ho, M.-C., Chiang, C.-M., Chou, P.-C., Chang, K.-F., & Lee, C.-Y. (2008). Optimal sun-shading design for enhanced daylight illumination of subtropical classrooms. *Energy and Building*, *40*(10), 1844–1855. doi:10.1016/j.enbuild.2008.04.012

Hobbs, H., Hunker, K., Demircay, V., Rodriguez, T., & Issa, R. (2015). A semi-immersive virtual environment preference study of four interior architectural geometries. *Of Architectural Research,* 369.

Hong, T., Lee, M., Yeom, S., & Jeong, K. (2019). Occupant responses on satisfaction with window size in physical and virtual built environments. *Building and Environment*, *166*, 106409. doi:10.1016/j.buildenv.2019.106409

Hong, Y., & Michalatos, P. (2016). LumiSpace: A VR architectural daylighting design system. In SIGGRAPH ASIA 2016 Virtual Reality Meets Physical Reality: Modelling and Simulating Virtual Humans and Environments (pp. 1–2). doi:10.1145/2992138.2992140

Huang, Q., Yang, M., Jane, H., Li, S., & Bauer, N. (2020). Trees, grass, or concrete? The effects of different types of environments on stress reduction. *Landscape and Urban Planning*, *193*, 103654. doi:10.1016/j.landurbplan.2019.103654

Hwang, J., Li, W., Stough, L. M., Lee, C., & Turnbull, K. (2021). People with disabilities' perceptions of autonomous vehicles as a viable transportation option to improve mobility: An exploratory study using mixed methods. *International Journal of Sustainable Transportation*, *15*(12), 924–942. doi:10.1080/15568318.2020.1833115

Imottesjo, H., & Kain, J.-H. (2022). The Urban CoCreation Lab—an integrated platform for remote and simultaneous collaborative urban planning and design through web-based desktop 3D modeling, head-mounted virtual reality and mobile augmented reality: Prototyping a minimum viable product and developing specifications for a minimum marketable product. *Applied Sciences (Basel, Switzerland)*, *12*(2), 797. doi:10.3390/app12020797

Iqbal, M. A., Asrafuzzaman, S. K., Arifin, M. M., & Hossain, S. K. A. (2016). Smart home appliance control system for physically disabled people using kinect and X10. *2016 5th International Conference on Informatics, Electronics and Vision (ICIEV),* (pp. 891–896). IEEE.

Islam, S., Hasan, S., Antu, A. C. P., Islam, M., & Ahmed, F. T. (2021). Prototype Design and Development of a Smart Home. *2021 International Conference on Engineering and Emerging Technologies (ICEET)*, (pp. 1–6). IEEE. 10.1109/ICEET53442.2021.9659769

Israr, A., & Poupyrev, I. (2011). Tactile brush. *Proceedings of the SIGCHI Conference on Human Factors in Computing Systems*, (pp. 2019–2028). IEEE. 10.1145/1978942.1979235

Jakob, D. (2022). Voice Controlled Devices and Older Adults–A Systematic Literature Review. *International Conference on Human-Computer Interaction*, (pp. 175–200). IEEE. 10.1007/978-3-031-05581-2_14

Jeon, J. Y., & Jo, H. I. (2019). Three-dimensional virtual reality-based subjective evaluation of road traffic noise heard in urban high-rise residential buildings. *Building and Environment*, *148*, 468–477. doi:10.1016/j.buildenv.2018.11.004

Jeon, J. Y., & Jo, H. I. (2020). Effects of audio-visual interactions on soundscape and landscape perception and their influence on satisfaction with the urban environment. *Building and Environment*, *169*, 106544. doi:10.1016/j.buildenv.2019.106544

Jiang, L., Masullo, M., Maffei, L., Meng, F., & Vorländer, M. (2018). How do shared-street design and traffic restriction improve urban soundscape and human experience?—An online survey with virtual reality. *Building and Environment*, *143*, 318–328. doi:10.1016/j.buildenv.2018.07.005

Jiang, X., Kurihara, T., Torii, H., & Tsubota, K. (2018). Progress and Control of Myopia by Light Environments. Eye & Contact Lens: Science &. *Clinics and Practice*, *44*(5), 273–278. doi:10.1097/ICL.0000000000000548 PMID:30048342

Jo, H. I., & Jeon, J. Y. (2021). Urban soundscape categorization based on individual recognition, perception, and assessment of sound environments. *Landscape and Urban Planning*, *216*, 104241. doi:10.1016/j.landurbplan.2021.104241

Jo, H. I., Jeon, J. Y., & Polack, J.-D. (2019). *Soundscape Cognition for User Behavior in Urban Parks.*

Jordana Casamitjana, F. (2021). *Luminaria* (Patent No. ES1257950U).

Kapppers, A. M. L., & Plaisier, M. A. (2022). *Guidance for the Design of Vibrotactile Patterns for Use on the Human Back.*, doi:10.1007/978-3-031-06249-0_5

Kauppi, A., Wikström, J., Sandblad, B., & Andersson, A. W. (2006). Future train traffic control: Control by re-planning. *Cognition Technology and Work*, *8*(1), 50–56. doi:10.100710111-005-0019-3

Kaynezhad, P., Tachtsidis, I., & Jeffery, G. (2016). Optical monitoring of retinal respiration in real time: 670 nm light increases the redox state of mitochondria. *Experimental Eye Research*, *152*, 88–93. doi:10.1016/j.exer.2016.09.006 PMID:27664904

Kit, D., Katz, L., Sullivan, B., Snyder, K., Ballard, D., & Hayhoe, M. (2014). Eye Movements, Visual Search and Scene Memory, in an Immersive Virtual Environment. *PLoS One*, *9*(4), e94362. doi:10.1371/journal.pone.0094362 PMID:24759905

Kokkinara, E., Slater, M., & López-Moliner, J. (2015). The Effects of Visuomotor Calibration to the Perceived Space and Body, through Embodiment in Immersive Virtual Reality. *ACM Transactions on Applied Perception*, *13*(1), 1–22. doi:10.1145/2818998

Krupiński, R. (2020). Virtual reality system and scientific visualisation for smart designing and evaluating of lighting. *Energies*, *13*(20), 5518. doi:10.3390/en13205518

Kumar, N., Rahman, S. S., & Dhakad, N. (2021). Fuzzy Inference Enabled Deep Reinforcement Learning-Based Traffic Light Control for Intelligent Transportation System. *IEEE Transactions on Intelligent Transportation Systems*, *22*(8), 4919–4928. doi:10.1109/TITS.2020.2984033

Lanca, C., Teo, A., Vivagandan, A., Htoon, H. M., Najjar, R. P., Spiegel, D. P., Pu, S.-H., & Saw, S.-M. (2019). The Effects of Different Outdoor Environments, Sunglasses and Hats on Light Levels: Implications for Myopia Prevention. *Translational Vision Science & Technology*, *8*(4), 7. doi:10.1167/tvst.8.4.7 PMID:31360613

Lanier, J. (1992). Virtual reality: The promise of the future. *Interactive Learning International*, *8*(4), 275–279.

Lee, J.-Y., Han, P.-H., Tsai, L., Peng, R.-D., Chen, Y.-S., Chen, K.-W., & Hung, Y.-P. (2017). Estimating the simulator sickness in immersive virtual reality with optical flow analysis. In SIGGRAPH Asia 2017 Posters (pp. 1–2). doi:10.1145/3145690.3145697

Li, R., & Xu, D. (2020). Distribution of landscape architecture based on 3D images and virtual reality rationality study. *IEEE Access : Practical Innovations, Open Solutions*, *8*, 140161–140170. doi:10.1109/ACCESS.2020.3010097

Li, R. Y. M. (2022). Smart Home, Robots, and Robotic Arms for Elderly and Disabled Persons: A Lab Experiment Research Agenda. In Current State of Art in Artificial Intelligence and Ubiquitous Cities (pp. 91–103). Springer.

Li, Y., Yabuki, N., & Fukuda, T. (2022). Measuring visual walkability perception using panoramic street view images, virtual reality, and deep learning. *Sustainable Cities and Society*, *86*, 104140. doi:10.1016/j.scs.2022.104140

Lu, Y., Hasegawa, Y., Tan, J. K. A., & Lau, S.-K. (2022). Effect of audio-visual interaction on soundscape in the urban residential context: A virtual reality experiment. *Applied Acoustics*, *192*, 108717. doi:10.1016/j.apacoust.2022.108717

Mahmoudzadeh, P., Afacan, Y., & Adi, M. N. (2021). Analyzing occupants' control over lighting systems in office settings using immersive virtual environments. *Building and Environment*, *196*, 107823. doi:10.1016/j.buildenv.2021.107823

Mannion, P., Duggan, J., & Howley, E. (2016). An Experimental Review of Reinforcement Learning Algorithms for Adaptive Traffic Signal Control. In *Autonomic Road Transport Support Systems* (pp. 47–66). Springer International Publishing., doi:10.1007/978-3-319-25808-9_4

Marques, A. P., Ramke, J., Cairns, J., Butt, T., Zhang, J. H., Muirhead, D., Jones, I., Tong, B. A. M. A., Swenor, B. K., Faal, H., Bourne, R. R. A., Frick, K. D., & Burton, M. J. (2021). Global economic productivity losses from vision impairment and blindness. *EClinicalMedicine, 35*, 100852. doi:10.1016/j.eclinm.2021.100852 PMID:33997744

Megalingam, R. K., Nair, R. N., & Prakhya, S. M. (2011). Automated voice based home navigation system for the elderly and the physically challenged. *13th International Conference on Advanced Communication Technology (ICACT2011)*, (pp. 603–608). IEEE. 10.1109/WIRELESSVITAE.2011.5940832

Mountjoy, E., Davies, N. M., Plotnikov, D., Smith, G. D., Rodriguez, S., Williams, C. E., Guggenheim, J. A., & Atan, D. (2018). Education and myopia: assessing the direction of causality by mendelian randomisation. *BMJ*, k2022. doi:10.1136/bmj.k2022

Mouratidis, K., & Hassan, R. (2020). Contemporary versus traditional styles in architecture and public space: A virtual reality study with 360-degree videos. *Cities (London, England), 97*, 102499. doi:10.1016/j.cities.2019.102499

Moyano, D. B., & González Lezcano, R. A. (2021). *Indoor Lighting Workplaces*., doi:10.4018/978-1-7998-7279-5.ch012

Mtshali, P., & Khubisa, F. (2019). A smart home appliance control system for physically disabled people. *2019 Conference on Information Communications Technology and Society (ICTAS)*, (pp. 1–50). IEEE. 10.1109/ICTAS.2019.8703637

Narayanan, K. L., Ram, C. R. S., Subramanian, M., Krishnan, R. S., & Robinson, Y. H. (2021). IoT based Smart Accident Detection & Insurance Claiming System. *2021 Third International Conference on Intelligent Communication Technologies and Virtual Mobile Networks (ICICV)*, (pp. 306–311). IEEE. 10.1109/ICICV50876.2021.9388430

Nasar, J. L., & Bokharaei, S. (2017). Lighting modes and their effects on impressions of public squares. *Journal of Environmental Psychology, 49*, 96–105. doi:10.1016/j.jenvp.2016.12.007

Natapov, A., & Fisher-Gewirtzman, D. (2016). Visibility of urban activities and pedestrian routes: An experiment in a virtual environment. *Computers, Environment and Urban Systems, 58*, 60–70. doi:10.1016/j.compenvurbsys.2016.03.007

Natephra, W., Motamedi, A., Fukuda, T., & Yabuki, N. (2017). Integrating building information modeling and virtual reality development engines for building indoor lighting design. *Visualization in Engineering, 5*(1), 1–21. doi:10.118640327-017-0058-x

Nederveen Pieterse, J. (2021). Decentering Rome. In Connectivity and Global Studies (pp. 79–87). Springer International Publishing. doi:10.1007/978-3-030-59598-2_6

Nocera, F., lo Faro, A., Costanzo, V., & Raciti, C. (2018). Daylight Performance of Classrooms in a Mediterranean School Heritage Building. *Sustainability, 10*(10), 3705. doi:10.3390u10103705

Obaid, T., Rashed, H., el Nour, A. A., Rehan, M., Saleh, M. M., & Tarique, M. (2014). ZigBee based voice controlled wireless smart home system. *International Journal of Wireless & Mobile Networks, 6*(1), 47–59. doi:10.5121/ijwmn.2014.6104

Organization, W. H., & Bank, W. (2011). *World report on disability 2011 (p. Summary also available in Braille)*. World Health Organization.

Palumbo, L., Rampone, G., Bertamini, M., Sinico, M., Clarke, E., & Vartanian, O. (2020). Visual preference for abstract curvature and for interior spaces: Beyond undergraduate student samples. *Psychology of Aesthetics, Creativity, and the Arts*.

Parameshachari, B. D., Gopy, S. K., Hurry, G., & Gopaul, T. T. (2013). A study on smart home control system through speech. *International Journal of Computers and Applications*, *69*(19).

Park, J., & Chowdhury, S. (2018). Investigating the barriers in a typical journey by public transport users with disabilities. *Journal of Transport & Health*, *10*, 361–368. doi:10.1016/j.jth.2018.05.008

Pathak, P., Pal, P. R., Shrivastava, M., & Ora, P. (2019). Fifth revolution: Applied AI & human intelligence with cyber physical systems. *International Journal of Engineering and Advanced Technology*, *8*(3), 23–27.

Pencheva, E., Atanasov, I., & Trifonov, V. (2022). Identity Management in Future Railway Mobile Communication System. *Applied Sciences (Basel, Switzerland)*, *12*(9), 4293. doi:10.3390/app12094293

Piderit Moreno, M., & Labarca, C. (2015). Methodology for Assessing Daylighting Design Strategies in Classroom with a Climate-Based Method. *Sustainability*, *7*(1), 880–897. doi:10.3390u7010880

Pielot, M., & Boll, S. (2010). Tactile Wayfinder. Comparison of Tactile Waypoint Navigation with Commercial Pedestrian Navigation Systems (pp. 76–93). doi:10.1007/978-3-642-12654-3_5

Pope, N. J., & Denton, M. L. (2020). Low irradiance light exposure alters the activity of key enzymes in the mitochondrial electron transport chain. In M. R. Hamblin, J. D. Carroll, & P. Arany (Eds.), *Mechanisms of Photobiomodulation Therapy XV* (p. 13). SPIE. doi:10.1117/12.2546624

Prasad, M., Taele, P., Goldberg, D., & Hammond, T. A. (2014). HaptiMoto. *Proceedings of the SIGCHI Conference on Human Factors in Computing Systems,* (pp. 3597–3606). IEEE. 10.1145/2556288.2557404

Prasad, M., Taele, P., Olubeko, A., & Hammond, T. (2014). HaptiGo: A navigational; *2014 IEEE Haptics Symposium (HAPTICS),* (pp. 339–345). IEEE. 10.1109/HAPTICS.2014.6775478

Qu, C., Cao, W., Fan, Y., & Lin, Y. (2010). Near-infrared light protect the photoreceptor from light-induced damage in rats. *Advances in Experimental Medicine and Biology*, *664*, 365–374. doi:10.1007/978-1-4419-1399-9_42 PMID:20238037

Rashid, H., & Osman, S. bin, Hassan, N., Ahmed, I. U., Das, R., & Karim, M. M. (2017). A new design approach of home automation system for patients with physical disability to reduce water wastage and power consumption using renewable energy. *2017 4th International Conference on Advances in Electrical Engineering (ICAEE),* (pp. 770–774). IEEE.

Rockcastle, S. F., Chamilothori, K., & Andersen, M. (2017). *An experiment in virtual reality to measure daylight-driven interest in rendered architectural scenes*.

Rodriguez, F., Garcia-Hansen, V., Allan, A., & Isoardi, G. (2021). Subjective responses toward daylight changes in window views: Assessing dynamic environmental attributes in an immersive experiment. *Building and Environment*, *195*, 107720. doi:10.1016/j.buildenv.2021.107720

Saw, S.-M. (2002). Near-Work Activity, Night-lights, and Myopia in the Singapore-China Study. *Archives of Ophthalmology*, *120*(5), 620. doi:10.1001/archopht.120.5.620 PMID:12003612

Scarfe, P., & Glennerster, A. (2015). Using high-fidelity virtual reality to study perception in freely moving observers. *Journal of Vision (Charlottesville, Va.)*, *15*(9), 3. doi:10.1167/15.9.3 PMID:26161632

Scorpio, M., Laffi, R., Masullo, M., Ciampi, G., Rosato, A., Maffei, L., & Sibilio, S. (2020). Virtual reality for smart urban lighting design: Review, applications and opportunities. *Energies*, *13*(15), 3809. doi:10.3390/en13153809

Shaik, A., Bowen, N., Bole, J., Kunzi, G., Bruce, D., Abdelgawad, A., & Yelamarthi, K. (2018). Smart Car: An IoT Based Accident Detection System. *2018 IEEE Global Conference on Internet of Things (GCIoT),* (pp. 1–5). IEEE. 10.1109/GCIoT.2018.8620131

Shemesh, A., Talmon, R., Karp, O., Amir, I., Bar, M., & Grobman, Y. J. (2017). Affective response to architecture–investigating human reaction to spaces with different geometry. *Architectural Science Review*, *60*(2), 116–125. doi:10.1080/00038628.2016.1266597

Shinhmar, H., Hogg, C., Neveu, M., & Jeffery, G. (2021). Weeklong improved colour contrasts sensitivity after single 670 nm exposures associated with enhanced mitochondrial function. *Scientific Reports*, *11*(1), 22872. doi:10.103841598-021-02311-1 PMID:34819619

Simpson, G., Sinnis-Bourozikas, A., Zhao, M., Aseeri, S., & Interrante, V. (2018). A virtual reality investigation of the impact of wallpaper pattern scale on qualitative spaciousness judgments and action-based measures of room size perception. *International Conference on Virtual Reality and Augmented Reality,* (pp. 161–176). IEEE. 10.1007/978-3-030-01790-3_10

Soranzo, A., & Wilson, C. (2014). *Virtual environments in visual perception: applications and challenges*.

Stamps, A. E. III. (2011). Effects of area, height, elongation, and color on perceived spaciousness. *Environment and Behavior*, *43*(2), 252–273. doi:10.1177/0013916509354696

Stamps, A. E. III, & Krishnan, V. (2006). Spaciousness and boundary roughness. *Environment and Behavior*, *38*(6), 841–872. doi:10.1177/0013916506288052

Sunehra, D., & Tejaswi, V. (2016). Implementation of speech based home automation system using Bluetooth and GSM. *2016 International Conference on Signal Processing, Communication, Power and Embedded System (SCOPES),* (pp. 807–813). Springer. 10.1109/SCOPES.2016.7955552

Sutherland, I. E. (1965). *The ultimate display. Multimedia: From wagner to virutal reality*. Norton.

Szemes, P. T., Joo-Ho Lee, Hashimoto, H., & Korondi, P. (2003). Guiding and communication assistant for disabled in intelligent urban environment. *Proceedings 2003 IEEE/ASME International Conference on Advanced Intelligent Mechatronics (AIM 2003),* (pp. 598–603). ACM. 10.1109/AIM.2003.1225162

Tabrizian, P., Baran, P. K., Smith, W. R., & Meentemeyer, R. K. (2018). Exploring perceived restoration potential of urban green enclosure through immersive virtual environments. *Journal of Environmental Psychology*, *55*, 99–109. doi:10.1016/j.jenvp.2018.01.001

Tarr, M. J., & Warren, W. H. (2002). Virtual reality in behavioral neuroscience and beyond. *Nature Neuroscience*, *5*(S11), 1089–1092. doi:10.1038/nn948 PMID:12403993

Torii, H., Ohnuma, K., Kurihara, T., Tsubota, K., & Negishi, K. (2017). Violet Light Transmission is Related to Myopia Progression in Adult High Myopia. *Scientific Reports*, *7*(1), 14523. doi:10.103841598-017-09388-7 PMID:29109514

Turner, P. L., & Mainster, M. A. (2008). Circadian photoreception: Ageing and the eye's important role in systemic health. *The British Journal of Ophthalmology*, *92*(11), 1439–1444. doi:10.1136/bjo.2008.141747 PMID:18757473

Vamshi, B., Mittal, V. K., & Vineeth, K. V. S. (2017). Wireless voice-controlled multi-functional secure ehome. *2017 International Conference on Advances in Computing, Communications and Informatics (ICACCI)*, 2235–2240. 10.1109/ICACCI.2017.8126178

van der Linden, J., Johnson, R., Bird, J., Rogers, Y., & Schoonderwaldt, E. (2011). Buzzing to play. *Proceedings of the SIGCHI Conference on Human Factors in Computing Systems,* (pp. 533–542). IEEE. 10.1145/1978942.1979017

van Leeuwen, J. P., Hermans, K., Jylhä, A., Quanjer, A. J., & Nijman, H. (2018). Effectiveness of virtual reality in participatory urban planning: A case study. *Proceedings of the 4th Media Architecture Biennale Conference,* (pp. 128–136). IEEE. 10.1145/3284389.3284491

Vigouroux, N., Vella, F., Lepage, G., & Campo, E. (2022). Usability Study of Tactile and Voice Interaction Modes by People with Disabilities for Home Automation Controls. *International Conference on Computers Helping People with Special Needs*, (pp. 139–147). IEEE. 10.1007/978-3-031-08645-8_17

Vittori, F., Pigliautile, I., & Pisello, A. L. (2021). Subjective thermal response driving indoor comfort perception: A novel experimental analysis coupling building information modelling and virtual reality. *Journal of Building Engineering*, *41*, 102368. doi:10.1016/j.jobe.2021.102368

von Castell, C., Oberfeld, D., & Hecht, H. (2014). The effect of furnishing on perceived spatial dimensions and spaciousness of interior space. *PLoS One*, *9*(11), e113267. doi:10.1371/journal.pone.0113267 PMID:25409456

Wang, C., Lu, W., Ohno, R., & Gu, Z. (2020). Effect of wall texture on perceptual spaciousness of indoor space. *International Journal of Environmental Research and Public Health*, *17*(11), 4177. doi:10.3390/ijerph17114177 PMID:32545379

Wilson, C. J., & Soranzo, A. (2015). The Use of Virtual Reality in Psychology: A Case Study in Visual Perception. *Computational and Mathematical Methods in Medicine*, *2015*, 1–7. doi:10.1155/2015/151702 PMID:26339281

Winterbottom, M., & Wilkins, A. (2009). Lighting and discomfort in the classroom. *Journal of Environmental Psychology*, *29*(1), 63–75. doi:10.1016/j.jenvp.2008.11.007

Wong, M. O., Du, J., Zhang, Z. Q., Liu, Y. Q., Chen, S. M., & Lee, S. H. (2019). An experience-based interactive lighting design approach using BIM and VR: A case study. *IOP Conference Series. Earth and Environmental Science*, *238*(1), 012006. doi:10.1088/1755-1315/238/1/012006

Woźniak, M. P., Dominiak, J., Pieprzowski, M., Ładoński, P., Grudzień, K., Lischke, L., Romanowski, A., & Woźniak, P. W. (2020). Subtletee: Augmenting Posture Awareness for Beginner Golfers. Proceedings of the ACM on Human-Computer Interaction, 4(ISS), 1–24. 10.1145/3427332

Wu, Q., Wu, J., Shen, J., Yong, B., & Zhou, Q. (2020). An Edge Based Multi-Agent Auto Communication Method for Traffic Light Control. *Sensors (Basel)*, *20*(15), 4291. doi:10.339020154291 PMID:32752055

Xu, C., Oberman, T., Aletta, F., Tong, H., & Kang, J. (2020). Ecological validity of immersive virtual reality (IVR) techniques for the perception of urban sound environments. *Acoustics (Basel, Switzerland)*, *3*(1), 11–24. doi:10.3390/acoustics3010003

Xu, M., David, J. M., & Kim, S. H. (2018). The Fourth Industrial Revolution: Opportunities and Challenges. *International Journal of Financial Research*, *9*(2), 90. doi:10.5430/ijfr.v9n2p90

Yin, J., Yuan, J., Arfaei, N., Catalano, P. J., Allen, J. G., & Spengler, J. D. (2020). Effects of biophilic indoor environment on stress and anxiety recovery: A between-subjects experiment in virtual reality. *Environment International*, *136*, 105427. doi:10.1016/j.envint.2019.105427 PMID:31881421

Yue, C. Z., & Ping, S. (2017). Voice activated smart home design and implementation. 2017 2nd International Conference on Frontiers of Sensors Technologies (ICFST), 489–492.

Zitouni, R., Petit, J., Djoudi, A., & George, L. (2019). IoT-Based Urban Traffic-Light Control: Modelling, Prototyping and Evaluation of MQTT Protocol. *2019 International Conference on Internet of Things (IThings) and IEEE Green Computing and Communications (GreenCom) and IEEE Cyber, Physical and Social Computing (CPSCom) and IEEE Smart Data (SmartData),* (pp. 182–189). IEEE. 10.1109/iThings/GreenCom/CPSCom/SmartData.2019.00051

Chapter 13
The Urban Context as a Support for Energy Efficiency:
Mild Climate Cities

Jesica Fernandez-Agüera
https://orcid.org/0000-0002-8582-6009
Universidad de Sevilla, Spain

Samuel Domínguez-Amarillo
https://orcid.org/0000-0002-9177-8736
Universidad de Sevilla, Spain

Miguel Ángel Campano
https://orcid.org/0000-0002-0221-4657
Universidad de Sevilla, Spain

Pedro Bustamante
Universidad de Sevilla, Spain

ABSTRACT

This chapter focuses on the impact that urban development has had on mid-climate cities, with high consumption of natural resources, significant waste production and environmental impact, and encroachment on productive or wild territories. In these cities, buildings are dependent on considerable energy consumption to achieve internal comfort and habitability. Considering cities as urban ecosystems allows us to study them in a way that allows us to propose new strategies to improve the efficiency of urban systems, reducing their impact on the habitability of buildings and the city itself, as well as reducing their ecological footprint. In this chapter, the authors will discuss aspects of the urban climate that affect the well-being of citizens inside and outside buildings, such as natural lighting, sunlight, natural ventilation, and wind, and how planning can improve them.

DOI: 10.4018/978-1-6684-6924-8.ch013

1. INTRODUCTION

One of the processes with the greatest ecological impact of our society is the urban growth on the territory, especially as developed in the last 150 years. The process —accelerated in the fifties of the last century— generated an extraordinary expansion of urbanization throughout the planet, fundamentally linked to the growth of world population growth and the economic boom after the second world war (Domínguez-Amarillo et al., 2016).

The "diffuse city" growth model has mostly been followed (Bretagnolle et al., 2000). Suburbs, polygons, scattered over the territory, with commercial, industrial, and leisure centers organized around transport nodes (Li & Gong, 2016). This is a model with high consumption of resources, (soil, energy, water, etc.), with high waste production and an increasing environmental impact on its near- and far environment (Clark et al., 2018). Urban growth dynamics is an unstoppable process with high consumption of energy, primary resources, and productive and/or wild territory. This dynamic highlights the need to undertake one of the greatest challenges such as generating models of sustainable urban development.

The architectural types mostly in use in the twentieth century city - even today - follow the principles of design of the "International Style" with very similar city layouts for any place on the planet and usually based on prototypical solutions (Helleman & Wassenberg, 2004; Lang, 2009). They show more often a common indifference to climate, geographical, and cultural context as for local identity (Hebbert, 2014; Verlie, 2020). In most cases, buildings are highly dependent on mechanical solutions for environmental conditioning with a high associated energy consumption for thermal comfort, habitability, and operation. It is not until the last decades of this century, as consequences of successive energy crises, that concern for energy efficiency has started to become part of the building agenda. Based on a systemic analysis, some authors point to the growing inefficiency of the current urban model (MAHMOUD et al., 2021; Vijayan et al., 2021).

Most of the urban areas where the population develops its normal life not only have a significant impact on the biotope but, more often, even negative effects on its citizens (de Sa et al., 2022). The citizens work in environments with limitations to natural lighting and to access to a steady flow of clean air, suffer from noise and other related damages. In many cases, city inhabitants do not have individual capacity to adapt and control their nearby environment, depending on general schedules, thus increasing the problems of adaptation and perception of the quality of the environment. Usually, this situation worsens due to lack of visual contact with open outdoor spaces. Efficient and healthy urban development should encourage their buildings to have sufficient access to and use of natural light, adequate rates of fresh air, fostering a significant number of hours of natural ventilation operation, and to have outdoor environments free of air pollutants, such as smoke, particulate matter, and toxic gases (Audrey & Batista-Ferrer, 2015; Satterthwaite, 1993).

To maximize psychological comfort, they must have a visual connection with open spaces, preferably landscaped or natural exteriors (Jabbar et al., 2022; Prospero & Health, 2010). After the recent health crisis of COVID-19, and its confinement and limitation of citizens' movements episodes -mandatory lockdowns, stay-at-home orders and the like, the population has become aware of the importance of buildings with open envelopes and the benefits provided by structures that facilitate the entry of air and natural light. After this social shock, many reflection processes on the quality of current built environments have been started (Lehberger et al., 2021; Poortinga et al., 2021).

2. THE CLIMATE AND URBAN CONTEXT OF CITIES IN MILD CLIMATE CITIES

Climate-sensitive urban design is a prerequisite for sustainable urban development: it aims for twofold: First, the design must allow the comfort outdoors and the environmental quality of the open space, increasing the opportunities for the development of outdoor activities, generating spaces-of-refuge, as well as other factors supporting an active life of the urban mesh. Second, the configuration must act on the building construction, contributing -to a considerable extent, to buffer and adjust the heating and cooling needs in buildings, reducing the use of electric lighting and mechanical HVAC systems, and supporting the capability to enjoy an adequate quality of the interior atmosphere. [12]

Climate-sensitive urban design is most effective at the urban mesoscale, where:

- The geometry of built areas can be designed and optimized to improve shaded and sun protection areas.
- The possibility of making an adequate selection of materials on the surfaces of buildings and streets, to the adequate adoption of reflectivity and absorptivity to maximize albedo or thermal absorption, as well as to optimize the thermal mass of these elements.
- Proper control of street orientation and green areas can lead to more comfortable and healthy outdoor conditions (even further providing climate shelters).

2.1. Weather Conditions

The most important climatic groups of the Mediterranean area —as typical mild climate urban areas— can be clustered on 6 climatic classes (Andrade & Contente, 2020; Deliège & Nicolay, 2016; Kottek et al., 2006):

- Oceanic Mediterranean climate: occurs throughout the region of Atlantic influence, which softens temperatures and brings remarkable humidity to the region. It is divided into: 1a Humid, 1b Subhumid and 1c hyper humid.
- Subtropical Mediterranean climate: typical of the Mediterranean coast, it is characterized by mild temperatures and absence of frost. It is divided into: 2a Subhumid and 2b Humid.
- Subcontinental Mediterranean climate of warm summers: it is characterized by high average annual temperatures, very warm summers, and cool winters with occasional frosts. It has only one variant: 3a
- Subcontinental Mediterranean climate of cold winters: its summers are temperate/mild, and very cold winters, with a high number of frosts. It is divided into 4a Subhumid and cold, 4b Dry and cold, 4c subhumid and mild, 4d Wet and 4 and hyper humid.
- Continental Mediterranean climate: it is characterized by cold and long winters, and noticeably short and not extremely hot summers, where much of its precipitation is in the form of snow. It is divided into: 5a of High-Mountain, 5b dry highlands and 5c of mid-mountains.
- Sub-desert Mediterranean climate: it is characterized by its mild temperatures, absence of frost and extremely low rainfall. It is divided into: 6a soft and 6b cold.

2.2 Climate With Significant Daily Thermal Oscillation

One of the most characteristic factors of temperate zones along with highly solar radiation dominance and moderate temperature range is the effect of thermal oscillations, both annual and daily —especially the latter.

This thermal amplitude oscillates around the human thermal band of comfort, as one of the most specific characteristics of these regions. The correct understanding of this factor and the impact on the conditions of both outdoor space and buildings indoor and their envelopes provides a fundamental tool for taking advantage of climate opportunities, which are not usually present in other regions.

The value of the thermal oscillation at ground level depends on the following factors:

- The average temperature.
- Average humidity.
- The wind regime (intensity, duration, variation, temperature, etc.).
- The proximity of large bodies of water, such as the sea.

In general, climates that correspond to coastal areas or near the sea have lower thermal oscillations, due to the moderating or softening effects of the water mass. On the contrary, climates in more inland areas usually have a strong thermal oscillation both daily and annual.

An important effect, which is evident in large contemporary urban areas, is the reduction or damping of amplitude due to energy storage caused by the masses and materials of buildings and urbanized spaces (heat island effect). In more densely built areas, daily thermal oscillations are significantly attenuated, reducing opportunities for climate use, such as night-time cooling, or intensifying the negative effects of solar radiation in the warm period.

2.3 Climate Change and Affection to the Mild Climate City

Although climate change affects multiple aspects of biotopes and far-reaching repercussions on human life, urban areas face specific challenges. The city as natural support of buildings must assess those effects on the existing building stock -and future one— as the city open spaces of the city (Roaf et al., 2010). The actual potentials and weaknesses of the city areas need to be addressed. This must be overcome especially in the already existing urban areas, to design appropriate strategies for adaptation and to avoid the use of inadequate or inefficient techniques (CIBSE, 2005) —with the consequent consumption of resources.

In the projections of climate change scenarios the weight of winter-heating is likely to decrease to the steady rise of cooling needs (Domínguez-Amarillo, Fernández-Agüera, Sendra, et al., 2019). This should foster the evolution of common retrofit techniques towards those focusing on the variable-temperature regime and its periodic oscillation. The search for high and passive environments will contribute to the development of low energy buildings (NZEB: *near zero energy buildings*). In the climate change scenarios, there is foreseen and intensification on the effects affecting building environment overheating – buildings and public spaces as more extreme temperature range, heat, and cold wave events, etc.

The buildings operating costs are expected to significatively increase and may ultimately drive economically unviable to part of the building stock (Holmes & Hacker, 2007). Therefore, the assessment of climate change against the future evolution of existing buildings must become a fundamental aspect of the study and gain importance in the coming years (Jentsch et al., 2008).

Most buildings in southern Europe or other typical temperate areas, especially housing stock—show high figures of "*naturally ventilated*" operation annual hours in (Carbon Trust, 2007). They also primarily rely on passive systems for cooling control in the warm months. However, it has been identified that energy consumption related to the thermal conditioning of buildings is increasing gradually (Domínguez-Amarillo, Fernández-Agüera, Peacock, et al., 2019), although with heterogeneous distribution and unsteady pace (Sendra et al., 2013).

3. BASIC PRINCIPLES OF ENERGY EFFICIENCY OF THE URBAN DESIGN IN MILD CLIMATES

The energy sustainability of urban design for cities of mild climate and medium latitude depends mainly on passive solar design, the use of natural energy opportunities, and the promotion of the incorporation of on-site renewable energy on site, both in buildings and in urban facilities.

The climate responsible strategies are far from been recent, having been an inherent to vernacular architecture and traditional city generation (Domínguez-Amarillo, Samuel; & Fernandez-Aguera, 2020). Beyond was in the foundation of the hygienist principles of the urban reform in the XIX.s (Ponce Herrero & Dávila Linares, 1998) as in the *Modern Movement* (Aguilera, 2015; Bastlund, 1967; Mumford & Restrepo, 2007) and the avant-garde proposals of the early twentieth century (Butti & Perlin, 1905).

The shape and orientation of the building are fundamental in optimizing its passive response in climatic environment such as that of the city in a temperate climate, of which the most representative example is the Mediterranean city. At the urban level, planners must foresee the structure and urban layout and the position and shape of the buildings, to know the areas of shade and radiation, their evolution, and behavior at separate times of the year. Likewise, other aspects such as the control of wind in the plot, for its correct use, as well as other aspects related to the energy storage and rejection, etc.

The urban design must determine, in coordination with other aspects and requirements of the urban concept, what road layout street dimension are needed, such as shape and position of the trees, control of wind turbulence, the arrangement of water sheets, surfaces, and pavement characteristics, and the use of gardening and vegetation. This approach allows to modulate the climatic and energy behavior of the outdoor space, supporting the activity of the city itself as well as the buildings themselves.

The approach to the principles of urban energy saving and efficiency must reflect a set of coordinated aspects:

- Regulate solar radiation and use of its thermal energy.
- Allow natural ventilation and take advantage of wind dynamics.
- Maximize natural lighting, both indoors and in urban areas.
- Allow adequate insulation and shielding against inclement weather.
- Optimize the dissipative capacity, reflection, and inertia of surfaces.
- Establish techniques of natural cooling: ventilation and evaporative cooling, especially with the help of vegetation.
- Allow the adequate incorporation and exploitation of renewable energy systems in their built elements.

For a correct application of these strategies, it is essential to reflect in the urban configuration (i.e., use of shade, access to solar radiation during cold periods, management of thermal wave oscillation, etc.).

4. REGULATE SOLAR RADIATION AND USE OF ITS THERMAL ENERGY

4.1 Solar Geometry

Solar geometry represents the apparent paths of the Sun in the sky, as well as its position at different dates and times of the year to predict its interaction with planes and volumes in space - built fabrics and surfaces of the city, depending on their relative location.

Geometric simplification assimilates that solar movement occurs in a translation movement on the surface of a sphere whose center is the Earth. Given the small size of this compared to the celestial sphere, the plane of the horizon is replaced by a parallel one that passes through the center of the Earth. The path of the Sun depends on the point from which we are observing it, determined by the latitude (angular distance between the equator and the parallel of the place).

The solar rays strike with different inclinations on each part of the Earth. This generates differences in climate and geographic landscape. The Mediterranean region and similar temperate zones lie between the tropics (+/-23° 27') and the polar circles (+/-66° 33'). At this latitude, the Sun only spends one day at the zenith: during the summer solstice. The rest of the solar trajectories are of lower height, so there is less total radiation. Winter days are quite different from summer days and the four seasons are clearly distinguished, which especially characterizes the cities of this region. This aspect indicates the need for dynamic design and even urban zoning, to allow differentiated comfort areas throughout the annual cycle.

It is very useful to design different shadows use a solar chart. A solar chart is a two-dimensional graphical representation of the position of the Sun in the sky for a specific location at each latitude. By choosing a date and time, the corresponding solar angle and azimuth is deduced. There are two types of solar chart: Fisher Chart or stereographic, which bases the projection of the path of the sun on a hemisphere; this is the most used for ease of use. The second is the Cylindrical Solar Charter, which bases its projection on a half-cut cylinder. The main advantage is that it represents the horizon around the observer, which allows for a study of facades directly and their sunbathing. With these data, we can evaluate what type of protection can be implemented to offer thermal protection in hot hours and seasons or how to take advantage of that same energy during the colder months or in less warm hours. The main contribution of the solar graphs is to help defining and designing variables such as the geometry of the façade elements or the orientation so that they play an essential role in the face of sun protection.

In typical Mediterranean regions, with latitudes around 40° (for areas in the northern hemisphere), we find solar profiles with these characteristics:

- The surfaces and areas facing north only present solar incidence in the early and late hours of the day during the summer. They receive virtually no direct radiation throughout the year. This orientation is recommended for spaces that need constant diffused light, as well as for spaces where a prolonged daytime presence is not performed. During the cold months, they do not receive gains from solar radiation, so they do not present accumulation potential, and, in outdoor spaces, they tend to be cold and shady areas.
- In the south orientation, there is a prolonged solar incidence at all hours, except the first and last hours of the day during the summer. It receives the sun all year round throughout the day. This orientation is recommended for spaces where the main activities and presence of the day develop, especially during cold months. A feature of special interest at this latitude is the change in height of the solar path between the winter and summer periods, which allows for an easy design of solar

protections for both facades and outdoor spaces. A useful design will block the sun during the summer and to foster penetration of radiation and light during the winter period.

- The east and west orientations, although very abundant in typical contemporary urban planning, are the ones with the worst capacity for solar use and control. They present little effective exposure during the winter months due to the advance of the azimuth of the ortho and the sunset and the low solar height — overly sensitive to blockage by other urban elements. However, they have a significant load in the warm months, with high intensity of radiation due to their almost normal incidence to the vertical surfaces of this orientation (with substantial risk of overheating and periods of glare).

These reflections can be applied to southern hemisphere locations only by alternating north to south in characterization.

The study of shading and solar geometry allows a critical analysis of the behavior on solar radiation of the different surfaces of the building and the exterior areas of the city. Roofs and courtyards should also be accurately assessed to achieve an optimal design with optimization between solar control and energy gains and losses.

Often buildings are erected in open areas where there are no other buildings interfere, but commonly other buildings generate shadows and blocks, altering the solar control itself. Based on the calculation of the own and remote shadows, the need for light control and glare on the facades is determined, as well as the optimal thermal insulation needs, namely the balance between solar gains and heat losses in winter. Designers also know the importance of planning the project with the appropriate orientation of the building and know how to take advantage of the sun to thermal comfort and light..

These same considerations must be applied in outdoor area design, both for public and private use, but conforming the open spaces system of the urban plot. In the Mediterranean city, a solar design that allows maximum insolation in cold periods must prevail, alternating the promotion of shade and radiation rejection (albedo) in warm periods while ensuring adequate lighting levels.

The design of the urban configuration must always have a double approach: the urban space and the configuration of the built volumes. They will be considered for the design of the open space itself: streets, squares, garden areas, as well as other spaces of relationship in the city. Primary design must allow buildings to apply these solar design strategies. To fulfill this task, it is necessary to optimize orientations of the plots and blocks, the separations between the different buildings and their relationship with the height, the determination of the maximum effective volume, as well as the interferences between them and other factors that affect both the built and the open space.

Apart for some interesting examples, the former considerations are not embedded in the current or recent workflow of new city production. Conventional or 'routine urbanism' far from large public operations of prestige - development of action units, expansions, new neighborhoods, etc. - usually does not pay special attention to efficiency of the design or its passive potential, in many cases gripped by the requirements of the maximum productivity of buildable surface, property structures, and other socio-political considerations. Today it is still sadly common to develop city areas with orientations of the plots eminently east-west, with high-rise buildings in the south, thus generating screen to buildings of lower height in the north (blocking not only solar access to the building envelopes but integration of solar renewable energy system). The design of open spaces: gardens, squares... — that remain cold and shady during winter and very exposed during the summer are profuse.

4.2 Solar Accessibility: The Right to the Sun

The concept of solar access in the design of the city is based on the capacity to create urban areas that ensure enough sun exposure during the necessary periods, either daily or seasonal. This concept must be applied to both the open spaces of the city and the buildings that make it up. The lack or by-contrast the overexposure to this sunstroke causes lack of comfort, unhealthy spaces, affects the use and actual activity of urban spaces —shady streets or over-irradiated squares, and a higher energy consumption than desirable due to the lack of use of natural energy (Capeluto & Shaviv, 2001).

The conflict or debate about access to the sun or "solar rights" versus urbanism and city design is not something new, but has arisen since the beginning of the formalization of urban science and contemporary doctrines of the city.

There is a certain controversy from city designers about the limitations to safeguard solar access. There is a widespread concern on the rigid application that would put in check the idea of freedom in the design of cities, aggravated by the risk of homogenization. This movement becomes understood as a limitation to the construction of high-rise buildings and the rigid tendency towards low rise cities, thus generating itself an obstacle to the achievement of sustainability in the urban structure (Lepore, 2017).

However, it is a principle marked as a priority from the beginning of Architecture, and then.... surprisingly forgotten?

Perhaps the oldest example is Mohenjo-Daro —in the Indus Valley— (2500 BC). It was characterized by a grid plan with streets oriented exactly from north to south and from east to west, and with waste collection systems already very advanced (Iqbal, 2021). The straight and wide streets, along the main axes of the city, therefore, were not intended for circulating assets, but were kept in narrow and winding lanes to better defend against the sun or wind. In ancient Egypt, El-Lahun (Horváth, 2009) is a settlement built to house laborers and slaves who worked on the construction of a nearby pyramid; and had a checkerboard design (1).

4.3 Passive Solar Design

Passive solar design (PSD) proposes optimizing the shape, envelope and orientation of a building, volume, or urban area to maximize solar gain from autumn to spring, while minimizing it during the warmer part of summer. At the same time, daylight is maximized at all times, which adds to the overall well-being and comfort of the occupants (Crosbie, 1998).

One of the fundamental measures to avoid overheating or discomfort indoors is to prevent solar radiation from reaching the building and its interior, especially its masses, during the summer and to allow entry into the building during the winter (Givoni, 1994). The ideal ratio would be approximately twice as much radiation gain in the winter as in the summer.

For this, it is essential that the urban design and the resulting plot allow the development of these strategies starting from the shape of the plots. As a rule, it could be applied that, for mid-latitudes and temperate climate, to maximize solar gain during the heating season, most of the openings of a building should be oriented to the south (+/- 30 °) seeking the minimum shadows of 9 to 3 p.m.

From the works of Olgyay (Olgyay, 1963), we can synthesize the following:

- All elongated shapes in a north-south direction work less efficiently than the square shape.
- The optimal form in all temperate climates is the elongated one in an east-west direction.

Figure 1. Map of the city of the pyramid of Sesostris II at El-Lahoun
(1889-90, licensed under the Creative Commons)

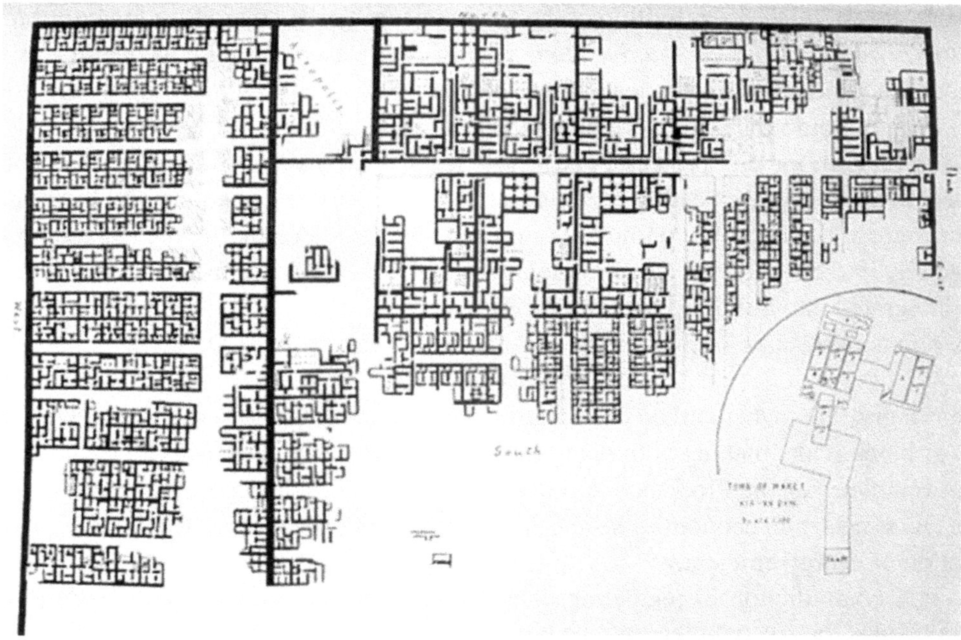

- At latitudes from 32 ° to 56 °, the south of the building receives three times more radiation in winter than the east and west sides of the building. During summer on the east and west sides will receive more radiation than on the south wall.
- A reduced form factor is recommended for cold climates (between 0.5 and 0.8), compared to values above 1.2 for hot climates.
- Orientation plays a decisive role in the thermal behavior of the building, regardless of the shape it has.
- The roof is one of the parts with greater exposure in a building, so the solutions in which it has less extension are better.

There are other factors that must be considered in a complementary way.

- The increase in the spacing ratio between buildings decreases the shading potential on the facades, which explains the increase in cooling demand. [3]
- The orientation of a deviated building to the east (east to south - usually 15 ° from east to south) is more effective, because in this way the western façade absorbs less heat from the sun in summer in hot and dry climates.

4.4 The Solar Envelope Concept: Solar Energy

The technique of the "solar envelope" is proposed by Knowles from the University of Southern California, as a mechanism to ensure the correct or maximum access to the sun of all users of the city, without implying the elimination of buildings in height or highly homogeneous type plots, allowing multiple models of urban density (Knowles, 1981, 2003).

In his work, he establishes a definition of the solar envelope as *"a container to regulate development within the limits derived from the relative motion of the Sun",* establishing it as the area of volumetric movement within which the building can be established without casting a certain amount of shade on nearby buildings or outdoor spaces to be protected (Knowles, 1981).

This 'Solar Law' in the city project, in any of its formalizations or definitions, establishes a fundamental aspect to allow passive heating of buildings in winter, ensure certain natural lighting in interior spaces, and improve the comfort conditions of citizens on the street and in open spaces. Another key factor, especially in recent years, is to allow solar collection capacity for thermal and photovoltaic systems, both integrated into buildings and city facilities.

The key points of this approach could be summarized in (Knowles, 2003):

- There is a grey area where urban design guidelines and building regulations overlap, especially at block or block scale, making both planning and building design ineffective.
- The morphology of the block is configured in relation to traditional limitations such as terrain, distances, streets, and economic aspects. These elements that require, at this scale, a greater consideration of energy efficiency.
- There is a contradiction in regulating, encouraging, and demanding the adoption of strategies based on solar energy and planning the city with rules that deny solar access.
- In the case of access to solar energy, these are borderline; whose actions – the location of the house, the outbuildings and vegetation, its size and height – will determine the extent of its ability to take advantage of sunlight.
- The solar envelope is a maximum volume whose shape is determined by the relative motion of the sun.
- Buildings designed within this volume, at critical hours of the day, will not shade adjacent plots.

5 ALLOW NATURAL VENTILATION AND TAKE ADVANTAGE OF WIND DYNAMICS

5.1 Wind in the Energy Efficiency of the City

Climatic conditions and human comfort are affected in urban environments by the action of air currents and the wind. These dynamic effects are clearly related to the morphology of the buildings and the elements that alter the natural topography of the area.

The winds in the urban environment are significantly modified by the different obstacles and reliefs of the city, with a less affection —usually— in the peripheral areas and greater affections in downtown areas. Changes in wind direction and speed and their relationship with sunlight and warming of urban surfaces are key to understanding climate effects in the city (Reiter, 2010).

The concept of comfort of urban spaces is relatively recent but is identified as a fundamental factor for the creation of living and vertebrate cities, where the city can support activities and social life (Nikolopoulou et al., 2001). Wind speed for urban spaces for citizens' use is one of the most relevant environmental parameters for the usability and well-being of users, as well as for providing adequate environments in buildings and the city as in (Stathopoulos, 2006; Walton et al., 2007). The dynamics of wind in the areas of the city are, together with the solar radiation received —direct or indirect— are aspects directly related to the design and urban conformation and, therefore, susceptible to be optimized (Reiter, 2010).

Similarly, vegetation, together with built obstacles, has effects on wind dynamics: speed, direction, and turbulence. These elements modify the laminar regime of the air, especially in the lower layers (Szkordilisz & Zöld, 2016). The wind, when colliding with an obstacle, is deflected both vertically and horizontally, which when concentrated, greater flow of the laminar wind increases its speed in the upper part, but decreases in the lower part. This can be used in favor, since it is possible to use architectural or vegetal barriers, controlling their permeability indices to moderate wind speed (Bustamante et al., 2014).

Finally, after the transformative process of the industrial revolution, which translates into a strong alteration of the atmospheric quality of cities and their surroundings, health and pollution have become critical aspects in the well-being of these areas. The continuous movement of air in the city is a fundamental necessity to ensure the dilution and dispersion of urban pollutants (gases from traffic combustion and heating, emission of particles, etc.). Therefore, ensuring the correct dynamics of the wind is one of the basic climatic factors to ensure adequate air quality in urban areas (Bustamante Oleart, 2020).

5.2 The Role of Urban Canyons

An urban canyon is an open space of the city enclosed by buildings on one of its sides, mainly on two sides in the case of streets, creating an environment like a natural canyon. Modification of the characteristics of the atmospheric boundary layer by the presence of this geometric singularity in the topography of the city area is called the urban canyon effect (2). This effect becomes more evident the higher the height of the buildings. The different urban canyons affect the local conditions of the city, including temperature, wind, light, and even the reception of telecommunication signals.

An aspect of great interest for the environmental health of urban space is that the presence of laminar and turbulent flows has a direct effect on the air quality of the space. Specifically, by concentrating locally generated pollutants and avoiding their atmospheric dilution (Vardoulakis et al., 2003).

The probability of urban canyoning increases with aspect ratio (0.7 being usually the level beyond which we can assume that there is a risk of accumulation of pollutants). Since there is stagnant air near the base of the canyon, air recirculation is often poor (Afiq et al., 2012).

Typical parameters of air movement in urban areas are (Nunez & Oke, 1977)

- Both the speed and direction of the winds that act on the area are modified.
- The vertical wind speed approaches zero at the canyon roof level.
- Shear production and dissipation are high at roof level, and a thin and strong layer of shear is created at the height of the building.
- The kinetic energy of turbulence is greater near the building downwind than near the building downwind because of stronger wind shear.
- The resulting flow patterns within the canyon depend on the direction of the wind with respect to the direction of orientation of the street.

Figure 2. The effect of a street canyon on winds; after Oake, 1977
(Source: RoshiniA. Lic. Creative Commons)

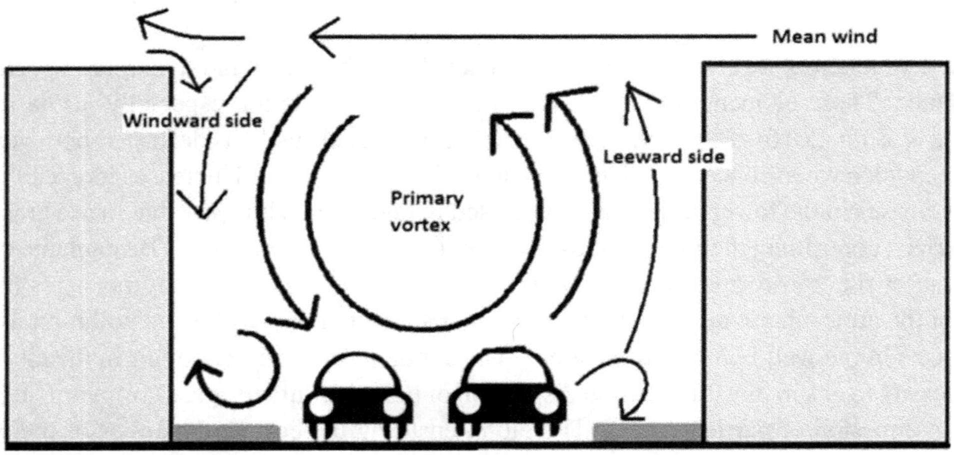

5.3 Behavior of Urban Canyons

The prevailing wind direction is fundamental in the formation of canyons.

a) Perpendicular wind:

In the case of wind directions eminently perpendicular to the direction of the street, there is a greater probability of this occlusion behavior. The flow of air in motion over buildings does not allow mixing and exchange with air masses occluded in the street between surfaces (Sini et al., 1996) as a vertically rotating wind flow is created with a primary vortex centered within the street canyons.

The typical behavior will depend, fundamentally, on the aspect ratio of the barrel, as stated (Kovar-Panskus et al, 2002; Baik & Kim, 1999).

An aspect that must be considered to understand the turbulence regime of the canyon is the type and intensity of road traffic within it. There is a significant difference between pedestrian streets, one-way or two, as this increases turbulence in the lower half and reduces the intensity of recirculation flow within the canyon (Pirjola et al., 2012).

b) Parallel wind:

Conversely, in the action of parallel winds, a channeling effect is observed where winds tend to direct and accelerate through the canyon (Nunez & Oke, 1977).(Nunez & Oke, 1977)When the width of the street is not uniform, the formation of the Venturi effect is observed when the air is channeled, increasing speed. Behavior along the street can be significantly different for short and long barrels, as corner vortices have a greater influence on the former(Kastner-Klein et al., 2001).

5.4 Effects of Winds Dynamics and the Urban Canyon on the Environment of the City

a) Effects on urban temperature:

Urban canyons contribute to the urban heat island effect, allowing the temperature inside the canyon to increase between 2 and 4 ° C to the surrounding areas. To evaluate the temperature phenomena within the pipe, the irradiance, the angle of solar incidence, the albedo of the surface, the emissivity, its orientation, and the sky vision factor [SVF] must be considered.

On the main geometric factors that affect the production of the urban form, the following considerations of interest for the city of temperate climate and mid-latitudes can be indicated:

i. About SVF:
   - Urban canyons with high SVF cool quickly in the night periods because there is more space between the celestial vault - the radiation sink - available to absorb the heat stored by the buildings. However, they run the risk of increased thermal uptake and storage in daylight hours - greatly influenced by their orientation and ability to block the solar path. In warm periods, spaces with high SVF can increase thermal discomfort, especially in the absence of trees and local shades (Krüger et al., 2011).
   - When the SVF is reduced, the barrel will store less heat during the day –depending on its thermal capacity, but, on the contrary, it will tend to store it for longer with less nocturnal release and, therefore, increased the heat island effect of that area. Proper control of the SVF can contribute to reducing air temperature in the state(Bourbia & Boucheriba, 2010)

ii. Aspect ratio
   - For a hot and dry climate, increasing the height-to-width ratio (H/W) can moderately decrease the air temperature. In relation to the increase in SVF, the increase in width tends to increase user discomfort (Ali Toudert & Mayer, 2006).
   - A high aspect ratio can produce a higher percentage of shadow cast over the space with a more comfortable wind chill in the (Andreou, 2014).

iii. Orientation
   - In general, the north-south orientation of the urban canyon usually offers better thermal conditions for the occupants (with normal aspect ratios) (Ali Toudert & Mayer, 2006; Andreou, 2014; Bourbia & Boucheriba, 2010; Targhi & Van Dessel, 2015).
   - Intermediate or diagonal orientations can present similarity in thermal conditions with the North-South orientation and, in particular, offer a shorter time of discomfort than the East-West orientation, which can be identified as the one with the worst thermal response in the warm period and the generation of heat island effect(Ali Toudert & Mayer, 2006).

iv. Vertical profile shape
   - The presence of urban layouts with an asymmetrical profile or the appearance of dilations in the streets in the form of open spaces can help design better shading, which in turn, can improve comfort conditions (Ali Toudert & Mayer, 2006)
   - The mixture of buildings of different heights contributes to improving the operation of the canyon, through openings (Bahgat et al., 2019).

b) Air quality

As discussed previously, temperature and wind modification affect the air quality inside the street canyon. This is especially affected by its turbulence and the present air flows.

- When the wind is directed parallel to the street, the effect of channeling and venturi appears, so the dispersion capacity of pollutants increases - an improvement of removal.
- In the opposite case, with perpendicular wind, the vortex flow formed within the canyon tends to confine the airflow, reduce the dispersion of pollutants, and increase pollution concentrations within the canyon.
- When there is a phenomenon marked by canyons, especially with the formation of internal vortices, there is a risk of entrapment, not only of the contamination of local origin but of that which is incorporated by the wind. This can cause circulation within the street, which significantly worsens its environmental quality.
- The pollution columns generated in the volume of the street, at the surface level, are pushed to the leeward side of the canyon by the flow of the vortex. In general, surface-level pollution concentrations tend to be highest on the leeward side of the street; special attention should be paid to locating activities with sensitive or vulnerable occupants in these areas of the street.
- Lower secondary vortices can generate stagnation effects of pollutants on sidewalks, especially on the wind side.

6. MAXIMIZE NATURAL LIGHTING, BOTH INDOORS AND IN URBAN AREAS

Maximize natural lighting can significantly reduce the need for artificial lighting and the associated energy consumption. There are some strategies for maximizing natural lighting both indoors and in urban areas:

- Building orientation: Buildings should be oriented to maximize the amount of natural light that enters the building throughout the day. This can be achieved by aligning the building with the sun's path and minimizing obstructions such as neighboring buildings or trees. This orientation was discussed more detailed in the sections 5.1 and 5.2.
- Daylighting: Daylighting is the strategic placement of windows, skylights, and other openings in a building to maximize natural light and reduce the need for artificial lighting. Daylighting strategies should be carefully planned to avoid glare and excessive heat gain or loss. These strategies should be compatible with termal comfort (Ruiz et al., 2021; Acosta et al., 2019; Campano et al., 2015).
- Light-colored surfaces: Light-colored surfaces reflect more sunlight and can help to increase the amount of natural light in urban areas. This can be achieved by using light-colored building materials, pavements, and roofs.
- Urban design: Urban design strategies such as the placement of buildings, trees, and other urban elements should be carefully planned to maximize natural light in public spaces.

7. OPTIMIZE THE DISSIPATIVE CAPACITY, REFLECTION, AND INERTIA OF SURFACES

Optimizing the dissipative capacity, reflection, and inertia of urban surfaces involves using materials, textures, colors, and shapes that can enhance the thermal and visual properties of the built environment.

It is important to improve the dissipative capacity of materials. The ability of a surface to dissipate heat and reduce the urban heat island effect can be improved by using materials that have a high thermal conductivity, such as concrete, asphalt, and natural stone. Additionally, the use of shading devices and green roofs can help reduce the amount of solar radiation that is absorbed by surfaces.

Other good practice could be include reflective materials. The reflectivity of a surface can be improved by using materials that have a high albedo, such as white or light-colored concrete, or reflective coatings on roofs and pavements. This helps to reduce the amount of solar radiation that is absorbed by surfaces and contributes to the urban heat island effect.

The texture and color of surfaces can also impact their thermal and visual properties. For example, rough and porous surfaces can increase the surface area for heat exchange and improve thermal comfort. Additionally, lighter colors can reflect more sunlight and reduce the urban heat island effect.

Other important characteristic of the used materials is the inertia. The ability of a surface to store and release heat can be improved by using materials that have a high thermal mass, such as concrete and stone. This can help to maintain a more stable temperature in buildings and reduce the need for heating and cooling.

Overall, optimizing the dissipative capacity, reflection, and inertia of surfaces requires a comprehensive approach that considers a range of factors, such as materials, textures, colors, and shapes. It also involves balancing the need for thermal comfort and energy efficiency with other design considerations, such as aesthetics and functionality. (Yinghong, 2015 and Kim, 2016) provides an overview of the role of urban surfaces in shaping the built environment, and includes strategies for optimizing their dissipative capacity, reflection, and inertia.

8. ESTABLISH TECHNIQUES OF NATURAL COOLING

Establishing techniques of natural cooling that use ventilation and evaporative cooling can help to reduce the energy consumption of buildings and improve thermal comfort. Here are some ways to establish these techniques:

i. Natural ventilation: Natural ventilation relies on the movement of air through a building to cool it down. This can be achieved through passive ventilation, such as opening windows and doors, or through the use of mechanical ventilation systems that circulate air. To optimize natural ventilation, it is important to consider the building orientation, wind patterns, and the placement of windows and vents (see in previous sections). Additionally, incorporating greenery in and around the building can help to create a more favorable microclimate and promote air movement.
ii. Evaporative cooling: Evaporative cooling uses the process of evaporation to cool air, and can be achieved through the use of evaporative coolers, misting systems, or through the use of plants and vegetation. Plants and vegetation can help to create shade, reduce the amount of solar radiation that

is absorbed by surfaces, and release moisture into the air through transpiration, which can help to cool the surrounding environment.

iii. Green roofs: are one example of how vegetation can be used to help cool buildings through evaporative cooling. A green roof is a type of roof that is partially or completely covered with vegetation, typically consisting of a layer of soil, a drainage layer, and a layer of plants. The vegetation and soil on the roof can absorb and evaporate water, which can help cool the air around the building. Here are some examples and references on green roofs for evaporative cooling:

A study by Wong et al. (2019) found that green roofs can reduce the heat island effect in urban areas and improve thermal comfort. The study found that green roofs can reduce the surface temperature of roofs by up to 40°C, and that the effect can extend to surrounding areas, reducing the air temperature by up to 3°C. A study by Kolokotsa et al. (2014) found that green roofs can significantly reduce indoor temperatures in buildings. The study found that green roofs can reduce indoor temperatures by up to 4.6°C, and that the effect is greater in buildings with less insulation.

An example of a green roof system designed specifically for evaporative cooling is the Hydrotech Garden Roof Assembly. This system uses a layer of moisture-retaining soil and a layer of vegetation to facilitate evapotranspiration and cool the air around the building. A study by Dvorak and Vranayova (2018) found that the Hydrotech system was effective in reducing the surface temperature of roofs and improving thermal comfort in a residential building. Another example of a green roof system designed for evaporative cooling is the Xeroflor Green Roof System. This system uses a combination of drought-tolerant plants and a moisture-retaining substrate to facilitate evapotranspiration and cool the air. A study by Jim et al. (2019) found that the Xeroflor system was effective in reducing the surface temperature of roofs and improving thermal comfort in a commercial building.

iv. Facade greening: is another technique for using vegetation to help cool buildings through evaporative cooling. Facade greening involves growing climbing plants, vines, or other vegetation on the exterior walls of a building to provide shading and evaporative cooling. A study by Liu et al. (2020) found that facade greening can significantly reduce the surface temperature of walls and improve thermal comfort. The study found that facade greening can reduce the surface temperature of walls by up to 25°C and reduce the air temperature by up to 5°C.

9. ALLOW THE ADEQUATE INCORPORATION AND EXPLOITATION OF RENEWABLE ENERGY SYSTEMS

To allow the adequate incorporation and exploitation of renewable energy systems in their built elements, the following approaches can be taken: integration of renewable energy systems, such as solar panels, wind turbines, or geothermal systems, into the design of buildings can help to reduce energy consumption and improve sustainability. Architects and engineers can collaborate to incorporate these systems into the building design to optimize their performance and ensure they are aesthetically integrated into the building. Different types of archetypes can optimise the photovoltaic systems (Fernández-Agüera et al., 2021).

Proper orientation and shading of buildings can help to maximize the potential for renewable energy systems. For example, solar panels should be oriented towards the sun and should not be shaded by nearby buildings or trees, explained in the task 5.4 before. Proper shading of windows can also reduce the cooling load on buildings, which can increase the effectiveness of renewable energy systems (Murshed et al, 2018).

10. CONCLUSION AND RECOMMENDATIONS

On the design of the city under the concepts of passive solar design and active use of natural energies:

- Climate or climate-responsible design strategies are not new or have emerged with current environmental concerns or climate change. These have been part of the vernacular heritage of the traditional city, having been at the base of the hygienist principles of the s. XIX and the modern movement – although its application was largely diluted during *Modern Movement* development.
- The same way that the shape and orientation of the surfaces of the city are fundamental to optimize the passive response of a building in each climatic environment. At an urban scale, planning must foresee that the structure and urban layout, as well as the position and shape of the buildings, enabling their correct orientation and the optimization of natural ventilation, controlling unwanted winds, and fostering adequate shade strategies.
- Urban design must not only determine the layout of the road layout and the size of the streets, but also specify the shape and position of the trees, the control of wind turbulence, the arrangement of water sheets, the treatment of surfaces and pavements and the use of vegetation to temper the "heat island" effect.
- Understand and extract the keys to the various types of urban fabric that have developed locally.
- The contemporary city faces the challenge of climate change, with a special predominance of overheating, where the heat island effect plays a significant role. Cooling should be established as the dominant condition to be considered for energy efficiency.
- From an urban layout that allows for the correct arrangement of buildings, architecture must be built according to the principle of energy saving and efficiency. The design of the urban configuration must:
    - Maximize natural lighting and ventilation.
    - Regulate solar radiation.
    - Allow active use of solar loads in buildings and urban elements (photovoltaic and thermal systems).

ACKNOWLEDGMENT

This research was funded by the *III Plan Propio de Docencia and Contrato de Acceso* (3PPD-US) and the *VI Plan Propio de Investigación* (PPI-US) from the Universidad de Sevilla (SPAIN).

The authors wish to express their thanks for technical support provided to the research project. *CARE-Light_Lite: Biodynamic lighting for circadian rhythm regulation* (Ref PI-0136-2019). The authors thank all those who collaborated on this research project. The authors also want to thank to Junta de Andalucía and the University of Seville for providing test cell and experimental facilities for the research.

REFERENCES

Acosta, I. J., & Campano, M. 1 Á., Domínguez Amarillo, S., Fernández-Agüera, J.(2019) Minimum Daylight Autonomy: A New Concept to Link Daylight Dynamic Metrics with Daylight Factors. En: LEUKOS - Journal of Illuminating Engineering Society of North America.

Afiq, W., Che Sidik, N. A., & Saqr, K. (2012). Effects of buildings aspect ratio, wind speed and wind direction on flow structure and pollutant dispersion in symmetric street canyons: A review. *International Journal of Mechanical and Materials Engineering*, *7*, 158–165.

Aguilera, A. V. (2015). El bosque en la ciudad: La invención del urbanismo moderno en la Ciudad de México (1870-1930). Amérique Latine Histoire et Mémoire. Les Cahiers ALHIM. *Les Cahiers ALHIM*, *29*(29), 29. Advance online publication. doi:10.4000/alhim.5237

Ali Toudert, F., & Mayer, H. (2006). *Effects of Street Design on Outdoor Thermal Comfort.*

Andrade, C., & Contente, J. (2020). Köppen's climate classification projections for the Iberian Peninsula. *Climate Research*, *81*, 71–89. doi:10.3354/cr01604

Andreou, E. (2014). The effect of urban layout, street geometry and orientation on shading conditions in urban canyons in the Mediterranean. *Renewable Energy*, *63*, 587–596. doi:10.1016/j.renene.2013.09.051

Audrey, S., & Batista-Ferrer, H. (2015). Healthy urban environments for children and young people: A systematic review of intervention studies. *Health & Place*, *36*, 97–117. doi:10.1016/j.healthplace.2015.09.004 PMID:26457624

Bahgat, R., Reffat, R. M., & Elkady, S. L. (2019). Energy Efficiency Design Guide for Optimal Urban Features of Open Spaces in Residential Complexes. *The Academic Research Community Publication*, *3*(1), 136–152. doi:10.21625/archive.v3i1.436

Bastlund, K. (1967). *José Luis Sert: Architecture city planning urban design*. Les Éditions d'Architecture.

Blasco, J. A. (2016, February 20). *Urban Networks: Panorama del urbanismo europeo en la década de 1950 (la transición del pesimismo de posguerra a la esperanza por un mundo mejor)*. Urban Networks. https://urban-networks.blogspot.com/2016/02/panorama-del-urbanismo-europeo-en-la.html

Bourbia, F., & Boucheriba, F. (2010). Impact of street design on urban microclimate for semi arid climate (Constantine). *Renewable Energy*, *35*(2), 343–347. doi:10.1016/j.renene.2009.07.017

Bretagnolle, A., Mathian, H., Pumain, D., & Rozenblat, C. (2000). *Long-term dynamics of European towns and cities: Towards a spatial model of urban growth.* Cybergeo., doi:10.4000/cybergeo.566

Bustamante, C., Jans, M., & Higueras, E. (2014). El comportamiento del viento en la morfología urbana y su incidencia en el uso estancial del espacio público, Punta Arenas, Chile. *AUS*, *15*(15), 28–33. doi:10.4206/aus.2014.n15-06

Bustamante Oleart, C. (2020). La historia del viento en las ciudades = The history of the wind in the cities. *Cuadernos de Investigación Urbanística*, *132*(132), 1. doi:10.20868/ciur.2020.132.4510

Butti, K., & Perlin, J. (1905). *A Golden Thread: 2500 Years of Solar Architecture and Technology.*

Campano, M. Á., Acosta, I. J., Fernández-Agüera, J., & Sendra, J. J. (2015). Towards finding the optimal location of a ventilation inlet in a roof monitor skylight, using visual and thermal performance criteria, for dwellings in a Mediterranean climate. Journal of Building Performance Simulation, 4, 226–238.

Capeluto, I. G., & Shaviv, E. (2001). On the use of 'solar volume' for determining the urban fabric. *Solar Energy*, *70*(3), 275–280. doi:10.1016/S0038-092X(00)00088-8

Carbon Trust. (2007). *Technical Guide CTG005—Air conditioning: Maximising Comfort, Minimising Energy Consumption*. Carbon Trust.

CIBSE. (2005). *Climate Change and the Indoor Environment: Impacts and Adaptation, CIBSE TM36*. The Chartered Institution of Building Services Engineers.

Clark, G., Moonen, T., & Nunley, J. (2018). *Europe and its Urban Development, 1970 to 2020* (City Transformed, p. 40). European Investement Bank. https://www.eib.org/en/essays/the-story-of-your-city

Crosbie, M. J. (Ed.). (1998). *The Passive Solar Design and Construction Handbook*. John Wiley & Sons.

de Sa, T. H., Mwaura, A., Vert, C., Mudu, P., Roebbel, N., Tran, N., & Neira, M. (2022). Urban design is key to healthy environments for all. *The Lancet. Global Health*, *10*(6), e786–e787. doi:10.1016/S2214-109X(22)00202-9 PMID:35561710

Deliège, A., & Nicolay, S. (2016). Köppen–Geiger Climate Classification for Europe Recaptured via the Hölder Regularity of Air Temperature Data. *Pure and Applied Geophysics*, *173*(8), 2885–2898. doi:10.100700024-016-1339-3

Domínguez-Amarillo, S., Fernández-Agüera, J., Peacock, A., & Acosta, I. (2019). Energy related practices in Mediterranean low-income housing. *Building Research and Information*. doi:10.1080/09613218.2019.1661764

Domínguez-Amarillo, S., Fernández-Agüera, J., Sendra, J. J., & Roaf, S. (2019). The performance of Mediterranean low-income housing in scenarios involving climate change. *Energy and Building*, *202*, 109374. doi:10.1016/j.enbuild.2019.109374

Domínguez-Amarillo, S., Sendra, J. J., Fernández-Agüera, J., & Escandón, R. (2017). *La construcción de la vivienda social en Sevilla y su catalogación.1939-1979* (U. de Sevilla, Ed.). Editorial Universidad de Sevilla. https://us.odilotk.es/opac?id=00027396%0A

Domínguez-Amarillo, S., Sendra, J. J., & Oteiza San José, I. (2016). La envolvente térmica de la vivienda social: El caso de Sevilla, 1939 a 1979. In Editorial CSIC (Consejo Superior de Investigaciones Científicas). Editorial Consejo Superior de Investigaciones Científicas.

Dvorak, P., & Vranayova, Z. (2018). Application of green roof systems for the improvement of energy performance of buildings. *Energy and Building*, *158*, 1140–1149.

Fernández-Agüera, J., Domínguez, S., García, N., & Campano, M. Á. *Analysis of Building Archetypes for Optimising New Photovoltaic Energy Facilities: A Case Study.* Sustainability, 13(21). doi:10.3390u132112249

Givoni, B. (1994). *Passive and Low Energy Cooling of Buildings*. John Wiley & Sons.

Hebbert, M. (2014). Climatology for city planning in historical perspective. *Urban Climate, 10*, 204–215. doi:10.1016/j.uclim.2014.07.001

Helleman, G., & Wassenberg, F. (2004). The renewal of what was tomorrow's idealistic city. Amsterdam's Bijlmermeer high-rise. *Cities (London, England), 21*(1), 3–17. doi:10.1016/j.cities.2003.10.011

Holmes, M. J., & Hacker, J. N. (2007). Climate change, thermal comfort and energy: Meeting the design challenges of the 21st century. *Energy and Building, 39*(7), 802–814. doi:10.1016/j.enbuild.2007.02.009

Horváth, Z. (2009). Temple(s) and town at el-Lahun: A study of ancient toponyms in the el-Lahun papyri. In D. P. Silverman, W. Kelly Simpson, & J. Wegner (Eds.), Archaism and Innovation: Studies in Middle Kingdom Egypt (p. 457).

Iqbal, S. (2021). Energy Efficiency in Architecture Design in Mohenjo-Daro. In N. Mohareb, A. Versaci, Y. Mahgoub, S. Maruthaveeran, & F. Alberti (Eds.), *Cities' Vocabularies: The Influences and Formations* (pp. 203–208). Springer International Publishing. doi:10.1007/978-3-030-51961-2_15

Jabbar, M., Yusoff, M. M., & Shafie, A. (2022). Assessing the role of urban green spaces for human well-being: A systematic review. *GeoJournal, 87*(5), 4405–4423. doi:10.100710708-021-10474-7 PMID:34305268

Jenofonte. (1993). *Recuerdos de Sócrates; Económico; Banquete; Apología de Sócrates. Editorial Gredos.*

Jentsch, M. F., Bahaj, A. B. S., & James, P. A. B. (2008). Climate change future proofing of buildings—Generation and assessment of building simulation weather files. *Energy and Building, 40*(12), 2148–2168. doi:10.1016/j.enbuild.2008.06.005

Jim, C. Y., Li, X., Xu, Y., & Chow, W. T. (2019). Potential thermal benefits of xeroflor green roofs for building energy conservation in a sub-tropical city. *Urban Forestry & Urban Greening, 44*, 126389.

Kastner-Klein, P., Fedorovich, E., & Rotach, M. W. (2001). A wind tunnel study of organised and turbulent air motions in urban street canyons. *Journal of Wind Engineering and Industrial Aerodynamics, 89*(9), 849–861. doi:10.1016/S0167-6105(01)00074-5

Knowles, R. L. (1981). *Sun Rhythm Form*. MIT Press.

Knowles, R. L. (2003). The solar envelope: Its meaning for energy and buildings. *Energy and Building, 35*(1), 15–25. doi:10.1016/S0378-7788(02)00076-2

Kolokotsa, D., Santamouris, M., & Akbari, H. (2014). Passive cooling of buildings by using green and blue roofs. *Advances in Building Energy Research, 8*(1), 9–30.

Kottek, M., Grieser, J., Beck, C., Rudolf, B., & Rubel, F. (2006). World map of the Köppen-Geiger climate classification updated. *Meteorologische Zeitschrift (Berlin), 15*(3), 259–263. doi:10.1127/0941-2948/2006/0130

Krüger, E. L., Minella, F. O., & Rasia, F. (2011). Impact of urban geometry on outdoor thermal comfort and air quality from field measurements in Curitiba, Brazil. *Building and Environment, 46*(3), 621–634. doi:10.1016/j.buildenv.2010.09.006

Lang, J. (2009). International urban design: Theory and practice. *Proceedings of the Institution of Civil Engineers. Urban Design and Planning, 162*(1), 7–17. doi:10.1680/udap.2009.162.1.7

Lehberger, M., Kleih, A.-K., & Sparke, K. (2021). Self-reported well-being and the importance of green spaces – A comparison of garden owners and non-garden owners in times of COVID-19. *Landscape and Urban Planning, 212*, 104108. doi:10.1016/j.landurbplan.2021.104108 PMID:36569995

Li, X., & Gong, P. (2016). Urban growth models: Progress and perspective. *Science Bulletin, 61*(21), 1637–1650. doi:10.100711434-016-1111-1

Liu, Y., Chen, H., Tang, Y., Yang, X., & Zhang, J. (2020). Effects of facade greening on the urban microclimate and building energy performance. *Building and Environment, 176*, 106868.

Mahmoud, M., Cheikh, N., Cerny, O., Gerard, F., & Lemoine, P. (2021). The road to energy efficiency (p. 164). Policy Department for Economic, Scientific and Quality of Life Policies Directorate-General for Internal Policies.

Mumford, E., & Restrepo, L. D. E. (2007). *El discurso del CIAM sobre el urbanismo*. 21.

Murshed, S. M., Ahmed, S., & Rasul, M. G. (2018). Integration of renewable energy into building and urban design: A literature review. *Renewable & Sustainable Energy Reviews, 82*, 1325–1336.

Nikolopoulou, M., Baker, N., & Steemers, K. (2001). Thermal comfort in outdoor urban spaces: Understanding the human parameter. *Solar Energy, 70*(3), 227–235. doi:10.1016/S0038-092X(00)00093-1

Nunez, M., & Oke, T. R. (1977). The Energy Balance of an Urban Canyon. *Journal of Applied Meteorology and Climatology, 16*(1), 11–19. doi:10.1175/1520-0450(1977)016<0011:TEBOAU>2.0.CO;2

Olgyay, V. (1963). *Design with Climate: Bioclimatic Approach to Architectural Regionalism*. Princeton University Press.

Pirjola, L., Lähde, T., Niemi, J. V., Kousa, A., Rönkkö, T., Karjalainen, P., Keskinen, J., Frey, A., & Hillamo, R. (2012). Spatial and temporal characterization of traffic emissions in urban microenvironments with a mobile laboratory. *Atmospheric Environment, 63*, 156–167. doi:10.1016/j.atmosenv.2012.09.022

Ponce Herrero, G., & Dávila Linares, J. M. (1998). Medidas higienistas y planes de reforma urbana en el tránsito de los siglos XIX al XX en las principales ciudades de la provincia de Alicante. *Investigaciones Geográficas, 20*(20), 141. doi:10.14198/INGEO1998.20.07

Poortinga, W., Bird, N., Hallingberg, B., Phillips, R., & Williams, D. (2021). The role of perceived public and private green space in subjective health and wellbeing during and after the first peak of the COVID-19 outbreak. *Landscape and Urban Planning, 211*, 104092. doi:10.1016/j.landurbplan.2021.104092 PMID:36540159

Prado, R. G. (1998). La herencia moderna. Astrágalo. *Cultura de la Arquitectura y la Ciudad, 8*, 35–44.

Prospero, F., & Health, R. (2010). *Healthy Open Spaces*. Research Gate. doi:10.13140/2.1.2568.0169

Reiter, S. (2010). Assessing Wind Comfort in Urban Planning. *Environment and Planning. B, Planning & Design, 37*(5), 857–873. doi:10.1068/b35154

Roaf, S., Crichton, D., Nicol, F., Rudge, J., & Kovats, S. (2010). Adapting Buildings and Cities for Climate Change. In Adapting Buildings and Cities for Climate Change. doi:10.1016/B978-1-85617-720-7.00007-3

Ruiz, A., Campano, M. Á., Acosta, I. J., & Luque, Ó. (2021). Partial Daylight Autonomy (DAp): A new lighting dynamic metric to optimize the design of windows for seasonal use spaces. *Applied Sciences (Basel, Switzerland)*, *11*(17), 11. doi:10.3390/app11178228

Satterthwaite, D. (1993). The impact on health urban environments. *Environment and Urbanization*, *5*(2), 87–111. doi:10.1177/095624789300500208 PMID:12318602

Sendra, J. J. J., Domínguez-Amarillo, S., Bustamante, P., León, A. L., Bustamante Rojas, P., & Leon, A. L. (2013). Energy intervention in the residential sector in the south of spain: Current challenges. *Informes de la Construcción*, *65*(532), 457–464. doi:10.3989/ic.13.074

Sini, J.-F., Anquetin, S., & Mestayer, P. G. (1996). Pollutant dispersion and thermal effects in urban street canyons. *Atmospheric Environment*, *30*(15), 2659–2677. doi:10.1016/1352-2310(95)00321-5

Source Weather Data Formats. (n.d.). Auxiliary Programs—EnergyPlus 8.3. https://bigladdersoftware.com/epx/docs/8-3/auxiliary-programs/source-weather-data-formats.html

Stathopoulos, T. (2006). Pedestrian level winds and outdoor human comfort. *Journal of Wind Engineering and Industrial Aerodynamics*, *94*(11), 769–780. doi:10.1016/j.jweia.2006.06.011

Szkordilisz, F., & Zöld, A. (2016). Effect of Vegetation on Wind-Comfort. *Applied Mechanics and Materials*, *824*, 811–818. . doi:10.4028/www.scientific.net/AMM.824.811

Targhi, M. Z., & Van Dessel, S. (2015). Potential Contribution of Urban Developments to Outdoor Thermal Comfort Conditions: The Influence of Urban Geometry and Form in Worcester, Massachusetts, USA. *Procedia Engineering*, *118*, 1153–1161. doi:10.1016/j.proeng.2015.08.457

Vardoulakis, S., Fisher, B., Pericleous, K., & Gonzalez-Flesca, N. (2003). Modelling air quality in street canyons: A review. *Atmospheric Environment*, *37*(2), 155–182. doi:10.1016/S1352-2310(02)00857-9

Verlie, B. (2020). Intergenerational Climate Injustice within the Urban Planning Profession. *Planning Theory & Practice*.

Vijayan, M., Patil, A., Kapse, V., & Bahadure, S. (2021). Assessing the Energy Efficiency Practices in Cities Across the World. *Current Science*, *121*(3), 372. doi:10.18520/cs/v121/i3/372-383

Walton, D., Dravitzki, V., & Donn, M. (2007). The relative influence of wind, sunlight and temperature on user comfort in urban outdoor spaces. *Building and Environment*, *42*(9), 3166–3175. doi:10.1016/j.buildenv.2006.08.004

Wong, N. H., Tan, A. Y. K., Tan, P. Y., & Wong, N. C. (2019). *Green roofs and walls for a more sustainable urban environment*. Springer.

Yinghong, Q. (2015). A review on the development of cool pavements to mitigate urban heat island effect. *Renewable & Sustainable Energy Reviews*, *52*, 445–459. doi:10.1016/j.rser.2015.07.177

ADDITIONAL READINGS

Adapting Buildings and Cities for Climate Change: A 21st Century Survival Guide. Sue Roaf, David Crichton, and Fergus Nicol. (2009). Routledge.

Climate Considerations in Building and Urban Design. Baruch Givoni. (1998). John Wiley & Sons.

Design with climate. Bioclimatic approach to architectural regionalism. Victor Olgyay. Princeton University Press, 1963 (Rev. Ed. 2015).

Sun Rhythm Form. Ralph L. Knowles. (1985). MIT Press.

KEY TERMS AND DEFINITIONS

Albedo: The percentage of radiation that any surface reflects relative to the incident radiation.

Aspect ratios: Are determined by the ratio of building heights to street width.

Carbon footprint: is an environmental indicator that aims to reflect "the totality of greenhouse gases (GHG) emitted by direct or indirect effect of an individual, organization, event or product". Such environmental impact is measured by conducting a GHG emissions inventory or a life cycle analysis according to the type of footprint, following recognized international standards, such as ISO 2007. ISO 14069, ISO 14067, PAS 2050 or GHG Protocol, among others.

Compactness: The ratio of the volume enclosed by the thermal envelope (V) of the building (or part of the building) to the sum of the heat exchange surfaces of that envelope ($A=\sum Ai$). It is expressed in m^3/m^2.

NZEB: Near Zero Energy Buildings.

NZEB: Near Zero Energy Buildings.

Orientation: Position or direction of buildings with respect to a cardinal point.

The sky vision factor (FVS): Denotes the ratio of radiation received by a flat surface to that of the entire hemispheric radiant environment [2] and is calculated as the fraction of sky visible from the ground. SVF is a dimensionless value ranging from 0 to 1

Urban canyon: Narrow street with tall, continuous buildings on both sides of the road. But now the term urban canyon is used more broadly, and the geometric details of the street canyon are used to categorize them. The most important geometric detail about a street cannon is the ratio between the height of the barrel (H) and the width of the barrel (W), H/W, which is defined as the aspect ratio. The aspect ratio value can be used to classify street guns as follows: **Normal barrel**: Aspect ratio ≈ 1 and no major openings in the barrel walls. **Avenue canyon:** Aspect ratio <0.5 **Deep Canyon:** Aspect ratio ≈ 2

Urban heat island: This is the name given to the urban area significantly warmer than its surrounding rural environment, because of human constructions and activities. This effect is associated with surface changes linked to urbanization, which alter runoff and decrease subsoil moisture, and the effects of building materials (such as asphalt and concrete) on heat retention. Also playing a significant role are the modification of the surface albedo -caused by the retention of outgoing radiation in buildings-, as well as changes in atmospheric composition due to emissions of gases and particles. Finally, there is an added factor, which is anthropogenic heat – from air conditioning systems, engines, etc. – which, according to some studies, can even be of the same order of magnitude as the heat received by radiation.

ENDNOTES

1 After the COVID-19 crisis not only the benefits on health security of locating activities in the outdoor environment have been highly appreciated but the positive effect both for physical health and mental of citizens. Such the potential for revaluation and structuring of urban areas linked to citizen activities is a trend.

2 This concept, widely developed by S. Roaf (Roaf et al., 2010), indicates the need for today's cities to provide protection and refuge spaces against extreme weather events —such as heat waves. Theses phenomes have a greater probability of occurring in the coming years because of Climate Change.

3 The spacing ratio is measured as the ratio of the distance between adjacent buildings to the front length of the building.

Chapter 14
The Waste of Today's Architecture Will Become the Materials for the Architecture of the Future

Anya Montserrat Pulido Cavada
https://orcid.org/0000-0002-1510-5580
Universidad CEU San Pablo, Spain

ABSTRACT

Today, 55% of the world's population lives in large cities or dense urban areas, large concrete jungles whose constructions are responsible for between five and ten percent of the world's carbon dioxide. It is estimated that by 2050 this proportion will grow to 68%. Is the society of this decade prepared to deal with this congestion? And society 30 years from now? Inequality, waste generation, consumption and resource depletion in front of the headline that has been sold in recent years: 'Smart cities, zero emissions and technologies that surpass science fiction'. 'The residues of today's architecture will be the materials of the architecture of the future' This headline makes us reflect on whether we are really thinking, not only about the reuse of materials and the design of mobile structures, but also about the great cost of returning to the environment that have a large part of the materials used in the architecture of the XXI century.

INTRODUCTION

Today, the mean global temperature has increased at least 1.0ºC compared to pre-industrial times and it is estimated it will reach 1.5oC between 2030 and 2050 if it continues to increase at the current rate. This warming could lead to devastating impacts, such as extreme droughts, sea level rise, marine heat-waves and the loss of biodiversity, among other (New et al., 2022; O'Neill et al., 2022). With increased risks to the health, safety, livelihood and economic growth of people and countries globally. According to the Intergovernmental Panel on Climate Change (ipcc) it is not inconsistent to assume that"warming

DOI: 10.4018/978-1-6684-6924-8.ch014

caused by anthropogenic emissions from the pre-industrial period to the present will last for centuries to millennia and will continue to cause further long-term changes in the climate system..." (Masson-Delmotte et al., 2018).

Reconciling the effects of climate change with the projected growth in human population and subsequent urban areas poses a big challenge. It is a fact that cities will continue to grow at an accelerated rate, and therefore, probably in an uncontrolled and unequal manner. According to a report published by the Department of Economic and Social Affairs of the United Nations, more than 65% of the world's population will live in urban areas by 2050 (Dodman et al., 2022), with a figure that exceeds 6.6 billion inhabitants. However, it will be the low- and middle-income countries that will develop the fastest, where more than 90% of the population will settle in less developed regions such as India, Nigeria, Bangladesh or the Democratic Republic of Congo (Cissé et al., 2022).

The growth of cities brings with it an increased risk from natural disasters and extreme weather events. About 20% of the world's population resides in large coastal cities, affected by storm surges and rising sea levels. Furthermore, 90% of urban expansion in developing countries occurs in risk areas and through unplanned and uncontrolled settlements (Baraya, 2022; Cissé et al., 2022; Dodman et al., 2022; Mirzabaev et al., 2022; Serrano Yuste, 2015; Souza, 2021; Stouhi, 2021).

Is this decade's society prepared to deal with this congestion? And the society of 30 years from now? Inequality, waste generation, consumption and depletion of resources confronts the selling headlines of recent years: 'Smart cities, zero emissions and technologies that go beyond science fiction'.

Indisputably, risk exposure faced by each population, each infrastructure, each socioeconomic system and each cultural asset varies widely between regions and within them, for not all settlements have the same requirements. Accordingly, impacts faced by each settlement due to climate change must be taken into account (O'Neill et al., 2022). Impacts on food and water systems, on infectious diseases, on the increasing mobility of the population from rural to more developed urban areas, and consequently, on changes in distribution and urban planning. Many people today live in unsafe homes within polluted environments. People who suffer from chronic illnesses or struggle against a context of poverty, insecurity and scarcity of jobs and educational opportunities (Masson-Delmotte et al., 2018; New et al., 2022; O'Neill et al., 2022). As many have asserted, the pandemic that began in early 2020 has been a 'wake-up call' towards future urban models. Climate change has not only violently altered the planet's biodiversity, it has exacerbated the lack of drinking water, the reproduction rate of increasingly destructive pests, the intensity and frequency of floods and droughts (Dodman et al., 2022). Food scarcity has led to a whole wave of diseases that threaten our health and well-being and that are increasingly affecting informal and high-density settlements where social distancing is minimal and hygiene is a commodity for the very few (New et al., 2022).

According to the European Respiratory Society (ERS), "a 6% increase in mortality in Europe due to respiratory infections is predicted for every degree that the temperature rises". Famine, desertification, floods, scarcity of resources, viruses... things at the time where theoretical exercises have now become a reality (Cissé et al., 2022).

Anticipating the transformation of ecosystems and population growth, it is beyond doubt that the resources we have are coming to an end. "The current overexploitation of natural resources is generating a huge deficit, since every year 20% more than can be regenerated is consumed and that percentage does not stop growing" warns the World Wide Fund for Nature (WWF) (Dodman et al., 2022).

One of the stated purposes of the Intergovernmental Panel on Climate Change is to "making cities and settlements inclusive, safe, resilient and sustainable" (O'Neill et al., 2022); but how can this goal be achieved? As it is well known, one of the purposes of the European Union is, with a view to 2050, to reduce greenhouse gas emissions by 80% compared to 1990 levels. However, estimates indicate that 33% of the built-up park it is yet to be built for 2050. This helps in appreciaing how our built environment is beginning to outpace our natural environment].

A fun fact: drylands cover about 45-47% of the entire Earth's surface and are home to about three billion people. In recent decades, 6% of megacities have settled in arid areas and 2% in hyper-arid desert areas. Deserts and semi-arid areas have already been affected by climate change, with vast areas affected by desertification and surface warming (Mirzabaev et al., 2022). Global drylands, with a surface warming of between 1.2ºC and 1.3ºC, have surpassed warming on humid lands, expanding the area of drylands by 4% between 1948 and 2004. In addition to surface warming, natural dryland's surface produced between 75% and 90% of global atmospheric dust in the early 2000s along with other human and agricultural land. Many of its inhabitants are at risk of experiencing cardiovascular and respiratory disease (Masson-Delmotte et al., 2018).

Another fun fact: sand runs out. Among many of the present and future environmental emergencies, the depletion of sand is one nobody talks about. In 2010, the world surface covered by cement was comparable to one million square kilometres, that is, twice the surface occupied by Spain (Hodgson et al., 2022; LePan, 2021; Niranjan, 2021). Considering the aforementioned data on the inevitable urban growth and that the materials most used in construction are cement, concrete and mortar (which require sand for their composition), we can now also include the illegal trade in sand to the list of problems.

"The central problem is that we don't understand the material well enough "comments Louise Gallagher, from the Global Sand Observatory in Geneva; "we still know very little about the consequences of sand mining. Sometimes we don't even know where it comes from, how much comes from the rivers. We have no idea." (Deutsche, 2021)

Sand mining is not limited to the exploitation of deserts and quarries. In recent years, due to progressive exhaustion of mined sand, seas and rivers have begun to be exploited, ferociously affecting the biodiversity in both environments. Sand mining in India has pushed the Gangetic gharial crocodile to the brink of extinction, according to an article published in the journal Nature in 2019 (Niranjan, 2021).

Giving a simple example of the demand for this material, about 200 tons of sand are needed for an average-sized house and 30,000 tons for 1km of highway. In the last 20 years, the global demand for cement has increased by 60% and by 437% in China (Hodgson et al., 2022).

Human beings do not stop sponsoring the loss of biological productivity, ecological integrity and the value that the natural environment has to themselves.

The role of building in today's climate crisis is undeniably, and alarmingly, high. The construction sector accounts for 30% of the national energy consumption (Delmastro et al., 2022); Between the production, execution and operation of buildings, the sector is one of the largest emitters of greenhouse gases.

A clear example of this is cement. This material accounts for almost one tenth of industrial water use, and 75% of this tenth, occurs in regions that suffer frequent droughts. However, it is not only the carbon footprint that this material has, but the direct and indirect consequences its use generates such as social inequality, criminal activity, and the 'heat island' effect the reasons that might begin to tip the balance from the benefits that favored its use. According to Marta Olazabal and María Ruíz de Gopegui, researchers at the Basque Center for Climate Change (BC3) in the magazine Landscape and Urban Planning, "as they are currently propose, climate change adaptation plans of the largest cities worldwide are not going to achieve effective results in the medium and long term, as they are currently proposed" (Sanz et al., 2019).

Many are those who have begun to propose theories, models and assays for an architecture that can ensure a level of safety and good management in the face of extreme weather events. But from which resources does this architecture benefits from? Are we going to be able to benefit from them in the next 10 years? What about in 50?

Analysis

'Residues from current architecture will be the materials of the architecture of the future'. East

This headline makes us reflect on whether we are really thinking beyond traditional end-of-life options such as reusing materials and the design of mobile structures. Are we also thinking about the enormous cost of returning to the environment a large part of the materials used by the 21st century architecture (Souza, 2021). In recent years, what has reverberated in our ears the most is 'sustainable construction', referring to that architecture that we must achieve but that we have not yet consolidated. An architecture that leaves aside toxic substances in the manufacturing of construction materials, that limits the impact on the natural environment and that reduces energy consumption (New et al., 2022).

Net-Zero Buildings, Resiliency, Green Star Certification, LEED Certification, EDGE Certification, alternative building materials, among many others. A long list of goals to be achieved while the countdown continues to advances, getting us closer to a point of no return.

Many have chosen to go back in time and recover the identity of men and their environment. In retrospect, vernacular architecture has left great clues for solutions adopted in diverse geographical contexts and that respond to the physical and cultural environment characteristics of these contexts. It reflects the identity of a region and a culture that collects and transforms the resources offered by the environment (Baraya, 2022; Cao, 2020; Cissé et al., 2022; Dejtiar, 2021; Dodman et al., 2022; Goy, 2022; Guerrero Baca, 2007; Martino, 2021; Masson-Delmotte et al., 2018; Mirzabaev et al., 2022; New et al., 2022; O'Neill et al., 2022; Serrano Yuste, 2015; Souza, 2019; Souza, 2021; Stouhi, 2021).

Is the desire then to fly towards mitigation, adaptation and sustainable development in synergy with vernacular architecture and indigenous knowledge?

Maricarmen Tapia, architect and researcher associated with the USC, explains that "it is important how the pandemic takes us back to the 19th century, when the idea of health was born in urban planning... cities must be healthy, not only in terms of hygiene but also mentally and with communities in mind" (Hermida, 2020).

Throughout history, methods for earth construction has adapted to varying planning, application and construction techniques, building architectonic masterpieces (Guerrero Baca, 2007). The Great Chinese Wall (500 B.C) commissioned during the Ming dynasty is made from a wood framework, earth, adobe and stone. The Shibam city has earth buildings reaching 65m in height, while over 300 earth mosques still stand along the river Niger, inspired by the Great Mosque of Djenne (Guerrero Baca, 2007; Molina Contreras, 2020; Tutor Vicente, 2015).

Since time immemorial, man has built with the materials that the environment supplied him with and which made up the landscape, thus modeling constructions in accordance with the climate and environment of each region. An architecture that today we would associate with the concept

'Materials at Zero Kilometers' (Souza, 2021).

However, since the time of industrialization, the rejection of traditional construction materials and techniques has been transmitted and favoured. Such is the case of earth. This material has been used in many parts of the world over the years both for its accessibility and cost; for its versatility and for the history of tradition it possesses (Tutor Vicente, 2015). Today there is a struggle to introduce this material to the great cities dominated by concrete and steel; the reflection of modernity and industrial and architectural progress of the last decades.

Architectures such as the City of Sana'a in Yemen dating from the 11th century, the ruins of the city of Paquimé in Mexico from 700 AD or the citadel of Arg-é Bam in southwestern Iran from the period 224 to 637 AD, considered a one of the largest constructions in the world on land, reflect the great durability of this material and its great resistance (Maldonado Ramos et al., 2003; Olmedo Rodríguez, ; Paniagua Padilla, 2015; Yuste, 2018). What naked truth is behind this material? Many settlements throughout the globe have colonize territories, allowing the introduction of a series of anthropic elements that have been integrated into the landscape and have gradually shaped popular rural architecture. Due to the presence of very diverse lithologies, the use of different materials has been made possible; reasons of utility, time, economy, etc., have allowed the knowledge of the environment to use the nearby materials avoiding seasonal and transport costs (De Schiller & Martin Evans, 2020; Maldonado Ramos et al., 2003; Yuste, 2018). This was the case of the tapial, an architecture composed of clay, silt, sand and gravel; one of the many construction techniques with earth that was transferred by romanization to many countries in Europe.

There has been a growing interest in recent years for the tapia construction technique in terms of projects and research form universities and institutions, despite not having resurfaced since the 10th century. Great progress has been made in modernizing traditional earth construction techniques to adapt them to current design and construction needs (Bestraten et al., 2011). However, there is still a long way ahead of industrializing and mechanizing its use. Is it lawful to forget a material that has not evolved apace with society? Is the perception of scarcity and poverty attached to this material true, or has it been imposed by man and his eagerness to envision an architecture that is increasingly 'futuristic'? Here then we have the great paradox.

Another notorious concept in recent years is the term 'Bioconstruction', alluding to a form of construction that respects the natural environment and the live it harbors (Molina Contreras, 2020). Now, what potential does this type of construction has to face the imminent climate crisis?

"Our home, how we build it, with what materials and how we use it, can contribute to saving CO2 emissions in many ways. The design of the house, taking into account the specific characteristics of the place, the choice of materials, water management systems, waste, the application of renewable energy... are basic aspects. For example, a conventional house in which 3 people live can emit about 21 tons of CO2/year. The same house, built under the bioconstruction criteria, will only emit 7 tons of CO2/year" according to Toni Marín, editor of EcoHabitar and member of the Spanish Association of Bioconstruction (Valdés Kuri & Ricalde de Jager, 2006).

The influence of the natural environment in the earth walls of popular architecture is indisputable. But is it possible to promote its use beyond the countryside or developing countries, but in the large cities of the future? Well, sometimes moving forward means going back to our origins, without having to lose the benefits of knowledge gained with practice over the centuries.

Jean Dethier, architect, historian and author of the volume 'earth architectures', exposes "it is then paradoxical that today a holistic relationship between man, his built environment and nature is claimed, as well as the eco-responsible use of resources" denouncing how governments and politics have made this type of construction difficult in recent years (Margalejo, 2022).

Since 2015, the maximum temperatures in record have been exceeded each year around the globe (Masson-Delmotte et al., 2018). Consequently, there has been an increase in temperature within dense urban areas have occurred. In these urban areas, where the surface of vegetation is minimal, and materials with great thermal inertia give off the stored heat of the day, cause temperature differences of eight degrees with respect to other parts of the city. Materials, the urban fabric and the building model are key for the heat island effect, another of the climatic risks that in recent years has been punishing a large number of urban centers (Baraya, 2022; Cao, 2020; Cissé et al., 2022; Dejtiar, 2021; Dodman et al., 2022; Guerrero Baca, 2007; Martino, 2021; Masson-Delmotte et al., 2018; Mirzabaev et al., 2022; Molina Contreras, 2020; New et al., 2022; O'Neill et al., 2022; Serrano Yuste, 2015; Souza, 2021; Stouhi, 2021; Tutor Vicente, 2015).

"In Mexico City, at six in the morning on some days in March, we have found differences of 10ºC between the city center and the rural area... It is important to point out that this phenomenon is a product of the way in which the city has grown and not something typical of meteorological issues"explains Dr. Elda Luyando, a researcher in the Climate Change and Solar Radiation group at the UNAM Center for Atmospheric Sciences (Luyando López, 2020).

The continuous and increasing use of household appliances and devices that consume energy and release heat such as printers, computers, light bulbs, etc. They turn the problem into a vicious circle where the solution to reach indoor comfort temperature is to install cooling systems that consume even more energy and radiate even more heat (Dodman et al., 2022).

High temperatures are one of the main causes of mortality in cities. Transportation, asphalt, glass, lighting and air conditioning systems go hand in hand with respiratory illnesses, dryness and heat stroke. People spend more than 90% of their time indoors, and as climate change shakes us, the environmental conditions in which today's buildings were designed to function are fast changing (Cissé et al., 2022; Dodman et al., 2022; O'Neill et al., 2022).

They paint the streets of Los Angeles to lower the ambient temperature. It is estimated that the measure manages to reduce between 10oC and 12oC. (Blancaret, 2022)

How to cool a megacity of 16 million inhabitants. The Pakistani city of Karachi suffered a heat wave five years ago with temperatures above 45 degrees... A businessman in this town has proposed to reduce high temperatures through the construction of urban forests. (Autocosmos News, 2021)

Paris uses the Seine River to cool its most emblematic places. (Ferrer, 2022)

Toronto is studying the cooling system from the deep water of Lake Ontario to cool hospitals, data centers, educational campuses, government buildings, commercial and residential buildings. (Euronews, 2020)

These are some of the headlines that keep appearing in newspapers and newscasts in recent years. It is clear that heat waves are becoming more frequent and deadlier, and are going to increase. Mark Watts, executive director of 'C40 Cities', warns that "Cities that are used to heat have to prepare for even longer periods of sweltering heat, and colder cities have to prepare for levels of extreme heat that they are not used to." (2022)

But it is precisely these enclaves where there is the greatest potential for mitigation. (Pierre-Louis, 2018) Cities emit between 60% and 80% of greenhouse gases and consume practically the same percentages of energy, which makes them a strategic point where to propose and carry out strategies that comply with future climate commitments. (Cissé et al., 2022; Dodman et al., 2022; O'Neill et al., 2022)

One of these strategies, as previously mentioned, is to include earth as a construction material in dense urban areas and not limit its use to rural dwellings belonging to so-called third world countries; introduce this new material in a highly technical environment and economy that is increasingly disconnected from its cultural identity.

There are many benefits to this element as a construction material, but they are poorly known and little disclosed.

1. According to records from five independent organizations, the average global temperature during the first months of 2018 rose by 0.98 degrees compared to the average temperature that existed in the second half of the 19th century. This is reflected in the use of climate control systems to manage this rise in temperatures. According to a report by the International Energy Agency, "The number of air conditioners in the world will skyrocket from 1.6 billion units today to 5.6 billion by mid-century. By 2050, air conditioning systems will use the same amount of electricity that China currently needs for all its activities." (Pierre-Louis, 2018) Earth balances the indoor climate. The use of earth in construction and structural elements can favor the absorption of pollutants and humidity faster and in a greater proportion than any other construction material - between 40% and 80% more. - Thus protecting organic materials such as wood and being able to reduce, and even eliminate, the use of artificial air conditioning systems thanks to its excellent thermal behavior, if a good architectural design is considered. (Baraya, 2022; Cao, 2020; Dejtiar, 2021; Martino, 2021; Serrano Yuste, 2015; Souza, 2021; Stouhi, 2021)
2. The construction industry registers one of the highest consumption of energy and raw materials, generating a high percentage of greenhouse gas (GHG) emissions. The production of cement generates 5% of global GHG emissions, followed by other materials such as steel, brick and those derived from plastic. (Delmastro et al., 2022) This is without accounting on the great consumption that the extraction of minerals and ores required to obtain them. Research by the European Union to develop new materials that are less energy demanding and thus with reduced the footprint is currently being carried out. Compared to the energy required for a block of concrete (e.g., 600-800 KWh/m3) or natural sand (e.g.., 45 KWh/m3) earth is considered a low energy input material (e.g., 5-10 KWh/m3) (Baraya, 2022; Cao, 2020; Cissé et al., 2022; Dejtiar, 2021; Dodman et al., 2022; Goy, 2022; Guerrero Baca, 2007; Martino, 2021; Masson-Delmotte et al., 2018; Mirzabaev et al., 2022; Molina Contreras, 2020; New et al., 2022; O'Neill et al., 2022; Serrano Yuste, 2015; Souza, 2019; Souza, 2021; Stouhi, 2021).
3. According to Enhassi, Bernd and Ehsan (2014), the most significant impacts within construction comes from dust, noise and air pollution, and operations that require the removal of vegetation, generating a negative impact on the health of workers which can developed in cardiovascular and respiratory problems, loss of sleep, cancer, and hearing impairment among others (Baraya, 2022; Cao, 2020; Cissé et al., 2022; Dejtiar, 2021; Delmastro et al., 2022; Deutsche, 2021; Dodman et al., 2022; Enhasin et al., 2014; Goy, 2022; Hodgson et al., 2022; LePan, 2021; Martino, 2021; Mirzabaev et al., 2022; Niranjan, 2021; Pierre-Louis, 2018; Seguí, n.d.; Serrano Yuste, 2015; Souza, 2019; Souza, 2021; Stouhi, 2021).
4. One of the advantages of building with earth is its low production cost, because a good design can avoid the use of insulation, coatings and waterproofing, as well as low extraction and transportation

costs, because most of the soils suitable for This type of construction are often at the site, with the soil excavated for the foundations can be used in the construction (Molina Contreras, 2020).

5. As the overexploitation of resources increases, so does the complexity and variety of materials used, and with it the production of waste. The construction and demolition industry is the sector that generates the most waste (Baraya, 2022; Cao, 2020; Dejtiar, 2021; Delmastro et al., 2022; Deutsche, 2021; Dodman et al., 2022; Enhasin et al., 2014; Goy, 2022; Hodgson et al., 2022; LePan, 2021; Martino, 2021; Mirzabaev et al., 2022; Niranjan, 2021; Pierre-Louis, 2018; Seguí, n.d.; Serrano Yuste, 2015; Souza, 2019; Souza, 2021; Stouhi, 2021). This limits the reuse and recycling of waste derived from constructions works, which ends in landfills. We find ourselves in an infinite chain to which a link is added every day, every hour and every minute. Contrastingly, earth is characterized by having a low return cost to the environment, one of the main objectives to be achieved by the future architecture. Earth, like other natural materials such as wood, has a recyclable nature. If it has not been mixed with cement, lime or other chemical additives, during construction the material can be fully integrated into nature after dissolving in water. This feature not only reduces waste, but also to saves energy and promotes a circular economy in building with the full life cycle of the material (De Schiller & Martin Evans, 2020; Javier Castilla Pascual & Núñez Martí, 2005; Yuste, 2018).

Currently, one of the biggest challenges of sustainable construction is achieving a 100% degradable material with practically zero cost for its return to the environment. At present, there are numerous research groups that have proposed and experimented with mixtures and stabilizers in order to obtain a 100% biodegradable earth (Olmedo Rodríguez, n.d.). Although there are many countries that lack regulations for Building with earth (although in many it is beginning to be drafted, as in Spain), in many, it is required for mixtures of earth used to build walls, to contain a minimum of 15% cement, lime or plaster as a stabilizer. (De Schiller & Martin Evans, 2020; Javier Castilla Pascual & Núñez Martí, 2005; Yuste, 2018) But what would be the benefit of earth with this type of stabilizers?

Stabilizing earth for construction entails the addition of foreign components to the earth and its natural condition in order to enrich its mechanical properties and its stability in the presence of water. Depending on how these elements affect the earth, three types are distinguished: (1) consolidation stabilizers, (2) friction stabilizers and (3) waterproofing stabilizers (De Schiller & Martin Evans, 2020; Javier Castilla Pascual & Núñez Martí, 2005; Molina Contreras, 2020; Tutor Vicente, 2015).

Consolidation stabilizers help clays in the binding action they exert on inert Earth particles. This provides flexibility to the mix, increasing compression resistance and reducing cracking by the expansion and contraction of the earthen wall. However, all these parameters will depend on the quality of the Earth and its additives, as well as on the amount of each component included in the mixture.

The best stabilizer for consolidation, whose effectiveness has been validated over the centuries is (hydraulic) lime; chemically known as calcium hydroxide. Its addition increases the compressive and shear resistance of the wall, obtaining increases in simple compression resistance of up to 15kg/cm2. Additionally, this additive is capable of reducing the levels of water absorption and, therefore, its possible shrinkage upon drying without modifying the porosity of the Earth. With this additive, the best responses were achieved with a mixture of 4% and 8% lime. Although lime has many constructive, economic and ecological qualities, it is worth mentioning that this material can produce a lot of heat, tending to dry the soil quickly dry the earth with the risk of expansion (Molina Contreras, 2020; Tutor Vicente, 2015).

Cement is another widely used stabilizers and the main competitor of lime. It helps to reduce the liquid limit and to increase the plastic index the mixture workability. However, its use prevents the return of the earth mix to the environment at the end of the building's useful life, making this material difficult to recycle and with the potential to become toxic in low proportions (Guerrero Baca, 2007).

Clearly, earth construction requires first have a great understanding of the weather and the location where it is going to be carried out. Second, a minimum understanding of the methods for earth architecture, given that a large part of the countries of the world lacks regulations for buildings that use this technique (Guerrero Baca, 2007); largely because its construction may not be entirely feasible. However, where natural earth do not meet the ideal conditions for this type of construction, empirical means have traditionally been developed to determine the most appropriate proportions, using natural and biodegradable stabilizers in parallel. These types of aggregates are gaining prominence and, although they are not exploited or regulated, they exist and are being used (Molina Contreras, 2020).

Many stabilizers have been used in many countries and cultures that have worked and shaped earth structures throughout centuries. However, how these were used is one of the great unknowns, for it is difficult to propose regulatory guidelines in places where the tradition that gave rise to this practice has been forgotten or never existed (Baraya, 2022; Cao, 2020; Cissé et al., 2022; Dejtiar, 2021; Dodman et al., 2022; Guerrero Baca, 2007; Martino, 2021; Masson-Delmotte et al., 2018; Mirzabaev et al., 2022; Molina Contreras, 2020; New et al., 2022; O'Neill et al., 2022; Serrano Yuste, 2015; Souza, 2021; Stouhi, 2021; Tutor Vicente, 2015).

There are various organic stabilizers that can fulfill binding functions being stabilizers by consolidation. Some examples, include polymers extracted from plants such as cacti or succulents, as well as animal proteins extracted from milk, blood or eggs. These components have been used throughout history in various regions and by various cultures, but due to the lack of documentation and intergenerational knowledge transfer, their practice has been abandoned. In countries like Mexico or Peru other types of stabilizers are still used (Cao, 2020; Dejtiar, 2021; Martino, 2021). A tradition on the use of the prickly pear cactus' pulp – baba de nopal – as an adhesive to work construction earth, to plaster walls and lime paints surviving since pre-colonial times.

Among the friction stabilizers, fibers stand out. Fibers create a net-like structure to which earth particles adhere, controlling their expansion, displacement and retraction during setting. In the same way, a system of microcracks is created that modifies the cracking patterns derived from changes in humidity and ambient temperature, preventing the structure from collapsing (Cao, 2020; Martino, 2021). These fibers can be of vegetable origin, such as straw from different grasses, coconut husks, corn stalks, conifers' needles, pita or sisal fibers, or wood shavings. Some cultures have used materials of animal origin, such as sheep or goat wool, horsehair, llama hair and even human hair.

These types of fibrous stabilizers have extensive qualities for durability, resistance and plasticity; functioning as joints that confer flexibility to the structures in the event of possiblewall failure due to overloads or seismic movements.

Finally, stabilizers for waterproofing are other set of elements used to regulate the contact of the clay with water. Historically, the components that have shown the best results when it comes to acting as water 'repellents' are fats of both animal (e.g., beef tallow or milk) and vegetable origin (e.g., sunflower, linseed and olive oil) and bituminous materials such as asphalt.

Considering both in isolation and together, all these stabilizers have shown great results throughout their construction tradition (2020).

RESULTS

In the last three decades, different developing trends in architecture have developed. Architecture studios such as Studio Anna Heringer, Hive Earth Studio or Edra Arquitectura, and research groups such as Centro Tierra, Uni-Terra or International Center for Earth Construction are dedicated to the investigation, implementation and dissemination of knowledge related to earthen architecture and its use together with other local materials.

Currently, construction with earth is done alongside research by research both by a large part of developing countries and by more developed countries such as the United States, Australia, France and Germany. This research focuses mainly on experimental projects, improvements in composition, additives and new compositional and aesthetic concepts. Among the projects carried out by research institutions, we can highlight the Lyon experimental city of L'Isle d'Abeau, "Le domaine de la Terre", mostly carried out using the mud wall technique under the supervision of the CRATerre laboratory of the University of Grenoble; or the housing Project promoted German government, where the University of Kassel has collaborated. In Spain, the experimental project of 10 earthen houses in Amayuelas (Palencia) is not yet approved due to the lack of regulations in Europe for construction with earth. All these projects reflect a great interest in achieving an ecological architecture that generates the least possible environmental impact, provides comfort from the point of view of climate and air quality, and is quick to build with a certain level of interest in social housing and architectures for to "developing" countries where there is a need for cheap, fast and easy-to-build housing (Goy, 2022; Seguí, n.d.; Souza, 2019).

One of the most recent trends both in Europe and in other middle and low income countries is the incorporation of wooden or bamboo rods to adobe constructions as reinforcements. This internal structure incorporated into earthen walls can increase their resistance to both compression and shear, and alleviate concerns about their stability in the face of earthquakes. This is a main motivator in many countries for reinforcing adobe walls to increase their traction resistance. Several universities in countries such as Israel, Peru, France and Mexico have already began experimenting with certain variants of this type of construction with earth on urban land (Dodman et al., 2022).

In other countries characterized by hydromagmatic zones, research is beginning on the advantages and disadvantages of volcanic ash and its impact on the production of certain construction materials, such as adobe. Currently, traditional cement is being replaced by pulverized volcanic rocks, which can reduce the energy needed to make concrete by up to 16% (Baraya, 2022; Serrano Yuste, 2015). Adding volcanic deposits can:

1. Reduce the amount of sand, partly alleviating its great demand; sand, together with gravel, represents the largest volume of material extracted worldwide (Mirzabaev et al., 2022).
2. Reduce cement as a stabilizer, which represents 5% of global CO2 emissions.

In countries such as Germany, Australia, Brazil, Canada, Colombia, Spain, the United States, France and Portugal, wall construction has gained rapid momentum, once again recovering this material in order to use it in modern structures with a language that responds to the needs of today's citizens. But despite its growing popularity, conquering this material still requires breaking down numerous cultural, psychological, aesthetic, technological and technical, structural, economic and legislative walls (Enhasin et al., 2014).

After the pandemic that began in 2020 due to COVID-19, modular architecture and dry construction began to gain ground due to its speed in terms of execution, the lower tax burden and for being a commitment to sustainable architecture. The popularity of pre-engineered and pre-fabricated buildings is growing and Nordic countries such as Sweden already build around 90% of their homes in pre-fabricated wood. They follow the example of countries like Japan that have built with wooden pre-assemblies for over a century. Now, construction with earth has been incorporated, taking a step forward in the manufacturing processes. Contemporary construction with earth, traditional building techniques have been annexed to modern dry construction techniques to produce prefabricated elements that minimize construction time (Gatti, 2012):

- **WEM Radiant Panel.** These are heating elements for interior wall cladding made by the German company Wem in 2008. This prefabricated panel is made from a mixture of earth, straw and natural additives together with a 16 x 2mm plastic or metal pipe which acts as the centerpiece of the drywall system.
- **Cannapanel.** This is a prefabricated panel produced by The Cannabric company since 2010. The panel is made of stabilized earth, straw and hemp fiber and is produced by mechanical pressing on an assembly line. These panels are capable of improving the thermal-acoustic-bioclimatic comfort of indoor environments and reduce the environmental impact of their manufacture. Use of the panels allows savings on air conditioning and design costs. In some instances, the use coatings or waterproofing might not be necessary, depending on the location.
- **Lehmo Precast Wall Blocks.** The prefabrication of elements in rammed earth represents a great advance in this technique, especially considering that the tradition of putting this type of structure into work is very elaborate and has practically fallen into oblivion. Prefabrication of these elements allows for the construction of higher quality factories and decreased construction times, although costs may increase due to transportation and elevation requirements. This Australian company makes mud walls of only 6 cm to cover stoves and chimneys, so the mud wall ceases its structural function and becomes a surrounding element.
- **ERDEN Radiant Prefabricated Wall.** The introduction of installations inside the tapial further justifies the concept of tapial prefabrication. The ERDEN company, located in Austria, produces prefabricated radiant walls, turning the wall into a design element. In the Vigilus Mountain Resort project in Lana (Italy) carried out in 2003, the rammed earth takes on the function of dividing wall, heat emitting element, thermal accumulator and regulator of environmental humidity thanks to its great thermal behavior.
- **The Calls Design Competition.** The Project carried out in the United Kingdom by the Italian architect Davide Marchetti foresees the use of mud panels, confining them under a metal structure that modulates different panels and provides anchorage as in a classic ventilated facade. The panel isolates and protects the building from solar radiation while allowing air and light to penetrate inside the building, enabling to lighten the weight of the ground panel.
- **Wall Paving ERDEN.** This Austrian company produces different types of compacted earth paving for interiors and exteriors using the rammed earth technique, offering different types of finishes and designs. The earth is arranged on the surface to be carried out and once leveled it is compacted with a vibratory plate. It is finished by a layer of wax, necessary for cleaning.

In addition, digital media have created a new archetype that is driving earthen architecture even further. Although it is rare to think that construction is the second most lagging industry in the digital age after agriculture, this sector has one of the worst records in adapting new technologies, which implies losses of up to 60% in the largest part of the projects. Rodrigo Broering, president of the civil association BIM Forum Brazil, remarked that "Technology is the easiest part, because it supports the process and not the other way around, you have to change your mentality, because we are talking about transformation and this implies an evolution in the way of doing things" (C40 Cities, 2022; Delmastro et al., 2022; Deutsche, 2021; Enhasin et al., 2014; Gatti, 2012; Goy, 2022; Hermida, 2020; Hodgson et al., 2022; LePan, 2021; Luyando López, 2020; Margalejo, 2022; Martino, 2021; Niranjan, 2021; Pierre-Louis, 2018; Pierre-Louis, 2018; Sanz et al., 2019; Seguí, n.d.; Souza, 2019; Valdés Kuri & Ricalde de Jager, 2006). The digital era is giving rise to new methods for the development of architecture with earth, including construction processes such as:

- **Stone Spray.** A method that employs a jet spray system that deposits the soil mix and liquid binder to solidify the soil granules.
- **D_Shape.** An innovative technique based on the construction of three-dimensional printing that uses a stereolithography system. This construction technique allows to built conglomerate structures of any shape and size automatically and quickly and without the use of dies or moulds, which would be more difficult to carry out with traditional construction techniques if not at a high price and in prohibitive time.
- **Contour Crafting.** This manufacturing technology developed by Professor Behrokh Khoshnevis of the Institute of Information Sciences at the University of Southern California, Tbuilds in layers through 3D printing. The system uses computer control to create whole structures or smaller components with smooth planar and free-form surfaces that can be made using different materials, including earth.

These technologies bring earth closer to the 21st century advances in construction materials and promote research and development into its use, helping to achieve a construction detached from the perceptions of 'humble' or 'architecture of poverty'.

More and more technicians and individuals from industrialized countries are becoming aware of earth as a construction material of its bioclimatic benefits, its plastic qualities and its contemporary nature. Contributing to the desire to achieve an increasingly sustainable architecture, the continuous search for new construction materials is providing new solutions and new lessons to learn reviving a construction technique that many considered already forgotten, even lost. The architect Marcelo Gianotti, specialist in Habitat, former co-director of the Fadu-UNL Social Housing Institute, teacher and researcher at the Faculty of Architecture and Urbanism, argued that "construction with earth is an ancient technique usually associated with poorer sectors for the solution of their habitat, but in recent times, and thanks to an increase in the awareness of environmental issues, it has evolved into the idea of a 'constructive culture'. A more integrative insight that transcends technique to relate with a 'cultural process', one that is accepted by other social classes that identify themselves with new days of living more sustainably".

CONCLUSION

The renaissance of this material has not happened on a single geographical area, but throughout the world. Zero emissions building is possible anywhere in the world and the dissemination and materialization of this fact is clearly expanding among developed countries. This represents an incentive for developing countries that look up in search of a constructive reinvention and identity.

As previously mentioned, the impacts of climate change will not cease, rather they will increase over the years; loss of livelihoods, food insecurity, malnutrition, permanent impacts on health and labor productivity together with the loss of life and land are irreversible.

Earth is a material whose comeback does not need to be a return to the world of the lost life of the senses. The path of construction with earth from today to the future requires research in various fields. Most prominently the industrialization and mechanization for process optimization; additives to stabilize, waterproof and protect from forces to which earth structure could be subjected; the introduction of lightening agents that do not compromise the resistance of the material's resistance, and the possibilities of incorporating waste from different industries such as rubble or ashes. All this research should be backed by regulations that allows incorporating this material in the construction industry.

In short, it seeks to give way to creativity on how the use of Earth could be promoted in large cities, transferring what once was the construction material of a large part of Europe's landscape. A material that, despite having shaped the first houses and cities of man, has fallen into ambiguity.

Could this material become the 'builder of the future'?

REFERENCES

Baraya, S. (2022). *Adobe: el material reciclable más sostenible.* Archdaily. Available at: https://www.archdaily.cl/cl/944575/adobe-el-material-reciclable-mas-sostenible

Bestraten, S., Hormías, E., & Altermir, A. (2011). Construcción con tierra en el siglo XXI. *Informes de la Construcción, 63*(523), 5–20. doi:10.3989/ic.10.046

C40 Cities. (2022). *C40 and IFRC urge cities to prepare for more dangerous and deadly heatwaves.* Available at: https://www.c40.org/news/global-day-heat-action-cities-prepare-heatwaves/

Cao, L. (2020). *Cómo se construyen los muros de tierra apisonada.* Archdaily. https://www.archdaily.cl/cl/933445/como-se-construyen-los-muros-de-tierra-apisonada

Cissé, G., McLeman, R., Adams, H., Aldunce, P., Bowen, K., Campbell-Lendrum, D., Clayton, S., Ebi, K. L., Hess, J., Huang, C., Liu, Q., McGregor, G., Semenza, J., & Tirado, M. C. (2022). Health, Wellbeing, and the Changing Structure of Communities. In *Climate Change 2022: Impacts, Adaptation and Vulnerability". IPCC.* World Meteorological Organization.

De Schiller, S., & Martin Evans, J. (2020). Construcción con Tierra Nº9. Centro de Investigación Hábitat y Energía, CIHE, SI, FADU, UBA.

Dejtiar, F. (2021). *'No se usan en las grandes ciudades solo por no estar normados': nuestros lectores opinan sobre materiales.* Archdaily. https://www.archdaily.cl/cl/967698/no-se-usan-en-las-grandes-ciudades-solo-por-no-estar-normados-nuestros-lectores-opinan-sobre-materiales-locales

Delmastro, C., De Bienassis, T., Goodson, T., Lane, K., Le Marois, J., Martinez-Gordon, R., & Husek, M. (2022). *Buildings.* International Energy Agency (IEA). https://www.iea.org/reports/buildings

Deutsche, W. (2021). Global Sand Mining is destroying the planet and costing lives. *EcoWatch.* https://www.ecowatch.com/sand-mining-climate-crisis-2651083582.html

Dodman, D., Hayward, B., Pelling, M., Castan Broto, V., Chow, W., Chu, E., Dawson, R., Khirfan, L., McPhearson, T., Prakash, A., Zheng, Y., & Ziervogel, G. (2022). Cities, Settlements and Key Infrastructure. In *Climate Change 2022: Impacts, Adaptation and Vulnerability.* IPCC World Meteorological Organization.

Enhasin, A., Kochendoerfer, B., & Rizq, E. (2014). Evaluación de los impactos medioambientales de los proyectos de construcción. *Revista Ingeniería de Construcción, 29*(3), 234-254. https://www.scielo.cl/scielo.php?script=sci_arttext&pid=S0718-50732014000300002

Gatti, F. (2012). *Arquitectura y construcción en tierra. Estudio comparativo de las técnicas contemporáneas en tierra.* Universidad Politécnica de Catalunya. https://core.ac.uk/download/pdf/41807254.pdf

Goy, M. (2022). Construir con tierra: todo lo que hay que saber de un material que se redescubre. *El Litoral.* https://www.ellitoral.com/area-metropolitana/construccion-tierra-barro-tecnologia-btc-ingeniero-tecnologica-utn_0_lkGlCoGayF.html

Guerrero Baca, L. F. (2007). Arquitectura de tierra. Hacia la recuperación de una cultura constructiva. *Pontificia Universidad Javeriana Bogotá, 20*(2), 182-201.

Hermida, P. (2020). *En busca de una ciudad más amable tras la COVID.* El Correo Gallego. https://www.elcorreogallego.es/galicia/en-busca-de-una-ciudad-mas-amable-tras-la-covid-YB5245357

Hodgson, D., Hugues, P., & Vass, T. (2022). *Cement.* International Energy Agency (IEA). https://www.iea.org/reports/cement

Javier Castilla Pascual, F., & Núñez Martí, P. (2005). *Estudio para la recuperación de la técnica del tapial en la construcción tradicional de la provincia de Albacete.* Actas del Cuarto Congreso Nacional de Historia de la Construcción.

Jerez García, O., & Sánchez López, L. (2002). La arquitectura geográfica manchega: recurso y compromiso educativo. *Espacio, Tiempo y Forma, Serie VI, Geografía, 15*, 129-145.

LePan, N. (2021). *How much of Earth's surface is covered by each country – in one graphic.* World Economic Forum. https://www.weforum.org/agenda/2021/01/earth-surface-ocean-visualization-science-countries-russia-canada-china/

Luyando López, E. (2020). *El clima como experimento urbano.* Revista de la universidad de México. https://www.revistadelauniversidad.mx/articles/b3bfbc5d-6505-4f33-a7ab-2330a0c2cde6/el-clima-como-experimento-urbano

Maldonado Ramos, L., Fernando Vela, C., & David Rivera, G. (2003). *Nuevas aplicaciones de la tierra como material de construcción.* Memoria de Investigaciones, Universidad Politécnica de Madrid.

Margalejo, I. (2022). *La tierra es el material del futuro en arquitectura: volvemos a los orígenes.* Arquitectura y Diseño. https://www.arquitecturaydiseno.es/arquitectura/tierra-es-material-futuro-arquitectura-volvemos-a-origenes_7518

Martino, G. (2021). *Más allá de la tierra y el bambú: tecnologías locales y grandes ciudades*. Archdaily. https://www.archdaily.cl/cl/967841/mas-alla-de-la-tierra-y-el-bambu-tecnologias-locales-y-grandes-ciudades

Masson-Delmotte, V., Zhai, P., Pörtner, O., Roberts, D., Skea, J., Shukla, P., Pirani, A., Moufouma-Okia, W., Péan, C., Pidcock, R., Connors, S., Matthews, J. B. R., Chen, Y., Zhou, X., Gomis, M. I., Lonnoy, E., Maycock, T., Tignor, M., & Waterfield, T. (2018). *Special Report on the impacts of global warming of 1.5°C above pre-industrial levels and related global greenhouse gas emission pathways, in the context of strengthening the global response to the threat of climate change, sustainable development, and efforts to eradicate poverty.* World Meteorological Organization.

Mirzabaev, A., Stringer, L. C., Benjaminsen, T. A., Gonzalez, P., Harris, R., Jafari, M., Stevens, N., Tirado, C. M., & Zakieldeen, S. (2022). Deserts, Semiarid Areas and Desertification. In *Climate Change 2022: Impacts, Adaptation and Vulnerability*. World Meteorological Organization.

Molina Contreras, D. K. (2020). *La tierra como material de construcción, propiedades y estabilizantes* [Tesis doctoral]. Universidad Santo Tomás.

New, M., Reckien, D., Viner, D., Adler, C., Cheong, S.-M., Conde, C., Constable, A., Coughlan de Perez, E., Lammel, A., Mechler, R., Orlove, B., & Solecki, W. (2022). Decision-Making Options for Managing Risk. In Climate Change 2022: Impacts, Adaptation and Vulnerability. World Meteorological Organization.

Niranjan, A. (2021). *The world is running out of sand*. Deutsche Welle (DW). https://www.dw.com/en/sand-crisis-shortage-supply-mafia/a-56714226

NZS 4297. (1998). *Engineering design of earth buildings*. Building Code Compliance Documents B1 (VM1), B2 (AS1).

O'Neill, B., Van Aalst, M., Zaiton Ibrahim, Z., Berrang Ford, L., Bhadwal, S., Buhaug, H., Diaz, D., Frieler, K., Garschagen, M., Magnan, A., Midgley, G., Mirzabaev, A., Thomas, A., & Warren, R. (2022). Poverty, Livelihoods and Sustainability Development. In *Climate Change 2022: Impacts, Adaptation and Vulnerability*. World Meteorological Organization.

Olmedo Rodríguez, A. (2020). *Evaluación de estrategias arquitectónicas para la consecución del nuevo modelo energético* [Tesis doctoral]. Universidad de Valladolid.

Paniagua Padilla, D. (2015). *Interpretación bioclimática de la arquitectura vernácula*. Monografía.

Pierre-Louis, K. (2018). El calentamiento que general el aire acondicionado. *The New York Times*. https://www.nytimes.com/es/2018/05/18/espanol/aire-acondicionado-calentamiento-global.html

Pierre-Louis, K. (2018). The world wants air-conditioning. That could warm the world. *The New York Times*. https://www.nytimes.com/2018/05/15/climate/air-conditioning.html

Sanz, E., Olazabal, M., & Sainz de Murieta, E. (2019). *Planificación de la adaptación al cambio climático en las ciudades españolas: evaluando su sostenibilidad y efectividad a largo plazo*. Basque Centre for Climate Change (BC3). https://www.researchgate.net/publication/337059161_Planificacion_de_la_adaptacion_al_cambio_climatico_en_las_ciudades_espanolas_Evaluando_su_sostenibilidad_y_efectividad_a_largo_plazo

Seguí, P. (n.d.). *La tierra que busca su protagonismo en la arquitectura.* Ovacen. https://ovacen.com/la-tierra-que-busca-su-protagonismo-en-la-arquitectura/

Serrano Yuste, P. (2015). *Tierra comprimida y normativa para construir edificios.* Certificados Energéticos. https://www.certificadosenergeticos.com/tierra-comprimida-normativa-construir-edificios

Souza, E. (2019). *Colores de la tierra: los increíbles diseños de los muros de barro en Ghana.* Archdaily. https://www.archdaily.cl/cl/914727/colores-de-la-tierra-los-increibles-disenos-de-los-muros-de-tapia-en-ghana

Souza, E. (2021). *Materiales a 0km: preservando el medio ambiente y las culturas locales.* Archdaily. https://www.archdaily.mx/mx/958897/materiales-a-0-km-preservando-el-medio-ambiente-y-las-culturas-locales

Stouhi, D. (2021). *Las ciudades tienen cada vez más jóvenes, ¿están preparadas?* Archdaily. https://www.archdaily.cl/cl/968540/las-ciudades-tienen-cada-vez-mas-jovenes-estan-preparadas

Tutor Vicente, M. (2015). *La recuperación de la tierra pisada en la arquitectura contemporánea* [Tesis doctoral]. Universidad de Zaragoza.

Valdés Kuri, L., & Ricalde de Jager, A. (2006). *Experiencias rumbo a la sustentabilidad.* Ecohábitat. https://www.academia.edu/13447041/Ecohabitat_Experiencias_rumbo_a_la_sustentabilidad

Yuste, B. (2018). *Arquitectura de Tierra. Caracterización de los tipos edificatorios* [Tesis doctoral]. Universidad Politécnica de Madrid.

Chapter 15
Urban Health as a New Vector to Characterise Vulnerable Neighbourhoods:
Zaramaga Neighbourhood in Vitoria-Gasteiz (Spain)

Emilia Román López
https://orcid.org/0000-0001-6746-2793
Universidad Politécnica de Madrid, Spain

Ester Higueras García
https://orcid.org/0000-0002-0182-8884
Universidad Politécnica de Madrid, Spain

Rafael Córdoba Hernández
https://orcid.org/0000-0001-7878-2055
Universidad Politécnica de Madrid, Spain

Elisa Pozo Menéndez
https://orcid.org/0000-0001-5420-7849
Universidad Politécnica de Madrid, Spain

ABSTRACT

For decades, public administrations have been working on rigorous analysis to identify and delimit vulnerable neighbourhoods in order to prioritize their regeneration and rehabilitation actions. The progress and improvements have been significant, mainly in Euskadi (Spain), thanks to an alignment of economic investment with an exhaustive knowledge based on the articulation of indicators that integrate social, economic, environmental, and urban data into a digital open access platform (GeoEuskadi). However, despite all these plans and actions, most vulnerable neighbourhoods continue to have these challenges. This situation has made the Government of Euskadi contract a pilot plan with the aim of establishing a new methodology to characterise vulnerable residential areas. The new methodology has focused on urban health and well-being, combining quantitative and qualitative data, and the analyses for this goal are presented in this chapter.

DOI: 10.4018/978-1-6684-6924-8.ch015

INTRODUCTION

This chapter presents a new approach to urban regeneration of residential neighbourhoods, based on the concept of urban health, understood as a complete state of well-being, both physical and psychological, individual and social, and therefore encompassing a very holistic people-based approach (World Health Organization, 1946).

The chapter begins with a critical view of neighbourhood regeneration in Europe, whose successes have been assessed and contrasted on numerous occasions, but in which there is also a relevant critical view, as it is shown that, despite these initiatives, many of the existing problems persist in most cases for decades. It is in this sense that the health vector of people living in the neighbourhoods appears as an interesting opportunity to approach regeneration with a new people-centred approach. Urban planning and health have always gone hand in hand (García-González et al., 2022); it should be remembered that urban planning was created in the 19th century in the face of the serious epidemiological problems generated by the Industrial Revolution in the urban population, and that it was the Sanitary Laws that were the first to seek a solution to tackle them. In this sense, the research presented here provides a methodology adapted and based on the recently published *Guide for Planning Healthy Cities* (Fariña Tojo et al., 2022) commissioned by the Spanish Ministry of Health, which understands how urban planning can address this challenge, thanks to a comprehensive approach based on three strategic lines (cities for walking, nature in the city and spaces for coexistence), the analysis of which is structured into a series of questions organised into these three main working groups.

This research proposes a combined methodology of quantitative and qualitative assessments, with a series of tools (conventional and innovative, based on Geographic Information Systems, GIS) to successfully address all these synergies, as complementarity and interactions are one of the main characteristics present from a health point in residential neighbourhoods. The chapter ends with a pilot case in the Zaramaga neighbourhood, located in the town of Vitoria-Gasteiz, where this method has been carried out, combining a quantitative and qualitative assessment, to arrive at a health-based characterisation of the neighbourhood under study. The strengths of this new approach allow a series of actions to be established within an Urban Health Action Plan that simultaneously help to prevent and promote more active urban lifestyles in less polluted and comfortable urban environments, as well as help to achieve the SDG 3 and SDG 11 targets in vulnerable European residential neighbourhoods (Sartorius, 2006).

REGENERATION: A LONG EUROPEAN HISTORY WITH A MULTITUDE OF APPROACHES AND METHODS

Urban regeneration processes, in most European countries, are instruments for the comprehensive renovation of neighbourhoods that bring together a series of complex problems that cannot be solved sectorally. Since 1960, the renovation of residential neighbourhoods has progressively evolved thanks to the incorporation of not only physical-spatial policies, but also social, educational and employment policies, from the URBAN programmes of the European Union (URBAN I, URBAN II) (de Gregorio Hurtado, 2015). Indeed, the idea of urban regeneration is closely linked to the idea of transversality and complexity, so that in the 21st century it has fitted in perfectly with the concept of sustainability firstly (Aguado, 2018; Naciones Unidas, 1987; Robert Goodland, 1997) and now with the Sustainable Development Goals (Naciones Unidas, 2015) and those of the New Urban Agenda (Naciones Unidas, 2017).

Both France and the United Kingdom were pioneers in neighbourhood regeneration processes, beyond the rehabilitation of building envelopes, where other strategic multidisciplinary processes were gradually incorporated, which are now considered essential for such integrated approaches. In France, Germany, and the UK, over 30 years of neighbourhood regeneration policies and plans can be studied, providing an extraordinary source of data for academic reflection and new actions needed to advance the most successful actions. One of the main findings is the ability to account for the influence of context in shaping society's responses to different problems (Couch et al., 2011). Each country's policies and plans reflect key national priorities, such as social exclusion in France, spatial inequalities in Germany, or land-use efficiency in the UK. In the case of the UK, for example, there are a large number of successful regeneration projects, with appropriate contributions to local regeneration strategies through a variety of community services and by encouraging community involvement (Bailey, 2012). However, following the case of the English experiences, critical voices have also emerged in these processes, stating that actions aimed at implementing and achieving sustainability have become political instruments, used within the urban political discourse and constrained by market-based solutions (Lombardi et al., 2011).

Understanding the new dynamics now referring to current concepts, such as the Sustainable Development Goals and the New Urban Agenda, it seems necessary to reflect on the neighbourhood renovation strategies carried out in recent years in order to draw up new, more transversal and integrated actions to solve the problems of residential neighbourhoods built massively between 1950 and 1980 in Europe, which currently reflect insufficient habitability conditions in different aspects, which also implies impacts on the health of citizens, and which appear under the denomination of vulnerable neighbourhoods.

HEALTH AND WELL-BEING AS A VECTOR FOR NEW REGENERATION OF RESIDENTIAL NEIGHBOURHOODS

Considering the definition of health as a state of complete well-being, there are multiple spatial, social and lifestyle relationships directly related with spatial planning, regeneration of space and urban design (HUDU Land Use Consultants, 2007). Indeed, urban environments with major built-up spaces, lack of green areas, air pollution stemming from traffic and acoustic pollution have a direct impact on people's health, creating an environment in which people live under high pressure, in psychological or physical discomfort, which may lead to chronic diseases or the deterioration in the quality of life (Dumbaugh & Rae, 2009; Woodcock et al., 2007). In this context, the health vector seems appropriate to propose a new analysis method as well as urban action plans that can be linked to the promotion of health, through more active, healthier lifestyles (Sallis et al., 2008), as well as to health prevention through unpolluted and unharmful urban environments. In this sense, the guidelines and manuals for healthy streets and neighbourhoods published in several countries such as UK, USA, Canada, or Spain, have been consulted and adapted to the previous needs to produce an innovative methodology to consider the neighbourhoods from a transversal concept of the people's health (Higueras García, 2015; Román López et al., 2022). Urban areas can provide healthy living environments; indeed, they can improve health via their various elements, provision of services, cultural or aesthetic attributes (Córdoba Hernández & Martí Guitera, 2022; Kirdar, 1997). A conceptual framework for urban health was suggested by this author, for whom the core concept is that urbanisation does not occur in a vacuum. Multiple drivers and pathways affect the urban setting and its social and physical environments (Kjellstrom & Mercado, 2008).

WHO defines the quality of life as the subjective perception that an individual has within a cultural context that considers a person's aims, expectations, rules and concerns (WHO, 1999). It is, therefore, a concept that is also related to the physical health of people, their psychological state, their level of independence, their social relations, as well as their relationship with the environment. This is why it seems appropriate to propose a new way to characterise vulnerable urban areas from a health point of view, as most of them concentrate an ageing population, and buildings with low energy efficiency, limited accessibility, lack of green areas and a high presence of motorised mobility. This is the basis for this innovative methodology, which focuses on the well-being and health of people (Barton & Grant, 2006).

URBAN DETERMINANTS OF HEALTH FOR RESIDENTIAL NEIGHBOURHOODS

The urban environment conditions the health of the people who live in it, and in the same way society's activities and lifestyles condition aspects of the built environment that have an impact on the physical and mental health of its residents. The urban structure, mobility, distribution of green areas, presence of polluting activities... are, among others, variables that directly and indirectly affect the physical and mental health of the resident population. Given these premises, how can an urban diagnosis be made based on the health of a neighbourhood? We propose to start from the urban determinants of health, in order to understand the intrinsic relationships between the urban environment and people's quality of life and well-being.

It should also be noted that in cities there are significant differences between one area and another in terms of air quality, noise, water quality, presence of green areas and their accessibility, design of public spaces, etc. All these extrinsic factors condition the quality of life and life expectancy of the people who live there, which are known as the urban determinants of health. Cities are created by humans, and cities determine people's well-being and quality of life (Córdoba Hernández, 2022; Corraliza & Collado, 2011). In this sense, the WHO identifies the determinants of health in five major groups: material circumstances, social cohesion and psychosocial, behavioural or biological factors of each person, biophysical factors of each person, social, economic, behavioural and other factors. Numerous authors state that the real pandemic of Western societies in the 21st century is sedentary lifestyles and isolation, (Arocha Rodulfo, 2019; Rueda Martínez de Santos, 2005) from which the main causes of adult morbidity and mortality derive (Edwardson et al., 2012). These pathologies are closely related to urban design, land use distribution, density, and access to urban green spaces (HUDU Land Use Consultants, 2007).

The methodology aims to improve the urban-related health conditions of all inhabitants but recognises that not all personal health issues are related to this. It is assumed that any condition can be improved, although only general ones are considered. Of course, there would then be specific factors (poorly located industries, power lines, contaminated soil, and water...) which would have to be studied independently and which, in some cases, would be the main problem. However, this research tries to focus exclusively on those aspects related to lifestyle, making it impossible or possible to improve them.

One of the most important variables, is the impact of cars on certain illnesses, due above all to the air pollution they produce, the noise of traffic, encouraging a sedentary lifestyle and street accidents and insecurity. There is some evidence in the bibliography that the pollution produced by motor vehicles would affect diseases of the respiratory system in general, lung cancer and diseases of the upper aerodigestive tract. In turn, circulatory system diseases, cerebrovascular diseases and diabetes could be related to sedentary lifestyles and noise. Vulnerable groups such as children and older adults must be specially identified in each urban residential area. This must be considered in this urban health characterization.

At the same time, the lack of physical exercise, is one of the causes of which almost all authors point to as being due to the lack of green spaces being close by (green pockets). In addition, mental illness is caused not only by the lack of green areas in the nearby environment, but also by the absence of places for people to live together (the most important of which are precisely these nearby green areas). This is one of the main elements to determine the health characterisation of the neighbourhood proposed in this chapter.

PLANS, PROGRAMMES, AND GOOD PRACTICES IN URBAN PLANNING AND HEALTH: THEORETICAL AND PRACTICAL REVIEW

Understanding health and well-being as an opportunity to positively transform residential neighbourhoods in the 21st century, the question is how to establish the key indicators that help in this task, in order to characterise residential neighbourhoods from a health perspective and, subsequently, to suggest proposals for their improvement.

In 2020, the authors of this chapter, researchers from the Universidad Politécnica de Madrid, carried out an extensive literature review of manuals, plans, programmes and good practices worldwide that considered urban health as a preventive and well-being element in residential neighbourhoods. The work was published in the article *Guidelines for Healthier Public Spaces for the Elderly Population: Recommendations in the Spanish Context* (Higueras García et al., 2021). A systematic bibliographic review of the scientific literature was carried out, according to the PRISMA method (Liberati et al., 2009; Potchter et al., 2022). The search for studies was made on Scopus, Web of Knowledge, Google Scholar and Science Direct. This has been complemented with a manual search that included the bibliographic references cited in the articles, focusing on those published between 2000 and June 2018. Most of the plans and good practices found came from the United Kingdom, Canada, and the United States. Despite the wide range of key words and the large number of references consulted, it was possible to establish three conclusive, common lines, which encompass the dual need to prevent and promote people's health through urban planning. These three lines are as follows:

- Active mobility of people for their daily activities, understanding that cardiovascular diseases and obesity are the result of sedentary urban lifestyles. This requires minimum conditions for streets and urban spaces to be safe and attractive.
- It stresses the importance of the presence of vegetation in neighbourhoods, considering this to be highly beneficial for its micro-climatic contributions to improve thermal comfort and making it possible to be in urban public spaces; filtering and improving air quality, bringing humidity to the environment, and providing a psychological improvement and reducing urban stress for all people. It is not only vegetation, but this must be complemented by Nature-Based Solutions, as they come from closing water and urban matter cycles. Permeable, light-coloured surface finishes, and sustainable urban drainage systems (SUDS) are of great importance in this respect. The environmental benefits of green spaces have been verified and contrasted by numerous authors (Aram et al., 2019; Higueras García, 2006; Louv, 2010; Shanahan et al., 2015; Sukopp & Werner, 1991; Ulrich, 1983; Wilson & O., 1984).

- The third line is related to social cohesion, which is key to the reduction of isolation and unwanted loneliness of the urban population, which can be encouraged through the design of public spaces where there are activities and meeting places for all, especially for older adults, young people, and children.

The Spanish Healthy Cities Planning Guide

The Healthy Cities Planning Guide[1] (Fariña Tojo et al., 2022) was drafted in 2002, as part of the framework of the Agreement for the promotion of the Spanish Network of Healthy Cities and the local implementation of the Strategy for Health Promotion and Prevention, signed by the Ministry of Health and the Spanish Federation of Municipalities and Provinces (FEMP). The first conceptual part establishes the relationship between urban planning and health, understanding how, over time, urban society has suffered a series of pathologies and illnesses that have been tackled, in most cases, with public health care policies and plans and various planning measures in which zoning is one of the relevant actions. It is in the 21st century that the idea of preventing and promoting people's health through urban design and the planning of public spaces, the basic element of the aforementioned Guide, appears for the first time. In this sense, variables such as density, the presence of urban green areas, mobility and the distribution of land uses are seen as determining elements for healthy neighbourhoods.

Figure 1. Guide for planning healthy cities
Source: Ministry of Health (Government of Spain) (2022)

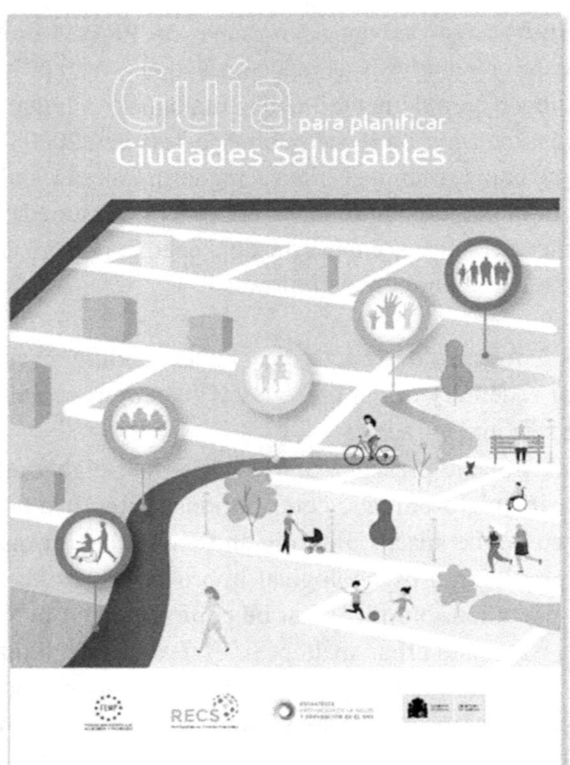

In this way, the guide sets out three complementary lines of action to improve the health conditions of residents in urban environments, in line with the conclusions of previous work carried out by the research team:

- Walkable neighbourhoods, which represent the idea of being able to walk from one point to another in the daily routines and activities. Walking is an essential activity to improve our physical and mental health, as well as contributing to a more sustainable environment. The promotion of a more active mobility, including both walking and cycling, requires the redistribution of the public space to reduce the space for motorised vehicles and to create safer, friendlier streets and paths. Specific variables to make this walkability possible include urban density, complexity, thermal comfort of streets, non-noisy areas, security, identity, appropriate land use distribution and urban connection with other urban areas (Health promotion achieved).
- Improvement of nearby urban green areas and new nature-based solutions, to increase nature and greenery in the neighbourhoods. There is high evidence of the physical and physiological benefits that proximity to green spaces bring both for mental and physical well-being. The increase of nature areas also contributes to the reduction of pollution, and the improvement of air quality as well as the urban micro-climate (Health prevention achieved).
- Creation of spaces for intergenerational coexistence. The availability of these kind of spaces contributes to more equitable and solidary cities, as it supports the elimination of isolation and loneliness (Health promotion and prevention achieved).

These three main ideas are characterised and assessed in the Guide through a series of urban planning and urban design variables, as shown in Figure 2.

In order to present an efficient, quick method to characterise each of the three main strategic lines, the Guide articulates and distributes 72 simple, specific questions among these thematic areas. These have been the basis for structuring the quantitative and qualitative characterisation and assessment proposed in this research, on the understanding that only from this dual approach is it possible to tackle the variables of a complex environment, such as the urban environment, and its influence on health, understood as a complete state of well-being, physical and psychological, individual and social, of the population, as established by the WHO.

THE NEED FOR A TWO-PRONGED APPROACH: MIXED QUANTITATIVE AND QUALITATIVE FOCUS

Consideration of the health vector, from an urban planning point of view, implies the need to combine quantitative and qualitative approaches for a number of reasons. Firstly, from the WHO's own definition (complete state of individual and social well-being), collecting urban data and real illnesses that have a direct or indirect impact on people's health is necessary. However, subjective perception, both at individual and collective level, needs to be addressed by consulting the people who have direct experience of the urban environment, hence the need to carry out focus groups and questionnaires to help determine these issues. According to Formi and De Grande (2020): "From the subsidiarity of the qualitative to the quantitative and the incompatibility of methods, more than half a century ago, we moved on to discuss and propose ways of integration". In addition, according to Creswell (2014),

Figure 2. Graphic scheme of the three lines of action for planning healthier cities, including the main elements for each line
Source: Adapted from Fariña Tojo et al. (2022, p. 12)

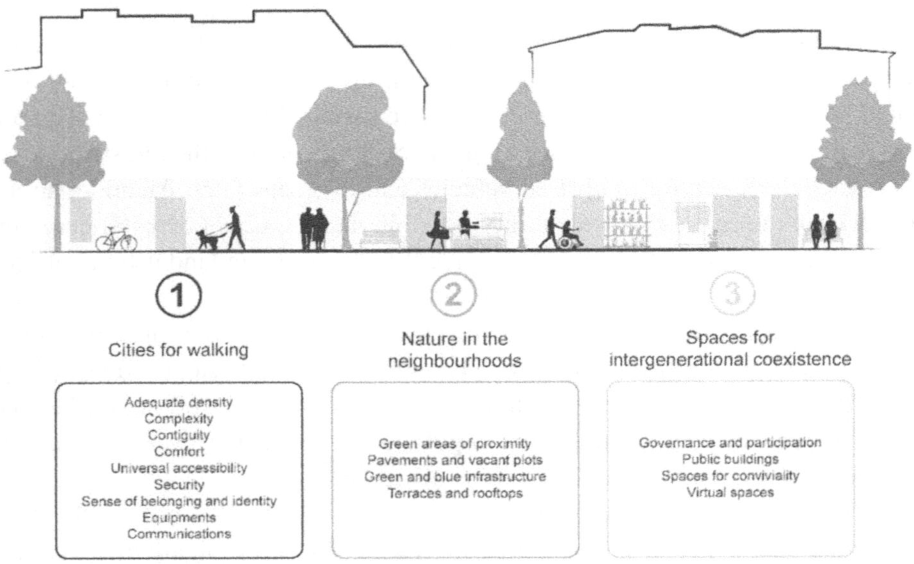

a leading proponent of mixed methods, who defines them as those in which the researcher gathers quantitative and qualitative data, integrates them and then makes interpretations based on combining the strengths of both. This dual quantitative and qualitative approach to study provides a better understanding of complex research problems.

Quantitative and qualitative analyses are common practice in analysing urban problems, appropriate to the complexity and wide variety of interconnected variables. Whether from energy efficiency (Ali et al., 2021), from green spaces (Ouzir et al., 2021), air quality (Engel-Cox et al., 2004), ecosystem services (Córdoba Hernández, 2021; Haase et al., 2014), health promotion from urban green spaces (Zhang et al., 2021), poverty and inequality (Vakulabharanam & Motiram, 2012) or even for decision making (Lwin et al., 2012). In view of this evidence, it is therefore appropriate to address the methodology for the health characterisation of residential neighbourhoods by combining quantitative data, present in large spatial data infrastructures such as GeoEuskadi[2] and in official health data portals; with qualitative data, obtained by means of two media: questionnaires and focus groups. Finally, it is proposed to complement the dual approach with essential field work, shared between technicians and neighbours.

THE OPPORTUNITY TO REGENERATE VULNERABLE NEIGHBOURHOODS IN EUSKADI THROUGH URBAN HEALTH AND WELL-BEING

The Context of Regeneration in Euskadi

In the Autonomous Community of the Basque Country in Spain (hereafter referred to as Euskadi), urban regeneration policies, plans and programmes have been pursued over a long period of time and within a broad institutional framework (Álvarez Mora & Camerin, 2019). The methodological systematisation to tackle both the rehabilitation of buildings and the regeneration of neighbourhoods was rigorously approached by Ruiz Palomeque (2018) thanks to a method of integral systematisation of the problems and projects for the rehabilitation of the building stock, which had its first examples in the open block estates of several neighbourhoods in Zaragoza (Spain).

Law 3/2015 on Housing, in Euskadi, articulated the actions in the special regime on urban regeneration and renovation, whose name in Euskadi is the "Urban Regeneration Area", which in turn defined new techniques to promote urban preservation with a joint, integrated character (including social, economic and environmental measures) and thus be able to meet the real urban needs of residential neighbourhoods. Regeneration and renewal action on the urban environment redefines and reinstates previously separate concepts and, by updating and combining them, enables new scenarios for more inclusive urban planning action. However, neither the Urban Regeneration Law nor the Housing Law establishes a closed model, nor do they formulate specific techniques for the definition of these actions (Cerezo Ibarrondo, 2019), which can vary greatly from one neighbourhood to another and can compromise the success of their actions.

VULNERABLE NEIGHBOURHOODS IN EUSKADI

In a global context where urbanisation processes of the territories are constantly accelerating, Euskadi stands out as a particularly urban territory in one of the European regions with the highest degree of urban concentration. With more than 75% of the population living in the 3 large urban areas of the region, the urban occupation of its territory represents only 7%, concentrated on the Cantabrian coast, in three cities: Bilbao and San Sebastian, and in the interior plains of Alava in Vitoria-Gasteiz.

In this context, Euskadi's Urban Agenda Bultzatu 2050 sets very ambitious goals where sustainability, equality, health and development are framed within the 17 SDGs and the region's environmental conditions.

In Euskadi, intensive work has been carried out to determine the state of residential neighbourhoods using a vulnerability index, which combines environmental, building, social and economic elements, all of which are active on the GeoEuskadi platform.[3] This is an open data viewer which, thanks to a powerful database that is continuously updated, determines the vulnerability of the census sections of Euskadi according to density, socio-demographic and socio-economic variables, accessibility and the condition of buildings. The data come from the Provincial Councils of Vizcaya, Guipúzcoa and Álava, the local councils and the state statistics institute. All this information is provided in Euskadi's 1,742 census sections.

The different information supplied by the geoportal is provided through 19 large groups of information: geographical names, basic cartography, boundaries, locations, environment, water, agriculture, territorial and urban planning, security, health, citizen services, housing, society, culture, economy, employment, information related to historical memory or geotechnics. All this information was accessible free of charge in a cartographic form. However, for the processing of this data using GIS tools, the information had to be requested in a shapefile format from the Basque Government, who authorised its use.

This powerful database was used to assess vulnerability and found that certain inequalities and dysfunctionalities persist over time in some urban areas. In other words, despite the efforts of the regional and local administration, vulnerable neighbourhoods continue to show the worst rates decade after decade. This evidence makes it necessary to address new cross-cutting methodologies to reverse the situations of vulnerability identified, which often go beyond the mere physical intervention of urbanisation or rehabilitation of buildings (de la Puerta Rueda, 2018; Grijalba Aseguinolaza, 2017). In this context, the research proposal is based on the health and well-being of the people living in the neighbourhoods, as an analytical and propositional vector to determine new actions to eliminate these persistent situations of vulnerability in residential neighbourhoods. Firstly, from the vulnerability and health characterisation of neighbourhoods, which is the main aim of this chapter.

SELECTION CRITERIA FOR THE PILOT CASE

Given the need and opportunity to consider the health vector as a new element for the characterisation of vulnerable residential neighbourhoods in Euskadi, and in view of the existence of a total of 1,742 census sections, grouped into residential neighbourhoods, it is necessary to establish selection criteria for the prioritisation of the areas of intervention.

The selection criteria are based, firstly, on the existing morbidity and mortality data in the three Basque provinces, selecting those diseases, according to the scientific literature, which have a more direct association with urban conditions. The selected diseases are listed below[4]:

- Diseases of the circulatory system
- Diseases of the respiratory system
- Cerebrovascular diseases
- Ischemic heart disease
- Diabetes
- Lung cancer
- Acute respiratory diseases, pneumonia, and influenza
- Chronic obstructive pulmonary disease
- Suicide
- Cancer of the upper aerodigestive tract
- Regarding the issue of mental illness, the number of suicides has been taken into account as an indicator, also aligned with the work already conducted in Euskadi.

Euskadi has data on each of these diseases, differentiated by sex, which has helped to determine which vulnerable neighbourhoods have worse data on these variables.

All these variables have been studied for both male and female population across Euskadi and it has been found that each disease has a different area of incidence within the urban areas. Given the results, it was initially proposed by this research to create a scorecard, using Geographic Information Systems, with three variables:

- Probability of Relative Risk of Mortality for men.
- Probability of Relative Risk Mortality for females.
- Sum of the mortality ratios for the 10 indicated diseases.

This last variable allows us to assess where diseases accumulate the most overall. Since we do not have the absolute values of the incidence of diseases, this is the only way to analyse where the cases of these 10 diseases concentrate in residential areas.

Figure 3. Control panel 1: Probability of relative risk of mortality
Source: Compiled by the authors

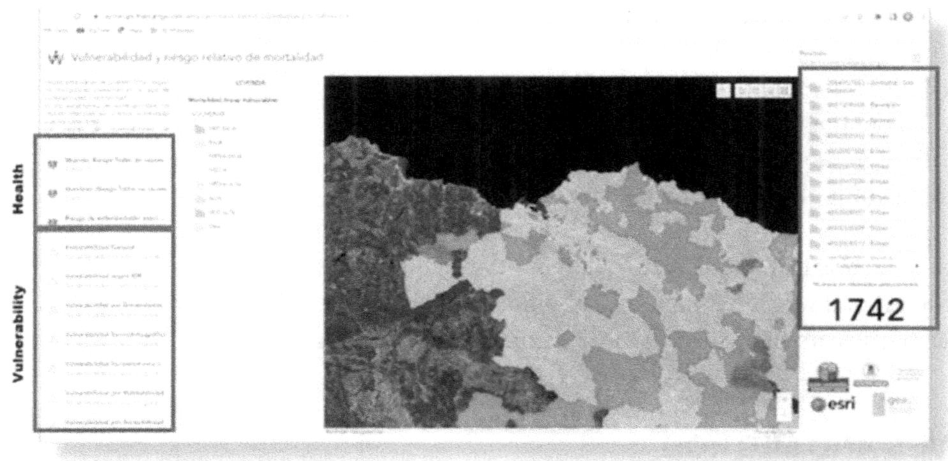

This control panel enables us to:

- Adjust the above variables by means of scroll bars.
- Filter the information for each of the three Basque provinces (Vizcaya, Guipúzcoa, Álava).
- List the most affected census sections, both on an individual level with their census section code and using their number on the right-hand panel.

To obtain a better identification of the urban areas, this information is completed with other variables related to the urban context such as the Vulnerable Areas of Euskadi and land use patterns. The first one corresponds to an information layer provided by the Basque Government which has vulnerability indices according to different aspects such as measurements, habitability, accessibility, etc. The second is part of the Land Occupation Information System in Spain (SIOSE), which is the land occupation database in Spain. It is generated at a scale of 1:25,000, but its most updated version dates from 2014.

Thanks to all this information, a new control panel was configured to visualize and compare the variables from the different data sources, to select future study areas according to the indicators present in the vulnerability and mortality layer. In the mortality parameters, lower values are less vulnerable than higher values. This allows a vulnerability gradient for all indicators to be established according to their mortality, in urban areas, located between very high and very low, establishing five other intermediate values (high, medium high, medium, medium low and low).

This tool also has a map on which we can request information by clicking on it, carry out other actions such as searching for an address or obtaining a list of the census sections that meet the requirements established in the aforementioned filters, as well as the total number of elements that meet the requirements. Thus, the methodology designed, through a control panel, allows the vulnerable areas to be combined, with all the indicators used for their determination (socio-economic, demographic, accessibility, housing conditions, etc.) with the mortality risks associated with the 10 selected diseases, choosing census sections that meet the parameters established through the previous filtering to deliver this research goal.

Therefore, the selection criteria for the pilot case were as follows:

- Socially vulnerable area of the list of vulnerable neighbourhoods in Euskadi
- Area with a high ageing rate
- Area with high unemployment and economic constraints
- Mainly residential area
- Area with high mortality of the 10 diseases selected above
- Urban areas of high population density.

With these selection criteria, the case study for the health-based characterisation of a vulnerable residential neighbourhood was the Zaramaga neighbourhood in Vitoria-Gasteiz, province of Álava (Spain), whose characteristics are explained in more detail in the following points.

OBJECTIVES AND METHOD

From the framework of people's health and well-being outlined above, this research aims to characterise vulnerable neighbourhoods, in line with the targets set out in "SDG 3-Health and Well-being" and "SDG 11-Sustainable Communities". Two main objectives are set:

- To carry out a diagnosis based on the urban determinants of health for the residents of a vulnerable neighbourhood.
- To spatialise the determining factors and health determinants in the selected vulnerable urban area, by means of dynamic analytical mapping, along the three key lines established (cities for walking, nature in the neighbourhoods and new spaces for intergenerational coexistence).

METHODOLOGY

In order to meet these objectives, and as mentioned in previous points, it is necessary to establish a method that brings together quantitative and qualitative data, applying a mixed methodology, so that both objective and subjective assessments can be recorded. Table 1 shows how they are combined in each of the two objectives:

Table 1. Objectives and methodology applied

Objective	Quantitative Method	Qualitative Method
Carry out a diagnosis based on the urban determinants for health of the people living in the neighbourhood	GeoEuskadi Viewer GIS (Geographical Information System) mapping analysis Fieldwork (Field *Maps* and *QuickCapture* tools) ©ESRI	Questionnaires Focus Group Neighbourhood walks
Specialise the determining factors and health determinants in the selected vulnerable urban area, through dynamic analytical mapping.		

Source: Compiled by the author (2023)

Therefore, the mixed method for the health-based characterisation of vulnerable neighbourhoods will follow this sequence; first an analysis from the quantitative approach, with information derived mostly from the GeoEuskadi geospatial data platform, combined with the qualitative approach, centred on questionnaires, focus groups and neighbourhood walks with neighbours. All these steps provide sufficient data to draw up the SWOT (Strengths-Weaknesses-Opportunities-Threats) map, focusing on urban health, and thus be able to establish the characterisation of the vulnerable neighbourhood of Zaramaga, in Vitoria-Gasteiz (Euskadi).

Both the quantitative and qualitative methods are structured along the three main strategic lines explained above.

RESULTS AND METHODOLOGICAL APPROACHES TO DATA COLLECTION AND DATA PROCESSING IN THE ZARAMAGA CASE STUDY

The Zaramaga neighbourhood has a population of 12,349 inhabitants,[5] being one of the most densely populated in the city and is located to the north of the historic quarter. The indices of social, economic and environmental vulnerability in some of the census sections that make up the neighbourhood make it a priority neighbourhood for action, in addition to problems in the public space, which are reflected in the health diagnosis of the neighbourhood, as shown below.

Specifically, the area selected as the object of study is located between Molinuevo Park, Santa Isabel Cemetery and El Boulevard Shopping Centre, bordering to the north with one of the main industrial areas of Vitoria-Gasteiz. In total, there are 10 census sections, with an area of 56.1 hectares, 4,872 dwellings and a population of 9,921 inhabitants (80% of the total population of the neighbourhood).

As mentioned before, results were obtained in various formats for the questions recommended by the Guide.

Firstly, spatial analysis maps of the main problems and opportunities of the neighbourhood were obtained in GIS format, in each of the three complementary lines: a map of the walkability of the

Table 2. Mixed method analysis for the urban characterisation of residential neighbourhoods from a health perspective

<table>
<tr><th colspan="6">Mixed Analysis Method for Urban Characterisation From a Health Perspective</th></tr>
<tr><th colspan="3">Quantitative</th><th colspan="3">Qualitative</th></tr>
<tr><td>Field work
Field Maps
Quick capture</td><td colspan="2">GIS Analysis
GeoEuskadi</td><td colspan="2">Online Questionnaire
Neighbourhood residents</td><td>Focus Group
Neighbourhood walks</td></tr>
<tr><th colspan="6">SWOT</th></tr>
<tr><th colspan="2">Cities for walking</th><th colspan="2">Nature in the neighbourhood</th><th colspan="2">Coexistence spaces</th></tr>
<tr><td colspan="2">Weaknesses
Threats
Strengths
Opportunities</td><td colspan="2">Weaknesses
Threats
Strengths
Opportunities</td><td colspan="2">Weaknesses
Threats
Strengths
Opportunities</td></tr>
<tr><th colspan="6">Urban health characterisation</th></tr>
</table>

Source: Own compilation (2023)

Figure 4. Geographical location of the study area
Source: Compiled by the author

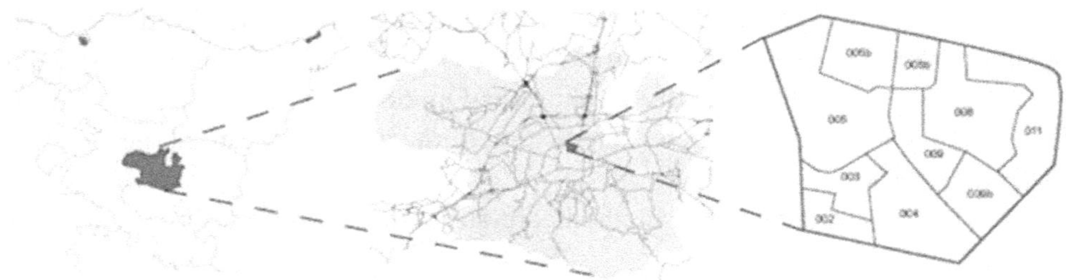

Figure 5. Description of the field of study
Source: Compiled by the authors

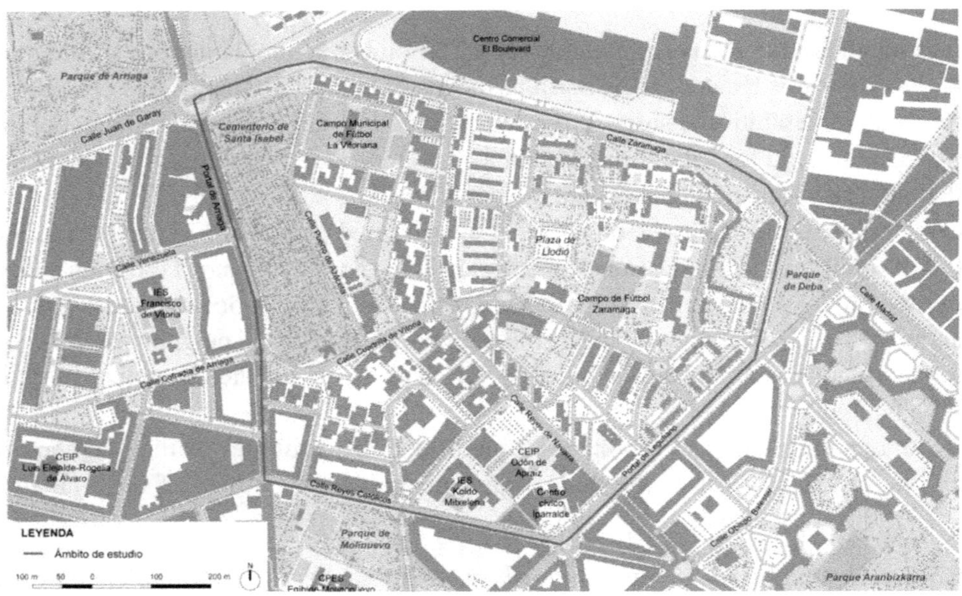

neighbourhood and the main barriers, deficiencies, weaknesses and critical points according to the determining elements; a map of the structure of the neighbourhood's green areas, considering the quantity, quality and accessibility of these in relation to the entrances of all the houses in the neighbourhood; and the open spaces and small squares, open or closed meeting places that the neighbours have available to carry out various activities together.

Questionnaires were then carried out among the residents and population of the neighbourhood in order to determine their individual and subjective conditions. The analysis of the different age groups, gender and the ageing population revealed important nuances that will be taken into account in the Integrated Health Action Plan. In addition to the individual questionnaires, two important activities were carried out with the neighbours; firstly, the creation of focal work groups, where the importance and necessity of urban planning from a health perspective was explained to them, and where all their opinions could be collected. The second activity consisted of a joint visit to the neighbourhood between neighbours and the research team, where different aspects related to the daily activities of the population were discussed, the maintenance of some urban spaces or parks, and even concerns, insecurities and conflicts were recorded, which would not have been detected if it had not been for this walk. The possibility of recording all this field information using mobile devices and the creation of an accessible, open online map is one of the great contributions for this type of work, which is inventoried in this way, characterised, completed and in a dynamic format for other successive stages of improvement of the neighbourhood.

QUANTITATIVE APPROACH

This first approach is conducted by exploiting the databases available on the websites of the public administrations. In this case, as mentioned above, one of the main ones is GeoEuskadi, belonging to the Basque Government.

The analysis and characterisation of each of the chosen neighbourhoods is structured according to the questions raised in the *Guide for Planning Healthy Cities*. Some of them are resolved using Geographic Information Systems, but others require another type of analysis, more focused on field visits and work with neighbours and local agents, as will be seen below.

Below are some of the cartographies developed using GIS technologies, which provide answers to the questions set out in the *Guide,* and which are integrated, through a web application, in the GeoEuskadi geospatial data platform.

Two tools were developed, with different scopes, to collect more participatory technical data:

- The first one (QuickCapture, ©ESRI), is aimed at the simple, orderly capture of images, which are geolocated and classified according to whether they are strengths or weaknesses in each of the three strategic lines proposed in the project. This tool could also be used by the citizens themselves, given its simplicity, for the preparation of a collaborative cartography.
- The second one of a more technical nature (Field Maps, ©ESRI), allows for data collection where, in addition to geolocated images, a more specific classification can be made, in subcategories belonging to the three main strategic lines, as well as in collecting written observations or with voice recordings, sounds, videos or files associated with each issue analysed.

Figure 6. Green areas and maximum noise thresholds in the Zaramaga neighbourhood, Vitoria-Gasteiz
Source: compiled by the author, based on GIS analysis and data from GeoEuskadi

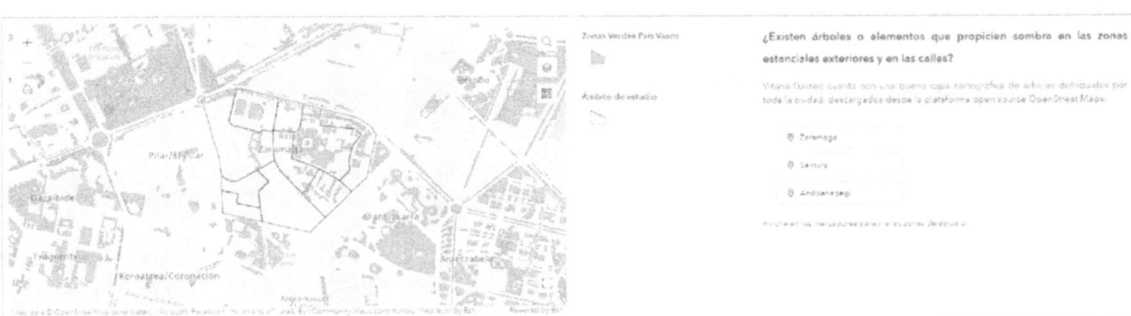

During the visits, the weaknesses, strengths and singularities found were mapped, sorted according to the three strategic lines, using the traffic light code (red-weakness, green-strength, yellow-singularity).

All the data were updated and shared through online cartographies, where filters, selection by attributes and other operations required for subsequent office work, which aim to analyse and characterise the neighbourhood, can be carried out.

The data collection carried out with these tools allows the visualisation, georeferencing, organisation and management of the information collected during the fieldwork. Specific queries can be made, and thematic filters can be applied, depending on the technical objective pursued. This allows very rich, flexible, and varied databases to be created, with truly diverse information.

For example, during the fieldwork (using the Field Maps tool) 275 data in the form of entities were captured in the *Cities for Walking* strategic line. Of these, 119 belong to strengths present in the neighbourhood (green circles) and 155 to weaknesses detected along these lines (red circles). As for the singularities (yellow circles) only one has been detected.

A high percentage of the strengths found in the area belong to thematic areas related to the sense of belonging and identity, mainly through physical symbolic elements, such as artistic manifestations found on façades, party walls, shop windows, etc. The high number of strengths found in the area of comfort and convenience (climatic, topographical, visual and acoustic) is also very significant. This is due, among other things, to the high presence of vegetation and urban trees in the neighbourhood. On the other hand, it is an area that is well connected to the rest of the city by public transport and the main roads.

With regard to weaknesses, in this same strategic line, various problems were found in the neighbourhood. Some are related to universal accessibility, the contiguity of public spaces and streets, lack of comfort (climatic, visual, etc.) and convenience, due to the absence of urban trees and/or shading elements in some streets and public spaces, high presence of empty premises on the ground floor of buildings, lack of maintenance and cleanliness of public space, noise pollution, mainly in the perimeter streets of the neighbourhood, subjective feeling of insecurity due to the lack of lighting at night, lack of activity, complex legibility of public space, conflicts between pedestrians and bicycle users due to the current design of the bicycle lane, etc.

Figure 7. QuickCapture. Fieldwork applications in Zaramaga neighbourhood (Vitoria-Gasteiz)
Source: Compiled by the authors based on ©ESRI

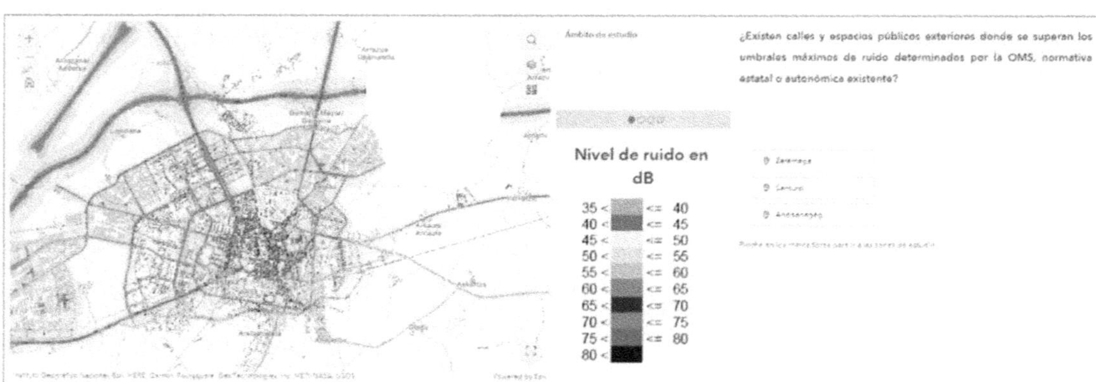

Figure 8. Strengths, broken down by thematic areas, in the strategic line of walkable cities/neighbourhoods
Source: Compiled by the authors based on ©ESRI

QUALITATIVE APPROACH

Regarding health in vulnerable neighbourhoods, the subject of the study, there is no doubt of the importance of citizen's knowledge from the diagnosis phase itself. No one better than the users of the urban space themselves can express from their direct experience, the relationships between their physical and mental health and the daily living conditions in those urban areas that present previously identified factors of vulnerability.

And it is also the people who are fully involved in the urban life of the neighbourhood who are best able to articulate, through collective thinking and dialogue, the objectives, and possible solutions to address the health problems identified.

From a technical point of view, the aim is to create the conditions for the expression of experiences and the identification of objectives and solutions by citizens in an operational, articulated, and methodical manner.

This valuable qualitative contribution is introduced into the project in two ways: an online questionnaire and two Focus Groups.

Figure 9. Weaknesses, broken down by thematic areas, in the strategic line of walkable cities/neighbourhoods
Source: Compiled by the authors based on ©ESRI

ONLINE QUESTIONNAIRE

With the support of Geographic Information Systems, an online questionnaire has been designed (Survey 123, ESRI), and adapted on paper for those population groups that have more difficulties with the use of technologies. The purpose was to find out the neighbours' subjective perception, its place and areas identified with respect to issues related to urban health prevention and promotion. The conceptual framework developed in the first phase of the study was used to design a survey, focusing on the three urban factors that most clearly affect the physical and mental health of residents (walkability, green areas and coexistence places).

With regards to the standard type of neighbourhood considered in the formulation of the questions, specific attention was paid to aspects such as population density, the presence of facilities and activities, the proximity of shops and the existence of meeting places.

In relation to mobility, it was also considered important to pay attention, from the health point of view, to the mode of travel between residence and work, considering that both the length of the journeys

Figure 10. Online questionnaire for qualitative data collection
Source: Compiled by the authors

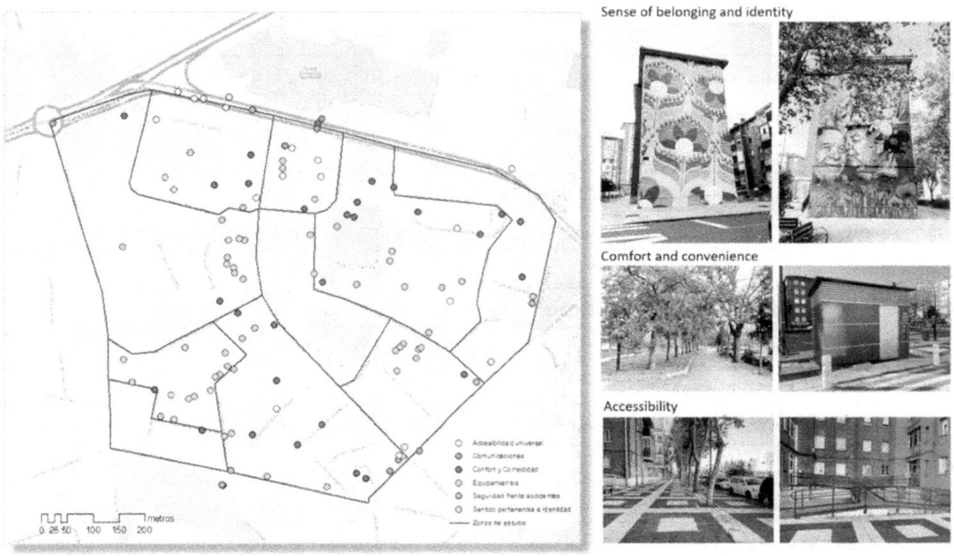

and the modes of transport used constitute a relevant factor in terms of the quality of daily life and, therefore, the health of the population.

The questionnaire was structured in two parts. The first part was aimed at finding out the profile of the person: age range, gender, profession/studies, location of residence, whether they work/study in the neighbourhood. The second focused on the characterisation of the neighbourhood from an approach based on the three basic strategic lines to achieve a healthy city: neighbourhoods for walking nature in the neighbourhoods and urban spaces for coexistence.

Some of the questions for each line are specified below, where, depending on the initial answer (yes/no), alternatives are displayed to help determine the reason for each answer:

The dissemination of the questionnaire was carried out with the support of the administration and local agents in each of the areas analysed. After data collection, a detailed analysis of the data was carried out, using graphs and summary tables that organise and summarise the key questions collected.

The questionnaire was answered by 347 people who live in the neighbourhood. Of these, 54% were women and 46% men. The distribution in terms of age groups was fairly balanced (22.77% were under 18 years old; 11.82% between 18-25 years old; 21.33% between 26-40 years old; 12.97% between 41-65 years old; 12.97% between 66-75 years old and 17.87% were over 75 years old). Although this distribution does not represent the current population profile of the area (with a predominance of older people), the results obtained are very interesting in terms of establishing programmes and projects in the medium and long term and, furthermore, have been complemented by the information provided by the focus groups where, as will be seen below, there has been a predominance of older groups.

Some of the key issues obtained by this method were the following:

Regarding *Neighbourhoods for walking*, an extremely high percentage of the population who completed the questionnaire walk to basic facilities related to education, health, social support, sport, or culture (94%). The same is true for people who buy food, pharmaceuticals and/or necessities in the

Table 3. Online questionnaire. Selection of main questions

Online questionnaire. Selection of main questions.
1. Neighbourhoods for walking
• Do you usually walk to basic facilities related to education, health, social support, sport or culture?
• Do you buy food, pharmaceuticals and/or basic necessities in the shops in your neighbourhood?
• Do you feel safe[6] in your neighbourhood?
• Are the streets in your neighbourhood comfortable and convenient?
• Do you have accessibility problems[7] when moving around the streets, squares and parks in your neighbourhood?
2. Nature in the neighbourhoods
• Do you consider that there is enough vegetation and green areas[8] in your neighbourhood?
• Do you visit green spaces in your neighbourhood?
• Do you visit green spaces outside your neighbourhood?
• Do you think that the green areas in your neighbourhood promote physical activity for everyone[9]?
3. Urban spaces for coexistence
• Do you regularly use basic facilities related to education, health, social support, sport or culture?
• Do the basic facilities have multiple and intergenerational uses[10]?
• Do you have relatives, friends, or acquaintances in the neighbourhood?
• Are there meeting places in the neighbourhood to socialise with family, friends or acquaintances?
• Do you feel safe in the meeting places?
• Do the outdoor public spaces have elements and facilities that encourage you to stay there[11]?

Source: Compiled by the authors

Figure 11. Location of the respondents to the questionnaire
Source: Compiled by the authors with data from the Survey 123, ©ESRI

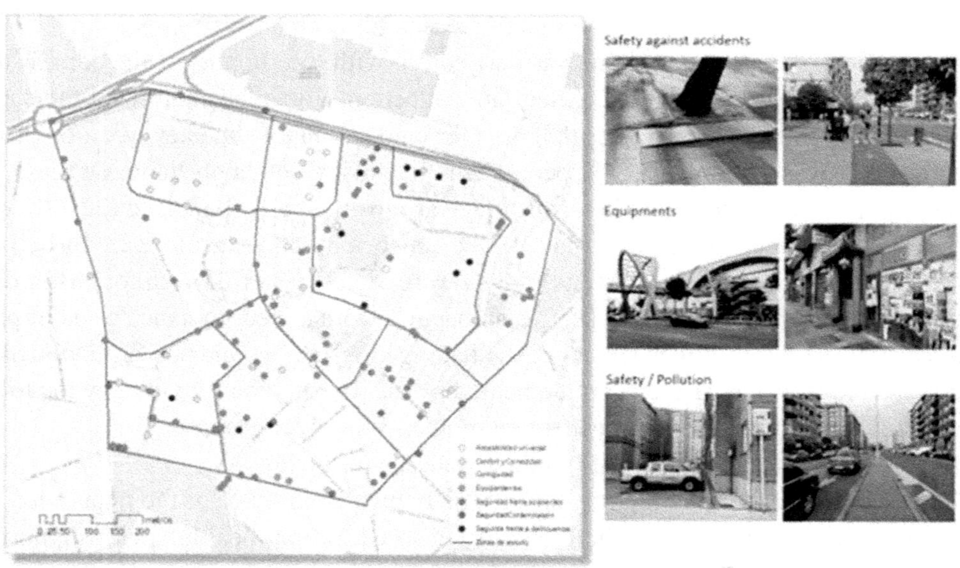

neighbourhood shop (87.90%). This is due, among other things, to the inherent physical conditions of the area, which has very few slopes and gradients and, in general, spacious pavements. There is also a high percentage who feel safe in the neighbourhood (73.78%). The reasons why some people feel insecure are diverse, such as crime, empty streets and lack of urban life, traffic, or fear of accidents in public space. Other issues also arise, such as the lack of or inadequate lighting of spaces at night, lack of maintenance of pavements and public spaces in general, the presence of bicycles and scooters on pavements, and accessibility problems. All of them result in people tripping and falling, especially older adults, who need auxiliary aids for personal mobility, such as canes, crutches, wheelchairs, walkers, etc.

Regarding *Nature in the neighbourhoods*, a high number of people living in the neighbourhood (93.37%), who completed the questionnaire, consider that there are enough green areas and vegetation. Also, a high percentage (87.03%) visit them quite often.

A high percentage of respondents (73.79%) visit green spaces outside the neighbourhood. When specifying where they go, they visit areas related to Vitoria-Gasteiz green ring, such as the Salburua wetland, Olarizu dehesa, Gorbea Natural Park, Armentia forest, San Juan de Arriaga Park or the green areas of Zabalgana. They are also frequent visitors to green areas in the city centre.

In the area of *Spaces for co-existence* a high proportion of the people who completed the questionnaire (89.63%) regularly use the basic facilities related to education, health, social support, sport or culture. 63.98% think that these facilities are multi-purpose and for different age groups. Practically all the people (98.27%) have relatives, friends or acquaintances in the neighbourhood and think that there are meeting places to get in touch with them (97.78%). The places where they meet are mainly open spaces, such as squares and parks, cafés, restaurants, txocos or similar, in the community centre, supermarkets and markets, places of worship, sports centres and other places, such as shopping centres and association premises.

Figure 12. Frequency of visits to green spaces in the neighbourhood
Source: Compiled by the authors with data from the Survey 123, ©ESRI

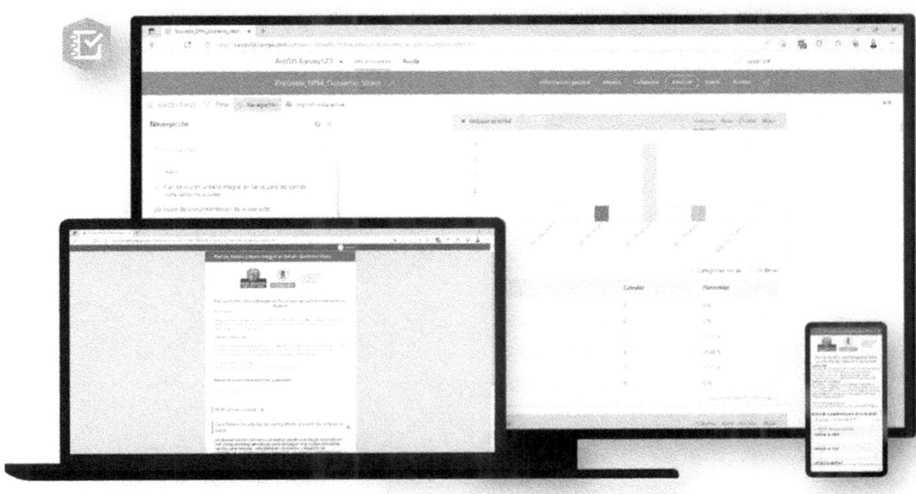

FOCUS GROUPS AND NEIGHBOURHOOD WALKS

In relation to the participation process, the specific identification of the areas of action is essential, especially in view of the face-to-face workshops, which are intended to complement the online questionnaire, but also to provide valuable details that cannot be found in the large databases available or in a technical inspection visit, as they are provided by the people who for years have known, enjoyed and suffered the strengths and weaknesses of their neighbourhoods. One of the main advantages of these study areas for the participation process is that there are already consolidated contacts between the administrations involved in the interventions and local civil society agents. In this sense, the Community Centres, which have already been set up, play a fundamental role.

In the next stage of the participation process, preliminary contacts were made with these local agents to promote the survey among neighbours, as well as to design each of the participatory events in the most appropriate way for each of the contexts. The process was based on focus groups, made up of key local agents such as representatives of neighbourhood associations, community centres, senior citizens' centres, health centres, street educators (who work with adolescents), schools, etc.

A first session was organised, where the strengths and weaknesses of the neighbourhood were discussed with respect to the three strategic lines proposed in the project, and in accordance with some of the questions worked on in the online questionnaire.

After this first characterisation, a second focus group was carried out by means of an exploration walk with the participants, where they located, on their own journeys through the area, issues and concerns that have been discussed on previous days, or even new issues that have arisen in the debates established during the activity.

Figure 13. Focus Group organised in the neighbourhood of Zaramaga, Vitoria-Gasteiz
Source: Compiled by the authors, 2022

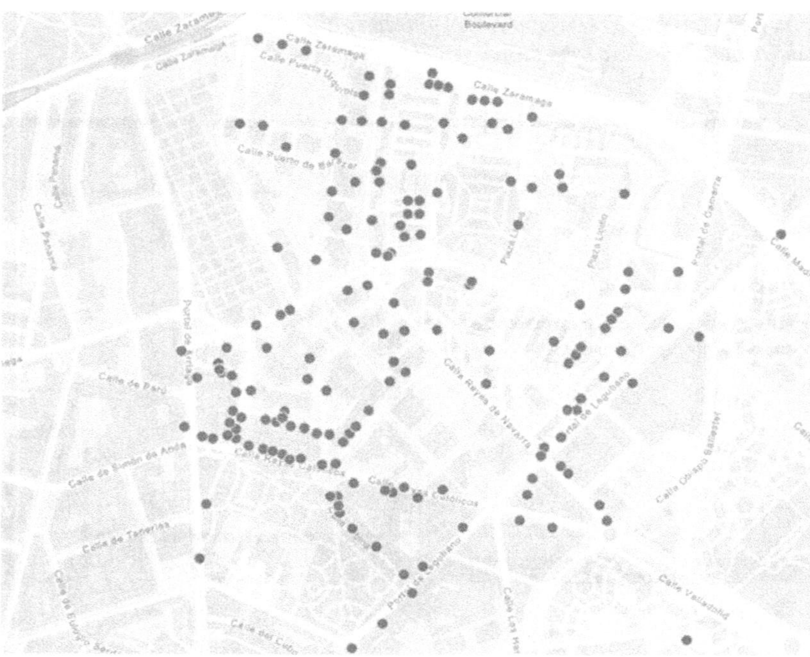

The fieldwork tools developed and explained in previous sections were also used here, allowing all the information provided by the residents of the neighbourhood to be mapped and geo-referenced. In this second meeting, ideas, actions, and strategies for the improvement of the neighbourhood were also shared.

Figure 14. Exploration walks carried out in the Zaramaga neighbourhood, Vitoria-Gasteiz
Source: compiled by the authors, 2022

After these processes, the information that was obtained regarding the general view of the neighbourhood, as perceived by the population, brought together two driving forces: On the one hand, the feeling of chronic neglect. And on the other hand, the privilege of living in a green, peaceful environment: "*You look out of the window, and it looks like you live in a forest" / "Everybody opens the window and sees green*".

- In the *Neighbourhoods to Walk line*, there is a sense that the neighbourhood is in decline and very run-down. There are problems of accessibility, lack of maintenance and perceived insecurity, which discourage self-care, especially in the older population, through adequate and continuous physical exercise, as part of an integral health concept. Bicycles on the pavement in squares, on perimeter roads or in streets within the neighbourhood pose a clear danger to people walking on the pavement (especially older people).
- Regarding the *introduction of nature in the neighbourhood*, the opinion of the residents is that, in general, it has an excellent quality and quantity of green spaces. It is considered a privilege to live in this environment. But it is necessary to care for and maintain this valuable heritage which, without good cleaning and maintenance guidelines, can lead to problems. For example, accumulation of leaves in wet weather are dangerous (slips and falls, concealment of holes and obstacles in the pavement). For this reason, frequent leaf removal is considered necessary, mainly in autumn-winter. Another aspect commented on is the presence of many empty, unreplaced or unpaved tree surrounds, which are points of danger in terms of falls and tripping.
- Lastly, in the line of *spaces for coexistence*, they point out that there are few conflicts, but also little intergenerational coexistence. The traditional spaces are missed: the fronton, the parish church, the markets that no longer exist. Teenagers and young people do not want to share spaces with families and do not adapt to the offer of municipal centres. They want exclusivity and autonomy in their activities. There are also mental health concerns among older people, due to unwanted

Figure 15. Older people strolling through the streets of Zaramaga, 2022
Source: Compiled by the author

loneliness and the high number of people who are used to being cooped up at home and end up not going out or seeing much of anyone during the day.

THE CHARACTERISATION OF THE NEIGHBOURHOOD FROM A HEALTH PERSPECTIVE

The convergence of the previous analyses has allowed us to establish the characterisation of the Zaramaga neighbourhood, from the perspective of public space and the health of its residents. Understanding health as the complete state of well-being established by the World Health Organisation, quantitative tools have made it possible to establish a diagnosis based on the extrinsic causes that condition this well-being. However, given the subjective and intrinsic nature of the residents' perception of well-being, it has been necessary and relevant to establish complementarity with quantitative analyses, using the tools that have been presented. In this way, the health characterisation of the Zaramaga neighbourhood is presented, which is the first step in the second phase of an Integrated Health Action Plan to resolve the problems encountered.

As a starting point for interpreting the results of the synthetic and comparative SWOT, it should be emphasised that the objective of this diagnosis is not so much, or not only, an analysis of the quality of the public space in the Zaramaga neighbourhood, but above all, of the way in which the conditions of this space affect the health of the residents, whether in a positive or negative way.

This is particularly relevant for some issues, such as accessibility, for which, in terms of health, it is advisable to take into account the overlap between the interior space of the building and the public space itself, beyond the delimitations in terms of ownership and who manages it. This is an important issue to consider when developing programmes and action plans, which must necessarily include integrated management measures, taking into account buildings and the urban environment as a whole. A key problem in this regard is the lack of lifts or the existence of architectural barriers in the interior common spaces of the building, such as the frequent flights of stairs or jumps in level between the lift exit and the street doorway, or between the doorway and the street level itself.

Another key issue, which goes beyond the objectives of this work but which is important to emphasise, is the lack of energy efficiency of buildings, with very inefficient envelopes and installations, which lead to a lack of comfort inside the dwellings and, therefore, associated pathologies that can have very serious consequences for the health of the people who live in them.

With regard to the different tools and approaches used, it should be noted that, due to their specific nature, they allow the different conditions considered to be identified with greater or lesser ease: thus, fieldwork allows a direct approach to the weaknesses and strengths visible at micro scale in the public space itself, but not so much to those issues that can be considered opportunities or threats, which in many cases depend on external factors or conditions that are not directly observable at present and at that micro-scale.

This reinforces the importance of a qualitative approach, and in particular participatory tools such as focus groups, as they allow easier access to latent threats and opportunities, both subjective and objective, through the experiences shared and discussed by the participants.

With regard to the mapping and quantitative data available, their analysis in the office makes it possible to complete and complement the data provided by fieldwork and qualitative tools by identifying weaknesses and strengths on a larger scale, as well as to identify threats and opportunities due mainly to issues such as the location and density of existing facilities in the neighbourhood and its surroundings, the urban morphology of public space or the conditions of continuity of mobility networks in all modes of transport.

It has become clear that there are aspects that are detected in one or more ways. In general, the importance of the participation of the residents of the neighbourhood in this analysis and diagnosis phase is emphasised, in order to complement the problems detected with other methodologies, such as cartographic

Figure 16. Urban Health characterisation of Zaramaga´s neighbourhood
Source: Compiled by author

analysis (GIS) or field work, but also to highlight other types of issues that can only be detected through direct experience of the area, lived in first person. For example, there are many contributions from the questionnaires, focus groups and neighbourhood walks related to the condition of maintenance and use of the neighbourhood's outdoor spaces that can hardly be characterised and analysed with the rest of the tools applied. This is particularly the case in the area of coexistence spaces, where the contribution of citizen participation and field work is essential.

This demonstrates the importance, for the urban characterisation of the neighbourhood from a health point of view, of using different tools and methodologies that allow a quantitative and qualitative analysis of the area, as their complementarity is clearly demonstrated.

STRENGTHS AND LIMITATIONS OF THE RESEARCH

Address the urban regeneration of residential neighbourhoods from a health perspective seems very timely from several points of view. Firstly, the approach is cross-cutting, integrated, holistic and complex, variables that are key to both sustainability and the strategies of the New Urban Agenda (United Nations, 2017). This approach also overcomes some of the limitations found in the studies of previous years, thanks to the spatialisation and use of GIS methodologies, which makes it possible to study the dynamics of neighbourhoods over extended periods of time, and can help in the design of new plans, policies or programmes adapted to these contexts.

The existence of the *Guide for planning healthy cities*, from the planning and design of urban public spaces, has been a great help to address, in an orderly, integrated manner, the analysis and diagnosis, and is a flexible and accessible methodological proposal to proceed in residential neighbourhoods. The synthetic and specific nature of the questions has allowed two complementary approaches: on the one hand, technicians or specialists can answer them and map them from the analysis of spatial data in a GIS platform-form; on the other hand, it is also possible to gather information by asking groups of different profiles (residents, students, associations, etc.) and thus obtain their perception of the neighbourhood from the possibilities for walking it has, from the existence of nature and its real accessibility and from the meeting spaces, which are truly points of coexistence and socialisation.

On the other hand, this methodology has some weaknesses, the first of which is the need to set up a multidisciplinary team of experts, which is a major investment and sometimes unattainable in certain local contexts. Furthermore, the existence or non-existence of open data or the ease of access to municipal information is a constraint when undertaking a full cartographic analysis, so it is recommended to assess the availability of existing data and resources before undertaking the cartographic analysis process.

In turn, the work has focused on the extrinsic conditions of residential areas, from public space, green areas and community spaces and facilities, but excluded from the analysis are buildings, where dampness, air quality, lack of solar access, low energy efficiency, etc., mean that important chronic pathologies can occur due to the large number of hours that people remain in enclosed spaces, especially older adults, so this study should be complemented by considering the condition of housing, as well as the work spaces of the resident population.

Table 4. Tools and methodologies for the urban characterisation from a health point of view

Description	SWOT	Methodologies/Tools Used				Priority Groups
		Digital Cartography	Questionnaire	G. Focal Points and Walks	Field Work	
SPACES OF COEXISTENCE FOR ALL: There is not much intergenerational coexistence.	W			x		All
SPACES OF COEXISTENCE FOR ALL: We miss the traditional spaces, such as the fronton, parish church, markets that no longer exist. Adolescents and young people want exclusivity and autonomy in their activities.	W			x		Young people
SPACES OF COEXISTENCE FOR ALL: Sports parks tend to be used exclusively by federated players.	W			x		Children and young people
SENSE OF BELONGING AND IDENTITY: Many of the meeting spaces are unnamed or not clearly identified.	W			x	x	All
UNWANTED LONELINESS: Shops and the market used to be the daily meeting place, especially for women, but this is in decline in the inner areas of the neighbourhood, concentrating on the side streets and the Boulevard.	W		x	x		All
UNWANTED LONELINESS: In older people there are concerns about mental health, due to unwanted loneliness.	T			x		Older adults
SPACES OF COEXISTENCE FOR ALL: In some parks there is competition and lack of integration between different cultural groups.	T			x		All
SPACES OF COEXISTENCE FOR ALL: Young people and adults tend to make a lot of use of terraces and bars.	S		x	x	x	All
SPACES OF COEXISTENCE FOR ALL: Outdoor public spaces have elements and facilities that make them feel comfortable and encourage them to stay in them.	S		x		x	All
SPACES OF COEXISTENCE FOR ALL: There is little conflict. The usual problems of coexistence, such as the "botellón", do not occur because young people go to the city centre or the shopping centre.	S			x		All

continued on following page

Table 4. Continued

Description	SWOT	Methodologies/Tools Used				Priority Groups
		Digital Cartography	Questionnaire	G. Focal Points and Walks	Field Work	
SPACES OF COEXISTENCE FOR ALL: Zuberoa square, in front of Iparralde Community Centre, attracts a lot of people during the week in good weather. It is one of the vital nodes of Zaramaga.	S			x	x	All
EQUIPPED PARKS: The healthy psychomotricity park in the centre of the neighbourhood, located in the Plaza de Llodio, is highly valued.	S			x		Older adults
EQUIPPED PARKS: The murals on the walls and façades of buildings are elements of neighbourhood identity and help to identify places in the neighbourhood.	S			x	x	All
PHYSICAL VENUES: Most of the population uses the basic facilities of the neighbourhood (health, social support, sport, culture, education, etc.)	S		x	x	x	All
UNWANTED LONELINESS: Most of the population has relatives, friends or acquaintances in the neighbourhood.	S		x			All
UNWANTED LONELINESS: There are many small sites, little parks, cosy places that invite you to meet and talk.	S			x	x	All
FACILITIES AND EQUIPMENT: The area has important facilities such as a school, sports areas, a centre for older adults (BIZAN) and Iparralde Community Centre	S	x		x	x	All
SPACES OF COEXISTENCE FOR ALL: At weekends, the attraction is in the sports venues and shopping centres. The Boulevard fills up on Saturdays with young people from all over Vitoria.	O			x		Young people
UNWANTED LONELINESS: Pets are elements of coexistence and indicators of the loneliness index.	O			x		All

Source: compiled by the authors.

CONCLUSION

An Integral Urban Health Plan is proposed for Euskadi´s vulnerable neighbourhoods with specific proposals related to the three lines of action established in the research methodology. The main conclusions of the proposed Action Plan are the following.

First, it is a comprehensive Plan focused and proposed for people and from people. This change of vision, from buildings (presented in the first neighbourhood rehabilitation actions of the 1960s) to regeneration with new social and economic measures, now moves from an internal vision based on the well-being of people through prevention and the promotion of more active lifestyles of the residents of the neighbourhoods.

Despite the existence of major chronic diseases in urban areas, they can be summarised in the urban lifestyles of sedentary lifestyles and individualism that have an impact on the physical and mental illnesses of urban residents. In this sense, by planning and redesigning public and green spaces in neighbourhoods, it is possible to reverse these deficiencies. Thanks to a design that encourages active mobility for daily activities, an increase in nearby green areas and the provision of spaces for coexistence. It has been observed that these three complementary lines of action will help in prevention and people's health. This is important to note, as changing the urban conditions of the locality is almost never enough. In other words, urban conditions can make healthy living impossible or possible, and the aim is to ensure that they are not an impediment to achieving this. But once this objective has been achieved, it will be necessary to implement complementary measures that contribute to changing the way of life of the inhabitants. Generally, the problem arises because the objectives of urban planning and design rarely include health.

Once again, the importance of active, informed participation of the residents of the residential neighbourhoods has become evident. Through new dynamic recording and monitoring devices, it is possible not only to expand the form of the evidence but also to classify, sort and prioritise it according to different criteria. These tools are sophisticated and require powerful platforms, but it is also true that many localities already have geo-referenced planning systems, where the health vector can be a new transversal axis of great interest for both planners and residents.

The importance of the multidisciplinary approach in the regeneration of vulnerable neighbourhoods is important, as it involves planners, architects, environmentalists, sociologists, economists, lawyers and managers. If, in addition to all of these, the objective of preventing and promoting healthy neighbourhoods is inserted into this, the interaction with doctors, physiotherapists, psychologists, epidemiologists and allergists is added to the above, which is a great challenge in the integration of tools. In this sense, thanks to the visualisation and data recording platforms, an efficient and transversal way has been found that is well understood by all the disciplines involved.

The research has fulfilled the objectives of the work, as it has listed the main diseases derived from the urban environment regarding the chronic diseases of people; it has made a diagnosis in health, from the three strategic lines in which the healthy neighbourhoods are taken into account, and finally has established a necessary interface in accordance with the complementary actions to promote a more active life in the neighbourhoods and prevent the risk of disease by controlling air, noise and water pollution, incorporating green areas and new active spaces for intergenerational coexistence.

However, limitations have also been seen in the need to have open data platforms in the localities, to have teams of planners and doctors in preventive disease together with a clear political leadership that wants to take the risk of committing to integrated actions, and above all the need to have networks of neighbourhood associations that are committed, active, responsible and excited about their neighbourhood and with proposals and improvements that could be made now from the local administration, but that should be managed and maintained by the neighbours. Creating the virtuous circle of having actions and proposals demanded by them, which motivate them, involve them and are active and shared by a wide range of collectives.

Thanks to the dynamic tools, it will be possible to check the opportunity of the proposed actions and rectify those in which the necessary level of social satisfaction has not been reached by all. This first Pilot Plan will be a reference and replica of others that could be carried out in other vulnerable neighbourhoods in Euskadi, firstly, and then in other residential areas.

Health is a social construct; it is a universal desire, and it is necessary for neighbourhood regeneration to support these new methodologies focused on people's well-being; healthy people in healthier environments.

In this way, the triple objective of improving urban environmental conditions that cause a series of diseases in people is achieved; a new way of approaching the habitability of urban public spaces is established from thermal and acoustic comfort mainly for the resident population and, finally, a framework for an active, healthy lifestyle will be established, from the proposal of the network of intergenerational activities that will be organised in the neighbourhoods, as spaces of new social relationship.

The health-based characterisation of residential neighbourhoods has emerged as an extraordinary new strategy to address a new regeneration of residential neighbourhoods by addressing the intrinsic and extrinsic needs of their residents.

ACKNOWLEDGMENT

We would like to thank the Basque Government for their support in conducting the work, as well as the company ESRI-Spain for the development of technological tools and the consultancy Gea21-Grupo de Estudios y Alternativas, for their work and dedication in the participatory processes carried out. Also, the local agents, technicians, and workers of the offices of proximity, Iparralde Community Centre, senior citizens' centres (BIZAN Zaramaga), health centres, etc., as well as the residents of the neighbourhoods studied.

REFERENCES

Aguado, A. (2018). Desarrolo sostenible: 30 años de evolución desde el informe Brundtland. *Ciencia y Sociedad*, *19*(1), 27–37.

Ali, U., Shamsi, M. H., Hoare, C., Mangina, E., & O'Donnell, J. (2021). Review of urban building energy modeling (UBEM) approaches, methods and tools using qualitative and quantitative analysis. *Energy and Building*, *246*, 111073. doi:10.1016/j.enbuild.2021.111073

Álvarez Mora, A., & Camerin, F. (2019). La herencia del 'urban renewal' en los procesos actuales de regeneración urbanael recorrido Renovación-Regeneración a debate. *Ciudad y Territorio: Estudios Territoriales*, *199*, 5–26.

Aram, F., Higueras García, E., Solgi, E., & Mansournia, S. (2019). Urban green space cooling effect in cities. *Heliyon*, *5*(4), e01339. doi:10.1016/j.heliyon.2019.e01339 PMID:31008380

Arocha Rodulfo, J. I. (2019). Sedentarismo, la enfermedad del siglo xxi. *Clínica e Investigación en Arteriosclerosis*, *31*(5), 233–240. doi:10.1016/j.arteri.2019.04.004 PMID:31221536

Bailey, N. (2012). The role, organisation and contribution of community enterprise to urban regeneration policy in the UK. *Progress in Planning*, *77*(1), 1–35. doi:10.1016/j.progress.2011.11.001

Barton, H., & Grant, M. (2006). A health map for the local human habitat. *The Journal of the Royal Society for the Promotion of Health*, *126*(6), 252–253. doi:10.1177/1466424006070466 PMID:17152313

Cerezo Ibarrondo, Á. (2019). *La actuación de regeneración y renovación (aMU-RR) : Nueva forma de equidistribución y gestión en suelo urbanizado en los desarrollos urbanos de los años 60 y 70 del País Vasco*. Universidad Politécnica de Madrid. doi:10.20868/UPM.thesis.58338

Córdoba Hernández, R. (2021). La vulnerabilidad ecosistémica según el planeamiento en la protección del suelo de la Comunidad de Madrid. *Urbano*, *24*(43), 18–29. doi:10.22320/07183607.2021.24.43.02

Córdoba Hernández, R. (2022). Resiliencia territorial desde la perspectiva de la vulnerabilidad ecosistémica. Aplicación metodológica al planeamiento urbanístico de la Comunidad de Madrid. *Ciudades*, *25*(25), 181–200. doi:10.24197/ciudades.25.2022.181-200

Córdoba Hernández, R., & Martí Guitera, L. (2022). Ecosystem vulnerability due to urban growth policies. The role of regulatory ecosystem contributions in the land use planning. *SUPTM 2022: 1st Conference on Future Challenges in Sustainable Urban Planning & Territorial Management*, 4. 10.31428/10317/10599

Corraliza, J. A., & Collado, S. (2011). La naturaleza cercana como moderadora del estrés infantil. *Psicothema*, *23*(2), 221–226. PMID:21504673

Couch, C., Sykes, O., & Börstinghaus, W. (2011). Thirty years of urban regeneration in Britain, Germany and France: The importance of context and path dependency. *Progress in Planning*, *75*(1), 1–52. doi:10.1016/j.progress.2010.12.001

Creswell, J. W. (2014). *Qualitative and quantitative and mixed Methods approaches* (4th ed.). University of Nebraska-Lincoln.

de Gregorio Hurtado, S. (2015). Políticas urbanas de la Unión Europea desde la perspectiva de la planificación colaborativa: Las iniciativas comunitarias URBAN y URBAN II en España. *Cuadernos de Investigación Urbanística, 98*, 6–67. https://dialnet.unirioja.es/servlet/articulo?codigo=5217787&info=resumen&idioma=ENG

de la Puerta Rueda, I. (2018). El reto de la Regeneración Urbana Integral en barrios vulnerables. *Planur-E, 12*. https://www.planur-e.es/articulos/ver/el-reto-de-la-regeneraci-n-urbana-integral-en-barrios-vulnerables

Dumbaugh, E., & Rae, R. (2009). Safe urban form: Revisiting the relationship between community design and traffic safety. *Journal of the American Planning Association*, *75*(3), 309–329. doi:10.1080/01944360902950349

Edwardson, C. L., Gorely, T., Davies, M. J., Gray, L. J., Khunti, K., Wilmot, E. G., Yates, T., & Biddle, S. J. H. (2012). Association of Sedentary Behaviour with Metabolic Syndrome: A Meta-Analysis. *PLoS One*, *7*(4), e34916. doi:10.1371/journal.pone.0034916 PMID:22514690

Engel-Cox, J. A., Holloman, C. H., Coutant, B. W., & Hoff, R. M. (2004). Qualitative and quantitative evaluation of MODIS satellite sensor data for regional and urban scale air quality. *Atmospheric Environment*, *38*(16), 2495–2509. doi:10.1016/j.atmosenv.2004.01.039

Fariña Tojo, J., Higueras García, E., Román López, M. E., & Pozo Méndez, E. (2022). *Guía para planificar ciudades saludables*. https://www.sanidad.gob.es/profesionales/saludPublica/prevPromocion/Estrategia/docs/Guia_Planificar_Ciudades_Saludables.pdf

Forni, P., & de Grande, P. (2020). Triangulation and mixed methods in contemporary social sciences. *Revista Mexicana de Sociologia*, *82*(1), 159–189.

García-González, M. C., Higueras García, E., Gallego Gamazo, C., Pozo Menéndez, E., & Román López, E. (2022). Prevención en salud desde el diseño del espacio público. El proyecto URB_HealthS como experiencia de transferencia de conocimiento. *Ciudades*, *25*(25), 59–78. doi:10.24197/ciudades.25.2022.59-78

Goodland, R. (1997). *Medio ambiente y desarrollo sostenible: más allá del informe Brundtland*. https://dialnet.unirioja.es/servlet/libro?codigo=1253

Grijalba Aseguinolaza, O. (2017). *La regeneración urbana en la CAPV. Divergencias entre el discurso y la realidad*. Universidad del País Vasco. http://hdl.handle.net/10810/26891%09

Haase, D., Larondelle, N., Andersson, E., Artmann, M., Borgström, S., Breuste, J., Gomez-Baggethun, E., Gren, Å., Hamstead, Z., Hansen, R., Kabisch, N., Kremer, P., Langemeyer, J., Rall, E. L., McPhearson, T., Pauleit, S., Qureshi, S., Schwarz, N., Voigt, A., . . . Elmqvist, T. (2014). A quantitative review of urban ecosystem service assessments: Concepts, models, and implementation. In Ambio (Vol. 43, Issue 4, pp. 413–433). doi:10.100713280-014-0504-0

Higueras García, E. (2006). *Urbanismo Bioclimático*. Gustavo Gili Editorial.

Higueras García, E. (2015). Barrios saludables. *Cuadernos de Investigación Urbanística*, *100*(100). Advance online publication. doi:10.20868/ciur.2015.100.3164

Higueras García, E., Román López, M. E., & Fariña Tojo, J. (2021). Guidelines for Healthier Public Spaces for the Elderly Population: Recommendations in the Spanish Context. In Javier Martinez, Claudia Andrea Mikkelsen, & R. Phillips (Eds.), Handbook of Quality of Life and Sustainability (pp. 35–51). Handbook of Quality of Life and Sustainability. doi:10.1007/978-3-030-50540-0_3

Kirdar, I. U. (1997). Tourism market segmentation for national tourism organisations and its practical importance for national tourism offices abroad [University of Surrey (United Kingdom)]. *PQDT - UK & Ireland*. https://www.proquest.com/dissertations-theses/tourism-market-segmentation-national/docview/301513276/se-2?accountid=159111

Kjellstrom, T., & Mercado, S. (2008). Towards action on social determinants for health equity in urban settings. *Environment and Urbanization*, *20*(2), 551–574. doi:10.1177/0956247808096128

Land Use Consultants, H. U. D. U. (2007). *Delivering Healthier Communities in London*. https://www.healthyurbandevelopment.nhs.uk/wp-content/uploads/2013/03/HUDU_Delivering_Healthier_Communities.pdf

Liberati, A., Altman, D. G., Tetzlaff, J., Mulrow, C., Gøtzsche, P. C., Ioannidis, J. P. A., Clarke, M., Devereaux, P. J., Kleijnen, J., & Moher, D. (2009). The PRISMA Statement for Reporting Systematic Reviews and Meta-Analyses of Studies That Evaluate Health Care Interventions: Explanation and Elaboration. *PLoS Medicine*, *6*(7), e1000100. doi:10.1371/journal.pmed.1000100 PMID:19621070

Lombardi, D. R., Porter, L., Barber, A., & Rogers, C. D. F. (2011). Conceptualising Sustainability in UK Urban Regeneration: A Discursive Formation. *Urban Studies (Edinburgh, Scotland)*, *48*(2), 273–296. doi:10.1177/0042098009360690

Louv, R. (2010). *Last child in the woods. Saving our children from nature-deficit disorder*. Atlantic B.

Lwin, K. K., Murayama, Y., & Mizutani, C. (2012). Quantitative versus Qualitative Geospatial Data in Spatial Modelling and Decision Making. *Journal of Geographic Information System*, *04*(03), 237–241. doi:10.4236/jgis.2012.43028

Naciones Unidas. (1987). *Report of the World Commission on Environment and Development: Our Common Future*. Oxford University Press.

Naciones Unidas. (2015). *Objetivos de Desarrollo Sostenible*. Author.

Naciones Unidas. (2017). *Nueva Agenda Urbana*. https://habitat3.org/wp-content/uploads/NUA-Spanish.pdf

Ouzir, M., Khalfallah, B., Dehimi, S., & Kadi Ahmed, A. (2021). Quantitative and qualitative assessment of urban green spaces in Boussaada City, Algeria using remote sensing techniques. *Journal of Geography and Regional Planning*, *14*(3), 123–133. doi:10.5897/JGRP2021.0831

Potchter, O., Cohen, P., Lin, T.-P., & Matzarakis, A. (2022). A systematic review advocating a framework and benchmarks for assessing outdoor human thermal perception. *The Science of the Total Environment*, *833*, 155128. doi:10.1016/j.scitotenv.2022.155128 PMID:35405233

Román López, E., Córdoba Hernández, R., & Eiroa Escalada, T. (2022). Thermal Comfort for Older Population in Spain: Diagnosis and Strategies for a Climate Change Scenario. In E. Pozo Méndez & E. Higueras García (Eds.), *Urban Design and Planning for Age-Friendly Environments Across Europe: North and South* (pp. 243–265). Springer. doi:10.1007/978-3-030-93875-8_12

Rueda Martínez de Santos, J. R. (2005). *Guía para la evaluación del impacto en la salud y en el bienestar de proyectos, programas o políticas extrasanitarias. Investigación Comisionada. Informe nº: Osteba D-05-04*. Servicio Central de Publicaciones del Gobierno Vasco.

Ruiz Palomeque, L. G. (2018). *Una Propuesta Metodológica para la Gestión Integral de la Rehabilitación Urbana*. Universidad Politécnica de Madrid. https://oa.upm.es/62657/

Sallis, J. F., Owen, N., & Fisher, E. B. (2008). Ecological models of health behavior. In K. Glanz, B. K. Rimer, & K. Viswanath (Eds.), *Health behavior and health education: Theory, research, and practice* (pp. 465–485). Jossey-Bass.

Sartorius, N. (2006). The Meanings of Health and its Promotion. *Croatian Medical Journal*, *47*(4), 662–664. PMID:16909464

Shanahan, D. F., Lin, B. B., Bush, R., Gaston, K. J., Dean, J. H., Barber, E., & Fuller, R. A. (2015). Toward Improved Public Health Outcomes From Urban Nature. *American Journal of Public Health*, *105*(3), 470–477. doi:10.2105/AJPH.2014.302324 PMID:25602866

Sukopp, H., & Werner, P. (1991). *Naturaleza en las ciudades*. Ministerio.

Ulrich, R. S. (1983). Aesthetic and Affective Response to Natural Environment. In I. Altman & J. F. Wohlwill (Eds.), *Behavior and the Natural Environment* (pp. 85–125). Springer US. doi:10.1007/978-1-4613-3539-9_4

Vakulabharanam, V., & Motiram, S. (2012). Understanding Poverty and Inequality in Urban India since Reforms: Bringing Quantitative and Qualitative Approaches Together. *Economic and Political Weekly, 47*(47/48), 44–52. https://www.jstor.org/stable/41720409

WHO. (1999). *Health for All in the 21st Century. The Health for All Policy Framework for the WHO European Region*. World Health Organisation.

Wilson, O. E. (1984). *Biophilia*. Harvard University Press.

Woodcock, J., Banister, D., Edwards, P., Prentice, A. M., & Roberts, I. (2007). Energy and transport. *Lancet, 370*(9592), 1078–1088. doi:10.1016/S0140-6736(07)61254-9 PMID:17868817

World Health Organization. (1946). *Preámbulo de la Constitución de la Organización Mundial de la Salud adoptado por la Conferencia Internacional de Salud*. https://www.who.int/suggestions/faq/en/

Zhang, L., Tan, P. Y., & Richards, D. (2021). Relative importance of quantitative and qualitative aspects of urban green spaces in promoting health. *Landscape and Urban Planning, 213*, 104131. doi:10.1016/j.landurbplan.2021.104131

ENDNOTES

1. More information at: https://www.sanidad.gob.es/profesionales/saludPublica/prevPromocion/Estrategia/docs/Guia_Planificar_Ciudades_Saludables.pdf
2. Reference geoportal of the Spatial Data Infrastructure of Euskadi, which aims to guarantee easy and efficient access to the geographic information of the Autonomous Community of Euskadi. More information at: https://www.geo.euskadi.eus/inicio/
3. https://www.geo.euskadi.eus/geobisoreaç
4. GeoEuskadi data consulted in 2022.
5. Source: Vitoria-Gasteiz City Council
6. Safety with regards to crime, traffic, and accidents.
7. Some accessibility problems are related to steep streets, narrow pavements, presence of stairs and tripping hazards, pavements in poor condition, etc.
8. Parks, gardens, tree-lined roads, etc.
9. For example, the park has playground equipment for children, exercise equipment for young people, adults and older adults, circuits, etc.
10. For example, uses such as: leisure, meetings, games, physical activity, learning, etc. for all age groups.
11. There are benches, toilets, fountains, shaded areas, picnic areas, trees, vegetation, adequate lighting, they are well maintained, clean, etc.

Compilation of References

Abbas, M., Gao, Y., & Sayyed Sadaqat Hussain, S. (2018). CSR and Customer Outcomes: The Mediating Role of Customer Engagement. *Sustainability*, *10*(11), 4243. doi:10.3390u10114243

Abd-Alhamid, F., Kent, M., Bennett, C., Calautit, J., & Wu, Y. (2019). Developing an innovative method for visual perception evaluation in a physical-based virtual environment. *Building and Environment*, *162*, 106278. doi:10.1016/j.buildenv.2019.106278

Abrahamse, W., Steg, L., Vlek, C., & Rothengatter, T. (2005). A review of Intervention Studies aimed at household energy conservation. *Journal of Environmental Psychology*, *25*(3), 273–291. doi:10.1016/j.jenvp.2005.08.002

Acharya, P., & Aithal, P. S. (2020). A Comparative Study of MPPT and PWM Solar Charge Controllers and their Integrated System. *Journal of Physics: Conference Series*, *1712*(1), 012023. doi:10.1088/1742-6596/1712/1/012023

Acosta, I. J., & Campano, M. l Á., Domínguez Amarillo, S., Fernández-Agüera, J.(2019) Minimum Daylight Autonomy: A New Concept to Link Daylight Dynamic Metrics with Daylight Factors. En: LEUKOS - Journal of Illuminating Engineering Society of North America.

Active City Hamburg. (n.d.). *Active City Hamburg*. Active City Hamburg. https://activecity.hamburg.de/

Active Well-being Initiative. (2017). *The 2017 Active Well-being Initiative White Paper on urbanisation, non-communicable diseases and the potential for cities to enhance the individual and collective well-being of their population.* Active Well-being Initiative. http://activewellbeing.org/wp-content/uploads/2017/09/AWI-White-Paper-2017.pdf

Adams, D., Novak, A., Kliestik, T., & Potcovaru, A.-M. (2021). Sensor-based Big Data Applications and Environmentally Sustainable Urban Development in Internet of Things-enabled Smart Cities. *Geopolitics, History, and International Relations*, *13*, 108.

Adams, T. (2016). *Sound Materials: a compendium of Sound Absorbing Materials for Architecture and Design.* Frame Publishers.

Adeniji, A. A., & Mash, B. (2016). Patients' perceptions of the triage system in a primary healthcare facility, Cape Town, South Africa. *African Journal of Primary Health Care & Family Medicine*, *8*(1), e1–e9. doi:10.4102/phcfm.v8i1.1148 PMID:27380788

ADEPT. (2019). *Oberbillwerder*. ADEPT. https://www.adept.dk/project/oberbillwerder-the-connected-city

Afiq, W., Che Sidik, N. A., & Saqr, K. (2012). Effects of buildings aspect ratio, wind speed and wind direction on flow structure and pollutant dispersion in symmetric street canyons: A review. *International Journal of Mechanical and Materials Engineering*, *7*, 158–165.

Aguado, A. (2018). Desarrolo sostenible: 30 años de evolución desde el informe Brundtland. *Ciencia y Sociedad*, *19*(1), 27–37.

Aguilera, A. V. (2015). El bosque en la ciudad: La invención del urbanismo moderno en la Ciudad de México (1870-1930). Amérique Latine Histoire et Mémoire. Les Cahiers ALHIM. *Les Cahiers ALHIM*, *29*(29), 29. Advance online publication. doi:10.4000/alhim.5237

AHKGA. (2018). *Australia active healthy kids global alliance*. Active Healthy Kids Global Alliance. Retrieved November 30, 2022, from https://www.activehealthykids.org/australia/

Ahmad, K., & Zabri, S. M. (2016). The Effect of Non-financial Performance Measurement System on Firm Performance. *International Journal of Economics and Financial Issues*, *6*(6S), 50–54.

Alam, S. M., & Islam, K. M. (2021). Examining the role of Environmental Corporate Social Responsibility in building Green Corporate Image and green competitive advantage. *International Journal of Corporate Social Responsibility*, *6*(1), 8. Advance online publication. doi:10.118640991-021-00062-w

Alanoğlu, M., & Demirtaş, Z. (2016). The Relationships between Organizational Learning Level, School Effectiveness and Organizational Citizenship Behavior. *Journal of Education and Training Studies*, *4*(4), 35–44. doi:10.11114/jets.v4i4.1262

Alavi, M., & Leidner, D. E. (2001). Review: Knowledge management and knowledge management systems. *Management Information Systems Quarterly*, *25*(1), 107–136. doi:10.2307/3250961

Albarracin, R., Eells, J., & Valter, K. (2011). Photobiomodulation protects the retina from light-induced photoreceptor degeneration. *Investigative Ophthalmology & Visual Science*, *52*(6), 3582–3592. doi:10.1167/iovs.10-6664 PMID:21421867

Aldrich, H., & Auster, E. R. (1986). Even dwarfs started small: Liabilities of age and size and their strategic implications. In B. M. Staw & L. L. Cummings (Eds.), *Research in Organizational Behavior* (Vol. 8, pp. 165–198). JAI Press.

Ali Toudert, F., & Mayer, H. (2006). *Effects of Street Design on Outdoor Thermal Comfort*.

Alías, F., & Alsina-Pagès, R. (2019). Ma. (2019). Review of Wireless Acoustic Sensor Networks for Environmental Noise Monitoring in Smart Cities. *Journal of Sensors*, *2019*, 1–13. doi:10.1155/2019/7634860

Ali, S. H., Al-Sultan, H. A., & al Rubaie, M. T. (2022). Fifth Industrial Revolution. International Journal of Business. *Management and Economics*, *3*(3), 196–212. doi:10.47747/ijbme.v3i3.694

Ali, U., Shamsi, M. H., Hoare, C., Mangina, E., & O'Donnell, J. (2021). Review of urban building energy modeling (UBEM) approaches, methods and tools using qualitative and quantitative analysis. *Energy and Building*, *246*, 111073. doi:10.1016/j.enbuild.2021.111073

Allam, Z., Moreno, C., Chabaud, D., & Pratlong, F. (2022). Proximity-Based Planning and the "15-Minute City": A Sustainable Model for the City of the Future. In *The Palgrave Handbook of Global Sustainability* (pp. 1–20). Springer International Publishing. doi:10.1007/978-3-030-38948-2_178-1

Alland, A. (1966). Jr. Medical Anthropology and the Study of Biological and Cultural Adaptation. *American Anthropologist*, *68*, 40–51. doi:10.1525/aa.1966.68.1.02a00040

Allwinkle, S., & Cruickshank, P. (2011). Creating Smart-er Cities: An Overview. *Journal of Urban Technology*, *18*(2), 1–16. doi:10.1080/10630732.2011.601103

AlMarshedi, A., Wanick, V., Wills, G. B., & Ranchhod, A. (2016). Gamification and behaviour. *Progress in IS*, 19–29. doi:10.1007/978-3-319-45557-0_2

Almasifar, N., Canbolat, T. Ö., Akhavan, M., & González-Lezcano, R. A. (2021, December 1). Proposing a new methodology for monument conservation "scope management" by the use of an analytic hierarchy process project management institute system and the ico-mos burra charter. *Sustainability (Switzerland)*. doi:10.3390/su132313174

Alonso, L., Gálvez, L., & de Luxán, S. (2006). Tabaco e Historia Económica. Estudios sobre fiscalidad, consumo y empresa (siglos XVII-XX), Fundación Altadis, Los libros de Altadis, nº 7, Madrid.

Álvarez Mora, A., & Camerin, F. (2019). La herencia del 'urban renewal' en los procesos actuales de regeneración urbanael recorrido Renovación-Regeneración a debate. *Ciudad y Territorio: Estudios Territoriales*, *199*, 5–26.

Alves-Pereira, M., & Castelo Branco, N. A. A. (2007). Vibroacoustic disease: Biological effects of infrasound and low-frequency noise explained by mechanotransduction cellular signalling. *Progress in Biophysics and Molecular Biology*, *93*(1–3), 256–279. doi:10.1016/j.pbiomolbio.2006.07.011 PMID:17014895

Amburgey, T., & Rao, H. (1996). Organizational ecology: Past, present, and future directions. *Academy of Management Journal*, *39*(5), 1265–1286. doi:10.2307/256999

Amirkhani, M., Garcia-Hansen, V., Isoardi, G., & Allan, A. (2018). Innovative window design strategy to reduce negative lighting interventions in office buildings. *Energy and Building*, *179*, 253–263. doi:10.1016/j.enbuild.2018.09.006

Amore, M. D., & Bennedsen, M. (2016). Corporate governance and green innovation. *Journal of Environmental Economics and Management*, *75*, 54–72. doi:10.1016/j.jeem.2015.11.003

Anderson, T. J., Saman, D. M., Lipsky, M. S., & Lutfiyya, M. N. (2015). A cross-sectional study on health differences between rural and non-rural U.S. counties using the County Health Rankings. *BMC Health Services Research*, *15*(1), 441. doi:10.118612913-015-1053-3 PMID:26423746

Andrade, C., & Contente, J. (2020). Köppen's climate classification projections for the Iberian Peninsula. *Climate Research*, *81*, 71–89. doi:10.3354/cr01604

Andre de la, P. (2016). Spirituality and healthcare: Towards holistic people-centred healthcare in South Africa. *Hervormde Teologiese Studies*, *72*(4), e1–e9.

Andreou, E. (2014). The effect of urban layout, street geometry and orientation on shading conditions in urban canyons in the Mediterranean. *Renewable Energy*, *63*, 587–596. doi:10.1016/j.renene.2013.09.051

Antin, J., & Churchill, E. F. (2011). Badges in social media: A social psychological perspective. *Paper presented at the CHI 2011*, Vancouver.

Antonioli, D., Mancinelli, S., & Mazzanti, M. (2013). Is environmental innovation embedded within high- performance organizational changes? The role of human resource management and complementarity in green business strategies. *Research Policy*, *42*(4), 975–988. doi:10.1016/j.respol.2012.12.005

Aram, F., Higueras García, E., Solgi, E., & Mansournia, S. (2019). Urban green space cooling effect in cities. *Heliyon*, *5*(4), e01339. doi:10.1016/j.heliyon.2019.e01339 PMID:31008380

Architectural Association School of Architecture Public Programme. (2022). AA School. https://www.aaschool.ac.uk/publicprogramme/whatson/so-farpractice-in-times-of-climate-crisis

Arendt, R. (1999). *Growing greener: putting conservation into local plans and ordinances*. Island Press.

Arkhangelskaya, I. V. (2017). The Principles Shaped The Perception Of Objects Of Industrial Heritage In Urban Space. *Vestnik Tomskogo Gosudarstvennogo Universiteta. Kul'turologiya i Iskusstvovedenie*, (26), 126–130. doi:10.17223/22220836/26/13

Armstrong, C. G., Shoemaker, A. C., McKechnie, I., Ekblom, A., Szabó, P., Lane, P. J., McAlvay, A. C., Boles, O. J., Walshaw, S., Petek, N., Gibbons, K. S., Quintana Morales, E., Anderson, E. N., Ibragimow, A., Podruczny, G., Vamosi, J. C., Marks-Block, T., LeCompte, J. K., Awâsis, S., & Crumley, C. L. (2017). Anthropological contributions to historical ecology: 50 questions, infinite prospects. *PLoS One*, *12*(2), e0171883. doi:10.1371/journal.pone.0171883 PMID:28235093

Arocha Rodulfo, J. I. (2019). Sedentarismo, la enfermedad del siglo xxi. *Clínica e Investigación en Arteriosclerosis*, *31*(5), 233–240. doi:10.1016/j.arteri.2019.04.004 PMID:31221536

Astolfi, A., Puglisi, G., Murgia, S., Minelli, G., Pellerey, F., Prato, A., & Sacco, T. (2019). Influence of Classroom Acoustics on Noise Disturbance and Well-Being for First Graders. *Frontier in psychology*. doi:10.3389/fpsyg.2019.02736

Ataguba, J. E., Day, C., & McIntyre, D. (2014). Monitoring and evaluating progress towards Universal Health Coverage in South Africa. *PLoS Medicine*, *11*(9), e1001686. doi:10.1371/journal.pmed.1001686 PMID:25243462

Atuahene-Gima, K. (2005). Resolving the capability: Rigidity paradox in new product innovation. *Journal of Marketing*, *69*(4), 61–83. doi:10.1509/jmkg.2005.69.4.61

Atuoye, K. N., Dixon, J., Rishworth, A., Galaa, S. Z., Boamah, S. A., & Luginaah, I. (2015). Can she make it? Transportation barriers to accessing maternal and child health care services in rural Ghana. *BMC Health Services Research*, *15*(1), 333. doi:10.118612913-015-1005-y PMID:26290436

Atwa, S. M. H., Ibrahim, M. G., Saleh, A. M., & Murata, R. (2019). Development of sustainable landscape design guidelines for a green business park using virtual reality. *Sustainable Cities and Society*, *48*, 101543. doi:10.1016/j.scs.2019.101543

Atz, U., Van Holt, T., & Douglas & Tensie, E. (2022). The Return on Sustainability Investment (ROSI): Monetizing Financial Benefits of Sustainability Actions in Companies. In *Sustainable Consumption and Production Volume II -Circular economy and beyond* (pp 303–354). Ranjula Bali Swain, Susanne Sweet.

Audrey, S., & Batista-Ferrer, H. (2015). Healthy urban environments for children and young people: A systematic review of intervention studies. *Health & Place*, *36*, 97–117. doi:10.1016/j.healthplace.2015.09.004 PMID:26457624

Awad Parada, T. (2015). *Arquitectura industrial tabacalera en la España peninsular: secaderos y fábricas*. [Tesis Doctoral, E.T.S. Arquitectura (UPM)]. doi:10.20868/UPM.thesis.38794

Awad Parada, T. (2015). *Arquitectura industrial tabacalera española: secaderos y fábricas*.

Awad Parada, T. (2017). *Celosías de ladrillo en los Secaderos de tabaco*

Awad Parada, T. (2021). *Permeability in bioclimatic modular facades Spanish sheds*.

Awad Parada, T. (2013). *Patrones y permeabilidad en los secaderos cacereños*. Accesit.

Awad T, Guardiola J. and Fraíz D. (2021). *Sustainable Construction: Improving Productivity through Lean Construction*.

Ayres, I., Raseman, S., & Shih, A. (2009). *Evidence from two large field experiments that peer comparison feedback can reduce residential energy usage*. NBER. doi:10.3386/w15386

Aytekin, A. (2018). Using hybrid method in selecting timber factory location. *Drvna Industrija*, *69*(3), 273–281. doi:10.5552/drind.2018.1736

Babu, K. M. C., & Vardhini, P. A. H. (2020). Brain Computer Interface based Arduino Home Automation System for Physically Challenged. *2020 3rd International Conference on Intelligent Sustainable Systems (ICISS)*, (pp. 125–130). IEEE.

Baeza Moyano, D., & González Lezcano, R. A. (2021). *Indor LED luminarie emittering the full visible spectrum of light* (Patent No. ES1274209U).

Baeza Moyano, D., & González Lezcano, R. A. (2021). *The Importance of Light in Our Lives.*, doi:10.4018/978-1-7998-7023-4.ch011

Baeza Moyano, D., & González Lezcano, R. A. (2022). Effects of infrasound on health: Looking for improvements in housing conditions. *International Journal of Occupational Safety and Ergonomics*, *28*(2), 809–823. doi:10.1080/10803548.2020.1831787 PMID:33019907

Baeza-Moyano, D., Arranz-Paraíso, D., Sola, Y., & González-Lezcano, R. A. (2022). Suitability of blue light filters for eye care. *The European Physical Journal Plus*, *137*(7), 817. doi:10.1140/epjp13360-022-03045-3

Bahgat, R., Reffat, R. M., & Elkady, S. L. (2019). Energy Efficiency Design Guide for Optimal Urban Features of Open Spaces in Residential Complexes. *The Academic Research Community Publication*, *3*(1), 136–152. doi:10.21625/archive.v3i1.436

Bai, J., Lu, J., & Lu, S. (2019). The influence of capital market distortion on environmental pollution: Based on the analysis of provincial spatial dynamic panel data. *J Nanjing Audit Univ*, *16*(1), 37–47.

Bailey, N. (2012). The role, organisation and contribution of community enterprise to urban regeneration policy in the UK. *Progress in Planning*, *77*(1), 1–35. doi:10.1016/j.progress.2011.11.001

Baines, T., Brown, S., Benedettini, O., & Ball, P. (2012). Examining green production and its role within the competitive strategy of manufacturers. *Journal of Industrial Engineering and Management*, *5*(1), 53–87. doi:10.3926/jiem.405

Bai, Y., Song, S., Jiao, J., & Yang, R. (2019). The impacts of government R&D subsidies on green innovation: Evidence from Chinese energy-intensive firms. *Journal of Cleaner Production*, *233*, 819–829. doi:10.1016/j.jclepro.2019.06.107

Balaguera, A., Carvajal, G. I., Albertí, J., & Fullana-i-Palmer, P. (2018). Life cycle assessment of road construction alternative materials: A literature review. *Resources, Conservation and Recycling*, *132*, 37–48. doi:10.1016/j.resconrec.2018.01.003

Ballim, F. (2017). The Un-making of the Group Areas Act: Local Resistance and Commercial Power in the Small Town of Mokopane. *South African Historical Journal*, *69*(4), 568–582. doi:10.1080/02582473.2017.1377760

Bamidis, P. D., Gabarron, E., Hors-Fraile, S., Konstantinidis, E., Konstantinidis, S., & Rivera, O. (2016). Gamification and behavioral change. *Participatory Health Through Social Media*, 112–135. doi:10.1016/B978-0-12-809269-9.00007-4

Banton, C., Potters, C., & Kvilhaug, S. (2022, 09 13). *Investopedia*. (D. Meredith, Editor) Investiopedia. https://www.investopedia.com/terms/r/rawmaterials.asp

Baraya, S. (2022). *Adobe: el material reciclable más sostenible.* Archdaily. Available at: https://www.archdaily.cl/cl/944575/adobe-el-material-reciclable-mas-sostenible

Barišić Marenić, Z., & Vukojevic, I. (2019). Adaptive reuse of zagreb tobacco factory buildings in the context of contemporary Urban regeneration. *Architektura a Urbanizmus*, *53*(1–2), 103–113.

Barnett, J. (2009). The way we were, the way we are the theory and practice of designing cities since 1956. A. Krieger, W.S. Saunders (Eds.), *Urban design*, University of Minnesota Press (2009), pp. 101-110 NED—New edition Retrieved from: https://www.jstor.org/stable/10.5749/j.ctttspsh.9View Record in ScopusGoogle Scholar

Barnett, J., & Adger, W. N. (2003). Climate dangers and atoll countries. *Climatic Change*, *61*(3), 321–337. doi:10.1023/B:CLIM.0000004559.08755.88

Barney, J. (1991). Firm resources and sustained competitive advantage. Journal of Management, 17(1), 99–120.

Barron, P., Padarath, A., Ranchod, S., Adams, C., Burger, R., Carvounesi, A., Stewart, J., Dreyer, K., Smith, A., & van Biljon, C. (2017). Twenty years of the South African Health Review; South Africa's hospital sector: old divisions and new developments. *Health Systems Trust, Durban.*

Barton, H., & Grant, M. (2006). A health map for the local human habitat. *The Journal of the Royal Society for the Promotion of Health, 126*(6), 252–253. doi:10.1177/1466424006070466 PMID:17152313

Basanta, H., Huang, Y.-P., & Lee, T.-T. (2017). Assistive design for elderly living ambient using voice and gesture recognition system. *2017 IEEE International Conference on Systems, Man, and Cybernetics (SMC)*, (pp. 840–845). IEEE. 10.1109/SMC.2017.8122714

Bastlund, K. (1967). *José Luis Sert: Architecture city planning urban design.* Les Éditions d'Architecture.

Bates, H. (2021). *5 Businesses Using Green Gamification to Save the World.* GivingForce. https://www.givingforce.com/blog/5-businesses-using-green-gamification-to-save-the-world

Bayrak, M., & Çadirci, K.BAYRAK. (2021). Mortal disseminated intravascular coagulopathy and cutaneous involvement in a COVID-19 positive patient; case report. *Anatolian Current Medical Journal, 3*(3), 259–261. doi:10.38053/acmj.930047

Beacher, R. (2018, July). Hamburgo. El Legado sigue vivo. *Olympic Review*, (107), 68–71.

Becker, M. C. (Ed.). (2008). Handbook of organizational routines. Cheltenham, UK: Edward Elgar Publishing Becker, M. C. (Ed.). (2008). Handbook of organizational routines. Cheltenham, UK: Edward Elgar Publishing. doi:10.4337/9781848442702

Beckereit, M., Holstein, C., Unkelbach, I., Mantell, J., & Beine, C. (2016). HAMBURGmachtSPORT: Kommentierung 2016. Eine Dekadenstrategie für den Hamburger Sport erstellt von der "Zukunftskommission Sport." *Hamburger Senat. Freie und Hansestadt Hamburg*. https://www.hamburg.de/contentblob/5924192/7b238ce5fd6ba7fb4487a33aa05eec4d/data/2016-04-29-dl-dekadenstrategie.pdf

Beckereit, M., Holstein, C., Unkelbach, I., Mantell, J., Kodolitsch, K., Troeder, M., & Hellberg, A. (2022). *Hamburger Sportbericht. Im Rahmen der Dekadenstrategie für den Hamburger Sport.* Hamburg: Zukunftskommission Sport. https://www.hamburg.de/contentblob/16314304/d1927b14bd5433d314e13c5c8dbd2023/data/2022-06-30-d-hamburger-sportbericht-2022.pdf

Beckereit, M., Unkelbach, I., Ploß, G., Wolf, R., Beyer, T., & Hinzpeter, C. (2011). HAMBURGmachtSPORT. Eine Dekadenstrategie für den Hamburger Sport ukunftskommission Sport. Hamburg: Der Hamburger Senat. https://www.hamburg.de/contentblob/3115782/3368559d735158cfe3237b3398651d11/data/2011-09-29-bis-bt-zukunftskommission-sport.pdf

Behavior Institute. (n.d.). *Gamification for behavior change - Studies, products, and examples.* Behavior Change Tactic. https://www.besci.org/tactics/gamification

Behörde für Inneres und Sport. Freien und Hansestadt Hamburg. (2016). *Erfahrungsbericht des Landesabstimmungsleiters, der Bezirksabstimmungsleitungen und des Statistischen Amts für Hamburg und Schleswig-Holstein.* Hamburg: Behörde für Inneres und Sport. Freien und Hansestadt Hamburg. https://www.hamburg.de/contentblob/5456574/4798e7c85a74fd64feaed2b03368069f/data/erfahrungsbericht-olympia-referendum-dl.pdf

Behörde für Wissenschaft, Forschung, Gleichstellung und Bezirke. Freie und Hansestadt Hamburg. (2019, August 12). *Fakultät der HAW Hamburg zieht nach Oberbillwerder. Neuer Campus in Bergedorf für die Life Sciences.* Freie und Hansestadt Hamburg. https://www.hamburg.de/pressearchiv-fhh/12787776/haw-hamburg-oberbillwerder/

Bellazzi, A., Bellia, L., Chinazzo, G., Corbisiero, F., D'Agostino, P., Devitofrancesco, A., Fragliasso, F., Ghellere, M., Megale, V., & Salamone, F. (2021). Virtual reality for assessing visual quality and lighting perception: A systematic review. *Building and Environment*, 108674.

Belz, F.-M., & Peattie, K. (2010). Sustainability marketing: An innovative conception of marketing. *Marketing Review St. Gallen*, *27*(5), 8–15. doi:10.100711621-010-0085-7

Benedict, M., & McMahon, E. T. (2006). *Green infrastructure: linking landscape and communities.* Island Press.

Benner, M. J., & Tushman, M. L. (2003). Exploitation, exploration, and process management: The productivity dilemma revisited. *Academy of Management Review*, *28*(2), 238–256. doi:10.2307/30040711

Berkes, F., & Folke, C. (Eds.). (1998). *Linking Social and Ecological Systems: Management Practices and Social Mechanisms for Building Resilience.* Cambridge University Press.

Bernroider, E. (2002). Factors in SWOT analysis applied to micro, small-to-medium, and large software enterprises: An Austrian study. *European Management Journal*, *20*(5), 562–573. doi:10.1016/S0263-2373(02)00095-6

Berry, J. W. (2004). An Ecocultural Perspective on the Development of Competence. In R. Sternberg & E. Grigorenko (Eds.), *Culture and Competence: Contexts of Life Success* (pp. 3–22). American Psychological Association. doi:10.1037/10681-001

Bertalanffy, Ludwig von (1968): Teoría general de los sistemas. (1976). Fondo de Cultura Económica.

Bestraten, S., Hormías, E., & Altermir, A. (2011). Construcción con tierra en el siglo XXI. *Informes de la Construcción*, *63*(523), 5–20. doi:10.3989/ic.10.046

Bharadwaj, A., Shaw, S. B., & Goldreich, D. (2019). Comparing Tactile to Auditory Guidance for Blind Individuals. *Frontiers in Human Neuroscience*, *13*, 443. doi:10.3389/fnhum.2019.00443 PMID:31920601

Bi, K., Huang, P., & Wang, X. (2016). Innovation performance and influencing factors of low-carbon technological innovation under the global value chain: A case of Chinese manufacturing industry. *Technological Forecasting and Social Change*, *111*, 275–284. doi:10.1016/j.techfore.2016.07.024

Bilski, B. (2017a). Exposure to infrasonic noise in agriculture. *Annals of Agricultural and Environmental Medicine*, *24*(1), 86–89. doi:10.5604/12321966.1233897 PMID:28378979

Birnholtz, J. P., Cohen, M. D., & Hoch, S. V. (2007). Organizational character: On the regeneration of Camp Poplar Grove. *Organization Science*, *18*(2), 315–332. doi:10.1287/orsc.1070.0248

Blasco Abad, J. A., Lahoz Palacio, C. F., & Martínez-Arrarás Caro, C. (2022). *Hacia la ciudad activa: Estrategias urbanas para hacer las ciudades más vivibles y saludables.* Dykinson. doi:10.2307/j.ctv2zp4v16

Blasco, J. A. (2016, February 20). *Urban Networks: Panorama del urbanismo europeo en la década de 1950 (la transición del pesimismo de posguerra a la esperanza por un mundo mejor).* Urban Networks. https://urban-networks.blogspot.com/2016/02/panorama-del-urbanismo-europeo-en-la.html

Blecher, M., Pillay, A., Patcharanarumol, W., Panichkriangkrai, W., Tangcharoensathien, V., Teerawattananon, Y., Pannarunothai, S., & Davén, J. (2016). Guest Editorial: Health financing lessons from Thailand for South Africa on the path towards universal health coverage. *South African Medical Journal*, *106*(6), 533–534.

Bliege Bird, R., & Codding, B. F. (2022). Promise and peril of ecological and evolutionary modelling using cross-cultural datasets. *Nature Ecology & Evolution*, *6*(1), 6–8. doi:10.103841559-021-01579-w PMID:34697456

Boeing, P. (2016). The allocation and effectiveness of China's R&D subsidies—Evidence from listed firms. *Research Policy*, *45*(9), 1774–1789. doi:10.1016/j.respol.2016.05.007

Boff, L. (1999). *Saber Cuidar: Ética do humano – compaixão pela terra*. Editora Vozes.

Bokharaei, S., & Nasar, J. L. (2016). Perceived spaciousness and preference in sequential experience. *Human Factors*, *58*(7), 1069–1081. doi:10.1177/0018720816650068 PMID:27230490

Bonyar, A., Geczy, A., Krammer, O., Santha, H., Illes, B., Kaman, J., Szalay, Z., Hanak, P., & Harsanyi, G. (2017). A review on current eCall systems for autonomous car accident detection. *2017 40th International Spring Seminar on Electronics Technology (ISSE),* (pp. 1–8). IEEE. 10.1109/ISSE.2017.8000985

Borland, H., & Lindgreen, A. (2013). Sustainability, epistemology, ecocentric business, and marketing strategy: Ideology, reality, and vision. *Journal of Business Ethics*, *117*(September), 173–187. doi:10.100710551-012-1519-8

Bosnyak, D., Aziz Mahmoud, N., Wagenmann, T., Carballeira, A., & Gomez-Agustina, L. (n.d.). *The book of acoustics:vmaking people happy at work*. BAUX AB.

Boubakri, N., Cosset, J. C., & Saffar, W. (2013). The role of state and foreign owners in corporate risk-taking: Evidence from privatization. *Journal of Financial Economics*, *108*(3), 641–658. doi:10.1016/j.jfineco.2012.12.007

Bourbia, F., & Boucheriba, F. (2010). Impact of street design on urban microclimate for semi arid climate (Constantine). *Renewable Energy*, *35*(2), 343–347. doi:10.1016/j.renene.2009.07.017

Boyle, M., Kay, J., & Pond, B. (2001). Monitoring in support of policy: an adaptive ecosystem approach. In T. Munn (Ed.), *Encyclopedia of Global Environmental Change* (Vol. 4, pp. 116–137). Wiley and Son.

Bozzoli, M. E. (2000). A role for anthropology in sustainable development in Costa Rica. *Human Organization*, *59*(3), 275–279. doi:10.17730/humo.59.3.eu5h42p81wk26578

BPIE. (2011). *Europe's buildings under the microscope - A country-by-country review of the* July 28, 2022, from https://bpie.eu/wp-content/uploads/2015/10/HR_EU_B_under_microscope_study.pdf

Bradford, M., & Florin, J. (2003). Examining the role of innovation diffusion factors on the implementation success of enterprise resource planning systems. *International Journal of Accounting Information Systems*, *4*(3), 205–225. doi:10.1016/S1467-0895(03)00026-5

Brandstrom, J., & Saidani, M. (2022, October 15). Comparison between circularity metrics and LCA: A case study on circular economy strategies. *Journal of Cleaner Production*, *371*, 33537. doi:10.1016/j.jclepro.2022.133537

Brau S.J. (2016). Lean Manufacturing 4.0: La Evolución Tecnológica del Lean. *Guía Práctica sobre la Correcta Utilización de Tecnología en Proyectos Lean.*

Braun, B. (2014). A new urban dispositive? Governing life in an age of climate change. *Environment and Planning. D, Society & Space*, *32*(1), 49–64. doi:10.1068/d4313

Brauns, M. & Wallis, M. (2014). Performance management and public policy: the case of the health sector in South Africa. *Administratio publica, 22*(1), 149-170.

Brenner, B., & Lisman, T. (2018). Hemostasis and Thrombosis in Extreme Physiological and Pathological Conditions. *Seminars in Thrombosis and Hemostasis*, *44*(07), 615–616. doi:10.1055-0038-1666826 PMID:30253425

Bressi, S., Fiorentini, N., Huang, J., & Losa, M. (2019). Crumb Rubber Modifier in Road Asphalt Pavements: State of the Art and Statistics. *Coatings*, *9*(6), 384. doi:10.3390/coatings9060384

Bretagnolle, A., Mathian, H., Pumain, D., & Rozenblat, C. (2000). *Long-term dynamics of European towns and cities: Towards a spatial model of urban growth.* Cybergeo., doi:10.4000/cybergeo.566

Brokāne, N., & Strode, A. (2018). Heritage of industrial architecture in nowadays' cultural environment. *Arts and Music in Cultural Discourse. Proceedings of the International Scientific and Practical Conference*. 10.17770/amcd2017.2823

Bronzini, R., & Piselli, P. (2016). The impact of R&D subsidies on firm innovation. *Research Policy*, *45*(2), 442–457. doi:10.1016/j.respol.2015.10.008

Brooks, S., Hedman, J., Henningsson, S., Sarker, S., & Wang, X. (2018). Antecedents and effects of green IS adoptions: Insights from Nordea. *Journal of Cases on Information Technology*, *20*(4), 32–52. doi:10.4018/JCIT.2018100103

Bruns-Berentelg, J. (2017, May). HafenCity, 21st Century, Urban Development, Continuity & Transformation. Presented at *the UPSI – BVS / REALTY 2017*, Brussels. Brussels.

Bucherer, E., Eisert, U., & Gassmann, O. (2012). Towards systematic business model innovation: Lessons from product innovation management. *Creativity and Innovation Management*, *21*(2), 183–198. doi:10.1111/j.1467-8691.2012.00637.x

Buechel, B., Emrich, E., & Pohlkamp, S. (2016). Nobody's Innocent: The Role of Customers in the Doping Dilemma. *Journal of Sports Economics*, *17*(8), 767–789. doi:10.1177/1527002514551475

Burdea, G., Richard, P., & Coiffet, P. (1996). Multimodal virtual reality: Input-output devices, system integration, and human factors. *International Journal of Human-Computer Interaction*, *8*(1), 5–24. doi:10.1080/10447319609526138

Burguillo, J. C. (2010). Using game theory and competition-based learning to stimulate student motivation and performance. *Computers & Education*, *55*(2), 566–575. doi:10.1016/j.compedu.2010.02.018

Bustamante Oleart, C. (2020). La historia del viento en las ciudades = The history of the wind in the cities. *Cuadernos de Investigación Urbanística*, *132*(132), 1. doi:10.20868/ciur.2020.132.4510

Bustamante, C., Jans, M., & Higueras, E. (2014). El comportamiento del viento en la morfología urbana y su incidencia en el uso estancial del espacio público, Punta Arenas, Chile. *AUS*, *15*(15), 28–33. doi:10.4206/aus.2014.n15-06

Butti, K., & Perlin, J. (1905). *A Golden Thread: 2500 Years of Solar Architecture and Technology*.

C40 Cities. (2022). *C40 and IFRC urge cities to prepare for more dangerous and deadly heatwaves*. Available at: https://www.c40.org/news/global-day-heat-action-cities-prepare-heatwaves/

Cai, M., Lan, Z., Zhang, Z., & Wang, H. (2019). Evaluation of road traffic noise exposure based on high-resolution population distribution and grid-level noise data. *Building and Environment*, *147*, 211–220. doi:10.1016/j.buildenv.2018.08.037

Cainelli, G., D'Amato, A., & Mazzanti, M. (2020). Resource efficient eco-innovations for a circular economy: Evidence from EU firms. *Research Policy*, *49*(1), 103827. doi:10.1016/j.respol.2019.103827

Cajee, L. (2014). Eco-Cultural Tourism: A Tool for Environmental, Cultural and Economic Sustainability (A Case Study of Darap Village, West Sikkim). *SHS Web Conf.*, 12, 01029. 10.1051hsconf/20141201029

Campano, M. Á., Acosta, I. J., Fernández-Agüera, J., & Sendra, J. J. (2015). Towards finding the optimal location of a ventilation inlet in a roof monitor skylight, using visual and thermal performance criteria, for dwellings in a Mediterranean climate. Journal of Building Performance Simulation, 4, 226–238.

Cao, L. (2020). *Cómo se construyen los muros de tierra apisonada*. Archdaily. https://www.archdaily.cl/cl/933445/como-se-construyen-los-muros-de-tierra-apisonada

Cao, H., & Cao, W. (2019). Study on the Slow-Release Effect of Social Responsibility on Financing under the Node of Enterprise Life Cycle. *Procedia Manufacturing*, *30*, 619–626. doi:10.1016/j.promfg.2019.02.087

Cao, X., Deng, M., Song, F., Zhong, S., & Zhu, J. (2019). Direct and moderating effects of environmental regulation intensity on enterprise technological innovation: The case of China. *PLoS One*, *14*(10), e0223175. doi:10.1371/journal.pone.0223175 PMID:31589643

Cao, X., & Hsu, Y. (2021). The Effects of Soundscapes in Relieving Stress in an Urban Park. *Land (Basel)*, *10*(12), 1323. doi:10.3390/land10121323

Capeluto, I. G., & Shaviv, E. (2001). On the use of 'solar volume' for determining the urban fabric. *Solar Energy*, *70*(3), 275–280. doi:10.1016/S0038-092X(00)00088-8

Carayannis, E. G., & Provance, M. (2008). Managing firm innovativeness: Towards a composite index built on firm innovative posture, propensity and performance attributes. *International Journal of Innovative Research and Development*, *1*(1), 90–107. doi:10.1504/IJIRD.2008.016861

Carbon Trust. (2007). *Technical Guide CTG005—Air conditioning: Maximising Comfort, Minimising Energy Consumption*. Carbon Trust.

Carneiro, J. P., Aryal, A., & Becerik-Gerber, B. (2019). Influencing occupant's choices by using spatiotemporal information visualization in Immersive Virtual Environments. *Building and Environment*, *150*, 330–338. doi:10.1016/j.buildenv.2019.01.024

Carotenuto, R., Pezzimenti, F., della Corte, F. G., Iero, D., & Merenda, M. (2021). Ranging with Frequency Dependent Ultrasound Air Attenuation. *Sensors (Basel)*, *21*(15), 4963. doi:10.339021154963 PMID:34372207

Carpintero, S., Maraña, V., & Barcham, R. (2010). Benefits of urban light rail trains: A perspective from Spain. *WIT Transactions on the Built Environment*, *111*, 239–248. doi:10.2495/UT100221

Carreiro, M., Andrade, M. A. P., & Dias, M. S. (2017). Cognition and evaluation of architecture environments based on geometric contour references and aesthetic judgements. *22nd International Conference of the Association for Computer-Aided Architectural Design Research in Asia*, (pp. 581–591). IEEE. 10.52842/conf.caadria.2017.581

Caswell, B., Klein, E. S., Alleway, H. K., Ball, J., Cardinale, M., Eero, M., & Thurstan, R. H. (2020). Something old, something new: 200 years of a blue growth agenda. *Fish and Fisheries*, *21*, 774–796. doi:10.1111/faf.12460

Centro de Coordinación de Alertas y Emergencias Sanitarias. (2021). *Enfermedad por el coronavirus (COVID-19). 04.01.2021* (No. 283). Dirección General de Salud Pública. Secretaria de Estado de Sanidad. Ministerio de Sanidad. Gobierno de España. https://www.lamoncloa.gob.es/serviciosdeprensa/notasprensa/sanidad14/Paginas/2021/04012021_datoscovid19.aspx

Cerezo Ibarrondo, Á. (2019). *La actuación de regeneración y renovación (aMU-RR) : Nueva forma de equidistribución y gestión en suelo urbanizado en los desarrollos urbanos de los años 60 y 70 del País Vasco*. Universidad Politécnica de Madrid. doi:10.20868/UPM.thesis.58338

Chamilothori, K., Wienold, J., & Andersen, M. (2019). Adequacy of immersive virtual reality for the perception of daylit spaces: Comparison of real and virtual environments. *Leukos*, *15*(2–3), 203–226. doi:10.1080/15502724.2017.1404918

Chang, C. (2011). The influence of corporate environmental ethics on competitive advantage: The mediation role of green innovation. *Journal of Business Ethics*, *104*(3), 361–370. doi:10.100710551-011-0914-x

Chang, C.-W., Tseng, T.-H., & Woodside, A. G. (2013). Configural algorithms of patient satisfaction, participation in diagnostics, and treatment decisions' influences on hospital loyalty. *Journal of Services Marketing*, *27*(2), 91–103. doi:10.1108/08876041311309225

Chang, J. C. (2020). Disseminated intravascular coagulation: New identity as endotheliopathy-associated vascular microthrombotic disease based on in vivo hemostasis and endothelial molecular pathogenesis. *Thrombosis Journal, 18*(1), 25. doi:10.118612959-020-00231-0 PMID:33061857

Chan, S. H. M., Qiu, L., Esposito, G., & Mai, K. P. (2021). Vertical greenery buffers against stress: Evidence from psychophysiological responses in virtual reality. *Landscape and Urban Planning, 213*, 104127. doi:10.1016/j.landurbplan.2021.104127

ChArGED. (n.d.). Check.energy µ spare Einfach Energiekosten Ein. checkenergy. *Charged.* http://www.charged-project.eu/

Charron, R., Wiggin, H., Voehl, F., & Harrington, H. J. (2014). *The Lean Management Systems Handbook.* Productivity Press, Taylor & Francis. doi:10.1201/b17201

Chen, C. C., Shih, H. S., Shyur, H. J., & Wu, K. S. (2012). A business strategy selection of green supply chain management via an analytic network process. *Computers & Mathematics with Applications (Oxford, England), 64*(8), 2544–2557. doi:10.1016/j.camwa.2012.06.013

Chen, H. L., & Hsu, W. T. (2009). Family ownership, board independence, and R&D investment. *Family Business Review, 22*(4), 347–362. doi:10.1177/0894486509341062

Chen, H., Lin, H., & Zou, W. (2020). Research on the regional differences and influencing factors of the innovation efficiency of China's high-tech industries: Based on a shared inputs two-stage network DEA. *Sustainability, 12*(8), 3284. doi:10.3390u12083284

Chen, K.-H., Wang, J.-S., Lin, M.-H., & Chang, W.-Y. (2018). The Influence of Learning Organization on Organizational Innovation and Organizational Performance Relationship: The Case of Ecology Industry. *Ekoloji, 27*(106), 329–335.

Chen, M., Lin, J., & Wu, S. (2011). Potential of recycled fine aggregates powder as filler in asphalt mixture. *Construction & Building Materials, 25*(10), 3909–3914. doi:10.1016/j.conbuildmat.2011.04.022

Chen, S., & Golley, J. (2014). 'Green' productivity growth in China's industrial economy. *Energy Econ, 44*, 89–98. doi:10.1016/j.eneco.2014.04.002

Chen, Y. W., Saggi, N., Benitez-Amado, J., & Gang, K. (2015). IT Capabilities and Product Innovation Performance: The Roles of Corporate Entrepreneurship and Competitive Intensity. *Information & Management, 52*(6), 643–657. doi:10.1016/j.im.2015.05.003

Chen, Y., Cui, Z., & Hao, L. (2019). Virtual reality in lighting research: Comparing physical and virtual lighting environments. *Lighting Research & Technology, 51*(6), 820–837. doi:10.1177/1477153518825387

Chen, Y.-G., Cheng, J.-N., & Sato, M. (2017). Effects of school principals' leadership behaviors: A comparison between Taiwan and Japan. *Educational Sciences: Theory and Practice, 17*(1), 145–173.

Chen, Y., Nondahl, D. M., Schubert, C. R., Klein, B. E. K., Klein, R., & Cruickshanks, K. J. (2017). The Relation between Sleep Disruption and Cataract in a Large Population-Based Study. *Ophthalmic Epidemiology, 24*(2), 111–115. doi:10.1080/09286586.2016.1259640 PMID:28139160

Chen, Y.-W., Milstein, T., Anguiano, C., Sandoval, J., & Knudsen, L. (2012). Challenges and Benefits of Community-Based Participatory Research for Environmental Justice: A Case of Collaboratively Examining Ecocultural Struggles. *Environ. Commun, 6*(3), 403–421. doi:10.1080/17524032.2012.698291

Chen, Z., Zhang, X., & Chen, F. (2021). Do carbon emission trading schemes stimulate green innovation in enterprises? Evidence from China. *Technological Forecasting and Social Change, 168*, 120744. doi:10.1016/j.techfore.2021.120744

Chesbrough, H. (2007). Business model innovation: It's not just about technology anymore. *Strategy and Leadership, 35*(6), 12–17. doi:10.1108/10878570710833714

Chesbrough, H. (2010). Business model innovation: Opportunities and barriers. *Long Range Planning, 43*(2–3), 354–363. doi:10.1016/j.lrp.2009.07.010

Chin, J. M., & Chuang, C. P. (2015). The Relationships among School-Based Budgeting, Innovative Management, and School Effectiveness: A Study on Specialist Schools in Taiwan. *The Asia-Pacific Education Researcher, 24*(4), 679–693. doi:10.100740299-014-0220-3

Chiocchini, U. (2019). The Roman cistern of road Cristoforo Colombo, Rome, Italy: Operating mode and connection with the old Appian Way. *Archaeological and Anthropological Sciences, 11*(1), 321–336. doi:10.100712520-018-0606-x

Chiou, T., Chan, H. K., Lettice, F., & Chung, S. H. (2011). The influence of greening the suppliers and green innovation on environmental performance and competitive advantage in Taiwan. *Transportation Research: E-Logistics & Transportation, 47*(6), 822–836. doi:10.1016/j.tre.2011.05.016

Chiu, Y. B., & Lee, C. C. (2020). Effects of financial development on energy consumption: The role of country risks. *Energy Econ, 90*, 104833. doi:10.1016/j.eneco.2020.104833

Cho, J. H., & Sohn, S. Y. (2018). A novel decomposition analysis of green patent applications for the evaluation of R&D efforts to reduce CO2 emissions from fossil fuel energy consumption. *Journal of Cleaner Production, 193*, 290–299. doi:10.1016/j.jclepro.2018.05.060

Christensen, C. M. (1997). *The innovator's dilemma: When new technologies cause great firms to fail.* Harvard Business School Press.

Christiernsson, A., Geijer, M., & Malafry, M. (2021). Legal aspects on cultural values and energy efficiency in the built environment—A sustainable balance of public interests? *Heritage, 4*(4), 3507–3522. doi:10.3390/heritage4040194

Chui, W. S., & Wai, C. W. (2017). Gamification: Motivating Users' Energy Conservation Behaviour. *International Journal of Real Estate Studies, 11*(1), 37–42.

CIBSE. (2005). *Climate Change and the Indoor Environment: Impacts and Adaptation, CIBSE TM36*. The Chartered Institution of Building Services Engineers.

CIE. (2018). *CIE S 026/E:2018 CIE System for Metrology of Optical Radiation for ipRGC-Influenced Responses to Light*. CIE. doi:10.25039/S026.2018

Cioni, C., Di Sivo, M., & Ladiana, D. (2019). Use of bim technology as a safety tool in the restoration phase of buildings: Case study of the faÇade of the "royal tobacco factory" in seville, spain. In WIT Transactions on the Built Environment, 192, 291–303 WITPress. doi:10.2495/BIM190251

Cissé, G., McLeman, R., Adams, H., Aldunce, P., Bowen, K., Campbell-Lendrum, D., Clayton, S., Ebi, K. L., Hess, J., Huang, C., Liu, Q., McGregor, G., Semenza, J., & Tirado, M. C. (2022). Health, Wellbeing, and the Changing Structure of Communities. In *Climate Change 2022: Impacts, Adaptation and Vulnerability". IPCC*. World Meteorological Organization.

Clark, G., Moonen, T., & Nunley, J. (2018). *Europe and its Urban Development, 1970 to 2020* (City Transformed, p. 40). European Investement Bank. https://www.eib.org/en/essays/the-story-of-your-city

Clausen, T. H., & Rasmussen, E. (2012). Parallel business models and the innovativeness of research-based spin-off ventures. *The Journal of Technology Transfer, 38*(6), 836–849. doi:10.100710961-012-9294-3

Cohen-Rosenthal, E. (2000). A walk on the human side of industrial ecology. *The American Behavioral Scientist*, *44*(4), 245–264. doi:10.1177/0002764200044002007

Cole, M. B., Wright, B., Wilson, I. B., Galárraga, O., & Trivedi, A. N. (2018). Medicaid expansion and community health centers: Care quality and service use increased for rural patients. *Health Affairs*, *37*(6), 900–907. doi:10.1377/hlthaff.2017.1542 PMID:29863920

Colomina, B. (2021). *Arquitectura de rayos X*. Puente Editores.

Comín, F., & Martín Aceña, P. (1991). *Historia de la empresa pública en España*. Espasa-Calpe.

Corbusier, L. (2013 -18th edition). Œuvre complète - Les 5 points d'une architecture nouvelle. In W. B. Stonorov (Ed.). Birkhäuser. 1 doi:0.1515/97830356

Córdoba Hernández, R., & Martí Guitera, L. (2022). Ecosystem vulnerability due to urban growth policies. The role of regulatory ecosystem contributions in the land use planning. *SUPTM 2022: 1st Conference on Future Challenges in Sustainable Urban Planning & Territorial Management*, 4. 10.31428/10317/10599

Córdoba Hernández, R. (2021). La vulnerabilidad ecosistémica según el planeamiento en la protección del suelo de la Comunidad de Madrid. *Urbano*, *24*(43), 18–29. doi:10.22320/07183607.2021.24.43.02

Córdoba Hernández, R. (2022). Resiliencia territorial desde la perspectiva de la vulnerabilidad ecosistémica. Aplicación metodológica al planeamiento urbanístico de la Comunidad de Madrid. *Ciudades*, *25*(25), 181–200. doi:10.24197/ciudades.25.2022.181-200

Cordts, P., Cotten, S. R., Qu, T., & Bush, T. R. (2021). Mobility challenges and perceptions of autonomous vehicles for individuals with physical disabilities. *Disability and Health Journal*, *14*(4), 101131. doi:10.1016/j.dhjo.2021.101131 PMID:34147414

Corman, F., & Meng, L. (2015). A Review of Online Dynamic Models and Algorithms for Railway Traffic Management. *IEEE Transactions on Intelligent Transportation Systems*, *16*(3), 1274–1284. doi:10.1109/TITS.2014.2358392

Corraliza, J. A., & Collado, S. (2011). La naturaleza cercana como moderadora del estrés infantil. *Psicothema*, *23*(2), 221–226. PMID:21504673

Costa, J. P., Wehbe, R. R., Robb, J., & Nacke, L. E. (2013). Time's up. *Proceedings of the First International Conference on Gameful Design, Research, and Applications*. ACM. 10.1145/2583008.2583012

Couch, C., Sykes, O., & Börstinghaus, W. (2011). Thirty years of urban regeneration in Britain, Germany and France: The importance of context and path dependency. *Progress in Planning*, *75*(1), 1–52. doi:10.1016/j.progress.2010.12.001

Cowley, B., Moutinho, J. L., Bateman, C., & Oliveira, A. (2011). Learning principles and interaction design for 'green my place': A massively multiplayer serious game. *Entertainment Computing*, *2*(2), 103–113. doi:10.1016/j.entcom.2011.01.001

Cram, S. (2016). Wild and Scenic Wasteland: Conservation Politics in the Nuclear Wilderness. *Environmental Humanities*, *7*(1), 89–105. doi:10.1215/22011919-3616344

Cree, R. A., Okoro, C. A., Zack, M. M., & Carbone, E. (2020). Frequent Mental Distress Among Adults, by Disability Status, Disability Type, and Selected Characteristics— United States, 2018. *MMWR. Morbidity and Mortality Weekly Report*, *69*(36), 1238–1243. doi:10.15585/mmwr.mm6936a2 PMID:32914770

Creswell, J. W. (2014). *A concise introduction to mixed methods research*. SAGE publications.

Creswell, J. W. (2014). *Qualitative and quantitative and mixed Methods approaches* (4th ed.). University of Nebraska-Lincoln.

Crichton, F., Chapman, S., Cundy, T., & Petrie, K. J. (2014). The Link between Health Complaints and Wind Turbines: Support for the Nocebo Expectations Hypothesis. *Frontiers in Public Health*, *2*. Advance online publication. doi:10.3389/fpubh.2014.00220 PMID:25426482

Cronin, J. J. Jr, & Taylor, S. A. (1992). Measuring service quality: A reexamination and extension. *Journal of Marketing*, *56*(3), 55–68. doi:10.1177/002224299205600304

Crosbie, M. J. (Ed.). (1998). *The Passive Solar Design and Construction Handbook*. John Wiley & Sons.

Cuatrecasas, L. (2017). *Ingeniería de Procesos y de Planta: Ingeniería Lean*. Bresca.

Cui, J., Dai, J., Wang, Z., & Zhao, X. (2022). Does environmental regulation induce green innovation? A panel study of chinese listed firms. *Technological Forecasting and Social Change*, *176*, 121492. doi:10.1016/j.techfore.2022.121492

Dabestani, R., Shahin, A., Shirouyehzad, H., & Saljoughian, M. (2017). A comparative study of ordinary and fastidious customers' priorities in service quality dimensions. *Total Quality Management & Business Excellence*, *28*(3-4), 331–350. doi:10.1080/14783363.2015.1082420

Daft, R. L. (2016) Organization theory and design (10th ed.), South-Western College Publishing. Göksoy S (2015) Distributed Leadership in Educational Institutions. Journal of Education and Training Studies, 3(4): 110-118. doi:10.11114/jets.v3i4.851

Dahake, S. (2020). The making of fluid ecocultural identities in urban India. In T. Milstein & J. Castro-Sotomayor (Eds.), *Routledge Handbook of Ecocultural Identity* (pp. 333–350). Routledge. doi:10.4324/9781351068840-20

Dai, Q., Cai, W., Shi, W., Hao, L., & Wei, M. (2017). A proposed lighting-design space: Circadian effect versus visual illuminance. *Building and Environment*, *122*, 287–293. doi:10.1016/j.buildenv.2017.06.025

Dai, Q., Hao, L., Lin, Y., & Cui, Z. (2016). Spectral optimization simulation of white light based on the photopic eye-sensitivity curve. *Journal of Applied Physics*, *119*(5), 053103. doi:10.1063/1.4941396

Damanpour, F. (1992). Organizational size and innovation. *Organization Studies*, *13*(3), 375–402. doi:10.1177/017084069201300304

Dankov, K. (2021). *5 businesses using green gamification to save the world*. GivingForce. Retrieved September 5, 2022, from https://www.givingforce.com/blog/5-businesses-using-green-gamification-to-save-the-world

Darroch, J. (2005). Knowledge management, innovation, and firm performance. *Journal of Knowledge Management*, *9*(3), 101–115. doi:10.1108/13673270510602809

Daryl Slack, J. (2008). Resisting ecocultural studies. *Cultural Studies*, *2008*(22), 477–497. doi:10.1080/09502380802012575

Dauda, L., Long, X., Mensah, C. N., Salman, M., Boamah, K. B., Ampon-Wireko, S., & Dogbe, C. S. K. (2021). Innovation, trade openness and CO2 emissions in selected countries in Africa. *Journal of Cleaner Production*, *281*, 125143. doi:10.1016/j.jclepro.2020.125143

Dávideková, M., & Greguš ml, M. (2017). Concept of Dynamic Advertisement Composition Model Tailored to Customers´ Needs Based on Interactive Customer Input. *Procedia Computer Science*, *109*, 1016–1021. doi:10.1016/j.procs.2017.05.449

Davis, L. J., & Morris, D. B. (2007). Biocultures Manifesto. *New Literary History*, *38*(3), 411–418. doi:10.1353/nlh.2007.0046

Day, R. M. (1998). *Beyond eco-efficiency: Sustainability as a driver for innovation.* Washington: World Resources Institute Sustainable Enterprise Initiative. Dechezlepr^etre, A., Neumayer, E., & Perkins, R. (2015). Environmental regulation and the cross-border diffusion of new technology: Evidence from automobile patents. *Research Policy, 44*(1), 244–257. doi:10.1016/j.respol.2014.07.017

Day, S., Cornell, J., & Malherbe, N. (2019). Discourses of 'service delivery protests' in South Africa: An analysis of talk radio. *Critical Discourse Studies*, 1–18.

Dayton, P. K., Tenger, M. J., Edwards, P. B., & Riser, K. L. (1998). Sliding Baselines, Ghosts and Reduced Expectations in Kelp Forest Communities. *Ecological Applications, 8*(2), 309–322. doi:10.1890/1051-0761(1998)008[0309:SBGARE]2.0.CO;2

de Gregorio Hurtado, S. (2015). Políticas urbanas de la Unión Europea desde la perspectiva de la planificación colaborativa: Las iniciativas comunitarias URBAN y URBAN II en España. *Cuadernos de Investigación Urbanística, 98*, 6–67. https://dialnet.unirioja.es/servlet/articulo?codigo=5217787&info=resumen&idioma=ENG

De Juan, A., & Wegner, E. (2019). Social Inequality, State-centered Grievances, and Protest: Evidence from South Africa. *The Journal of Conflict Resolution, 63*(1), 31–58. doi:10.1177/0022002717723136

de la Puerta Rueda, I. (2018). El reto de la Regeneración Urbana Integral en barrios vulnerables. *Planur-E, 12*. https://www.planur-e.es/articulos/ver/el-reto-de-la-regeneraci-n-urbana-integral-en-barrios-vulnerables

de Oña, J., Calvo, F. J., Garach, L., de Oña, R., & López, G. (2010). How to Expand Subway and Urban Railway Networks: Light Rail Extensions in Madrid, Spain. *Transportation Research Record: Journal of the Transportation Research Board, 2146*(1), 10–17. doi:10.3141/2146-02

De Reuver, M., Bouwman, H., & Haaker, T. (2013). Business model roadmapping: A practical approach to come from an existing to a desired business model. *International Journal of Innovation Management, 17*(01), 1340006. doi:10.1142/S1363919613400069

de Sa, T. H., Mwaura, A., Vert, C., Mudu, P., Roebbel, N., Tran, N., & Neira, M. (2022). Urban design is key to healthy environments for all. *The Lancet. Global Health, 10*(6), e786–e787. doi:10.1016/S2214-109X(22)00202-9 PMID:35561710

De Schiller, S., & Martin Evans, J. (2020). Construcción con Tierra Nº9. Centro de Investigación Hábitat y Energía, CIHE, SI, FADU, UBA.

De WaalA. A. (2006). The characteristics of high performance organization. https://ssrn.com/abstract=931873

Dejtiar, F. (2021). *'No se usan en las grandes ciudades solo por no estar normados': nuestros lectores opinan sobre materiales.* Archdaily. https://www.archdaily.cl/cl/967698/no-se-usan-en-las-grandes-ciudades-solo-por-no-estar-normados-nuestros-lectores-opinan-sobre-materiales-locales

del Rey, R., Uris, A., Alba Fernández, J., & Candelas, P. (2017). Characterization of Sheep Wool as a Sustainable Material for Acoustic Applications. *Materials (Basel), 10*(11), 1277. doi:10.3390/ma10111277 PMID:29112133

Deliège, A., & Nicolay, S. (2016). Köppen–Geiger Climate Classification for Europe Recaptured via the Hölder Regularity of Air Temperature Data. *Pure and Applied Geophysics, 173*(8), 2885–2898. doi:10.100700024-016-1339-3

Delmas, M. A., & Lessem, N. (2014). Saving power to conserve your reputation? the effectiveness of private versus public information. *Journal of Environmental Economics and Management, 67*(3), 353–370. doi:10.1016/j.jeem.2013.12.009

Delmas, M. A., & Montes-Sancho, M. J. (2010). Voluntary agreements to improve environmental quality: Symbolic and substantive cooperation. *Strategic Management Journal, 31*(6), 575–601.

Delmastro, C., De Bienassis, T., Goodson, T., Lane, K., Le Marois, J., Martinez-Gordon, R., & Husek, M. (2022). *Buildings*. International Energy Agency (IEA). https://www.iea.org/reports/buildings

DeLosh, E. L., Busemeyer, J. R., & McDaniel, M. A. (1997). Extrapolation: The sine qua non for abstraction in function learning. *Journal of Experimental Psychology. Learning, Memory, and Cognition*, *23*(4), 968–986. doi:10.1037/0278-7393.23.4.968 PMID:9231439

Deming, D. (2020). The Aqueducts and Water Supply of Ancient Rome. *Ground Water*, *58*(1), 152–161. doi:10.1111/gwat.12958 PMID:31667822

Deng, F., & Chen, C. H. (2020). R&D Input Intensity and Green Innovation Efficiency in China - a Threshold Study Based on Environmental Regulation. *Indust. Technol. Econ.*, *2*, 30–36. doi:10.3969/j.issn.1004-910X.2020.02.004

Deng, Q., & Ji, S. (2015). Organizational green IT adoption: *Concept and evidence. Sustainability*, *7*(12), 16737–16755. doi:10.3390u71215843

Deng, Y., Zhao, Y., Lin, F., & Zang, L. (2022). Influence of structure and material on the vibration modal characteristics of novel combined flexible road wheel. *Defence Technology*, *18*(7), 1179–1189. doi:10.1016/j.dt.2021.05.016

Department of Statistics. (2014). *Statistical Yearbook of Interior*. DOS. http://sowf.moi.gov.tw/stat/year/list.htm

Der Freien und Hansestadt Hamburg. (2016). *Mitteilung des Senats an die Bürgerschaft Masterplan ActiveCity (MPAC) – Für mehr Bewegung in Hamburg Haushaltsplan 2016* (No. 21/6800). Hamburg: Senat. Freie und Hansestadt Hamburg. https://www.hamburg.de/contentblob/7472822/ab9b4fa02dbfdad4540e1b27eaa3a230/data/mitteilung-senat.pdf

Desjeux, P. (2001) *Trans. of the Royal Society of Trop. Med. and Hygiene 95*(3) 239–43. NIH.

Deterding, S., Dixon, D., Khaled, R., & Nacke, L. (2011). From game design elements to gamefulness. *Proceedings of the 15th International Academic MindTrek Conference on Envisioning Future Media Environments - MindTrek '11*. ACM.10.1145/2181037.2181040

Deterding, S., Sicart, M., Nacke, L., O'Hara, K., & Dixon, D. (2011). Gamification. using game-design elements in non-gaming contexts. *Proceedings of the 2011 Annual Conference Extended Abstracts on Human Factors in Computing Systems - CHI EA '11*. ACM.10.1145/1979742.1979575

Deutsche, W. (2021). Global Sand Mining is destroying the planet and costing lives. *EcoWatch*. https://www.ecowatch.com/sand-mining-climate-crisis-2651083582.html

DH. (2013). *Health Technical Memorandum 08-01. Acoustics*. Department of Health and Social Care.

Diana, M., Schiraldi, L., Liu, Y.-Y., Memeo, R., Mutter, D., Pessaux, P., & Marescaux, J. (2016). High intensity focused ultrasound (HIFU) applied to hepato-bilio-pancreatic and the digestive system—Current state of the art and future perspectives. *Hepatobiliary Surgery and Nutrition*, *5*(4), 329–344. doi:10.21037/hbsn.2015.11.03 PMID:27500145

Díaz, J., López-Bueno, J. A., López-Ossorio, J. J., Gónzález, J. L., Sánchez, F., & Linares, C. (2020). Short-term effects of traffic noise on suicides and emergency hospital admissions due to anxiety and depression in Madrid (Spain). *The Science of the Total Environment*, *710*, 136315. doi:10.1016/j.scitotenv.2019.136315 PMID:31923678

Dicianno, B. E., Sivakanthan, S., Sundaram, S. A., Satpute, S., Kulich, H., Powers, E., Deepak, N., Russell, R., Cooper, R., & Cooper, R. A. (2021). Systematic review: Automated vehicles and services for people with disabilities. *Neuroscience Letters*, *761*, 136103. doi:10.1016/j.neulet.2021.136103 PMID:34237416

Dietz, T., Ostrom, E., & Stern, P. L. (2003). The Struggle to Govern the Commons. *Science*, *302*(5652), 1907–1912. doi:10.1126cience.1091015 PMID:14671286

DiMaggio, P., & Powell, W. W. (1983). The iron cage revisited: Collective rationality and institutional isomorphism in organizational fields. *American Sociological Review*, *48*(2), 147–160. doi:10.2307/2095101

Dirección General de Tráfico. (2021, August 21). *En 2020 fallecieron 1.370 personas en accidentes de tráfico.* [Nota de prensa]. https://www.dgt.es/comunicacion/notas-de-prensa/en-2020-fallecieron-1.370-personas-en-accidentes-de-trafico/

Dodman, D., Hayward, B., Pelling, M., Castan Broto, V., Chow, W., Chu, E., Dawson, R., Khirfan, L., McPhearson, T., Prakash, A., Zheng, Y., & Ziervogel, G. (2022). Cities, Settlements and Key Infrastructure. In *Climate Change 2022: Impacts, Adaptation and Vulnerability.* IPCC World Meteorological Organization.

Doherty, J., Kirigia, D., Okoli, C., Chuma, J., Ezumah, N., Ichoku, H., Hanson, K., & McIntyre, D. (2018). Does expanding fiscal space lead to improved funding of the health sector in developing countries?: Lessons from Kenya, Lagos State (Nigeria) and South Africa. *Global Health Action*, *11*(1), 1461338–1461311. doi:10.1080/16549716.2018.1461338 PMID:29768107

Dolan, P., Hallsworth, M., Halpern, D., King, D., Metcalfe, R., & Vlaev, I. (2012). Influencing behaviour: The mindspace way. *Journal of Economic Psychology*, *33*(1), 264–277. doi:10.1016/j.joep.2011.10.009

Domínguez-Amarillo, S., Sendra, J. J., & Oteiza San José, I. (2016). La envolvente térmica de la vivienda social: El caso de Sevilla, 1939 a 1979. In Editorial CSIC (Consejo Superior de Investigaciones Científicas). Editorial Consejo Superior de Investigaciones Científicas.

Domínguez-Amarillo, S., Sendra, J. J., Fernández-Agüera, J., & Escandón, R. (2017). *La construcción de la vivienda social en Sevilla y su catalogación.1939-1979* (U. de Sevilla, Ed.). Editorial Universidad de Sevilla. https://us.odilotk.es/opac?id=00027396%0A

Domínguez-Amarillo, S., Fernández-Agüera, J., Peacock, A., & Acosta, I. (2019). Energy related practices in Mediterranean low-income housing. *Building Research and Information*. doi:10.1080/09613218.2019.1661764

Domínguez-Amarillo, S., Fernández-Agüera, J., Sendra, J. J., & Roaf, S. (2019). The performance of Mediterranean low-income housing in scenarios involving climate change. *Energy and Building*, *202*, 109374. doi:10.1016/j.enbuild.2019.109374

Donato, P., & Link, M. W. (2013). AMA Marketing Research: The Gamification of Marketing Research

Dong, M., & Jin, G. (2021). Analysis on the Protection and Reuse of Urban Industrial Architecture Heritage. In IOP Conference Series: Earth and Environmental Science (Vol. 787). IOP Publishing Ltd. doi:10.1088/1755-1315/787/1/012175

du Gay, P. (2000) In praise of bureaucracy: Weber, organization, ethics. London: Sage. doi:10.4135/9781446217580

du Gay, P. (1994). Colossal immodesties and hopeful monsters. *Organization*, *1*(1), 125–148. doi:10.1177/135050849400100114

Du, K., Cheng, Y., & Yao, X. (2021). Environmental Regulation, Green Technology Innovation, and Industrial Structure Upgrading: The Road to the Green Transformation of Chinese Cities. *Energy Econ*, *98*, 105247. doi:10.1016/j.eneco.2021.105247

Dulskaia, I., Bellini, F., Zabal, R., Garcia Pañella, O., & D'Ascenzo, F. (2017). Gamification as an instrument for organizational behaviour change during the meeting: Case study «ROBATIEMPOS». *Proceedings of the International Conference on Business Excellence, 11*(1), 359–367. 10.1515/picbe-2017-0039

Dumbaugh, E., & Rae, R. (2009). Safe urban form: Revisiting the relationship between community design and traffic safety. *Journal of the American Planning Association*, *75*(3), 309–329. doi:10.1080/01944360902950349

Dvorak, P., & Vranayova, Z. (2018). Application of green roof systems for the improvement of energy performance of buildings. *Energy and Building*, *158*, 1140–1149.

Eckerberg, K., & Joas, M. (2004). Multi-level Environmental Governance: A Concept under Stress? *Local Environment*, *9*(5), 405–412. doi:10.1080/1354983042000255315

EDF. (2019). *Business and the fourth wave of environmentalism.* Environmental Defense Fund. https://www.edf.org/sites/default/files/Business-and-the-Fourth-Wave-of-Environmentalism_2019.pdf

Edwards, P., & Tsouros, A. D. (2006). *Promoting Physical Activity and Active Living in Urban Environments: The Role of Local Governments.* World Health Organization. Regional Office Europe.

Edwards, M., Chevillotte, F., Bécot, F.-X., Jaouen, L., & Totaro, N. (2020). Polynomial relations for cylindrical wheel stiffness characterization for use in a rolling noise prediction model. *Acta Acustica (Les Ulis)*, *4*(2), 4. doi:10.1051/aacus/2020003

Edwardson, C. L., Gorely, T., Davies, M. J., Gray, L. J., Khunti, K., Wilmot, E. G., Yates, T., & Biddle, S. J. H. (2012). Association of Sedentary Behaviour with Metabolic Syndrome: A Meta-Analysis. *PLoS One*, *7*(4), e34916. doi:10.1371/journal.pone.0034916 PMID:22514690

Edwards, P., & Tsouros, A. D. (2008). *A healthy city is an active city: A physical activity planning guide.* World Health Organization.

EEA. (2013). *Achieving energy efficiency through behaviour change: What does it take?* European Environment Agency. https://www.eea.europa.eu/publications/achieving-energy-efficiency-through-behaviour

Eells, J. T., DeSmet, K. D., Kirk, D. K., Wong-Riley, M., Whelan, H. T., ver Hoeve, J., Nork, T. M., Stone, J., & Valter, K. (2008). *Photobiomodulation for the Treatment of Retinal Injury and Retinal Degenerative Diseases.*, doi:10.1007/978-0-387-71809-5_5

Ehrenfeld, J. R. (2000). Industrial ecology: Paradigm shift or normal science? *The American Behavioral Scientist*, *44*(2), 229–244. doi:10.1177/00027642000044002006

Eiadat, Y., Kelly, A., Roche, F., & Eyadat, H. (2008). Green and competitive? An empirical test of the mediating role of environmental innovation strategy. *Journal of World Business*, *43*(2), 131–145. doi:. jwb.2007.11.012 doi:10.1016/j

Eitler, T. W., McMahon, E., & Thoerig, T. (2013). *Ten principles for building healthy places.* Urban Land Institute.

Elçi, E., Yalçın, N., & Ünaldı, S. (2021). Internet of Things based Smart Home System Design for Individuals with Disabilities. *2021 6th International Conference on Computer Science and Engineering (UBMK),* (pp. 619–622).

Elhelf, I. A. S., Albahar, H., Shah, U., Oto, A., Cressman, E., & Almekkawy, M. (2018). High intensity focused ultrasound: The fundamentals, clinical applications and research trends. *Diagnostic and Interventional Imaging*, *99*(6), 349–359. doi:10.1016/j.diii.2018.03.001 PMID:29778401

Elith, J. (2006). *Ecography*, *292*, 129–151. doi:10.1111/j.2006.0906-7590.04596.x

Elkington, J. (2018, June 25). *25 Years Ago I Coined the Phrase "Triple Bottom Line." Here's Why It's Time to Rethink It.* HBR. https://hbr.org/2018/06/25-years-ago-i-coined-the-phrase-triple-bottom-line-heres-why-im-giving-up-on-it

Ellen Macarthur Foundation. (n.d.). Circular economy introduction: https://ellenmacarthurfoundation.org/topics/circular-economy-introduction/overview

Elliott, L. R., van Erp, J. B. F., Redden, E. S., & Duistermaat, M. (2010). Field-Based Validation of a Tactile Navigation Device. *IEEE Transactions on Haptics*, *3*(2), 78–87. doi:10.1109/TOH.2010.3 PMID:27788115

El-Tantawy, S., Abdulhai, B., & Abdelgawad, H. (2013). Multiagent Reinforcement Learning for Integrated Network of Adaptive Traffic Signal Controllers (MARLIN-ATSC): Methodology and Large-Scale Application on Downtown Toronto. *IEEE Transactions on Intelligent Transportation Systems*, *14*(3), 1140–1150. doi:10.1109/TITS.2013.2255286

Elver Boz, T., Demirkan, H., & Urgen, B. A. (2022). Visual perception of the built environment in virtual reality: A systematic characterization of human aesthetic experience in spaces with curved boundaries. *Psychology of Aesthetics, Creativity, and the Arts*. doi:10.1037/aca0000504

Engel-Cox, J. A., Holloman, C. H., Coutant, B. W., & Hoff, R. M. (2004). Qualitative and quantitative evaluation of MODIS satellite sensor data for regional and urban scale air quality. *Atmospheric Environment*, *38*(16), 2495–2509. doi:10.1016/j.atmosenv.2004.01.039

Engels, F. (2020). *La situación de la clase obrera en Inglaterra*. Akal.

Enhasin, A., Kochendoerfer, B., & Rizq, E. (2014). Evaluación de los impactos medioambientales de los proyectos de construcción. *Revista Ingeniería de Construcción, 29*(3), 234-254. https://www.scielo.cl/scielo.php?script=sci_arttext&pid=S0718-50732014000300002

Epstein, M. J., & Young, S. D. (1999). Greening' with EVA. *Management Accounting*, *80*(1), 45–49.

Ertan, S., Lee, C., Willets, A., Tan, H., & Pentland, A. (1998). A wearable haptic navigation guidance system. Digest of Papers. *Second International Symposium on Wearable Computers (Cat. No. 98EX215),* (pp. 164–165). IEEE. 10.1109/ISWC.1998.729547

Esty, D. C., & Winston, A. S. (2006). *Green to Gold*. Yale University Press.

Etzion, D. (2007). Research on organizations and the natural environment, 1992-present: A review. *Journal of Management*, *33*(4), 637–664. doi:10.1177/0149206307302553

Europe, W. H. (2018). *Environmental noise guidelines for the European region.* WHO. https://www.who.int/europe/activities/providing-environmental-noise-guidelines-for-the-european-region

European Commission. (2011). *Hamburg, winner 2011: European Green Capital, an initiative of the European Commission: Green cities – Fit for life*. LU: Publications Office of the European Union. https://data.europa.eu/doi/10.2779/64936

European Commission. (2017). *Report on the blue growth strategy towards more sustainable growth and jobs in the blue economy*. European Commission.

Everett, J. L. (1985). *Culture and ecology in the analysis of organizations*. [PhD Thesis, University of Colorado at Boulder].

Fan, L.-H., Gao, L., Liu, X., Zhao, S.-H., Mu, H.-T., Li, Z., Shi, L., Wang, L.-L., Jia, X.-L., Ha, M., & Lou, F.-G. (2017). Patients' perceptions of service quality in China: An investigation using the SERVQUAL model. *PLoS One*, *12*(12), e0190123. doi:10.1371/journal.pone.0190123 PMID:29272312

Fariña Tojo, J., Higueras García, E., Román López, M. E., & Pozo Méndez, E. (2022). *Guía para planificar ciudades saludables*. https://www.sanidad.gob.es/profesionales/saludPublica/prevPromocion/Estrategia/docs/Guia_Planificar_Ciudades_Saludables.pdf

Farr, D. (2008). *Sustainable urbanism—urban design with nature.* John Wiley & Sons.

Fatima, T., Malik, S. A., & Shabbir, A. (2018). Hospital healthcare service quality, patient satisfaction and loyalty: An investigation in context of private healthcare systems. *International Journal of Quality & Reliability Management*, *35*(6), 1195–1214. doi:10.1108/IJQRM-02-2017-0031

Feeken, C., Wasmann, M., Heuten, W., Ennenga, D., Müller, H., & Boll, S. (2016). ClimbingAssist. *Proceedings of the 2016 ACM International Joint Conference on Pervasive and Ubiquitous Computing: Adjunct*, (pp. 57–60). ACM. 10.1145/2968219.2971417

Feldman, M. S. (2016). Past, Present, and future. In J. Howard-Grenville, C., Rerup, A., Langley, & H., Tsoukas (Eds.). Organizational Routines: How They are Created, Maintained, and Changed (pp. 23-46) Oxford: Oxford University Press

Feng, C., Shi, B., & Kang, R. (2017). Does Environmental Policy Reduce Enterprise Innovation?—Evidence from China. *Sustainability*, *9*(6), 872. Advance online publication. doi:10.3390u9060872

Feng, C., Zeng, H., Sun, Y., Tao, L., Ji, H., & Cai, Z. (2022). Design of Monitoring and Controlling System for Smart Home. *Journal of Physics: Conference Series*, *2160*(1), 012001. doi:10.1088/1742-6596/2160/1/012001

Fernández-Agüera, J., Domínguez, S., García, N., & Campano, M. Á. *Analysis of Building Archetypes for Optimising New Photovoltaic Energy Facilities: A Case Study.* Sustainability, 13(21). doi:10.3390u132112249

Fernandez-Antolin, M.-M., Manuel del Río, J., & González-Lezcano, R. A. (2022). Building Performance Simulations and Architects against Climate Change and Energy Resource Scarcity. *Earth (Waukesha, Wis.)*, *3*(1), 31–44. doi:10.3390/earth3010003

Ferreira, J., Afonso, J., Monteiro, V., & Afonso, J. (2018). An Energy Management Platform for Public Buildings. *Electronics (Basel)*, *7*(11), 294. doi:10.3390/electronics7110294

Figueiro, M. G., Sahin, L., Kalsher, M., Plitnick, B., & Rea, M. S. (2020). Long-Term, All-Day Exposure to Circadian-Effective Light Improves Sleep, Mood, and Behavior in Persons with Dementia. *Journal of Alzheimer's Disease Reports*, *4*(1), 297–312. doi:10.3233/ADR-200212 PMID:33024938

Figueiro, M., Steverson, B., Heerwagen, J., Yucel, R., Roohan, C., Sahin, L., Kampschroer, K., & Rea, M. (2020). Light, entrainment and alertness: A case study in offices. *Lighting Research & Technology*, *52*(6), 736–750. doi:10.1177/1477153519885157

Fink, D., & Mayes, J. (2021). *Too loud! Non-occupational noise exposure causes hearing loss. 040002.* ASA. doi:10.1121/2.0001436

Fiorini, C. V. (2022). Railway noise in urban areas: Assessment and prediction on infrastructure improvement combined with settlement development and regeneration in central Italy. *Applied Acoustics*, *185*, 108413. doi:10.1016/j.apacoust.2021.108413

Flammini, F., de Donato, L., Fantechi, A., & Vittorini, V. (2022). *A Vision of Intelligent Train Control.*, doi:10.1007/978-3-031-05814-1_14

Foko, T. T., Legare, L., & Maremi, K. (2017). Addressing Service Delivery in Rural Areas through Deployment of Information and Communication Technology Platforms. n 2017 IST-Africa Week Conference (IST-Africa), (pp. 1-9). IEEE.

Folke, C., Hahn, T., Olsson, P., and Norberg, J. (2005). Adaptive Governance of Social–ecological Systems. *Annual Review of Environment and Resources*, in press (will be published in October 2005).

Food and Agriculture Organization. (2017). *Food and agriculture organization blue growth initiative: Partnering with countries to achieve the sustainable development goals.* United Nations.

Forni, P., & de Grande, P. (2020). Triangulation and mixed methods in contemporary social sciences. *Revista Mexicana de Sociologia*, *82*(1), 159–189.

Frank, L. D., Andresen, M. A., & Schmid, T. L. (2004). Obesity relationships with community design, physical activity, and time spent in cars. *American Journal of Preventive Medicine*, *27*(2), 87–96. doi:10.1016/j.amepre.2004.04.011 PMID:15261894

Fraternali, P., Cellina, F., Herrera, S., Krinidis, S., Pasini, C., Rizzoli, A. E., Rottondi, C., & Tzovaras, D. (2018). A socio-technical system based on gamification towards Energy Savings. *2018 IEEE International Conference on Pervasive Computing and Communications Workshops (PerCom Workshops)*. IEEE. doi10.1109/PERCOMW.2018.8480405

Fraternali, P., & Gonzalez, S. L. (2019). An augmented reality game for Energy Awareness. *Lecture Notes in Computer Science*, *11754*, 629–638. doi:10.1007/978-3-030-34995-0_57

Fraval, S. E., van Middelaar, C. G., Ridoutt, B., & Opio, C. (2019). Life Cycle Assessment of Food Products. In Encyclopedia of food security and sustainability (Vol. 3, pp. 488-496). doi:10.1016/B978-0-08-100596-5.22221-X

Freie und Hansestadt Hamburg. (n.d.). *Active City Hamburg. Sport & Aktivitäten in Hamburg*. Apple. https://apps.apple.com/de/app/active-city-hamburg/id1481226913

Freire Silva, M. J. (2014). Permeabilidad, mixtura y escala: Tres "Cosas Urbanas" en HafenCity. *VI Seminario Internacional de Investigación en Urbanismo, Barcelona-Bogotá,* Pontificia Universidad Javeriana de Bogotá. 10.5821iiu.6093

Fujii, H. (2016). Decomposition analysis of green chemical technology inventions from 1971 to 2010 in Japan. *Journal of Cleaner Production*, *112*, 4835–4843. doi:10.1016/j.jclepro.2015.07.123

Fujii, H., & Managi, S. (2016). Research and development strategy for environmental technology in Japan: A comparative study of the private and public sectors. *Technological Forecasting and Social Change*, *112*, 293–302. doi:10.1016/j.techfore.2016.02.012

Fukada, S., Osafune, T., Sano, Y., Matsumoto, Y., Shimura, M., Kamiakito, N., Hama, H., & Hayashi, K. (2016). Characteristics of Bridge Vibration and Infrasound due to Moving Different Types of Trucks. *INTER-NOISE and NOISE-CON Congress and Conference Proceedings, 253*(2), 6016–6023.

Fulton, L. B., Lee, J. Y., Wang, Q., Yuan, Z., Hammer, J., & Perer, A. (2020). Getting playful with explainable AI: Games with a purpose to improve human understanding of AI. *Extended Abstracts of the 2020 CHI Conference on Human Factors in Computing Systems*. 10.1145/3334480.3382831

Fusheini, A., & Eyles, J. (2016). Achieving universal health coverage in South Africa through a district health system approach: Conflicting ideologies of health care provision. *BMC Health Services Research*, *16*(1), 558. doi:10.118612913-016-1797-4 PMID:27717353

Gabriel, N. (2014). Urban political ecology: Environmental imaginary, governance, and the non-human. *Geography Compass*, *8*(1), 38–48. doi:10.1111/gec3.12110

Gadenne, D. L., Kennedy, J., & McKeiver, C. (2009). An empirical study of environmental awareness and practices in SMEs. *Journal of Business Ethics*, *84*(1), 45–63. doi:10.100710551-008-9672-9

Gao, Z., Jia, Y., Liu, S., & Zhang, X. (2021). Micro-displacement Measurement of High-Speed Railway Bridge Based on Vector Network Analyzer. *2021 IEEE 15th International Conference on Electronic Measurement & Instruments (ICEMI),* (pp. 420–425). IEEE. 10.1109/ICEMI52946.2021.9679535

Gao, X., Lyu, Y., Shi, F., Zeng, J., & Liu, C. (2019). The impact of financial fac-tor market distortion on green innovation efficiency of high-tech industry. *Ekoloji*, *28*(107), 3449–3461.

Gárate Ojanguren, M. (1994). *Comercio ultramarino e Ilustración*. La Real Compañía de La Habana. Colección La Ilustración Vasca.

García de Paredes Andujar, J. (2008). *El cultivo del tabaco Virginia en España*. CETARSA.

García París, J. (1991). Intercambio y difusión de plantas de consumo entre el Nuevo y el Viejo Mundo. Ministerio de Agricultura, Pesca y Alimentación.

García-González, M. C., Higueras García, E., Gallego Gamazo, C., Pozo Menéndez, E., & Román López, E. (2022). Prevención en salud desde el diseño del espacio público. El proyecto URB_HealthS como experiencia de transferencia de conocimiento. *Ciudades*, *25*(25), 59–78. doi:10.24197/ciudades.25.2022.59-78

Garcia, J. (2021). Gibraltar and the European Union: In and out. *The Round Table*, *110*(3), 384–394. doi:10.1080/00358533.2021.1933728

García, Ó., Alonso, R., Prieto, J., & Corchado, J. (2017). Energy efficiency in public buildings through context-aware social computing. *Sensors (Basel)*, *17*(4), 826. doi:10.339017040826 PMID:28398237

Garcia-Valle, G., Arranz-Paraiso, S., Serrano-Pedraza, I., & Ferre, M. (2021). Estimation of Torso Vibrotactile Thresholds Using Eccentric Rotating Mass Motors. *IEEE Transactions on Haptics*, *14*(3), 538–550. doi:10.1109/TOH.2020.3048290 PMID:33378262

García-Valle, G., Ferre, M., Breñosa, J., Aracil, R., Sebastian, J. M., & Giachritsis, C. (2016). *Design and Development of a Multimodal Vest for Virtual Immersion and Guidance*., doi:10.1007/978-3-319-42324-1_25

Gartner. (2012, November 12). *Gamification: Engagement strategies for business and IT*. Gartner. Retrieved November 28, 2022, from https://www.gartner.com/en/documents/2246217

Gartner. (2014). *Gartner reveals how Gamification Drives Digital Business*. Gartner. https://www.gartner.com/en/newsroom/press-releases/2014-04-08-gartner-reveals-how-gamification-drives-digital-business

Gatti, F. (2012). *Arquitectura y construcción en tierra. Estudio comparativo de las técnicas contemporáneas en tierra.* Universidad Politécnica de Catalunya. https://core.ac.uk/download/pdf/41807254.pdf

Ge, B., Yang, Y., Jiang, D., Gao, Y., Du, X., & Zhou, T. (2018). An empirical study on green innovation strategy and sustainable competitive advantage: Path and boundary. *Sustainability*, *10*(10), 3631. doi:10.3390u10103631

Genell, A., Västfjäll, D., Kleiner, M., & Hedlund, A. (2006). Components in Evaluation of cOmplex Interior Truck Sounds. *Journal of Low Frequency Noise, Vibration and Active Control*, *25*(4), 227–237. doi:10.1260/026309206779884865

George, G., & Bock, A. J. (2011). The business model in practice and its implications for entrepreneurship research. *Entrepreneurship Theory and Practice*, *35*(1), 83–111. doi:10.1111/j.1540-6520.2010.00424.x

Ghatee, M. A., Taylor, W. R., & Karamian, M. (2020). The Geographical Distribution of Cutaneous Leishmaniasis Causative Agents in Iran and Its Neighboring Countries, A Review. *Frontiers in Public Health*, *8*, 111–113. doi:10.3389/fpubh.2020.00011 PMID:32391301

Ghotbabadi, A. R., Feiz, S., & Baharun, R. (2015). Service quality measurements: A review. *International Journal of Academic Research in Business & Social Sciences*, *5*(2), 267. doi:10.6007/IJARBSS/v5-i2/1484

Giblett, R. (2012). Nature is ordinary too: Raymond Williams as the founder of ecocultural studies. *Cultural Studies*, *26*(6), 922–933. doi:10.1080/09502386.2012.707221

Gibson, C. B., & Birkinshaw, J. (2004). The antecedents, consequences, and mediating role of organizational ambidexterity. *Academy of Management Journal*, *47*(2), 209–226. doi:10.2307/20159573

Gilbert, B., & Graff Zivin, J. (2014). Dynamic salience with intermittent billing: Evidence from Smart Electricity Meters. *Journal of Economic Behavior & Organization*, *107*, 176–190. doi:10.1016/j.jebo.2014.03.011

Gill, Z. M., Tierney, M. J., Pegg, I. M., & Allan, N. (2010). Low-energy dwellings: The contribution of behaviours to actual performance. *Building Research and Information*, *38*(5), 491–508. doi:10.1080/09613218.2010.505371

Gilson, L., Elloker, S., Olckers, P., & Lehmann, U. (2014). Advancing the application of systems thinking in health: South African examples of a leadership of sensemaking for primary health care. *Health Research Policy and Systems*, *12*(1), 30. doi:10.1186/1478-4505-12-30 PMID:24935658

Giménez, M., Beersma, D., Daan, S., Pol, B., Kanis, M., van Norren, D., & Gordijn, M. (2016). Melatonin and Sleep-Wake Rhythms before and after Ocular Lens Replacement in Elderly Humans. *Biology (Basel)*, *5*(1), 12. doi:10.3390/biology5010012 PMID:26891336

Givoni, B. (1994). *Passive and Low Energy Cooling of Buildings*. John Wiley & Sons.

Global Active City Label. (n.d.). Active Well-being Initiative. http://activewellbeing.org/global-active-city/

Golden, S. D., & Earp, J. A. L. (2012). Social Ecological Approaches to Individuals and Their Contexts: Twenty Years of Health Education & Behavior Health Promotion Interventions. *Health Education & Behavior*, *39*(3), 364–372. doi:10.1177/1090198111418634 PMID:22267868

Goldfarb, K. E. (2016). 'Coming to Look Alike': Materializing Affinity in Japanese Foster and Adoptive Care. *Social Analysis*, *60*(2), 47–64. doi:10.3167a.2016.600204

Golea, D. G., & Ştefan Cozma, L. (2021). The Use of Piezoelectric Materials for the Purpose of Creating Infrasound and Ultrasound Sources for Terrorist Acts. SSRN Electronic Journal. doi:10.2139/ssrn.3852014

Gollier, C. (2002). Discounting an uncertain future. *Journal of Public Economics*, *85*(2), 149–166. doi:10.1016/S0047-2727(01)00079-2

Gómez Hinojosa, J. F. (1990). De la ecología a la ecofilía: Apuntes para una ecología liberadora'. *Pasos (El Sauzal)*, *30*(July–August).

Gonçalves de Lassio, J., & Naked Haddad, A. (2016). Life cycle assessment of building construction materials: Case study for a housing complex. *Revista de la Construcción*, *15*(2), 69–77. Advance online publication. doi:10.4067/S0718-915X2016000200007

González Enciso, A. (2007). *Política económica y gestión de la Renta de tabaco en el s. SVIII*. ALTADIS.

González Enciso, A., & Torres Sánchez, R. (1999). *Tabaco y economía en el siglo XVIII*. Eunsa.

González, I. B., Pedraza Melo, N. A., Lavín Verástegui, J., & Monforte García, G. (2017). Service quality and users satisfaction assessment in the health context in Mexico. [Universidad del Valle]. *Cuadernos Americanos*, *33*, 36–47.

Goodland, R. (1997). *Medio ambiente y desarrollo sostenible: más allá del informe Brundtland*. https://dialnet.unirioja.es/servlet/libro?codigo=1253

Gordois, A., Cutler, H., Pezzullo, L., Gordon, K., Cruess, A., Winyard, S., Hamilton, W., & Chua, K. (2012). An estimation of the worldwide economic and health burden of visual impairment. *Global Public Health: An International Journal for Research, Policy and Practice*, *7*(5), 465–481. doi:10.1080/17441692.2011.634815 PMID:22136197

Goy, M. (2022). Construir con tierra: todo lo que hay que saber de un material que se redescubre. *El Litoral*. https://www.ellitoral.com/area-metropolitana/construccion-tierra-barro-tecnologia-btc-ingeniero-tecnologica-utn_0_lkGlCoGayF.html

Grabiec, A. M., Łacka, A., & Wiza, W. (2022). Material, Functional, and Aesthetic Solutions for Urban Furniture in Public Spaces. *Sustainability*, *14*(23), 16211. doi:10.3390u142316211

Grace, M., Scott, A. J., Sadler, J. P., Proverbs, D. G., & Grayson, N. (2021). Exploring the smart-natural city interface; re-imagining and re-integrating urban planning and governance. *Emerald Open Res*, *2*(7), 7. Advance online publication. doi:10.35241/emeraldopenres.13226.2

Grafkina, M., Nyunin, B., & Sviridova, E. (2019). Environmental Monitoring and Simulation of Infrasound Generating Mechanism of Traffic Flow. *Journal of Ecological Engineering*, *20*(7), 90–97. doi:10.12911/22998993/109877

Gragson, T. L., & Blount Ben, G. (Eds.). (1999). *Introduction Ethnoecology: Knowledge, Resources, and Rights*. University of Georgia.

Graham, B., Reilly, W., Beinecke, F., Boesch, D., Garcia, T., Murray, C., & Ulmer, F. (2011). *Deep water: The Gulf oil disaster and the future of offshore drilling. Report to the President*. National Commission on the BP Deepwater Horizon Oil Spill and Offshore Drilling.

Greenfield, A. (2010). *Everyware: The dawning age of ubiquitous computing*. New Riders, public lecture, MIT. http://web.mit.edu/uricchio/Public/television/documentary/Greenfield_Everyware.pdf

Griffin, P. (July 2017). *The Carbon Majors Database CDP Carbon Majors report 2017*. CMD.

Grijalba Aseguinolaza, O. (2017). *La regeneración urbana en la CAPV. Divergencias entre el discurso y la realidad*. Universidad del País Vasco. http://hdl.handle.net/10810/26891%09

Grisé, E., Boisjoly, G., Maguire, M., & El-Geneidy, A. (2019). Elevating access: Comparing accessibility to jobs by public transport for individuals with and without a physical disability. *Transportation Research Part A, Policy and Practice*, *125*, 280–293. doi:10.1016/j.tra.2018.02.017

Grossberg, F., Wolfson, M., Mazur-Stommen, S., Farley, K., & Nadel, S. (2015). *Gamified Energy Efficiency Programs*. ACEEE. https://www.aceee.org/sites/default/files/publications/researchreports/b1501.pdf

Grossman, G. M., & Krueger, A. B. (1995). Economic growth and the environment. *The Quarterly Journal of Economics*, *110*(2), 353–377. doi:10.2307/2118443

Guardiola, J., & Reyes, J. M. (2019). Del Sistema al Prototipo y viceversa, revista Torroja. *Informes de la Construcción*, *71*, 555.

Guerrero Baca, L. F. (2007). Arquitectura de tierra. Hacia la recuperación de una cultura constructiva. *Pontificia Universidad Javeriana Bogotá, 20*(2), 182-201.

Guerrero, A. L., García, C., Pérez Laorga, F., & Guardiola, J. (2009) El Ingeniero del ICAI y el desarrollo Sostenible. Chapter 21: Edificación y Urbanismo, sistemas, métodos & tecnologías.

Gunderson, L. (1999). Resilience, Flexibility and Adaptive Management: Antidotes for Spurious Certitude? *Conservation Ecology*, *3*(1), 7. http://www.consecol.org/vol3/iss1/art7. doi:10.5751/ES-00089-030107

Guo, L. L., Qu, Y., & Tseng, M. L. (2017). The interaction effects of environmental regulation and technological innovation on regional green growth performance. *Journal of Cleaner Production*, *162*, 894–902. doi:10.1016/j.jclepro.2017.05.210

Gupeng, Z., & Xiangdong, C. (2012). The value of invention patents in China: Country origin and technology field differences. *China Economic Review*, *23*(2), 357–370. doi:10.1016/j.chieco.2012.02.002

Gustafsdottir, S. S., Fenger, K., Halldorsdottir, S., & Bjarnason, T. (2017). Social justice, access and quality of healthcare in an age of austerity: Users' perspective from rural Iceland. *International Journal of Circumpolar Health*, *76*(1), 1347476–1347479. doi:10.1080/22423982.2017.1347476 PMID:28762300

Gustafsson, A., Katzeff, C., & Bang, M. (2009). Evaluation of a pervasive game for domestic energy engagement among teenagers. *Computers in Entertainment*, *7*(4), 1–19. doi:10.1145/1658866.1658873

Haase, D., Larondelle, N., Andersson, E., Artmann, M., Borgström, S., Breuste, J., Gomez-Baggethun, E., Gren, Å., Hamstead, Z., Hansen, R., Kabisch, N., Kremer, P., Langemeyer, J., Rall, E. L., McPhearson, T., Pauleit, S., Qureshi, S., Schwarz, N., Voigt, A., . . . Elmqvist, T. (2014). A quantitative review of urban ecosystem service assessments: Concepts, models, and implementation. In Ambio (Vol. 43, Issue 4, pp. 413–433). doi:10.100713280-014-0504-0

Haider, Q. (2019). Nuclear fusion: holy grail of energy. In *Nuclear Fusion-One Noble Goal and a Variety of Scientific and Technological Challenges*. IntechOpen. doi:10.5772/intechopen.82335

Haines, A., McMichael, A. J., Smith, K. R., Roberts, I., Woodcock, J., Markandya, A., Armstrong, B. G., Campbell-Lendrum, D., Dangour, A. D., Davies, M., Bruce, N., Tonne, C., Barrett, M., & Wilkinson, P. (2009). Public health benefits of strategies to reduce greenhouse-gas emissions: Overview and implications for policy makers. *Lancet*, *374*(9707), 2104–2114. doi:10.1016/S0140-6736(09)61759-1 PMID:19942281

Hall, B., & Harhoff, D. (2012). Recent research on the economics of patents. In K. Arrow, & T. Bresnahan (Eds.), Annual review of economics, pp. 541−565. doi:10.3386/w17773

hamburg.de. (2018). *Hamburg ist Global Active City.* Offizielles Stadtportal für die Hansestadt Hamburg. https://www.hamburg.de/active-city/11684660/hamburg-ist-global-active-city/

hamburg.de. (n.d.). Active City Map. *Geoportal.* https://geoportal-hamburg.de/activecitymaps/index.html?filter=[%22name%22:%22Sportst%C3%A4tten%22,%22isSelected%22:true,%22rules%22:[]]

Hancke, G., Silva, B., & Hancke, G. Jr. (2012). The Role of Advanced Sensing in Smart Cities. *Sensors (Basel)*, *13*(1), 393–425. doi:10.3390130100393 PMID:23271603

Hannan, M. (2005). Ecologies of Organizations: Diversity and Identity. *The Journal of Economic Perspectives*, *19*(1), 51–70. doi:10.1257/0895330053147985

Hannan, M. T., & Freeman, J. (1989). *Organizational Ecology*. Harvard University Press. doi:10.4159/9780674038288

Hannan, M. T., & Freeman, J. H. (1977). The Population Ecology of Organizations. *American Journal of Sociology*, *82*(5), 929–963. doi:10.1086/226424

Hanson, D. I., James, R. S., & NeSmith, C. (2004). *Tire/pavement noise study.*

Harding, G. W., Bohne, B. A., Lee, S. C., & Salt, A. N. (2007). Effect of infrasound on cochlear damage from exposure to a 4kHz octave band of noise. *Hearing Research*, *225*(1–2), 128–138. doi:10.1016/j.heares.2007.01.016 PMID:17300889

Hardt, C., & Bogenberger, K. (2019). Usage of e-Scooters in Urban Environments. *Transportation Research Procedia*, *37*(November), 155–162. doi:10.1016/j.trpro.2018.12.178

Harris, M. A. (2019). Maintenance of behaviour change following a community-wide gamification based Physical Activity Intervention. *Preventive Medicine Reports*, *13*, 37–40. doi:10.1016/j.pmedr.2018.11.009 PMID:30510892

Hashimoto, K. (2013). *En no Shakaigaku: Fukushi Shakaigaku no Shitenkara.* Harvest-sha.

Hatimtai, M. H., & Hassan, H. (2018). The relationship between the characteristics of innovation towards the effectiveness of ICT in Malaysia productivity corporation. *Malaysian Journal of Communication*, *34*(1), 253–269. doi:10.17576/JKMJC-2018-3401-15

Hawn, O. V. (2012). Do actions speak louder than words? *The case of corporate social responsibility (CSR), 2012*(1), 14137.

Hebbert, M. (2014). Climatology for city planning in historical perspective. *Urban Climate*, *10*, 204–215. doi:10.1016/j.uclim.2014.07.001

He, L., Lin, Q., Zhong, L., Zeng, Q., & Song, J. (2022). Thromboelastography maximum amplitude as an early predictor of disseminated intravascular coagulation in patients with heatstroke. *International Journal of Hyperthermia*, *39*(1), 605–610. doi:10.1080/02656736.2022.2066206 PMID:35465816

Helleman, G., & Wassenberg, F. (2004). The renewal of what was tomorrow's idealistic city. Amsterdam's Bijlmermeer high-rise. *Cities (London, England)*, *21*(1), 3–17. doi:10.1016/j.cities.2003.10.011

Hendricks, S. J., Buch, E., Seekoei, E., Bossert, T., & Roberts, M. (2014). Decentralisation in South Africa: Options for district health authorities in South Africa. *South African Health Review*, *2014*(1), 59–72.

Hendry, J. (2014). *Science and Sustainability: Learning from Indigenous Wisdom*. Palgrave Macmillan. doi:10.1057/9781137430069

Hermida, P. (2020). *En busca de una ciudad más amable tras la COVID*. El Correo Gallego. https://www.elcorreogallego.es/galicia/en-busca-de-una-ciudad-mas-amable-tras-la-covid-YB5245357

Herpertz, G. U., Nykamp, L., & Radke, O. C. (2022). Letaler Hitzeschock mit disseminierter intravasaler Koagulopathie. *AINS - Anästhesiologie · Intensivmedizin · Notfallmedizin · Schmerztherapie*, *57*(01), 68–78. doi:10.1055/a-1508-0726

Herring, H. (2006). Energy efficiency—A critical view. *Energy*, *31*(1), 10–20. doi:10.1016/j.energy.2004.04.055

Herrmann, B., & Butler, B. E. (2021). Aging auditory cortex. In Assessments, Treatments and Modeling in Aging and Neurological Disease (pp. 183–192). Elsevier. doi:10.1016/B978-0-12-818000-6.00017-2

Heydarian, A., Carneiro, J. P., Gerber, D., Becerik-Gerber, B., Hayes, T., & Wood, W. (2014). *Immersive virtual environments: experiments on impacting design and human building interaction*.

Heydarian, A., Carneiro, J. P., Gerber, D., & Becerik-Gerber, B. (2015). Immersive virtual environments, understanding the impact of design features and occupant choice upon lighting for building performance. *Building and Environment*, *89*, 217–228. doi:10.1016/j.buildenv.2015.02.038

Heydarian, A., Carneiro, J. P., Gerber, D., Becerik-Gerber, B., Hayes, T., & Wood, W. (2015). Immersive virtual environments versus physical built environments: A benchmarking study for building design and user-built environment explorations. *Automation in Construction*, *54*, 116–126. doi:10.1016/j.autcon.2015.03.020

Heydarian, A., Pantazis, E., Wang, A., Gerber, D., & Becerik-Gerber, B. (2017). Towards user centered building design: Identifying end-user lighting preferences via immersive virtual environments. *Automation in Construction*, *81*, 56–66. doi:10.1016/j.autcon.2017.05.003

Heyd, T. (1995). Indigenous knowledge, emancipation, and alienation. *Knowledge and Policy*, *8*(1), 63–73. doi:10.1007/BF02698557

Heywood, H. (2015). *101 Rules of Thumb for Sustainable Buildings and Cities*. RIBA publishing. https://www.homelogic.co.uk/wool-insulation-pros-and-cons-the-great-debate

He, Z. L., & Wong, P. K. (2004). Exploration vs. exploitation: An empirical test of the ambidexterity hypothesis. *Organization Science*, *15*(4), 481–494. doi:10.1287/orsc.1040.0078

Hickel, J. (2020). *Less is More: How Degrowth Will Save The World*. Windmill.

Higueras García, E., Román López, M. E., & Fariña Tojo, J. (2021). Guidelines for Healthier Public Spaces for the Elderly Population: Recommendations in the Spanish Context. In Javier Martinez, Claudia Andrea Mikkelsen, & R. Phillips (Eds.), Handbook of Quality of Life and Sustainability (pp. 35–51). Handbook of Quality of Life and Sustainability. doi:10.1007/978-3-030-50540-0_3

Higueras García, E. (2006). *Urbanismo Bioclimático*. Gustavo Gili Editorial.

Higueras García, E. (2015). Barrios saludables. *Cuadernos de Investigación Urbanística, 100*(100). Advance online publication. doi:10.20868/ciur.2015.100.3164

Hill, K. (2007). Urban ecological design and urban ecology: an assessment of the state of current knowledge and a suggested research agenda. V. Novotny, P. Brown (Eds.), Cities of the future: towards integrated sustainable water and landscape management. IWA Publishing, London (2007), pp. 251-266

Hilliard, A., & Jamieson, G. A. (2008). Winning solar races with interface design. *Ergonomics in Design, 16*(2), 6–11. doi:10.1518/106480407X312374

Hobbs, H., Hunker, K., Demircay, V., Rodriguez, T., & Issa, R. (2015). A semi-immersive virtual environment preference study of four interior architectural geometries. *Of Architectural Research,* 369.

Hockerts, K. (2007). *Managerial perceptions of the business case for corporate social responsibility*. CBS Center for Corporate Social Responsibility.

Hodgson, D., Hugues, P., & Vass, T. (2022). *Cement*. International Energy Agency (IEA). https://www.iea.org/reports/cement

Hoffman, C. (2020). USB Type A Connector. Everything You Need to Know. *How To Geek*. https://www.howtogeek.com/690160/usb-type-a-connector-everything-you-need-to-know

Hoffmann, J. A. (2020). Memory, Waterways, and Ecocultural Identity. In T. Milstein & J. Castro-Sotomayor (Eds.), *The Routledge Handbook of Ecocultural Identity*. Routledge. doi:10.4324/9781351068840-9

Hoke, M. K., & Schell, L. M. (2020). Doing biocultural anthropology: Continuity and change. *American Journal of Human Biology, 2020*(32), e23471. PMID:32681558

Hollands, R. (2008). Will the real smart city please stand up? *Will the Real Smart City Please Stand Up, 12*(3), 303–320. doi:10.1080/13604810802479126

Holmes, M. J., & Hacker, J. N. (2007). Climate change, thermal comfort and energy: Meeting the design challenges of the 21st century. *Energy and Building, 39*(7), 802–814. doi:10.1016/j.enbuild.2007.02.009

Ho, M.-C., Chiang, C.-M., Chou, P.-C., Chang, K.-F., & Lee, C.-Y. (2008). Optimal sun-shading design for enhanced daylight illumination of subtropical classrooms. *Energy and Building, 40*(10), 1844–1855. doi:10.1016/j.enbuild.2008.04.012

Hong, Y., & Michalatos, P. (2016). LumiSpace: A VR architectural daylighting design system. In SIGGRAPH ASIA 2016 Virtual Reality Meets Physical Reality: Modelling and Simulating Virtual Humans and Environments (pp. 1–2). doi:10.1145/2992138.2992140

Hong, T., Lee, M., Yeom, S., & Jeong, K. (2019). Occupant responses on satisfaction with window size in physical and virtual built environments. *Building and Environment, 166*, 106409. doi:10.1016/j.buildenv.2019.106409

Hopwood, A. G. (2009). Accounting and the environment. *Accounting, Organizations and Society, 34*(3-4), 433–439. doi:10.1016/j.aos.2009.03.002

Hopwood, A. G. (2010). In memoriam, Anthony G. Hopwood, 1944-2010. *Accounting, Organizations and Society*, *35*(4), 496–497. doi:10.1016/j.aos.2010.05.002

Horváth, Z. (2009). Temple(s) and town at el-Lahun: A study of ancient toponyms in the el-Lahun papyri. In D. P. Silverman, W. Kelly Simpson, & J. Wegner (Eds.), Archaism and Innovation: Studies in Middle Kingdom Egypt (p. 457).

Horvath, G., A. (2006). Decision-support tool for assessing the environmental effects of constructing commercial buildings. *Journal of Architectural Engineering*.

Hoskisson, R. E., Gambeta, E., Green, C. D., & Li, T. X. (2018). Is my firm-specific investment protected? Overcoming the stakeholder investment dilemma in the resource-based view. *Academy of Management Review*, *43*(2), 284–306. doi:10.5465/amr.2015.0411

Howard-Grenville, J., Rerup, C., Langley, A., & Tsoukas, H. (2016). Introduction: Advancing a process perspective on routines by zooming out and zooming in. In J. Howard-Grenville, C., Rerup, A., Langley, & H., Tsoukas (Eds.). Organizational routines: how they are created, maintained, and changed (pp.1-22.) Oxford: Oxford University Press.

Howe, B. (2010). *Low frequency noise and infrasound associated with wind turbine generator systems: a literature review*.

Hu, A. G. Z., Zhang, P., & Zhao, L. (2017). China as number one? Evidence from China's most recent patenting surge. *Journal of Development Economics*, *124*, 107–119. doi:10.1016/j.jdeveco.2016.09.004

Huang, C. (2016). *Estimates of the value of patent rights in China. Innovation and IPRs in China and India*. Springer.

Huang, J., & Li, Y. (2017). Green innovation and performance: The view of organizational capability and social reciprocity. *Journal of Business Ethics*, *145*(2), 309–324. doi:10.100710551-015-2903-y

Huang, L., Wang, C., Chin, T., Huang, J., & Cheng, X. (2022). Technological knowledge coupling and green innovation in manufacturing firms: Moderating roles of mimetic pressure and environmental identity. *International Journal of Production Economics*, *248*, 108482. doi:10.1016/j.ijpe.2022.108482

Huang, M., Ding, R., & Xin, C. (2021). Impact of technological innovation and industrial-structure upgrades on ecological efficiency in China in terms of spatial spillover and the threshold effect. *Integrated Environmental Assessment and Management*, *17*(4), 852–865. doi:10.1002/ieam.4381 PMID:33325155

Huang, Q., Yang, M., Jane, H., Li, S., & Bauer, N. (2020). Trees, grass, or concrete? The effects of different types of environments on stress reduction. *Landscape and Urban Planning*, *193*, 103654. doi:10.1016/j.landurbplan.2019.103654

Hua, Y., Xie, R., & Su, Y. (2018). Fiscal spending and air pollution in Chinese cities: Identifying composition and technique effects. *China Economic Review*, *47*, 156–169. doi:10.1016/j.chieco.2017.09.007

Hud, M., & Hussinger, K. (2015). The impact of R&D subsidies during the crisis. *Research Policy*, *44*(10), 1844–1855. doi:10.1016/j.respol.2015.06.003

Hu, J., Pan, X., & Huang, Q. (2020). Quantity or quality? The impacts of environmental regulation on firms' innovation–Quasi-natural experiment based on China's carbon emissions trading pilot. *Technological Forecasting and Social Change*, *158*, 120122. doi:10.1016/j.techfore.2020.120122

Hüttel, B. A., Ates, Z., Schumann, J. H., Büttgen, M., Haager, S., Komor, M., & Volz, J. (2019). The influence of customer characteristics on frontline employees' customer need knowledge. *Journal of Services Marketing*, *33*(2), 220–232. doi:10.1108/JSM-11-2017-0367

Hwang, J., Li, W., Stough, L. M., Lee, C., & Turnbull, K. (2021). People with disabilities' perceptions of autonomous vehicles as a viable transportation option to improve mobility: An exploratory study using mixed methods. *International Journal of Sustainable Transportation, 15*(12), 924–942. doi:10.1080/15568318.2020.1833115

Hyatt, D. G., & Berente, N. (2017). Substantive or Symbolic Environmental Strategies? Effects of External and Internal Normative Stakeholder Pressures. *Business Strategy and the Environment, 26*(8), 1212–1234. doi:10.1002/bse.1979

IBA Hamburg GmbH. (2017). *Oberbillwerder. Wettbewerblicher Dialog. Vergabeunterlagen mit Aufgabenstellung und Verfahrensablauf.* Hamburg: IBA Hamburg GmbH. https://www.oberbillwerder-hamburg.de/wp-content/uploads/OBW_Aufgabenstellung_Wettbewerblicher_Dialog.pdf

IBA Hamburg GmbH. (2019). *The Connected City. Oberbillwerder—Hamburgs Neuer Stadtteil.* IBA Hamburg GmbH. https://www.oberbillwerder-hamburg.de/wp-content/files/Oberbillwerder_Folder.pdf

Iba, T., Connors, J. M., Levi, M., & Levy, J. H. (2022). Heatstroke-induced coagulopathy: Biomarkers, mechanistic insights, and patient management. *EClinicalMedicine, 44*, 101276. doi:10.1016/j.eclinm.2022.101276 PMID:35128366

IEA & UTCP. (2020). *Users TCP*. UsersTCP. https://userstcp.org/news/behavioural-insights-for-demand-side-energy-policy-and-programmes-report-published

IEA. (n.d.). *The potential of behavioural interventions for optimising energy use at home*. IEA. https://www.iea.org/articles/the-potential-of-behavioural-interventions-for-optimising-energy-use-at-home

Ilg, P. (2019). How to foster green product innovation in an inert sector. *Journal of Innovation & Knowledge, 4*(2), 129–138. doi:10.1016/j.jik.2017.12.009

Imottesjo, H., & Kain, J.-H. (2022). The Urban CoCreation Lab—an integrated platform for remote and simultaneous collaborative urban planning and design through web-based desktop 3D modeling, head-mounted virtual reality and mobile augmented reality: Prototyping a minimum viable product and developing specifications for a minimum marketable product. *Applied Sciences (Basel, Switzerland), 12*(2), 797. doi:10.3390/app12020797

Imperial, M. T. (1999). Institutional Analysis and Ecosystem-based Management: The Institutional Analysis and Development Framework. *Environmental Management, 24*(4), 449–465. doi:10.1007002679900246 PMID:10501859

Ingielewicz, R., Zagubień, A., & ... (2014). Infrasound noise of natural sources in environment and infrasound noise of wind turbines. *Polish Journal of Environmental Studies, 23*(4), 1323–1327.

Iqbal, M. A., Asrafuzzaman, S. K., Arifin, M. M., & Hossain, S. K. A. (2016). Smart home appliance control system for physically disabled people using kinect and X10. *2016 5th International Conference on Informatics, Electronics and Vision (ICIEV),* (pp. 891–896). IEEE.

Iqbal, S. (2021). Energy Efficiency in Architecture Design in Mohenjo-Daro. In N. Mohareb, A. Versaci, Y. Mahgoub, S. Maruthaveeran, & F. Alberti (Eds.), *Cities' Vocabularies: The Influences and Formations* (pp. 203–208). Springer International Publishing. doi:10.1007/978-3-030-51961-2_15

Iria, J., Fonseca, N., Cassola, F., Barbosa, A., Soares, F., Coelho, A., & Ozdemir, A. (2020). A gamification platform to foster energy efficiency in office buildings. *Energy and Building, 222*, 110101. doi:10.1016/j.enbuild.2020.110101

Işık, C., Sirakaya-Turk, E., & Ongan, S. (2019b). Testing the Efficacy of the Economic Policy Uncertainty Index on Tourism Demand in USMCA: Theory and Evidence. *Tourism Economics, 26*(8), 1344–1357. doi:10.1177/1354816619888346

Islam, S., Hasan, S., Antu, A. C. P., Islam, M., & Ahmed, F. T. (2021). Prototype Design and Development of a Smart Home. *2021 International Conference on Engineering and Emerging Technologies (ICEET),* (pp. 1–6). IEEE. 10.1109/ICEET53442.2021.9659769

ISO 8995/CIE S 008: 2003. Lighting of Indoor Work Places. International Commission on Illumination. Austria. (n.d.).

Israr, A., & Poupyrev, I. (2011). Tactile brush. *Proceedings of the SIGCHI Conference on Human Factors in Computing Systems*, (pp. 2019–2028). IEEE. 10.1145/1978942.1979235

Issa, H., & Jabbouri, R. (2022). Green Innovation in the MENA Healthcare Industry: A Knowledge-Based View. [IJTHI]. *International Journal of Technology and Human Interaction*, *18*(1), 1–26. doi:10.4018/IJTHI.299072

Ivanov, N. I., Boiko, I. S., & Shashurin, A. E. (2017). The Problem of High-Speed Railway Noise Prediction and Reduction. *Procedia Engineering*, *189*, 539–546. doi:10.1016/j.proeng.2017.05.086

Izadifar, Z., Izadifar, Z., Chapman, D., & Babyn, P. (2020). An Introduction to High Intensity Focused Ultrasound: Systematic Review on Principles, Devices, and Clinical Applications. *Journal of Clinical Medicine*, *9*(2), 460. doi:10.3390/jcm9020460 PMID:32046072

Jabbar, M., Yusoff, M. M., & Shafie, A. (2022). Assessing the role of urban green spaces for human well-being: A systematic review. *GeoJournal*, *87*(5), 4405–4423. doi:10.100710708-021-10474-7 PMID:34305268

Jachimowicz, J. M., Hauser, O. P., O'Brien, J. D., Sherman, E., & Galinsky, A. D. (2018). The critical role of second-order normative beliefs in predicting energy conservation. *Nature Human Behaviour*, *2*(10), 757–764. doi:10.103841562-018-0434-0 PMID:31406290

Jackson, A., Humber, S., Idzikowski, I., & Kyle, T. (2021). Environmental Wellbeing: Engineering healthier spaces post Covid-19. *Plus journal-Foster and partners.*

Jackson, J. B. C., Kirby, M. X., Berger, W. H., Bjorndal, K. A., Botsford, L. W., Bourque, B. J., Bradbury, R. H., Cooke, R., Erlandson, J., Estes, J. A., Hughes, T. P., Kidwell, S., Lange, C. B., Lenihan, H. S., Pandolfi, J. M., Peterson, C. H., Steneck, R. S., Tegner, M. J., & Warner, R. R. (2001). Historical overfishing and the recent collapse of coastal ecosystems. *Science*, *293*(5530), 629–638. doi:10.1126cience.1059199 PMID:11474098

Jacobsen, K. H., & Hasumi, T. (2014). Satisfaction with healthcare services in South Africa: Results of the national 2010 General Household Survey. *The Pan African Medical Journal*, *18*, 172. doi:10.11604/pamj.2014.18.172.4084 PMID:25422690

Jakob, D. (2022). Voice Controlled Devices and Older Adults–A Systematic Literature Review. *International Conference on Human-Computer Interaction*, (pp. 175–200). IEEE. 10.1007/978-3-031-05581-2_14

James, S., & Miza, T. M. (2015). Perceptions of professional nurses regarding introduction of the Batho Pele principles in State hospitals. *Curationis*, *38*(1), 1–e9. doi:10.4102/curationis.v38i1.1128 PMID:26016696

James, T. L., Villacis Calderon, E. D., & Cook, D. F. (2017). Exploring patient perceptions of healthcare service quality through analysis of unstructured feedback. *Expert Systems with Applications*, *71*, 479–492. doi:10.1016/j.eswa.2016.11.004

Janda, K. B. (2011). Buildings don't use energy: People do. *Architectural Science Review*, *54*(1), 15–22. doi:10.3763/asre.2009.0050

Jang, S. H., Kim, R. H., & Lee, C. W. (2016). Effect of u-healthcare service quality on usage intention in a healthcare service. *Technological Forecasting and Social Change*, *113*, 396–403. doi:10.1016/j.techfore.2016.07.030

Javed, S. A., Liu, S., Mahmoudi, A., & Nawaz, M. (2019). Patients' satisfaction and public and private sectors' health care service quality in Pakistan: Application of grey decision analysis approaches. *The International Journal of Health Planning and Management*, *34*(1), e168–e182. doi:10.1002/hpm.2629 PMID:30160783

Javier Castilla Pascual, F., & Núñez Martí, P. (2005). *Estudio para la recuperación de la técnica del tapial en la construcción tradicional de la provincia de Albacete.* Actas del Cuarto Congreso Nacional de Historia de la Construcción.

Jeffery, R. D., & Brett Horner, BA, C. M. A. (2014). Industrial wind turbines and adverse health effects. *Canadian Journal of Rural Medicine*, *19*(1), 21. PMID:24398354

Jenofonte. (1993). *Recuerdos de Sócrates; Económico; Banquete; Apología de Sócrates. Editorial Gredos.*

Jensen, C. B., & Miho, I. (2016). Attuning to the Webs of En: Ontography, Japanese Spirit Worlds, and the 'Tact' of Minakata Kumagusu. *HAU*, *6*(2), 149–172. doi:10.14318/hau6.2.012

Jentsch, M. F., Bahaj, A. B. S., & James, P. A. B. (2008). Climate change future proofing of buildings—Generation and assessment of building simulation weather files. *Energy and Building*, *40*(12), 2148–2168. doi:10.1016/j.enbuild.2008.06.005

Jeon, J. Y., & Jo, H. I. (2019). Three-dimensional virtual reality-based subjective evaluation of road traffic noise heard in urban high-rise residential buildings. *Building and Environment*, *148*, 468–477. doi:10.1016/j.buildenv.2018.11.004

Jeon, J. Y., & Jo, H. I. (2020). Effects of audio-visual interactions on soundscape and landscape perception and their influence on satisfaction with the urban environment. *Building and Environment*, *169*, 106544. doi:10.1016/j.buildenv.2019.106544

Jerez García, O., & Sánchez López, L. (2002). La arquitectura geográfica manchega: recurso y compromiso educativo. *Espacio, Tiempo y Forma, Serie VI, Geografía*, *15*, 129-145.

Jewell, C. (2016). *How gamification is saving Brisbane renters thousands on energy bills.* The Fifth Estate. https://thefifthestate.com.au/home-and-lifestyle/how-gamification-is-saving-brisbane-renters-thousands-on-energy-bills/

Jiang, Z., Wang, Z., and Lan, X. (2021). How Environmental Regulations Affect Corporate Innovation? the Coupling Mechanism of Mandatory Rules and Voluntary Management. *Technol. Soc.*, *65*, 101575. doi:. 2021.101575 doi:10.1016/j.techsoc

Jiang, L., Masullo, M., Maffei, L., Meng, F., & Vorländer, M. (2018). How do shared-street design and traffic restriction improve urban soundscape and human experience?—An online survey with virtual reality. *Building and Environment*, *143*, 318–328. doi:10.1016/j.buildenv.2018.07.005

Jiang, W., Wang, A. X., Zhou, K. Z., & Zhang, C. (2020). Stakeholder relationship capability and firm innovation: A contingent analysis. *Journal of Business Ethics*, *167*(1), 111–125. doi:10.100710551-019-04161-4

Jiang, X., Kurihara, T., Torii, H., & Tsubota, K. (2018). Progress and Control of Myopia by Light Environments. Eye & Contact Lens: Science &. *Clinics and Practice*, *44*(5), 273–278. doi:10.1097/ICL.0000000000000548 PMID:30048342

Jiang, X., Savchenko, O., Li, Y., Qi, S., Yang, T., Zhang, W., & Chen, J. (2019). A Review of Low-Intensity Pulsed Ultrasound for Therapeutic Applications. *IEEE Transactions on Biomedical Engineering*, *66*(10), 2704–2718. doi:10.1109/TBME.2018.2889669 PMID:30596564

Jiaping, C., Jing, L., & Yaohong, W. (2020). Supplying space for innovation from the old factory from the perspective of land rent residual: Comparison between Guangzhou and Shenzhen. *Tropical Geography*, *40*(5), 795–807. doi:10.13284/j.cnki.rddl.003273

Jim, C. Y. (1999). A planning strategy to augment the diversity and biomass of roadside trees in urban Hong Kong. *Landscape and Urban Planning*, *44*(1), 13–32. doi:10.1016/S0169-2046(98)00113-3

Jim, C. Y., Li, X., Xu, Y., & Chow, W. T. (2019). Potential thermal benefits of xeroflor green roofs for building energy conservation in a sub-tropical city. *Urban Forestry & Urban Greening*, *44*, 126389.

Jiménez M, Espinosa Mª M., Domínguez M., Romero M. and Awad T.(2021) Adaptation of the Lean 6S Methodology in an Industrial Environment under Sustainability and Industry 4.0 Criteria.

Jo, H. I., Jeon, J. Y., & Polack, J.-D. (2019). *Soundscape Cognition for User Behavior in Urban Parks.*

Jo, H. I., & Jeon, J. Y. (2021). Urban soundscape categorization based on individual recognition, perception, and assessment of sound environments. *Landscape and Urban Planning*, *216*, 104241. doi:10.1016/j.landurbplan.2021.104241

Johann, M. (2015). *Services Marketing*. [Thesis, Warsaw School of Economics]. https://scholarworks.wmich.edu/honors_theses/2741

Johnson, S. (2007). The ghost map: The story of London's most terrifying epidemic and how it changed science, cities, and the modern world. New York: Riverhead.

Johnston, P. (2019, July 30). *How gamification can influence environmental behaviour*. The Fifth Estate. https://thefifthestate.com.au/urbanism/environment/how-gamification-can-influence-environmental-behaviour/

Jones, L. P., Turvey, S. T., Massimino, D., & Papworth, S. K. (2020). Investigating the implications of shifting baseline syndrome on conservation. *People and Nature*, *2*(4), 1131–1144. doi:10.1002/pan3.10140

Jordan, G. (1994). *Tobacco in History: The cultures of dependence*. Paperback.

Jordana Casamitjana, F. (2021). *Luminaria* (Patent No. ES1257950U).

Kallinikos, J. (2001). 'bureaucracy: Exploring organization forms in the age of contingency. Paper presented at the 17th EGOS Colloquium, The Odyssey of Organizing, 5–7 July, Lyon. (Organization, special issue on Bureaucracy, 2003). 616. *Organization Studies*, *24*(4).

Kamimura, A., Ashby, J., Myers, K., Nourian, M. M., & Christensen, N. (2015). Satisfaction with healthcare services among free clinic patients. *Journal of Community Health*, *40*(1), 62–72. doi:10.100710900-014-9897-8 PMID:24912587

Kango, R., Hadiyanto, E. H. P., & Pongtuluran, E. H. (2021). Design and Implementation of Smart Bench Integrated Solar Cell for Public Space Electricity Saving. *International Journal Papier Advance and Scientific Review*, *2*(2), 72–81. doi:10.47667/ijpasr.v2i2.121

Kapp, K. M. (2012). *The gamification of learning and instruction: Game-based methods and strategies for training and Education*. Pfeiffer.

Kapppers, A. M. L., & Plaisier, M. A. (2022). *Guidance for the Design of Vibrotactile Patterns for Use on the Human Back*., doi:10.1007/978-3-031-06249-0_5

KARRES + BRANDS. (n.d.). *Oberbillwerder: Europe's most sustainable urban masterplan*. Karres and Brands. https://www.karresenbrands.com/news/oberbillwerder-europes-most-sustainable-urban-masterplan

Kastner-Klein, P., Fedorovich, E., & Rotach, M. W. (2001). A wind tunnel study of organised and turbulent air motions in urban street canyons. *Journal of Wind Engineering and Industrial Aerodynamics*, *89*(9), 849–861. doi:10.1016/S0167-6105(01)00074-5

Kauppi, A., Wikström, J., Sandblad, B., & Andersson, A. W. (2006). Future train traffic control: Control by re-planning. *Cognition Technology and Work*, *8*(1), 50–56. doi:10.100710111-005-0019-3

Kaynezhad, P., Tachtsidis, I., & Jeffery, G. (2016). Optical monitoring of retinal respiration in real time: 670 nm light increases the redox state of mitochondria. *Experimental Eye Research*, *152*, 88–93. doi:10.1016/j.exer.2016.09.006 PMID:27664904

Kempera, J. A., & Ballantine, P. W. (2019). What do we mean by sustainability marketing? *Journal of Marketing Management*, *35*(3–4), 277–309. doi:10.1080/0267257X.2019.1573845

Kiang, H. C., & Malone-Lee, L. C. (2017). *An assessment framework for monitoring cities' sustainability*. CENTRE FOR SUSTAINABLE ASIAN CITIES NATIONAL UNIVERSITY OF SINGAPORE. https://cde.nus.edu.sg/csac/wp-content/uploads/sites/29/2019/11/Full-template-for-Benchmark-Booklet.pdf

Kilbourne, W., McDonagh, P., & Prothero, A. (1997). Sustainable consumption and the quality of life: A macromarketing challenge to the dominant social paradigm. *Journal of Macromarketing*, *17*(1), 4–24. doi:10.1177/027614679701700103

Kim, C. E., Shin, J.-S., Lee, J., Lee, Y. J., Kim, M., Choi, A., Park, K. B., Lee, H.-J., & Ha, I.-H. (2017). Quality of medical service, patient satisfaction and loyalty with a focus on interpersonal-based medical service encounters and treatment effectiveness: A cross-sectional multicenter study of complementary and alternative medicine (CAM) hospitals. *BMC Complementary and Alternative Medicine*, *17*(1), 174–112. doi:10.118612906-017-1691-6 PMID:28351389

Kim, M., Chang, S. I., Seong, J. C., Holt, J. B., Park, T. H., Ko, J. H., & Croft, J. B. (2012). Road Traffic Noise. *American Journal of Preventive Medicine*, *43*(4), 353–360. doi:10.1016/j.amepre.2012.06.014 PMID:22992352

Kinfack, E. C., & Akinboade, O. A. (2015). Financial development, economic growth and millennium development goals in South Africa: Is there a link? *International Journal of Social Economics*, *42*(5), 459–479. doi:10.1108/IJSE-01-2013-0006

King, D., Greaves, F., Exeter, C., & Darzi, A. (2013). 'Gamification': Influencing health behaviours with games. *Journal of the Royal Society of Medicine*, *106*(3), 76–78. doi:10.1177/0141076813480996 PMID:23481424

Kirdar, I. U. (1997). Tourism market segmentation for national tourism organisations and its practical importance for national tourism offices abroad [University of Surrey (United Kingdom)]. *PQDT - UK & Ireland*. https://www.proquest.com/dissertations-theses/tourism-market-segmentation-national/docview/301513276/se-2?accountid=159111

Kitchin, R. (2014). The real-time city? Big data and smart urbanism. *GeoJournal*, *79*(1), 1–14. doi:10.100710708-013-9516-8

Kit, D., Katz, L., Sullivan, B., Snyder, K., Ballard, D., & Hayhoe, M. (2014). Eye Movements, Visual Search and Scene Memory, in an Immersive Virtual Environment. *PLoS One*, *9*(4), e94362. doi:10.1371/journal.pone.0094362 PMID:24759905

Kittinger, J. N., McClenachan, L., Gedan, K. B., & Blight, L. K. (2015). *Marine historical ecology in conservation: Applying the past to manage for the future*. University of California Press.

Kjellstrom, T., & Mercado, S. (2008). Towards action on social determinants for health equity in urban settings. *Environment and Urbanization*, *20*(2), 551–574. doi:10.1177/0956247808096128

Klette, T. J., Møen, J., & Griliches, Z. (2000). Do subsidies to commercial R&D reduce market failures? Microeconometric evaluation studies. *Research Policy*, *29*(4–5), 471–495. doi:10.1016/S0048-7333(99)00086-4

Klocke, E., Kastens, B., & de Buhr, K. (2012). *Hamburg – European Green Capital 2011. Final Report.* Hamburg: Behörde für Stadtentwicklung und Umwelt. https://ec.europa.eu/environment/europeangreencapital/wp-content/uploads/2011/04/Doku-Umwelthauptstadt-engl-web.pdf

Knowles, R. L. (1981). *Sun Rhythm Form*. MIT Press.

Knowles, R. L. (2003). The solar envelope: Its meaning for energy and buildings. *Energy and Building*, *35*(1), 15–25. doi:10.1016/S0378-7788(02)00076-2

Ko, Y.-C., Zigan, K., & Liu, Y.-L. (2021). Carbon capture and storage in South Africa: A technological innovation system with a political economy focus. *Technological Forecasting and Social Change, 166*, 120633. . techfore. 2021. 120633 doi:10.1016/j

Kogut, B., & Zander, U. (1992). Knowledge of the firm, combinative capabilities, and the replication of technology. *Organization Science, 3*(3), 383–397. doi:10.1287/orsc.3.3.383

Kok, G., Lo, S. H., Peters, G.-J. Y., & Ruiter, R. A. C. (2011). Changing energy-related behavior: An intervention mapping approach. *Energy Policy, 39*(9), 5280–5286. doi:10.1016/j.enpol.2011.05.036

Kokkinara, E., Slater, M., & López-Moliner, J. (2015). The Effects of Visuomotor Calibration to the Perceived Space and Body, through Embodiment in Immersive Virtual Reality. *ACM Transactions on Applied Perception, 13*(1), 1–22. doi:10.1145/2818998

Kolokotsa, D., Santamouris, M., & Akbari, H. (2014). Passive cooling of buildings by using green and blue roofs. *Advances in Building Energy Research, 8*(1), 9–30.

Konis, K., Mack, W. J., & Schneider, E. L. (2018). Pilot study to examine the effects of indoor daylight exposure on depression and other neuropsychiatric symptoms in people living with dementia in long-term care communities. *Clinical Interventions in Aging, 13*, 1071–1077. doi:10.2147/CIA.S165224 PMID:29881263

Koštial, P., & Krmela, J., Frydr\`yšek, K., & Ružiak, I. (2012). The chosen aspects of materials and construction influence on the tire safety. *Composites and Their Properties, 13*, 265–298.

Koszarny, Z., & Jankowska, D. (1998). Wystepowanie i ocena halasow niskiej czestotliwosci w budynkach mieszkalnych. *Roczniki Panstwowego Zakladu Higieny, 3*(49), 347–363. PMID:9930028

Kottack, C. P. (1999). The new ecological anthropology. *American Anthropologist, 101*(1), 23–35. doi:10.1525/aa.1999.101.1.23

Kottek, M., Grieser, J., Beck, C., Rudolf, B., & Rubel, F. (2006). World map of the Köppen-Geiger climate classification updated. *Meteorologische Zeitschrift (Berlin), 15*(3), 259–263. doi:10.1127/0941-2948/2006/0130

Kousar, S., Sabri, P. S. U., Zafar, M., & Akhtar, A. (2017). Technological factors and adoption of green innovation-moderating role of government intervention: A case of SMEs in Pakistan. *Pakistan Journal of Commerce and Social Sciences, 11*(3), 833–861.

Krüger, E. L., Minella, F. O., & Rasia, F. (2011). Impact of urban geometry on outdoor thermal comfort and air quality from field measurements in Curitiba, Brazil. *Building and Environment, 46*(3), 621–634. doi:10.1016/j.buildenv.2010.09.006

Kruk, M. E., Kelley, E., Syed, S. B., Tarp, F., Addison, T., & Akachi, Y. (2017). Measuring quality of health-care services: What is known and where are the gaps? *Bulletin of the World Health Organization, 95*(6), 390–390. doi:10.2471/BLT.17.195099 PMID:28603302

Krupar, S., & Ehlers, N. (2020). Biocultures: A critical approach to mundane biomedical governance. *Culture, Theory & Critique, 61*(4), 440–456. doi:10.1080/14735784.2020.1857810

Krupiński, R. (2020). Virtual reality system and scientific visualisation for smart designing and evaluating of lighting. *Energies, 13*(20), 5518. doi:10.3390/en13205518

Kull, K. (1998). Semiotic Ecology: Different Natures in the Semiosphere. *Sign Systems Studies, 26*(1), 344–371. doi:10.12697/SSS.1998.26.15

Kumar, N., Rahman, S. S., & Dhakad, N. (2021). Fuzzy Inference Enabled Deep Reinforcement Learning-Based Traffic Light Control for Intelligent Transportation System. *IEEE Transactions on Intelligent Transportation Systems*, *22*(8), 4919–4928. doi:10.1109/TITS.2020.2984033

Kumar, R. (2018). The Delhi declaration 2018:"Healthcare for all rural people"–Alma Ata revisited. *Journal of Family Medicine and Primary Care*, *7*(4), 649. doi:10.4103/jfmpc.jfmpc_217_18 PMID:30234032

Kunapatarawong, R., & Martínez-Ros, E. (2016). Towards green growth: How does green innovation affect employment? *Research Policy*, *45*(6), 1218–1232. doi:10.1016/j.respol.2016.03.013

Lahoz, C. F., & Blasco, J. A. (2023). Healthy Cities in the 21st Century: Toward the Active City. In Green Research, Developments, and Programs. Sustainable and Healthy Building Environments (Roberto Alonso González Lezcano, pp. 75–98). New York: Nova Science Publishers. doi:10.52305/TKOH1520

Lanca, C., Teo, A., Vivagandan, A., Htoon, H. M., Najjar, R. P., Spiegel, D. P., Pu, S.-H., & Saw, S.-M. (2019). The Effects of Different Outdoor Environments, Sunglasses and Hats on Light Levels: Implications for Myopia Prevention. *Translational Vision Science & Technology*, *8*(4), 7. doi:10.1167/tvst.8.4.7 PMID:31360613

Land Use Consultants, H. U. D. U. (2007). *Delivering Healthier Communities in London*. https://www.healthyurbandevelopment.nhs.uk/wp-content/uploads/2013/03/HUDU_Delivering_Healthier_Communities.pdf

Landschaftsarchitekten, F. (2018). *Grün Vernetzen. Fachkarte für das Landschaftsprogramm—Erläuterungen -*. Behörde für Umwelt und Energie, Amt für Naturschutz, Grünplanung und Energie. Freie und Hansestadt Hamburg. https://www.hamburg.de/contentblob/12763874/85efe919b45682d9d973d70ee378af0e/data/d-fachkarte-gruen-vernetzen-erlaeuterungen.pdf

Lang, J. (2009). International urban design: Theory and practice. *Proceedings of the Institution of Civil Engineers. Urban Design and Planning*, *162*(1), 7–17. doi:10.1680/udap.2009.162.1.7

Lanier, J. (1992). Virtual reality: The promise of the future. *Interactive Learning International*, *8*(4), 275–279.

Larsen, O. N., & Radford, C. (2018). *Acoustic Conditions Affecting Sound Communication in Air and Underwater.*, doi:10.1007/978-1-4939-8574-6_5

Launonen, H., Tisov, A., Germini, A. M., Olivadese, R., Koroleva, K., Lukasik, M., Malamou, A., Arabsolgar, D., Zacharis, E., & Garbi, A. (2019). Exploitation of the European research projects aiming to achieve a behavior change for energy saving through innovative IT solutions. *Sustainable Places*, *2019*, 13. Advance online publication. doi:10.3390/proceedings2019020013

Le Boterf, G. (1999). *L'ingénierie des compétences*. Éditions d'Organisation.

Lebrusán, I., & Toutouh, J. (2020). Using Smart City Tools to Evaluate the Effectiveness of a Low Emissions Zone in Spain: Madrid Central. *Smart Cities*, *3*(2), 456–478. doi:10.3390martcities3020025

Lee, J.-Y., Han, P.-H., Tsai, L., Peng, R.-D., Chen, Y.-S., Chen, K.-W., & Hung, Y.-P. (2017). Estimating the simulator sickness in immersive virtual reality with optical flow analysis. In SIGGRAPH Asia 2017 Posters (pp. 1–2). doi:10.1145/3145690.3145697

Lee, I.-M., Shiroma, E. J., Lobelo, F., Puska, P., Blair, S. N., & Katzmarzyk, P. T. (2012). Effect of physical inactivity on major non-communicable diseases worldwide: An analysis of burden of disease and life expectancy. *Lancet*, *380*(9838), 219–229. doi:10.1016/S0140-6736(12)61031-9 PMID:22818936

Leff, E. (1995). *Green Production*. Guilford Press.

Lehberger, M., Kleih, A.-K., & Sparke, K. (2021). Self-reported well-being and the importance of green spaces – A comparison of garden owners and non-garden owners in times of COVID-19. *Landscape and Urban Planning, 212*, 104108. doi:10.1016/j.landurbplan.2021.104108 PMID:36569995

Lehmann, S. (2010). *The principles of green urbanism: transforming the city for sustainability*. Routledge.

Leonard, W. R. (2020). Re-examining Biocultural Approaches in Human Biology. *American Journal of Human Biology, 32*(4), e23475. doi:10.1002/ajhb.23475 PMID:32885558

LePan, N. (2021). *How much of Earth's surface is covered by each country – in one graphic*. World Economic Forum. https://www.weforum.org/agenda/2021/01/earth-surface-ocean-visualization-science-countries-russia-canada-china/

Leurquin, J. (2000). Hunter J. et Ralston I. (éd.) : The Archaelogy of Britain. An Introduction from the Upper Palaeolithic to the Industrial Revolution (L'archéologie en Grande-Bretagne depuis le Paléolithique supérieur jusqu'à la révolution industrielle). L'Anthropologie, 104(1), 176. doi:10.1016/S0003-5521(00)90017-7

Levi, M. (2018). Hemostasis and Thrombosis in Extreme Temperatures (Hypo- and Hyperthermia). *Seminars in Thrombosis and Hemostasis, 44*(07), 651–655. doi:10.1055-0038-1648231 PMID:29920620

Lévi-Strauss, C. (1962). *La Pensée Sauvage*. Plon.

Le, Y., Hollenhorst, S., Harris, C., McLaughlin, W., & Shook, S. (2006). Environmental management: A study of Vietnamese hotels. *Annals of Tourism Research, 33*(2), 545–567. doi:10.1016/j.annals.2006.01.002

Li, R. Y. M. (2022). Smart Home, Robots, and Robotic Arms for Elderly and Disabled Persons: A Lab Experiment Research Agenda. In Current State of Art in Artificial Intelligence and Ubiquitous Cities (pp. 91–103). Springer.

Liberati, A., Altman, D. G., Tetzlaff, J., Mulrow, C., Gøtzsche, P. C., Ioannidis, J. P. A., Clarke, M., Devereaux, P. J., Kleijnen, J., & Moher, D. (2009). The PRISMA Statement for Reporting Systematic Reviews and Meta-Analyses of Studies That Evaluate Health Care Interventions: Explanation and Elaboration. *PLoS Medicine, 6*(7), e1000100. doi:10.1371/journal.pmed.1000100 PMID:19621070

Li, J., Pan, S. Y., Kim, H., Linn, J. H., & Chiang, P. C. (2015). Building green supply chains in eco-industrial parks towards a green economy: Barriers and strategies. *Journal of Environmental Management, 162*, 158–170. doi:10.1016/j.jenvman.2015.07.030 PMID:26241931

Likos International. (n.d.). Likos International. https://www.liko-acoustics.com/en/acoustic-panels

Lin, Y. X., Sha, K. C., & Wang, J. (2020). Practical Experience and Inspiration of Foreign Emission Permit System. *Environ. Impact. Assess., 42*(1), 14–16. CNKI: SUN:SXHS.0.2020-01-004.

Li, N. B. (2019). Environmental Regulation and Corporate Green Technology Innovation - a Conditional Process Analysis. *Inn. Mong. Soc. Sci. Chin. Ed, 40*(6), 109–115. doi:10.14137/j.cnki.issn1003-5281.2019.06.016

Lin, C. Y., & Ho, Y. H. (2010). The influences of environmental uncertainty on corporate green behavior: An empirical study with small and medium-size enterprises. *Social Behavior and Personality, 38*(5), 691–696. doi:10.2224bp.2010.38.5.691

Lindgardt, Z., Reeves, M., Stalk, G., & Deimler, M. S. (2009). *Business model innovation: When the game gets tough, change the game*. The Boston Consulting Group.

Lin, J., Wu, H.-M., & Wu, H. (2021). Could government lead the way? Evaluation of Chi na's patent subsidy policy on patent quality. *China Economic Review, 69*, 101663. doi:10.1016/j.chieco.2021.101663

Lin, Z., Zhang, G., Xiao, X., Au, C., Zhou, Y., Sun, C., Zhou, Z., Yan, R., Fan, E., Si, S., Weng, L., Mathur, S., Yang, J., & Chen, J. (2022). A Personalized Acoustic Interface for Wearable Human–Machine Interaction. *Advanced Functional Materials*, *32*(9), 2109430. doi:10.1002/adfm.202109430

Li, R., & Xu, D. (2020). Distribution of landscape architecture based on 3D images and virtual reality rationality study. *IEEE Access : Practical Innovations, Open Solutions*, *8*, 140161–140170. doi:10.1109/ACCESS.2020.3010097

Li, S., Song, X., & Wu, H. (2015). Political connection, ownership structure, and corporate philanthropy in China: A strategic-political perspective. *Journal of Business Ethics*, *129*(2), 399–411. doi:10.100710551-014-2167-y

Little, C. (2015). The 'Mosquito' and the transformation of British public space. *Journal of Youth Studies*, *18*(2), 167–182. doi:10.1080/13676261.2014.944119

Liu, J., Zhao, M., & Wang, Y. (2020). Impacts of government subsidies and environmental regulations on green process innovation: A nonlinear approach. *Technology in Society*, *63*, 101417. doi:10.1016/j.techsoc.2020.101417

Liu, L., Jiang, J., Bian, J., Liu, Y., Lin, G., & Yin, Y. (2021). Are Environmental Regulations Holding Back Industrial Growth? Evidence from China. *Journal of Cleaner Production*, *306*, 127007. doi:10.1016/j.jclepro.2021.127007

Liu, W., Liu, Y., Twum, P., & Li, S. (2016). National equity of health resource allocation in China: Data from 2009 to 2013. *International Journal for Equity in Health*, *15*(1), 68. doi:10.118612939-016-0357-1 PMID:27093960

Liu, X., Dou, L., Zhang, H., Sun, Y., & Yuan, B. (2015). Analysis of context factors in compulsory and incentive strategies for improving attraction and retention of health workers in rural and remote areas: A systematic review. *Human Resources for Health*, *13*(1), 61. doi:10.118612960-015-0059-6 PMID:26194003

Liu, Y., Chen, H., Tang, Y., Yang, X., & Zhang, J. (2020). Effects of facade greening on the urban microclimate and building energy performance. *Building and Environment*, *176*, 106868.

Liu, Y., Wang, A., & Wu, Y. (2021). Environmental regulation and green innovation: Evi-dence from China's new environmental protection law. *Journal of Cleaner Production*, *297*, 126698. doi:10.1016/j.jclepro.2021.126698

Li, W., & Zheng, M. (2016). Is it substantive innovation or strategic innovation? Impact of macroeconomic policies on micro-enterprises' innovation. *Economic Research Journal*, *4*, 60–73.

Li, X., & Gong, P. (2016). Urban growth models: Progress and perspective. *Science Bulletin*, *61*(21), 1637–1650. doi:10.100711434-016-1111-1

Li, Y., Yabuki, N., & Fukuda, T. (2022). Measuring visual walkability perception using panoramic street view images, virtual reality, and deep learning. *Sustainable Cities and Society*, *86*, 104140. doi:10.1016/j.scs.2022.104140

Li, Z., Liao, G., Wang, Z., & Huang, Z. (2018). Green loan and subsidy for promoting clean production innovation. *Journal of Cleaner Production*, *187*, 421–431. doi:10.1016/j.jclepro.2018.03.066

Lobo, D. (2014, January 21). ULI Global Awards for Excellence: Hafen City, Hamburg, Germany. *Urban Land Magazine*. https://urbanland.uli.org/planning-design/hafen-city-hamburg-germany/

Loewenstein, G., & Prelec, D. (1992). Anomalies in intertemporal choice: Evidence and an interpretation. *The Quarterly Journal of Economics*, *107*(2), 573–597. doi:10.2307/2118482

Lombardi, D. R., Porter, L., Barber, A., & Rogers, C. D. F. (2011). Conceptualising Sustainability in UK Urban Regeneration: A Discursive Formation. *Urban Studies (Edinburgh, Scotland)*, *48*(2), 273–296. doi:10.1177/0042098009360690

Looyestyn, J., Kernot, J., Boshoff, K., Ryan, J., Edney, S., & Maher, C. (2017). Does gamification increase engagement with online programs? A systematic review. *PLoS One, 12*(3), e0173403. Advance online publication. doi:10.1371/journal.pone.0173403 PMID:28362821

López, J. M., Alonso, J., Asensio, C., Pavón, I., Gascó, L., & de Arcas, G. (2020). A Digital Signal Processor Based Acoustic Sensor for Outdoor Noise Monitoring in Smart Cities. *Sensors (Basel), 20*(3), 605. doi:10.339020030605 PMID:31979005

Lou, K., Xiao, P., Kang, A., Wu, Z., & Dong, X. (2022). Effects of asphalt pavement characteristics on traffic noise reduction in different frequencies. *Transportation Research Part D, Transport and Environment, 106*, 103259. doi:10.1016/j.trd.2022.103259

Lounis, S., Kotsopoulos, D., Bardaki, C., Papaioannou, T. G., & Pramatari, K. (n.d.). 1st International GamiFIN Conference. In *CEUR Workshop Proceedings* (2017th ed., Vol. 1857, pp. 129–134). Pori, Finland; Elsevier.

Lourens, G. (2012). The National Core Standards and evidence-based nursing: Professional practice. *Professional Nursing Today, 16*(1), 3–4.

Loures, L., & Panagopoulos, T. (2007). Sustainable reclamation of industrial areas in urban landscapes. *WIT Transactions on Ecology and the Environment, 102*, 791–800. doi:10.2495/SDP070752

Louv, R. (2010). *Last child in the woods. Saving our children from nature-deficit disorder.* Atlantic B.

Luo, Y., Salman, M., & Lu, Z. (2021). Heterogeneous impacts of environmental regulations and foreign direct investment on green innovation across different regions in China. *The Science of the Total Environment, 759*, 143744. doi:10.1016/j.scitotenv.2020.143744 PMID:33341514

Lu, Y., Hasegawa, Y., Tan, J. K. A., & Lau, S.-K. (2022). Effect of audio-visual interaction on soundscape in the urban residential context: A virtual reality experiment. *Applied Acoustics, 192*, 108717. doi:10.1016/j.apacoust.2022.108717

Luyando López, E. (2020). *El clima como experimento urbano*. Revista de la universidad de México. https://www.revistadelauniversidad.mx/articles/b3bfbc5d-6505-4f33-a7ab-2330a0c2cde6/el-clima-como-experimento-urbano

Lwin, K. K., Murayama, Y., & Mizutani, C. (2012). Quantitative versus Qualitative Geospatial Data in Spatial Modelling and Decision Making. *Journal of Geographic Information System, 04*(03), 237–241. doi:10.4236/jgis.2012.43028

Lyle, J. T. (1985). *Design for human ecosystems: landscape, land use, and natural resources.* Van Nostrand.

MacCallum, L., Howson, N., & Gopu, N. (2016). *Design to move. A Physical Activity Action Agenda. A Guide for City Leaders.* The American College of Sports Medicine (ACSM). NIKE, Inc. The International Council of Sport Science and Physical Education (ICSSPE).

Ma, H., & Li, L. (2021). Could environmental regulation promote the technological innovation of China's emerging marine enterprises? Based on the moderating effect ofgovernment grants. *Environmental Research, 202*, 111682. doi:10.1016/j.envres.2021.111682 PMID:34270994

Mahmoud, M., Cheikh, N., Cerny, O., Gerard, F., & Lemoine, P. (2021). The road to energy efficiency (p. 164). Policy Department for Economic, Scientific and Quality of Life Policies Directorate-General for Internal Policies.

Mahmoud, A. B., Ekwere, T., Fuxman, L., & Meero, A. A. (2019). Assessing Patients' Perception of Health Care Service Quality Offered by COHSASA-Accredited Hospitals in Nigeria. *SAGE Open, 9*(2), 215824401985248. doi:10.1177/2158244019852480

Mahmoudzadeh, P., Afacan, Y., & Adi, M. N. (2021). Analyzing occupants' control over lighting systems in office settings using immersive virtual environments. *Building and Environment*, *196*, 107823. doi:10.1016/j.buildenv.2021.107823

Makron . (2022, 12 02). Recycled Cellulose Fiber Insulation Production brochure. https://makron.com/en/industries/industrial-circular-economy-solutions/recycled-cellulose-insulation-technology/

Maldonado Ramos, L., Fernando Vela, C., & David Rivera, G. (2003). *Nuevas aplicaciones de la tierra como material de construcción*. Memoria de Investigaciones, Universidad Politécnica de Madrid.

Malen, J., & Marcus, A. A. (2019). Environmental externalities and weak appropriability: Influences on firm pollution reduction technology development. *Business & Society*, *58*(8), 1599–1633. doi:10.1177/0007650317701679

Mandavilli, S., Rys, M. J., & Russell, E. R. (2008). Environmental impact of modern roundabouts. *International Journal of Industrial Ergonomics*, *38*(2), 135–142. doi:10.1016/j.ergon.2006.11.003

Mannion, P., Duggan, J., & Howley, E. (2016). An Experimental Review of Reinforcement Learning Algorithms for Adaptive Traffic Signal Control. In *Autonomic Road Transport Support Systems* (pp. 47–66). Springer International Publishing., doi:10.1007/978-3-319-25808-9_4

Manulik, S., Rosińczuk, J., & Karniej, P. (2016). Evaluation of health care service quality in Poland with the use of SERVQUAL method at the specialist ambulatory health care center. *Patient Preference and Adherence*, *10*, 1435–1442. doi:10.2147/PPA.S108252 PMID:27536075

Mao, Y., & Robinson, D. (2019). Three pillars of sustainability: In search of conceptual origins. *Sustainability Science*, *14*(3), 681–695. doi:10.100711625-018-0627-5

Maran, T. (2018). Two Decades of Ecosemiotics in Tartu. *Sign Systems Studies*, *46*(4), 630–639. doi:10.12697/SSS.2018.46.4.11

Maran, T., & Kull, K. (2014). Ecosemiotics: Main Principles and Current Developments. *Geografiska Annaler. Series B, Human Geography*, *96*(1), 41–50. doi:10.1111/geob.12035

Marcuse, H. (1972). *Counterrevolution and Revolt*. Boston Beacon Press.

Margalejo, I. (2022). *La tierra es el material del futuro en arquitectura: volvemos a los orígenes*. Arquitectura y Diseño. https://www.arquitecturaydiseno.es/arquitectura/tierra-es-material-futuro-arquitectura-volvemos-a-origenes_7518

Marinova, M., Feradova, H., Gonzalez-Carmona, M. A., Conrad, R., Tonguc, T., Thudium, M., Becher, M. U., Kun, Z., Gorchev, G., Tomov, S., Strassburg, C. P., Attenberger, U., Schild, H. H., Dimitrov, D., & Strunk, H. M. (2021). Improving quality of life in pancreatic cancer patients following high-intensity focused ultrasound (HIFU) in two European centers. *European Radiology*, *31*(8), 5818–5829. doi:10.100700330-020-07682-z PMID:33486605

Markman, A. (2018, October 11). *Why people aren't motivated to address climate change*. Harvard Business Review. https://hbr.org/2018/10/why-people-arent-motivated-to-address-climate-change

Marques, A. P., Ramke, J., Cairns, J., Butt, T., Zhang, J. H., Muirhead, D., Jones, I., Tong, B. A. M. A., Swenor, B. K., Faal, H., Bourne, R. R. A., Frick, K. D., & Burton, M. J. (2021). Global economic productivity losses from vision impairment and blindness. *EClinicalMedicine*, *35*, 100852. doi:10.1016/j.eclinm.2021.100852 PMID:33997744

Martella, R. (2022). *Now is the time for businesses to act on Global Sustainability*. World Economic Forum. https://www.weforum.org/agenda/2022/05/global-sustainability-corporations-lead-net-zero/

Martino, G. (2021). *Más allá de la tierra y el bambú: tecnologías locales y grandes ciudades*. Archdaily. https://www.archdaily.cl/cl/967841/mas-alla-de-la-tierra-y-el-bambu-tecnologias-locales-y-grandes-ciudades

Marwan, Z., & Abdul, H. (2016). Effect of organizational culture, leadership behavior, achievement motivation, and job satisfaction on performance of lecturer at Private university in the Province of Aceh. *IOSR Journal of Humanities and Social Science*, *21*(4), 33–45.

Masco, J. (2006). *The Nuclear Borderlands: The Manhattan Project in Post–Cold War New Mexico*. Princeton University Press. doi:10.1515/9781400849680

Masino, J., Pinay, J., Reischl, M., & Gauterin, F. (2017). Road surface prediction from acoustical measurements in the tire cavity using support vector machine. *Applied Acoustics*, *125*, 41–48. doi:10.1016/j.apacoust.2017.03.018

Masson-Delmotte, V., Zhai, P., Pörtner, O., Roberts, D., Skea, J., Shukla, P., Pirani, A., Moufouma-Okia, W., Péan, C., Pidcock, R., Connors, S., Matthews, J. B. R., Chen, Y., Zhou, X., Gomis, M. I., Lonnoy, E., Maycock, T., Tignor, M., & Waterfield, T. (2018). *Special Report on the impacts of global warming of 1.5°C above pre-industrial levels and related global greenhouse gas emission pathways, in the context of strengthening the global response to the threat of climate change, sustainable development, and efforts to eradicate poverty.* World Meteorological Organization.

Matheus, N. M. & Sastry, M. (2023). Design and Simulation of a Floating Solar Power Plant for Goreagab Dam, Namibia. In *Human Agro-Energy Optimization for Business and Industry.* IGI-Global. doi:10.4018/978-1-6684-4118-3.ch001

Mathieu-Huart, A., de Lentdecker, C., Riviere, G., Sissoke, F., & Rousselle, C. (2014). French Agency for Food, Environmental and Occupational Health and Safety (ANSES) health reference values (RV). *Archives des Maladies Professionnelles et de l'Environnement*, *75*(3), 292–301. doi:10.1016/j.admp.2014.01.008

Maung, W. M., Nakata, H., Miura, M., Miyasaka, M., Kim, Y.-K., Kasugai, S., & Kuroda, S. (2021). Low-Intensity Pulsed Ultrasound Stimulates Osteogenic Differentiation of Periosteal Cells In Vitro. *Tissue Engineering. Part A*, *27*(1–2), 63–73. doi:10.1089/ten.tea.2019.0331 PMID:32164486

Mayo, X., Del Villar, F., & Jiménez, A. (2017). *X Termometro del Sedentarismo en Espana: Informe sobre la inactividad física y el sedentarismo en la población adulta española* (*Vol. 1*). Madrid, Spain: Observatorio de la Vida Activa y Saludable de la Fundación España Activa. Centro de Estudios del Deporte, Universidad Rey Juan Carlos, CSIC.

Mayosi, B. M., & Benatar, S. R. (2014). Health and Health Care in South Africa— 20 Years after Mandela. *The New England Journal of Medicine*, *371*(14), 1344–1353. doi:10.1056/NEJMsr1405012 PMID:25265493

Mazibuko. (2019). *Epidemic and the health of African Nations.* Pretoria: Published by the Mapungubwe Institute for Strategic Reflection (MISTRA).

Mazurek, G. (2018). Basic channel parameters of ultrasound transmission in air. *2018 22nd International Microwave and Radar Conference (MIKON),* 607–609. 10.23919/MIKON.2018.8405300

McClenachan, L., & Kittinger, J. N. (2013). Multicentury trends and the sustainability of coral reef fisheries in Hawai'i and Florida. *Fish and Fisheries*, *14*(3), 239–255. doi:10.1111/j.1467-2979.2012.00465.x

McClintock, P. (2014, March). *Box office milestone: 'Frozen' becomes No. 1 animated film of all time.* Hollywood Reporter. https://www.hollywoodreporter.com/news/box-office-milestone-frozen-becomes-692156

McCool, W. C., Vernon, K. B., Yaworsky, P. M., & Codding, B. F. (2022). Subsistence strategy mediates ecological drivers of human violence. *PLoS One*, *17*(5), e0268257. doi:10.1371/journal.pone.0268257 PMID:35604917

McCormick, K. (2018). *The business case for Healthy Buildings: Insights from Early Adopters*. Urban Land Institute. https://www.buildup.eu/en/practices/publications/business-case-healthy-buildings-insights-early-adopters

McCormick, T. (2013). ANTHROPOLOGY OF AN IDEA GAMIFICATION. *Foreign Policy*, *201*, 26–27.

McElroy, A. (1990). Biocultural Models in Studies of Human Health and Adaptation. *Medical Anthropology Quarterly*, *4*(3), 243–265. doi:10.1525/maq.1990.4.3.02a00010

McHarg, I. (1996). *Design with nature*. The Natural History Press.

McLeroy, K. R., Bibeau, D., Steckler, A., & Glanz, K. (1988, Winter). An ecological perspective on health promotion programs. *Review Health Educ Q*, *15*(4), 351–377. doi:10.1177/109019818801500401 PMID:3068205

Megalingam, R. K., Nair, R. N., & Prakhya, S. M. (2011). Automated voice based home navigation system for the elderly and the physically challenged. *13th International Conference on Advanced Communication Technology (ICACT2011),* (pp. 603–608). IEEE. 10.1109/WIRELESSVITAE.2011.5940832

Mendoza-Castejon, D., Fraile-García, J., Diaz-Manzano, M., Fuentes-Garcia, J. P., & Clemente-Suárez, V. J. (2020). Differences in the autonomic nervous system stress status of urban and rural school teachers. *Physiology & Behavior*, *222*, 112925. doi:10.1016/j.physbeh.2020.112925 PMID:32417231

Merçon, J., Vetter, S., Tengö, M., Cocks, M., Balvanera, P., Rosell, J. A., & Ayala-Orozco, B. (2019). From local landscapes to international policy: Contributions of the biocultural paradigm to global sustainability. *Global Sustainability*, *2*(e7), 1–11. doi:10.1017us.2019.4

Meyer, J. C., Schellack, N., Stokes, J., Lancaster, R., Zeeman, H., Defty, D., Godman, B., & Steel, G. (2017). Ongoing initiatives to improve the quality and efficiency of medicine use within the public healthcare system in South Africa; a preliminary study. *Frontiers in Pharmacology*, *8*, 751. doi:10.3389/fphar.2017.00751 PMID:29163151

Miller, K. (2022, 09 28). *The triple bottom line: what it is & why it's important*. Harvard Buisness School Online https://online.hbs.edu/blog/post/what-is-the-triple-bottom-line

Millington, N. (2013). Post-industrial imaginaries: Nature, representation and ruin in Detroit, Michigan. *International Journal of Urban and Regional Research*, *37*(1), 279–296. doi:10.1111/j.1468-2427.2012.01206.x

Milstein, T., & Castro-Sotomayor, J. (Eds.). (2020). *Routledge Handbook of Ecocultural Identity*. Routledge. doi:10.4324/9781351068840

Ming, Z., Desuo, C., Pangao, W., & Yongxiang, Z. (2014). Research on the Infrasound Generated by Busses. *Journal of Low Frequency Noise, Vibration and Active Control*, *33*(1), 1–11. doi:10.1260/0263-0923.33.1.1

Ministry of Urban Development and Environment and Ministry of Labour and Economic Affairs. (2006). *HafenCity Hamburg—The Masterplan*. HafenCity Hamburg GmbH in co-operation with the Ministry of Urban Development and Environment of the Free and Hanseatic City of Hamburg. https://edisciplinas.usp.br/pluginfile.php/5130780/mod_resource/content/0/Hafen%20City%20Hamburg_ASTOC.pdf

Mintzberg, H. (1979). *The structuring of organizations: A synthesis of the research*. Prentice Hall.

Mirzabaev, A., Stringer, L. C., Benjaminsen, T. A., Gonzalez, P., Harris, R., Jafari, M., Stevens, N., Tirado, C. M., & Zakieldeen, S. (2022). Deserts, Semiarid Areas and Desertification. In *Climate Change 2022: Impacts, Adaptation and Vulnerability*. World Meteorological Organization.

Molina Contreras, D. K. (2020). *La tierra como material de construcción, propiedades y estabilizantes* [Tesis doctoral]. Universidad Santo Tomás.

Møller, H., & Lydolf, M. (2002). A Questionnaire Survey of Complaints of Infrasound and Low-Frequency Noise. *Journal of Low Frequency Noise, Vibration and Active Control*, *21*(2), 53–63. doi:10.1260/026309202761019507

Monego, M., Fabris, M., Menin, A., & Achilli, V. (2017). 3-D Survey applied to industrial archaeology by tls methodology. In International Archives of the Photogrammetry, Remote Sensing and Spatial Information Sciences - ISPRS Archives (Vol. 42, pp. 449–454). International Society for Photogrammetry and Remote Sensing. doi:10.5194/isprs-archives-XLII-5-W1-449-2017

Montgomery, E., Bennett, J. W., & Scudder, T. (1973). The impact of human activities on the physical and social environments: New directions in anthropological ecology. *Annual Review of Anthropology*, *2*(1), 27–61. doi:10.1146/annurev.an.02.100173.000331

Morillas, J. M. B., Gozalo, G. R., González, D. M., Moraga, P. A., & Vílchez-Gómez, R. (2018). Noise Pollution and Urban Planning. *Current Pollution Reports*, *4*(3), 208–219. doi:10.100740726-018-0095-7

Morimoto, R. (2022). A wild boar chase: Ecology of Harm and Half-Life Politics in Coastal Fukushima. *Cultural Anthropology*, *37*(1), 69–98. doi:10.14506/ca37.1.08

Mosadeghrad, A. M. (2014). Factors influencing healthcare service quality. *International Journal of Health Policy and Management*, *3*(2), 77–89. doi:10.15171/ijhpm.2014.65 PMID:25114946

Mostafavi, M., & Doherty, G. (Eds.), *Ecological urbanism*. Lars Müller Publisher.

Motegi, N., Watson, D. S., & McKane, A. T. (2020). Enterprise Energy Management System Installation Case Study at a food processing plant. *Web Based Enterprise Energy and Building Automation Systems*, 101–108. doi:10.1201/9781003151234-13

Mountjoy, E., Davies, N. M., Plotnikov, D., Smith, G. D., Rodriguez, S., Williams, C. E., Guggenheim, J. A., & Atan, D. (2018). Education and myopia: assessing the direction of causality by mendelian randomisation. BMJ, k2022. doi:10.1136/bmj.k2022

Mouratidis, K., & Hassan, R. (2020). Contemporary versus traditional styles in architecture and public space: A virtual reality study with 360-degree videos. *Cities (London, England)*, *97*, 102499. doi:10.1016/j.cities.2019.102499

Moyano, D. B., & González Lezcano, R. A. (2021). *Indoor Lighting Workplaces*. doi:10.4018/978-1-7998-7279-5.ch012

Moyano, D. B., Paraiso, D. A., & González-Lezcano, R. A. (2022). Possible Effects on Health of Ultrasound Exposure, Risk Factors in the Work Environment and Occupational Safety Review. *Health Care*, *10*(3), 423. doi:10.3390/healthcare10030423 PMID:35326901

Mtshali, P., & Khubisa, F. (2019). A smart home appliance control system for physically disabled people. *2019 Conference on Information Communications Technology and Society (ICTAS)*, (pp. 1–50). IEEE. 10.1109/ICTAS.2019.8703637

Muller, M. (2021). Can We Use Ultrasound to Monitor and Diagnose Lung Diseases? *Acoustics Today*, *17*(4), 29. doi:10.1121/AT.2021.17.4.29

Mumford, E., & Restrepo, L. D. E. (2007). *El discurso del CIAM sobre el urbanismo*. 21.

Murphy, K. M., Shleifer, A., & Vishny, R. W. (1993). Why is rent-seeking so costly to growth? *The American Economic Review*, *83*(2), 409–414.

Murshed, S. M., Ahmed, S., & Rasul, M. G. (2018). Integration of renewable energy into building and urban design: A literature review. *Renewable & Sustainable Energy Reviews*, *82*, 1325–1336.

Musti, K. S. S. (2020b). Quantification of Demand Response in Smart Grids. *IEEE Int. Conf. INDISCON*, pp. 278-282. 10.1109/INDISCON50162.2020.00063

Musti, K. S. S. (2020a). *Circular Economy in Energizing Smart Cities*. Book Chapter in Handbook of Research on Entrepreneurship Development and Opportunities in Circular Economy., doi:10.4018/978-1-7998-5116-5.ch013

Musti, K. S. S., Iileka, H., & Shidhika, F. (2020). *Industry 4.0-Based Enterprise Information System for Demand-Side Management and Energy Efficiency*. Book Chapter in Novel Approaches to Information Systems Design. doi:10.4018/978-1-7998-2975-1.ch007

Naciones Unidas. (1987). *Report of the World Commission on Environment and Development: Our Common Future*. Oxford University Press.

Naciones Unidas. (2015). *Objetivos de Desarrollo Sostenible*. Author.

Naciones Unidas. (2017). *Nueva Agenda Urbana*. https://habitat3.org/wp-content/uploads/NUA-Spanish.pdf

Nagata, H., Satoh, Y., Gerrard, S., & Kytömäki, P. (2004). The dimensions that construct the evaluation of service quality in academic libraries. *Performance Measurement and Metrics*, Naidoo, S. (2012). The South African national health insurance: A revolution in health-care delivery! *Journal of Public Health*, *34*(1), 149–150.

Narayanan, K. L., Ram, C. R. S., Subramanian, M., Krishnan, R. S., & Robinson, Y. H. (2021). IoT based Smart Accident Detection & Insurance Claiming System. *2021 Third International Conference on Intelligent Communication Technologies and Virtual Mobile Networks (ICICV)*, (pp. 306–311). IEEE. 10.1109/ICICV50876.2021.9388430

Nasar, J. L., & Bokharaei, S. (2017). Lighting modes and their effects on impressions of public squares. *Journal of Environmental Psychology*, *49*, 96–105. doi:10.1016/j.jenvp.2016.12.007

Natapov, A., & Fisher-Gewirtzman, D. (2016). Visibility of urban activities and pedestrian routes: An experiment in a virtual environment. *Computers, Environment and Urban Systems*, *58*, 60–70. doi:10.1016/j.compenvurbsys.2016.03.007

Natephra, W., Motamedi, A., Fukuda, T., & Yabuki, N. (2017). Integrating building information modeling and virtual reality development engines for building indoor lighting design. *Visualization in Engineering*, *5*(1), 1–21. doi:10.118640327-017-0058-x

Nathali, B., Khan, M., & Han, K. (2018). Towards sustainable smart cities: A review of trends, architectures, components, and open challenges in smart cities. *Sustainable Cities and Society*, *38*, 697–713. doi:10.1016/j.scs.2018.01.053

Navarro, F. J. (2017). *Implementación de herramientas Lean Manufacturing en la planta de producción de un proveedor del sector automoción* [Master's thesis, Universitat Politècnica de Catalunya].

Ndubisi, F. (2002). *Ecological planning: a historical and comparative synthesis*. The Johns Hopkins University Press.

Ndubisi, F. (2014). *The ecological design and planning reader*. Island Press. doi:10.5822/978-1-61091-491-8

Nederveen Pieterse, J. (2021). Decentering Rome. In Connectivity and Global Studies (pp. 79–87). Springer International Publishing. doi:10.1007/978-3-030-59598-2_6

Nesta, L., Vona, F., & Nicolli, F. (2014). Environmental policies, competition and innovation in renewable energy. *Journal of Environmental Economics and Management*, *67*(3), 396–411. doi:10.1016/j.jeem.2014.01.001

Netting, R. M. (1974). Agrarian ecology. *Annual Review of Anthropology*, *3*(1), 21–56. doi:10.1146/annurev.an.03.100174.000321

Neumann, T. (2021). Does it pay for new firms to be green? An empirical analysis of when and how different greening strategies affect the performance of new firms. *Journal of Cleaner Production*, *317*, 128403. doi:10.1016/j.jclepro.2021.128403

Neupane, D., & Seok, J. (2020). A Review on Deep Learning-Based Approaches for Automatic Sonar Target Recognition. *Electronics (Basel)*, *9*(11), 1972. doi:10.3390/electronics9111972

New, M., Reckien, D., Viner, D., Adler, C., Cheong, S.-M., Conde, C., Constable, A., Coughlan de Perez, E., Lammel, A., Mechler, R., Orlove, B., & Solecki, W. (2022). Decision-Making Options for Managing Risk. In Climate Change 2022: Impacts, Adaptation and Vulnerability. World Meteorological Organization.

Nicol, E., & Hanmer, L. A. (2015). Routine Health Information Systems in South Africa—Opportunities for Improvement. *Studies in Health Technology and Informatics*, *216*, 993. PMID:26262295

Nielsen, F. G. (2022). Perspectives and Challenges Related Offshore Wind Turbines in Deep Water. *Energies*, *15*(8), 2844. doi:10.3390/en15082844

Nikolopoulou, M., Baker, N., & Steemers, K. (2001). Thermal comfort in outdoor urban spaces: Understanding the human parameter. *Solar Energy*, *70*(3), 227–235. doi:10.1016/S0038-092X(00)00093-1

Niranjan, A. (2021). *The world is running out of sand.* Deutsche Welle (DW). https://www.dw.com/en/sand-crisis-shortage-supply-mafia/a-56714226

Noble, H., & Smith, J. (2015). Issues of validity and reliability in qualitative research. *Evidence-Based Nursing*, *18*(2), 34–35. doi:10.1136/eb-2015-102054 PMID:25653237

Nocera, F., lo Faro, A., Costanzo, V., & Raciti, C. (2018). Daylight Performance of Classrooms in a Mediterranean School Heritage Building. *Sustainability*, *10*(10), 3705. doi:10.3390u10103705

Nöth, W. (1998). Ecosemiotics. *Sign Systems Studies*, *26*(1), 332–343. doi:10.12697/SSS.1998.26.14

Nozawa, S. (2015). Phatic Traces: Sociality in Contemporary Japan. *Anthropological Quarterly*, *88*(2), 373–400. https://muse.jhu.edu/article/582266. doi:10.1353/anq.2015.0014

Nsamenang, A. B. (2015). Ecocultural Theories of Development. In J. Wright (Ed.), *International Encyclopedia of the Social & Behavioral Sciences* (Vol. 6, pp. 838–844). Elsevier. doi:10.1016/B978-0-08-097086-8.23205-4

NSF. (n.d.). *Behaviour Change - Research Overview*. Sustainable Healthy Cities Network. https://www.sustainable-healthycities.org/behaviour-change/

Nunez, M., & Oke, T. R. (1977). The Energy Balance of an Urban Canyon. *Journal of Applied Meteorology and Climatology*, *16*(1), 11–19. doi:10.1175/1520-0450(1977)016<0011:TEBOAU>2.0.CO;2

NZS 4297. (1998). *Engineering design of earth buildings*. Building Code Compliance Documents B1 (VM1), B2 (AS1).

O'Boy, D. J. (2020). Automotive wheel and tyre design for suppression of acoustic cavity noise through the incorporation of passive resonators. *Journal of Sound and Vibration*, *467*, 115037. doi:10.1016/j.jsv.2019.115037

O'Neil, D. (2018, September 16). The EU needs a stability and wellbeing pact, not more growth. *The Guardian*. https://www.theguardian.com/politics/2018/sep/16/the-eu-needs-a-stability-and-wellbeing-pact-not-more-growth

O'Neill, B., Van Aalst, M., Zaiton Ibrahim, Z., Berrang Ford, L., Bhadwal, S., Buhaug, H., Diaz, D., Frieler, K., Garschagen, M., Magnan, A., Midgley, G., Mirzabaev, A., Thomas, A., & Warren, R. (2022). Poverty, Livelihoods and Sustainability Development. In *Climate Change 2022: Impacts, Adaptation and Vulnerability*. World Meteorological Organization.

O'Reilly, C., & Tushman, M. (2004). The ambidextrous organization. *Harvard Business Review*, *82*, 74–83. PMID:15077368

Obaid, T., Rashed, H., el Nour, A. A., Rehan, M., Saleh, M. M., & Tarique, M. (2014). ZigBee based voice controlled wireless smart home system. *International Journal of Wireless & Mobile Networks*, *6*(1), 47–59. doi:10.5121/ijwmn.2014.6104

Odum, E. P. (1959). *Fundamentals of Ecology* (2nd ed.). W. B. Saunders.

OECD. (2017). *Tackling environmental problems with the help of behavioural insights*. OECD. doi:10.1787/9789264273887-en

Ogiemwonyi, O., Harun, A. B., Alam, M. N., & Othman, B. A. (2020). Do we care about going green? measuring the effect of green environmental awareness, green product value and environmental attitude on green culture. an Insight from Nigeria. *Environmental and Climate Technologies*, *24*(1), 254–274. doi:10.2478/rtuect-2020-0015

Oginga-Martins, J., & Sharifi, A. (2022). *World Cities Report 2022: Envisaging the Future of Cities.* United Nations Human Settlements Programme (UN-Habitat)

Olgyay, V. (1963). *Design with Climate: Bioclimatic Approach to Architectural Regionalism.* Princeton University Press.

Oller Alonso, M. (2021). *La Responsabilidad Social Corporativa de las empresas del mármol en la comarca del Almanzora, Almería (2019-2021): análisis de sus estrategias de comunicación integral.* Doctorado en Gestión de la Información y de la Comunicación en las Organizaciones Universidad de Murcia Escuela Internacional de Doctorado.

Olmedo Rodríguez, A. (2020). *Evaluación de estrategias arquitectónicas para la consecución del nuevo modelo energético* [Tesis doctoral]. Universidad de Valladolid.

Olorunfemi, S. (2016). Rural Road Infrastructural Challenges: An Impediment to Health Care Service Delivery in Kabba-Bunu Local Government Area of Kogi State, Nigeria. *Academic Journal of Interdisciplinary Studies, MCSER Publishing, Rome-Italy*, *5*(2), 35–44.

Oppong-Tawiah, D., Webster, J., Staples, S., Cameron, A.-F., Ortiz de Guinea, A., & Hung, T. Y. (2020). Developing a gamified mobile application to encourage sustainable energy use in the Office. *Journal of Business Research*, *106*, 388–405. doi:10.1016/j.jbusres.2018.10.051

Organization, W. H., & Bank, W. (2011). *World report on disability 2011 (p. Summary also available in Braille)*. World Health Organization.

Ostrom, E. (2005). Understanding Institutional Diversity, Princeton University Press, Princeton New Jersey, USA. Ovesson, P. (2003). Markhävdkartering 2002, Hävdtillståndet på betesmarker och slåtterängar inom Nedre Helgeåns våtmarksområde i Kristianstads Vattenrike. Länsstyrelsen i Skåne län, Kristianstads kommun, Högskolan i Kristianstad.

Ostrom, Q. T., Gittleman, H., Fulop, J., Liu, M., Blanda, R., Kromer, C., Wolinsky, Y., Kruchko, C., & Barnholtz-Sloan, J. S. (2015). CBTRUS statistical report: Primary brain and central nervous system tumors diagnosed in the United States in 2008-2012. *Neuro-Oncology*, *17*(suppl_4), iv1–iv62. doi:10.1093/neuonc/nov189 PMID:26511214

Otalora, M. L., Rosenbaum, M. S., & Orejula, A. R. (2018). Understanding health care service quality in developing Latin America. *Health Marketing Quarterly*, *35*(3), 167–185. doi:10.1080/07359683.2018.1514733 PMID:30588870

Ouyang, J., Gao, L., Yan, Y., Hokao, K., & Ge, J. (2009). Effects of improved consumer behavior on energy conservation in the urban residential sector of Hangzhou, China. *Journal of Asian Architecture and Building Engineering*, *8*(1), 243–249. doi:10.3130/jaabe.8.243

Ouzir, M., Khalfallah, B., Dehimi, S., & Kadi Ahmed, A. (2021). Quantitative and qualitative assessment of urban green spaces in Boussaada City, Algeria using remote sensing techniques. *Journal of Geography and Regional Planning*, *14*(3), 123–133. doi:10.5897/JGRP2021.0831

Palazzo, D. (1997). Sulle spalle di giganti. (On the Shoulders of Giants) Franco Angeli, Milano.

Palazzo, D., & Steiner, F. R. (2011). *Urban ecological design—a process for regenerative places*. Island Press.

Palmer, M. (2005). Understanding the workplace: A research framework for industrial archaelogy in Britain. *Industrial Archaeology Review*, *27*(1), 9–17. doi:10.1179/030907205X50441

Palumbo, L., Rampone, G., Bertamini, M., Sinico, M., Clarke, E., & Vartanian, O. (2020). Visual preference for abstract curvature and for interior spaces: Beyond undergraduate student samples. *Psychology of Aesthetics, Creativity, and the Arts*.

Pandolfi, J. M., Bradbury, R. H., Sala, E., Hughes, T. P., Bjorndal, K. A., Cooke, R. G., McArdle, D., McClenachan, L., Newman, M. J. H., Paredes, G., Warner, R. R., & Jackson, J. B. C. (2003). Global trajectories of the long-term decline of coral reef ecosystems. *Science*, *301*(5635), 955–958. doi:10.1126cience.1085706 PMID:12920296

Paniagua Padilla, D. (2015). *Interpretación bioclimática de la arquitectura vernácula*. Monografía.

Papaioannou, T. G., Kotsopoulos, D., Bardaki, C., Lounis, S., Dimitriou, N., Boultadakis, G., Garbi, A., & Schoofs, A. (2017). IOT-enabled gamification for energy conservation in public buildings. *2017 Global Internet of Things Summit (GIoTS)*. doi:10.1109/GIOTS.2017.8016269

Papaioannou, T., Dimitriou, N., Vasilakis, K., Schoofs, A., Nikiforakis, M., Pursche, F., Deliyski, N., Taha, A., Kotsopoulos, D., Bardaki, C., Kotsilitis, S., & Garbi, A. (2018). An IOT-based gamified approach for reducing occupants' energy wastage in public buildings. *Sensors (Basel)*, *18*(2), 537. doi:10.339018020537 PMID:29439414

Parameshachari, B. D., Gopy, S. K., Hurry, G., & Gopaul, T. T. (2013). A study on smart home control system through speech. *International Journal of Computers and Applications*, *69*(19).

Parasuraman, A., Zeithaml, V. A., & Berry, L. L. (1985). A Conceptual Model of Service Quality and Its Implications for Future Research. *Journal of Marketing*, *49*(4), 41–50. doi:10.1177/002224298504900403

Pardo Abad, C. J. (2020). Valuation of industrial heritage in terms of sustainability: Some cases of tourist reference in spain. *Sustainability (Switzerland)*, *12*(21), 1–23. doi:10.3390u12219216

Park, J., & Chowdhury, S. (2018). Investigating the barriers in a typical journey by public transport users with disabilities. *Journal of Transport & Health*, *10*, 361–368. doi:10.1016/j.jth.2018.05.008

Pasini, D., Reda, F., & Häkkinen, T. (2017). User engaging practices for energy saving in buildings: Critical Review and new enhanced procedure. *Energy and Building*, *148*, 74–88. doi:10.1016/j.enbuild.2017.05.010

Patel, P. C., Kohtamäki, M., Parida, V., & Wincent, J. (2015). Entrepreneurial orientation-as-experimentation and firm performance: The enabling role of absorptive capacity. *Strategic Management Journal*, *36*(11), 1739–1749. doi:10.1002mj.2310

Pathak, P., Pal, P. R., Shrivastava, M., & Ora, P. (2019). Fifth revolution: Applied AI & human intelligence with cyber physical systems. *International Journal of Engineering and Advanced Technology*, *8*(3), 23–27.

Paulson, S., D'Alisa, G., Demaria, F., & Kallis, G. (2020). *The Case for Degrowth*. Polity.

Pauly, D. (1995). Anecdotes and the Shifting Baseline Syndrome of Fisheries. *Trends in Ecology & Evolution*, *10*(10), 430. doi:10.1016/S0169-5347(00)89171-5 PMID:21237093

Peet, R., & Watts, M. (1996) Liberation ecology: development, sustainability, and environment in an age of market triumphalism in: Richard Peet & Michael Watts (Eds) Liberation Ecologies: Environment, Development, Social Movements. Routledge.

Pencheva, E., Atanasov, I., & Trifonov, V. (2022). Identity Management in Future Railway Mobile Communication System. *Applied Sciences (Basel, Switzerland)*, *12*(9), 4293. doi:10.3390/app12094293

Pentland, A. (2004, October). *Social Dynamics: Signals and Behavior. International Conference on Developmental Learning*, Salk Institute, San Diego, CA

Pentland, B. T., Hærem, T., & Hillison, D. (2011). The (N)Ever-Changing World: Stability and Change in Organizational Routines. *Organization Science*, *22*(6), 1369–1383. doi:10.1287/orsc.1110.0624

Pereira, J. P. A. M. (2019). *Gamification in building automation - the Human in the loop in a Cyber-Physical System* [Dissertation, Universidad Nova de Lisboa]

Pereira, V., Munjal, S., & Ishizaka, A. (2019, October). Outsourcing and offshoring decision making and its implications for businesses- A synthesis of research pursuing five pertinent questions. *Journal of Business Research*, *103*, 348–355. doi:10.1016/j.jbusres.2019.07.009

Petterson, M., Kensek, K., & Noble, D. (2017). Supple Skins: Considering the Relevance, Scalability, and Design Strategies for Façade System Resilience. *Journal of Architectural Education*, *71*(1), 34–45. doi:10.1080/10464883.2017.1260919

Pfaffenbichler, P., Emberger, G., & Shepherd, S. A. (2010). System dynamics approach to land use transport interaction modelling: The strategic model MARS and its application. *System Dynamics Review*, *26*(3), 262–282. doi:10.1002dr.451

Pfeffer, J., & Salancik, G. (1978). *The External Control of Organizations: A Resource Dependence Perspective*. Harper & Row.

Pham, V. H., Nguyen, V. T., Ly, C. D., Choi, J., Park, S., Mondal, S., Vo, T. H., Lim, H. G., & Oh, J. (2022). Development of fast photoacoustic and ultrasound imaging system based on slider-crank scanner for small animals and humans study. *Expert Systems with Applications*, *206*, 117939. doi:10.1016/j.eswa.2022.117939

Phan, H. Y. T., Yano, T., Sato, T., & Nishimura, T. (2010). Characteristics of road traffic noise in Hanoi and Ho Chi Minh City, Vietnam. *Applied Acoustics*, *71*(5), 479–485. doi:10.1016/j.apacoust.2009.11.008

Picado-Santos, L. G., Capitão, S. D., & Neves, J. M. C. (2020). Crumb rubber asphalt mixtures: A literature review. *Construction & Building Materials*, *247*, 118577. doi:10.1016/j.conbuildmat.2020.118577

Piderit Moreno, M., & Labarca, C. (2015). Methodology for Assessing Daylighting Design Strategies in Classroom with a Climate-Based Method. *Sustainability*, *7*(1), 880–897. doi:10.3390u7010880

Pielot, M., & Boll, S. (2010). Tactile Wayfinder. Comparison of Tactile Waypoint Navigation with Commercial Pedestrian Navigation Systems (pp. 76–93). doi:10.1007/978-3-642-12654-3_5

Pierre-Louis, K. (2018). El calentamiento que general el aire acondicionado. *The New York Times*. https://www.nytimes.com/es/2018/05/18/espanol/aire-acondicionado-calentamiento-global.html

Pierre-Louis, K. (2018). The world wants air-conditioning. That could warm the world. *The New York Times*. https://www.nytimes.com/2018/05/15/climate/air-conditioning.html

Pineo, R. (2019). Preface to the 2019 Special Issue on Public Healthcare in the Developing World. *Journal of Developing Societies*, *35*(1), 1–15. doi:10.1177/0169796X19826774

Pirjola, L., Lähde, T., Niemi, J. V., Kousa, A., Rönkkö, T., Karjalainen, P., Keskinen, J., Frey, A., & Hillamo, R. (2012). Spatial and temporal characterization of traffic emissions in urban microenvironments with a mobile laboratory. *Atmospheric Environment*, *63*, 156–167. doi:10.1016/j.atmosenv.2012.09.022

Pitra, G. M., & Musti, K. S. S. (2021). Duck Curve with Renewable Energies and Storage Technologies. *13th International Conference on Computational Intelligence and Communication Networks (CICN)*, (pp. 66-71). IEEE. 10.1109/CICN51697.2021.9574671

Plumwood, V. (1995). Nature, self and gender: feminism, environmental philosophy, and the critique of rationalism in: Christine Pierce & Donald VanDeVeer (Eds) People, Penguins and Plastic Trees. Belmond Wadsworth.

Pomey, M.-P., Hihat, H., Khalifa, M., Lebel, P., Néron, A., & Dumez, V. (2015). Patient partnership in quality improvement of healthcare services: Patients' inputs and challenges faced. *Patient Experience Journal*, *2*(1), 29–42. doi:10.35680/2372-0247.1064

Ponce Herrero, G., & Dávila Linares, J. M. (1998). Medidas higienistas y planes de reforma urbana en el tránsito de los siglos XIX al XX en las principales ciudades de la provincia de Alicante. *Investigaciones Geográficas*, *20*(20), 141. doi:10.14198/INGEO1998.20.07

Poortinga, W., Bird, N., Hallingberg, B., Phillips, R., & Williams, D. (2021). The role of perceived public and private green space in subjective health and wellbeing during and after the first peak of the COVID-19 outbreak. *Landscape and Urban Planning*, *211*, 104092. doi:10.1016/j.landurbplan.2021.104092 PMID:36540159

Pope, N. J., & Denton, M. L. (2020). Low irradiance light exposure alters the activity of key enzymes in the mitochondrial electron transport chain. In M. R. Hamblin, J. D. Carroll, & P. Arany (Eds.), *Mechanisms of Photobiomodulation Therapy XV* (p. 13). SPIE. doi:10.1117/12.2546624

Popp, D. (2019). Environmental Policy and Innovation: A Decade of Research. *International Review of Environmental and Resource Economics*, *13*(3–4), 265–337. doi:10.1561/101.00000111

Porter, M. E. (2000). Strategy and the internet. *Harvard Business Review*, *79*(3), 62–78. PMID:11246925

Porter, M. E., & Van der Linde, C. (1995). Toward a new conception of the environment-competitiveness relationship. *The Journal of Economic Perspectives*, *9*(4), 97–118. doi:10.1257/jep.9.4.97

Postel, S. (1994). Carrying capacity: Earth's bottom line. In L. R. Brown, A. T. Durning, C. Flavin, H. F. French, N. Lenssen, M. D. Lowe, A. Misch, S. Postel, M. Renner, P. Weber, & ... (Eds.), *State of the World* (pp. 3–21). W.W. Norton.

Potchter, O., Cohen, P., Lin, T.-P., & Matzarakis, A. (2022). A systematic review advocating a framework and benchmarks for assessing outdoor human thermal perception. *The Science of the Total Environment*, *833*, 155128. doi:10.1016/j.scitotenv.2022.155128 PMID:35405233

Powles, A. E. J., Martin, D. J., Wells, I. T. P., & Goodwin, C. R. (2018). Physics of ultrasound. *Anaesthesia and Intensive Care Medicine*, *19*(4), 202–205. doi:10.1016/j.mpaic.2018.01.005

Prado, R. G. (1998). La herencia moderna. Astrágalo. *Cultura de la Arquitectura y la Ciudad*, *8*, 35–44.

Prasad, M., Taele, P., Goldberg, D., & Hammond, T. A. (2014). HaptiMoto. *Proceedings of the SIGCHI Conference on Human Factors in Computing Systems,* (pp. 3597–3606). IEEE. 10.1145/2556288.2557404

Prasad, M., Taele, P., Olubeko, A., & Hammond, T. (2014). HaptiGo: A navigational; *2014 IEEE Haptics Symposium (HAPTICS),* (pp. 339–345). IEEE. 10.1109/HAPTICS.2014.6775478

Praticò, A. (2015). *The analysis of the new strategic area of Hamburg: The redevelopment project of the Hafencity's waterfront*. Research Gate. doi:10.13140/RG.2.2.36784.56322

Preite, M. (2021). Recovered factories: Industrial heritage reuse in Italy. *Ural'skij Istoriceskij Vestnik*, *71*(2), 55–64. doi:10.30759/1728-9718-2021-2(71)-55-64

Premier, A., GhaffarianHoseini, A., & GhaffarianHoseini, A. (2022). Solar-powered smart urban furniture: Preliminary investigation on limits and potentials of current designs. *Smart and Sustainable Built Environment*, *11*(2), 334–345. doi:10.1108/SASBE-09-2021-0152

PRE-Sustainability. (n.d.). Life Cycle Assessment. https://pre-sustainability.com/articles/life-cycle-assessment-lca-basics/

Pretty, J. (2011). Interdisciplinary progress in approaches to address social-ecological and ecocultural *systems. Environmental Conservation*, *38*(2), 127–139. doi:10.1017/S0376892910000937

Preuss, L. (2007). Contribution of purchasing and supply management to ecological innovation. *International Journal of Innovation Management*, *11*(4), 515–537. doi:10.1142/S1363919607001850

Proestakis, A., di Sorrentino, E. P., Brown, H. E., van Sluijs, E., Mani, A., Caldeira, S., & Herrmann, B. (2018). Network interventions for changing physical activity behaviour in Preadolescents. *Nature Human Behaviour*, *2*(10), 778–787. doi:10.103841562-018-0436-y PMID:30886902

Prospero, F., & Health, R. (2010). *Healthy Open Spaces*. Research Gate. doi:10.13140/2.1.2568.0169

Prothero, A., Dobscha, S., Freund, J., Kilbourne, W. E., Luchs, M. G., Ozanne, L. K., & Thøgersen, J. (2011). Sustainable consumption: Opportunities for consumer research and public policy. *Journal of Public Policy & Marketing*, *30*(1), 31–38. doi:10.1509/jppm.30.1.31

Qi, S., Zhou, C., Li, K., & Tang, S. (2021). The impact of a carbon trading pilot policy on the low-carbon international competitiveness of industry in China: An empirical analysis based on a DDD model. *Journal of Cleaner Production*, *281*, 125361. doi:10.1016/j.jclepro.2020.125361

Qu, C., Cao, W., Fan, Y., & Lin, Y. (2010). Near-infrared light protect the photoreceptor from light-induced damage in rats. *Advances in Experimental Medicine and Biology*, *664*, 365–374. doi:10.1007/978-1-4419-1399-9_42 PMID:20238037

Rahim, A., Eladwiah, R., & Abdul Rahman, A. (2013). Resource-based framework of green IT capability toward firms 'competitive advantage. *Resource (Saint Joseph, Mich.)*, *6*, 18–2013.

Ramson, P., Govender, P., & Naidoo, K. (2016). Recruitment and retention strategies for public sector optometrists in KwaZulu-Natal Province, South Africa. *African Vision and Eye Health*, *75*(1), e1–e10. doi:10.4102/aveh.v75i1.349

Ranger-Moore, J. (1997). Bigger may be better, but is older wiser? Organizational age and size in the New York life insurance industry. *American Sociological Review*, *62*(6), 903–921. doi:10.2307/2657346

Rani, P. (2019). Strategy Implementation in Organizations: A Conceptual Overview pushpa rani. *Management*, *14*(3), 205–218. doi:10.26493/1854-4231.14.205-218

Rappaport, R. A. (2000). *Pigs for the Ancestors: Ritual in the Ecology of a New Guinea People*. Waveland Press.

Rashid, H., & Osman, S. bin, Hassan, N., Ahmed, I. U., Das, R., & Karim, M. M. (2017). A new design approach of home automation system for patients with physical disability to reduce water wastage and power consumption using renewable energy. *2017 4th International Conference on Advances in Electrical Engineering (ICAEE)*, (pp. 770–774). IEEE.

Raworth, K. (2012). A safe and just space for humanity: Can we live within the doughnut? Oxfam Policy and Practice. *Climate Change and Resilience*, *8*, 1–26.

Raza, U., Kulkarni, P., & Sooriyabandara, M. (2017). Low Power Wide Area Networks: An Overview. *IEEE Communications Surveys and Tutorials*, *19*(2), 855–873. doi:10.1109/COMST.2017.2652320

Recio, A., Linares, C., Banegas, J. R., & Díaz, J. (2016). Road traffic noise effects on cardiovascular, respiratory, and metabolic health: An integrative model of biological mechanisms. *Environmental Research*, *146*, 359–370. doi:10.1016/j.envres.2015.12.036 PMID:26803214

Reich, D. (2018). *Who We Are and How We Got Here: Ancient DNA and the New Science of the Human Past*. Oxford University Press.

Reichstein, C., & Härting, R.-C. (2018). Potentials of changing customer needs in a digital world – a conceptual model and recommendations for action in tourism. *Procedia Computer Science*, *126*, 1484–1494. doi:10.1016/j.procs.2018.08.120

Reinmoeller, P., & Van Baardwijk, N. (2005). The link between diversity and resilience. *MIT Sloan Management Review*, *46*(4), 61–64.

Reiter, S. (2010). Assessing Wind Comfort in Urban Planning. *Environment and Planning. B, Planning & Design*, *37*(5), 857–873. doi:10.1068/b35154

Ren, S., Sun, H., & Zhang, T. (2021). Do environmental subsidies spur environmental? innovation? Empirical evidence from Chinese listed firms. *Technological Forecasting and Social Change*, *173*, 121123. doi:10.1016/j.techfore.2021.121123

Roaf, S., Crichton, D., Nicol, F., Rudge, J., & Kovats, S. (2010). Adapting Buildings and Cities for Climate Change. In Adapting Buildings and Cities for Climate Change. doi:10.1016/B978-1-85617-720-7.00007-3

Roberts, C. M. (2007). *The unnatural history of the sea*. Island Press.

Rockcastle, S. F., Chamilothori, K., & Andersen, M. (2017). *An experiment in virtual reality to measure daylight-driven interest in rendered architectural scenes.*

Rockfon Grodan. (n.d.). Grodan 101. https://www.grodan101.com/about-grodan/

Rodriguez, F., Garcia-Hansen, V., Allan, A., & Isoardi, G. (2021). Subjective responses toward daylight changes in window views: Assessing dynamic environmental attributes in an immersive experiment. *Building and Environment*, *195*, 107720. doi:10.1016/j.buildenv.2021.107720

Rogers, C. S., Jones, M. S., McConkey, S., Spehar, B., van Engen, K. J., Sommers, M. S., & Peelle, J. E. (2020). Age-Related Differences in Auditory Cortex Activity During Spoken Word Recognition. *Neurobiology of Language*, *1*(4), 452–473. doi:10.1162/nol_a_00021 PMID:34327333

Rogers, E. M. (2003). Elements of diffusion. *Diffusion of Innovations*, *5*, 1–38.

Rokhina, E., Lens, P., & Virkutyte, J. (2009). Low-frequency ultrasound in biotechnology: State of the art. *Trends in Biotechnology*, *27*(5), 298–306. doi:10.1016/j.tibtech.2009.02.001 PMID:19324441

Román López, E., Córdoba Hernández, R., & Eiroa Escalada, T. (2022). Thermal Comfort for Older Population in Spain: Diagnosis and Strategies for a Climate Change Scenario. In E. Pozo Méndez & E. Higueras García (Eds.), *Urban Design and Planning for Age-Friendly Environments Across Europe: North and South* (pp. 243–265). Springer. doi:10.1007/978-3-030-93875-8_12

Ross, C. K., Frommelt, G., Hazelwood, L., & Chang, R. W. (1987). The role of expectations in patient satisfaction with medical care. *Journal of Health Care Marketing*, *7*(4). PMID:10302171

Rueda Martínez de Santos, J. R. (2005). *Guía para la evaluación del impacto en la salud y en el bienestar de proyectos, programas o políticas extrasanitarias. Investigación Comisionada. Informe nº: Osteba D-05-04*. Servicio Central de Publicaciones del Gobierno Vasco.

Ruiz Palomeque, L. G. (2018). *Una Propuesta Metodológica para la Gestión Integral de la Rehabilitación Urbana*. Universidad Politécnica de Madrid. https://oa.upm.es/62657/

Ruiz, A., Campano, M. Á., Acosta, I. J., & Luque, Ó. (2021). Partial Daylight Autonomy (DAp): A new lighting dynamic metric to optimize the design of windows for seasonal use spaces. *Applied Sciences (Basel, Switzerland)*, *11*(17), 11. doi:10.3390/app11178228

Rybnov, Y., Spivak, A. A., Kharlamov, V. A., & Soloviev, A. v. (2018). Infrasound noises of megapolis. In O. A. Romanovskii, & G. G. Matvienko (Eds.), *24th International Symposium on Atmospheric and Ocean Optics: Atmospheric Physics* (p. 26). SPIE. 10.1117/12.2502335

Saemann, E.-U. (2008). Contribution of the tyre to further lowering tyre-road noise. *Acoustics (Basel, Switzerland)*, 5429–5434.

Sailer, M., Hense, J. U., Mayr, S. K., & Mandl, H. (2017). How gamification motivates: An experimental study of the effects of specific game design elements on psychological need satisfaction. *Computers in Human Behavior*, *69*, 371–380. doi:10.1016/j.chb.2016.12.033

Salimath, M. S. & Jones, R. (2011). *Population ecology theory: implications for sustainability.* Emerald Group Publishing Limited.

Salimath, M., & Jones, R. III. (2011). Population ecology theory: Implications for sustainability. *Management Decision*, *49*(6), 874–910. doi:10.1108/00251741111143595

Sallis, J. F., Owen, N., & Fisher, E. B. (2008). Ecological models of health behavior. In K. Glanz, B. K. Rimer, & K. Viswanath (Eds.), *Health behavior and health education: Theory, research, and practice* (pp. 465–485). Jossey-Bass.

Sánchez-Montañés, B., & Castilla, M. V. (2020). Resilience factories. An opportunity for industrial heritage: La trinidad case study. *Architecture. City and Environment*, *15*(43), 1–18. doi:10.5821/ace.15.43.9192

Sanquist, T. F. (2008). Human factors and energy use. *HFES Bulletin*, *51*(11), 1–3.

Santoro, G., Vrontis, D., Thrassou, A., & Dezi, L. (2018). The Internet of Things: Building a knowledge management system for open innovation and knowledge management capacity. *Technological Forecasting and Social Change*, *136*, 347–354. doi:10.1016/j.techfore.2017.02.034

Santos, J., Spector, B., & Van der Heyden, L. (2009). *Toward a theory of business model innovation within incumbent firms*. INSEAD. doi:10.2139srn.1362515

Sanz, E., Olazabal, M., & Sainz de Murieta, E. (2019). *Planificación de la adaptación al cambio climático en las ciudades españolas: evaluando su sostenibilidad y efectividad a largo plazo.* Basque Centre for Climate Change (BC3). https://www.researchgate.net/publication/337059161_Planificacion_de_la_adaptacion_al_cambio_climatico_en_las_ciudades_espanolas_Evaluando_su_sostenibilidad_y_efectividad_a_largo_plazo

Saremi, P. (2020). Environmental Pollution and ways to Reduce Contamination with use of Environmental Engineering Techniques in Metropolises of Developing Countries. International Journal of Environment. *Agricultural Biotechnology*, *5*(3), 566–581. doi:10.22161/ijeab.53.9

Sartorius, N. (2006). The Meanings of Health and its Promotion. *Croatian Medical Journal*, *47*(4), 662–664. PMID:16909464

Sastry, M. K. S. (2007). Integrated Outage Management System: An effective solution for power utilities to address customer grievances. *International Journal of Electronic Customer Relationship Management*, *1*(1), 30–40. doi:10.1504/IJECRM.2007.014424

Sastry, M. K. S., & Sahadeo, A. (2015). Distributed Cloud Computing Based GIS Solution for Electrical Power Utility Asset Management. *Int. Conf. on Computational Intelligence and Communication Networks,* (pp. 832-838). IEEE. 10.1109/CICN.2015.169

Satterthwaite, D. (1993). The impact on health urban environments. *Environment and Urbanization*, *5*(2), 87–111. doi:10.1177/095624789300500208 PMID:12318602

Saud, S., Chen, S., Haseeb, A., Khan, K., & Imran, M. (2019). The Nexus between Financial Development, Income Level, and Environment in Central and Eastern European Countries: A Perspective on Belt and Road Initiative. *Environmental Science and Pollution Research International, 26*(16), 16053–16075. doi:10.100711356-019-05004-5 PMID:30968296

Saw, S.-M. (2002). Near-Work Activity, Night-lights, and Myopia in the Singapore-China Study. *Archives of Ophthalmology, 120*(5), 620. doi:10.1001/archopht.120.5.620 PMID:12003612

Scarfe, P., & Glennerster, A. (2015). Using high-fidelity virtual reality to study perception in freely moving observers. *Journal of Vision (Charlottesville, Va.), 15*(9), 3. doi:10.1167/15.9.3 PMID:26161632

Schaffers, H., Komninos, N., Pallot, M., Trousse, B., Nilsson, M., & Oliveira, A. (2011). Lecture Notes in Computer Science: Vol. 6656. *Smart Cities and the Future Internet: Towards Cooperation Frameworks for Open Innovation.* Springer. doi:10.1007/978-3-642-20898-0_31

SchmidtC.SchneiderY.SteffenS.StreitzD. (2020). Capital misal-location and innovation. *Available at* SSRN 3489801. doi:10.2139/ssrn.3489801

Schnarch, B. (2004). Ownership, control, access, and possession (OCAP) or self-determination applied to research: A critical analysis of contemporary First Nations research and some options for First Nations communities. *Journal of Aboriginal Health, 1*, 80–97.

Schomer, P. D. (2013). Comments on Recently Published Article, "Concerns about Infrasound from Wind Turbines. *Acoustics Today, 9*(4), 7. doi:10.1121/1.4827009

Schuurman, D., Marez, L. D., & Ballon, P. (2016). The impact of living lab methodology on open innovation contributions and outcomes. *Technology Innovation Management Review, 6*(1), 7–16. doi:10.22215/timreview/956

Scorpio, M., Laffi, R., Masullo, M., Ciampi, G., Rosato, A., Maffei, L., & Sibilio, S. (2020). Virtual reality for smart urban lighting design: Review, applications and opportunities. *Energies, 13*(15), 3809. doi:10.3390/en13153809

Scudder, T. (1973). The Human Ecology of Big Projects: River Basin Development and Resettlement. [Section 3 in Montgomery, Bennett, and Scudder (1973)] In B. J. Siegel, A. R. Beals, & S. A. Tyler (Eds.), *Annual Review of Anthropology.* Annual Reviews Inc.

Scudder, T., & Colson, E. (1982). From Welfare to Development: A Conceptual Framework for the Analysis of Dislocated People in Involuntary. In A. Hansen & A. Oliver-Smith (Eds.), *Migration and Resettlement: The Problems and Responses of Dislocated People* (pp. 267–287). Westview Press, Westview Special Study.

Seebode, D., Jeanrenaud, S., & Bessant, J. (2012). Managing innovation for sustainability. *R & D Management, 42*(3), 195–206. doi:10.1111/j.1467-9310.2012.00678.x

Seguí, P. (n.d.). *La tierra que busca su protagonismo en la arquitectura.* Ovacen. https://ovacen.com/la-tierra-que-busca-su-protagonismo-en-la-arquitectura/

Sele, K., & Grand, S. (2016). Unpacking the dynamics of ecologies of routines: Mediators and their generative effects in routine interactions. *Organization Science, 27*(3), 722–738. doi:10.1287/orsc.2015.1031

Sendra, J. J. J., Domínguez-Amarillo, S., Bustamante, P., León, A. L., Bustamante Rojas, P., & Leon, A. L. (2013). Energy intervention in the residential sector in the south of spain: Current challenges. *Informes de la Construcción, 65*(532), 457–464. doi:10.3989/ic.13.074

Senkubuge, F., Modisenyane, M., & Bishaw, T. (2014). Strengthening health systems by health sector reforms. *Global Health Action, 7*(1), 1–7. doi:10.3402/gha.v7.23568 PMID:24560261

Sens, L., Neuling, U., & Kaltschmitt, M. (2022). Capital expenditure and levelized cost of electricity of photovoltaic plants and wind turbines – Development by 2050. *Renewable Energy*, *185*, 525–537. doi:10.1016/j.renene.2021.12.042

Serrano Yuste, P. (2015). *Tierra comprimida y normativa para construir edificios*. Certificados Energéticos. https://www.certificadosenergeticos.com/tierra-comprimida-normativa-construir-edificios

Shafei, I., Walburg, J., & Taher, A. (2019). Verifying alternative measures of healthcare service quality. *International Journal of Health Care Quality Assurance*, *32*(2), 516–533. doi:10.1108/IJHCQA-05-2016-0069 PMID:31017062

Shafieisabet, N., Doostisabzi, B., & Azharianfar, S. (2017). An Assessment of Villagers' Satisfaction with the Quality of Construction-Related Services Based on the SERVQUAL Model. *Current Urban Studies*, *5*(01), 20–34. doi:10.4236/cus.2017.51002

Shafiq, M., Naeem, M. A., Munawar, Z., & Fatima, I. (2017). Service Quality Assessment of Hospitals in Asian Context: An Empirical Evidence From Pakistan. *INQUIRY: The Journal of Health Care Organization, Provision, and Financing*, *54*, 46958017714664. PMID:28660771

Shahadan, A., & Oliver, R. (2016). Elementary School Leaders' Perceptions of Their Roles in Managing School Curriculum: A Case Study. *Educational Research Review*, *11*(18), 1785–1789.

Shahin, A., & Samea, M. (2010). Developing the Models of Service Quality Gaps: A Critical Discussion. *Business Manaagement and Strategy*, *1*(1), 1–11. doi:10.5296/bms.v1i1.395

Shahrul, N. S., & Normah, M. (2015). Digital version newspaper: Implication towards printed newspaper circulation in Malaysia. *Malaysian Journal of Communication*, *31*(2), 687–701.

Shahzad, F., Lu, J., & Fareed, Z. (2019). Does firm life cycle impact corporate risk taking and performance? *Journal of Multinational Financial Management*, *51*, 23–44. doi:10.1016/j.mulfin.2019.05.001

Shaik, A., Bowen, N., Bole, J., Kunzi, G., Bruce, D., Abdelgawad, A., & Yelamarthi, K. (2018). Smart Car: An IoT Based Accident Detection System. *2018 IEEE Global Conference on Internet of Things (GCIoT)*, (pp. 1–5). IEEE. 10.1109/GCIoT.2018.8620131

Shameli, A., Althoff, T., Saberi, A., & Leskovec, J. (2017). How gamification affects physical activity. *Proceedings of the 26th International Conference on World Wide Web Companion - WWW '17 Companion*. IEEE. 10.1145/3041021.3054172

Shanahan, D. F., Lin, B. B., Bush, R., Gaston, K. J., Dean, J. H., Barber, E., & Fuller, R. A. (2015). Toward Improved Public Health Outcomes From Urban Nature. *American Journal of Public Health*, *105*(3), 470–477. doi:10.2105/AJPH.2014.302324 PMID:25602866

Shang, Z., Zhao, & Zhang. (2019). Obtaining High-Resolution Seabed Topography and Surface Details by Co-Registration of Side-Scan Sonar and Multibeam Echo Sounder Images. *Remote Sensing*, *11*(12), 1496. doi:10.3390/rs11121496

Sheep wool insulation. (n.d.). Sheep Wool. https://www.sheepwoolinsulation.com/

Shemesh, A., Talmon, R., Karp, O., Amir, I., Bar, M., & Grobman, Y. J. (2017). Affective response to architecture–investigating human reaction to spaces with different geometry. *Architectural Science Review*, *60*(2), 116–125. doi:10.1080/00038628.2016.1266597

Shi, C. K. (2019). Exploring the Evolutionary Trajectory of Corporate Green Technology Innovation under Environmental Regulatory Constraints. *J. Econ. Res.*, *13*, 15–16. doi:10.3969/j.issn.1673-291X.2019.13.007

Shinhmar, H., Hogg, C., Neveu, M., & Jeffery, G. (2021). Weeklong improved colour contrasts sensitivity after single 670 nm exposures associated with enhanced mitochondrial function. *Scientific Reports*, *11*(1), 22872. doi:10.103841598-021-02311-1 PMID:34819619

Sidze, E. M., Beekink, E., & Maina, B. W. (2015). Challenges associated with tracking resources allocation for reproductive health in sub-Saharan African countries: The UNFPA/NIDI resource flows project experience. *Reproductive Health*, *12*(1), 39. doi:10.118612978-015-0033-8 PMID:26012472

Silva, A. S., & Ghisi, E. (2014). Uncertainty analysis of user behaviour and physical parameters in residential building performance simulation. *Energy and Building*, *76*, 381–391. doi:10.1016/j.enbuild.2014.03.001

Simberloff, D. (2018). Nature, Culture, and Natureculture: The Role of Nonnative Species in Biocultures. In R. Rozzi, R. H. May Jr, F. S. Chapin III, F. Massardo, M. C. Gavin, I. J. Klaver, A. Pauchard, M. A. Nunez, & D. Simberloff (Eds.), *From Biocultural Homogenization to Biocultural Conservation* (pp. 207–218). Nature. doi:10.1007/978-3-319-99513-7_12

Simon H.A., (1968) The Science of the artificial.

Simon, J., Jahn, M., & Al-Akkad, A. (2012). Saving energy at work. *Proceedings of the 11th International Conference on Mobile and Ubiquitous Multimedia - MUM '12*. ACM. d10.1145/2406367.2406379

Simpson, G., Sinnis-Bourozikas, A., Zhao, M., Aseeri, S., & Interrante, V. (2018). A virtual reality investigation of the impact of wallpaper pattern scale on qualitative spaciousness judgments and action-based measures of room size perception. *International Conference on Virtual Reality and Augmented Reality,* (pp. 161–176). IEEE. 10.1007/978-3-030-01790-3_10

Sini, J.-F., Anquetin, S., & Mestayer, P. G. (1996). Pollutant dispersion and thermal effects in urban street canyons. *Atmospheric Environment*, *30*(15), 2659–2677. doi:10.1016/1352-2310(95)00321-5

Slater, D., & Tonkiss, F. (2001). *Market society: Markets and modern social theory*. Polity Press.

Smagowska, B., & Pawlaczyk-Łuszczyńska, M. (2013). Effects of Ultrasonic Noise on the Human Body—A Bibliographic Review. *International Journal of Occupational Safety and Ergonomics*, *19*(2), 195–202. doi:10.1080/10803548.2013.11076978 PMID:23759188

Smartnet. (2019). DataSmart Cities: Empowering Cities through Data. *SmmartNet.* https://smartnet.niua.org/data-smart-cities

Sneideriene, A., & Rugine, H. (2019). Theoretical approach on the green technologies development. *Regional Formation and Development Studies*, *2*(28), 124–134.

Sole, R. V., & Bascompte, J. (1995). Spatial Self Organization Self-Organization in complex Ecosystems Princeton University Press. Pág. 84 – 125

Somoza-Medina, X., & Monteserín-Abella, O. (2021). The sustainability of industrial heritage tourism far from the axes of economic development in Europe: Two case studies. *Sustainability (Switzerland)*, *13*(3), 1–27. doi:10.3390u13031077

Son, Y., Shin, H., Kim, D., Park, Y., Noh, J., Choi, K., Choi, J., & Kim, Y. (2015*). Rocking Drones with Intentional Sound Noise on Gyroscopic Sensors.* 24th USENIX Security Symposium (USENIX Security 15). USENIX. https://www.usenix.org/conference/usenixsecurity15/technical-sessions/presentation/son

Soranzo, A., & Wilson, C. (2014). *Virtual environments in visual perception: applications and challenges.*

Source Weather Data Formats. (n.d.). Auxiliary Programs—EnergyPlus 8.3. https://bigladdersoftware.com/epx/docs/8-3/auxiliary-programs/source-weather-data-formats.html

Souza, E. (2019). *Colores de la tierra: los increíbles diseños de los muros de barro en Ghana.* Archdaily. https://www.archdaily.cl/cl/914727/colores-de-la-tierra-los-increibles-disenos-de-los-muros-de-tapia-en-ghana

Souza, E. (2021). *Materiales a 0km: preservando el medio ambiente y las culturas locales.* Archdaily. https://www.archdaily.mx/mx/958897/materiales-a-0-km-preservando-el-medio-ambiente-y-las-culturas-locales

Spee, P., Jarzabkowski, P., & Smets, M. (2016). The influence of routine interdependence and skillful accomplishment on the coordination of standardizing and customizing. *Organization Science*, *27*(3), 759–781. doi:10.1287/orsc.2016.1050

Spirn, A. W. (2011). *Ecological urbanism: a framework for the design of resilient cities.* Anne Whistonspirn. https://annewhistonspirn.com/pdf/spirn_ecological_urbanism-2011.pdf

Stamps, A. E. III. (2011). Effects of area, height, elongation, and color on perceived spaciousness. *Environment and Behavior*, *43*(2), 252–273. doi:10.1177/0013916509354696

Stamps, A. E. III, & Krishnan, V. (2006). Spaciousness and boundary roughness. *Environment and Behavior*, *38*(6), 841–872. doi:10.1177/0013916506288052

Stathopoulos, T. (2006). Pedestrian level winds and outdoor human comfort. *Journal of Wind Engineering and Industrial Aerodynamics*, *94*(11), 769–780. doi:10.1016/j.jweia.2006.06.011

Steenkamp, A. J. (1995). The South African Constitution of 1993 and the Bill of Rights: An Evaluation in Light of International Human Rights Norms. *Human Rights Quarterly*, *17*(1), 101–126. doi:10.1353/hrq.1995.0010

Steiner, F. R. (1991). *The living landscape: an ecological approach to landscape planning.* McGraw-Hill.

Steiner, F. R. (2001). *Human ecology: following nature's lead.* Island Press.

Steiner, F. R. (2016). *Human ecology: how nature and culture shape our world.* The Island Press.

Steinzor, R. (2012). The case for abolishing centralized white house regulatory review. *Michigan Journal of Environmental & Administrative Law*, *1*(1.1), 209. doi:10.36640/mjeal.1.1.case

Stewart, T. A., & O'Connell, P. (2017). (201)7. HOW TO MEET YOUR CUSTOMER'S NEEDS—AND YOUR OWN: UNDERSTANDING SERVICE DESIGN ARCHETYPES. *Leader to Leader*, *2017*(84), 48–54. doi:10.1002/ltl.20291

Stiglitz, J. (2015). *Globalization and its discontents.* Penguin.

Stinson, L. (2017, June 8). Apple's architect says the future of offices must be flexible. *Wired.* https://www.wired.com/2017/06/apples-architect-says-future-offices-must-flexible/

Stokols, D. (1996). Translating social ecological theory into guidelines for community health promotion *American Journal of Health Promotion* Mar-Apr;10(4):282-98. doi:10.4278/0890-1171-10.4.282

Stokols, D. (1992). Establishing and maintaining healthy environments: Toward a social ecology of health promotion. *The American Psychologist*, *47*(1), 6–22. doi:10.1037/0003-066X.47.1.6 PMID:1539925

Stone, M. (2003). Is sustainability for development anthropologists? *Human Organization*, *62*(2), 93–99. doi:10.17730/humo.62.2.9cfam6hd6e04yac8

Stouhi, D. (2021). *Las ciudades tienen cada vez más jóvenes, ¿están preparadas?* Archdaily. https://www.archdaily.cl/cl/968540/las-ciudades-tienen-cada-vez-mas-jovenes-estan-preparadas

Sueyoshi, T., & Goto, M. (2012). Efficiency-based rank assessment for electric power industry: A combined use of data envelopment analysis (DEA) and DEA-discriminant analysis (DA). *Energy Economics*, *34*(3), 634–644. doi:10.1016/j.eneco.2011.04.001

Sukopp, H., & Werner, P. (1991). *Naturaleza en las ciudades*. Ministerio.

Sumaedi, S., Yarmen, M., & Yuda Bakti, I. G. M. (2016). Healthcare service quality model. *International Journal of Productivity and Performance Management*, *65*(8), 1007–1024. doi:10.1108/IJPPM-08-2014-0126

Sun, L., Miao, C., & Yang, L. (2017). Ecological-economic efficiency evaluation of green technology innovation in strategic emerging industries based on entropy weighted G. Lian, A. Xu and Y. Zhu *Journal of Innovation & Knowledge, 7.*

Sunehra, D., & Tejaswi, V. (2016). Implementation of speech based home automation system using Bluetooth and GSM. *2016 International Conference on Signal Processing, Communication, Power and Embedded System (SCOPES),* (pp. 807–813). Springer. 10.1109/SCOPES.2016.7955552

Sung, N.-J., & Lee, J.-H. (2019). Association between Types of Usual Source of Care and User Perception of Overall Health Care Service Quality in Korea. *Korean Journal of Family Medicine*, *40*(3), 143–150. doi:10.4082/kjfm.17.0093 PMID:30419631

Sun, X., Chen, Z., & Huang, L. (2020). Effects of factor price distortion on industrial environmental efficiency: Evidence from environmental pollution in China. *Polish Journal of Environmental Studies*, *29*(5), 3803–3812. doi:10.15244/pjoes/116104

Sun, X., Zhou, X., Chen, Z., & Yang, Y. (2020b). Environmental efficiency of electric power industry, market segmentation and technologi-cal innovation: Empirical evidence from China. *The Science of the Total Environment*, *706*, 135749. doi:10.1016/j.scitotenv.2019.135749 PMID:31940733

Su, Q., Deng, X., Liu, Z., Tan, C., & Dong, F. (2022). Phase fraction measurement of oil–gas–water three-phase flow with stratified gas by ultrasound technique. *Measurement Science & Technology*, *33*(7), 075302. doi:10.1088/1361-6501/ac60f6

Sutherland, I. E. (1965). *The ultimate display. Multimedia: From wagner to virutal reality.* Norton.

Swinburn, B. A., Kraak, V. I., Allender, S., Atkins, V. J., Baker, P. I., Bogard, J. R., Brinsden, H., Calvillo, A., De Schutter, O., Devarajan, R., Ezzati, M., Friel, S., Goenka, S., Hammond, R. A., Hastings, G., Hawkes, C., Herrero, M., Hovmand, P. S., Howden, M., & Dietz, W. H. (2019). The Global Syndemic of Obesity, Undernutrition, and Climate Change: The Lancet Commission report. *Lancet*, *393*(10173), 791–846. doi:10.1016/S0140-6736(18)32822-8 PMID:30700377

Szemes, P. T., Joo-Ho Lee, Hashimoto, H., & Korondi, P. (2003). Guiding and communication assistant for disabled in intelligent urban environment. *Proceedings 2003 IEEE/ASME International Conference on Advanced Intelligent Mechatronics (AIM 2003),* (pp. 598–603). ACM. 10.1109/AIM.2003.1225162

Szkordilisz, F., & Zöld, A. (2016). Effect of Vegetation on Wind-Comfort. *Applied Mechanics and Materials*, *824*, 811–818. . doi:10.4028/www.scientific.net/AMM.824.811

Tabrizi JS, Goshayie EH, Doshmangir L, Yousefi M. (2018)The Barriers to Implementation of New Public Management Strategies in Iran's Primary Health Care: A Qualitative Study. *J Liaquat Uni Med Health Sci. 17*(01), 08-17. . doi:10.22442/jlumhs.181710542

Tabrizian, P., Baran, P. K., Smith, W. R., & Meentemeyer, R. K. (2018). Exploring perceived restoration potential of urban green enclosure through immersive virtual environments. *Journal of Environmental Psychology*, *55*, 99–109. doi:10.1016/j.jenvp.2018.01.001

Taherdoost, H. (2016). Validity and reliability of the research instrument; how to test the validation of a questionnaire/survey in research. *International Journal of Academic Research in Management (IJARM) 5*(3), 28-36.

Tai, H., Khairalseed, M., & Hoyt, K. (2019). 3D H-scan ultrasound imaging system and method for acoustic scatterer size estimation: Preliminary studies using phantom materials. 2019 IEEE International Ultrasonics Symposium (IUS), (pp. 1515–1518). IEEE.. 10.1109/ULTSYM.2019.8926174

Tainter, J. A. (2008). Collapse and Sustainability: Rome, the Maya, and the Modern World. *Archeological Papers of the American Anthropological Association*, *24*(1), 201–214. doi:10.1111/apaa.12038

Talari, S., Shafie-khah, M., Siano, P., Loia, V., Tommasetti, A., & Catalão, J. (2017). A Review of Smart Cities Based on the Internet of Things Concept. *Energies*, *10*(4), 1–23. doi:10.3390/en10040421

Talotte, C., Gautier, P.-E., Thompson, D. J., & Hanson, C. (2003). Identification, modelling and reduction potential of railway noise sources: A critical survey. *Journal of Sound and Vibration*, *267*(3), 447–468. doi:10.1016/S0022-460X(03)00707-7

Tan, K. S., & Eze, U. C. (2008). An empirical study of internet-based ICT adoption among Malaysian SMEs. *Communications of the IBIMA*, *1*, 1–12.

Targhi, M. Z., & Van Dessel, S. (2015). Potential Contribution of Urban Developments to Outdoor Thermal Comfort Conditions: The Influence of Urban Geometry and Form in Worcester, Massachusetts, USA. *Procedia Engineering*, *118*, 1153–1161. doi:10.1016/j.proeng.2015.08.457

Tarr, M. J., & Warren, W. H. (2002). Virtual reality in behavioral neuroscience and beyond. *Nature Neuroscience*, *5*(S11), 1089–1092. doi:10.1038/nn948 PMID:12403993

Technacy Solutions. (2017, August 24). *Apple's architect says the future of offices must be flexible*. Technacy Solutions. https://www.technacysolutions.com/apples-architect-says-the-future-of-offices-must-be-flexible/

Teece, D. J. (2016). Dynamic capabilities and entrepreneurial management in large organizations: Toward a theory of the (entrepreneurial) firm. *European Economic Review*, *86*, 202–216. doi:10.1016/j.euroecorev.2015.11.006

Teece, D. J., Pisano, G., & Shuen, A. (1997). Dynamic capabilities and strategic management. *Strategic Management Journal*, *18*(7), 509–533. doi:10.1002/(SICI)1097-0266(199708)18:7<509::AID-SMJ882>3.0.CO;2-Z

Temesgen, A., Storsletten, V., & Jakobsen, O. (2021). Circular economy – reducing symptoms or radical change? *Philosophy of Management*, *20*(March), 37–56. doi:10.100740926-019-00112-1

Teshnizi, S. H., Aghamolaei, T., Kahnouji, K., Teshnizi, S. M. H., & Ghani, J. (2018). Assessing quality of health services with the SERVQUAL model in Iran. A systematic review and meta-analysis. *International Journal for Quality in Health Care*, *30*(2), 82–89. doi:10.1093/intqhc/mzx200 PMID:29408970

Thatte, A. A. (2007). *Competitive advantage of a firm through supply chain responsiveness and SCM practices* [Doctoral dissertation, The University of Toledo].

The intergovernmental Panel on Climate Change. (2022). IPCC. https://www.ipcc.ch/

Thompson, G. F., & Steiner, F. R. (Eds.). (1997). *Ecological design and planning*. John Wiley & Sons, Inc.

Ting, L. S. bin Mohammed, A. H., & Wai, C. W. (2011). 2011 International Conference on Social Science and Humanity. In *Promoting Energy Conservation Behaviour: A Plausible Solution to Energy Sustainability Threats* (*Vol. 5*). Singapore; IACSIT Press.

Titrek, O. (2015). The Level of Innovation Management of School Principals' in Turkey. *Anthropologist*, *19*(2), 449–456. doi:10.1080/09720073.2015.11891679

Toffler, A. (1970). *Future shock*. Random House.

Toledo, V. M. (1997) Sustainable development at the village community level: a Third World perspective in: Fraser Smith (Ed.) Environmental Sustainability Boca Raton St. Lucie Press pp. 233–250 doi:10.1201/9781420048742.ch11

Tolliver, C., Fujii, H., Keeley, A. R., & Managi, S. (2021). Green innovation and finance in Asia. *Asian Economic Policy Review*, *16*(1), 67–87. doi:10.1111/aepr.12320

Tong, T. W., He, W., He, Z. L., & Lu, J. (2014). Patent regime shift and firm innovation: Evidence from the second amendment to China's Patent Law. *Academy of Management Annual Meeting Proceedings*, *2014*(1) 14174–14174.

Tonin, R., Brett, J., & Colagiuri, B. (2016). The effect of infrasound and negative expectations to adverse pathological symptoms from wind farms. *Journal of Low Frequency Noise, Vibration and Active Control*, *35*(1), 77–90. doi:10.1177/0263092316628257

Torii, H., Kurihara, T., Seko, Y., Negishi, K., Ohnuma, K., Inaba, T., Kawashima, M., Jiang, X., Kondo, S., Miyauchi, M., Miwa, Y., Katada, Y., Mori, K., Kato, K., Tsubota, K., Goto, H., Oda, M., Hatori, M., & Tsubota, K. (2017). Violet Light Exposure Can Be a Preventive Strategy Against Myopia Progression. *EBioMedicine*, *15*, 210–219. doi:10.1016/j.ebiom.2016.12.007 PMID:28063778

Torii, H., Ohnuma, K., Kurihara, T., Tsubota, K., & Negishi, K. (2017). Violet Light Transmission is Related to Myopia Progression in Adult High Myopia. *Scientific Reports*, *7*(1), 14523. doi:10.103841598-017-09388-7 PMID:29109514

Tornatzky, L. G., & Klein, K. J. (1982). Innovation characteristics and innovation adoption-implementation: A meta-analysis of findings. *IEEE Transactions on Engineering Management*, *29*(1), 28–45. doi:10.1109/TEM.1982.6447463

Transsolar Energietechnik Gmb, H. (2019). Oberbillwerder Masterplan, Hamburg, Deutschland. *Transsolar.* Www.transsolar.com https://transsolar.com/de/projects/hamburg-oberbillwerder-masterplan

Trikootam, S. C., & Hornikx, M. (2019). The wind effect on sound propagation over urban areas: Experimental approach with an uncontrolled sound source. *Building and Environment*, *149*, 561–570. doi:10.1016/j.buildenv.2018.11.037

Trope, Y., & Liberman, N. (2010). Construal-level theory of psychological distance. *Psychological Review*, *117*(2), 440–463. doi:10.1037/a0018963 PMID:20438233

Truong, Y., Mazloomi, H., & Berrone, P. (2021). Understanding the impact of symbolic and substantive environmental actions on organizational reputation. *Industrial Marketing Management*, *92*, 307–320. doi:10.1016/j.indmarman.2020.05.006

Tufail, Y., Matyushov, A., Baldwin, N., Tauchmann, M. L., Georges, J., Yoshihiro, A., Tillery, S. I. H., & Tyler, W. J. (2010). Transcranial Pulsed Ultrasound Stimulates Intact Brain Circuits. *Neuron*, *66*(5), 681–694. doi:10.1016/j.neuron.2010.05.008 PMID:20547127

Turner, P. L., & Mainster, M. A. (2008). Circadian photoreception: Ageing and the eye's important role in systemic health. *The British Journal of Ophthalmology*, *92*(11), 1439–1444. doi:10.1136/bjo.2008.141747 PMID:18757473

Tushingham, S., Hopt, J., Christiansen, C., Bommelyn, M. L., Green, J., Peterson, M. R., Steinruck, S., & Stewart, C. (2020). In the footsteps of Amelia Brown: Collaborative historical ecology at Shin-yvslh-sri~, a Tolowa village on the north coast of California. *Journal of Island & Coastal Archaeology*, *15*(1), 3–27. doi:10.1080/15564894.2018.1539789

Tutor Vicente, M. (2015). *La recuperación de la tierra pisada en la arquitectura contemporánea* [Tesis doctoral]. Universidad de Zaragoza.

Tyler, W. J., Tufail, Y., Finsterwald, M., Tauchmann, M. L., Olson, E. J., & Majestic, C. (2008). Remote Excitation of Neuronal Circuits Using Low-Intensity, Low-Frequency Ultrasound. *PLoS One*, *3*(10), e3511. doi:10.1371/journal.pone.0003511 PMID:18958151

Ulrich, R. S. (1983). Aesthetic and Affective Response to Natural Environment. In I. Altman & J. F. Wohlwill (Eds.), *Behavior and the Natural Environment* (pp. 85–125). Springer US. doi:10.1007/978-1-4613-3539-9_4

UNEP. (2020). *2020 Global Status Report for Buildings and Construction*. Global Alliance for Buildings and Construction. https://wedocs.unep.org/bitstream/handle/20.500.11822/34572/GSR_ES.pdf?sequence=3

UNEP. (2021). *Global Status Report for Buildings and Construction: Towards a Zero emission, Efficient and Resilient Buildings and Construction Sector*. Global ABC. https://globalabc.org/sites/default/files/2021-10/GABC_Buildings-GSR-2021_BOOK.pdf

United Nations Development Programme. (2023). UNDP. https://www.undp.org/

United Nations Environment Programme. (2012). *Green economy in a blue world: Synthesis report*. United Nations.

United Nations General Assembly. (2017). Resolution 71/312 Our ocean, our future: Call for action. In *Resolution adopted by the general assembly on 6 July 2017*. United Nations.

United Nations. (1987). *Our Common Future. Report of the World Commission on Environment and Development*. Oxford University Press.

United Nations. (2021). *Sustainable Development Goals*. UN. https://www.un.org/sustainabledevelopment/es/objetivos-de-desarrollo-sostenible/

United Nations.Department of Economic and Social Affairs. (n.d.). Sustainable Development. https://sdgs.un.org/goals

US EIA. (2017, September 14). *International Energy Outlook 2017*. https://www.eia.gov/. https://www.eia.gov/outlooks/ieo/pdf/0484(2017).pdf

Vakulabharanam, V., & Motiram, S. (2012). Understanding Poverty and Inequality in Urban India since Reforms: Bringing Quantitative and Qualitative Approaches Together. *Economic and Political Weekly*, *47*(47/48), 44–52. https://www.jstor.org/stable/41720409

Valdés Kuri, L., & Ricalde de Jager, A. (2006). *Experiencias rumbo a la sustentabilidad*. Ecohábitat. https://www.academia.edu/13447041/Ecohabitat_Experiencias_rumbo_a_la_sustentabilidad

Vallianatos, M. (2015). Uncovering the early history of Big Data and the "Smart City". Los Angeles. *Boom: A Journal of California*. https://boomcalifornia.org/2015/06/16/uncovering-the-early-history-of-big-data-and-the-smart-city-in-la/

Vamshi, B., Mittal, V. K., & Vineeth, K. V. S. (2017). Wireless voice-controlled multi-functional secure ehome. *2017 International Conference on Advances in Computing, Communications and Informatics (ICACCI)*, 2235–2240. 10.1109/ICACCI.2017.8126178

van der Geest, L. G. M., Lam-Boer, J., Koopman, M., Verhoef, C., Elferink, M. A. G., & de Wilt, J. H. W. (2015). Nationwide trends in incidence, treatment and survival of colorectal cancer patients with synchronous metastases. *Clinical & Experimental Metastasis*, *32*(5), 457–465. doi:10.100710585-015-9719-0 PMID:25899064

van der Linden, J., Johnson, R., Bird, J., Rogers, Y., & Schoonderwaldt, E. (2011). Buzzing to play. *Proceedings of the SIGCHI Conference on Human Factors in Computing Systems*, (pp. 533–542). IEEE. 10.1145/1978942.1979017

Van der Ryn, S., & Cowan, S. (2007). *Ecological design: tenth anniversary edition*. Island Press.

van Leeuwen, J. P., Hermans, K., Jylhä, A., Quanjer, A. J., & Nijman, H. (2018). Effectiveness of virtual reality in participatory urban planning: A case study. *Proceedings of the 4th Media Architecture Biennale Conference*, (pp. 128–136). IEEE. 10.1145/3284389.3284491 van Rensburg, H. C. J. (2014). South Africa's protracted struggle for equal distribution and equitable access - still not there. *Human Resources for Health*, *12*(1), 26–26. doi:10.1186/1478-4491-12-26 PMID:24885691

van Someren, E. J. W., Kessler, A., Mirmiran, M., & Swaab, D. F. (1997). Indirect bright light improves circadian rest-activity rhythm disturbances in demented patients. *Biological Psychiatry*, *41*(9), 955–963. doi:10.1016/S0006-3223(97)89928-3 PMID:9110101

Vardoulakis, S., Fisher, B., Pericleous, K., & Gonzalez-Flesca, N. (2003). Modelling air quality in street canyons: A review. *Atmospheric Environment*, *37*(2), 155–182. doi:10.1016/S1352-2310(02)00857-9

Veber, T., Tamm, T., Ründva, M., Kriit, H. K., Pyko, A., & Orru, H. (2022). Health impact assessment of transportation noise in two Estonian cities. *Environmental Research*, *204*, 112319. doi:10.1016/j.envres.2021.112319 PMID:34740439

Verlie, B. (2020). Intergenerational Climate Injustice within the Urban Planning Profession. *Planning Theory & Practice*.

Vigouroux, N., Vella, F., Lepage, G., & Campo, E. (2022). Usability Study of Tactile and Voice Interaction Modes by People with Disabilities for Home Automation Controls. *International Conference on Computers Helping People with Special Needs*, (pp. 139–147). IEEE. 10.1007/978-3-031-08645-8_17

Vijayan, M., Patil, A., Kapse, V., & Bahadure, S. (2021). Assessing the Energy Efficiency Practices in Cities Across the World. *Current Science*, *121*(3), 372. doi:10.18520/cs/v121/i3/372-383

Visser, M., & Togt, K. (2016). Learning in Public Sector Organizations: A Theory of Action, Approach. *Public Organization Review*, *16*(2), 235–249. doi:10.100711115-015-0303-5

Vittori, F., Pigliautile, I., & Pisello, A. L. (2021). Subjective thermal response driving indoor comfort perception: A novel experimental analysis coupling building information modelling and virtual reality. *Journal of Building Engineering*, *41*, 102368. doi:10.1016/j.jobe.2021.102368

von Castell, C., Oberfeld, D., & Hecht, H. (2014). The effect of furnishing on perceived spatial dimensions and spaciousness of interior space. *PLoS One*, *9*(11), e113267. doi:10.1371/journal.pone.0113267 PMID:25409456

Von Pressentin, K. B., Mash, B. J., & Esterhuizen, T. M. (2017). Examining the influence of family physician supply on district health system performance in South Africa: An ecological analysis of key health indicators. *African Journal of Primary Health Care & Family Medicine*, *9*(1), e1–e10. doi:10.4102/phcfm.v9i1.1298 PMID:28470076

Wai, C. W. (2009). The conceptual model of Energy Awareness Development Process: The Transferor segment. *2009 3rd International Conference on Energy and Environment (ICEE)*. ICEEE. 10.1109/ICEENVIRON.2009.5398630

Walborn, A., Rondina, M., Mosier, M., Fareed, J., & Hoppensteadt, D. (2019). Endothelial Dysfunction Is Associated with Mortality and Severity of Coagulopathy in Patients with Sepsis and Disseminated Intravascular Coagulation. *Clinical and Applied Thrombosis/Hemostasis*, *25*, 107602961985216. doi:10.1177/1076029619852163 PMID:31140293

Wales, W. J. (2016). Entrepreneurial orientation: A review and synthesis of promising research directions. *International Small Business Journal*, *34*(1), 3–15. doi:10.1177/0266242615613840

Walker, P. (2005). Political ecology: Where is the ecology? *Progress in Human Geography*, *29*(1), 73–82. doi:10.1191/0309132505ph530pr

Wallace-Wells, D. (2019). *The uninhabitable earth: Life after warming*. Tim Duggan Books.

Walton, D., Dravitzki, V., & Donn, M. (2007). The relative influence of wind, sunlight and temperature on user comfort in urban outdoor spaces. *Building and Environment*, *42*(9), 3166–3175. doi:10.1016/j.buildenv.2006.08.004

Wang, F. Z., Jiang, T., & Guo, X. C. (2018). Government Quality, Environmental Regulation and Corporate Green Technology Innovation. *Sci. Res. Manage, 39* (1), 26–33.

Wang, C., Lu, W., Ohno, R., & Gu, Z. (2020). Effect of wall texture on perceptual spaciousness of indoor space. *International Journal of Environmental Research and Public Health, 17*(11), 4177. doi:10.3390/ijerph17114177 PMID:32545379

Wang, D., Schacht, A., Leng, Z., Leng, C., Kollmann, J., & Oeser, M. (2017). Effects of material composition on mechanical and acoustic performance of poroelastic road surface (PERS). *Construction & Building Materials, 135*, 352–360. doi:10.1016/j.conbuildmat.2016.12.207

Wang, K. H., Umar, M., Akram, R., & Caglar, E. (2021). Is technological innovation making world "Greener"? An evidence from changing growth story of China. *Technological Forecasting and Social Change, 165*, 120516. doi:10.1016/j.techfore.2020.120516

Wang, K., & Jiang, W. (2021). State ownership and green innovation in China: The con-tingent roles of environmental and organizational factors. *Journal of Cleaner Production, 314*, 128029. doi:10.1016/j.jclepro.2021.128029

Wang, Q.-Z., Wang, N.-N., Tseng, M.-L., Huang, Y.-M., & Li, N.-L. (2020). Waste tire recycling assessment: Road application potential and carbon emissions reduction analysis of crumb rubber modified asphalt in China. *Journal of Cleaner Production, 249*, 119411. doi:10.1016/j.jclepro.2019.119411

Wang, X., Shuster, W., Pal, C., Buchberger, S., Bonta, J., & Avadhanula, K. (2011). Low impact development design—Integrating suitability analysis and site planning for reduction of post-development stormwater quantity. *Sustainability, 2*(8), 2467–2482. doi:10.3390u2082467

Wang, Y., Sun, X., & Guo, X. (2019). Environmental regulation and green productivity growth: Empirical evidence on the Porter Hypothesis from OECD industrial sectors. *Energy Policy, 132*, 611–619. doi:10.1016/j.enpol.2019.06.016

Wasserman, H., Chuma, W., & Bosch, T. (2018). Print media coverage of service delivery protests in South Africa: A content analysis. *African Studies, 77*(1), 145–156. doi:10.1080/00020184.2018.1426312

Wehr, R., Fuchs, A., & Breuss, S. (2021). Statistical tyre/road noise modelling based on continuous 3D texture data. *Acta Acustica (Les Ulis), 5*, 52. doi:10.1051/aacus/2021040

Weick, K. E. (1969). *The Social Psychology of Organizing*. McGraw Hill.

Wei, J., & Zuo, Y. (2018). The certification effect of R&D subsidies from the central and local governments: Evidence from China. *R & D Management, 48*(5), 615–626. doi:10.1111/radm.12333

WeinsteinG. (2013). The 1905 Relativity Paper and the "Light Quantum" https://arxiv.org/abs/1307.2132

Weiss, J. F., & Anisimova, T. (2019). The innovation and performance effects of well- designed environmental regulation: Evidence from Sweden. *Industry and Innovation, 26*(5), 534–567. doi:10.1080/13662716.2018.1468240

Weng, M. H., & Lin, C. Y. (2011). Determinants of green innovation adoption for small and medium-size enterprises (SMES). *African Journal of Business Management, 5*(22), 9154–9163.

Weston, A. (2009). *The incompleat eco-philosopher: essays from the edges of environmental ethics*. State University of New York Press.

Westwood, R., & Low, D. R. (2003). The multicultural muse: Culture, creativity, and innovation. *International Journal of Cross Cultural Management, 3*(2), 235–259. doi:10.1177/14705958030032006

Whelan, T., Zappa, B., Zeidan, R., & Fishbein, G. (2022). (2017, 10 13). *Harvard Business Review.* [from How to Quantify Sustainability's Impact on Your Bottom Line.]. *Retrieved, 11*, 2.

Whittaker, S., Linegar, A., Shaw, C., & Spieker, N. (2011). Quality standards for healthcare establishments in South Africa. *South African Health Review*, *2011*(1), 59–67.

WHO. (1999). *Health for All in the 21st Century. The Health for All Policy Framework for the WHO European Region.* World Health Organisation.

Wiley, A. S., & Cullin, J. M. (2016). What Do Anthropologists Mean When They Use the Term Biocultural? *American Anthropologist*, *2016*(118), 554–569. doi:10.1111/aman.12608

Willermet, C. (2016). Biological Anthropology in 2015: Open Access, Biocultural Interactions, and Social Change. *American Anthropologist*, *118*(2), 118. doi:10.1111/aman.12529

Wilson, A. (2016). Making the case for Green Building. *BuildingGreen*. https://www.buildinggreen.com/feature/making-case-green-building

Wilson, O. E. (1984). *Biophilia*. Harvard University Press.

Wilson, C. J., & Soranzo, A. (2015). The Use of Virtual Reality in Psychology: A Case Study in Visual Perception. *Computational and Mathematical Methods in Medicine*, *2015*, 1–7. doi:10.1155/2015/151702 PMID:26339281

Winchester, M. S., & King, B. (2018). Decentralization, healthcare access, and inequality in Mpumalanga, South Africa. *Health & Place*, *51*, 200–207. doi:10.1016/j.healthplace.2018.02.009 PMID:29709650

Winterbottom, M., & Wilkins, A. (2009). Lighting and discomfort in the classroom. *Journal of Environmental Psychology*, *29*(1), 63–75. doi:10.1016/j.jenvp.2008.11.007

Wolf, E. (1972). Ownership and political ecology. *Anthropological Quarterly*, *45*(3), 201–205. doi:10.2307/3316532

Womack, J. P., & Jones, D. T. (2005). *Lean thinking: cómo utilizar el pensamiento Lean para eliminar los despilfarros y crear valor en la empresa*. Grupo Planeta GBS.

Wong, M. O., Du, J., Zhang, Z. Q., Liu, Y. Q., Chen, S. M., & Lee, S. H. (2019). An experience-based interactive lighting design approach using BIM and VR: A case study. *IOP Conference Series. Earth and Environmental Science*, *238*(1), 012006. doi:10.1088/1755-1315/238/1/012006

Wong, N. H., Tan, A. Y. K., Tan, P. Y., & Wong, N. C. (2019). *Green roofs and walls for a more sustainable urban environment*. Springer.

Woodcock, J., Banister, D., Edwards, P., Prentice, A. M., & Roberts, I. (2007). Energy and transport. *Lancet*, *370*(9592), 1078–1088. doi:10.1016/S0140-6736(07)61254-9 PMID:17868817

World Commission on Environment and Development. (1987). *Our common future*. Oxford University Press.

World Health Organization Assembly. (1998). *WHA51.18: Noncommunicable disease prevention and control. Resolution.* (No. Agenda item 13.18). Fifty-fifth World Health Assembly. Geneva: World Health Organization, WHO. https://apps.who.int/gb/ebwha/pdf_files/WHA55/ewha5523.pdf

World Health Organization Assembly. WHO. (2002). *WHA55.23: Diet, physical activity and health. Resolution.* (No. Agenda item 13.11). Fifty-fifth World Health Assembly. Geneva: World Health Organization. https://apps.who.int/gb/ebwha/pdf_files/WHA55/ewha5523.pdf

World Health Organization, (2010). Global recommendations on physical activity for health. WHO.

World Health Organization. (1946). *Preámbulo de la Constitución de la Organización Mundial de la Salud adoptado por la Conferencia Internacional de Salud.* https://www.who.int/suggestions/faq/en/

World Health Organization. (2022). *Global status report on physical activity 2022*. Geneva: World Health Organization. https://apps.who.int/iris/bitstream/handle/10665/363607/9789240059153-eng.pdf?sequence=1&isAllowed=y

Woźniak, M. P., Dominiak, J., Pieprzowski, M., Ładoński, P., Grudzień, K., Lischke, L., Romanowski, A., & Woźniak, P. W. (2020). Subtletee: Augmenting Posture Awareness for Beginner Golfers. Proceedings of the ACM on Human-Computer Interaction, 4(ISS), 1–24. 10.1145/3427332

Wu, M. (2018, March 8). *Gamification from a company of pro gamers*. LinkedIn. https://www.linkedin.com/pulse/20140923144022-66703918-gamification-from-a-company-of-pro-gamers

Wu, A. (2017). The signal effect of Government R&D subsidies in China: Does ownership matter? *Technological Forecasting and Social Change*, *117*, 339–345. doi:10.1016/j.techfore.2016.08.033

Wu, H. Y., Tsai, A., & Wu, H. S. (2019). A Hybrid Multi-Criteria Decision Analysis Approach For Environmental Performance Evaluation: An Example Of The Tft-Lcd Manufacturers In Taiwan. [EEMJ]. *Environmental Engineering and Management Journal*, *18*(3), 597–616. doi:10.30638/eemj.2019.056

Wu, Q., Wu, J., Shen, J., Yong, B., & Zhou, Q. (2020). An Edge Based Multi-Agent Auto Communication Method for Traffic Light Control. *Sensors (Basel)*, *20*(15), 4291. doi:10.339020154291 PMID:32752055

Wurlod, J. D., & Noailly, J. (2018). The impact of green innovation on energy intensity: An empirical analysis for 14 industrial sectors in OECD countries. *Energy Econ*, *71*, 47–61. doi:10.1016/j.eneco.2017.12.012

Xiang, X., Liu, C., & Yang, M. (2022). Who is financing corporate green innovation? *International Review of Economics & Finance*, *78*, 321–337. doi:10.1016/j.iref.2021.12.011

Xiao, R., Wu, Z., & Hamari, J. (2021). Internet-of-gamification: A review of literature on IOT-enabled gamification for user engagement. *International Journal of Human-Computer Interaction*, *38*(12), 1113–1137. doi:10.1080/10447318.2021.1990517

Xia, W., Kuniyil Ajith Singh, M., Maneas, E., Sato, N., Shigeta, Y., Agano, T., & Ourselin, S., J. West, S., & E. Desjardins, A. (. (2018). Handheld Real-Time LED-Based Photoacoustic and Ultrasound Imaging System for Accurate Visualization of Clinical Metal Needles and Superficial Vasculature to Guide Minimally Invasive Procedures. *Sensors (Basel)*, *18*(5), 1394. doi:10.339018051394 PMID:29724014

Xie, P. F. (2015). A life cycle model of industrial heritage development. *Annals of Tourism Research*, *55*, 141–154. doi:10.1016/j.annals.2015.09.012

Xie, R., Yuan, Y., & Huang, J. (2017). Different Types of environmental regulations and heterogeneous influence on "Green" productivity: Evidence from China. *Ecological Economics*, *132*, 104–112. doi:10.1016/j.ecolecon.2016.10.019

Xie, X., Hoang, T. T., & Zhu, Q. (2022). Green process innovation and financial performance: The role of green social capital and customers' tacit green needs. *Journal of Innovation & Knowledge*, *7*(1), 100165. doi:10.1016/j.jik.2022.100165

Xing, X., Wang, J., & Tou, L. (2019). The relationship between green organization identity and corporate environmental performance: The mediating role of sustainability exploration and exploitation innovation. *International Journal of Environmental Research and Public Health*, *16*(6), 921. doi:10.3390/ijerph16060921 PMID:30875787

Xu, C., Oberman, T., Aletta, F., Tong, H., & Kang, J. (2020). Ecological validity of immersive virtual reality (IVR) techniques for the perception of urban sound environments. *Acoustics (Basel, Switzerland)*, *3*(1), 11–24. doi:10.3390/acoustics3010003

Xu, D., Zhou, K. Z., & Du, F. (2019). Deviant versus aspirational risk taking: The effects of performance feedback on bribery expenditure and R&D intensity. *Academy of Management Journal*, *62*(4), 1226–1251. doi:10.5465/amj.2016.0749

Xue, F., Chen, Q., Chan, K. C., & Yi, Z. (2021). Is corporate social responsibility value relevant? Evidence from a quasi-natural experiment of anti-corruption campaign. *Journal of Business Research*. Advance online publication. doi:10.1016/j.jbusres.2021.11.020

Xu, M., David, J. M., & Kim, S. H. (2018). The Fourth Industrial Revolution: Opportunities and Challenges. *International Journal of Financial Research*, *9*(2), 90. doi:10.5430/ijfr.v9n2p90

Xu, Q., Zhu, L., Zheng, G., & Wang, F. (2007). Haier's Tao of innovation: A case study of the emerging total innovation management model. *The Journal of Technology Transfer*, *32*(1–2), 27–47.

Xu, Z., Frankwick, G. L., & Ramirez, E. (2016). Effects of big data analytics and traditional marketing analytics on new product success: A knowledge fusion perspective. *Journal of Business Research*, *69*(5), 1562–1566. doi:10.1016/j.jbusres.2015.10.017

Yang, S. & Zeng, G. (2018) The ecological innovation effect of environmental regulation: From the perspective of regional differences. *Ecological Economy*, *34*(9), 41-49.

Yang, R., Liu, Y., Liu, Y., Liu, H., & Gan, W. (2019). Comprehensive public transport service accessibility index-a new approach based on degree centrality and gravity model. *Sustainability (Switzerland)*, *11*(20), 5634. doi:10.3390u11205634

Yang, T., Hu, L., Xiong, X., Petru, M., Tayyab Noman, M., Mishra, R., & Militký, J. (2020). Sound Absorption Properties of Natural Fibers. *Sustainability*, *12*(20), 8477. doi:10.3390u12208477

Yinghong, Q. (2015). A review on the development of cool pavements to mitigate urban heat island effect. *Renewable & Sustainable Energy Reviews*, *52*, 445–459. doi:10.1016/j.rser.2015.07.177

Yin, J., Yuan, J., Arfaei, N., Catalano, P. J., Allen, J. G., & Spengler, J. D. (2020). Effects of biophilic indoor environment on stress and anxiety recovery: A between-subjects experiment in virtual reality. *Environment International*, *136*, 105427. doi:10.1016/j.envint.2019.105427 PMID:31881421

Yokum, D., Lauffenburger, J. C., Ghazinouri, R., & Choudhry, N. K. (2018). Letters designed with Behavioural Science Increase Influenza Vaccination in Medicare beneficiaries. *Nature Human Behaviour*, *2*(10), 743–749. doi:10.103841562-018-0432-2 PMID:31406294

Yongming, Z. (2010). How Our Village Becomes "Ecocultural". In W. Ascher, & J. Heffron (eds.) Cultural Change and Persistence, Press, Washington, D.C. doi:10.1057/9780230117334_7

Young, M. (2016). Private vs. public healthcare in South Africa. Honors Theses. 2741. https://scholarworks.wmich.edu/honors_theses/2741

Young, T., Garner, P., Clarke, M., & Volmink, J. (2016). Series: Clinical Epidemiology in South Africa. Paper 1: Evidence-based health care and policy in Africa: past, present, and future. *Journal of Clinical Epidemiology*, *83*, 24–30. doi:10.1016/j.jclinepi.2016.06.006 PMID:27349186

Yue, C. Z., & Ping, S. (2017). Voice activated smart home design and implementation. 2017 2nd International Conference on Frontiers of Sensors Technologies (ICFST), 489–492.

Yu, G.-X., Li, Z.-M., Zhou, X.-L., & Li, C.-L. (2011). Crumb Rubber–Modified Asphalt: Microwave Treatment Effects. *Petroleum Science and Technology*, *29*(4), 411–417. doi:10.1080/10916460903394102

Yuste, B. (2018). *Arquitectura de Tierra. Caracterización de los tipos edificatorios* [Tesis doctoral]. Universidad Politécnica de Madrid.

Yu, Z., Fung, B. C. M., Haghighat, F., Yoshino, H., & Morofsky, E. (2011). A systematic procedure to study the influence of occupant behavior on building energy consumption. *Energy and Building*, *43*(6), 1409–1417. doi:10.1016/j.enbuild.2011.02.002

Yu, Z., Khan, S. A. R., Ponce, P., & Jabbour, A. B. L. (2022). Factors affecting carbon emissions in emerging economies in the context of a green recovery: Implications for sustainable development goals. *Technological Forecasting and Social Change*, *176*, 121417. doi:10.1016/j.techfore.2021.121417

Zailani, S., Iranmanesh, M., Nikbin, D., & Jumadi, H. B. (2014). Determinants and environmental outcome of green technology innovation adoption in the transportation industry in Malaysia. *Asian Journal of Technology Innovation*, *22*(2), 286–301. doi:10.1080/19761597.2014.973167

Zan, L., & Lusiani, M. (2011). Managing Change and Master Plans: Machu Picchu Between Conservation and Exploitation. *Arch*, *7*(2), 329–371. doi:10.100711759-011-9167-7

Zaw, A. K., Myat, A. M., Thandar, M., Htun, Y. M., Aung, T. H., Tun, K. M., & Han, Z. M. (2020). Assessment of Noise Exposure and Hearing Loss Among Workers in Textile Mill (Thamine), Myanmar: A Cross-Sectional Study. *Safety and Health at Work*, *11*(2), 199–206. doi:10.1016/j.shaw.2020.04.002 PMID:32596016

Zedler, J. B., & Stevens, M. L. (2018). Western and Traditional Ecological Knowledge in Ecocultural Restoration. *San Francisco Estuary and Watershed Science*, *16*(3), 1–18. doi:10.15447fews.2018v16iss3art2

Zhang, H., Jovcic, D., Lin, W., & Far, A. J. (2016). Average value MMC model with accurate blocked state and cell charging/discharging dynamics. *2016 4th International Symposium on Environmental Friendly Energies and Applications (EFEA)*. IEEE. 10.1109/EFEA.2016.7748768

Zhang, J., Cenci, J., Becue, V., & Koutra, S. (2021, January 1). The overview of the conservation and renewal of the industrial belgian heritage as a vector for cultural regeneration. *Information (Switzerland). MDPI AG*. doi:10.3390/info12010027

Zhang, D. (2022). Environmental Regulation and Firm Product Quality Improvement: How Does the Green Washing Response? *International Review of Financial Analysis*, *80*, 102058. doi:10.1016/j.irfa.2022.102058

Zhang, D. G., & Lu, Y. Q. (2017). Impact of market segmentation on energy efficiency. *China Popul Resour Environ*, *27*(1), 65–72.

Zhang, J., Cenci, J., Becue, V., Koutra, S., & Ioakimidis, C. S. (2020). Recent evolution of research on industrial heritage in Western Europe and China based on bibliometric analysis. *Sustainability (Switzerland)*, *12*(13), 5348. doi:10.3390u12135348

Zhang, J., Zhang, N., & Bai, S. (2021). Assessing the carbon emission changing for sus- tainability and high-quality economic development. *Environmental Technology & Innovation*, *22*, 101464. doi:10.1016/j.eti.2021.101464

Zhang, L., Tan, P. Y., & Richards, D. (2021). Relative importance of quantitative and qualitative aspects of urban green spaces in promoting health. *Landscape and Urban Planning*, *213*, 104131. doi:10.1016/j.landurbplan.2021.104131

Zhang, W., He, L., & Yuan, H. (2021). Enterprises' decisions on adopting low-carbon technology by considering consumer perception disparity. *Technovation*, *102238*. doi:10.1016/j.technovation.2021.102238

Zhang, Y., Sun, J., Yang, Z., & Li, S. (2018). Organizational learning and Green innovation: Does environmental proactivity matter? *Sustainability*, *10*(10), 3737. doi:10.3390u10103737

Zhao, W., Liu, X., Shan, Y., & He, T. (2021). Design and simulation of Helmholtz resonator assembly used to attenuate tire acoustic cavity resonance noise. *INTER-NOISE and NOISE-CON Congress and Conference Proceedings, 263*(6), 942–953. 10.3397/IN-2021-1706

Zhao, X., Shang, Y., & Song, M. (2020). Industrial structure distortion and urban ecological efficiency from the perspective of green entre-preneurial ecosystems. *Socio-Economic Planning Sciences*, *72*, 100757. doi:10.1016/j.seps.2019.100757

Zhou, B. (2016). Lean principles, practices, and impacts: A study on small and medium-sized enterprises SMEs. *Annals of Operations Research*, *241*(1-2), 1–2, 457–474. doi:10.100710479-012-1177-3

Zhou, K. Z., Gao, G. Y., & Zhao, H. (2017). State Ownership and firm innovation in China: An integrated view of institutional and efficiency logics. *Administrative Science Quarterly*, *62*(2), 375–404. doi:10.1177/0001839216674457

Zhou, P., Ang, B. W., & Poh, K. L. (2008). Measuring environmental performance under different environmental DEA technologies. *Energy Economics*, *30*(1), 1–14. doi:10.1016/j.eneco.2006.05.001

Zitars, J., Spadafore, B., Coulombe, S., Riemer, M., Dreyer, B., & Whitney, S. (2021). Understanding the psycho-environmental potential functions of a green building to promote employee health, wellbeing and productivity: A theoretical perspective. *Building and Environment*, *205*, 108268. doi:10.1016/j.buildenv.2021.108268

Zitouni, R., Petit, J., Djoudi, A., & George, L. (2019). IoT-Based Urban Traffic-Light Control: Modelling, Prototyping and Evaluation of MQTT Protocol. *2019 International Conference on Internet of Things (IThings) and IEEE Green Computing and Communications (GreenCom) and IEEE Cyber, Physical and Social Computing (CPSCom) and IEEE Smart Data (SmartData),* (pp. 182–189). IEEE. 10.1109/iThings/GreenCom/CPSCom/SmartData.2019.00051

Zott, C., & Amit, R. (2010a). Business model innovation: Creating value in times of change (No. D/870). IESE Business School

Zvolenský, P., Grenčík, J., Pultznerová, A., & Kašiar, Ľ. (2017). Research of noise emission sources in railway transport and effective ways of their reduction. *MATEC Web of Conferences, 107*, 00073. 10.1051/matecconf/201710700073

About the Contributors

Roberto Alonso González-Lezcano is a PhD in Industrial Engineering, Postgraduate Diploma in Plant Engineering, Postgraduate Diploma in University Didactics, Master in Mathematical Engineering Extraordinary Doctorate Award. Assistant Professor of the Department of Architecture and Design, in the area of Facilities at the Higher Polytechnic School of the CEU San Pablo University. He has been teaching at Building Installations, Electromechanics and Materials, Physics, Mathematics, Mechanical Engineering and Mechanics of Continuous Media and Theory of Structures. Accredited Professor by the ACAP in the figures of Professor Hired Doctor, Professor Doctor of Private University and Tenured Professor. A six-year research period recognized by the CNEAI. He has taught in undergraduate and master's degrees at the Carlos III University of Madrid, Camilo José Cela University, European University of Madrid, Antonio de Nebrija University,Technical University of Madrid and Alfonso X El Sabio University. He has published several books and articles concerning the areas of Energy, Installations and Continuous Media Mechanics.

* * *

Daniel Arranz-Paraiso PhD in Pharmaceutical Technology, Master in Pharmacy and Degree in Pharmacy from the Complutense University of Madrid. Researcher in charge of galenic development at Medicinal Gardens S.L. (Baïa Food Co.) by CDTi NEOTEC competitive project. Collaborator in galenic development and external formulation consultant with PINISAN S.L. Collaborating professor at the University CEU San Pablo within the area of knowledge of Pharmaceutical Technology. His research career is multidisciplinary: research on the generation of reversible models of malabsorption in laboratory mice, studies and galenic development of classical formulations, development of patents for new galenic devices for the application of formulations (ES2518740 B2 and P202230466). And currently developing a career focused on the study and design of medical devices type medical device with its corresponding intellectual property protection and detailed analysis of the potential benefits, hazards and risks that these structures can bring to the user. I am currently a member of the Spanish Society of Industrial and Galenic Formulation.

Sandra Arranz-Paraíso obtained her Bachelor of Science degree in psychology, with the Grade Extraordinary Prize, in 2016, and her Master of Science degree in methodology in 2018, both from the Complutense University of Madrid (UCM) in Madrid, Spain. She is currently pursuing a Ph.D. degree in experimental and applied psychology, with a research focus on studying the inhibitory mechanisms that underlie visual motion perception. At present, she is an assistant at the Complutense University of

Madrid. From 2016 to 2020, Sandra collaborated with the Centre for Automation and Robotics—CAR (UPM-CSIC). Her research interests include haptic and visual perception, psychophysics, presence and realism of virtual environments, methods, and statistics.

Tamar Awad has a PhD in Architecture by Polytechnic University of Madrid. Assistant Professor of the Department of Mechanical engineering of ICAI Comillas Pontificial University. Professor of product design department at ESNE. Researcher of Spanish tobacco factories and sustainable and bioclimatic architecture.

David Baeza Moyano has a Master´s Degree in higher education and professional training. PhD at Universidad San Pablo CEU. Master's Degree in Renewable Energy from Universidad CEU San Pablo. Bachelor's Degree in Pharmacy from Universidad Complutense de Madrid. Bachelor's Degree in Optics from Universidad Complutense de Madrid. Diploma in Orthopedics from Universidad Complutense de Madrid. Adjunct Professor in the Faculty of Pharmacy Universidad CEU San Pablo, Madrid of Photometry, Acoustics and Radiometry. Member of the institutional research group ARIE (EC01/0720). Universidad CEU San Pablo. Member of the research international project JRP-n12 Metrology for wearable light loggers and optical radiation dosimeters. Member of J 14 (CIE-ISO) Integrative Lighting. ISO 8995 CIE S 008/E Lighting of indoor workplaces; JTC 20 (D6/D2) Wearable alpha-opic dosimetry and light logging. Ángel Herrera 2021 Award for Best Research project, for his work "Development on Utility Model of LED Luminaires integrative light emitters for harmony and well-being of people". Third price in the cathegory Dispositives with the proyect Biosanitarian LED lamps. GO HEALTH AWARDS 2019.

Vinod Bijlani is an AI & IoT expert with a passion for sustainability. He has contributed to the design and implementation of smart city projects and established intelligent public transportation and traffic ecosystems in Singapore, India and the U.S. He has over 22 years of experience in creating solutions and is a distinguished inventor with 25 patents in AI and ML technologies.

Pedro Bustamante is a PhD in Architecture. Associate Professor of Architecture at the School of Architecture of the University of Seville. Member of the University Institute of Architecture and Building Sciences.

Miguel Ángel Campano is a Tenured Associate Professor (Profesor Titular de Universidad) at the Higher Technical School of Architecture of Seville. Architect specialized in the field of advanced building facilities, hygrothermal comfort, energy efficiency, daylighting and circadian stimulation. He stands out in the design of HVAC systems and in the environmental conditioning of architectonical spaces.

Rodney Chakwesha is with Department of Electrical Engineering, Namibia University of Science and Technology. He has a bachelors degree in Electrical and Computer Engineering with a major in Power Systems Engineering. His research interests include Energy Systems, Smart Cities, Urban infrastructure development.

Rafael Córdoba Hernández is an architect specializing in planning and the environment and Doctor of Architecture from the Universidad Politécnica de Madrid (UPM). Member of Planners for Climate Action (P4CA) of the Climate Change Planning Unit of UN-HABITAT and associate professor of the Department of Urban and Territorial Planning of the Universidad Politécnica de Madrid, of the Master in Historic Gardens and Ecosystem Services of Green Infrastructure of the Universidad Politécnica de Madrid and of the Master in Land Policy and Sustainable Urban Development of the UNED-Lincoln Institute of Land Policy Chair of Cambridge (Massachusetts). He combines his professional activities with the drafting of general planning, development and management at different scales and the intervention as a legal expert in urban-environmental processes throughout the national territory. His line of research focuses on the analysis of urban vulnerability, territorial resilience, and the role of urban planning in the face of the new challenges arising from the environmental, social and economic crisis we are suffering.

Laura de Azcárate Rodríguez is an Acoustic Designer and Architect, Founder at SoundScape Studio in Madrid which specialises in sustainable architecture and Acoustic Design. She finished her Master's degree of Architecture at San Pablo CEU University and a Bachelor of Music in Madrid. She also holds an MSc in Environmental and Architectural Acoustics from London South Bank University. As an Architect and Music teacher specialised in Acoustics she pursues an international Design career trying to merge Architecture, Acoustics, Sustainability and Research.

Samuel Domínguez-Amarillo is a Vice Dean in the School of Architecture and Associate Professor in the Department of Architectural Engineering at the University of Seville, Spain. He is senior researcher of the research group TEP-130: Architecture, Heritage, and Sustainability of the Andalusian Scientific Research. In his professional career he acts as Expert Consultant on Hi-performance systems for buildings and in the assessment of sustainability and energy efficiency of buildings and their urban environment. He has extensive background as adviser on environmental control for Cultural Heritage, with a wide portfolio of national and international projects.

Jessica Fernandez-Agüera is senior researcher at the University of Seville with extensive experience in indoor air quality and environmental control in buildings. Her research focus on the architectural-environment control for inhabitants' health comfort and wellness. She has participated in multiple R&D projects, both national and international, being author of several international research publications. She is leading the UE-FEDER Project "UnCOVER: Evaluation of the protection capacity against pollution of Early Childhood Education Centers in Andalusia". Related to this work she is editing the book " Guidelines on ventilation, thermal comfort and indoor air quality in schools ". She has conducted awareness campaigns on indoor and outdoor air quality and developed activities and training materials for children between 4 to 10 years old, educators and public officials. She is developer of the Covid Risk airborne tool (). The app proposes a method for simulating disease airborne propagation via aerosols and to assess indoor infection risk.

Skhumbuzo Gcabashe holds a Diploma and Bachelor of Technology in Public Administration and is currently doing a PhD in Public administration at the Durban University of Technology in Durban campus. His research interests include Service delivery, Governance and Public Policy. He is a member of the South African Association in Public Administration and Management.

Ester Higueras is architect (1988) and PhD (1997) who collaborates in several research groups on bioclimatic and healthy built environment. Since 1997 she has developed several works based on bioclimatic aspects from the focus on the local microclimate and the thermal comfort. Dra. Higueras has carried out projects for environmental municipal ordinances, urban regeneration plans for public spaces, projects for sustainable, green and blue infrastructures and urban health and well bieing design.

Carlos Lahoz, born in Madrid in 1976, received his degree in Architecture and Urbanism by the ETSAM (Escuela Técnica Superior de Arquitectura de Madrid) in 2002. In 2015 he obtains a Ph. D. in Architecture from the Universidad San Pablo CEU with the thesis Towards the Conscious Space. The Influence of New Communication Technologies on the Sociability in Public Space. In terms of his academic life, he develops a research and teaching activity as a faculty of the School of Architecture at the Universidad San Pablo CEU in Madrid, the Universidad de Salamanca and the Politecnico di Milano, institutions where he imparts lectures in the fields of Urbanism, Landscape and Territorial and Metropolitan Planning. He is also the director of the Smart Cities Laboratory of the Universidad San Pablo CEU. In parallel to his academic work, after several years of work experience in international architectural firms such as Foster and Partners, in 2006 he joined Taller de Ideas as a partner where he has accomplished a variety architectural and urban projects in Spain, Europe, North of Africa and the Middle East. Additionally, in 2010 he founded URBAN NETWORKS with the mission of promoting the creative transformation of cities and territories. In recent years, his career, both in the field of urban planning and architecture, has been very focused on the field of sports, health and quality of life, with special dedication to the design of active cities. Carlos Lahoz, in the past, has been director of Design LAAB (Laboratory of Advanced Architecture and Bioclimatism) of the Fundación Metropoli and of the Madrid Think Tank, a joint initiative of the COAM (the Madrid Association of Architects), the City Council and the Regional Government. having been Vice Dean of the COAM from 2015 to 2019. He has also been part of the jury of numerous competitions in Architecture and Urbanism and has participated in congresses and conferences in different forums. Currently, Carlos Lahoz is also Trustee of the Fundación Arquitectura.

Noluthando Shirley Matsiliza is a Professor of Public Administration at Fort Hare University. Her research interests include Public Policy Implementation, Governance, leadership Monitoring and Evaluation and Development Management. She is involved in teaching, research conduct, and postgraduate supervision at UFH. Prof Matsiliza has published from international and National journals focusing on multidisciplinary research issues and edited a book. She is also mentoring students and staff in their areas of specialisation. Noluthando is an assistant Editor of the Journal of Local Government Research and Innovation. She is a member of the South African Association in Public Administration and Management and the Association of Schools and Departments in Public Administration and Management.

K. S. Sastry Musti is presently with Namibia University of Science and Technology, Windhoek, Namibia. He has than 30 years of professional experience. He obtained his BTech in Electrical Engineering from JNTU, Kakinada (A.P.) in 1990, MTech and PhD from NIT, Warangal in the years 1996 and 2002 respectively. Some of his earlier employments include University of the West Indies, St Augustine, Trinidad, ESIGELEC, Rouen, France and Sophia University, Tokyo, Japan. His research interests include Power and Energy Systems, Information Systems and Engineering Education.

Elisa Pozo Menéndez is an urban architect with specialisation in Sustainable Cities (UPEM-IFU, 2014) and Environment and Bioclimatic Architecture (MAYAB-UPM, 2019). She is architect, urban planner and researcher at Matia Instituto Gerontológico. She is currently finishing her PhD in Sustainability and Urban Regeneration at the Polytechnic University of Madrid on healthy ageing and cities, where she also collaborates in research projects of the Department of Urban and Regional Planning. She is co-author of the "Guía para planificar Ciudades Saludables" published by the Spanish Ministry of Health and the FEMP. In 2022 she was selected in the ranking of the "35 under 35" most influential people in Spain and Madrid in the world of engineering and architecture and in 2020 she received the third Talento Joven-Carné Joven award from the Community of Madrid in the category of Solidarity for her work with older people.

Anya Pulido Cavada is a recent architecture graduate from San Pablo CEU University in Madrid (Spain) and enrolled in the first year of the PhD programme in Composition, History and Technique in Architecture and Urbanism.

Omar Vargas-González is Professor and Head of Systems and Computing Department at Tecnologico Nacional de Mexico Campus Ciudad Guzman, professor at Telematic Engineering at Centro Universitario del Sur Universidad de Guadalajara with a master degree in Computer Systems. Has been trained in Innovation and Multidisciplinary Entrepreneurship at Arizona State University (2018) and a Generation of Ecosystems of Innovation, Entrepreneurship and Sustainability for Jalisco course by Harvard University T.H. Chan School of Health. At present conduct research on diverse fields such as Entrepreneurship, Economy, Statistics, Mathematics and Information and Computer Sciences. Has colaborated in the publication of over 20 scientific articles and conducted diverse Innovation and Technological Development projects.

Index

I

L

M

N

O

P

R

S

T

U

V

W

Premier Reference Source
Tax Audit and Taxation in the Paradigm of Sustainable Development
TAX

Premier Reference Source
Controlling Epidemics With Mathematical and Machine Learning Models

Premier Reference Source
School-Museum Relationships and Teaching Social Sciences in Formal Education

Premier Reference Source
Sociological Perspectives on Sustainable Development and Poverty Reduction in Rural Populations

www.ingramcontent.com/pod-product-compliance
Lightning Source LLC
LaVergne TN
LVHW062111300926
849161LV00010B/2435